中國文化及名勝指南

MAGNIFICENT CHINA
A Guide to Its Cultural Treasures

衣上征塵雜酒痕
遠遊無處不銷魂
此身合是詩人未
細雨騎驢入劍門

喜聞思謀編著中國文化及名勝指南查東方出版社書
說為詩誌賀
黃永玉乙丑於香港

Petra Häring Kuan
Yu-Chien Kuan

中國文化及名勝指南

MAGNIFICENT CHINA

A Guide to Its Cultural Treasures

CHINA
BOOKS
& Periodicals, Inc.
San Francisco

Photographed by Mo Beiquan

The original German version is published by
Verlag W. Kohlhammer GmbH, Stuttgart, West Germany
under the title of *China*.

German edition copyright © 1983, 1987
Verlag W. Kohlhammer GmbH.

Revised English edition copyright © 1987, 1988
Joint Publishing (H.K.) Co., Ltd.

Co-published by
Joint Publishing (H.K.) Co., Ltd.
9 Queen Victoria Street, Hong Kong
and
China Books & Periodicals, Inc
2929 Twenty-fourth Street
San Francisco, CA94110, U.S.A.

First American hardcover edition published May, 1987
Paperback edition published September, 1988

Printed by
C & C Joint Printing Co. (H.K.) Ltd.
75 Pau Chung Street, Kowloon, Hongkong.

ISBN 0-8351-2044-9

Contents

Part One

Introduction   1

Part Three

Description of Cities and Provinces

Jiangzi (Gyangze)
Taiwan Province

Appendices

Preface

China is the oldest country in the world which has to this day remained a cultural and political entity without a break in tradition. The revolutionary events of the last decades, despite all the changes, reconfirm the basic unity of past and present. Without knowledge of the past, present-day China remains an enigma. And the living present offers much in the way of explanation of tradition.

Besides conveying necessary information to travelers in China, this art and travel guide aims at explaining this relationship of the past to the present. Chinese art is perhaps the best vehicle for making China and the general human values of Chinese culture clear to the China visitor who otherwise is not familiar with the country. This guide was written by Dr. Kuan Yu-Chien and his wife Petra Häring-Kuan. Both authors are well-qualified for the task: Dr. Kuan is a sinologist who is well versed in the Chinese culture of the past and present; Petra Häring-Kuan is also a sinologist and, as a result of her experiences in China, can judge what a foreign visitor needs to know about traveling there. This book will certainly help many visitors to better understand and appreciate China.

Prof. Dr. Wolfgang Franke

Notes and Acknowledgements

'How would you like to write an art and travel guide for us?' This question was the beginning of an adventure for us. Many friends and acquaintances had asked us for tips and information about trips to China. So we did not hesitate for long and agreed. We considered ourselves to be experienced enough to handle the task. After all, we had already seen the most important places of interest in the course of our own travels, and in addition to that, I had traveled extensively in China during the first thirty years of my life. But soon the first problems arose. Of course I had visited the Imperial Palace in Peking dozens of times, but how many halls were located on the middle axis? Or the Lingyin Si temple in Hangzhou that we like so well — when was it built? I spent three years in western China — how could I have forgotten where the golden Zongkaba statue stands in the Ta'er Si monastery in Qinghai? These questions and similar ones caused us quite a few headaches; so we began an extensive search for material. We mobilized all our relatives and friends in China and soon after received information from all over the country. Then we ourselves embarked on a long tour of China. Things were running smoothly — I made inquiries and gathered information and my wife took notes and collected material. As soon as the first suitcase was full, we realized that we had enough material for several books and that we would exceed the page limit set by the publisher. What now? Should we just fleetingly mention the famous tourist spots and give detailed descriptions of the lesser known ones — those only accessible to people not traveling with a group? Being Chinese, there was no doubt in my mind that my country was the most beautiful in the world. Where else is there a remote temple whose little bronze bells, tinkling in the wind, can be heard for miles? Where else can one see knotty pines estimated at being centuries old — where else if not in China? So, I was in favor of describing all interesting sites, irrespective of how inaccessible they are. But my wife quickly brought me back down to earth. We had to make concessions and only describe the places which are easiest to reach. Some cities and attractions are open to all tourists; in order to gain entrance to many others you need a travel permit which is relatively easy to obtain. Some places one may only visit if accompanied by a Chinese citizen or if one is an overseas Chinese; these places, however, will soon be open to everyone — for example the Wutai Shan mountains. Please do not regard it as being impolite or discriminatory if you are not allowed to enter certain places. It is often concern for the tourist which dictates these rules. In many cases, unsatisfactory lodging and transportation or the demands made on a foreign guest's constitution are the reasons for refusing entrance. And another thing: Who doesn't want to show his country from its best and most beautiful side? Although, as my wife and I have discovered, you can argue about what is beautiful. A newly restored hall is to me a welcome sight; on the other hand, my wife delights in seeing a weatherworn temple. In passing new buildings, I am glad to see that modernization is continuing in China. My wife likes to wander through winding streets in the old sections of cities and astonishes my Chinese relatives and friends by excitedly reaching for her camera to photograph these ancient sights. As you can see, Eastern and Western points of view do sometimes differ.

We have just mentioned Taiwan briefly. Inclusion of specific descriptions of existing conditions and places of interest would have meant exceeding the limits of this work.

It originally took us two years to compile the material and put it down on paper. It would have taken longer if we had not had help and support from my friends and colleagues. Special thanks go to our parents Elisabeth and Georg Häring, who offered us all possible assistance in the writing and revising of the manuscript. Our appreciation goes to Vera and Oskar Claussen for generously offering us the use of their vacation home in Switzerland during the summer months, where the magnificent surroundings made our task of writing about a fascinating country easy.

We would like to express our gratitude to the local representatives of the Chinese travel agency Lüxingshe and also to my Chinese relatives and friends for their support and encouragement.

Finally, the German edition of this book appeared on the market at the end of 1983. At this time, the general manager of Joint Publishing Co., Hongkong, Mr. Shaw Tse, saw it when visiting the International Bookfair in Frankfurt and suggested that we publish it in English. This idea was great, but who was going to translate it into English?

Suddenly we thought of our good American friend, Janet Delmas, who has a B.A. and an M.A. in German language and literature and has also studied Chinese. Janet, her friend Catherine Badger, who has a B.A. in linguistics and an M.A. in linguistics and German language and literature and has had translating experience, my student, Janey Gaventa, who is working toward a B.A. in German and Chinese (also Americans) and Peter Jagenteufel, a German who received his M.A. in English from an American university, were all members of the translating team. They worked day and night. They were conscientious in their work, discussing it with us frequently. Their warm friendship and enthusiasm moved us very much.

During our cooperation with them, we discovered that the situation in China has changed a lot within the last two years. The original version of the book would not satisfy the readers. Therefore, my wife and I made up our minds to visit China again in order to revise the book. In the summer of 1984 — the hottest summer in the past twenty years — we climbed from one mountain to another, visited interesting sites and talked to the people. We started in the very South, in the provinces of Guangdong and Fujian, and moved gradually to the East, North, then to the Northwest and, at last, to the Southwest. We traveled by train, plane, bus and ship. We visited China in 1979, 1981, 1983, 1984, 1985 and 1986; my wife also went to China in 1975 and 1977. Each time we were there, we received new impressions. Especially in 1984, we could hardly believe how much China had changed in such a short time! On the streets you could see a lot of people wearing brightly colored and fashionable clothing. Depending on your mood, you could spend a pleasant afternoon at a teahouse, taking in the performance of local opera troupes, go to open-air dance floors or stroll through the outdoor free markets.

We will have achieved our purpose in writing this book if it helps in making the reader a bit more familiar with Chinese culture and customs.

Kuan Yu-Chien

Part One

Introduction

National Conditions

Location, Size, Borders, Capital, National Flag, National Emblem

CHINA is situated in the southeastern part of the Eurasian continent and is bordered in the east by the Pacific Ocean. It covers an area of 9,560,900 km² and is the third largest country in the world, being surpassed in size only by the Soviet Union and Canada. The country stretches for about 5,500 km from the Heilong Jiang river in the north, near the city of Mohe, to the Zengmu Reef of the Nansha Islands in the South China Sea and for about 5,200 km from the Pamir Highlands in the far west to the junction of the rivers Heilong Jiang and Wusuli Jiang (Ussuri) in the east.

Its land frontier measures 28,000 km and is shared by North Korea in the east, the People's Republic of Mongolia in the north, the Soviet Union in the northeast and northwest, Afghanistan, Pakistan, India, Nepal and Bhutan in the west and southwest, and Burma, Laos and Vietnam in the south. The Chinese coast is more than 18,000 km long and is bounded by the Gulf of Bohai, the Yellow Sea, the East and South China Seas. More than 5,000 islands dot the China coast, the largest of which is Taiwan (35,788 km²), followed by the island of Hainan (34,380 km²).

Politically, China is divided into 22 provinces (including Taiwan), five autonomous regions and the three municipalities of Beijing (Peking), Tianjin and Shanghai, which are directly under the central government.

Capital: The capital of the People's Republic of China is Beijing (Peking).

National flag: The national flag has five yellow, five-pointed stars on the upper left part on a field of red. The red color of the flag symbolizes revolution. The five yellow stars represent the great unity of the revolutionary peoples under the leadership of the Communist Party of China.

National emblem: The national emblem is with the famous gate, Tianan Men, in the center, illuminated by five stars and encircled by stalks of grain and a cogwheel.

Topography

China's land surface slopes from west to east and can be divided into three zones: The Qinghai-Tibet-Plateau has an average altitude of over 4,000 m. The greatest highland area of the world is located here — the "Roof of the World" — with an average elevation of over 5,400 m. This zone covers an area of 2,200,000 km². The second zone begins east of the Kunlun Mountains and has a mean altitude ranging from 1,000 — 2,000 m. The Tarim Basin, the Mongolian Highlands, the Loess Plateau of the Sichuan Basin and the Yunnan-Guizhou Plateau are part of this region. East of this, the third zone begins with hardly any elevations exceeding 500 m. The relief levels off in an eastward direction toward the China Sea. This has traditionally been the agricultural region of the country. Here Chinese culture and civilization developed, and it is today the most densely populated area.

The most important rivers flow from west to east, following the topography of the land: the Huanghe, Yellow River, is 4,848 km long and the Changjiang (Yangtze) is 5,983 km in length.

China's topography is characterized by harsh contrasts and varied landscapes. The Mt. Qomolangma, Mount Everest, on the China/Nepal border has an elevation of 8,848 m, the highest mountain in the world. The Turfan Depression in the autonomous region of Xinjiang is the lowest point in China — 155 m below sea level.

Climate

China's climate is determined by the interplay between seasonally changing monsoons — the winter monsoon, polar continental air masses from Siberia which cause cold, arid winters, and the summer monsoon, the tropical Pacific air masses which cause hot summers. Due to China's size — an expanse of land covering more than 35 degrees of latitude — and complex topography, there are pronounced variations in climate from region to region. Extremely cold, dry Siberian winds blow over the Mongolian Plateau seaward into North China from September to April. In the south they are blocked by parallel mountain ranges such as Qinling in Shaanxi, Dabie Shan in Anhui/Henan/Hubei and Nanling in southern Hunan.

From April to September, tropical winds from the Pacific and Indian Oceans sweep into China from the south. This is the so-called summer monsoon and is the most important

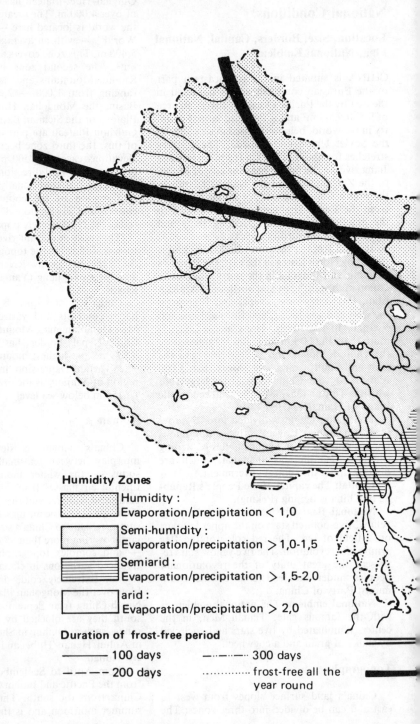

Climate Map

Humidity Zones

Humidity :
Evaporation/precipitation < 1,0

Semi-humidity :
Evaporation/precipitation > 1,0-1,5

Semiarid :
Evaporation/precipitation > 1,5-2,0

arid :
Evaporation/precipitation > 2,0

Duration of frost-free period

——— 100 days   —·—·— 300 days

— — — 200 days   ············· frost-free all the
year round

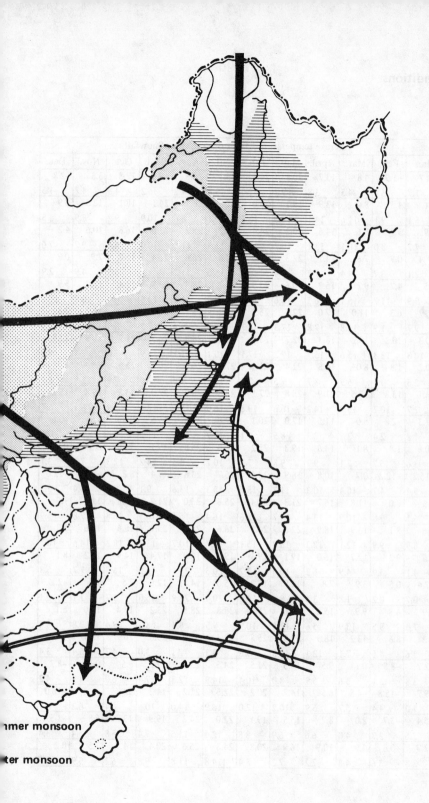

mer monsoon

ter monsoon

Climate Conditions

	Average temperature / Days of rainfall or Snowfall											
	Jan.	Feb.	Mar.	April.	May.	Jun.	Jul.	Aug.	Sept.	Oct.	Nov.	Dec.
Beijing	−4.7	−1.9	4.8	13.7	20.1	24.8	26.1	24.8	19.9	12.8	3.8	−2.8
	1.7	3.8	4.5	3.8	9.2	11.0	13.8	14.2	6.2	4.8	4.2	1.5
Shanghai	3.1	4.3	8.4	13.9	19.1	23.0	27.8	28.1	24.1	18.1	12.5	5.9
	8.1	9.1	11.6	14.1	14.0	12.5	10.1	8.6	10.9	9.2	8.9	8.5
Nanjing	1.9	3.7	8.6	14.6	20.3	24.4	28.2	28.2	23.0	16.8	10.6	4.2
	7.2	8.0	10.1	13.1	10.7	10.0	11.3	11.8	10.0	8.4	9.2	7.0
Jinan	−1.4	0.9	7.6	14.7	22.3	26.6	27.6	26.6	21.4	15.7	7.9	0.9
	2.1	3.7	4.4	7.2	5.4	6.6	15.0	11.7	8.2	5.5	4.9	2.9
Hangzhou	3.5	4.7	9.2	15.2	20.6	23.9	28.7	28.4	23.8	17.6	12.2	5.9
	9.9	11.7	15.1	16.5	15.6	14.0	10.0	11.1	12.8	10.5	10.9	10.6
Nanchang	5.1	6.3	11.0	17.0	22.6	25.3	29.7	29.7	25.4	19.3	13.2	7.3
	9.7	11.9	16.8	17.8	17.3	14.7	8.6	8.9	7.3	8.9	10.3	10.5
Fuzhou	10.3	10.3	13.2	18.3	22.7	25.0	28.8	28.3	26.3	21.7	17.9	12.9
	10.8	13.3	15.6	15.7	17.2	17.1	10.1	11.1	11.9	7.0	7.4	9.2
Zhengzhou	−0.2	1.8	8.0	14.6	21.4	26.4	27.8	26.3	20.5	15.0	7.9	1.7
	2.5	4.2	5.9	8.7	7.5	7.1	11.7	9.8	11.0	7.9	5.8	2.2
Guangzhou	13.1	13.8	17.5	21.9	25.8	27.1	28.3	28.2	27.0	23.8	19.8	15.2
	7.7	10.7	15.0	14.2	16.6	19.8	16.0	15.5	12.4	5.9	6.1	6.7
Lanzhou	−7.3	−2.8	5.0	11.5	17.0	20.1	22.0	21.0	15.5	9.6	1.3	−5.6
	1.2	2.4	3.7	7.3	8.5	9.1	12.7	10.6	11.5	7.4	2.6	0.8
Xi'an	−0.8	1.8	8.1	13.6	19.3	25.2	26.8	25.8	19.1	13.6	6.6	0.6
	3.6	5.7	7.1	9.7	9.8	7.6	10.7	8.3	14.2	12.3	7.4	3.1
Urumqi	−15.2	−12.2	0.7	10.8	18.9	23.4	25.7	23.8	17.4	8.2	−2.6	−12.0
	5.4	4.7	10.4	10.3	11.7	15.7	18.3	13.6	9.1	7.0	6.4	5.3
Chengdu	5.5	7.0	11.8	16.7	21.3	23.4	25.6	25.0	21.2	16.8	11.7	7.2
	6.1	9.0	10.9	13.4	14.7	15.6	16.4	15.4	16.5	16.8	7.8	5.9
Chongqing	7.6	9.1	13.9	18.9	22.6	24.9	28.6	28.6	23.9	18.6	13.6	9.3
	8.9	9.9	12.1	12.3	18.8	15.1	10.7	10.7	13.7	18.3	14.6	10.7
Kunming	7.5	9.3	12.7	16.0	19.1	19.3	19.8	19.0	17.4	14.9	11.2	8.1
	4.1	3.9	4.9	6.2	10.0	17.7	20.5	21.1	15.5	16.8	7.7	5.3
Lhasa	−2.4	0.5	3.9	7.8	11.9	15.2	15.0	14.1	12.6	7.5	1.5	−2.1
	0.7	0.2	1.8	3.6	8.6	14.8	20.4	21.9	15.0	3.7	1.1	0.1
Wuhan	2.9	4.8	9.9	15.8	21.6	25.5	28.8	28.5	23.2	17.4	11.0	5.1
	7.0	9.5	13.9	15.6	12.8	10.9	9.5	8.4	8.4	9.4	10.8	8.4
Guilin	8.2	8.8	13.2	18.3	23.8	25.8	28.3	27.9	25.8	20.7	15.1	10.1
	3.6	4.5	7.1	12.1	10.0	9.8	8.3	7.11	3.0	4.7	5.4	3.4
Shenyang	12.7	−8.8	0.1	9.5	17.5	21.5	24.5	23.8	17.2	9.5	0.1	−8.7
	3.8	3.1	3.6	5.9	8.0	10.4	14.9	12.3	7.4	6.0	4.9	4.2
Harbin	19.7	−15.8	−4.8	6.5	14.7	20.2	22.5	21.2	14.2	5.8	−6.2	−16.0
	7.0	4.4	5.7	5.9	10.2	12.0	16.9	14.0	10.6	6.4	6.2	6.1
Dalian	−5.4	−3.7	2.0	8.7	15.5	19.1	22.0	24.2	19.9	13.7	5.8	−1.5
	2.8	2.7	4.0	6.6	6.9	8.8	12.4	11.5	7.4	55.8	5.4	3.4
Qingdao	−2.7	−0.6	4.9	10.9	16.9	20.8	24.8	25.6	20.4	14.5	7.5	0.2
	2.8	3.6	4.8	7.2	7.2	8.4	14.8	11.8	9.8	6.2	5.9	3.7

Climate

| | Maximum temperature / Minimum temperature | | | | | | | | | | | |
	Jan.	Feb.	Mar.	April.	May.	Jun.	Jul.	Aug.	Sept.	Oct.	Nov.	Dec.
Beijing	10.2	18.5	24.4	30.9	38.3	40.6	38.7	35.9	32.3	29.8	19.6	13.9
	-17.8	-27.4	-12.3	-2.9	2.5	10.0	15.3	12.2	3.7	-3.2	-12.3	-18.3
Shanghai	18.9	23.6	27.4	33.3	35.5	34.7	37.1	38.2	36.3	31.3	28.5	23.0
	-8.8	-8.4	-3.3	0.3	5.7	11.5	18.5	18.2	12.0	2.3	-3.4	-9.0
Nanjing	17.7	23.3	27.9	32.8	34.8	36.0	38.0	40.5	37.4	33.1	26.5	23.1
	-11.0	-13.0	-3.2	0.0	5.0	11.8	16.8	17.4	9.4	-0.2	-4.4	-11.5
Jinan	15.9	21.5	26.2	33.0	38.1	40.5	39.0	37.7	34.7	31.3	24.0	18.2
	-16.7	-13.6	-10.3	-1.9	4.2	11.1	17.7	15.1	6.9	0.3	-9.1	-16.0
Hangzhou	23.9	28.3	29.2	33.7	36.5	35.6	38.9	38.5	36.3	32.3	29.7	26.5
	-8.0	-9.6	-1.9	0.7	9.0	14.1	19.4	18.8	12.0	2.3	-1.4	-6.5
Nanchang	20.8	28.6	28.6	33.4	36.5	37.7	40.6	39.7	38.6	34.1	28.1	26.1
	-7.6	-6.7	-0.1	2.4	10.7	17.2	20.9	20.5	13.3	6.4	1.1	-5.2
Fuzhou	27.0	27.5	30.2	33.0	35.7	38.0	39.0	39.0	38.2	33.0	31.5	29.6
	-1.1	0.1	2.5	6.3	12.9	17.1	21.5	21.0	15.0	11.2	6.6	1.5
Zhengzhou	17.6	23.9	31.8	33.1	40.8	42.3	43.0	40.6	35.9	32.6	25.1	19.9
	-15.8	-14.4	-10.2	-2.8	6.3	12.2	17.0	14.6	5.0	-0.2	-6.3	-12.4
Guangzhou	27.1	27.5	29.6	32.1	36.0	36.6	37.5	37.0	37.6	33.6	32.4	29.6
	0.1	1.3	3.3	7.7	14.7	18.9	21.6	21.1	15.5	16.6	7.0	1.8
Lanzhou	12.6	15.5	27.5	31.5	32.9	36.7	35.7	34.8	30.9	25.0	18.9	16.2
	-21.7	-17.6	-9.4	-8.6	2.1	4.6	9.7	6.5	1.5	-3.8	-14.9	-17.4
Xi'an	15.2	20.7	27.9	30.8	37.0	41.7	41.0	39.6	33.7	28.8	21.6	17.5
	-13.8	-18.7	-5.1	-4.0	5.1	11.6	16.9	12.7	5.4	-0.7	-6.1	-11.3
Urumqi	7.0	10.6	21.6	31.2	35.7	40.9	40.3	40.7	37.0	30.2	16.7	12.5
	-32.0	-29.5	-23.7	-8.9	0.7	6.0	10.7	9.0	-0.2	-10.6	-20.5	-32.0
Chengdu	16.3	20.8	27.6	30.8	34.0	35.3	35.0	35.1	34.8	26.8	23.8	20.3
	-4.3	-3.2	-1.0	2.9	8.6	14.6	17.1	16.5	11.6	6.8	1.4	-3.0
Chongqing	18.7	21.6	31.8	36.4	38.9	39.3	40.4	40.3	39.5	30.8	25.1	21.5
	-16.5	-13.8	-9.7	-8.1	-2.7	3.5	5.5	3.7	3.1	-6.7	-10.5	-15.8
Kunming	21.6	22.2	25.9	29.0	31.2	28.9	28.4	27.5	28.4	25.7	24.2	20.6
	-5.1	-1.3	-0.1	0.5	6.0	9.2	12.3	8.8	7.1	3.6	0.6	-4.6
Lhasa	20.9	24.9	29.6	32.7	36.0	37.8	38.2	38.7	36.2	32.9	26.2	22.2
	-16.5	-13.8	-9.7	-8.1	-2.7	3.5	5.5	3.7	3.1	-6.7	-10.5	-15.8
Wuhan	20.9	24.9	29.6	32.7	36.0	37.8	38.2	38.7	36.2	32.9	26.2	22.8
	-17.3	-14.8	-3.3	-0.3	7.2	14.2	17.3	18.0	10.1	1.5	-3.3	-8.2
Guilin	27.6	26.8	31.3	33.1	34.7	37.4	38.2	38.1	38.5	34.4	29.9	27.6
	-4.5	-3.6	1.5	4.0	12.4	13.0	21.5	18.3	12.9	8.8	2.7	-1.2
Shenyang	7.3	13.4	19.8	28.6	32.7	35.2	34.4	35.7	30.6	27.5	19.4	13.4
	-30.5	-27.2	-19.3	-12.5	0.2	3.6	13.9	11.3	1.0	-8.3	-20.1	-30.2
Harbin	4.2	11.0	17.1	27.9	34.0	35.4	34.5	32.9	28.5	25.8	15.2	6.2
	-38.1	-33.0	-28.4	-12.7	-3.2	4.9	11.1	8.6	-1.1	-11.9	-26.1	-35.7
Dalian	7.7	9.5	17.3	23.3	28.2	32.0	33.7	34.4	36.6	24.7	18.8	13.5
	-21.1	-17.3	-11.8	-4.2	3.7	11.2	15.0	14.5	6.4	1.0	-12.7	-19.0
Qingdao	13.4	16.4	23.5	28.1	33.9	34.2	35.9	36.9	31.2	26.0	20.8	17.3
	-15.6	-17.2	-9.7	-2.8	1.9	7.1	14.9	13.4	3.1	-1.1	-9.0	-16.8

source of rain. Part of the humidity precipitates in the mountains and hilly country in southeast and southern China. The air masses penetrate inland as far as the Mongolian Plateau and the eastern edge of the Tibetan Plateau.

The front where the two air masses meet is of great significance to the climate of central and northern China. This occurs in North China in the summer and results in heavy precipitation in this area. The winds diminish in the fall and the frontal zone moves farther south to central China, causing heavy rainfall which often leads to flooding.

The variability of rainfall is a problem for China's farmers. In North China, 80—90% of the annual precipitation falls in the summer months. The variability, however, exceeds 50% in this area; droughts often occur as a result. The rate of variability in South China is only 40%. Southeast China receives the most rainfall due to the fact that this area is also hit by typhoons from July to September.

It can be said in general that northeast China is influenced by Siberian air, all of eastern China has a mild to subtropical climate and the South lies in a tropical climate zone.

Flora and Fauna

There are approximately 32,000 species of seed plants in China, more than 2,000 of which are utilizable. Of the 2,800 species of trees, many are of economic importance such as tung oil trees, camphor trees, cedar, rubber and cacao trees. Traditional crops include cotton, millet, wheat, rice, soybeans, rape, sugar cane and tea as well as tropical plants such as coffee, oil palm trees, sisal and pepper. China can roughly be divided into two zones along a diagonal running from the southwest to the northeast, according to its vegetation: the dry Northwest and the humid Southeast.

The Northwest with its Daxing'an Mountains is part of the cold coniferous region. Here larch, fir and pine grow. The mountainous area along the Chinese-Korean border is a mixed woodland consisting of elm, maple, birch, linden and ash, among others. Oak forests are found in the areas of Liaodong and Shandong. Farther south along the lower and middle Changjiang and in Sichuan, are the subtropical evergreen forests. Several of the species there originated in the tertiary period, for example the ginkgo and the metasequoia trees. There are tropical rain forests in the South from Yunnan to Guangdong. Bananas, litchi, longyan, mango, coffee, sugar cane and industrial crops such as rubber trees, oil and cocoanut palm trees grow here.

Throughout the year, the steppe of the Northeast Plain and the eastern part of the Mongolian Plateau are covered with grasses (goat and feather grasses). The highly fertile pasture land is ideal for raising livestock. Alpine meadow areas are found in the east-central and southern parts of the Qinghai-Tibet Plateau where glacial waters have created numerous marshes, lakes and meadows with succulent grasses and flowers. In the valleys of these plateaus, cold-resistant grains such as spring barley and hardy types of vegetables prevail.

The desert area of northwestern Tibet lies at an altitude of 5,000 m. Only short shrubs and bushes grow here. In the oases of the desert regions of Xinjiang, Gansu and the Qaidam Basin of Qinghai, there is also vegetation.

The natural environment and the variety of vegetation have provided favorable conditions for the development of diverse forms of animal life and have prevented species which cannot be found in any other parts of the world from becoming extinct. Worthy of note are the Chinese paddle-fish (Psephurus gladius, up to 2 m long) of the Changjiang, the small species of alligator in eastern and central China and the giant salamandar in western China. A variety of animals are found in the mountains and valleys on the Sichuan/Tibet border, an area in which the giant panda also lives.

Squirrel, sable, red fox, tiger, leopard, black bear, musk-deer, sika and red deer inhabit northeastern China.

The grass and desert steppe is the home of central Asian animals which can adapt to the extreme conditions of this region: the desert jerboa and marmot. The two-humped wild camel (Bactrian camel) and the Mongolian wild horse still live in the Mongolian highlands as well as the onager (Asiatic wild ass) and antelope. The higher-lying steppe areas of western China are inhabited by the Tibetan wild ass and the wild yak.

The tropical rain forests are inhabited by numerous bird species, also by monkey, mongoose, the tree shrew, tiger, elephant, sambar (deer), muntjac (deer), civet and leopard.

Mineral Resources

China is rich in mineral resources. Most significant is the presence of bituminous coal and lignite. There are huge coal producing areas in the northern provinces of Heilongjiang, Jilin, Liaoning, Hebei, Shanxi and Shandong.

The country also has large crude oil reserves at its diposal, primarily in the Northeast, in Xinjiang, Gansu, Qinghai, Hebei and Sichuan. Iron ore is also significant.

In addition to these reserves, China has a plentiful supply of manganese, tungsten, bauxite, antimony and tin. The tungsten and antimony reserves are believed to be the largest in the world. There are also reserves of copper, cobalt, nickel, lead, zinc, aluminum, uranium, gold and important phosphates.

Agricultural Regions

Although the vast country of China covers an area of 9.56 million km^2, only about 11% of the land is suitable for agricultural use. Mountain ranges, deserts and steppes make up a large part of the country. Because cultivable land is at a minimum and the climate is unfavorable, China has been plagued by innumerable famines throughout its long history. Since ancient time, the Chinese have endeavored to improve conditions by terracing, building irrigation systems, reaping multiple harvests and double cropping. Today, thanks to extensive dike construction projects and the improvement and modernization of agricultural techniques, adequate food production is largely ensured.

The most important agricultural regions are: The Northeast Plain where millet, corn, sugar beets, soybeans and wheat are cultivated; the North China Plain, the main agricultural region, where the soil has been enriched by deposits from the Huanghe and Huaihe rivers and where wheat, corn, barley, millet, peanuts, sweet potatoes and cotton are grown here; the Plains of the Middle and Lower Changjiang and the southern part of the country, which are the main rice producing regions yielding two harvests annually, and the Sichuan Basin, a fertile region, where products such as rice, wheat, sugar beets and rape are abundant.

Demography

According to historical sources, it is estimated that as early as 800 BC, in the first centuries of the Zhou Dynasty, there were about 13.7 million people living in China. It is assumed that at the end of the Western Han Dynasty, the population had reached a total of 59.6 million. Most of the inhabitants were concentrated in the semi-arid provinces of the North and Northwest. Beginning in the 8th century, the Changjiang Basin and the southern provinces were settled. More than half of the population lived in these new areas. In the early 12th century, China had around 100,000,000 inhabitants. As a result of uninterrupted invasions from the north, the population at the beginning of the 13th century had diminished by 40%. After the founding of the Ming Dynasty in the 14th century, a census was taken, the result of which was 59.9 million people. From the 15th century on, the population figures continued to increase. This development was, however, interrupted in the middle of the 17th century by wars and natural catastrophes. The number of inhabitants tripled from the end of the 17th to the early part of the 19th century:

1762: more than 200 million; 1803: 302 million; 1834: 401 million. The growth in population which began at the end of the 17th century was not accompanied by a corresponding increase in food production, which soon led to disasterous famines. China suffered from internal unrest and external pressures and was hit by natural disasters starting in the middle of the 19th century; the result was not only a stagnation, but a decrease in population.

After the founding of the People's Republic, a census was taken in 1953, using modern poll-taking methods. The result — 583 million — exceeded previous estimates. According to the census figures, 87% of the population lived in the rural areas of the traditionally densely populated regions of the North China Plain and the Changjiang Basin. The estimated population figure in 1964 was 694 million.

Results of the census of July 1982 (according to an official communiqué from the Central Office of Statistics of Oct. 27, 1982): China had a total population of 1,031,882,511.

Inhabitants in the 29 provinces, municipalities and autonomous regions (excluding Taiwan, Jinmen, Mazu and other islands off the coast of Fujian Province, Hongkong and Macao) numbered 1,008, 175, 288.

The population figures increased 45.1% within the last 18 years with an average annual growth rate of 2.1%

Female/male ratio: 48.5% female, 51.5% male.

Nationalities: The national minorities make up 6.7% of the population, the Han Chinese 93.3%. A comparison of the figures from 1964 shows an increase of 43.8% in the Han population and 68.4% in that of the minorities.

Educational levels of the population: 4,414,495 people out of the 1,008,175,288 have graduated from college; 1,602,474 are studying at present or have studied at a university

China's Major Crops

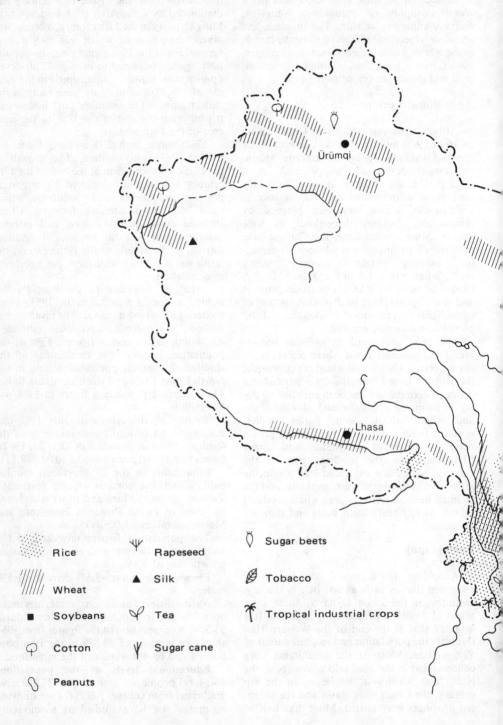

Ürümqi

Lhasa

:::: Rice

⅄ Rapeseed

/// Wheat

▲ Silk

■ Soybeans

⌇ Tea

⌾ Cotton

⋎ Sugar cane

⬭ Peanuts

⥾ Sugar beets

⌸ Tobacco

🌴 Tropical industrial crops

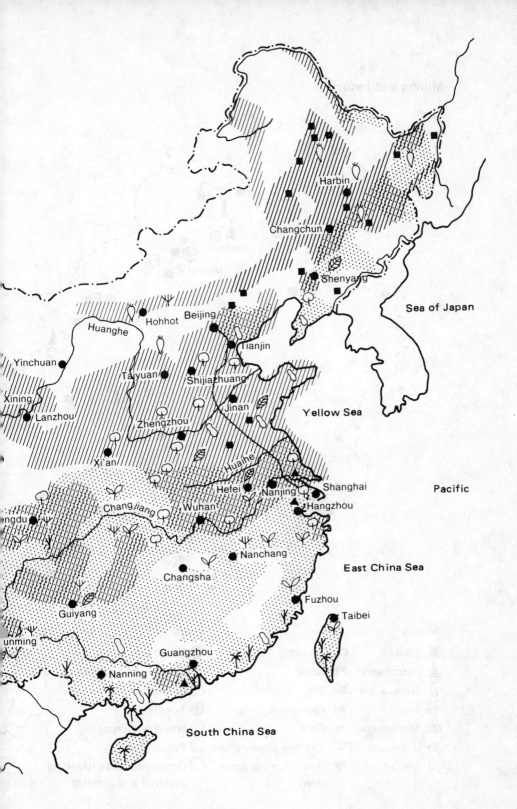

Sea of Japan

Harbin

Changchun

Shenyang

Huanghe

Hohhot

Beijing

Tianjin

Yinchuan

Taiyuan

Shijiazhuang

Jinan

Yellow Sea

Xining

Lanzhou

Zhengzhou

Xi'an

Huaihe

Hefei

Nanjing

Shanghai

Pacific

Chang Jiang

Wuhan

Hangzhou

ngdu

Nanchang

East China Sea

Changsha

Fuzhou

Guiyang

Taibei

unming

Guangzhou

Nanning

South China Sea

Mining and Industry

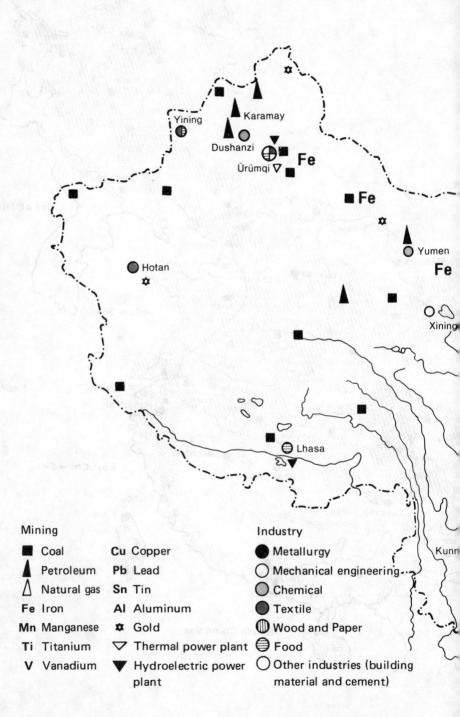

Yining

Karamay

Dushanzi

Ürümqi Fe

Fe

Yumen

Fe

Hotan

Xining

Lhasa

Kunn

Mining

- ■ Coal
- ▲ Petroleum
- △ Natural gas
- **Fe** Iron
- **Mn** Manganese
- **Ti** Titanium
- **V** Vanadium

- **Cu** Copper
- **Pb** Lead
- **Sn** Tin
- **Al** Aluminum
- ✿ Gold
- ▽ Thermal power plant
- ▼ Hydroelectric power plant

Industry

- ● Metallurgy
- ◐ Mechanical engineering
- ◯ Chemical
- ◯ Textile
- ▥ Wood and Paper
- ⊜ Food
- ◯ Other industries (building material and cement)

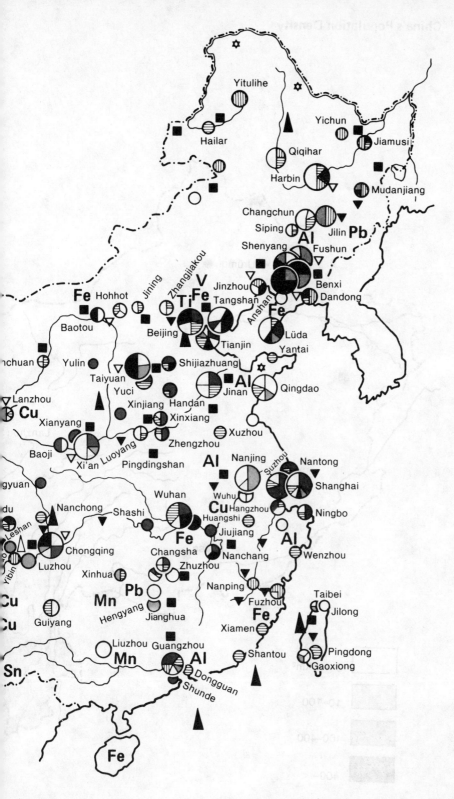

China's Population Density

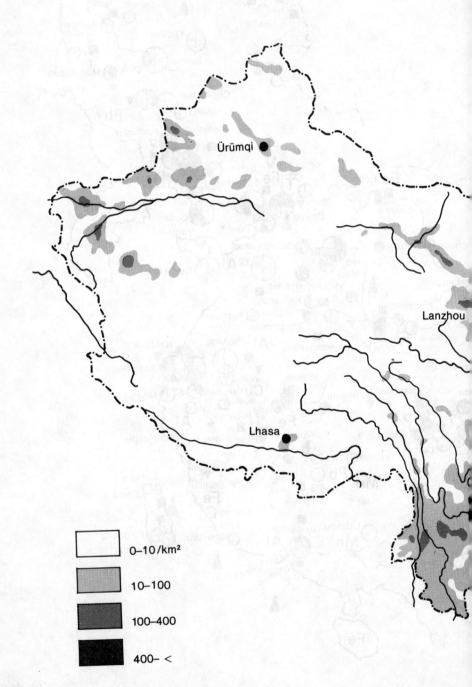

0–10 /km²

10–100

100–400

400– <

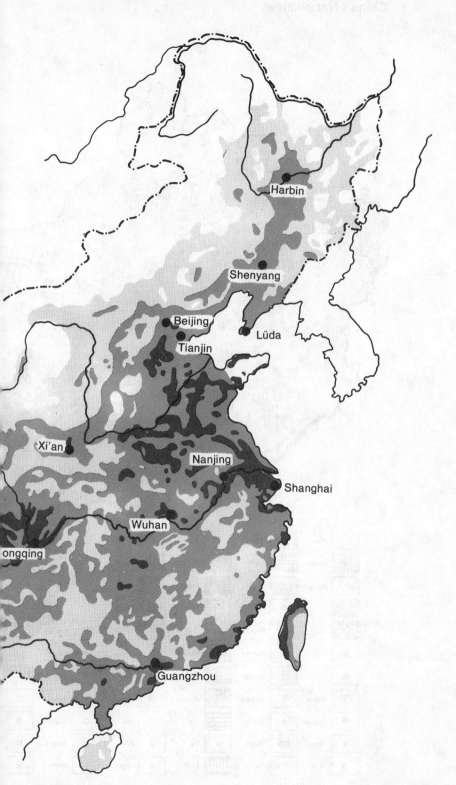

Harbin

Shenyang

Beijing

Lüda

Tianjin

Xi'an

Nanjing

Shanghai

Wuhan

ongqing

Guangzhou

China's Nationalities

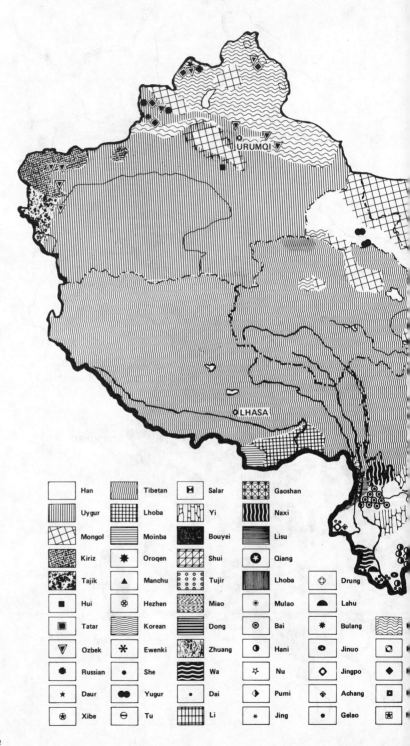

Han		Tibetan		Salar		Gaoshan				
Uygur		Lhoba		Yi		Naxi				
Mongol		Moinba		Bouyei		Lisu				
Kiriz		Oroqen		Shui		Qiang				
Tajik		Manchu		Tujir		Lhoba		Drung		
Hui		Hezhen		Miao		Mulao		Lahu		
Tatar		Korean		Dong		Bai		Bulang		
Ozbek		Ewenki		Zhuang		Hani		Jinuo		
Russian		She		Wa		Nu		Jingpo		
Daur		Yugur		Dai		Pumi		Achang		
Xibe		Tu		Li		Jing		Gelao		

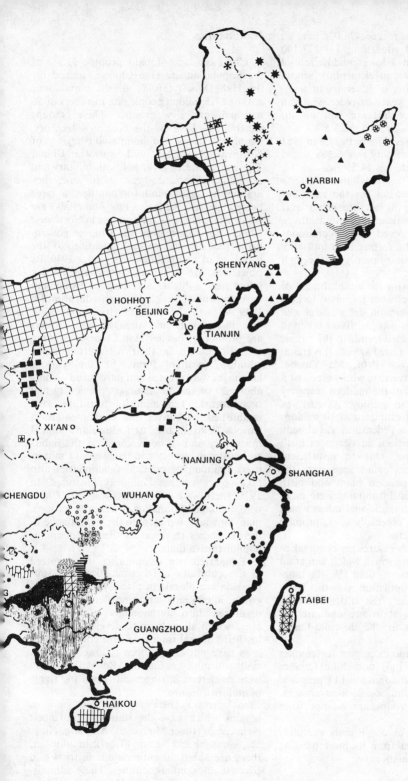

without finishing a degree; 66,478,028 have an upper middle school education; 178,277,140 have graduated from a lower middle school and 355,160,310 have an elementary school education. The number of illiterates or semi-illiterates (people 12 years or older who can read and write very little or not at all) decreased from 38.1% in 1964 to 23.5%.

Birth and death rates: The birth rate in 1981 was $20.91^0/_{00}$, the mortality rate $6.36^0/_{00}$ and the natural growth rate was $14.55^0/_{00}$.

Total urban population: 20.6% (206,588,582). The reason for the explosive population increase in the last three centuries is the difference in the ratio of births to deaths, a consequence of improved social conditions and medical care. The former high mortality rate of $30^0/_{00}$ was due primarily to the high infant mortality rate.

In the years following the establishment of the People's Republic, what promised to be a rapid increase in population size was still seen positively because this was justifiably taken to be the sign of an upward trend. In the fifties, however, protest was raised against this trend. Among the critics was Prof. Ma Yinchu, Rector of Beijing University, who warned of a surplus of laborers that the modern economy was in no position to employ. As early as 1957, this excess was estimated at 10 million. The Chinese Women's Federation was already among the most tenacious advocates of birth control at that time. Due to insufficient housing, city dwellers could appreciate the need for regulated pension plans and birth control, whereas rural inhabitants were more closely bound up with traditional values which stated that children, especially sons, promise good luck and prosperity.

Today, consistent measures are being taken to control population growth which aim at an annual growth rate of less than 1%; the long-term goal is zero population growth. These measures include the free distribution of contraceptives, free abortions and sterilization. Late marriages and the one-child-family are also encouraged.

There are economic incentives for couples who decide to have only one child; families with more than two children must be prepared to accept material and social disadvantages. National minority groups are exempt from these measures.

Only the success of consistently executive steps can save China from its most pressing problem — overpopulation.

Nationalities

China is a land of many peoples. 93.3% of the population are Han Chinese, named for the Han Dynasty; 6.7% of the population, almost 67.5 million people, are members of 56 national minority groups. These groups inhabit 50—60% of the country's territory, mainly the steppe and mountainous regions of Northeast, Northwest and Southwest China. These areas are of great political, military and economic importance because, for one, they are border areas, and for another, a large percentage of China's raw materials are concentrated here — for example in Northwest China. For this reason, the Chinese government has devoted careful attention to the problems of nationalities policy since 1949. Its objectives are economic improvements for minorities, a higher standard of living and development of health care and education (in 1949, 95% of the minority group population was illiterate). Ethnic languages and cultures are promoted; besides Han Chinese, children are also taught in their native tongue. In addition, written forms of the various languages were created and introduced — only about 20 of the 50 languages previously had such forms. Ten minority institutes were established to convey the fundamentals in various fields such as agriculture and animal husbandry and to do research on the habits and customs, history and languages of minorities. Training of political functionaries also takes place in these minority institutes. In 1978, there were over 800,000 cadre in China who belonged to national minority groups, many of whom were sent to the highest governmental bodies to represent their autonomous administrative units.

Equal treatment of minorities is guaranteed in the consitution. Discrimination and suppression are illegal. In places where minority group inhabitants are prevalent, they are organized into autonomous administrative areas which allow them to develop according to their cultural traditions. But constitutional laws have not always been followed — especially during the Cultural Revolution there were numerous infringements upon the rights of minority groups.

At present there are five autonomous regions which have the status of provinces: Neimenggu (Inner Mongolia), Xinjiang, Ningxia, Guangxi and Xizang (Tibet); in addition, there are about 30 autonomous districts and over 70 autonomous counties. These administrative areas are irrevocably part of the territory of the People's Republic of China as stated in the constitution, and their inhabitants are not entitled to make common political decisions with the same or related nationalities in neighboring countries.

The largest group among the national minorities is the Zhuang, numbering around 12 million people, who mainly inhabit the areas of Guangxi, Yunnan and Guangdong. They belong to the Dai family, speak a Sino-Tibetan language, and most earn a living planting rice.

With about 6.5 million people, the Huis are the second largest group. They are not an ethnic, but rather a religious minority group which adopted the Islamic faith when it was introduced in China in the 7th century. The Huis live mainly in Ningxia, Gansu, Henan, Hebei, Qinghai, Shandong, Yunnan, Xinjiang, Beijing and Tianjin. They speak Han Chinese and use Chinese characters.

The Uighurs, with a population of about 5.5 million, live in Xinjiang. They are a light-complected Turkic people and speak a language which belongs to the Altaic language family.

The Yis (ca. 4.8 million) live in Sichuan, Yunnan, Guizhou and Guangxi. Most of them are farmers; some raise livestock.

The ca. 3.9 million members of the Miao minority inhabit Guizhou, Hunan, Yunnan, Guangxi, Sichuan, Guangdong and Hubei.

The Tibetans, numbering around 3.4 million, live in Tibet, Qinghai, Sichuan, Gansu and Yunnan.

The Mongols, formerly a nomadic people, are scattered throughout China. Approximately 2.6 million members of this national minority live in Inner Mongolia, Xinjiang, Liaoning, Jilin, Heilongjiang, Gansu, Qinghai, Hebei and Henan.

Also numbering about 2.6 million, the Manchus live in Liaoning, Jilin, Heilongjiang, Hebei, Beijing and Inner Mongolia. Descendants of the warriors who conquered China in the 17th century and founded the Qing Dynasty, they have been totally assimilated into Chinese culture.

Social Structure

Imperial China — 1911:
The social hierarchy of Imperial China consisted of four classes:

1. intellectuals   3. craftsmen
2. peasants   4. merchants

Actors, beggars, prostitutes and slaves were not officially included in the hierarchy.

Any intellectual who had passed the imperial examinations could obtain a position in either the central or the local government and was guaranteed power, social standing and exclusive privileges.

Peasants made up the most substantial part — 80% — of Chinese society. Agriculture was considered the only productive livelihood and was always preferred above other means of earning. Although peasants ranked high in the social hierarchy — second place — they were often the victims of state and private exploitation since they constituted the most important tax paying group. They often led a life on the edge of existence. Their misery was the fuel for unrest and uprisings which permeated Chinese history.

The occupation of craftsman was a hereditary one. Sons born into this class were not allowed to pursue a profession of their own choosing. They were either employed in a family business, worked for state or private large-scale businesses or earned a living as traveling craftsmen. Due to the fact that their services could be requisitioned from time to time, much of their own working time was lost. It was not until the 16th century that compulsory service could be replaced by payment of a tax. Merchants were on the bottom rung of the social ladder, whether rich or poor. According to Confucian values, expertise in the area of economy was unimportant. Merchants and craftsmen were mostly denied the privilege of advancing directly to the elite class and, as a consequence, well-to-do merchants endeavored to help their children attain high office by sending them to study the classics. There were times when even children of this class were prohibited from holding official positions and other times when such positions could be purchased.

Modern China:
At the beginning of the 20th century, the hierarchical social structure began to totter. The position of the merchants in the cities had changed significantly in their favor. A labor class began to develop in industrial factories. New ideas were brought home by students returning from abroad.

The fall of the Qing Dynasty sealed the fate of the Confucian-oriented social structure. New China rejected the traditional classification system; after the establishment of the People's Republic of China in 1949, the system was based on Mao Zedong's class analysis of 1926:

1. landlords — compradors
2. national bourgeoisie (middle bourgeoisie)
3. petty bourgeoisie = peasants owning land, independent craftsmen; intellectuals = students, elementary school

teachers, lesser officials, clerks, lawyers, small traders

4. semi-proletariat = semi-tenants, poor peasants, craftsmen, shop assistants, peddlers;

Today, more than thirty years after the revolution, the conversion to a modern revolutionary society is considered to be essentially complete.

The Family and the Role of Women in Imperial and Modern China

The family was the smallest social and economic unit in traditional China. It provided safety and security for each member, as far as economically possible, but demanded from each his subordination to the head of the family, the father. After the father's death, this position was usually assumed by the eldest son.

Relationships to family members and to outsiders were determined by the five rules which governed human relationships according to Confucian ethics. These rules demanded that each person accept the authority of his superior:

ruler — subject

father — son

husband — wife

older brother (sister) — younger brother (sister)

older friend — younger friend

With the exception of the last relationship, violation of these rules was considered a criminal offense. Social status, sex and age left no one in doubt about his position within society, his rights or his duties.

Within this strictly-ordered patriarchal, hierarchical system, women were doomed to economic dependence and absolute obedience. As girls, they were subordinate to their fathers, as wives, to their husbands and as widows, to their eldest sons. Women had no right to education; among numerous other virtues, they were expected to demonstrate submissiveness, chastity and obedience. The development of the custom of footbinding in the 9th/10th centuries caused women to be even more tied to the home.

Marriages were contracted for material reasons. Generally with the help of matchmakers, the parents arranged the bride's price, her dowry and all other conditions. In general, the young couple had never met before, and it was not until the marriage ceremony was over, did they see each other for the first time. After marriage, the woman was considered part of her husband's family and was under the authority of her mother-in-law. Especially in rural areas, marriage mostly provides the husband's family with cheap additional labor.

Unlike a man, a woman did not have the right to leave her partner, unless she could prove that he was guilty of a criminal act. On the other hand, a man could divorce his wife merely on the grounds of talkativeness. He was also allowed to have secondary wives and concubines under his roof. This was a sign of prosperity. A secondary wife was subordinate to a principle wife and frequently came from a poorer family. She could, however, assume a more privileged status if, for example, the husband's chief wife did not provide him with male offspring but she bore him a son. At some periods of feudalism a woman, being widowed, did not have the right to remarry.

Even before the Revolution of 1911, demands were made for the equal treatment of women. Gradually, schools and universities opened their doors to women. A young girl often had to wage bitter battles within her family before she succeeded in asserting her right to be educated.

After the founding of the People's Republic of China, the role of women changed to a great extent. The Marriage Law of May 1, 1950, ensured equality between men and women. Its 'General Principles' state:

Art. 1: The feudal marriage system, based on arbitrariness and compulsion, which gave the husband precedence over the wife and which ignored the interest of children, has been abolished. The new, demoratic marriage system, based on free choice of partner, monogamy, equality of rights for both sexes and protection of the lawful rights of women and children, is now in effect.

Art. 2: Polygamy, concubinage, child engagements, encroachments upon the right of widows to remarry and the demand for money and presents in connection with marriages are forbidden.

Of marriage contracts it says in Art. 3: Marriages are based on the purely voluntary decisions of both parties. No party may compel nor may any third party interfere.

Art. 4: A marriage may only take place if the man has reached the age of 20 and the woman, the age of 18 years.

Some of these regulations were already anchored in the Civil Law Book of 1930 under the National Government, but the new law had never expressly been publicized at the time. In 1950, on the contrary, all means of propaganda were used to acquaint people in the country with the new guidelines.

Of course, it did take years until people — especially the older generation in rural areas — accepted and adhered to the new laws and were willing to abandon old customs.

Much turmoil was caused by the new divorce law. Of the petitioners for divorce in the first two years, 82% were women.

The Women's Federation, founded in the spring of 1949, was significantly instrumental in determining revolutionary development in the lives of women. This was facilitated by the support provided by the state or by the work unit or responsible administrative unit within each residential district.

Women's equality is not confined to a position in the family, but is to be realized particularly in the working world, where women are constitutionally ensured equal pay. Women as well as men are supposed to contribute to the socialist development of the country. All professions are open to them. In order to relieve women from household duties, nurseries, kindergartens and cantines have been established. In addition, husbands are urged to help with housework.

Constitution

The first constitution of the People's Republic was passed in 1954. In 1975, the National People's Congress ratified a second constitution with was heavily influenced by the spirit of the Cultural Revolution.

On December 4, 1982, a new constitution was adopted, which attempts to take into consideration previous miscalculations and unforeseen developments and make corrections. It is divided into four chapters that follow the preamble: General Principles; Fundamental Rights and Duties of Citizens; Structure of the State; National Flag, National Emblem and the Capital. The *Preamble* states that the fundamental duty of the Chinese people in the coming years will be to 'concentrate all its energy on socialist modernization. Under the leadership of the Chinese Communist Party and guided by Marxism-Leninism and the ideas of Mao Zedong, the people of all nationalities in China will continue to adhere to the democratic dictatorship of the people and follow the way of socialism, to constantly improve socialist institutions, to develop socialist democracy, to perfect the socialist legal system and, through self-reliance and hard work, to modernize industry, agriculture, national defense and science and technology step by step, to make China a socialist country with a highly-developed civilization and highly-developed democracy.' The constitution is the basic law of the land and is the highest authority.

The *General Principles* are divided into 32 articles. They state, among other things, that: 'All power in the People's Republic of China belongs to the people. The organs through which the people exercise state power are the National People's Congress and the local people's congresses at various levels.' These 'are constituted by democratic elections, are responsible to the people and are under the people's supervision'.

The section ' *Fundamental Rights and Duties of Citizens* ' contains 24 articles. The equality of all citizens before the law, freedom of religion, speech, press, assembly and demonstration, among other things, are laid down in this section. Every citizen who has reached the age of 18 is eligible for election and has the right to vote.

In the section on *'State Structure'*, the functions and powers of the governmental bodies are set down:

'The *National People's Congress* is the highest organ of state power. Its permanent body is the Standing Committee of the National People's Congress.' The National People's Congress is made up of representatives elected by the provinces, the autonomous regions, the municipalities and army units. Its term of office is five years. The National People's Congress is empowered to: amend the constitution; elect the president and vice-president of the People's Republic of China; decide on the choice of the premier of the State Council upon recommendation of the president of the People's Republic; elect the chairman of the Central Military Commission; examine and approve plans for economic and social development and reports on their implementation; examine and approve the state budget and the report of its implementation. Laws and resolutions may be passed by a majority vote of all representatives. The National People's Congress elects the members of its Standing Committee and has the power to remove them from office.

'The *State Council* of the People's Republic of China, the Central People's Government, is the executive body of the highest organ of state power and the highest organ of state administration.' Its term of office is the same as that of the National People's Congress.

The State Council exercises the following functions and powers: stipulating administrative measures; drawing up ordinances and

The Administrative Levels and Units of the People's Republic of China (as of 7/1/1984)

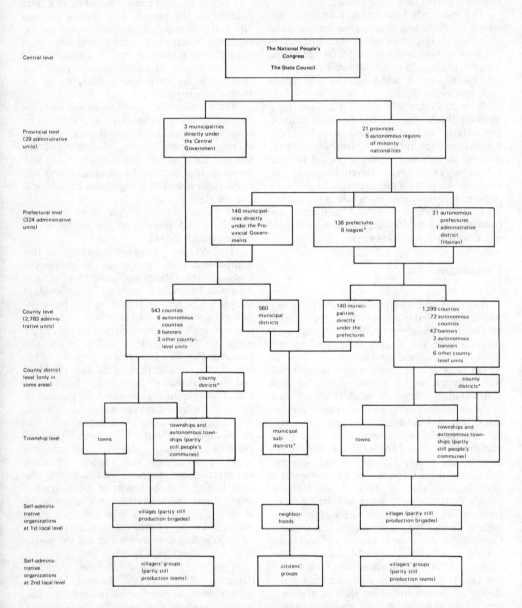

| Central level | The National People's Congress / The State Council |

Provincial level (29 administrative units)
- 3 municipalities directly under the Central Government
- 21 provinces / 5 autonomous regions of minority nationalities

Prefectural level (324 administrative units)
- 148 municipalities directly under the Provincial Governments
- 136 prefectures / 8 leagues*
- 31 autonomous prefectures / 1 administrative district (Hainan)

County level (2,783 administrative units)
- 543 counties / 6 autonomous counties / 9 banners / 3 other county-level units
- 560 municipal districts
- 140 municipalities directly under the prefectures
- 1,399 counties / 72 autonomous counties / 42 banners / 3 autonomous banners / 6 other county-level units

County district level (only in some areas)
- county districts*
- county districts*

Township level
- towns
- townships and autonomous townships (partly still people's communes)
- municipal sub-districts*
- towns
- townships and autonomous townships (partly still people's communes)

Self-administrative organizations at 1st local level
- villages (partly still production brigades)
- neighborhoods
- villages (partly still production brigades)

Self-administrative organizations at 2nd local level
- villagers' groups (partly still production teams)
- citizens' groups
- villagers' groups (partly still production teams)

* Prefectures, leagues, county districts and municipal subdistricts have no people's congresses and people's governments. Rather, they are lead by administrative offices whose cadre are appointed by the governments of the respective next-higher administrative unit.
From: P. Schier, Hamburg 1985

The Organization of the State Apparatus

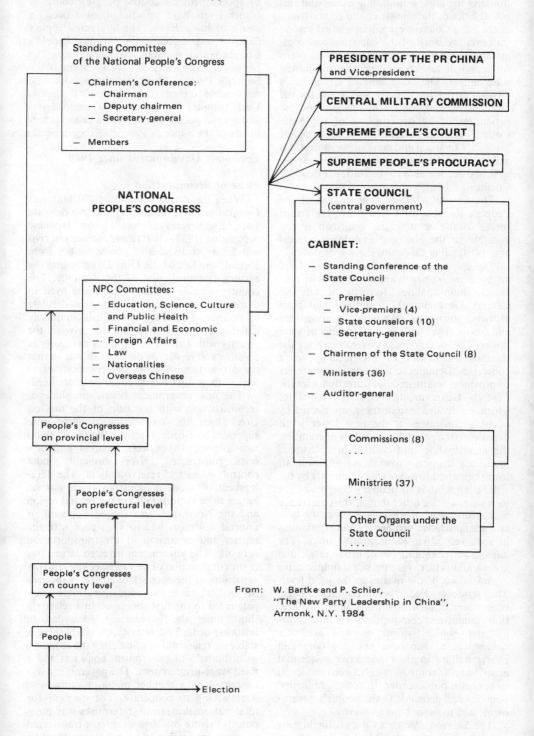

Standing Committee of the National People's Congress

- Chairmen's Conference:
  - Chairman
  - Deputy chairmen
  - Secretary-general
- Members

NATIONAL PEOPLE'S CONGRESS

NPC Committees:
- Education, Science, Culture and Public Health
- Financial and Economic
- Foreign Affairs
- Law
- Nationalities
- Overseas Chinese

People's Congresses on provincial level

People's Congresses on prefectural level

People's Congresses on county level

People

→ Election

PRESIDENT OF THE PR CHINA and Vice-president

CENTRAL MILITARY COMMISSION

SUPREME PEOPLE'S COURT

SUPREME PEOPLE'S PROCURACY

STATE COUNCIL (central government)

CABINET:

- Standing Conference of the State Council
  - Premier
  - Vice-premiers (4)
  - State counselors (10)
  - Secretary-general
- Chairmen of the State Council (8)
- Ministers (36)
- Auditor-general

Commissions (8)
. . .

Ministries (37)
. . .

Other Organs under the State Council
. . .

From: W. Bartke and P. Schier,
"The New Party Leadership in China",
Armonk, N.Y. 1984

regulations and proclamations of decisions and instructions in accordance with the constitution and the laws; establishing duties and responsibilities of the ministries and commissions of the State Council; exercising unified leadership over the work of the ministries and commissions; drawing up and instrumenting plans for economic and social development and the state budget. The State Council establishes a General Office for Finance and Trade for the examination and control of receipts and expenditures of all departments of the State Council, of local governments at all levels, of the state's financial and currency organizations and of enterprises and institutions. It is responsible and accountable to the National People's Congress.

The *Central Military Commission* of the People's Republic of China heads the armed forces of the country. Its chairman is responsible to the National People's Congress and its Standing Committee.

The local people's congresses and *local people's governments* are established in provinces, municipalities (directly under the Central Government), counties, municipal districts, townships, autonomous townships and towns. They are the local organs of state power. The local people's governments are the standing authorities of the local people's congresses. Deputies to the people's congresses of provinces, municipalities (directly under the Central Government), and municipalities which are divided into districts, are elected by people's congresses at the next lower level; deputies to the people's congresses of counties, the municipalities not divided into districts, municipal districts, townships, autonomous townships and towns are elected directly by the voters. The duties of people's congresses are to ensure, among other things, the observance and enforcement of the constitution, the laws and administrative ordinances and regulations in their respective administrative units. The *administrative committees* of urban residential areas and rural areas are the self-administrative organizations of the masses at the local level. The residents elect their chairmen. These committees in turn establish popular arbitration committees, committees for public security and public hygiene as well as other committees to supervise public affairs and public welfare in their respective residential areas, to settle controversies between residents, to maintain public order, to convey residents' opinions and demands to the people's governments and to submit suggestions.

The *Supreme People's Court* is the highest judicial authority in the People's Republic of China. It supervises the administration of justice by local people's courts at all levels and by special people's courts; people's courts at higher levels have jurisdiction over people's courts at lower levels. The Supreme People's Court is responsible to the National People's Congress and its Standing Committee. The highest agency for public prosecution is the Supreme People's Procuratorate; it is likewise responsible to the National People's Congress. Local people's procuratorates at various levels and special people's procuratorates are subordinate to the Supreme People's Procuratorate.

Economic Development since 1949

Phase of Reconstruction

When the People's Republic of China was founded in 1949, the country was in a desolate state. Eight years of war against Japanese occupation (1937—1945) and four years of civil war followed decades of power politics from abroad, the fall of the Qing Dynasty and the ensuing chaotic period of the Republic. The country was devastated, the people lived in destitution and despair and the desolate economy and currency system had completely collapsed. It was necessary to provide the country with a stable government as rapidly as possible and repair the damages of war so that the production of food and commodities as well as their distribution could be guaranteed.

The new government began the phase of reconstruction with the help of the masses. Great hydraulic engineering projects were supposed to finally avert the danger of flood catastrophes. Dikes were repaired and new ones constructed, rivers brought under control, dams and reservoirs built. The development of modern industry, which was no longer to be concentrated in the coastal region and the Northeast, and the development of mineral resources had to keep pace with the repairs and expansion of the transportation network. The government invested large sums in the construction of new railway lines and the expansion of the network of roads. In the area of medical care and education, mass campaigns led to the first successes. In a relatively short time, the government succeeded in restoring order and security, in establishing a stable currency and in stimulating the economy with the help of government contracts and a fixed wage-price system. The government was supported by a number of businessmen who were willing to cooperate. The moment for total nationalization of enterprises was postponed. Private concerns were to be transferred to state ownership step by step and their former owners compensated through the payment of dividends. The exceptions were banks, the coal and steel industries, railroads and the assets of foreign firms and capitalists which were transferred to state control without compensation.

The new government did not always feel obligated to honor contracts that the National Government had signed with foreign countries, and so some contracts which had been drawn up to the advantage of foreign partners were declared invalid.

The government filled the most important administrative positions with Communist cadre, but otherwise it drafted administrative personnel of the National Government.

The land reform which took place in the rural areas on June 28, 1950, made great changes in the social strata unavoidable. According to official figures, 70% of the rural population were poor peasants and farm workers. Land-owners and rich peasants who made up only about 10% of the rural population owned in some areas up to 70—80% of the land. A large number of the poor peasants were tenant farmers who, due to unfair leases, were often not even able to produce enough for subsistence. The leases demanded from the tenants 40—70% of their annual harvest, and not seldom lease payments had to be made ahead of time in the form of half the annual yield. In extreme cases, payments were demanded years ahead of time. It is therefore not surprising that land reform was welcomed by a large percentage of the rural population. The program provided for uncompensated expropriation of the great landowners whose property was to be divided up among the peasants. The government proceeded cautiously, without forcing the egalitarianism which had been feared at the beginning. There were still differences in the size of individual plots. The majority of the peasants could only produce enough for their own needs. Only middle and rich peasants could produce a surplus for the markets. In 1952, the phase of reconstruction was considered to be complete. Industry could boast figures which corresponded to the highest of those in the period before the war. In the area of agriculture, the harvests were good.

First Five-Year Plan (1953—1957) and Collectivization of Agriculture

While the great powers of the West continued to be sceptical about the new government in Beijing, the Soviet Union declared itself willing to participate in the development of China through economic cooperation. In December 1949, Mao Zedong led a delegation to Moscow for two months of negotiations. On February 14, 1950, the representatives of both countries signed a friendship and assistance pact. With the help of Russian experts, the first five-year plan came into existence. It was modelled after the Soviet's own five-year plan and placed sole emphasis on the rapid development of heavy industry. The neglect of agriculture and the production of consumer goods had to be taken in stride. In 1953, the first five-year plan went into effect but, due to organizational failings, did not bear fruit until 1955. The most important projects in the following years were the construction of iron and steel works, the expansion of the machine industry and energy production. Coal was of great significance here. Development of existing coal mines and the opening of new ones was in the foreground. The intensive search for new sources of energy resulted in the discovery of various oil fields.

The new economic plan made state control over production and consumption necessary and called for the nationalization of private concerns. The state, due to its monopoly on raw materials and its role as contractor and customer, had made private companies dependent on it in any case. Since 1954, the position of the state had continually been strengthened by capital investments and conversion of private enterprises into joint state-private enterprise. The state took over the administration of enterprises, and owners lost decision-making powers but were compensated by the payment of dividends. Even during the course of the first five-year plan, nationalization of private firms was largely complete. Former owners, at one time partners, worked in the meantime mostly as managers and received a settlement in the form of annual interest at a fixed rate of 5% of their share of capital.

In the area of agriculture there were also innovations. The smallholder system soon revealed its disadvantages: non-profitable production and the lack of possibilities to modernize it. Many peasants could not earn enough for a minimal existence due to a lack of machines and fertilizers, and so they sold their land to rich peasants. For this reason, the trend toward the creation of new social strata could be anticipated. Therefore, as far back as the end of 1951, opinions were voiced that the collectivization process in agriculture should be speeded up. This was to take place on three levels: creation of community groups for mutual help, and the creation of semi-socialist and of socialist production cooperatives. The cooperatives were made up of about 200 families. Within the collective system, private ownership of property was not allowed. Peasant families were left only a small plot on which they could raise vegetables for their own tables and a couple of pigs or small livestock. The means of production were in the hands of the collective and were distributed by the cooperative management, which also set up the production plan and work norms.

Production cooperatives were divided into several brigades to which work was assigned according to the production plan. Payment of the brigade members was calculated according to a work-point system in which points were earned for completed work.

At the end of 1956, collectivization was complete and included 96% of all agricultural households.

The new collective system had both advantages and disadvantages. The former included the optimal mobilization of all available labor and the distribution of the means of production according to plan. A disadvantage was the frequent emergence of indifference toward collective work and property.

The first five-year plan led to the rapid growth of heavy industry. In many areas the calculated output was exceeded by far. In comparison, agriculture registered a low growth rate which had a negative effect on investments made in the industrial sector and which convinced politicians, even before the five-year plan had run its course, that the Soviet model, which placed priority on the development of heavy industry, was not suitable for China, a land whose economy was based on agriculture.

Period of the 'Three Red Banners' (1958 — 1960) and the Phase of Consolidation (1961 — 1965)

In 1958, the second five-year plan was put into effect, but it was interrupted by the phase of the 'Three Red Banners': the 'Great Leap Forward' in the area of industry, the creation of people's communes in the area of agriculture, and in the area of ideology, the socialist general line. The 'Great Leap Forward' drew worldwide attention to the development of domestic policies in China. It was an attempt to hasten industrialization in the whole country through extensive decentralization and to reach a growth rate of 20—23%, mainly in the sector of steel, coal and energy production. To help increase steel output, the so-called backyard blast furnaces came into

existence — altogther about 600,000 of them — at which members of all professions worked. Numerous small industrial factories and workshops were created as subcontractors for the industrial and agricultural sectors. In the field of agriculture, the creation of communes represented a further step toward socialist transformation. A commune consisted of about 30 fully socialist production cooperatives. By the end of 1959, there were 24,000 people's communes in which 98% of the rural population lived. People's communes were divided into brigades, and brigades into production teams. The creation of the communes amounted to total collectivization. Private ownership was to be abolished — from household items to the farmhouse itself and the small piece of privately owned land — everything became the property of the collective. The goal was the maximal utilization of land, machines and manpower. Millions of people were mobilized for big economic projects like the construction of reservoirs and dams and terracing as well as for reclamation of cultivatable land. Where technology was lacking, masses of people were to take its place. On the principle of 'walking on two legs', the government tried to further development in agriculture and industry simultaneously by using both modern and traditional methods. The centrally administered economic system in use up to this point did not seem to be suited for the realization of such ambitious plans. Decentralization was supposed to lead to spontaneity and creative cooperation at the local level. It was to ensure that all available local resources would be drawn upon — manpower as well as technology, energy and raw materials. The administration of economic and socio-political affairs was transferred to the local level, both in rural and in urban areas.

Production showed a marked increase during the first year, especially in industry. This could not, however, be attributed to the new measures but to the completion of various big projects from the phase of the first five-year plan. In the following years, production decreased. The entire program ended in failure. Today, the Communist Party attributes this to a 'lack of understanding of the patterns of natural law which determine economic development as well as the basic economic conditions'. (See: 'Resolution concerning several questions in the history of our party since the founding of the People's Republic of China', adopted by the 6th plenum meeting of the XI Central Committee of the Chinese Communist Party on June 27,

1981.)

Various factors caused the failure of the 'Three Red Banners', for instance the lack of capable personnel who were equal to the task of the new additional administrative work. Decentralization gave the local economic units planning and production freedom. Government officials were not able to coordinate the individual local units with each other which resulted in mistakes in planning. Millions of people were busy at backyard blast furnaces which, however, produced iron of such a poor quality that it was seldom good enough to be used in industry; at best it could be used for the production of agricultural tools. The expectations regarding small businesses proved to be too high. The quality of their wares was often deficient and did not meet the expected standards. Unsuitably high production costs made many concerns unprofitable. The millions of laborers who were assigned jobs in industry were no longer available to work in agriculture; this led to bottlenecks in providing the workers in the city with food. Also, the people's communes had proved to be too big and administratively too difficult to oversee. They had to be reduced in size: from a total of 24,000, the number was increased to 74,000. The peasantry was not prepared for total collectivization and felt degraded in their positions as farm workers. Altogether the haste with which the individual measures had been implemented evoked resistance in all classes of the population. In the years from 1959—61, natural catastrophes plagued the country. Food production came to a standstill, which resulted in famines in 1961—62. Matters were complicated in 1960 when, as a result of ideological conflict, it came to a break with Moscow and a withdrawal of all Soviet experts. Industrial complexes which had been started could not be completed because the specialists had also taken their plans with them. The country was faced with a major economic crisis. Mao Zedong turned in his resignation as the head of state. Under the leadership of his successor, Liu Shaoqi, the government met this catastrophe by calling off the campaign and returning to a moderate program. Private plots were permitted, production teams adapted to the traditional village units and were provided with more authority, material incentives and, here and there, free markets were tolerated. Funds for agriculture were won through cuts in the industrial sector. The prevailing slogan was: 'Agriculture is the foundation, industry the managing factor of the economy'. Priorities in industry had to be postponed. Reductions in heavy industry led to the closing of several factories and to discontinuation of a number of projects which had been started. On the other hand, branches of industry that produced directly for the agricultural sector were considered important, for example those which produced fertilizer and farming equipment. Soon the first indications of improvement in the economic situation became visible. The shock of the 'three bitter years' (1960—1962) had been withstood. Again it was possible to increase spending for industrial projects, but caution was taken not to repeat the mistakes of the last few years. From 1962 on, industry was able to show an annual growth rate of approximately 10%. In 1965, the 1958 level had been reached and even surpassed.

The Cultural Revolution and Its Consequences (1966 — 1976)

In 1966, a new compaign — the 'Great Proletarian Cultural Revolution' was kindled and attracted worldwide attention. This movement was strongest in the cities, industrial regions and administrative organs and only influenced the agricultural sector to a lesser extent.

Mao Zedong had to remain in the background due to his failure in the 'Great Leap Forward'. The pragmatic economic line of the years 1961—65 had been a resumption of the program before 1958 and had been able to register considerable success. The discussion about economic policy was, however, not over. The line followed by Liu Shaoqi which allowed, if necessary, falling back upon capitalist methods such as material incentives, was rejects by the followers of Mao. In their opinion, material incentives should be substituted by ideological ones, the consciousness of the people had to be changed. As early as 1964, the mottos could be heard: 'In agriculture, learn from Dazhai', 'In industry, learn from Daqing'. Dazhai, formerly a poor village in Shanxi whose peasants had reclaimed a maximum of cultivatable land from their barren ground through extensive terracing, was considered a model brigade. In Daqing, Liaoning, workers had tapped an oil field under the most difficult conditions and had begun production. Success was achieved in both places without material incentives. Mao and his followers were of the opinion that increased achievement was dependent on the transmission of ideology.

Mao's support in his fight against Liu Shaoqi came from young people in the 'Red

Guard' who undertook the spreading of his ideas. The Cultural Revolution reached its pinnacle in 1967. The 'Red Guard' did not remain solely in the streets but, since the winter of 1966, had penetrated factories and workshops. There were clashes with the workers, walkouts, superiors were attacked and a wave of purges took place among leaders and management. Creation of factions and fighting between them inside the factories caused a standstill in most of industry. The transportation system partly collapsed; trains and buses were often confiscated by the 'Red Guard'. Transportation difficulties caused bottlenecks in the delivery of raw materials which, in turn, affected industry. There were also problems in providing the urban population with food, coal and electricity. In these critical times, it was, above all, Zhou Enlai who took pains to restore orderly conditions and return to disciplined work in the factories. It took until September, 1967 until industrial production could gradually be ensured again, thanks to intervention of the army.

In 1968, the 'Red Guard' also attempted to further their cause in rural areas. But the Central Committee immediately took precautionary measures which made it clear that major changes were unwelcome. Private ownership, meaning private plots, were to remain untouched. Agriculture was given continued priority. Experiments were too risky. Regional disturbances among the peasantry did arise in spite of this.

In the area of industry, the utmost was done for the development of small industry, not only in urban, but also in rural areas, in order to break down the barriers between city and country. Due to the expansion of industry and the opening of new installations, losses incurred by short-term shut-downs, walkouts and strikes could be compensated. The end of the Cultural Revolution showed that the values advocated by Liu Shaoqi could not be waived and that a return to pragmatism was inevitable. On the whole, the Cultural Revolution did not produce as catastrophic consequences as were the result of the 'Great Leap Forward'. There was, of course, substantial damage done, but the annual growth rate at the beginning of the seventies was equivalent to that of the phase on consolidation of the years 1962—65, and a stable increase was attained. This is not as true for the agricultural sector, however, as for the industrial, such as in the area of petroleum production, the chemical, electronic and machine industries. In agriculture the attempt was made to increase production by implementing large irrigation projects and expanding farmland.

New Policy Beginning 1976

After the collapse of the so-called Gang of Four (Jiang Qing, Zhang Chunqiao, Yao Wenyuan and Wang Hongwen) in 1976, more was brought to light concerning the proportions of the Cultural Revolution which officially had lasted 10 years. According to a report by Hua Guofeng in February 1978, under the influence of the Gang of Four between 1974 and 1976, losses amounting to billions were incurred, which was almost the ruin of the country. In spite of this, it can well be said that the sociopolitical consequences were even worse than the economic ones.

New emphasis was to be placed on economic policies. In 1978, the leadership adopted a ten-year plan (1976—1985) which was based on a concept of Zhou Enlai's — submitted in 1975 — and which focused on economic development and modernization. In the same year, the government approved the program of the 'Four Modernizations', which provides for the modernization of agriculture, industry, defense and science and technology. This foresaw the development of a strong socialist economy in China by the year 2,000. The class struggle advocated by Mao would have to yield to the primacy of economic development; professional qualifications and achievement would be duly honored; the opening of the country to the West would acquaint the country with modern management and technology and intensify trade. The importation of goods necessary to expedite economic growth would be financed by the export of raw materials such as petroleum and coal. Newly established organizations endeavored to intensify contact to countries abroad. Individual export companies and businesses were granted more extensive powers of authority. Trade agreements with Japan and the European Community were signed and numerous delegations were sent abroad to explore the market. However, since the goals were set too high, the party voted in April 1979 to make a number of changes in the general plan. The new guidelines were: regulate, transform, align and raise standards. The goal was to stabilize the entire economic situation and to strengthen political unity, vitality and stability. Economic cooperation and technical exchange with foreign countries were not to endanger the independence and self-reliance of the country but were to be the result of their own efforts. It was agreed that in the industrial sector, the development of light industry should be accelerated. The branches of heavy industry which served light industry and agriculture were expanded.

A number of measures had been taken in agriculture: the raising of the purchase price of agrarian products and by-products, introduction of the system of production responsibility, reinstatement or expansion of private plots of land, the permission of market trade and promotion of additional means of income.

The *responsibility system* or 'the contract system according to production' had been established in more than 90% of the production teams throughout China. To date, it has proved to be a viable system. Its sphere of teams made land available to small groups formed voluntarily by peasants or individual households. They contracted the amount to be produced and delivered and the output value on which their payments were based.

The major forms of the responsibility system can be summarized as follows: '(1) Peasants or groups are paid according to fixed jobs and work norms; (2) Peasants or groups are paid according to a special line of work and the result of the harvest; (3) Production teams assign output quotas to individual able-bodied labourers under the unified administration of production teams; (4) *bao chan dao hu*, or, "fixing output quotas on a household basis", (5) *bao gan dao hu*, ie, each household retains everything produced on the land assigned to it after paying taxes and contributing its shares to the accumulation and public welfare funds as a member of the collective. Same in nature as they are, these forms differ a little from each other in the contracting methods. The first three forms mean that production teams contract out their production tasks such as farming, tractor-ploughing, livestock-raising, and orchard keeping to peasant groups, individual labourers or households and then distribute the final reward among the peasants of the teams in a unified way. All of the three forms take unified management as a prerequisite, yet the degree of unification varies. While some production teams only put agricultural machinery and water conservancy projects under unified administration, other teams may place other aspects of agricultural production under unified management.

The last two forms of the responsibility system are mainly adopted by the poorer communes and production teams which have little agricultural machinery, water conservancy facilities, and side-line occupations, except farmland. These teams assign their farmland to individual households and then distribute the produce within fixed output quotas in a unified way while peasants retain what they have over-produced. This form is known as *bao chan dao hu*. If the households only pay taxes to the state and contribute to the collective accumulation without unified distribution of their remaining products, the form is called *bao gan dao hu*. Compared with the first three forms, therefore, the last two involve more decentralized management.'

(Source: Wang Xiyu, China's responsibility system in agricultural production, in 1982/83 China Official Annual Report, Hongkong 1982, S. 575)

The responsibility system allows the peasants — now being masters of their own affairs — a high degree of freedom in their decision making, and in practice, it leads to profitable and disciplined farming. The Chinese leaders reported repeatedly that a significant increase in the peasants' willingness to achieve and in record harvests has been registered due to these measures. Long-existing flaws in the collective economy caused by egalitarianism in distribution have been overcome.

In December 1981, the Premier of the State Council, Zhao Ziyang, announced the guidelines for future economic development. He stressed the significance of agriculture. It was the basis of the Chinese economy, its development, the key to all-round economic growth. Investments in this sector could not be made on a large scale, but they should be increased. The principles of socialist collectivization and the common ownership of the basic means of production should be strictly adhered to.

In the industrial sector, priority would be given to the development of the consumer goods industry. It should function efficiently on low investments and augment employment. The accelerated development of the consumer goods industry would be beneficial to heavy industry.

Zhao Ziyang made public the guidelines for the energy sector: finding more sources of energy, being frugal in consumption. The most important sources of energy are petroleum and coal. The Chinese leadership complained of an astonishing waste of energy; savings should therefore be made and oil gradually replaced by coal. Obsolete plants and production processes using a high amount of energy are to be technically altered. The oil saved is to be used domestically or exported, and the profits used for the development of the energy industry. In the long run, the processing of crude oil ought to be raised to a higher level and its petrochemical multi-purpose use promoted. At the same time, the transportation system must be expanded. This includes expansion of railroad lines and seaports, improvement of inland navigation and further increase of road construction.

Another important point in the new guidelines is adherence to the open door policy. International economic and technical exchange is to be intensified. In order to accelerate economic development, foreign funds, especially credit at low-interest rates under favorable conditions, would be necessary. They are intended for the development of basic equipment for the energy industry and transportation system.

On the basis of equality and mutual aid, foreign investments are also considered welcome. Mines and factories should be built as joint efforts. The tapping of new oil fields is also planned in cooperation with foreign firms.

Since 1980 a lot of Chinese and foreign investors have established corporations, called *joint ventures*. The participants in a joint venture share the profits between them and bear losses and risks together. They help to transfer modern technology, expand the export and increase China's foreign exchange.

In border provinces such as Guangdong and Fujian, Special Economic Zones have been established. Experiments are carried out here in an attempt to hasten modernization with the help of modern foreign technology, foreign capital, foreign managerial experience and technical personnel. Four different forms of foreign investment are known in the Special Economic Zones: 1. Enterprises started by foreign investors. 2. Joint ventures. 3. Coproduction enterprises: capital and equipment are supplied by one party, land and manpower by the other. 4. Processing with supplied foreign equipment, materials and models and compensation trade. China's first Special Economic Zone was established in Shenzhen, near Guangzhou, in May 1980.

The outstanding success of the responsibility system in agriculture has motivated Chinese leadership into carrying out an all-encompassing reform in economic structure. There are to be no more companies which operate at a loss and are dependent upon state subsidies and delivery of raw materials. The state is not to lead them by the hand any longer. Companies must openly compete on the market and respond to consumer wishes. They are directly exposed to the market's dictates, according to the principle: 'Where goods are manufactured, there is competition.'

System of Education

For a period of ten years, intellectuals and technical experts had been criticized and despised, and the anti-intellectual educational policy led to an enormous decline in standards and quality in research and teaching. The situation changed fundamentally after the Cultural Revolution and the fall of the radical leftists around Jiang Qing. The sciences and research, especially, are now once again considered extremely important under the policy of the four modernizations (the modernization of agriculture, industry, defense and science and technology). In the school curricula, political subject matter has increasingly had to give way to the natural sciences and mathematics. The re-introduction of grading, testing and competition has created achievement-oriented institutions of education. Whereas a proletarian background and the right political and ideological consciousness used to be two of the criteria of admission to the universities, today, strict entrance examinations determine eligibility. Intellectuals have experienced an incredible increase in political standing; the new leaders have recognized their importance for the development of a modern China.

Summary of the Chinese system of education:

Children attend pre-schools from three to six years of age. Here, they are taught the basics of hygiene, language and arithmetic, which is supposed to prepare them for elementary school. The subjects of painting, singing, dancing and physical education are an important part of pre-school instruction. It is estimated that only about one-quarter of all Chinese children can pass through this first phase of education due to a lack of pre-schools.

General enrollment in elementary school usually takes place at six or seven years of age. According to offical figures, about 93% of all school-age children attend school — a high percentage in view of the geographic conditions and the isolation of large regions of the country. Instruction at elementary schools lasts five to six years; a compulsory sixth year for all schools is planned. Class time amounts to about 26 hours on five-and-a-half days per week. In addition, there are about 10 hours of extracurricular activities such as sports and productive work. Major subjects are Chinese, math and a foreign language; minor subjects are natural history, music, art, political science and history — in the upper grades also physics, chemistry, biology and geography. The language of instruction is standard Chinese.

Major Agricultural Products

	1949 10,000t	1952 10,000t	1979 10,000t	1981 10,000t	1982 10,000t	1983 10,000t
Grain	11,320.00	16,390.00	33,211.00	32,502.00	35,343.00	38,728.00
Rice	4,865.00	6,845.00	14,375.00	14,396.00	16,124.00	16,887.00
Wheat	1,380.00	1,815.00	6,273.00	5,964.00	6,842.00	8,139.00
Soybeans	510.00	950.00	746.00	933.00	903.00	976.00
Cotton	44.40	130.40	220.70	296.80	359.80	463.70
Oil	256.40	419.30	643.50	1,020.50	1,181.70	1,055.00
Peanut Oil	126.80	231.60	282.20	382.60	391.60	395.10
Vegetable Oil	73.40	93.20	240.20	406.50	565.60	428.70
Sesame Oil	32.60	48.10	41.70	51.00	34.20	34.90
Hemp	3.70	30.60	108.90	126.00	106.00	101.90
Sugar Cane	264.20	711.60	2,150.80	2,966.80	3,688.20	3,114.10
Sugar Beets	19.10	47.90	310.60	636.00	671.20	918.20
Tobacco	4.30	22.20	80.60	127.90	184.80	115.10
Tea	4.10	8.20	27.70	34.30	39.70	40.10

Major Industrial Products

		1949	1952	1957	1977
Coal	mill. t	32.00	66.00	131.00	550.00
Crude Oil	mill. t	0.12	0.44	1.46	93.64
Natural Gas	mill. cbm	7.00	8.00	70.00	12,120.00
Electricity	bill. kwh	4.30	7.30	19.30	223.40
Iron	mill. t	0.25	1.93	5.94	25.05
Steel	mill. t	0.16	1.35	5.35	23.74
Wood	mill. cbm	5.67	11.20	27.87	49.67
Cement	mill. t	0.66	2.86	6.86	55.65
Fertilizer	1000 t	6.00	39.00	151.00	7,238.00
Automobiles	per 1000	–	–	7.90	125.40
Tractors	per 1000	–	–	–	99.30
Televisions	per 1000	–	–	–	284.60
Radios	per 1000	4.40	17.00	352.00	10,494.00
Cameras	per 1000			0.10	246.60
Cotton Material	bill. m	1.89	3.83	5.05	10.15
Sugar	1000 t	199.00	451.00	864.00	1,815.00
Bicycles	per 1000	14.00	80.00	806.00	7,427.00
Sewing Machines	per 1000		66.00	278.00	4,242.00
Wrist Watches	per 1000			0.40	11,043.00
		1978	**1981**	**1982**	**Jan.-Sept. 1984***
Coal	mill. t	618.00	622.00	666.00	561.00
Crude Oil	mill. t	104.05	101.22	102.12	84.59
Natural Gas	mill. cbm	13,730.00	12,740.00	11,930.00	8,993.00
Electricity	bill. kwh	256.60	309.30	327.70	276.70
Iron	mill. t	34.79	34.17	35.51	29.96
Steel	mill. t	31.78	35.60	37.16	32.28
Wood	mill. cbm	51.62	49.42	50.41	–
Cement	mill. t	65.24	82.90	95.20	88.31
Fertilizer	1000 t	8,693.00	12,390.00	12,781.00	11,120.00
Automobiles	per 1000	149.10	176.00	196.00	223.00
Tractors	per 1000	113.50	53.00	40.00	50.00
Televisions	per 1000	517.30	5,394.00	5,920.00	6,926.00
Radios	per 1000	11,677.00	40,570.00	17,240.00	17,879.00
Cameras	per 1000	178.90	623.00	742.00	899.00
Cotton Material	bill. m	11.03	14.27	15.35	10.22
Sugar	1000 t	2,267.00	3,170.00	3,384.00	2,560.00
Bicycles	per 1000	8,540.00	17,450.00	24,200.00	20,784.00
Sewing Machines	per 1000	4,865.00	10,390.00	12,860.00	7,042.00
Wrist Watches	per 1000	13,511.00	28,720.00	33,010.00	26,743.00

*January – September *Daily News Guangming Ribao*, October 22, 1984.

Approximately 88% of all those who have successfully completed elementary school go on to middle school.

Pupils attend general education middle schools for five years, as a rule. These schools are divided into a two to three-year lower level and a two to three-year upper level. There are 28—29 hours of class per week and an additional 10—12 hours of activities such as sports, political instruction and practical work. Major subjects are Chinese, math and a foreign language; minor subjects are physics, chemistry, biology, geography, political science, history, music art and physical education. Middle schools prepare pupils to attend higher schools or to take up a vocation. Successful completion of a middle school education is comparable to a high school diploma and makes the pupil eligible to take the national university entrance exams. Only about 40% make the transition from the lower to the upper middle school level; of these, about 4% attend a university and 10% attend vocational middle schools after graduation.

Eighty-six percent begin working.

Special middle schools: Students attend special courses for two to five years in areas such as engineering, medicine, economics and finance. In order to attend a special middle school, one must have successfully completed a general education middle school and passed an entrance exam.

Technical schools: These schools offer two to three-year courses of study for students training to become skilled workers. These are usually in a factory's own training centers.

Agricultural and vocational middle schools: These schools are open to the graduates of the lower level of middle schools. They mainly teach subjects pertaining to agricultural techniques and technical sciences.

Universities and colleges: Students attain eligibility to study at a university by passing the three-day national entrance exams, which take place once a year during the summer. A further requirement is that the applicant should not be older than 25 and that he is single. Exceptions are made in special cases.

History

Chronological Table of Chinese History

Xia		ca. 2100 — ca. 1600 BC
Shang		ca. 1600 — ca. 1100 BC
Zhou		ca. 1100 — 221 BC
Western Zhou	ca. 1100 — 771 BC	
Eastern Zhou	770 — 221 BC	
Chunqiu, Spring and Autumn Period	770 — 476 BC	
Zhanguo, Period of Warring States	475 — 221 BC	
Qin		221 — 206 BC
Han		206 BC — 220 AD
Western Han	206 BC — 8 AD	
Wang Mang Period	8 — 23	
Eastern Han	25 — 220	
San Guo, Three Kingdoms		220 — 280
Wu	220 — 280	
Shu	220 — 261	
Wei	220 — 265	
Jin		265 — 420
Western Jin	265 — 316	
Eastern Jin	317 — 420	
Sixteen Kingdoms	304 — 439	
Northern and Southern Dynasties		420 — 589
Northern Wei	386 — 534	
Eastern Wei	534 — 550	
Northern Qi	550 — 577	North
Western Wei	535 — 557	
Northern Zhou	557 — 581	
Song	420 — 479	
Qi	479 — 502	
Liang	502 — 557	South
Chen	557 — 589	

Sui		581 —	618
Tang		618 —	907
Wu Dai, Five Dynasties and		907 —	960
Ten Kingdoms		902 —	979
Song		960 —	1279
Northern Song	960 — 1127		
Southern Song	1127 — 1279		
Liao (Khitan)		907 —	1125
Xi Xia, Western Xia		1032 —	1227
Jin		1115 —	1234
Yuan		1271 —	1368
Ming		1368 —	1644
Period of Reign:			
Hongwu	1368 — 1398		
Jianwen	1399 — 1402		
Yongle	1403 — 1424		
Hongxi	1425		
Xuande	1426 — 1435		
Zhengtong	1436 — 1449		
Jingtai	1450 — 1456		
Tianshun	1457 — 1464		
Chenghua	1465 — 1487		
Hongzhi	1488 — 1505		
Zhengde	1506 — 1521		
Jiajing	1522 — 1566		
Longqing	1567 — 1572		
Wanli	1573 — 1620		
Taichang	1620		
Tianqi	1621 — 1627		
Chongzhen	1628 — 1644		
Qing		1644 —	1911
Period of Reign:			
Shunzhi	1644 — 1661		
Kangxi	1662 — 1722		
Yongzheng	1723 — 1735		
Qianlong	1736 — 1795		
Jiaqing	1796 — 1820		
Daoguang	1821 — 1850		
Xianfeng	1851 — 1861		
Tongzhi	1862 — 1874		
Guangxu	1875 — 1908		
Xuantong	1909 — 1911		
Republic of China		1912 —	1949
People's Republic of China		founded: October 1, 1949	

Prehistoric Period

In 1929, excavations southwest of Beijing revealed the remains of pre-historic man (Peking Man = Sinanthropus pekinensis) and his tools. They were estimated at being 400,000—500,000 years old. The remains of even more highly developed beings have been found in many parts of China, for example on the Zhujiang River in Guangdong Province, in the Changjiang Valley in Hubei and on the Huanghe in Shanxi; but little is known about them.

The finds from the early Stone Age are the first to convey more information about the people of that time. Tribal communities settled, lived in villages which were sometimes surrounded by deep trenches and began to cultivate the soil and raise animals. These were matriarchal societies. Land, dwellings and livestock belonged to the whole tribe; all members of the tribe were equal. It was only later, as the development of agriculture and livestock breeding continued, that these communities became patriarchal. Gradually private ownership and social strata evolved. Pottery was invented. First, painted ceramics were found in Henan Province and then delicate, black ceramics in Shandong. After this, the finds became more frequent. They probably originate from the time of the mythical rulers (3rd century BC). Ancient Chinese historians report of them in numerous legends. The first dynasty was the Xia Dynasty which had settled in the fertile valley of the Huanghe. The first lunar calendar was supposedly invented here and was continuously improved later. It is still called the Xia calendar today.

Shang Dynasty ca. 1600—ca. 1100 BC

The first dynasty recorded in written documents and evidenced by excavational finds is the Shang Dynasty. Its sphere of influence at first included only the northern region of today's Henan Province but later expanded to west Shanxi and Shandong, Jiangsu.

The leader was a king who had unlimited rule. He was followed in the social hierarchy by the aristocracy, scribes and clergy, craftsmen, peasants and slaves. An early form of feudalism developed. The Shang rulers frequently waged war on neighboring clans, being superior to them in their possession of bronze weapons and chariots with spiked wheels. Prisoners were taken captive and became slaves or were used for sacrifices to the dead.

Farming, probably done by bonded slaves, was the basis of the state. In the cities, which were surrounded by high clay embankments, the noblemen and craftsmen lived in rectangular houses made of pounded clay. Not only weapons, but also ritual vessels were cast from bronze. Pottery was made from white porcelain; material was woven from hemp and silk.

Belief in gods of nature and ancestral cults played a special role in the lives of the populace. Scribes and priests versed in astronomy performed sacrificial rituals. In Anyang, graves of kings were discovered which contained, in addition to instruments, many beheaded slaves. They were supposed to be of service to the deceased in a later life. Besides this, tens of thousands of oracle bones engraved with characters, oracle questions were found. These bones were placed into a fire and answers to corresponding questions were read from the cracks made by heat. Such oracle texts were also found on tortoise shells.

Zhou Dynasty ca. 1100—221 BC

Around the year 1100 BC, the Zhou clans conquered the Shang. They were nomadic shepherds who came from the area of present-day Shanxi Province. Out of the necessity to administrate the vast regions, a feudal system developed. Individual fiefs were created and conferred upon members of the tribe, clan leaders or loyal noblemen by the king. In return, the feudal estate holders were to support the king in times of war, make payments in the form of natural produce and see to the management of the king's lands.

This system functioned in the first 300 years so well that the Zhou rulers succeeded in expanding their area of influence to the Changjiang. At first the fiefs consisted of large or small rectangularly plotted garrisoned cities surrounded by land, in which the established population continued to live. With time, they developed into inheritable principalities.

The Zhou, as former vassals of the Shang, were acquainted with their culture and adopted it. Also with respect to religion, they oriented themselves to the Shang traditions, but they did add their own celestial religion. The highest god was heaven; the king, as the 'Son of Heaven', was the mediator between heaven, earth and the people. He alone received the heavenly mandate to rule; he alone made the sacrifices. Human sacrifices were forbidden and consultation of the bone oracle abandoned. In that way, the priests of the Shang became superfluous. Due to the fact that they were the only ones who could read and write, many helped the noblemen with the administration of the fiefs or taught etiquette.

The capital of the Zhou was located near what is today known as Xi'an; it was destroyed and the king killed by foreign enemies and dissatisfied fief holders in 771 BC. With this, the Western Zhou period ended. The son of the slain king retreated to the second capital, Luoyang, in present-day Henan Province, but was completely powerless. He, as well as his successor, were only nominal heads of state, holy sovereigns.

The ruling tribes had developed into a feudal noble class which was becoming more and more powerful and whose members continually fought among themselves; the larger tribes overthrew the smaller. Federations temporarily combined to form a 'hegemony', but the fight for predominance continued. Out of the numerous, small semi-states, seven larger kingdoms arose in the 4th century BC. This 'Period of Warring States' continued from 475—221 BC until only one was left — the state of Qin. China derives its name from it.

In spite of continuous wars, the economy,

crafts, trade and an active intellectual life had developed. Land could be sold, iron instruments were made, irrigation systems built, land taxes collected, coined currency and the first laws were introduced. A new class of scholars arose, consisting of landless nobles and officers.

The political and social upheaval generated many schools of thought which advocated different philosophic views and reacted in a variety of different ways to the problems of the time. They are called the 100 schools of philosophy. The most significant included the Daoists, Confucians, Mohists and Legalists (see page 55). Their teachings would influence Chinese thought for millenia.

Qin Dynasty 221—206 BC

The Prince of Qin, thanks to his legalist advisors, controlled the most powerful state; in 221 BC, all other princes had been defeated. He proclaimed himself sovereign under the title of Qin Shihuang (First Emperor of Qin) of the united Chinese Empire which he expanded to south of Canton. Xianyang, near present-day Xi'an, became the capital, and the empire's territory was divided into prefectures which were under the strict central administration of officials who could be replaced at any time. The emperor rendered the nobility powerless and forced them to settle in the capital.

The differing weights and measures of the individual regions as well as the width of the axles of wagons were standardized and an official national currency was issued. The most important innovation, however, was the introduction of a unified form of writing. This made possible a written basis for understanding despite many dialects.

The emperor had wide streets and canals built. High taxes and harsh laws were introduced; peasants were forced to submit a large percentage of their harvests and had to render compulsory labor and military service. Because the northern part of the empire was under constant threat of foreign invasion, the emperor had the existing fortifications and ramparts connected by a wall. A single, 2,500-km-long wall was the result which, however, is not identical to the structure existing today. In addition, he had many palaces and a large mausoleum built for himself.

The trenchant measures taken in all areas evoked vehement criticism. The emperor believed he could protect himself from dissenters — above all, from Confucians — by burning all historical and literary books and by persecution. The entire population suffered under the laws and compulsory duties which became increasingly stricter. Soon rebellion and peasant uprisings followed, which brought about the end of the dynasty in 206 BC.

Han Dynasty 206 BC—220 AD

The victor of the revolt was Liu Bang, son of a peasant, who established the Han Dynasty in 206 BC which continued, with short interruptions, until 220 AD. The capital was Chang'an, today known as Xi'an. In order to strengthen his power, the emperor relaxed the harsh laws and rewarded his fighting companions and members of his clan with feudal estates which, however, were no longer inheritable. So the administrative structure at the beginning of the Han period was based on the prefectural divisions of the Qin and the local feudal estates. Gradually, under Legalist-Confucian influence, an official centralized state was created. Emperor Wudi founded an academy for officials in which Confucian principles were taught.

Since land could be bought, not only the nobility, but also families of merchants and officials owned property which was leased to tenants who were treated like bondsmen. In time, an entirely new upper class developed which endured for many centuries. Property owners who were of the same family or related by marriage formed large clans. They had enough money to finance time-consuming studies and to make it possible for individual family members to take part in the state examination. It was the goal of every clan to have as many relatives as possible in important government positions. Further ways to exercise influence presented themselves in the class of eunuchs who worked in the imperial harem, because they came from social circles that were obligated to the land owners.

The educated upper class cultivated literature, painting and calligraphy. Great new works in philosophy, history and literature were written. The most significant discovery, which took place about 100 BC, was the making of paper from plant fibers. Prior to this, wood, bamboo or silk had been used to write on. Arts and crafts developed further, especially lacquered work and jade cutting, as well as the silk industry. Trade in these products reached as far as the Occident. By way of the Silk Road and harbors in the South, Buddhism reached China in the 1st century. In the 2nd century, the seismograph was invented.

From the evidence found in tombs, conclusions can be drawn about life at that time. The rich families followed an extravagent death cult. Models of houses and towers were found. Scenes from social life are found on frescos, stone engravings and relief tiles.

After the death of the first emperor, his widow became regent for his nephew who had not yet come of age. During this time, the relatives of the empress held all important positions, so that power was in the hands of her family. Such a situation was to be repeated again and again up to the end of imperial times.

The first Han emperors strengthened the empire above all from within and maintained a defensive foreign policy. They made pacts with the 'Huns' who had built an equally strong empire in the North, based on a nomadic existence. The contracts provided for delivery of grain and silk by the Chinese and the discontinuation of raids by the 'Huns'. As the 'Huns' did not need much silk themselves, they sold the material which reached the Roman Empire by way of the Silk Road. Emperor Wudi was the first to change these policies. His troops fought against the 'Huns', conquered the Ordos Basin (the land on the northern Huanghe), large parts of the Tarim Basin in the West, North Korea, southern Manchuria and, in the South, the coastal regions around Canton and what is today North Vietnam.

But the wars were very costly. The emperor attempted to restore the state budget by establishing a state monopoly on iron, salt and coinage and by raising taxes. Again the free peasants were hard hit, because the land-owning families had succeeded in freeing themselves from having to make required crop payments and freeing those who were dependent upon them from state taxes and compulsory service. More and more peasants were forced to sell their land. There were disturbances everywhere, but they were kept under control. Nor could the usurpation of the throne by Wang Mang (8—23), who belonged to the clan of an empress, bring about a change. On the contrary, it caused the end of the Western Han Dynasty, increased chaos and led to a civil war, in the course of which Wang Mang was killed. It was not until the year 25 that a member of the former emperor's house managed to reinstate the Han Dynasty and end the civil war. The new capital was Luoyang, located east of old Chang'an; for this reason the following period is also called the Eastern Han period. After the long civil war, the economy initially prospered. Soon however, troops had to be sent into battle against the 'Huns' and defeated them in numerous campaigns. But the general state of the economy again suffered considerably, and the symptoms of decline increased after 150. Court intrigues, corrupt officials, a centralized government which continued to become weaker, battles for power between the empress's clans and the eunuchs, the concentration of land in the hands of a few rich families and the migration of peasants which reached incomprehensible limits, all led to catastrophe. In 184, the whole empire was caught up in a rebellion, that of the 'Yellow Turbans', caused by sectarianism. This uprising could probably have been put down, but the government was helpless and the generals fought among themselves for power. In 220, the emperor was forced to abdicate, and the three most powerful generals divided up the empire.

Three Kingdoms 220—280

During the next 360 years, an uninterrupted struggle for power took place among individual great families who were striving to unite the empire. The most powerful commander-in-chief, Cao Cao (155—220), founded the Wei Empire. After his death, his son proclaimed himself emperor in 221; his capital was Luoyang. The other two generals also immediately declared themselves emperors; one established the Shu Han Dynasty in the Southwest, in present-day Sichuan Province, with its capital in Chengdu, and the other — the Wu Dynasty — in the Southeast; its capital was what is today known as Nanjing.

The Wu Empire was sparsely populated. Very different climatic and soil conditions prevailed in this area. Native tribes cultivated primarily rice. The peasants who emigrated from the North, where wheat and millet were the main crops, were forced to adapt to these new conditions. There was only a very small upper class of Han Chinese. State revenues came mainly from trade; in order to expand this trade, new roads and ships were built.

In Shu Han, the silk industry, especially the production of brocade, was progressively flourishing. The main disadvantage of this empire, also, was its small population. In the long run, it was unable to offer resistance to the troops of Wei.

The Wei Empire was in possession of the fertile regions in the North but had lost a large percentage of the peasant population due to the chaotic conditions of the past centuries. Most of the peasants had abandoned their lands and become wandering vagabonds. The new emperor attempted to get them settled again. He expanded the peasant defense colonies which his father had created. Great armies were maintained to fight against the South. But it was mainly domestic problems that remained unsolved. The new ruling house did not have the means to triumph over the remaining powerful families. In 265, a member of the most influential clan succeeded in forcing the emperor to abdicate and established his own dynasty. He called it Jin.

Jin Dynasty 265—420

This dynasty was of short duration. The emperor had attained control with the help of his family, and so he had to show his gratitude. Again feudal estates were distributed which existed alongside the prefectures and districts. The new princes were allowed to have armies and appoint officials. In 280, the Jin conquered the Wu Empire and unified the whole country under a single government. After the death of the first emperor, a violent struggle for power broke out among the princes. Raids by various nomadic tribes from the North and Northwest which had grown stronger, made for further catastrophes. In 311, the capital Luoyang and in 316, the capital Chang'an fell into the hands of the 'barbarians'. The emperor was forced to surrender. That was the end of the Western Jin Dynasty. Many noblemen, officials and large estate owners fled to the South and supported a member of the Jin family in establishing the Eastern Jin Dynasty in 317. Nanjing was the new capital. This state existed until 420.

The Sixteen Kingdoms 304—439 and the Northern and Southern Dynasties 420—589

In North China, rulers continued to come from one nomadic tribe and then another for a period of 130 years. The 'Hun' Han Dynasty, as it was called in reference to former relations at the beginning of the Han period, initially governed the Northwest. The ruler, as emperor of China, wanted to pattern his court on that of the Han Chinese. In the Northeast, another Hun leader, a former slave who followed nomadic tradition, had seized power. In 329, he annexed the Northwest and governed the entire North, with the exception of the present-day province of Gansu. His dynasty was called the Zhao Dynasty (329—352). Today's Gansu Province was still ruled by a Chinese governor from the old Jin Dynasty. He founded the Liang Dynasty which lasted until 376. Many Chinese from the North had fled here. Trade

with Turkestan flourished. The merchants brought many Buddhist monks with them, who established monasteries in trading settlements. In the 4th century, which brought foreign rule, a period of migration and misery to the North, Buddhism spread, especially among the poor of the population. Many found refuge in the monasteries. The ruling houses also supported the new religion. With Buddhism, a new direction in the arts emerged. Cave temples and rock monasteries were built, decorated with murals, reliefs and statues which initially were reminiscent of their Indian and Central Asian origins and later exhibited their own Chinese style. The most famous cave temples are located at Yungang near Datong in Shanxi Province, at Longmen near Luoyang in Henan Province and in Dunhuang in present-day Gansu. They have been preserved and can be visited.

In 351, the leaders of the Tibetans founded the Qin Dynasty (351—394) and subjugated the proto-mongolian tribes which had meanwhile taken the place of the 'Huns' and brought the Liang Dynasty under their power. They now ruled the entire North. But, in order to control all of China, they had to conquer the South. The attempt failed in 383. Not long after, this empire also collapsed and was broken up into many small parts. The warlords formed new states, and the period of the Sixteen Kingdoms followed. In all of these states, a small upper class reigned, which was not supported by the people and which for the most part relied solely on its military power.

The numerous small kingdoms soon succumbed to a wave of raids by the nomads. The Toba, members of Turkish and Mongolian tribes, invaded from Inner Mongolia. They established the Northern Wei Dynasty in 386 and maintained their rule until 550. By 439 they already controlled the entire Huanghe Valley. The emperor adopted the governmental system of the Han and surrounded himself with Han Chinese officials. He instructed the Toba nobility to assume Chinese family names, to marry Han Chinese, to wear Chinese clothing and to speak their language. In the meanwhile, the other foreigners who had entered the country as nomads, had settled. They were all integrated into the Chinese culture in the course of generations.

Soon the Han Chinese had taken over the whole administration. New conflicts broke out among the sinicized aristocracy, the poor nomadic tribes and the exploited peasantry. Rebellions were put down, but the disintegration of the Northern Wei rule could not be hindered. Several short-lived dynasties followed, until a Chinese general succeeded in seizing power in 581 and founded the Sui Dynasty.

After the end of the Jin Dynasty in the South in 420, four other dynasties followed. One general contested another's throne. Battles between cliques of noble families were characteristic of this period. The gap between rich and poor widened. Cultural and intellectual life, which was promoted by the court and the rich, flourished. Confucianism suffered a severe setback, to the benefit of Buddhism and Daoism.

Sui Dynasty 581—618

The founder of the Sui Dynasty was a Chinese military leader, an aristocrat who came from the Northwest. He declared himself emperor in 581 and moved his capital to Chang'an. In only a few years, he succeeded in uniting the empire after 360 years of dissension. He created a new central government, ordered the distribution of abandoned lands among the peasants, levied taxes and had granaries for hard times built. His son began gigantic construction projects, for example, the famous Anji Bridge in Hebei Province, the oldest masonry arch bridge in the world which has weathered all natural catastrophes and is still in use today. Luoyang was restored and made the new capital. In the South, in present-day Yangzhou, another capital was built. His main achievement, however, was the construction of the Grand Canal, connecting the Haihe, Huanghe, Huaihe and Changjiang rivers. This made possible an active exchange of goods between the North and the South; it was mainly used for the transportation of grain.

The foreign policy of both emperors was also successful. The North was fortified against invasion, and North Tibet was annexed to the empire. An expeditionary army advanced as far as South Vietnam, but failed to conquer Korea. This marked the end of the dynasty. The wars, the great construction projects and the pomp and wastefulness of the last emperor had emptied the treasury. The people rebelled against the forced labor and military draft; riots broke out which the nobility also joined. The emperor was forced to flee to the South and was killed in 618.

Tang Dynasty 618—907

A Sui general, an aristocrat from North China who had participated in the peasant uprisings, declared himself emperor of the Tang Dynasty in 618. Not many years later, his son, Taizong, one of the more prominent Chinese ruling figures, succeeded him on the throne. In a very short time, they succeeded in restoring peace and order. Under their rule, the empire experienced a display of power and expansion it had never before known. Within only a few centuries, they subjugated the Turk peoples and established military protectorates in the Tarim Basin and in what is today Vietnam, occupied Afghanistan and brought Tibet and Korea under Chinese sovereignty.

The reforms introduced by the Sui were perfected and a new land distribution law initially helped the peasants. Production of grain and silk increased; the government warehouses were again replenished. Lease payments in the form of grain, silk and compulsory labor were made to the state. Villeinage could, however, be compensated by payment of certain amounts of cotton or silk material. The nobility, public officials, large estate owners and monasteries were exempt from these services. In the 8th century, the estates had prospered to such an extent — at the expense of the peasants — that the government had to introduce a new taxation system.

There were also innovations in administration. In lieu of the examination system for public officials which had originated in the Han period, a new system was introduced which remained valid until the beginning of the 20th century.

Up until now, the military had been under the control of provincial civilian administration; this changed in the 8th century. The commanding officers of military districts established on the borders, governor general — ships and general protectorates were put under the jurisdiction of public officials and the financial administration of their own districts. This increased the effectiveness of the army, which was converted to a professional army in 722, and at the same time gave the governors enormous power and the chance to dictate their own policy. These innovations also reached the innermost provinces of the empire and became the seed of the downfall of the dynasty.

The capital of the Tang Empire was Chang'an, at the gateway to the Silk Road. The city developed into an international metropolis whose population in the 8th century was over one million. Merchants who came with their caravans from West and Central Asia met here. Chang'an was also connected to the coastal regions in the South by waterways. The city was full of workshops and stores.

Foreigners established their own trading houses and lived in colonies. They not only lived in the capital, but also in other important trading centers. They brought various religions with them to China which were allowed to spread without hindrance.

The basis of all trade relations was the tribute system. Because the emperor, as the Son of Heaven, did not recognize any other ruler, each city that wished to enter into trade relations with China had to send an envoy to the court. They brought with them not only products of their countries, but also had to recognize Chinese sovereignty in writing. In return, they received gifts from the emperor amounting to the equivalent of their products. It was not until modern times that this system collapsed.

Not only merchants came to Chang'an, students from Korea, Japan, Persia and Arabia also came to the city to study astronomy, philosophy, medicine, history, politics, literature and art. The Chinese profited through contact to foreign peoples. In this way they learned how to produce sugar from sugarcane and how to press grapes. Persians and Arabs brought new fruits and plants with them to China.

Craftsmanship developed further. Chengdu in Sichuan and Yangzhou in Jiangsu were famous for their delicately-patterned silk and brocade material. Also the production of porcelain had made great progress. White ceramics with green, yellow or white glaze evolved out of the proto-porcelain of the Han period. The production of paper expanded as a result of new manufacturing methods.

During the reign of Taizong's successor, a woman reached a position of great power. After his death, under the name of Wu Zetian, she ruled for 20 years as the first and only empress of China. Not until after her death could the sovereignty of the Tang be reinstated.

Soon, under Emperor Xuanzong who was an appreciator of art and ruled for 40 years, the second blossoming of the Tang Dynasty began. It was the Golden Age of Chinese poetry and painting. Thousands of poems were composed according to certain rules. Tang poets like Li Bai, Du Fu and Bai Juyi became world-renowned. Also the murals of this time in temples and grottos are famous (see Dunhuang, page 394). The works of prominent portrait and landscape painters are still considered to be unique.

Buddhism had reached all social classes. There were innumerable monasteries and temples in the cities as well as in the countryside. Because the monasteries which were located at trading centers also served the merchants as banks, their economic power grew with the increase in foreign trade. They bought more and more land which was not subject to taxation. The metal from coins was used to make heavy Buddha figurines; the clergy neither had to pay taxes nor render service. They not only functioned as healers and fortune-tellers, but were also poets, calligraphers, painters or translators of countless texts.

An important invention of this time was printing. The oldest printed book in the world still in existence dates from the year 868.

In the years from 842—845, the emperor issued laws which forbade all foreign religions and confiscated their property. Buddhism was also affected by this, although it had meanwhile developed into a popular religion. The main reason for these measures was certainly more the necessity of procuring money and fear of an increase in power of the Buddhist monasteries than any religious hostility. Thousands of Buddhist monasteries and temples were secularized and many destroyed. The lands belonging to them were seized and monks and nuns were defrocked. Although Buddhism continued to be practiced by the people, it never quite recovered from this enormous setback.

The downfall of the dynasty began under the reign of Xuanzong, due to internal and foreign policy difficulties such as the rebellion of a military governor who wanted to usurp power in 755. A civil war caused the population great misery and could only be quelled by government troops with the help of outside forces.

The central government did attempt to stabilize the treasury and power with the help of reforms, a new system of taxation and the creation of a monopoly on salt, alcohol and tea, but the powerful governors were not totally loyal and only delivered part of their taxes. For this reason, the imperial court was not successful in consolidating its power again. Disputes between the various factions of officials and eunuchs made matters worse. The result was a destitute population and peasant uprisings and revolts which lasted for decades and brought about the collapse of the dynasty in 907.

Wu Dai, Five Dynasties 907—960 and Ten Kingdoms 902—979

Within the next 50 years, the empire was again divided into many parts. In the South, 10 independent kingdoms evolved from the former military districts. Here, unlike in the North, it was relatively peaceful and the area could develop culturally and economically. Besides the silk trade, the monopolized trading of tea, salt and porcelain expanded. The first light-colored porcelain was produced; many processes were involved in its manufacture, and it therefore had to be made in large-scale concerns.

Printing was also improved. A special innovation which served to further trade was the deposit receipt which came into use, the forerunner of paper money. For the deposit of copper money, certificates were issued which had the same cash value.

In the North, one warlord after another established short-lived dynasties. At the same time, non-Chinese dynasties were expanding in the North and Northwest, for example the Kingdom of Liao of the Khitan, a nomadic people from present-day Inner Mongolia, which lasted 200 years.

Song Dynasty 960—1279

In 960, for the first time, a general was elected by his officers to become emperor. He named his dynasty Song. While he was conquering one southern state after another during the next 20 years, thus uniting the empire on a smaller scale, the North remained in the hands of foreigners to whom tribute had to be paid in order to keep peace. In view of the reasons behind the fall of the Tang Dynasty, the new emperor completely reorganized the administration. Civil servants replaced military commanders and were placed under the authority of the central administration, thus creating a bureaucracy. The only ones to reach a position of power were those who had passed strict examinations based on Confucian classics.

State expenditures increased in the 11th century with the growth of the army, so that tax revenues were no longer sufficient. Those who had money bought land which was leased to tenants who had to pay rent totalling 40—50% of the harvest. It was a time in which the highest percentage of land was in the hands of a small class of people. There were property taxes, but one knew how to get around them. Property owned by officials was exempt from the most important taxes, and so the main burden of taxation was on the shoulders of the free peasants. If they were not able to pay, they were forced to turn their lands over to a large estate owner and work the land as a tenant, or they moved to another district and

disappeared. This led time and again to rebellion. Under Wang Anshi (1021—1086), reforms for the improvement of agriculture which were to the benefit of the small landholders but directed against monopolies, were boycotted by high officials, large estate owners and merchants with large businesses.

At the same time, the country was flourishing culturally. Confucian teachings were reinterpreted by influential philosophers like Zhu Xi and dogmatized; today this is known as Neo-Confucianism. Another innovation of the Song era was colloquial literature. Painting from this time is also of great significance. Besides other painting schools, there was also a painting academy at the imperial court which devoted itself to genre painting. Typical ceramics of the Song period called celadon, made from stoneware with a green glaze, are also famous. Toward the end of the Song era, the first blue and white porcelain was made.

In 1115, a vassal people of the Khitan, the Nüzhen, ancestors of the later Manchus, founded the Kingdom of Jin. As early as 1125, they had beaten the Khitan and pressed forward to the south. In 1127, they captured the Song capital, Kaifeng, thus bringing an end to the Northern Song Dynasty.

One of the emperor's brothers fled with several ministers to Nanjing and founded the Southern Song Dynasty there. Hangzhou was the capital from 1127—1279. The Jin stormed further toward the south, but Chinese troops were always able to stop them. Isolated battles were won by one side or the other. The emperor bought peace with the Jin by paying annual tribute. In spite of this, border incidents occurred again and again.

The south developed further economically. The planting and manufacturing of cotton increased, paper money became more widely used, shipbuilding and trade flourished in the southern ports. With the help of the compass, foreign trade continually advanced.

Meanwhile, in the North, the Mongols had invaded. The Jin were conquered by them in 1234 and, in 1279, so were the troops of the Southern Song. All of China was now under Mongolian rule.

Yuan Dynasty 1271—1368

In 1206, Genghis Khan was elected regent by the tribal leaders of Mongolian and Turkish sheepherding nomads. To expand his territory, he attacked neighboring states. He and his successors triumphed over the Jin. In 1260, his grandson Kublai Khan made present-day

Beijing his capital and, in 1271, founded the Yuan Dynasty. After long struggles, he defeated the last of the Southern Song troops in 1279. China was now an empire that stretched from Russia to Manchuria. Further campaigns against Japan and Indochina, extending as far as Java, followed with varying success, during which large parts of Southeast Asia came under Mongolian influence.

The administration of a civilized state like China at first presented difficulties to the Mongols. At the beginning, the Mongolian nobility wanted to turn the northern Chinese farm country into grazing land. But they tackled the problems and organized a new civil administration. The official languages were Mongolian and Chinese. The highest governmental positions were held by Mongols, aided by foreigners including Turks, Uighurs and Persians; among them were often merchants who were in the service of the state as well. The most famous foreigner at the imperial court was the son of a Venetian merchant, Marco Polo (1254—1324), who was in the service of Kublai Khan for 17 years. Foreigners were chiefly in control of finance. The Northern, but especially the Southern Chinese had what amounted to no rights at all. The rich landowners in the South were allowed to hold onto their lands, but lost all their positions and with them, their political influence. Foreign merchants had various privileges. They did not need to pay taxes and were allowed to use the trade roads which had been built and were equipped with mail stations. Most of the wealth they acquired was taken with them when they went back home. Domestic trade was the only option left to the Chinese merchants.

The new capital, today's Beijing, grew. Not only the emperor lived here with his court, but also many state officials and foreigners. Kublai had magnificent palaces erected. Poor peasants, forced laborers, did the building. In order to feed these people, the transportation system had to be improved, because most of the grain — chiefly rice — came from the South. Rivers and canals had to be built or regulated, coastal shipping and roads had to be improved. These extensive projects had a favorable effect on the economy of the united empire. The Mongols were tolerant of the different religions; they were very religious themselves. The court supported Lamaism, the Tibetan form of Buddhism. Still, other world religions made their way to China. At the beginning of the 14th century, the Pope sent Franciscan missionaries to Asia.

In the area of culture, musical dramas written in colloquial language were popular. The Tibetan pagoda, the dagoba, entered the architectural scene. In northern China, the art of hooking rugs was introduced.

In the long run, the Mongols and their foreign advisors were not in a position to govern this highly civilized agrarian state. The country was reduced to poverty. The result was a succession of hunger revolts that began in 1325 and did not seem as if they would ever end. At first they were directed at all rich people, later, at the Mongols in particular. Zhu Yuanzhang, a mendicant friar who came from an impoverished small peasant family, became the leader of the revolt movement in the years after 1350. He conquered Nanjing and the Southeast. The intellectuals and richer classes joined him. The goal of the rebellion was to expel the Mongols. In 1368, Beijing came under his control; the emperor fled to the steppe with his confidants.

Ming Dynasty 1368—1644

After conquering Beijing in 1368, Zhu Yuanzhang founded the Ming Dynasty and made Nanjing the capital. With a strict hand, he brought order to the central administration and placed the most important ministries under his personal control. In this way he achieved the most all-encompassing power that an emperor had ever had. Grand secretaries were his advisors. The training of officials was again based on Confucian teachings. But soon the eunuchs came into positions of increasing power and the rivalry with officials was rekindled. Beijing again became the capital under Zhu Yuanzhang's successors.

Laws were passed regarding a new distribution of property, and devastated areas in the North were resettled. Foreigners who resided in China had to adopt Chinese names and were only allowed to marry Chinese.

The Mongols were expelled but continued to attack intermittantly. Neither could they be defeated nor could the Chinese gain land. For this reason the attempt was made to protect the whole northern border militarily. In 1449, the Mongols invaded the country as far as Beijing. They were driven back, and the government — as a precautionary measure — had the Great Wall extended in the North. It is still in existence today. Nor was it peaceful in the South and the East. Japanese pirates frequently attacked the coastal provinces.

In order to supply the armies, military colonies — patterned on former ones — were created. But, contrary to plans, they were not self-sufficient, and so grain had to be supplied from the main farming areas in central China. Thanks to innovations (chiefly the use of a new type of rice which ripened in 60 days and could therefore be harvested twice a year), agriculture had progressed. Besides this, wheat and barley were also grown in rice-producing areas. In order to ensure an uninterrupted supply for the soldiers, the government had the grain transported by traders who received salt certificates for their work. They sold this salt with such large profits that their wealth increased immensely. When the government began paying for the grain delivery in currency, the merchants were no longer interested. Trade at this time experienced considerable prosperity. The planting of cotton was expanded, fabrics were already being produced in small factories — Shanghai was the center of this — and large porcelain manufacturing businesses evolved. Blue and white porcelain became increasingly popular.

The printing and selling of books flourished anew. The new readers, who were no longer exclusively learned officials, wanted another kind of reading matter. Novels and short stories were printed in the popular language. At the same time, censorship was introduced. Plays and the theater developed further.

In 1406, the emperor sent troops to Annam and Indochina to make the regions formerly under Mongolian influence dependent on the Ming. He also built up a fleet which advanced as far as the Persian coast and the Red Sea by way of the South Seas and Indochina. Its main purpose was to strengthen trading contacts. These voyages were soon brought to a halt because they were too costly. In 1517, the Portuguese first landed near Canton; the Spanish, Dutch and English followed.

Mutual trade relations proved, in the long run, to be quite unsatisfactory, because they were based on the tribute system which the Europeans rejected. In 1582, a Christian mission was started anew by the Jesuit Matteo Ricci. He was an astronomer and in this capacity attained entrance to the imperial court. Missionary activities were comparatively unimpressive.

Again rebellions and peasant revolts brought about the end of a dynasty. The struggles between officials and eunuchs came to a head, and there were also conflicts within the ranks of the officials; this led to mismanagement and rebellion. In addition to this, the empire had acquired an outside enemy. In Manchuria, where descendants of the Tungusic tribes lived and Mongols who had been driven out of China had settled, these tribes joined together and became very powerful. They took advantage of the chaos in the empire, occupied Beijing and, after only a few years, ruled the whole country.

Qing Dynasty 1644—1911

Manchuria was mainly populated by Tungusic tribes, Mongols and Chinese and was under Chinese military administration. After the peoples of Manchuria had united under the leadership of a strong tribal prince, who proclaimed himself Khan in 1616 and began to expand his sphere of influence, the Mongols soon joined him. His successor intervened in the rebellions in the Chinese empire and founded the Qing Dynasty in Beijing in 1644. The last Ming emperor had hanged himself, but the great rebel generals fought on, chiefly in southern China. None of them was in a position to establish a new government. There was no support from the upper class. The intellectuals had lost confidence and saw no alternative; many committed suicide during this time. The attempt by several princes of the Ming imperial house, together with loyal officials, to found a Southern Ming dynasty patterned on the Song Dynasty failed. Due to the fact that the Manchus did not disturb the property of the upper classes, a large proportion of them gradually went over to the side of the conquerors. But it took them almost four decades before the Manchus dominated the entire empire.

The administration was Manchu/Chinese, i.e. the most important offices were held by both a Manchu and a Chinese official, whereby the Chinese, unlike his counterpart, had to take the difficult state examinations. Like the Mongols, the Manchus also considered theirs a master race. The first laws were very degrading for the Chinese people because, under penalty of death, they were all forced to wear pigtails as a sign of subjugation. Marriages between Chinese and Manchus were forbidden.

The country began to flourish anew under the first Qing emperors. They were open-minded and put the economy and finances in order, regulated canals and rivers, repaired their dams and, in so doing, prevented great floods in the 17th and 18th centuries which previously had cost innumerable lives. The emperors recruited Chinese intellectuals to their courts, had great encyclopedias written and promoted literature and the arts. The Chinese language came increasingly into the foreground at the court, while Manchurian was almost forgotten by the end of the dynasty.

The emperor displayed generosity toward the missionaries, especially toward the Jesuits. They were allowed to work as scholars at the court and distinguished themselves in the areas of astronomy and calendrical science, which had always been important to the emperors. The enthusiastic reports sent by the foreigners to their own countries did not fail to influence the European arts in the Age of Enlightenment (Voltaire, Leibniz). Like their predecessors, they endeavored to spread Christianity by adapting to the Chinese way of life.

From the time the last rebels on Taiwan had to admit defeat in 1683, fighting took place only on the periphery of the empire. The Western Mongols rebelled, but they were defeated in 1697 by imperial troops. In 1724, Tibet was annexed to China and from 1757—59 East Turkestan. In addition, Korea, Indochina and Nepal were under Chinese sovereignty, so that by the end of the 18th century, China dominated all of Central and East Asia. At the same time, the Russians expanded their territory into Siberia.

Border conflicts with the Russian colonizers on the Amur were settled by a treaty in 1689 — the first one ever contracted with a European state. Two Jesuits served as interpreters for the Chinese. Internal peace and economic recovery which lasted into the middle of the 18th century, led to an enormous increase in population. Soon the country was unable to feed so many people. Cultivatable land was limited and the development of industry, to which the peasant population could have turned, was prevented by the upper class, on which the laboring class had always been dependent. The country began to become impoverished; money was increasingly concentrated in the hands of the merchants. Existing capital was invested in property. The downfall of the dynasty began to occur as early as the end of the 18th century. Unrest and rebellion broke out among the rural populations of different provinces as a consequence of the poor economic situation.

Overseas trade played only a minor role at that time. From 1685 on, it was permitted in several ports on the southeast coast and a maritime customs house was established in Canton. From 1760 on, business could only be conducted with a small group of concessioned merchants there. The English soon became the leading foreign business partners.

The Chinese sold mainly tea and silk, but did not know what to make of the European products. In order to increase their export and to achieve an active balance of trade, the English began trading with opium, which they could procure cheaply from India. This trade developed to such an extent that the Chinese government prohibited it. The result was that it was smuggled in ever-increasing amounts. In 1839, the government sent a high official to Canton who had the English stock of opium destroyed. The conflict intensified and led to the Opium War in 1840, in which European weapons proved to be superior. During the Peace of Nanjing, the first of the so-called Unequal Treaties was signed. In 1842, China, among other things, had to open five ports to western trade and pay reparations. In an additional contract, the most-favored-nation clause was drawn up which proved to be quite awkward for China. The clause states that all rights granted by China to other countries are automatically granted to England. The first exterritorial rights had to be acknowledged. After 1854, the maritime customs administration was in the hands of foreigners; the inspectors were, however, officially responsible to the Chinese government.

The traditional-thinking Chinese did not yet perceive what the consequences of these forced concessions would be. For them, trade was part of the tribute system to which foreign merchants had been subject for a thousand years. They considered the English to be barbarians who wanted to conquer the Chinese market by force. The western powers were not willing to adapt to the Chinese system nor to allow the Chinese emperor to decide whether trade was to be conducted or not. They were even less willing to accept his authority as the 'Son of Heaven'. They recognized and took advantage of China's military and domestic weakness and extorted rights for themselves which they otherwise would not have obtained. Minor inducement gave rise to armed conflict.

As early as the Taiping Rebellion, in 1856, war broke out against English and French contingents, who advanced to Beijing in 1860 and plundered and laid waste to the Imperial Summer Palace. After this, new concessions were demanded, such as the opening of other ports for trade, the establishment of diplomatic representation in Beijing, the concession of exterritorial rights and consular jurisdiction, free use of Chinese rivers for shipping, limitation of customs authority, permission to establish concessions, settlements and leased areas under foreign administration. The most-favored-nation clause became valid again. The opium trade also had to be permitted once more. The USA and Russia also received similar concessions.

Until now, trading interests had been in the foreground; these contracts were the first step toward creating semi-colonial conditions for parts of the country. Foreign merchants established themselves in the concessions and settlements of treaty ports, appeared for the most part to be arrogant and presumptuous, and their relations with the appropriate merchants and Chinese offices did not go beyond business matters. Otherwise they lived in complete isolation and were avoided and scorned by the inhabitants. On the other hand, there were constantly new conflicts and outbreaks of violence with the missionaries who, on the basis of treaties, were active in the entire country. In contrast to their Jesuit predecessors, they practiced their profession under the protection of their respective governments and did not need to adapt to Chinese conditions. Nor were they considerate of traditional customs in spreading the teachings of Christianity. Most of the converts came from the ranks of the poor, often only to get a bowl of rice, or were criminals who fled to the protection of the mission houses in order to evade the authorities. It was not until the turn of the century, when the missionaries began building more and more hospitals and schools which were also open to the non-baptized population, that their reputation gradually improved.

The riots which began at the end of the 18th century continued and were intensified by the decline of the economy and the currency. Religious sects and secret societies registered a great influx of members. In 1850, the situation came to a head. The Taiping Rebellion, a civil war which began in Guangxi Province and spread rapidly into central China, almost toppled the dynasty. Government troops were incapable of quelling the rebellion. It was the Chinese governors who took the initiative and, with the support of the upper class, formed a militia. With the help of European mercenaries, they succeeded in defeating the Taiping. It was convenient for the Western powers, who had just ended the second Opium War, to have the weak Qing government continue because they could force the most concessions from them. In 1864, Nanjing, the headquarters of the Taiping, fell. At the same time, there were violent rebellions in other provinces, among them the Muslim rebellions in Gansu, Shaanxi, Yunnan and Turkestan. The results of these riots were devastating. They not only took the lives of millions of people, but also caused heavy destruction. In almost half of the empire, agriculture had to be built up again from scratch.

Strengthened by the victory over the rebels, Chinese politicians began to undertake innovations, chiefly the modernization of the armed forces. Their efforts failed due to the orthodox system. The conservative court, above all the emperor's widow, rejected reforms. The Empress Dowager Cixi, who was appointed regent for a child emperor, had succeeded in creating her own sphere of influence by means of intrigue and retained it for almost 50 years.

China hardly had time to catch its breath, because the Western powers continued to advance. The Chinese protectorate of Vietnam fell to the French and Burma to the English; with the surrender of some Manchurian areas Russia obtained Vladivostok. Portugal got Macao, Germany got Jiaozhou along with Qingdao, Russia obtained Lüshun (Port Arthur) and Dalian, France got the Bay of Guangzhou, and England occupied or leased the area of Weihaiwei. In addition, these countries were promised their own spheres of influence. Also, Japan began to expand its territories. First the Ryukyu Islands were annexed; then the Japanese invasion of Korea caused a war in 1894—1895 in which China was badly defeated and had to relinquish Taiwan and recognize the independence of Korea as a result. Japan was victorious over Russia in the war for Manchuria in 1904/05, took Dalian with Lüshun and fortified its territories in southern Manchuria.

In this time of degradation and political weakness, many learned officials were in favor of profound reforms. Winning the young emperor's ears, the champion of a radical line, Kang Youwei, passed laws to introduce fundamental reforms in 1898, that provoked resistance from conservatives. The Empress Dowager reacted immediately, had the emperor imprisoned, banned him to his palace until death and took over the reins. Reformers who were not able to flee were executed.

As soon as 1900, there were renewed riots in North China. Droughts, flooding, economic distress and hatred of foreigners, especially the missionaries, led to the Boxer Rebellion, which initially was directed at the Manchus, but cleverly manipulated by the government to include foreigners. When the Boxers laid siege to the European legation quarters, the Western powers, upon whom the Chinese had declared war, sent an international army to free them. In the 'Boxer-Protocol' new concessions and high reparations were demanded.

The situation worsened steadily, so that even conservative court circles could no longer refuse to have anything to do with the reforms, the most important of which was the abolishment of the traditional examination system.

They were, however, too late to save the dynasty. The end was in sight.

The South had taken a very different path of development than the North in the previous decades. People were more open-minded, European ideas had entered through the treaty ports and, due to the trade with foreigners, a new middle class — the rich merchants — had formed. Their sons went abroad to study, most to Japan. It was here that young intellectuals founded the first revolutionary organizations which united to form a revolutionary alliance, electing Sun Yatsen, a young overseas Chinese doctor, to be their leader. The first attempts at a putsch were unsuccessful.

The most powerful man at this time was Yuan Shikai, who had the only modernly trained army at his disposal. In 1911, the central government wanted to put the railroad under state control and met with violent resistance. There were riots, a military putsch in Wuchang, and most provincial governors broke with Beijing. At the end of the year, Sun Yatsen was elected Provisional President of the Republic in Nanjing. He offered the presidency to the more powerful Yuan Shikai under the condition that he defended the Republic. Yuan Shikai accepted the offer, succeeded in persuading the Manchus to abdicate — after the Empress Dowager's death, there had been another child emperor — and in February of 1912, he became the first President of the Republic of China.

Republican Period 1912-1949

China, now a republic, was the scene of internal conflict; political and economic difficulties increased. In order to exist, new loans from foreign countries were continually needed which, on the other hand, meant making renewed concessions. Individual provinces became independent, and the goal of the new president, Yuan Shikai, was not the development of the Republic, but the founding of his own dynasty. Within a short period of time, he had attained dictatorial competencies, dissolved the parliament and was persecuting his political opponents. In 1913, Sun Yatsen fled to Japan. Yuan Shikai declared himself emperor in 1915. But such resistance was raised in China and abroad that he abolished the monarchy before his enthronment. He died in 1916.

After Yuan Shikai's death, the central government became less and less important. The period of fighting 'warlords' began; they also dominated the civil administration of their provinces, were partly supported by foreign

powers and had money and armies at their disposal. Durring the years from 1911—1927, in which they played a political role, chaotic conditions greatly increased. Inflation, corruption, plundering and looting were the characteristics of this time.

Foreign policy was just as bleak. Right after the downfall of the Manchus, Tibet came under English control and Outer Mongolia under Russian. After the start of World War I in Europe, Japan decided it was time to realize its imperialist plans and exercised increasing influence in Manchuria; the areas leased by the Germans, including Qingdao, were occupied. The Chinese government received 21 demands which would have made a Japanese protectorate out of China. Despite the inhabitants' great protests, part of the demands were met. Under pressure from the USA and Japan, China had to declare war on Germany in 1917; the country expected to win back the former German areas, but was disappointed by the Western powers because the Treaty of Versailles promised them to the Japanese.

This instigated a demonstration by thousands of students on May 4, 1919, on Tiananmen Square in Beijing, which caused a wave of protest in the whole population. In other cities, too, there were month-long protest marches, strikes and boycotts of Japanese goods. A strong national consciousness developed in all social classes, especially within the intellectual class, as a result of the pressure created by these events. China did not sign the Treaty of Versailles. It was not until the Washington Conference that Japan was forced to return Shandong Province in 1922. These were the years of violent revolution in all areas of intellectual life, summarily called the 'May 4th Movement'. The new intellectuals, most of whom had studied abroad, declared war on Confucianism and old traditions. The West became the model for all intellectual directions.

Beijing University had developed into the intellectual center of these new ideas. This was where Professors Chen Duxiu, editor of the magazine 'New Youth', and Li Dazhao, head of the university library, were engaged in Marxism-Leninism studies. In 1918, Li Dazhao founded the 'Society for the Study of Marxism' whose membership included students and several professors. Among them was a young library employee, Mao Zedong. Out of this Society, the Chinese Communist Party evolved in 1921. It was founded in Shanghai and its First Chairman was Chen Duxiu. Simultaneously, outside of China, Communist student groups were forming, i.e.

in Paris, under Zhou Enlai and in Germany, under Zhu De's leadership. The Soviet government acquired particular respect when it declined the privileges it had been allowed after World War I. Special treaties were made with Germany and Austria in 1920, in which both countries waived all special privileges.

After Yuan Shikai's death, Sun Yatsen returned to Shanghai. Due to the fact that his efforts to create a revolutionary government in Canton had failed and that he received no support from the USA, he was compelled to rely on the help of the Soviet Union. In 1923, political and military advisors came to Canton and reorganized the National People's Party (Kuomindang) which had evolved out of the revolutionary alliance of 1911, on the Soviet pattern. In addition, they aided China in establishing a military academy near Canton, later commanded by Chiang Kaishek.

Sun Yatsen laid down the 'Three Principles of the People' in his political platform: 1) nationalism, that is, national unity and independence, 2) democracy, the right of the people to elect their own government, and 3) social justice, the teachings of people's welfare and fair distribution of property. The realization of this platform was to take place in three stages: military government, provisional government under the political leadership of the National People's Party, legally elected government. The National People's Party, Guomindang, and the Communist Party, Gongchandang, formed an alliance which endured from 1923—1927. Sun Yatsen died in 1925, and conflicts arose between the different wings within the Party, which continued during the following campaign.

In the meantime, Chiang Kaishek had become increasingly influential. In 1926 he was given the job of undertaking a campaign into the North in cooperation with the Communist Party to eliminate the military authorities and to reunify the empire. After only one year, all of South and Central China had been conquered and the seat of government had been moved to Wuhan. The troops received support from the peasants to whom the Communist Party had promised a new distribution of land and changes in the tax system.

Communist influence grew, especially in the big cities in the Changjiang Valley. Since 1925, one strike had followed another in Shanghai. In 1926, Chiang Kaishek reduced the number of positions held by members of the Communist Party within the Guomindang. He finally decided in favor of the right wing in February of 1927. He secretly made an agreement with a well-known influential banker and

head of a secret society whom he knew; it ensured industrial manufacturers and merchants continued ownership of their property. After Shanghai, China's financial and industrial center, surrendered to his army without a fight, he proceeded to openly suppress the Communists. Thousands of Communists and workers' leaders were killed. Afterwards, he formed a right-wing nationalist government in Nanjing, supported by industrial and financial circles as well as by great estate owners to whom he had also made the promise that they could retain their property. Chiang Kaishek prohibited the Communist Party and, from that time on, persecuted all Communists. He expelled Soviet advisors and replaced them with German ones; land reform and other sociopolitical reforms existed only on paper. In December of 1927, he married a woman from a rich banker's family in Shanghai, the sister of Sun Yatsen's widow. Chiang Kaishek's troops advanced farther northward and occupied Beijing as early as June of 1928. The left wing of the National People's Party, which had temporarily formed an opposition government, severed its ties to the Communists and rejoined Chiang Kaishek. Nanjing remained the seat of the Nationalist Government.

Since it was a one-party-system, Chiang Kaishek held the reins tightly in his hands. He received support from the Western powers who wanted to keep Japanese expansion in check with the help of a strengthened China. In this way, the Nationalist Government gradually regained a part of the privileges set down in the Unequal Treaties — most important of all, control of maritime customs, which since the 'Boxer Protocol' of 1900, had had to be paid to several Western countries as reparations. The government began with the modernization of the country, especially the expansion of the transportation system; but Chiang Kaishek placed most emphasis on the development of an effective army of which he took direct control and which he continually employed to fight the Communists and rebelling warlords. The members of the Communist Party worked underground from this time on. While they were increasingly driven out of the cities, they succeeded in gaining the trust of the peasants in the countryside, who were disappointed by the reform policies which Chiang Kaishek had promised but had not delivered.

After the founding of the Communist Party, Mao Zedong returned to his home province Hunan where he inspired workers — chiefly peasants — with revolutionary ideas and organized them. He was convinced that it was not the proletariat, which was insignificant in size, that could carry out a revolution, but that the masses of this agrarian state of China, the peasantry, had to be the revolutionary power behind it. In this, he deviated from Moscow's orthodox Marxist line and was considered a renegade. When, in 1927, the autumn harvest uprising in Hunan, organized by Mao and directed against Chiang Kaishek's right wing, failed, he was barred from the Political Bureau. He fled to the Jinggangshan mountains between Hunan and Jiangxi. In July of 1927, Zhou Enlai and Zhu De had attempted to initiate a rebellion, but to no avail. They, too, marched with their troops to the Jinggangshan mountains and, together with Mao, formed the Red Army. This strictly disciplined army, for whom property theft from the civilian population, rape and manslaughter meant capital punishment, contributed considerably to creating a relationship of trust between themselves and the inhabitants. Mao and Zhu De established bases and soviets in the countryside in Southeast China and began putting land reform into practice by rigorously expropriating the great estate owners and rich peasants. In 1931, the First Congress of Soviets was held in Ruijin, Jiangxi, the capital of the largest soviet. Since 1930, Chiang Kaishek had been trying to surround and capture these areas in five campaigns; he was not successful until 1934. The Red Army had a difficult time secretly escaping the encirclement and began its legendary 'Long March' which ended a year later in the sparsely-populated northwest of Shaanxi Province. Of the 300,000 people who started out to travel more than 12,000 km, enduring great hardship through impassable terrain and constant pursuit by Guomindang troops, only one tenth reached the goal. Mao, who in the meantime had taken over the leadership of the Party, made camp in the city of Yan'an.

Japan had not given up striving to form a great East Asian empire under Japanese leadership. They occupied Manchuria in 1931—32, declared it an independent state, Manzhuguo, and set up a puppet government with the last Qing emperor at its head. Chiang Kaishek protested to the League of Nations without success. The Japanese expanded their territory southward and westward in the following years. But Chiang Kaishek considered his main task to be the elimination of Communists. A new encirclement was to begin at Xi'an at the end of 1936, but the Communist leadership in Yan'an were capable of persuading the commanders there to form an anti-Japanese united front. Angered,

Chiang Kaishek returned to his headquarters in Xi'an and was taken captive there. He was released but was forced into forming a united front with the Communists against the Japanese.

On July 7, 1937, the Japanese used a volley of shots between Chinese and Japanese troops on the Lugou Qiao (Marco Polo Bridge) near Beijing as an excuse to attack openly. They occupied Beijing and quickly captured Shanghai and Nanjing, which forced the Nationalist Government to move their capital first to Hankou and then to Chongqing in Sichuan Province. Not only members of the government fled from the Japanese, but also many members of the upper class and intellectuals. They attempted to take everything transportable with them.

Soon the Japanese had captured the entire coast and the whole eastern half of China, so that the western half was cut off from the importation of supplies; provisions could only reach them by way of the Burma Road, which was usually closed and, later, by air.

Japan set up a puppet government in the territories they occupied and made treaties with them. They put much faith in the new Nanjing government, which was led by a rival of Chiang Kaishek's. The united front was not maintained and soon split up. The tension between the Guomindang and the Communist Party continuously increased.

From 1939 on, there were continual armed conflicts. From their positions the Communist troops waged a guerilla war behind Japanese lines and interfered with troop supply lines. Chiang Kaishek's troops were much too weak to stop the well-equipped Japanese. After the Japanese attack on Pearl Harbor, the USA and Great Britain declared war on Japan. They recognized Nationalist China as an equal major power and relinquished all special rights afforded them by the Unequal Treaties. Though the economically weakened Chongqing government had been receiving material and financial support from the USA since 1941, Chiang Kaishek preferred to hold back part of his troops for the fight against the Communists, rather than to use them against the Japanese. Inflation and corruption prevailed in the areas he controlled, which made life for the population increasingly difficult. In August 1945, atom bombs fell on Hiroshima and Nagasaki. At the same time, Russia declared war on Japan and invaded Manchuria. Japan surrendered unconditionally.

The Nationalist Government now had the enormous task of taking over the administration of the entire area which had been freed from the Japanese. Its troops occupied the cities. In level territories the Communist Party succeeded in winning influence and power. In accordance with the Yalta Agreements, Russia occupied Manchuria. The Russians took advantage of the opportunity to dismantle the industrial complexes the Japanese had built and to transport them to the USSR. In spite of this, Chiang Kaishek requested that the Soviets retain their troops in Manchuria for a few more months due to the lack of transportation facilities for the occupation of Manchuria. The United States endeavored to persuade the Nationalists and Communists to form a coalition government under Chiang Kaishek. Mao Zedong traveled to Chongqing for negotiations in 1946, but they failed due to the deep animosity between the two sides.

Whereas the Communist Party won the sympathy of a great percentage of the population in the areas administered by them — mainly as a result of land reform — mismanagement, inflation and corruption increased to a great degree in the regions controlled by the Nationalists. Mao's troops constantly gained strength from the weapons abandoned by the Japanese in North China and the increasing numbers of deserters from the Guomindang army. After capturing Manchuria and North China, they began their last great offensive on a broad front in September 1948 and conquered the entire empire from the North within one year. Chiang Kaishek fled with his government, the treasury and a large number of his followers to Taiwan. On October 1, 1949, Mao Zedong proclaimed the People's Republic of China in Beijing.

People's Republic

On October 1, 1949 on Tiananmen Square in Beijing, Mao Zedong announced the establishment of the People's Republic of China. The Soviet Union recognized the new state one day after its founding. In February of 1950, Soviet and Chinese government representatives signed a friendship and assistance pact in Moscow. Russian experts came to China; Chinese students went to the Soviet Union to study at Russian universities.

National reconstruction was completed by 1952. The administrative functions of the People's Liberation Army were turned over to Party-dominated control in different parts of the country. Large estates were divided, land reform was carried out successfully. Financial and economic management was made uniform in the whole country, a stable currency created, the rule of high finance eliminated and large concerns nationalized. Political and economic grievances in the administration and companies were to be remedied, which was why the two campaigns were carried out: 'Struggle against the Three Evils' — corruption, waste and bureaucratism (1951) and the 'Struggle against the Five Evils' — bribery, tax evasion, embezzlement of state property, fraud in fulfilling state contracts and theft of national economic information (1952). The first five-year plan began in 1953. Due to organizational shortcomings, it showed no effect until February of 1955; nevertheless, it yielded a surplus of 17% of its quota.

In September, 1954, the First National People's Congress met and adopted the constitution of the People's Republic of China.

For many Chinese, these first years of reconstruction, filled with excitement and infinite optimism for the young state, remain unforgettable.

In January of 1956, a conference of the Central Committee was to discuss the question of the intellectuals: guidelines were determined for work in education, science and culture. The policy 'let a hundred flowers blossom and a hundred schools of thought contend' was supposed to promote work in all areas. In 1957, a movement toward party alignment was introduced, and the people were encouraged to make suggestions to and offer criticism of the Party. When they did so, however, many of them were bitterly denounced and regarded as enemies who took advantage of the campaign to attack the leading role of the Party, and this was followed by a movement against rightist deviants from the party line. As later officially stated, the scope of the movement had been exceeded and a great number of patriotic individuals and intellectuals unjustly characterized as 'rightist elements'.

The three-year phase of the 'Three Red Banners' began in February of 1958. This included the 'Great Leap Forward', the socialist main line and the people's commune movement (see page 24). The policy of the 'Three Red Banners' did not produce the desired success; on the contrary, it plunged the country into a dangerous economic crisis. The break with the Soviet Union and bad weather added to the deteriorating situation and led to the 'three bitter years'. Thanks to the policy of consolidation which devoted special attention to agriculture, the economy had recovered relatively well by 1966.

In September of 1962, Mao Zedong denounced the great contradiction between the proletariat and the bourgeoisie in Chinese society. He accused several Party circles of striving to restore capitalism and, for that reason, a search for revisionism in the Party was necessary. From 1963—1965, a socialist education campaign was carried out. Strong forces within the Party leadership opposed the course pursued by Mao. From May of 1966 to October of 1976, the Chinese people experienced the Cultural Revolution, which, as the Party Leadership stated in 1981, caused the Party, country and people the most serious setbacks since the founding of the People's Republic.

At the beginning of 1974, Mao Zedong's wife, Jiang Qing and others initiated the 'movement of criticism of Lin Biao and Confucius' which was directed more against Zhou Enlai than against Lin Biao. Zhou Enlai became seriously ill in 1975 and could not continue his official duties alone. Deng Xiaoping took over in his stead. He endeavored to systematically correct the mistakes of the Cultural Revolution. Zhou Enlai died in January of 1976. In April of the same year, on the occasion of the Qingming festival, the Tiananmen incident took place. 200,000 people came together on Tiananmen Square in Beijing, in mourning for the deceased premier. During the gathering, protest was voiced against Jiang Qing's circle of supporters. Deng Xiaoping's removal from office followed. In September of 1976, Mao Zedong died; his widow, Jiang Qing, and her followers attempted to seize party and state power. At the beginning of October, under the leadership of Hua Guofeng, the 'Gang of Four' was overthrown. The Cultural Revolution was now officially at an end. Order was restored to education, science and culture, which had suffered the most during the movement.

Hua Guofeng was made First Vice Chairman of the Central Committee and Premier of the State Council.

The third plenary convention of the Eleventh Central Committee of the Chinese Communist Party in December of 1978 was a turning-point. It was determined that emphasis would be placed on the common goals of socialist modernization, development of socialist democracy and strengthening the socialist legal system.

Hua Guofeng resigned in November of 1980. Hu Yaobang became the new Party Chairman, Zhao Ziyang, the new premier of the State Council. Both men are considered to be pragmatists and supporters of Zhou Enlai.

Language

Modern standard Chinese, *Putonghua* (Mandarin), is based on the northern Chinese dialect, one of the eight dialects of the Han Chinese which include, for example, the Shanghai and Canton dialects. The difference in pronunciation is stupendous. If someone from Canton and someone from Shanghai meet and neither can speak the standard language, their only recourse is to use written language as a means of communication. Thanks to the modern school system, *Putonghua* is taught in the entire country, so that communication problems are gradually being reduced.

The eight main dialects are divided into innumerable sub-dialects.

Chinese originally consisted almost exclusively of one-syllable words and is therefore categorized as monosyllabic. There are a total of 411 syllables in the standard language which can be pronounced in four different tones. In the transcription 'Pinyin', in use in China since 1958, the tones are indicated in the form of strokes above the characters. The first tone is high and constant, the second ascending, the third descending and ascending, the fourth descending. Words having very different meanings can have the same pronunciation and the same intonation, but their orthographic representations differ. Take, for example, the syllable 'ma'; meanings vary with the different intonations. The meaning of the sentence "Má māma mà mǎ má" is: Is the pock-faced mother scolding the horse?

Colloquial language differs from the classical written language. The latter evolved three millenia ago from the colloquial language used at that time and played a decisive role in literature up until modern times. Since the characters have not changed in over two thousand years, it is still possible for modern Chinese to read works written in ancient times. The main differences were in the pronunciation of characters.

In contrast to the written language, the standard language consists to a large extent of polysyllabic words. Due to its logical grammatical structure, Chinese, apart from the writing of characters, is quite easy to learn. Chinese grammar has no inflexion and no differences in gender; temporal nouns and adverbs take over the function of expressing concrete time.

Literature

The oldest work in classical Chinese is the

Shijing, a collection of folk and court songs as well as temple hymns, which were sung from the beginning of the Zhou era until about the 6th century BC.

According to tradition, officials were ordered by the government to collect songs from all over the country, including love songs, wedding songs, dirges, psalms, hunting songs and songs about good and bad princes. They were sung, accompanied by musical instruments or by dancing, and their lines were usually four characters long. The interpretation of the songs was expected to yield many insights into the heart and life of the people. It was supposedly Confucius (551—479 BC) who selected 305 from 3000 folk songs to which so-called prologues were added as an aid to interpretation. The result was the *Shijing,* one of the five Confucian classics that influenced Chinese literature for over two millenia. The other four classics are:

Yijing, usually translated as the 'Book of Changes', a book of prophecy containing texts of oracles and their interpretations from the Zhou era.

Shujing, the 'Classic of History', contains documents, including speeches made by rulers to their own or enemy peoples. About half of this work originated in the early Zhou period, the other half consists of supplements which are even older but were not added until centuries later.

Liji, the 'Record of Rites', was probably written in the Period of the Warring States.

Chunqiu, the 'Spring and Autumn' Annals, is a concise chronological description of the history of the feudal state of Lu, where Confucius was born. He supposedly wrote this work himself. In later years it was supplemented by three commentaries, one of which — the *Zuozhuan* — achieved renown as a work in itself. These five classics were the foundation of Confucian education and training of officials. Their contents had to be studied and partly memorized. In addition, there was the so-called *Si Shu,* the Four Books, which, since the Song Dynasty, have also been part of the Confucian canon.

Lunyu, the 'Analects', is a record of Confucius' thoughts, opinions and sayings which were put together by his students and disciples after his death. With this work, the Confucians gave their teachings a unified foundation which was intended to check the fragmentation of their own school and strengthen their fight against other schools.

Zhongyong, the 'Doctrine of the Mean', written by Confucius' grandson, Kong Ji (492—431 BC), comprises Confucius' thoughts

about man's relationship to himself and to his fellow-man. Confucius professed that man should be true to himself and kind to his neighbors.

Daxue, 'Great Learning', is partly attributed to Zeng Can, an outstanding student of Confucius. It formulates the Confucian teachings of an individual's self-perfection.

Mengzi, named after the philosopher Mengzi (Mencius) (372–289 BC), contains notes of his own sayings and deeds collected by his students and is divided into 14 chapters. The most important message of this work is Mengzi's theory that human nature is basically good.

The fall of the Zhou Dynasty, the chaotic times of the Period of the Warring States, wars and misery had all contributed to the creation of a unique intellectual life, from which other philosophies, in addition to Confucianism, evolved. The basic works of the most important schools were:

Daodejing, the central work of Daoism, which was probably written at the end of the Period of the Warring States, and contains the sayings of Laozi, considered to be the founder of Daoism. Aside from Laozi, Zhuangzi (died ca. 370 BC), is considered to be the most significant Daoist. Several chapters in the collection of texts named after him had a lasting influence on philosophy and literature of later times due to their depth of thought and imagery.

Moism and the Legalist school also produced fundamental writings, such as *Mozi,* containing the teachings of Mo Di (ca. 480—390 BC) and those of the Legalist Han Feizi (ca. 280—233 BC). Also significant is the work of Xunzi (313—238 BC) who, together with Mengzi, was one of the most important Confucian thinkers of Chinese antiquity; he developed the teachings of the original evil nature of human beings.

In the field of poetry, in addition to the *Shijing,* songs of Chu *(Chuci)* should be mentioned — a collection of hymns and rhapsodies, most of which originated in the Changjiang river regions in South China and were sung in the local Chu dialect. The author of part of this work was supposedly Qu Yuan (ca. 332—295 BC), an official who became the victim of a plot and was banned. He finally sought death in exile and drowned himself. The longest and most important of his poems is *Lisao,* in which he makes known his disappointment and sadness over his own destiny and that of his country. The unhappy fate of this man and his suicide were the original basis of the Dragon Boat Festival. On the fifth day of the fifth month of the moon calendar, the people remembered Qu Yuan and threw rice wrapped in bamboo leaves into the rivers as an offering. Today it is a Chinese family custom to eat rice rolled in bamboo leaves on this day.

Chuci is divided into 15 chapters; *Lisao* is the first of them. Parts of the fourth chapter are also attributed to Qu Yuan. The other ones originated during the Han Dynasty; some are imitations of Qu Yuan's style. The *Chuci* follows a different poetic tradition than the *Shijing*. This is recognizable by the fact that its lines generally consist of six characters. The poetic power expressed in this work indicates that, from an artistic standpoint, the *Chuci* is more valuable than the *Shijing;* at any rate, it had a greater influence on later poetry.

After the unification of the empire under the short rule of the Qin and starting at the beginning of the Han Dynasty, literature took a new direction. The *fu,* a type of prose poem characterized by parallel lines and later by variation of rhymed and prose sections, followed the tradition of the songs of Chu. The most renowned poet of *fu* was Sima Xiangru (179—117 BC) who is considered to be the best poet of the Han period. As many other poets of that time, he also came from Chengdu in present-day Sichuan. Emperor Han Wudi, himself a student of the arts, had the talented poet brought to his court, where Sima Xiangru soon made a noteworthy career for himself.

Many *fu* poems served as a glorification of ruler and empire and, at the same time, as a medium of courtly society. This type of poem has often been criticized as being inferior due to its choice of theme. For example, objects of daily use such as tables or combs were described in flowery verse. On the other hand, *fu* poems were also characterized by their intimations, behind which criticism of the ruler's lack of moderation and extravagance was often hidden.

Another type of poetry is also significant — one that was quite popular during the Han Dynasty: *yuefu,* named after the imperial music bureau, *yuefu,* which collected songs and melodies from all parts of the empire — also those from distant border regions. A group of court poets wrote new verses for many of these melodies — traditional texts were also used — and they were published as songs and ballads by the authorities. These songs were simply called *yuefu.* Especially well-known and loved were the *yuefu* from the South; their popularity continued until modern times, and their content can still be heard today in China, for example in operas. The most remarkable and the longest *yuefu* of

that time was *kongque dongnan fei,* The Peacock Flies to the Southeast, the story of a happy, young newly wedded couple, forced to separate by the husband's mother, who finally commit suicide out of despair. Most *yuefu* texts from the Han period consist of lines of five characters. They were the forerunners of a new type of poem, the *gushi,* ancient style poems.

During the Western Han Dynasties under the rule of Wudi (140—87 BC), Confucians reached a position of political power and respect. The emperor favored Confucian teachings because they ensured his position of power. He proclaimed new state ethics which were based on Confucian principles. The most important Confucian of that time was Dong Zhongshu. He wrote *Chunqiu fanlu*, Luxuriant Dew of Chunqiu, in which he portrayed, among other things, the foundations of future policy — the interrelationship of heaven, emperor and people and cosmic references to life on earth. He also developed the characteristics of a general and a higher education system.

One of the greatest achievements of Chinese literature is its historical writings. Exemplary works of this type were written as early as the Western Han Dynasty. *Shiji* by the palace scribe Sima Qian (145—86 BC) contains a history of China since primitive times. It is divided into imperial annals, tables, proceedings, feudal princes and biographies of famous people. It encompasses more than 520,000 characters, is written in narrative prose and deals with a 2,000-year period of time, beginning with the legendary epoch up until the time of Emperor Wudi. the preliminary work had been done by his father; and Sima Qian continued to bring it to fruition. It took 18 years to complete the project. The *Shiji* became a model for following dynasty histories. The first one written after it was *Qian Han Shu,* History of the Early Han Dynasty, by Ban Gu. The preliminary work on this book had also been done by Ban Gu's father. Ban Gu continued the work and, after his death, his sister completed it. 800,000 characters were used and 229 years of the Han Dynasty were covered. It is divided into imperial annals, tables, proceedings and biographies.

The end of the Han period marked a change in the field of literature which, up until then, had been strongly influenced by Confucianism. Power struggles, wars, empire divisions and invasions by peoples from the North were reasons why the empire had not been left in peace for over three centuries. Accounts of the population's misery and despair are found in the *yuefu* songs of the outgoing Han and Wei eras. They lament about the shortness and bitterness of life as a result of war's confusion. The contents frequently reflect the fate of individuals, telling of the suffering of unhappy women, orphaned children and distressed officials.

Despite the chaos of the times, this period was especially significant culturally. A number of brilliant poets lived during this time, for example Cao Zhi, the son of the renowned general and chancellor Cao Cao. His brother, Cao Pi, took the throne after the fall of the Han and declared himself ruler of the Wei Dynasty. All three, father as well as both of his sons, were noteworthy poets; Cao Zhi was the most notable of them. They gathered the best poets of their time at their courts, seven of whom made literary history as the 'Seven Poets of the Jian'an Period'. This was the period from 196—219 at the close of the Han era, the time of the dynasty's decline. The poets who were active at this time turned away from Confucian-influenced themes. The artistic, aesthetic aspect moved into the foreground. The melody of the language, elegant phrases, new subjects, were what was pleasing. A frequent topic was friendship. Lines mainly consisted of five syllables. This new style is generally known as the Jian'an style.

The dangerous life in unstable times and the increasing surveillance of the remarks made by men of letters and scholars, led many educated people in the middle of the 3rd century to believe that it was easier not to worry about the fate of the empire any more, but to seek diversion and oblivion in the seclusion of the mountains and forests, especially with wine and entertainment, to lead a satisfying life and to engage in *Qingtan,* Pure Conversation, about the fundamental questions of life. The most famous poets of this period were the 'Seven Wise Men of the Bamboo Forest', named for their common meeting place. Among them were Liu Ling, a drinker devoted to Daoism, Ji Kang and Xiang Xiu, both experimenters in alchemy, and Shan Tao, also a Daoist. Their poems frequently reflect a kind of escape from the world; they influenced the poets of the period when the empire was divided into a Northern dynasty and a Southern one. That North China was ruled by foreigners was intolerable for many writers, so they fled to the South of the country. Here, numerous cultural centers developed. The magnificent scenery of the South, abundant vegetation, bizarre mountains, quiet valleys and lakes inspired the artists. Many of them — poets as well as painters — devoted themselves to nature in their works.

Tao Yuanming (Tao Qian 365—427) was one of the most outstanding literary men of this time and is China's first great pastoral poet. In his early years, he began his career as an official, but he was not completely happy with administrative work. He retreated to his country home, cultivated flowers — mainly chrysanthemums — and devoted himself to poetry, music and — not lastly — wine. His attitude toward life was often compared to that of the Daoist Zhuangzi. His poems, written in a style which was easy to understand, were the model for many generations of poets after him. Over a hundred of his poems have survived, among them, prose poems and other works of prose. One of his most famous works is the *Taohuayuan Ji.* It is the story of a fisherman who travels along the river in his boat and suddenly comes upon a remote area. The fisherman sees rich fields, tidy houses, clear ponds and magnificent mulberry trees and bamboo groves. People had lived there for centuries, content and on good terms with each other. Their ancestors had moved there during the Qin Dynasty. Since that time, they had no longer had contact with the empire. It was, so to speak, a dreamland into which the author had had his fisherman travel and to which the fisherman never returned, because he could not find it a second time. It was China's first utopia; the poet set down on paper his conception of an ideal society.

A notable work from the Northern and Southern Dynasties is the anthology of literature *Wenxuan*. It encompasses works by 127 authors from the outgoing Zhou period to the beginning of the 6th century. *Wenxuan* was compiled by Xiao Tong (501—531), crown prince and oldest son of Xiao Yan, the founder of the Liang Dynasty. Tradition portrays Xiao Tong as being not only a prominent scholar, but also an exemplary and exceptionally benevolent ruler.

After the empire had again been united under the short-lived Sui Dynasty, literary life blossomed anew. The following Tang Dynasty has been designated the Golden Age of literature. A number of the Tang emperors were themselves noteworthy poets and became promoters of literature. They had libraries built, rare works collected from all over the country and many copies made of them. They had the best poets of their time summoned to their courts where they became honored men. Since the composition of a poem and poetic description were part of the state examinations, there were a number of distinguished writers in the ranks of the officials. The second half of the Tang Dynasty saw war, hardship and chaos. Many poets captured the terrible events in their poems; others followed the example of their predecessors and withdrew from society.

The most important genre of Tang literature was poetry. Existing styles and structures were adopted and refined. General rules for verse composition were established. A new from evolved — the poem with a strict tonal meter — called *lüshi*. This type of poem, or one verse, consisted for example of eight lines, containing five or seven characters each. Lines three and four, five and six were parallel. Word order in the lines was strictly regulated by rules of tone. A further type was *jueju*, a short poem of only four lines, each line consisting of five or seven characters.

Even today, more than two thousand poets from the Tang Dynasty are known. Only the most famous will be mentioned here — first Li Bai and Du Fu. Both are among the most notable Chinese poets. Li Bai (Li Taibo 699—762) was an open, free-spirited man who was closely bound to nature and to wine. Upon recommendation, the emperor Xuanzong had him called to his court and gave him a position of honor. He only remained there two or three years because life at court did not suit him, and he found himself in danger of becoming a victim of intrigue. Li Bai recognized this danger in time and left the court. He embarked upon a long life of wandering, always accompanied by his best friend — wine. There are several versions of his death. The one which best suits his adventurous life full of drink, tells that he drowned during a boat trip while trying to embrace the moon which was reflected in the water.

Du Fu (712—770) who came from a family of lower officials, held a low office at court, but had to flee in the course of disturbances which were connected with the rebellion of 755. He later lived in Chengdu (where today his property may still be visited) and worked for the governor Yan Wu. Du Fu was a sharp observer of political and social conditions. Where he recognized injustice, he did not hesitate to criticize. In contrast to Li Bai, who was influenced by Daoism, Du Fu considered himself a strict Confucian. In spite of this, both were united by a profound friendship.

Bai Juyi (772—846) was a great admirer of Du Fu. He was a poet whose works were popular and widely known during his own lifetime. Bai Juyi had had a Confucian education but was not able to evade the influence of Buddhism and Daoism. He was a high

official and held a number of positions in the course of his life. Bai Juyi endeavored to find insights into the feelings and thoughts of the common people. He wanted his poems to be understood by all. They frequently contained criticism of the events of the times and drew attention to grievances. He is said to have always given his poems to an old washerwoman to be read before he publicized them. He changed parts that she could not understand and simplified them. He was especially successful with his *Xin Yuefu*, New Yuefu Poems, which found great approval — also in Japan — during his lifetime.

In the area of prose, Han Yu (768—824) was the most famous artist of the Tang Dynasty. He was both a philosopher and an official. Many generations of scholars to come regarded him and his works as being exemplary. Han Yu used the style of the philosophers and scholars of the Zhou and Han periods as a guide and rejected the prose style of the pre-Tang era which he found artificial, difficult to understand and bound by many rules. The written language had deviated from the spoken language increasingly and was only accessible to the educated who had mastered the literature of former times. This return to *guwen,* the classical literary style, a movement chiefly led by Han Yu, had a liberating effect. The strict sentence structure of *Pianwen,* the legal language which originated during the Han Dynasty, was no longer adhered to; rather, one could formulate as one wished, according to the content. This paved the way for the famous Tang novel. In this genre one often encounters stories of love, magic, ghosts and spirits — many based on old legends — but also descriptions of historical figures, heroes and warriors. The plots of Tang novels were often adapted to musical dramas in later dynasties. The authors usually came from the class of scholars who knew how to admirably combine what they had experienced with fiction. Though miraculous things happen in these short stories, they also offer valuable insights into the social and economic conditions of the time.

During the period of the decline of the Tang Dynasty and the Five Dynasties, scholars again retreated into private life and devoted themselves in their work to topics that had nothing to do with contemporary events. Numerous poems about nature and love have been handed down from this time. The Song era (960—1279) was a time of great weakness of foreign policy and constant threats from the so-called barbaric tribes, but despite this, there was also a remarkable development in the area of culture. Since printing was widespread and was continually being improved, the number of literary publications was considerably increased. In addition, the establishment of schools in every part of the country and admission of the sons from all social classes to the state examinations and to official careers soon had an effect on general literary creativity. The Song Dynasty emperors appreciated scholarship and literature. Among them were poets and painters who were patrons of the arts. Almost all types of poetry and prose were fostered during the Song era. In the field of prose, Ouyang Xiu and Su Dongpo were the ones to continue the classical style revived by Han Yu. Sima Guang and Zhu Xi followed suit.

Ouyang Xiu (1007—1072), a dignitary of the highest rank, was the author of the New Imperial Annals of the Tang and Five Dynasties, *Xin Tangshu* and *Xin Wudai Shi*. He possessed well-founded, comprehensive knowledge and devoted himself to the most diverse topics, such as old bronze and stone inscriptions and contemporary politics (he called for economic reforms). Ouyang Xiu opposed Buddhism; he was an orthodox Confucian. His literary works were also influenced by Confucianism.

Su Dongpo (1036—1101) is considered to be one of the greatest poets of the Song Dynasty. His outstanding works of poetry and prose influenced many later generations of authors.

Sima Guang (1019-1086) was the author of *Zizhi Tongjian,* one of the most widely read historical works in China, which offers a historical survey from the Period of the Warring States until the beginning of the Song Dynasty and, for this reason, replaced the study of the detailed dynasty annals. He wrote it in the classical style.

Zhu Xi (1130—1200), a patriotic official, was a poet as well as a philosopher. He retired from official life and founded a private academy. Zhu Xi is considered the perfecter of so-called neo-Confucianism.

Also of great importance was the poet, philosopher and politician Wang Anshi (1021—1086). He followed Legalist and Daoist principles. His Ten-thousand-Character Memorandum, in which he demands reform of the administrative system and a practical rather than literary education for officials, deserves special attention.

A new development in literature was introduced by the art of story telling in colloquial language. People gathered at market places, temple courtyards and other public places to hear story tellers. The narrators had a kind of notebook in which the story's plot was sketched along general lines. Not until later was more interest devoted to recording the stories. They were first written down in full in about the 12th century. This genre, called *huaben* style, opened up new possibilities to the artists. In spite of this, colloquial literature remained an exception within China's classical literary history, because it was the common people who read these works and not the educated class who were the actual supporters of standard literature.

Historical narratives which mainly dealt with the periods of the Three Kingdoms (220—280) and the Five Dynasties (907—960) were extremely popular. The stories about heroes like Liu Bei and Zhuge Liang live on today among the people. Love stories were just as common — stories which took place in the palace milieu and also in the urban middle classes. The most important genre of the Song era is *ci,* the intoned poem. In contrast to other types of poems, it followed no strict rules of meter, and its lines could contain up to 11 syllables; it was the melody to which the poem was written which was important. Frequent subjects were the joys and woes of love as well as the transience of life. Famous *ci* poets were Li Yu (937—978), the last emperor of the Southern Tang Dynasty, and Liu Yong, an official who knew his way around in the world of singing and dancing girls and wrote chiefly love songs. All other poets of the Song period promoted this popular form. The rulers of the Song Dynasty had not been able to maintain their position against their enemies in the North. In 1126 they fled south from the invaders and continued their sovereignty there for almost 150 years. The cultural center shifted to the South and would remain there even after the empire had been reunited.

Under the foreign rule of the Jin and Yuan dynasties, the use of colloquial language became more important. It was easier for the foreigners in power to speak simple conversational language than learned classical Chinese. Announcements written in the colloquial language could be understood by the common people. As early as the end phase of the Song period, the Confucians had had to employ the uncomplicated colloquial form to compete with the Buddhists. The latter principally used colloquial language in their propaganda writings, addressing themselves directly to the people, and were quite successful. Another reason for the increasing importance of colloquial language was the abolishment of the written state examinations by the Mongol rulers.

In the course of this development, *yuanqu,* the musical drama of the Yuan era, reached prominence. It had evolved out of the *zaju,* Mixed Theater (performances consisting of parts which were spoken and others which were sung) of the Song period; however, it was influenced by the music and the customs of the northern regions.

More than 1,700 musical dramas were written during the Yuan Dynasty; about ten percent have survived. One of the most famous works is *Xixiang Ji,* The Story of the Western Pavilion, based on a Tang novel. *Yuanqu* almost always consisted of four acts and was composed of dialogues and arias. It frequently opened with a prologue. The dialogues and arias followed colloquial language closely and, for that reason, could be understood by the common people. All arias in one act were sung in a certain key by the main actor. Almost all the plays have happy endings. The heroes come mainly from the middle and lower classes; and the subjects range from love stories to historical, Daoist and Buddhist themes, to plays about social topics.

One of the greatest dramatists of the Yuan period, considered by many to be the actual creator of the Yuan drama, is Guan Hanqing (1220—1300). Of the 64 plays he wrote, only 14 remain. The most renowned is *Dou E Yuan,* the Unjust Verdict on Dou E. The story is about a young widow who was sentenced to death because she supposedly had not remained chaste. After her death, her innocence is proven and her reputation restored.

Toward the end of the Yuan period, the Song era *zaju,* Mixed Theater, increased in importance also in South China. It was generally called *nanju* or *xiwen.* In contrast to the Yuan play, frequently called the Northern Drama, the Southern play had no constraining rules to follow, and it thus achieved vivacity and dramatic quality. It was not only a four-act play, but had stronger divisions and could number thirty or forty scenes altogether. The key could be changed within an act; arias were sung by one or more actors.

After the Mongolian rulers had been expelled, the Ming Dynasty (1368—1644) was founded. With it began a renewed consciousness of old styles and forms. Artists of the Ming era considered the masters of past epochs to be the examples to follow. Rival groups developed in the field of prose; they either used the works of the Qin and Han periods or those of the Tang and Song as guidelines. In this way, many imitations were created. Not until the end of the 16th century did a number of learned men voice the opinion that imitation

was meaningless and that they wanted to give new life to literature.

Real progress was made in the field of colloquial prose narratives. To some extent, themes from the storytellers, the Tang novels and the Yuan dramas were used. The most famous work is *Shuihu Zhuan* by Shi Nai'an and Luo Guanzhong, known under the title 'The Water Margin'.

It is a novel about thieves, based on the story of the historical Song Jiang and his robbers who lived during the Northern Song era in Shandong. The thieves, 108 in the novel, historically only 36, are declared enemies of greedy, brutal officials and friends of the suffering population. This story gained recognition after it was written and is still read with pleasure today. It has been translated into a number of Western languages.

Xiyou Ji and *Jin Ping Mei* were just as renowned. *Xiyou Ji* by Wu Cheng'en (1510—1580) is the story of Sun Wukong, the Monkey King. Strong Buddhist influence is evident in the work; traces of Daoism are also recognizable.

Jin Ping Mei contains a realistic presentation of the licentiousness and brutality frequently encountered in the upper circles of those days. The Manchurian Qing Dynasty followed the Ming. Many learned men were not willing to serve the foreign rulers. They retreated into private life and devoted themselves to the study of the classics and the composition of commentaries, taking pains to avoid any reference to the politics of the day. In the different literary genres, artists followed the traditions which had been passed down; but their works seldom reached the level of excellence of the centuries before.

Solely in the area of novel writing were new topics introduced during the Qing era. Authors directed their critique chiefly toward officialdom. The most famous work was *Honglou Meng,* The Dream of the Red Chamber, by Cao Xueqin, (1715–1763), which was written in colloquial language and describes the rise and fall of an official's family. The plot centers around a young couple whose marriage was prevented by deceit.

The political events of the early 19th century forced the Chinese to come to terms with Western thought. Numerous scientific and technical works were translated. But what interested scholars most were topics of philosophy, ethics and literature. Two men did exceptional work in this area — Yan Fu and Lin Shu. Yan Fu, who had studied in England, devoted himself mainly to the translation of philosophical and sociological works, among them T.H. Huxley's *Evolution and Ethics,* which made a deep impression on the Chinese reader. Lin Shu had never learned a foreign language and had to rely on oral translations. He did, however, succeed in rendering the contents of the works in an outstanding style and in interesting the Chinese reader in European literature. He accomplished a mammoth job, translating 171 books. Both translators still used the classical written language, the ancient prose style. Soon it was recognized, however, that new ideas, new knowledge, could not be expressed in the language of the first and second centuries. A modern person should not have to use an antiquated language.

Tendencies to modernize literature could not be checked toward the end of the 19th century. Due to China's weakness in relation to foreign powers, and to the incompetence of the Manchurian imperial court, the demand for far-reaching reforms and for renunciation of conservative thinking became more urgent at the beginning of the 20th century. A new medium appeared — numerous magazines in which colloquial literature was published. Novels written in the common tongue took a new turn. Their topics were contemporary problems; they offered unambiguous criticism of the basic evils of society and publicly exposed grievances in a sharp manner.

The revolution of 1911 brought down the hated ruling house; but the developments which the progressive scholars had expected from it did not come about. The old state examinations were abolished. Young people left the country en masse to study at foreign universities. An abundance of new information, impressions and stimuli poured indiscriminately into the country. The magazine *Xin Qingnian,* New Youth, started by Chen Duxiu (1879—1942) in Shanghai in 1915, was an instrument for the publication of western ideas. It became the organ of the *Baihua* Movement whose members were in favor of solely using colloquial language in literature. They were against empty phrases and classical quotations, against the old constricting rules of style and form. Literature was no longer only to serve a small class of educated people, but the masses. Besides Chen Duxiu, Hu Shi (1891—1962) was one of the most important supporters of the movement. Hu Shi had studied in the United States. After his return, he joined the *Baihua* Movement and published his ideas about modern literature in New Youth. Chen Duxiu and Hu Shi registered great success with their articles. Soon, noted representatives of science, research and literature joined them. Naturally there were also dissenting opinions and an opposing movement which considered support of *Baihua* to be traitorous to Chinese tradition. But, in the long run, they could not assert themselves against the trend of the times. The May 4th Movement in 1919 gave progressive powers a new lift. News about the negotiations of the Versailles Peace Conference had provoked the indignation of all classes of the population. A flood of protests and demonstrations engulfed the country. A new nationalism was inflamed and found suitable expression in the colloquial language. Speeches, articles, pamphlets were written in this language and could be understood by the common man.

The most prominent author of the following years was Lu Xun (1881—1936), today considered the greatest Chinese author of modern times. His stories gained fame in the literary world. His most renowned works are 'Diary of a Madman' and 'The True Story of Ah Q'.

In his stories, Lu Xun sided with the poor and oppressed. He spoke out against feudalism, the ruling class of rural landowners and publicly exposed superstition and ignorance. He also mocked the arrogance and stupidity of many intellectuals.

Also of significance for the literature of the 20th century are Lao She, Mao Dun, Shen Congwen, Ba Jin and Cao Yu. They took up the problems of their time, spoke out against feudalism and fascism, and relayed a dismal picture of social conditions in China. A turning point came in the literature in the liberated areas (liberated by the Chinese Communist Party from the Japanese). The authors did not only describe the conditions realistically, but also allowed components of Party policy to flow into their works by underlining the merits of the Communist Party and propagated their goals.

With the founding of the People's Republic of China in 1949 came a new development in literature. Most of the successful progressive writers of the 20's and 30's obtained high positions in the administration, which consequently hampered their literary work. The new guidelines which were set for writers held that literature was to serve the masses; the author was to write from a socialistic point of view.

Religion

The Chinese language does not have a term for the concept 'religion' in the occidental sense of the word; expressions such as 'school' or 'teachings' are used instead. There has never been a clearly definable religion in China; the ideas of a state church and clergy or religious wars are unknown.

Confucianism, often considered by Westerners to be a Chinese religion, was a philosophical doctrine, the purpose of which was to guarantee order within state and society. The Han emperors elevated it to a state doctrine; it was supported by an officialdom educated in its teachings and was fostered by various forms of observance and rites. The fate of Confucianism was determined by the loss of its supporters when the last dynasty fell. After 1911, it lost importance as a state doctrine.

Early on in China's history, people had reflected about the universe and man's place within it. According to these deliberations, the cosmos is a magnitude of harmony and order. It is not static, but active; its state is one of change and variation. Perpetual becoming and fading away, contracting and expanding, revolving and merging make up the cosmos and keep it in motion. *Dao,* the Way, guides the happening in the cosmos in its function as ordering principle and provides it with universal order. From within the *Dao,* the two elementary powers, *yin* and *yang,* function by means of reciprocal action and permutation as creators of all things. *Yang* and *yin* are two polar opposites in which all things can be classified: light - dark, day - night, life - death, male - female, strong - weak, good - evil, high -low, etc. In addition to this, there are the teachings of the five elements, *wu xing,* the five elements: wood, fire, earth, metal and water. These are also not static but, like *yin* and *yang,* basic powers which constantly react to one another and trigger nature's processes.

Dao, yin and *yang, wu xing* were the foundation of the Chinese view of the world up until the very recent past.

During the Shang Dynasty (ca. 1600—1100 BC), the highest supernatural power was personified by God (*Di* or *Shangdi*); presumably it was once a tribal god or perhaps a noble ancestor of the ruling house. In the writings of the philosophers of the late Zhou Dynasty — with the exception of those of Modi — this highest ruler in heaven was attributed an almost abstract character and was usually addressed only as 'Heaven'.

As early as the 14th century BC, there was a cult of ancestor worship within the aristocratic upper class. According to the conceptions of that day, the ancestors lived with the Supreme Ruler in heaven. If they were satisfied with their living descendants, they protected the clan and convinced the Ruler to reward the living with blessings; if they were dissatisfied, the opposite would happen. Sacrificial rites were part of taking care of the ancestors and were only performed by male offspring — the oldest sons or grandsons — in front of the ancestral tablets. For this reason it was necessary to insure that there were male offspring in a clan. Tending the graves was also part of ancestral worship. It was based on the belief that a person has two souls: the physical, which expires upon death, and the spiritual, which lives on. Good spirits, *shen,* were the souls that were satisfied with the honors their descendants bestowed upon them. Bad spirits or demons, *gui,* evolved from the souls of ancestors who had been wronged or who had been neglected by their descendants. If ancestral rites were not observed, good spirits could turn into dangerous 'hungry' demons who began a search for nourishment. Bad spirits, according to these ideas, worked on an individual basis. Good spirits could become gods, as for example on a local level, the protecting spirit of a place or district or the patron saint of a social class. Some reached a universal status and were popular throughout China, such as the earth god *Tudi,* or the guardian spirit of hearth, home and neighborhood. Spirits could also come from the animal world, the heavens and nature.

The time of the decline of the Zhou Dynasty was marked by political chaos, increasing social mobility and the perfection and popularization of the writing system. The first created an age of spirited, free thought, while the last provided for the recording and systemization of ideas. Both of the great philosophies — Confucianism and Daoism — developed.

Confucius had always considered himself to be a conveyor — moral values and the Way, the *Dao,* of the ancestors from the past which he idealized were to be reinstated in order to put an end to the chaos and the confusion of his time. He lay down behavioral norms to regulate human order and determined ceremonies and rites to regulate relationships between people within the family and society as well as in the area of religion. The most important aspects of his teachings were ancestor worship and subordinates' obedience to their superiors (see page 58). Though Confucius considered ancestor worship to be the honoring of one's own forefathers, a Confucius-cult developed which was in opposition to his beliefs. In the year 59, when Confucianism had already become the state doctrine, the Han emperor ordered regular sacrificial ceremonies for Confucius. In Qufu, Shandong, where Confucius was born and died, and also in other parts of the empire, temples were erected in his honor (see page 291).

This Confucian cult continued until the 20th century. Confucius had recognized Heaven as the highest god. The emperor was the highest being on earth and, as the Son of Heaven, responsible to Heaven. It was his duty alone to pay homage to heaven. The most important sacrificial act took place during the winter solstice. The last emperor's place of worship can be visited today in Beijing (see Temple of Heaven, page 138). These activities were not allowed to be witnessed by the common people. They had to find their own ways to practice religion.

Daoism placed value on individualism, anarchy and mystic experience. Daoists were seeking individual peace. They strove to become one with nature through *wuwei,* inactiveness, in order to let all that exists take its free, natural course. The goal was a life in harmony with the cosmos. Daoists endeavored to develop various techniques for longevity and immortality. The creator of Daoism is considered to be the legendary Laozi. The fundamental Daoist work, *Daodejing,* is attributed to him (see page 59).

Phenomenal religious activity developed during the Qin and Han Dynasties. Religious Daoism, above all the desire for immortality, spread; at the same time it was an age of superstition. This was the starting point for the development of the so-called folk religion. It united elements from all religious movements, especially from Daoism and Buddhism, and its adherents were mainly the masses. Many gods were created, such as gods of rain, city, earth, kitchen etc., who were honored and to whom sacrifices were made in order to gain their favor.

Daoism did not develop into a unified religious doctrine; the so-called masters of the different temples influenced the teachings in their distinct ways. In the 2nd century, Zhang Daoling became the first in the line of southern Daoist masters which still continues today. Fixed forms of worship developed, congregations were organized, monasticism developed and a comprehensive canon was established. The teachings also acquired elements of the folk religion. Independent Daoist congregations, sometimes led by charismatic leaders, were not seldom closely connected with political uprisings.

Foreign merchants brought Buddhism to China via India and Central Asia in the middle of the 1st century at the latest; and at first it was practiced mainly by foreigners. As early as 166, Buddhism was known at the Imperial Court. Emperor Huan of the Han Dynasty had a shrine in which a Buddhist god was honored, erected inside the palace. In the following centuries, Buddhist monks translated Indian sutras, (educational stories), and founded monasterial centers. At the beginning, celibacy was not accepted because it meant having no children, that is, no descendants who would make sacrifices to the ancestors. But, with time, more and more Chinese adopted the foreign religion and were willing to accept monastery life. At the end of the 4th century, the first Chinese monks went to India to visit the holy places of Buddhism and to collect new texts.

The decline and fall of the Han Dynasty at the beginning of the 3rd century and the following time of political division made traditional Confucian officialdom seem irrelevant. Daoism and Buddhism experienced a great boom. Secluded monastery life became attractive. Under foreign rule, Buddhism, as a non-Chinese religion, received state support.

During the first millenium, Buddhism's influence grew among Chinese thinkers, and it was a constant rival of Confucianism and Daoism. It affected philosophic thought, literature and art. Hundreds of thousands of men and women joined the orders and millions of believers supported them. Monasteries became rich and reached the pinnacle of their power by the Tang period.

The type of Buddhism propagated in China was *Mahayana,* which promised all people enlightenment and salvation, whether rich or poor, male or female, good or bad. This was in contrast to monastic Buddhism, *Hinayana,* which succeeded in Burma, Thailand, Laos and Cambodia. *Mahayana* not only propagated one's own salvation and the attainment of nirvana, but also sacrificing oneself for others. Honoring the charitable bodhisattvas, who held the highest rank before becoming a Buddha, became the focus because they were the ones who took pity on suffering people and made it possible for them to experience a good rebirth in the next life. *Mahayana* assimilated various Chinese gods, rites, forms of worship and superstition and for this reason offered all stages of religiosity. Different schools developed, based upon certain Buddhist writings and their interpretations, and maintained great monasteries. Among the most important was the *Tiantai* school, founded in 580, named for a mountain near Ningbo, Zhejiang, where the main monastery was located. Its central work was the Lotossutra, *Fahua Jing*. Another school is the school of the 'Pure Land' which was probably in existence as early as the 5th century. It is based on the belief that Buddha Amitabha mercifully saves people who call upon him for help. He demands only faith, no active demonstrations. This school had the largest number of adherents and is still active today. A second outstanding school was the school of *Chan* (Japanese *Zen*), which promised salvation through one's own perceptions following long meditation exercises.

Towards the middle of the Tang Dynasty, the enmity between Daoism/Confucianism and Buddhism manifested itself. Confucianism was again the state doctrine, so Confucian education was relevant. The state viewed Buddhist institutions with mistrust. The monasteries had become rich; besides possessing property, they also owned mills and oil presses. They did not have to pay taxes. Numerous donors had bequeathed their lands to them in order to avoid taxes and, in this roundabout way, to obtain revenue from the land. Since monks could not be forced to join the army nor to do compulsory service, the state lost thousands of young workers. In 845, over 200,000 monks and nuns were defrocked, hundreds of monasteries were destroyed and valuables confiscated. Buddhism in China was never really able to recover from this blow. Only the schools of *Chan* Buddhism and 'Pure Land' survived the persecution.

Mahayana and *Hinayana* Buddhism did not reach Tibet until the 7th century. Here various schools also developed. The most significant was the 'Yellow Sect' of the reformer Zongkaba (1357—1410). The highest representatives in the hierarchy of this sect have been called *Dalai Lama* since the 16th century. The Mongols and later the Manchus accepted the teachings of the 'Yellow Sect'. Under the rule of the Manchurian Qing Dynasty, sacred institutions of Tibetan Buddhism were established throughout the empire; this is known in the West as Lamaism.

Other foreign religions, such as Islam, were brought to China by way of the sea by Arabian and Persian merchants during the Tang era. During the Yuan Dynasty, this religion acquired many believers, and in the West and Northwest of the empire, it even became the dominant religion. Christian teachings came to China with the arrival of the Nestorians in the 6th century. A stele which can still be seen today in Xi'an tells of a Nestorian mission which was located in the empire's capital Chang'an in 635 (see page 380). During the Yuan Dynasty in the 13th century, Christian missionaries—Franciscan and Dominican monks—came to China. With the fall of the Yuan Dynasty, the Christian mission was finished for the time being. In the 16th century, the Jesuit Matteo Ricci (1552—1610) came to China and earned the good opinion of the emperor. Fifty years later there were supposedly 150,000 Christians in the country. The Jesuits were respected by the Chinese emperors, above all for their knowledge of mathematics and astronomy. A widespread Christian missionary movement began under the cover of Western countries' power politics in the 19th century.

Schools, hospitals and universities were built. But the imperialistic appearance and use of force by their governments were the doom of the missionaries. The anger and indignation directed toward Western power politics and oppression erupted in the Boxer Rebellion (1900—1901), in the course of which many Christians were killed. In the following decades, the Christian movement recovered again. But in spite of the successes which cannot be denied in the area of education and medicine, the Christian religion was not very successful in China.

After the founding of the People's Republic, freedom of religion was guaranteed in the constitution in 1954. However, above all during the Cultural Revolution, it was the Christians and Buddhists who were oppressed. Monasteries and churches were closed or used for other purposes. After the fall of the Gang of Four, things changed. Monasteries were reopened and were allowed to recruit young members. Christian churches held services again; study and researching of religion at educational establishments and institutes was again taken up.

Foundations of Philosophy

The foundations of Chinese philosophy were established between the 6th and 3rd centuries BC. The rulers of the Zhou Dynasty had lost some of their power; armed conflicts between feudal princes plunged the country into chaos and misery. In this atmosphere of violent struggle for power, intellectual life developed and diversified as it never would again. This period is called the 'Age of 100 Schools'. Advisors traveled from one feudal state to another, offering the rulers their services. At some courts there were dozens or even hundreds of such advisors, competing to formulate adequate measures to save and strengthen the country. These contests produced a number of philosophers who soon had a following and became the founders of schools. The four most important ones will be dealt with.

Confucianism

Confucianism was initiated by a scholar named Kong Qiu. The designation 'Master Kong', in Chinese Kong Fuzi, was latinized by the Jesuit fathers as Confucius. Confucius' family came from the lower nobility; his home was in the state of Lu, present-day Shandong. He was born in 551 BC and died in 479 BC. Perhaps he could be considered to be the first of the wandering advisors. Since his teachings were based on moral values, the princes who were occupied with armed conflicts hardly listened to him, and he remained more or less unsuccessful. Later he founded a type of private school in which he passed his teachings on to his pupils and prepared them for administrative positions. It was the students of these pupils who first collected Confucius' thoughts in the so-called *Lunyu*, 'Analects', creating the basis to which the later Confucian teachings referred.

The focus of this teachings was 'humanity' and 'nobility'. Integrity and benevolence were to determine the behavior of a virtuous person toward his fellow-man. Only a virtuous ruler would be able to bring order to his country and be a model of morality and integrity for his subjects. Confucius believed it was possible to attain the ideal societal order by reviving the culture and the ritual behavioral rules of the early Zhou period, which made necessary a thorough study and interpretation of the traditional texts of that time. In this way, several works were written — supposedly revised by Confucius — which later became classics of Chinese literature alongside *Lunyu*:

> *Shijing*, the Classic of Poetry, a collection of popular songs and courtly melodies from the early Zhou period, which were interpreted according to Confucian teachings.
> *Shujing*, the Classic of History, a collection of early historical annals.
> *Liji*, the Record of Rites, notes about rites, manners and customs.
> *Chunqiu*, the Spring and Autumn Annals, a chronicle of his home state Lu, in which the traditions of the early Zhou era were supposedly kept the longest.
> *Yijing*, the Book of Changes, a book of divination.

Confucius divided people into three categories:
1. The holy, (wisemen), who had reached the highest stage of extraordinary perfection.
2. The noble, a generally attainable stage, which could be reached through virtuous behavior, fulfillment of duties and humaneness.

In this context, five rules were formulated which were to lend order to human relationships.

Recognition of the authority of superiors was an obligation in the relations:

> ruler — subject
> father — son
> husband — wife
> elder brother — younger brother
> friend — friend

Love of children and brotherly love were values which were continually stressed in Confucian tradition and were considered to be the root of human kindness. That meant that Confucius did not judge a person by his origins, but by his moral integrity and perfection. According to Confucius, the noble should be wise, benevolent and courageous, not motivated by profit, but solely by integrity.

3. The common or insignificant

Confucius had not yet analyzed the question whether human nature was basically good or evil. His predecessors Mengzi and Xunzi did take up the problem.

Mengzi (372—289 BC), also known by his Latin name, Menzius, maintained that man is by nature good because he possesses four inherent virtues from the beginning: humanity, integrity, propriety and knowledge. For this reason he has an innate knowledge of good and the inborn capacity to do good. Education is required to maintain these virtues.

Xunzi (313—238 BC) believed however, that human nature is inherently bad; man is supposedly born with feelings of greed and envy. Since these characteristics result in conflicts and disagreements, rules of propriety and justice must be made in order to control the evil and train the good. Government by a virtuous ruler striving for order and welfare — what Confucius was aiming at — was also idealized by Mengzi and Xunzi. Whereas Mengzi desired a humane government and an exemplary humane ruler, Xunzi saw his goal to be a government based upon laws and, instead of moral examples, he called for discipline. This was why Xunzi was criticised by some Confucians and was accused of having ties to Legalist doctrine.

By the 3rd century BC, Confucianism had not had the chance to develop considerably, and during the Qin Dynasty, it was forced to give precedence to Legalism (see page 60). Not until after the fall of the Qin Dynasty, under Han rule in the 2nd century BC, did a court scholar, *Dong Zhongshu* (176—104 BC), succeed in creating a Confucian state doctrine which did, however, harbor Legalist factors, and which would become the foundation of the Chinese empire.

This doctrine of state was based on three aspects:

Religion: Confucius recognized heaven as a higher power and stressed ancestor worship. Man and the cosmos were closely bound and were in a state of harmony. If this harmony were destroyed by man, the universe would express its displeasure through signs which threatened disaster or through natural catastrophes. These warnings were meant for the ruler, as the representative of humanity, who either had to show improvement or was in danger of losing the 'mandate of heaven', the justification of his sovereignty.

Philosophy: In his attempts to revive the culture of the early Zhou Dynasty, Confucius analyzed its traditions and made them part of his teachings. Dong Zhongshu expanded these teachings with cosmological and Legalistic considerations when he created the Confucian state doctrine.

Social politics: In the early Han period, Confucianism was able to establish itself as a doctrine of state. This doctrine was upheld by loyal officials who were devoted to the emperor. Since studying Confucian texts and taking examinations were the only way to obtain a career as an official, candidates did not necessarily have to come from the aristocratic upper class, but could also be recruited from the lower classes. This reduced the influence of the hereditary aristocracy, and greater social mobility was the consequence. Those who in this way became part of the Confucian elite as officials remained firmly in a position of power until the end of the empire.

Daoism

As with other schools, the Daoists strove to find a way out of the disorder and misery of the times. The concept of Daoism comes from the word *Dao*, the 'Way', the 'source' from which all being originates. The legendary Laozi (6th century BC) is considered to be the founder of the Daoist school of thought; the central work about these teachings, *Daodejing,* the 'Book of Dao and its Influence' , is also attributed to him.

The focus of Daoism is *Dao*, which is absolute, beyond space and time, eternal. It generated the original forces *yin* and *yang. Yin* — female, weak — also stands for darkness, passivity; *yang* — male, strong — also re-

presents light and activity. The balance between these two forces results in harmony; their mutual interaction generates all forms of life.

In a world ruled by *Dao,* in which all things are in harmony with each other, it is not necessary for a ruler to intercede. Laozi's advice to him is to practice 'inactivity'. The more prudently a ruler governs, letting things take their course and only making his presence felt through the power of his virtue, the more possible it becomes to realize a life in harmony with *Dao.* — Laozi stressed the strength of the weak, their superiority, and compared them to water which, though soft and weak, was capable in the long run of hollowing out even stone.

Laozi rejected all kinds of rules and laws — they would only deform man and increase the number of wrongdoers. He was in favor of a life of moderation, quiet and simplicity and rejected all forms of avidity.

Apart from Laozi, Zhuangzi (4th century BC) is considered to be the most important representative of Daoism. He carried on Laozi's ideas, but paid little attention to his predecessor's wish to offer council about governing wisely. He was much more concerned with the relativity of all things; they are able to transform themselves at any time, nothing is absolute. If one found something beautiful, there was certain to be something more beautiful; if one found something ugly, there was certainly something even uglier. In this way, the beautiful becomes ugly and the ugly, beautiful. Zhuangzi's ideal human being can only find a way out of a life full of worries and troubles if he will free himself from his individuality, let things take their course without resistance and become a companion of nature. Free of all ties, he would let all contradictions pass him by and would be able to become one with the universe, changing freely in nature. These were the thoughts people found so attractive and exciting in the times of unrest and distress.

Mohism

The school of Mozi, founded by Mo Di (ca. 480—390 BC), propagated all-encompassing love and mutual gain. Mozi was familiar with Confucian teachings and became a severe critic of them. He condemned the hierarchical social order and the principle of the five human relationships which Confucius advocated. It would, due to a lack of love, lead to arrogance on the part of the superior towards his subordinate and would provoke hate and disaster.

For this reason, people should love and respect the parents, families and states of others as if they were their own.

Mozi strictly rejected wars of aggression but accepted defensive wars. His disciples supported the position of the weak and considered themselves to be champions of justice. Justice came from heaven and had to be exercised by people on earth. Mohists were the ones who advised small, threatened states in their defensive wars against larger ones.

Mozi advocated industry and thrift. In order to mitigate the suffering of the people and help them to earn a modest income, he welcomed everything that would contribute to their welfare and rejected everything which was of no use to them or did them harm. Costly burials which could plunge a family into debt and the long period of mourning which followed — Mozi considered this a waste of time and a deterrent to work — were in this category. He equally condemned the life of luxury and thought music and art useless.

In the 3rd century BC, Mohism was still more influential than Confucianism. It was not, however, agreeable to the ruling class and did not look after its own interests to the extent that Confucianism did. By the end of the 3rd century BC, the Mohists had become increasingly less important.

Legalism

The school of Legalism, also called the school of law, was oriented not toward moral values like humanity, justice, universal love as the proper means to govern a state, but instead advocated the formulation of general, binding laws which were the same for all and which — complemented by a system of rewards and punishments — strengthened the ruler's power and made it possible to control each individual. The goal was a militarily and economically strong state maintained by soldiers and peasants. Tendencies toward a legalistic philosophy developed relatively early. In the 7th century BC, the statesman Guanzi (Guan Zhong) propagated a constitutional state and stressed the importance of general material welfare. Two other notable representatives of Legalist ideas, Shen Buhai (ca. 400—337 BC) and Shang Yang (ca. 390—338 BC), lived in the 4th century BC. Shen Buhai had made a name for himself primarily by his methods of choosing and handling high dignitaries. Shang Yang favored strict laws which would strengthen sovereign powers and a system of rewards and punishments which he is said to have created.

Not until the 3rd century BC were the ideas and teachings of these men compiled by Han Feizi (ca. 280—233 BC) and the foundations of Legalism laid down. Han Feizi is considered the actual perfector of the Legalist philosophy. He was a student of the Confucian Xunzi and like Xunzi, he was convinced that man was basically evil. The only deterrent to injustice and crime was the threat of severe punishment. He held strict laws to be the only effective means of strong rule.

The first and last dynasty to govern according to Legalist principles was the short-lived Qin Dynasty, 221—206 BC. The state of Qin, originally a vassal state of the Western Zhou empire, succeeded in subjugating all feudal states and founding a new empire under its control. Emperor Qin Shihuang used Legalist principles to build up a centrally administered state and create a system of public officials which diminished the power of the feudal lords and continued to be the administrative basis for all later dynasties.

After the fall of the Qin empire, Legalism was immediately discredited and was bitterly opposed by Confucians. Although there were occasionally rulers who governed by Legalist principles, Legalism never again succeeded in being elevated to a state doctrine. But it cannot be denied that Confucian states of later dynasties repeatedly employed Legalist practices.

Art

Classical Architecture

The People's Republic of China has been engaged in restoring its cultural-historical monuments for quite a long time. More frequently than in earlier years, the visitor's attention is today directed towards the inheritance of traditional architecture, and he is proudly reminded of the brilliant artistic skill of past epochs' architects.

We know from our own experiences how much more worthwhile visits to houses, palaces and temple complexes can be if one has a certain amount of knowledge about architecture. For this reason, we would like to offer some background information about the development of architecture. In addition, we will concentrate on the creation of forms and structures of residential and religious buildings. Sketches will draw attention to noteworthy details such as roof decoration, ornamentation on doors, windows, terraces, etc.

Classical Chinese architecture is characterized by 3,500 years of continuity. As early as the 1st century BC, the important structural elements had been developed which would influence architecture up until the 20th century. The first evidence of wooden structures were found in the excavations of a settlement in Banpo Cun village near Xi'an, Shaanxi. This settlement dates back to the 5th-4th century BC and can be classified by the ceramic finds of the Yangshao Culture. Traces in house foundations point to a simple timber frame construction system (see page 379). The center of the first dynasty, the Xia Dynasty (21st—16th century BC), was located on the middle and lower course of the Yellow River. The Shang Dynasty followed in the 16th century BC; its high level of craftsmanship, exemplified by remains of outstanding bronze work, astounded later generations time and again. At that time people lived in village communities under the rule of a hierarchically structured tribal nobility. Land was distributed by the king to the nobles in the form of fiefs. The first movements toward forming a state were discernible toward the end of the Shang Dynasty. The beginnings of a class system are naturally evident in the architecture of the time. While the majority of the population continued to live in simple huts, the upper class lived in buildings characterized by complex building techniques. Interesting structures are recognizable in characters found on bronzes of the Shang era.

In Erlitou, near Luoyang, archaeologists found construction remains from the transition period between the Xia and Shang Dynasties. They indicate that one of the first important cities of Chinese civilization was located here. A terrace — 100 m long, 108 m wide and 0.8 m high — was uncovered on which the platforms of several representative buildings can be recognized. The complex was enclosed by a wall with a colonnade inside. Archaeologists refer to this find as a forerunner of future palace architecture. The most important elements of Chinese architecture were included in the complex at Erlitou: the terrace, several buildings forming the walled-in building complex, the platform, timber frame construction. Rulers lived in fortified cities which soon developed into centers of craftsmanship and trade.

The Zhou Dynasty followed the Shang. An interesting innovation was the use of fired roof tiles.

The second half of the Zhou Dynasty — also called the Eastern Zhou Dynasty — was divided into Chunqiu — Spring and Autumn periods — and Zhanguo — the Period of Warring States. The power of the ruling house of Zhou and the feudal system were considerably weakened; small, independent, rival states evolved from the fiefs. As at one time bronze casting had had a crucial effect on arms production, so the casting of iron revolutionized development in agriculture and trade. With the help of new tools such as saws and axes, more woods could be cleared for cultivation substantially faster; the system of community-managed agriculture was replaced by private ownership and private cultivation of the land. The division of labor and the production of goods influenced trade and opened up markets. With the invention of metal money came an economy based on currency. Innumerable trading and handicraft businesses opened branches in new places. Iron mines began operation and made their owners richer than members of princes' families. Great residences and palaces were built which were artistically decorated with reliefs, wood carvings and colorful paintings. Excavations have brought to light the luxury and splendor which surrounded the upper class at that time. Lacquerware, bronze vessels, carvings, jade and ceramics from this time are on display today in China's museums. The rivalry of the princes and the wars which resulted placed new demands on architecture. The construction of city walls, city gates, border fortifications (forerunners of the Great Wall) and signal towers were essential. Streets and bridges were built in the cities and the digging of canals served military as well as commercial purposes. Exact stipulations for the width of streets were made, expressed in the number of horse-drawn wagons that could be driven next to each other.

At the end of the Zhou period, there were only seven states left. One of these, the state of Qin, proved to be the strongest after a slow start; it subjugated the other six, uniting the empire under its leadership in 221 BC. The first

Characters from the Shang period

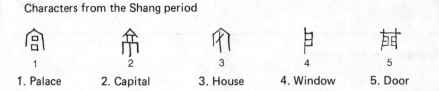

1. Palace   2. Capital   3. House   4. Window   5. Door

Piyong shrine, Han period

emperor of this united China, Qin Shihuang, developed incredible architectural activity. He gathered the best craftsmen from all parts of the country in the capital and had palaces and tombs built. Of about 700 palaces constructed under his rule, 270 were in the vicinity of the capital. The forced meeting of the artisans had the advantage of automatically bringing about the constructive exchange of building techniques, and a melting pot of southern, northern, eastern and western architectural and handicraft skills was the result. The continuing excavations at Xi'an, where the first capital of the empire was located, offer an impression of the technical perfection which had already been reached by that time. Further significant measures taken by Qin Shihuang were the connection of individual fortification complexes to form the Great Wall and the standardization of weights, measures and axle widths.

Qin dynasty rule was of short duration. As early as 206 BC, a peasant revolt tumbled the house of Qin and brought with it the Han Dynasty (206 BC—220 AD). Under the new rulers, the empire expanded to Central Asia. A centrally organized government with a hierarchy of officials evolved. The new system was built on the foundations of Confucian doctrine.

Contact with foreign countries made via the Silk Road was to affect the arts and skilled crafts in numerous ways. New houses and streets were built, and in the capital city Chang'an, northwest of present-day Xi'an, the palaces Weiyan Gong and Changle Gong were erected. The city was divided into nine sections and 160 streets. Twelve horse-drawn wagons could be driven next to one another on the main streets.

Much is known about the architecture of the Han period. Detailed clay models of buildings of all kinds, which were buried with the dead, prove that the art of construction at that time already included the foundations which later would only be further developed and refined. Reconstructions according to uncovered building remains and wall paintings in tombs complete the picture. One example is the reconstruction of a shrine from the Han period — 'Piyong' — on page 62.

Timber frame construction and a simple bracket system were already fully developed. Important building complexes were laid out on a north-south central axis in a walled-in courtyard, most often rectangular in shape.

The building of multi-storied houses and towers was an important architectural step; towers up to four stories high were especially

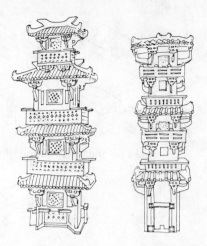

Clay models of towers from the Han period

popular in the second half of the Han Dynasty. They had diverse uses and, in addition, were a status symbol.

Adherents of Daoism liked to retreat there to practice exercises which were supposed to prolong life. At the upper levels they felt themselves removed from the earth. On rivers and lakes the tower constructions served as observation pavilions. People often enjoyed celebrating feasts in these buildings. They also functioned as watch towers.

Another important factor for the future development of architecture was the area of funerary architecture with its masonry construction. At the beginning, only hollow bricks were made; later, bricks were used which made it possible to form complicated vaults and domes. Doors were decorated with stone pillars and slabs.

After the fall of the Han Dynasty, wars, chaos and a succession of short-lived dynasties followed. Valuable edifices burned down, cities were reduced to ashes and ruin. Foreigners advanced from the north and made themselves the new rulers. People fled from the north to the area south of the Changjiang river, so that new cultural centers sprang up there. Buddhism, known in China since the Han Dynasty, found a foothold in the despairing population in these difficult times. The foreign rulers recognized Buddhism, which was also alien, as a welcome means of opposing Chinese Confucianism and Daoism. They fostered its propagation and financed numerous buildings. Even today, evidence of this development can be seen in the magnificent cave temples of Dunhuang in Gansu, Yungang in Shanxi, and Longmen in Henan.

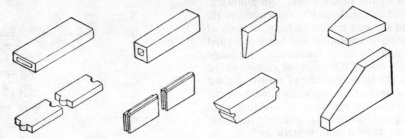

Bricks for the construction of vaults and domes in funerary architecture

Mass-produced wooden parts

Throughout the empire, in the cities as well as in the countryside, temples and monasteries were built. Buddhism had a reviving effect on architecture. Although temples were constructed according to the established principles of religious buildings, new accents were added in the interior decoration of the halls and pagodas. Pagodas were modelled on the Indian stupa. The impulse to realize it was there, but the style was not successful. Chinese building masters returned to their own tradition, namely towers from the Han Dynasty.

The short-lived Sui Dynasty (581—618), which put an end to the wars and reunited the empire, began, as the Qin Dynasty did, with a gigantic construction project. Besides the building of palaces and new sections of the Great Wall, the Grand Canal project — a waterway which was to connect the North with the South — was started.

Architecture reached a peak in the following Tang Dynasty (618—907). There are several small wooden structures remaining from this period; however, they are not representative of the perfection of Tang architecture. The excavations in present-day Xi'an — the former capital Chang'an — on the other hand, do give an impression of the brilliant success of Tang architects.

The architectural style of the Song Dynasty (960—1279) is characterized by elegance and sensitive design and by harmonious coloration. Two important architectural documents were written in these times: *Mujin*, 'Wood-working' and *Yingzao Fashi;* 'Fundamentals of Architecture'. With the help of these books, the amount of materials needed for a project could be estimated ahead of time. A type of

mass production of important parts was begun which considerably cut down on building time.

The end of the Song Dynasty again brought the country chaos and misery. Foreigners from the north invaded once again and established a new dynasty on Chinese territory. In 1279, the Mongols succeeded in uniting the empire under their leadership to found the Yuan Dynasty. Since the Mongols maintained close contact to the Tibetan lamaseries, the influence of Lamaism was soon noticeable. Tibetan Lamaist monks went to the court in Dadu, today's Beijing, to support the Mongols in the administration of government. Lamaism became the state religion. Numerous monasteries were built which distinctly reflect the influence of, or at times even totally incorporate, Tibetan style.

During the Yuan Dynasty, plays were especially popular. As a result, stages were built in temples, parks, palaces and in public squares. With the advance of Islam, a branch of temple architecture took on a new direction. The foreign, Islamic architectural style became accepted in contrast to Buddhism.

Under the new rule of the Ming Dynasty, traditions of Chinese architecture were continued and perfected. In the 17th century, the Manchurian Qing Dynasty took over the inheritance of the Ming, creating no noteworthy new structures, so that today, a good number of historically valuable complexes remain.

Timber Frame Construction

Since ancient times, timber frame construction had been used for the building of dwellings, halls and temples. The basic principle is that columns and beams fulfill static functions, while walls are only used to fill the spaces in between and to decorate. This technique gave each individual building an elegant, pleasing appearance and made a nice combination of buildings possible. Solid construction in stone was almost exclusively confined to ornamental walls, courtyard walls, terraces, balustrades, pagodas, funerary buildings, bridges and fortification complexes.

Of course, wooden structures naturally had the disadvantage of being less permanent than stone structures. Wood is more easily destroyed by fire than stone. For this reason, few wooden structures from the 1st millenium have survived. The oldest examples of timber frame construction date back to the Tang Dynasty (618—907). But there were a great many advantages which caused the Chinese to give preference to wood over stone for more than 3,500 years. Wood was easier to transport and work with than stone, because large, single pieces could be used and it was strong enough to support heavy tile roof constructions. It lent itself to the mass-production of standardized construction parts. A further advantage was the fact that statically unimportant parts could be moved at will or even entirely removed so that partitions between the supporting columns could simply be taken away during long warm summers. Wood was also pleasing from an aesthetic point of view because it could be carved beautifully to unite harmoniously with the columns.

The most important elements of a traditional Chinese building are the terrace on which the building rests and the roof which covers it. Both elements are symbols of the cosmos: the terrace represents the supporting earth and the roof, the heavens which cover all. Between the roof and the terrace are the column zone and the framework of which only the lower longitudinal beams and the bracket system are visible.

The platform or terrace protects the building from dampness and water. Its design depended on the type of building which was to be built. The height of the terrace was determined by the rank of the structure within the building complex. Main halls on the central axis stand on higher terraces than secondary halls and tower over them. Construction materials varied. The platforms of simple buildings were usually made of packed earth. Valuable halls, on the other hand, were erected on terraces made of bricks and a mixture of different materials. In building a terrace, first a hole was dug and the earth was firmly packed. The hole was then filled, layer by layer, with brick fragments, stones, earth, lime or other materials and each was packed hard. Terraces were decorated on the outside with stone slabs or bricks, column bases were sunk into its surface and steps leading up to it were built.

Column bases — usually of stone, although occasionally of bronze — protected the bottom of the wooden columns from dampness. They could be very simple, but were often artistically patterned.

The smallest unit of a building was a *jian,* 'interval' — a space bounded by four columns. Normally a building consisted of three to seven *jian.* The number of *jian* is odd because one *jian* was laid out on the middle axis. There are structures of only one *jian,* for example simple houses and pavilions, and great palace constructions of 11 *jian.* The wider the structure, the more rows of columns had to be built inside to support the crossbeams.

Columns, which could often be quite high, usually were made of pine. Particularly during the Ming Dynasty, precious southern Chinese *nanmu* wood — prized for its durability, length and strength — was preferred for the building of palaces. Years later the tree became rare, and finally, even magnificent structures had to be built with pine.

At the top, columns are connected by one or two longitudinal beams. Crossbeams run between these. The lower one penetrates the column and extends slightly beyond it. The second column is also connected by longitudinal beams. The upper crossbeam supports two small columns which support the next crossbeam. The highest crossbeam supports only a small column on which the ridge piece rests.

Imperial buildings, temples and villas belonging to high dignitaries have bracket systems between the column zone and the roof; the common man was not allowed to have them. Official regulations dictated to what extent this system could be used for particular structures. Originally the bracket system was supposed to support the overhang of the roof — the eaves — and to shift the bulk of the weight to the columns and beams. With time, it increasingly developed into a decorative element which not only ornamented the wall area, but was also used as ceiling decoration.

The bracket system consists of arms which run longitudinally and diagonally. Four arms extend out from a lower bracket and each leads in turn to smaller plates from which arms extend upward.

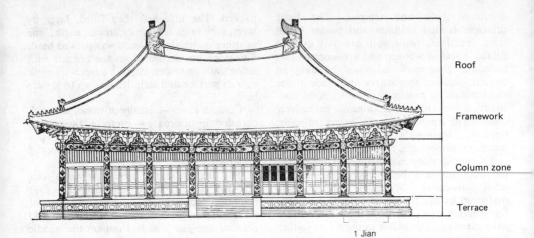

Roof

Framework

Column zone

Terrace

1 Jian

The four levels of a hall

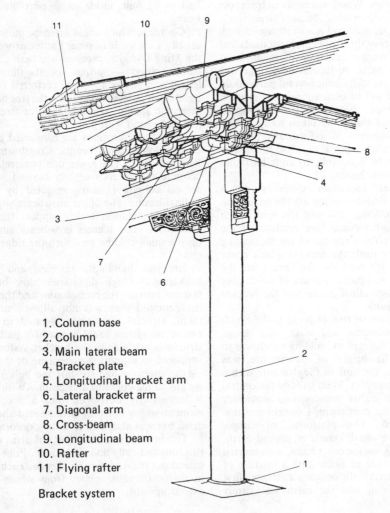

1. Column base
2. Column
3. Main lateral beam
4. Bracket plate
5. Longitudinal bracket arm
6. Lateral bracket arm
7. Diagonal arm
8. Cross-beam
9. Longitudinal beam
10. Rafter
11. Flying rafter

Bracket system

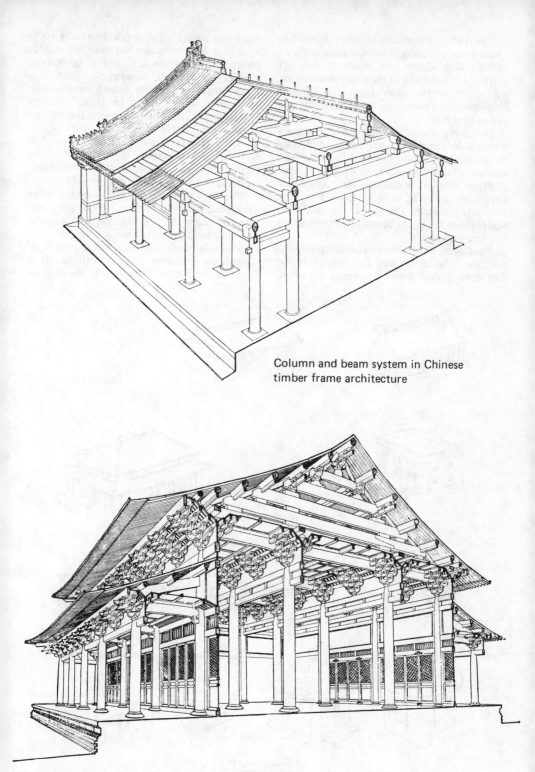

Column and beam system in Chinese timber frame architecture

Bracket system as a decorative element in hall construction

The roof of a traditional Chinese house has a wide eaves overhang. The increasing angle up to the ridge allows rain water to run off quickly; the outswing of the eaves ensures that the water drains away from the house's platform. Since there were no gutters, this was quite important.

In talking about types of roofs, one must distinguish between normal houses and state buildings. Normal houses usually had *xuanshan,* saddle or gabled roofs. In a number of places, one also encounters flat roofs which were built according to local styles. For more elaborate buildings, the *wudian,* hipped roof, was preferred; it could be modified to taste but had one basic form.

Pavilions were often constructed with *juanjian,* conical broach and broach roofs. The most simple ones were made of straw.

Mud was used for flat roofs. Normally roofs were tiled. Simple houses had roofs with slightly-fired gray tiles, the more well-to-do houses, palaces and temple complexes, roofs with black clay or colorfully glazed ceramic tile; yellow tiles were reserved for imperial palace buildings and, in some cases with special permission, for temple complexes.

The tiles were usually laid so that in the first row the hollow pointed upward, and in the second row the hollow pointed downward, covering the seam of the first row of tiles.

The tiles of noble structures had a more exaggerated curvature than the simple ones. The tiles along the edges usually had a round or semi-round decorated end.

The ridge ornamentation on the roofs of some state buildings is quite striking. It is found on both sides of the roof in the form of

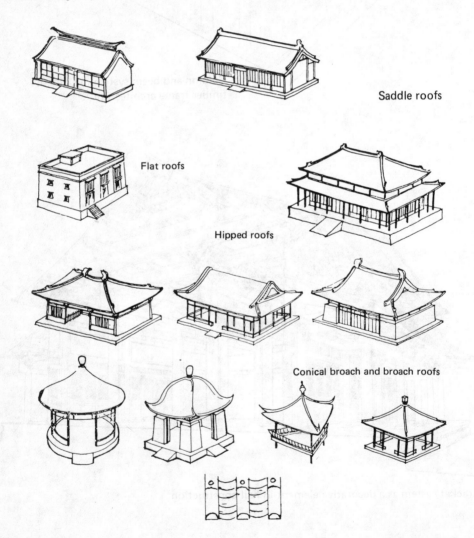

Saddle roofs

Flat roofs

Hipped roofs

Conical broach and broach roofs

Decorations on edge tiles

Chiwei, ridge decorations

sculptures made of glazed tiles — *chiwei*. These are representations of dragon-like animals which face each other with raised tails and seem to hold the ridge in their wide-open mouths. They are supposed to protect the building from bad luck.

Hipped roofs frequently feature small figures along the edges. At the bottom is a sculpture of a person riding a hen.

According to a legend, this is supposedly Prince Min of Qi, a tyrant who was defeated and killed by his enemies in the 3rd century BC. The inhabitants of Qi are said to have his likeness riding a hen on their roofs in order to mark his evil deeds. The hen cannot risk jumping from the roof due to its great burden, and retreat across the roof is also not possible because a dragon head with sharp horns is blocking the way.

Between these two sculptures there are other figures which function as magic symbols and protect the building from evil spirits. After the hen, the lowest figure, come the dragon, phoenix, lion, unicorn, celestial horse and dragon head. Up to 11 figures sometimes adorn the edges of a roof; the figures other than the hen and dragon head sometimes occur more than once.

In the course of the Qing Dynasty, the regulations were not adhered to as strictly, so that deviations from the norm are often visible. In addition, individual styles had developed in central and southern China. There, roofs extend even farther and feature more vivid ornamentation than in North China.

Since the supporting elements of Chinese timber frame construction are the columns, the purpose of walls is to divide, separate and fill

in. Simple houses were made of firmly packed loess or mud or of wood. Walls made of bricks and then plastered were more expensive. Doors and windows were built into the front of the structure.

The outside walls of the halls of extravagant palace and ritual buildings often consisted of wood. Here their filler function is particularly evident because in many cases, the walls are subdivided by windows and doors which are rich in artistic lattice work. An outstanding example is Qinian Dian, the Hall of Prayer for Good Harvests, in the complex of the Temple of Heaven in Beijing; its outside walls are made entirely of lattice work doors. The lower parts of these doors have wooden partitions decorated with carvings. The upper part consists of lattice work which has various patterns. In the cold months, rice paper was glued behind the lattices. Windows were decorated in the same way.

Columns

Wooden columns have been known in China for thousands of years. Since the Period of the Warring States, columns of state buildings have been placed on stone column bases. These were supposed to protect the wood from dampness and give the columns more stability. Column bases, rather simple at the beginning, became more ornamental with time. Besides stone, bronze was also used as a building material.

Solid Construction

Solid construction in China was far less

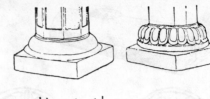

Column bases from the 5th-6th centuries

Column bases from the 10th-13th centuries

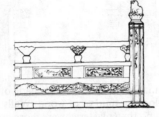

Balustrades as terrace decoration

significant than in Europe. Where there was enough wood, timber frame construction was always given priority. The exceptions were regions which were rich in loess and mud; solid construction has a long tradition there. Not until the end of the 19th century did solid construction become accepted in the building of houses.

The areas in which solid construction always predominated were in the building of terraces, walls, vaults, pagodas and gates. It must also be mentioned that the styles and methods were often determined by or had been copied from timber frame construction. Thus one often sees stone pagodas with curved roofs and bracket clusters which have absolutely no function in solid construction. Bricks were the predominant construction material.

Terraces were among the most important components of Chinese solid construction. They are found in ritual, religious and representative structures. They are designed on a large scale, having one, two or three levels, usually with white stone balustrades. One and two-tiered terraces are present in structures for high officials and within temple complexes. Three-tiered ones were only for imperial buildings.

Such terraces stand alone, like the Altar of Heaven in Tiantan, Temple of Heaven in Beijing. The best examples of this are the main halls of the Beijing Imperial Palace. The terraces are decorated with reliefs and sculptures. The balustrades with their posts and postheads are quite striking.

Walls

Walls are often seen in China surrounding palace and temple complexes and traditional houses. The open design of individual structures — the wide doors, windows and latticework walls, the many walkways and pavilions, which gave the buildings altogether a generous appearance, also made a sturdy wall to the outside necessary in order to form a closed unit. The building materials were either packed loess or mud, though in the last two dynasties, bricks were preferred. Solid, high walls were built around cities. The most famous of all walls is the Wanli Chang Cheng, the Great Wall (see page 156). The gates of the Great Wall and the city walls usually consisted of two parts: the actual gateway and a multi-storied superstructure. Gate constructions which were designed as defensive complexes were built of stone and brick. The towers which were not necessary for defense were made of wood.

Houses

The first stages of architectural development, as already mentioned, can be seen in Banpo Cun, Shaanxi. The traces of dwellings discovered there show rectangular or round pits with a diameter of from 4—7 m in which post holes can be seen. It is assumed that the posts supported a roof of straw or of similar

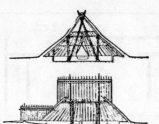

Dwellings in the 5th-4th centuries BC

(Cross-sections of dwelling)

material. The walls consisted of straw and a mixture of earth and lime.

Toward the end of the 4th century BC, people often no longer dug pits and built their houses on flat ground. Sometimes the houses were directly next to one another.

The classic *Yili* (presumably from the Period of the Warring States from 475—221 reports about the houses of the upper class in the 1st millenium BC as being structures which already contained the significant elements of Chinese architecture: a group of buildings surrounded by walls.

The armed conflicts of the last century of the Zhou Dynasty had a stimulating effect on architecture. As early as the time of the Han Dynasty (206BC—220AD) there were exact depictions of city houses. Clay models of residences were buried with the dead; they were supposed to be symbols of their worldly possessions. Thanks to these models, detailed knowledge about the construction of dwellings during the Han Dynasty exists. So there is no doubt that timber frame construction had already reached a high level. People preferred multi-storied houses. They kept pets on the ground floors, and the living quarters were on the next level.

Practically no evidence of dwellings from the centuries after the Han Dynasty remains; one must rely on reliefs. Some from the Northern Wei Dynasty (386—534) offer information about the design of buildings. Corridors connected individual buildings of the complex. Large windows and doors opened out into the courtyards. Ridges were decorated

Clay models from the Han period

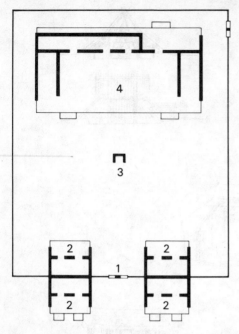

Song reconstruction of buildings from the 1st millenium

1. Main gate
2. Reception halls with back rooms
3. Courtyard
4. Main hall with adjoining and back rooms

with two *chiwei.* figures, which had been reserved for imperial structures during the Han Dynasty. Wealthy families erected temples inside their homes; this was a kind of status symbol at the time.

Murals in the caves at Dunhuang in Gansu depict houses from the Sui and Tang periods (6th—9th centuries). They are pictures of property belonging to high dignitaries and rich families and are characterized by elegance and generosity of scale. Corridors, doors and windows open wide into the courtyard. The beginnings of garden landscaping are visible.

Paintings are likewise the source of information about the lifestyle during the Song era. The works of the painter Wang Ximeng contain scenes which depict houses in rural surroundings.

Distinguished urban families subdivided their buildings within the complexes strictly into the categories of living room, bedroom, study etc. The government of the Northern Song Dynasty (960—1127) issued harsh regulations about how much expense was permissible in the bracket clusters, painted ceilings, carved windows and doors of imperial palaces, temple complexes and villas belonging to high dignitaries. Rich landowners and merchants who lived outside the capital were not subject to strict control. Thus magnificent estates were built, mainly south of the Changjiang river.

During the Ming Dynasty, the imperial court also issued concrete regulations as to the degree of ornamentation allowed. But during

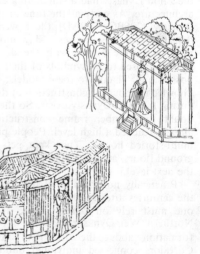

Houses from the Northern Wei period

this time, also, wealthy families knew how to get around the regulations. The houses of this epoch demonstrate strong regional differences. The Qing era adopted the designs and refined them. Individual types of houses are dealt with in the following paragraphs.

Traditional residential complexes were in principle planned for large families. Several generations lived 'under one roof': grandparents, parents, children and, in wealthy families, a large number of servants. As soon as the sons married, they moved with their wives into one of the adjacent buildings. Depending on how prosperous a family was, a male family member had other wives besides his main wife, and they also lived with their children within the complex. Married daughters left the home and joined their husbands' families.

The typical, traditional residential grounds consisted of a rectangular court divided into several units and corridors and surrounded by a wall. Naturally there were great differences — both regional and financial — as far as

design and lay out of buildings and courtyards were concerned. The simple house with courtyard, *siheyuan,* in North China has the following floorplan:

If the front part of the building was replaced by walls, it was referred to as a *sanheyuan.* A well-to-do family could expand its house to two courtyards.

The entrance is located on the right of the southern narrow side. The entrance gate is followed by a so-called *yingbi,* a screen wall which borders the walkway to the north. The purpose of this is to provide protection against evil spirits and certainly to obstruct the view into the courtyard. To the left, a passageway leads to the outer courtyard where the male servants lived and where the kitchen and storage rooms were situated. Through an inside gate one had access to the second court which was exclusively for the family. The female servants usually slept near the women they served.

Individual buildings varied in size and structure depending on the need for living

Sui and Tang period houses

Rural houses of the Song period

space. There were also differences in the use of buildings. Kitchens and storage rooms could be located in different places. Some residential complexes could accommodate several hundred people. They were not only built in a north-south direction, but also, if so desired, in an east-west direction.

As with all building complexes, residential ones were also surrounded by high outside walls. They shielded the buildings from the outside world. The women of the house only ventured out as far as the outer gateway to buy goods.

The courtyards were paved, windows and doors opened into the court. In winter, windows were covered with thick paper, usually only from the inside, sometimes from both sides. The paper was protected from rain and snow by the overhanging roof. Stone floors were not usually covered with carpets. The rooms were heated by charcoal — containers were filled with glowing coals outside the rooms and brought inside.

Floor heating was frequently built into palaces. Especially in the countryside — even today — the *kang,* a heatable brick bed, is used. It is heated from outside. Hot smoke is drawn into the *kang* which is used as a bench during the day and a warm place to sleep at night.

The courtyard houses were naturally quite cold during the biting north Chinese winters — despite the small 'ovens'. People protected themselves from the cold by wearing heavy, quilted clothing.

In the area south of the Changjiang river, the strict plan of the north Chinese house was not followed; several small building complexes were put next to each other. Corridors connected the individual buildings, small ponds, artificial mountains and bizarre rocks subdivided the courtyard. Residential com-

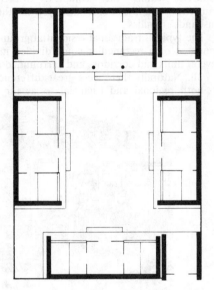

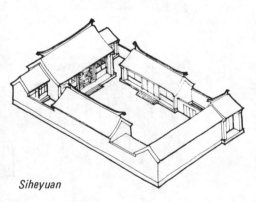

Siheyuan

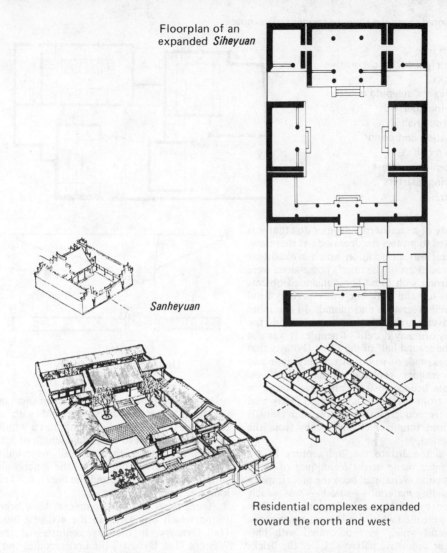

Floorplan of an
expanded *Siheyuan*

Sanheyuan

Residential complexes expanded
toward the north and west

plexes in Hangzhou and Suzhou are typical examples. Residential architecture reached a high level in Suzhou. Here one can even say that the living quarters, pavilions, libraries etc. were built around the gardens.

Funerary Buildings

The construction of funerary buildings occupies an important place in traditional architecture. In the last three decades, Chinese archaeologists have uncovered and investigated various tombs and have come to conclusions that offer new insights and unforeseen details of millenia old tomb architecture. One of the most spectacular finds was made near Xi'an, Shaanxi: the underground army in front of the tomb of the Emperor Qin Shi-

huang (259—210 BC).

Imperial funerary buildings played an important role in court ceremony. Emperors frequently returned to the last resting places of their ancestors, not only to make sacrifices to them and to commemorate them, but to ask for protection and the continuation of their power, since they were the guardians of the dynasty.

The millenia-old cross-shaped underground 'pit' tombs from the Shang Dynasty in Anyang, Henan are among the oldest graves to have been found.

A single or double coffin containing the body was placed in a wooden burial chamber decorated with carvings. With time the caskets were also richly decorated. Underneath the coffin there was usually a small pit containing

Traditional southern Chinese residential complex

1. Entrance
2. Courtyard with decorative rocks
3. Servants' sleeping quarters
4. Living quarters
5. Garden hall
6. Pavilion and pond
7. Main hall
8. Sleeping quarters
9. Living quarters
10. Kitchen

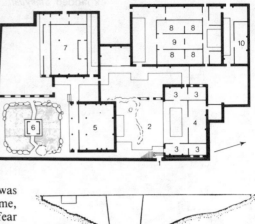

the body of a sacrificed person or dog that was supposed to protect the deceased. At that time, a funeral was an occasion which evoked fear and dread. Part of the ruler's possessions were also buried with him. These included objects of daily use and things he was especially fond of as well as servants and animals. In a number of graves, archaeologists have found the remains of many dozens of people. It was not until the second half of the Zhou Dynasty that offerings made of wood, metal, clay, jade and later ceramics replaced human sacrifices. Valuable bronze instruments were found in tombs from the late Zhou period. Clay and bronze reproductions of people and animals have been found chiefly in tombs from the Han period.

From the 3rd to the 2nd century BC, a change was made in the techniques of tomb construction. What had been the most important building material — wood — was widely replaced by brick. At the beginning, hollow bricks were used which could measure over one meter and which were decorated with bas-reliefs or geometric patterns. Later the bricks were more wieldy and were produced as a kind of fired brick.

This new construction material allowed architects to create underground tombs in which the magnificence of the earthly structures of the deceased could be reproduced.

The tomb of the first Chinese emperor Qin Shihuang is described by the historian Sima Qian (ca. 145—86 BC) as being a monumental complex. About 700,000 people were supposed to have worked on this structure. The results of the excavations in Lintong district, Shaanxi, seem to bear out these descriptions. About 1,200 m east of the actual grave is a 7,000-man army of lifesize terracotta figures. A 47-m-high grave mound still rises today above the not yet opened underground palace. The mound was

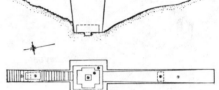

Underground 'pit' tomb

once shaped out of three layers packed earth in the form of a four-sided pyramid with a capped peak. At the base, the hill has a width of 345 m from east to west and a length of 350 m from north to south. Two walls were built around the burial complex — the inner wall with a length of 2.5 km and the outer, 6.3 km long (see page 382).

Three types of tomb complexes have been found which originated in the 400-year-long Han Dynasty. In the first centuries of the Western Han Dynasty, the underground 'pit' tombs still dominated; during the Eastern Han Dynasty, funerary complexes made of brick or cut stone superceded them in importance. Bricks, becoming handier in shape, were well-suited for use in the construction of domes and vaults. By now, underground burial complexes consisted of several main and secondary rooms. A cut stone tomb from the 3rd century, discovered in Yinan, Shandong, was built in a north-south direction and has a length of 8.7 m. It consists of three main rooms, situated one in back of the other on a north-south axis; to the east and west of the first two are annexes. Octagonal columns subdivided the front complex, a column base with bracket clusters, the back. The walls are decorated with reliefs.

Not only the underground burial chambers

Brick construction in funerary architecture

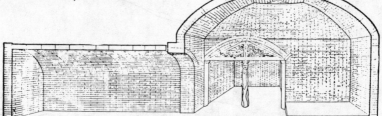

Cut stone tomb in Yinan

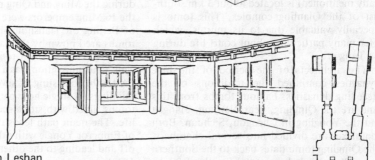

Rock cave tomb in Leshan

were magnificently equipped, the outside of the tomb complex was also festively designed. The path which usually led from the south to the grave mound was bordered by *que,* (honor towers) and stone figures of animals. At the end of this path stood stone steles and a sacrificial shrine or a memorial hall. The steep shaft which led to the underground palace was filled in after the burial. This type of tomb complex would not change significantly in its structure until the Qing Dynasty (1644—1911).

The third type of tomb complex from the Han period consists of chambers which were cut directly into steep cliff slopes. An example from the 1st century is the rock cave tomb Baiya in Leshan, Sichuan. It was laid out on a large scale and the design within distinctly shows the influence of timber frame construction. In this region, 56 tombs were built in an area 1 km long.

The excavation of Crown Prince Zhanghuai's tomb in Qianxian district, Shaanxi, caused a sensation. This tomb is situated about 100 km northwest of Xi'an and is one of the 17

secondary tombs of the Qianling complex, the last resting place of the third Tang emperor Gaozong (reigned from 650—683) and his wife, Empress Wu Zetian. The Qianling imperial tomb and also most of the secondary tombs fit in well with the natural surroundings of the Liangshan hills. The grave mound of Qianling is formed by the highest of the Liangshan hills, the North Hill. The design of the complex followed the fundamentals of Han period funerary architecture with many complementary additions. A square wall was built around the tomb complex and the corners were equipped with towers, each of the sides with a gate guarded by stone statues of animals. South of the North Hill or Tomb Hill, are the two South Hills on which two 8-m-high *que* — honor towers — once stood. Both towers together formed the first gate to the tomb complex. From here, a 4-km-long path led to the grave. Flanking the grave were ornamental columns, stone figures of animals and humans, steles as well as sculptures of kings of countries which were obligated to pay tribute. The south

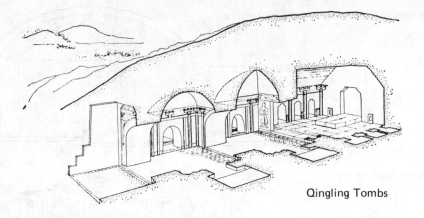

Qingling Tombs

gate and the Xiandian sacrificial hall followed in the north.

The Grave of Crown Prince Zhanghuai (already mentioned) is located about 3 km southeast of the Qianling complex. This tomb is especially valuable due to its murals, which offer many particulars about court life during the Tang era.

The architects of the period of the Five Dynasties continued the traditions of the preceding dynasties. Famous tombs from this time are the Qingling, near Nanjing, Jiangsu and the Yongling in Chengdu, Sichuan. Both complexes are divided into several chambers. The Qingling tomb dates back to the Southern Tang Dynasty. It has a total length of 22 m. The front and middle rooms were built of brick, the back one of natural stone. This underground complex also reflects the influence of timber frame construction in its design.

The Yongling tomb in Chengdu originated in the year 918. It was built directly into a 14-m-high hill and has a length of 23.5 m. Its peculiarity is a coffin platform — a stone terrace — the sides of which are decorated with beautiful reliefs.

The Song imperial tombs are relatively small. One reason for this might be that they were not built until after the emperor had passed away and had to be completed within seven months, the latest time allowed for the burial. The tombs are similar in design and furnishings. There was a fixed number of stone figures which lined the holy path.

In comparison, tombs like that of a merchant in Yuxian district, Henan, from the year 1099, were designed on an individual basis. This particular tomb is a brick construction with a height and design resembling a house. The walls are amply decorated with carvings and paintings, mostly scenes from the life and the surroundings of the deceased.

Funerary architecture reached its peak during the Ming and Qing periods. Thirteen of the 16 Ming emperors were buried 45 km north of Beijing on Tianshou Shan mountain. The tombs are known by the name of Shisan Ling, Thirteen Tombs. Each tomb is enclosed by a wall. One innovation was a complex in front of the tomb, consisting of several courtyards and buildings. A single holy path led to the thirteen tombs, lined with stone sculptures larger than life. The main path leads directly to the tomb of Emperor Yongle with other paths branching off and leading to the other 12 graves (see page 154).

Architects of the Qing era used the Ming period complexes as models. One significant change from the Ming era was the fact that the empress and secondary wives were no longer buried together with the emperor in one grave, but had their own tombs somewhere else. The tombs of the Qing rulers are located in Zunhua and Yixian, Hebei.

Que, Honor Towers

An interesting element of Chinese architecture is a kind of pillar or tower which was erected for decoration at either side of the entrance to palaces, ritual structures or tombs and was generally called a *que*. One of the best examples of this kind is located within the tomb complex of the prefect Gao Yi (died 209) in Ya'an in Sichuan.

It was constructed of stone and is 5.88 m high.

The first *que* appeared as early as the 6th century BC in front of palaces and tombs. Beginning in Han times, temple entrances were decorated with these pairs of towers which were often joined together by an arch or a roof to change it into a kind of front gate.

Architects from the Northern Wei Dynasty devoted special attention to the construction of *que*. Instead of two *que*, they often erected four, and behind them, an ornamental gate.

No fundamental changes in design were made in the Tang and Song Dynasties. The structures became more complex and included large gate constructions.

During the Ming and Qing Dynasties, the *que* was gradually replaced by the *pailou*, ornamental gate, *zhaobi*, screen wall, and *huabiao*, ornamental column. One of the last examples of *que* construction is in the *Wumen* gate at the Beijing Imperial Palace.

Pailou, Ornamental Gate

There are many places in China where the *pailou*, ornamental or ceremonial gate, with one, three or five arches can be seen. It probably originated in India, but Chinese architects usually built them in the traditional timber frame method. *Pailou* stand in broad view outside cities, in front of temple or tomb complexes and on park and palace grounds. They were frequently erected on imperial order to honor or commemorate a distinguished person.

Pagodas

Towers have been known in China since the Han era. In many places they were status symbols for well-to-do families or served as observation or signal towers. When Buddhism came to China in the 1st century, tower structures served religious purposes. They were considered to be symbols of Buddhist teachings which, visible from great distances, proclaimed the will to pass on the faith. The height of the pagoda played a significant role here.

At the start, the pagoda was the main building of a Buddhist temple. It contained relics of of a Buddha or a saint or holy Buddhist symbols and writings. Since the Northern Wei era at the latest, the central buildings of a temple complex have included a shanmen — mountain gate — and a main hall as well as a pagoda. In later centuries, pagodas were erected which had no connection with any temple. They were built to blend into the landscape, guided by the Daoist ideas of harmony and beauty. The pagoda soon became a preferred motif in painting and poetry. In the last centuries it developed into an element of landscape paintings which could not be left out.

They were built to beautify, to serve as observation towers in gardens and parks or as navigational guides for seamen on the coasts and along rivers. Some were no longer significant as symbols of Buddhism, but were merely an element used in landscaping. Daoism also occasionally borrowed the pagoda from Buddhism.

The first pagoda in China was supposed to have been erected in the second half of the 1st

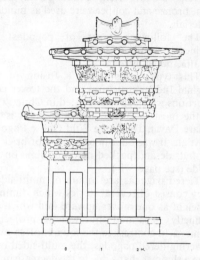

Que, honor tower, in Ya'an

Que as a gate structure

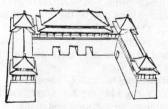

Que as a gate structure
Wumen gate in Beijing

century in Luoyang, which at that time was the imperial capital. The pagoda was the central building of the temple Baima Si, The White Horse Temple. The style of pagoda which developed in China evolved from the Indian shrine (stupa) and from the above mentioned tower structures. They were round in design, four-, six-, eight-, sometimes even twelve-sided. There were single and multi-storied pagodas; the number of stories was usually uneven. Wood, brick, glazed brick, stone, iron, bronze and copper were used as building materials.

The following types of pagodas are frequently seen in China:

Jita, tiered pagoda

This type seems to be a fusion of the original Indian structures and the tower constructions which already existed in China. One of the most renowned tiered pagodas is the square Dayan Ta, Large Wild Goose Pagoda, in Xi'an. It was built in 652 and is of brick on the outside and packed mud and lime on the inside (see page 378).

Tiered pagodas are square or multi-sided. They consist of several stories which diminish in height as one moves upward and which are distinctly separated by widely projecting cornices. In contrast to the square, often overpowering tiered pagodas, the multi-sided ones have a slimmer shape due to the decrease in height of the stories and a considerable increase in the number of stories.

Tianning ta, Heavenly Peace pagoda

This type of pagoda is named after the pagoda at Tianning Si monastery near Beijing. It can be divided into three parts: 1. base, 2. main body containing relics or Buddhist holy objects, 3. high, narrow superstructure with numerous low stories or rings.

Dieceng ta, ring pagoda

Ring pagodas are characterized by low stories and cornices which encircle the tower like rings. They are usually octagonal in design.

Cengta, storied pagoda

This type of pagoda has well-proportioned stories of almost uniform height and cornices which barely project outward. It towers practically straight up due to the minimal angle of incline. One often comes across storied pagodas as glazed pagodas. In the south and southeast of China they were usually made of stone.

Wailangceng ta, gallery pagoda

Gallery pagodas are an interesting further development of storied pagodas. Outside walkways encircle each story and are protected by overhanging eaves. This type of pagoda is

Tiered pagoda

prevalent in central China in the Changjiang region.

Muta, tomb pagoda

Relics of Buddhist saints were buried in tomb pagodas. This type can have many different shapes.

The memorial pagoda evolved from the tomb pagoda. Bodily remains were not interred here, but the deceased was commemorated. A further development was the *sutra column* into which inscriptions of holy Buddhist texts were carved.

Urn pagoda

The model for the urn pagoda must have been the funeral urn. Cremations are especially prevalent in the southern provinces. The highest development of the urn pagoda is the lama pagoda — dagoba — consisting of a base, a bulging urn, a neck with connecting rings, wide umbrella and capital. This kind of pagoda was popular in northern China during the Yuan and especially during the Ming era. There is a double blind door and above it, an inscribed tablet on the main body of the structure; this was probably borrowed from the older tomb pagoda.

Pagodas were distinguished from each other not only in shape but also in construction material, as for example liuli ta, glazed pagodas, the most famous examples of which originated in the Song and Qing eras. There are also shita, stone pagodas, tieta, iron pagodas, and tongta, bronze pagodas.

Cave Temples

The mighty cave temples in North China offer evidence of the advance of Buddhism

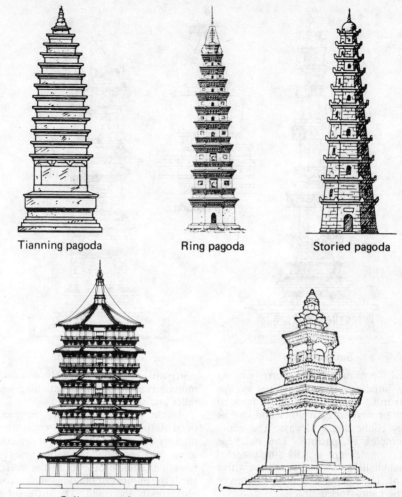

Tianning pagoda

Ring pagoda

Storied pagoda

Gallery pagoda

Tomb pagoda

into China via Central Asia. The most significant ones are the Mogao Caves near Dunhuang and the Maijishan Caves near Tianshui, Gansu, the Yungang Caves near Datong, Shanxi and the Longmen Caves near Luoyang, Henan.

The first cave temples were created in the 4th century along the trading routes between Central Asia and China. In 366, Buddhist monks cut caves into the mountain slopes near Dunhuang and built shrines. They were usually financed by donations from pilgrims.

The great cave temples of Yungang and Longmen originated from the 4th — 6th centuries during the Northern Wei Dynasty. The rulers of this dynasty were, with one exception, great supporters of Buddhism. Buddhist art also reached a peak during this period (see page 183 and 305).

Cave temple construction also flourished

again in the Tang era when caves, niches and sculptures were created by members of all social classes. The smallest sculptures are 2 cm high, the largest, up to 17 m.

Buddhist and Daoist Temple Complexes

There are no great differences in the floor plans and structure of Buddhist and Daoist temple complexes; on the contrary, Daoist temple architects used Buddhist structures as their models. In order to know to which of these two groups a temple belongs, one usually needs to find out its name and the name of the halls or the name of the person to whom it is dedicated.

Chinese temples are never single buildings. They always consist of a group of buildings following a fundamental pattern which, however, can be modified. The main buildings

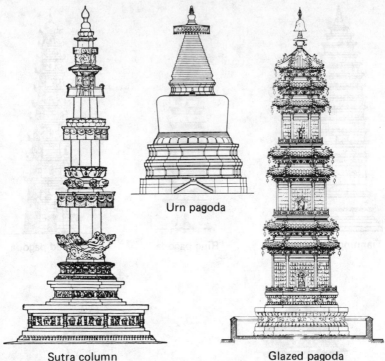

Urn pagoda

Sutra column

Glazed pagoda

and their symmetrically corresponding secondary buildings form individual groups and courtyards. These units stand in back of each other or next to each other and can be reached by connecting walkways. The entire temple complex is spacious. The buildings inside the complex are usually single-storied and the main halls, sometimes decorated with a double roof. The so-called towers, pavilions or halls can be multi-storied structures.

The Chinese temple complex was subject to great structural changes throughout the centuries. Different schools of thought produced different types of structures which conformed to the demands of the teachings and monastery life. A Buddhist monastery in the middle of the first millenium was designed in the shape of a large rectangle in a south-north direction. The entrance, usually a simple gateway in which both celestial guardians stood, led to the outer courtyard of the temple complex. The structures in this outer courtyard were limited to residential, administrative and labor buildings. Following the entrance gate in the north on the central axis, there was a second gateway which led to the inner courtyard. The limits of this rectangular inner court were defined by walls which encircled it or hall-like walkways. In the north, bell and drum towers rose to the left and the right, and in between stood the instruction hall. The inner

courtyard contained the holy objects of the monastery: the pagoda containing sealed-up relics and the Buddha hall.

In the following centuries, temples developed into quite extensive complexes. The number of main halls in the inner courtyard grew; the pagoda was sometimes moved toward the north or even to the outer courtyard; the number of buildings in this courtyard also greatly increased. The different schools had their temple complexes built to approximate more and more the structure of secular palace complexes. Sometimes monasteries came into the possession of other schools which changed and added to the complex according to their own principles. With time, a mixture of styles evolved that made it impossible to determine the school to which the monks of the monastery belonged just by looking at the building complex.

In the following paragraphs, the temple complexes which can still be visited today — their buildings and sacred representations — are described in more detail. As already mentioned, temple architects followed the basic principles of secular structures from the Tang Dynasty on. The complexes stand on a central axis — usually a south-north axis — east-west only as an exception. The main buildings are strung along this central axis, their broadest sides facing south or east. To the right and left of the main hall are secondary halls; all of these together form a structural entity. Next to the main axis there are sometimes lateral axes on which special halls, living quarters, work and storage buildings stand. The adaptability to natural surroundings, demonstrating the special Chinese bond with nature, is characteristic of many temple complexes — chiefly of mountain monasteries. An isolated environment had always been preferred as a site for such institutions. Like imperial tomb complexes, regions were chosen which had mountains, springs and streams close by. Mountains were supposed to protect the monasteries from the north and were considered symbols of eternity; springs and streams were symbols of purity. The natural surroundings influenced the structural development of the entire temple complex and the order and size of each individual group of buildings. Before construction began, the whole area was carefully investigated by a geomancer.

The most important and most frequently represented buildings inside a Buddhist temple complex:

The outer temple gate interrupts the temple's surrounding walls in the south of the complex, or, if it lies on an east-west axis, in the east, and offers access to the temple complex. It is either quite simple or it is a hall-like building with one middle and two side gateways or a pailou, ornamental gate. Above the middle entrance hangs an inscription with the name of the temple. These are often calligraphies by famous masters or influential people; some were even written by emperors. The path leads through the main gate hall to the main area of the monastery. The mighty statues of Erwang, the 'two kings' — the temple guardians — stand in this hall to the left and right. They watch over the actual temple entrance. They are frightening figures with threatening faces and strong, muscular bodies. One stares resentfully at the entering visitors and the other, at those departing and seems to be calling out something to them with wide-open mouth. The temple guardians, armed with a diamond club or diamond wedge, are always ready to destroy evil, sin and the enemy, and to protect the good. According to Buddhist tradition, the two are actually one single being having numerous manifestations. Erwang, also called 'Kings of Knowledge' (Mingwang), know the way to salvation. They remind the Buddhist believer of the significance and sanctity of the place and the principles of their teachings. They show the worthy the way to the shrine; the unworthy are

threatened and forbidden entrance. They are a symbol of Vairocana — the highest and absolute — and his infinite wisdom.

Zhonglou and gulou, bell and drum towers, are two corresponding two-storied pavilions — vertical structures with square-shaped floor-plans — which offer a contrast to the broad design of the halls. They are the characteristic landmark of a sacred building complex. The bell is rung at holy times of the day. Its sound symbolizes the holy teachings, giving the tortured souls consolation and keeping the believer on the right path. With thundering noise, the drum wards off the enemy — the powers which threaten absolute truth.

The first of the holy halls is usually the Tianwang Dian in which the statues of the four Celestial Kings — also called the guardians of the world — stand. They provide protection at all points of the compass for Buddhist teachings, Buddha and the congregation of believers. They carry arms and weapons with which they destroy evil and demons, guard Buddhist truth and serve the welfare of all. Each commands eight generals and their armies. The king of the northern cardinal point — the northern guardian of the world — is the yellow-skinned Duo Wen. In his right hand he holds an unfurled flag, the victory flag of Buddhist truth, which looks like a closed umbrella. It is his special duty to protect Buddhist truth. The white-skinned eastern guardian of the world, Zhi Gui, holds the heavenly lute with which he soothes restless people. He protects people and the world through the power of Dharma. The blue-skinned southern guardian of the world, Zeng Zhang, carries a sword and is ready to destroy evil and demons and to defend goodness. He promotes the good in people. The red-skinned western world guardian, Guang Mu, grasps a snake with his right hand and in the left, holds the pearl of perfection, wisdom and magical power which is only for the holy and withheld from evil beings. It is his special task to further the truth of Mahayana. The four celestial guardians watch over earthly happenings; nothing escapes them. They punish injustice, violence and vice and reward virtue and morality.

The representation of these four kings is not only typical for Buddhist temples, but also for Daoist and Lamaist ones.

Besides the four celestial guardians, the Buddha-to-be, Maitreya, is also in the hall in the form of a fat, genially laughing monk Budai. He is actually still a bodhisattva who, in his capacity as the future savior Buddha, is called Mile Fo. Still on earth today with monk's robes, beggar's sack and rosary, he will finally save the world in times to come. He is a symbol of harmony, love and joy. Maitreya, like a monk, has a bald head; his long earlobes are a symbol of great wisdom and human nobility, and the bushy eyebrows indicate happiness and wisdom. Laugh lines are at the corners of his friendly eyes and his wrinkled brow is a sign of experience and great knowledge. His round belly points to a great center of life behind his navel, which has grown to such proportions as a result of concentrated meditation and self-introspection. Frequently he is surrounded by six children who symbolize the five senses and thought. The monk sees through their perceptions and benevolently tolerates them while recognizing the absolute law of the world, Buddhist truth. The appearance of the monk Budai, according to legend, goes back to a monk who is said to be a magic person. He foretold good luck and bad. He did not follow the laws for fasting, ate what was given to him, slept wherever he ended up in the evening, paid no attention to asceticism and religious laws because he had already reached his goal from where he could look down upon the world of human beings. He had grown into the state of nirvana. But he renounced his own salvation and, after he had died and was buried, he appeared in the same form in another place. He is depicted with much respect in caves and temples. The earliest examples originated in the 5th century and can be seen today in the Yungang caves near Datong, Shanxi.

Behind the Maitreya statue stands the youthful warrior Weituo who faces the next hall. He is under the command of the celestial guardians as the leader of the heavenly host and protector of Buddhist truth. He is one of the southern celestial king's generals, but commands the other generals and heavenly legions. He has come to report to the four celestial kings who are full of admiration and respect for him because, in spite of his low position, he surpasses them in enlightenment, purity and chastity. According to tradition, Buddha personally gave him the task of protecting the holy teachings and truth. He faces the northern Buddha hall with the knowledge that Buddha is present, and his expression reflects his devotion, faith and loyalty.

Daxiong Baodian, the Treasure Hall of the Great Hero, is the most important hall in a Buddhist monastery — the actual shrine of the temple — because it is dedicated to the master of the world, Sakyamuni Buddha. It is often called just Dadian, Great Hall.

The path leads through the inner courtyard along the central axis up the steps to the terrace on which the holy hall stands. This hall frequently has a two-tiered roof. The color of the tiles may be yellow, with imperial permission, or green, with the permission of a prince; the traditional tile color of old temples is blue, seldom gray. The roof, the lower corners curving up, seems light and winged. The ridge beam usually has two dragons or fish at either end. The fish is the son of the dragon king, of whom it is said that he brings back life from the waters of the dead. Figures from fables are sometimes depicted at the slightly curved corners of the roof — an uneven number because uneven numbers are holy and correspond to the positive principle of Yang.

The hall's interior is just barely lit by daylight; in this, the sacred hall is unique. This makes the gold and multi-colored idols seem stately and secretive in subdued, dim lamplight and outside light. The center of the hall is dominated by one or more statues of Buddha sitting on a lotus throne on a terrace — the symbol of the Buddhist central world mountain Sumeru. The lotus blossom, which grows up out of swampy water, symbolizes absolute beauty, purity and immaculate knowledge. It rises on its stem, the symbol of the world axis, out of primeval waters. Often one comes across a group of three golden Buddha figures in the main hall, the so-called historical row: Buddhas of the past, present and future. In the middle sits the historical Buddha, Sakyamuni, teacher of people and gods, proclaimer of nirvana. To his right, on the west or south side, the Buddha of the past, Dipamkara who represents the many Buddhas of the past. To his left, the Buddha-to-be, Maitreya, the future savior. There is sometimes a group of five figures — Wuzhirulai, five wisdom Buddhas. The positions of the hands of the five Buddha statues show the five typical hand positions of Sakyamuni. The number 'five' has an even further-reaching and universal meaning. It stands for the five regions of the world (the cardinal points and the middle), the five elements (metal, wood, water, fire, earth), the five senses and the five parts of man (body, feeling, discrimination, ability, consciousness).

In some temple complexes only one Sakyamuni statue stands in the Great Hall.

Buddha statues are so similar that they are difficult to distinguish from each other at first glance. Normally, Buddha is depicted simply and without decoration, but in gold. He wears a plain monk's cowl which often leaves breast, shoulders and arms bare. He sits in a position of meditation with crossed legs, his right foot on his left knee and his left foot on his right knee, his eyes directed straight ahead or cast downwards. Sometimes Buddha is shown standing still. His face radiates harmony and strength. His long earlobes are striking, sign of the master and teacher, historically explainable by the Indian custom of wearing heavy ear jewelry. His hair is short and worn in curls twisted to the right, the protuberance at the top of his head symbolizes the highest level of enlightenment. His forehead is smooth and wide, between his delicately-winged eyebrows there is a small, white, world-illuminating tuft of hair where the third eye is located, normally represented in the shape of a shining point. He has dark blue eyes and a full, graciously smiling mouth. His body is well-proportioned his shoulders and limbs softly rounded. The individual Buddha representations can be distinguished only by the symbolic hand positions and the accompanying figures. A typical Sakyamuni pose shows him with his left hand in his lap, holding the alms bowl of the monk; his right hand resting on his right knee and almost touching the ground — a hint at his oath to bring the teachings of salvation to the unenlightened world after he had attained the great knowledge.

It is easier to recognize the Vairocana Buddha—unlike the other Buddhas, he wears jewelry, for example, a magnificent crown — or the Buddha Yaoshi Fo, the master of the art of healing, who holds fruit or containers of medicine in his hands and heals the sick. Yaoshi Fo reigns in the eastern paradise.

One often comes across the figure of Buddha Amitabha who is extremely important in Chinese Buddhist teachings. Amitabha is the lord of the western paradise. He offers believers the 'easy' way to salvation because he is merciful to those who call him in true faith. After death, he takes the deceased into his paradise and offers him salvation. From there he enters nirvana after aeons. Amitabha saves people from the 'hard' way: suffering, the endless rebirths and the effort of expending ones own energy on salvation.

The three Buddhas Sakyamuni, Yaoshi Fo and Omito Fo (Amitabha) form a trinity in some temples-Sakyamuni sitting in the middle, on the world axis, the master of healing to his left and Amitabha to his right.

The Buddha statues do not stand alone, but have an entourage of bodhisattvas, kings, priests and followers.

Unlike the Buddha figures, the bodhisattvas are richly bejewelled with costly crowns, jewels on their breasts and around their necks and arms. They are graceful and look upon the visitor with mild expressions, their hands often raised soothingly. Bodhisattvas are holy ones who, as many different beings, have achieved the maturity to reach nirvana. But they forego the highest goal of personal salvation—entry into nirvana—in order to show others the way to redemption, the way to becoming a Buddha. They are considered to be the mediators between the supreme and human beings, are called upon directly by people who suffer and are asked for help and beneficence.

Some of the most important bodhisattvas are:

Maitreya, the loving, the future savior, who is usually already represented as a Buddha.

Dizang, Ksitigarbha, the lord of earth and hell, rescues the unhappy and sets them free from the tortures of hell as soon as they recognize the truth and are converted by the horrors of the underworld. He reigns on the mountain Jiuhua Shan, Anhui Province, one of the four holy mountains of Buddhism. According to legend, Dizang was a daughter of a Brahman in an earlier life. After the death of her mother, she was concerned about her spiritual welfare and made daily sacrifices to Buddha. One day she became lost in meditation and her soul wandered into hell, where she learned that her mother was already delivered from its tortures. But, in this way, she gathered knowledge about suffering and pain in hell and decided to forever serve by freeing poor souls. This is how she became the bodhisattva Ksitigarbha.

Puxian, Samantabhadra, the bodhisattva who bestows happiness, lord of fire. According to legend, he came from India riding a white elephant (symbol of majesty and prudence) to present-day Sichuan Province and reigned there on Emei Shan, also a holy mountain of Buddhism.

Wenshu, Manjushri, lord of Wutai Shan (today's Shanxi Province), is the personification of greatest wisdom. According to tradition, he taught on Wutai Shan in the 1st century. He is often pictured riding a blue lion.

Guanyin, Avalokiteshrara, personification of compassion, goodness, wisdom and love, reigns on Putuo Shan mountain on an island in the middle of the ocean on the other side of Ningbo. Guanyin has the ability to appear in different forms, both male and female, and is often portrayed as a thousand armed bodhisattva in order to stress his unending goodness and unlimited willingness to help. Sometimes one sees him with 11 heads arranged like a crown on the lowest one. Legend has it that he once delivered a number of unfortunates from the tortures of hell and led them into Amitabha's paradise. No sooner had he accomplished this task, but the places in hell were already occupied again. Out of dismay at not being able to rescue all, his head split into 11 parts. But Amitabha Buddha formed a new head out of each of the parts so that Guanyin could better contemplate the salvation of all unfortunate beings and lead them into the kingdom of Amitabha.

In many temples, Guanyin is depicted as a female bodhisattva who brings the blessings of children because her help and love also extend into this area. Naturally there is also a legend about Guanyin: In one of her lives she was supposed to be Miaoshan, the daughter of an emperor. When the emperor wanted to marry her off, she refused because she wanted to follow the path of Buddha and joined a convent. Her father tried in vain to win his daughter back. Finally he became angry and had her beheaded. Miaoshan then descended into hell and later came to Putuo Shan, where she finally reached the first stage of becoming a Buddha through years of meditating and accomplishing good deeds. But for aeons she chose to forego her own salvation and became a merciful bodhisattva who bestowed blessings.

Necessary traditional utensils of the Buddhist altar include a bronze basin for the burning of incense, two candles and two flower vases. Musical instruments such as bells, drums, gongs, chimes and wooden clappers give the monks the sign to start or stop their singing.

The gods of the small Pantheon usually stand along the side walls. Gods by nature are superhuman but, unlike Buddha, not ultramundane. They have not yet attained great knowledge nor have they reached the state of nirvana. They surpass humans in power and longevity and, in the cycle of rebirth, they are at the top, but they still need instruction from the teacher of man and the gods, Buddha, in order to achieve nirvana after further rebirth.

The Cangjing Dian, sermon or instruction hall, often stands at the northern end of the inner courtyard. This hall is totally void of decoration and is dedicated to the study and interpretation of the holy Buddhist texts. Twice a month the congregation of monks meets here to listen to the abbot's address.

In important monasteries, there is frequently a hall of the 500 Luohan, Arhats, embodying the monk's ideal of early Hinayana Buddhism. They achieve their own salvation through meditation and asceticism. In historical Buddhist records, it is reported that 500 Luohan held council one year after Sakyamuni's death; they are considered to be something like fathers of the church.

In contrast to the generous bodhisattvas, the Luohan are selfishly concerned only with their own redemption. They live in solitude and seclusion and do not bother with the salvation of others; they do not show them the way to deliverance. Depictions of Luohans appear strange and partly grotesque to a western observer. They are often life-size statues which crowd each other along the walls and passage ways of the hall. Some are lost in meditation, others look down with friendly or amused expressions. They all have in common an expression of superiority and special freedom. Luohan statues are also sometimes found in the Buddha hall—usually 18 in number.

A pagoda is part of a Buddhist temple complex and is the most important sacred element among the Buddhist structures. Its origin was the Indian stupa, a commemorative monument. Relics, both physical (mortal remains of holy ones) and spiritual (texts) are walled up here (see page 80).

Garden Landscaping

The most important examples of Chinese garden landscaping are located in Beijing, Chengde and cities south of the Changjiang, such as Suzhou and Wuxi. The gardens in the north were imperial property: Beihai Park in Beijing (see page 131) and the Summer Palace, Yihe Yuan (see page 143) as well as the imperial summer residence in Chengde (see page 172). The gardens in the south usually belonged to high officials and wealthy merchants, many of whom spent their years of retirement there in leisure.

The traditions of Chinese garden landscaping have their origins far back in history. Historians report of magnificent gardens and parks as early as the Shang and Zhou eras. Often these were gigantic preserves in which all kinds of animals were kept and where the rulers enjoyed hunting.

On the parkgrounds and in gardens which still exist today, one finds a harmonious interplay between nature and architecture. Decorative constructions unite with cliffs, trees, flowers and hills to create artistic sceneries. Gardens were supposed to resemble a sequence of continually changing landscapes. The landscape was shown as a fluctuation between movement and repose. Paths wind through the grounds in a zigzag pattern, revealing new views of halls, trees, bridges, pavilions and hills. Even in the most confined places, architects succeeded in creating a succession of varying landscapes.

The most important natural elements of a garden are water—in any form: pond, lake, stream, river, waterfall; the movement of flowing water gave the garden pulsating life— cliffs, stones, trees, bushes and flowers. Landscapes were created in the shape of artificially built hills, valleys and terraces. Trees were planted: conifers, bamboo and above all, fruit trees—not for their fruit, but for their blossoms. Among the most popular flowers were the lotus, the summer flower and symbol of fertility; the chrysanthemum, the autumn flower, symbol of happiness, leisure and retreat; peonies, the spring flower, symbol of feminine beauty, love and affection; and orchids, symbol of love and beauty, fragrance and elegance.

Among the most important structures of garden grounds were walkways, pavilions and bridges. Timber frame construction played a decisive role here. Pavilion-like houses had neither a harsh nor domination effect, but rather blended effortlessly into the general surroundings. Above all, it is the walkways that are most noticeable in gardens. They traverse the complex, subdivide it, connecting the different groups of buildings, and lead the visitor to the most important points. There are different types of walkways—open on both sides, half-open and multi-storied ones. The most famous walkway in China is located at the Summer Palace in Beijing.

Pavilions were built in especially imposing places, such as at the top of a hill or in the middle of a lake on a small island. Open on all sides, they offer a good view and invite the visitor to take a short rest. Various types of bridges can be found on the grounds: flat stone slab bridges from which one can comfortably watch the fish in the water, high arched bridges and swinging bridges which subdivide and at the same time ornament the grounds.

The walls of the walkways and houses feature openings and gateways in many shapes: round, so-called moon gates, oval, angular, in the shape of vases and bottles etc. They offer a view into the next courtyard, into the next scene and often look like the frame around a landscape painting. The fine lattice work which can be seen in windows and as ornamentation on pavilions and walkways is attractive. Attention should be given to the artistic patterns of the stone and marble paths.

Painting

Traditional Chinese painting distinguishes itself from European painting in its means of expression, form and technique. The basic element of Chinese painting is the brush stroke. Variations in the breadth of a line give life to the drawings and stress contours. Dabs, lines and small areas of solid color complement the fundamental means of expression. Naturally there are many styles and also various schools of Chinese painting, but what they all have in common is the goal of creating a picture purely by using a brush and not by accurately reproducing the subject. In a book about painting techniques from the 12th century it says that one should not use a model when painting; one should impress the motif upon one's memory exactly and paint the picture from memory without interruption.

Of outstanding significance were pictures on silk and paper, followed by frescos, glass-painting and oil painting. The subjects can be roughly divided into the categories of portraits and figure painting, religious painting, landscapes and genre painting. Chinese painting differed from European in its perspective. While in European pictures the lines meet in back, at the vanishing point, in Chinese pictures they meet in the foreground and spacially include the viewer.

A further characteristic of Chinese paintings are the calligraphic inscriptions which can vary in form and content considerably — for instance, poems which refer to the depicted motif, personal dedications or just the seal and signature of the artist.

The history of Chinese painting is more than 2,500 years old. Among the oldest examples is a painted silk banner which was found in a tomb from the 2nd century BC in Mawangdui near Changsha, Hunan, in April, 1972. In the shape of a 'T', measuring ca. 200 x 90 cm and perfectly preserved, it depicts the journey into the next world of the royal woman who is buried in the tomb. Her own picture, creatures from the hereafter, flora and fauna are shown with delicate brushstrokes. The technique and feel for style which are recognizable in this picture indicate a high level of brush technique at that time.

With the state promotion of Confucianism during the Han Dynasty, portrait and figure painting developed. Pictures of influential persons of the past as well as illustrations of legendary anecdotes and classical texts had an educational function and were supposed to act as instructive examples of the Confucian fulfillment of duty.

Chaos and the division of the empire into different small states followed the end of the Han Dynasty, until at the end of the 6th century, China was again united. Very little has been preserved from that period which could offer comprehensive information about the development of painting. There were, however, already critical writings about painting. The only great painter of that time was Gu Kaizhi who lived from about 345—406, during the Eastern Jin Dynasty. He was the first to advocate the idea that in creating a picture, what matters most is the reproduction of feeling. He achieved this through the conscious use of shades of color. Among his most famous works is 'The Fairy of Luo River'; the subject is a poem by Cao Zhi from the period of the Three Kingdoms which sensitively mirrors the romantic feelings of the poet. With his work 'Admonitions of the Instructress to the Court Ladies' he illustrates a moralizing text from the 4th century. It is an example of didactic, Confucian painting. These works have, however, only been preserved as later reproductions of the originals or approximations of their styles. The search for new subjects and means of expression yielded the technique of shading which made the three-dimensional representation of objects possible. This technique, like various other arts, came to China from the western regions of India with the teachings of Buddhism and its iconography. It introduced Chinese artists to new ideas and initiated a period of religious and secular figure and portrait painting. Significant works of this time have been preserved in the caves of Dunhuang. Dunhuang, located on the route of pilgrimage to India, was the most important center for new ideas and foreign styles.

At the beginning of the Tang Dynasty, there were already artists who specialized in figure painting and were considered to be quite good: Wu Daozi, Yan Liben, Zhang Xuan and Zhou Fang. Concentration was on the representation of the smallest details. The exact description of a person's characteristics, a face, clothing, animals and landscape were the goal; reproduction of corporality and movement followed.

This development was at its zenith during the Tang Dynasty. Outstanding examples of this kind of painting are the murals in the tomb of Crown Prince Zhanghuai near Xi'an, Shaanxi (see page 383). Many artists were increasingly less concerned with color than with the descriptive power of the brush stroke. The aforementioned painter Wu Daozi, a master in the portrayal of human figures, used color sparingly and Zhang Xuan and Zhou Fang, who made names for themselves by depicting ladies of the palace, added only light mineral colors to their delicate brush strokes. A similar tendency is found in landscape painting, which began developing in the 9th century. The poet and painter Wang Wei, a representative of the so-called Southern School, became famous for his monochrome landscapes. Unlike the Southern School, which preferred calligraphic watercolors, the Northern School was characterized by its richness of color — although the colors did not necessarily correspond to natural ones — and the goal was to produce a decorative effect.

The tradition of scholar-painters began with Wang Wei. Besides professional painters, also educated laymen became active at this time.

The shift of interest from man to nature had already begun in the 9th century. Nature was no longer used as a background but a subject in itself. During the period of the Five Dynasties, many pictures of flowers, birds and animals were painted. Figure painting had reached its height in connection with Confucian and Buddhist teachings. Landscape painting was, however, influenced by Daoist thought. One trend which began in the 10th century did not attribute much importance to detail, but rather to unity. It was important to understand and describe the essence and character of the things portrayed. The study of everything that could be seen or heard in nature — listening to natural forces, rivers, trees and animals — gave artists a deep understanding of it. They seemed to grasp nature's soul, which stimulated them to create their works. A new conception of space developed. Shapes dissolved. Unoccupied space between the fore-and back-ground gave pictures dimension. The lack of color stressed its expressiveness.

During the Song Dynasty, 10th-13th century, this tendency to comprehend and portray the soul of an object continued. Artists did not restrict themselves to landscapes, but endeavored to fathom the nature of animals, plants, even villages and cities. Emperor Huizong (1082—1135) of the Song Dynasty, himself a famous painter and calligrapher, sought to probe into the world of birds and plants. The artist Wang Shen endeavored to portray the spirit of a village and Zhang Ziduan, the nature of life in the capital Kaifeng. The depiction of personal feelings about the portrayed objects became foremost and influenced painting into the 13th century. The landscape painters of the Yuan era who, following Daoist ideas, retreated into solitude to live in harmony with nature, became well-known. Their pictures, which were supplemented with calligraphy, were examples for the painters of the Ming period. The Yuan Dynasty had been founded by victorious Mongol tribes. It was foreign rule which, in the eyes of the artists, threatened the inheritance of the past centuries. It was a time to preserve tradition and to rediscover various former styles of painting.

During the Ming era, central China remained a hub of culture; thus most painters lived there. Among the most famous artists of that time were Tang Yin (1470—1523) and Qiu Ying (1509—1551). Tang Yin became famous for his portraits of elegant women. He developed his own technique of portrait painting. Qiu Ying was also a master at portraying women. He was a disciple of finely detailed drawing and was partial to shades of turquoise.

Painting hardly attained the level of the Tang and Song eras in the following centuries.

During the Qing Dynasty, artists with diverse styles were active. Even painters from Europe came to China and exchanged ideas with their Chinese colleagues. Among the most well-known of these Europeans was the Italian missionary Giuseppe Castiglione (1680—1766). His Chinese name was Lang Shining. He began his activities in China in 1715 and also studied Chinese painting, adding European methods of painting to his portraits. This technique was officially recognized by the court and was imitated.

The revolutionary upheavals which began at the start of the 20th century gave painting new impulses. One of the most famous painters of this time is Qi Baishi, whose works encompass an especially wide range of subjects. Besides shrimp, one of his most renowned and successful subjects, he also painted landscapes, figures, flora and fauna. He tried new color combinations and brush techniques. Another famous painter of the recent past is Li Keran, a student of Qi Baishi, who became known for his pictures of buffalo and young boys.

Many painters of this time attempted to combine traditional painting techniques with foreign ones as a result of Western and Japanese influences. Methods varied: while some only adopted the details of foreign painting techniques and composition, others adhered to them stylistically and formally. Some painters went abroad as art students, mainly to France, to study the fundamentals of Western painting.

After 1949, themes were determined chiefly by socialist motifs. Many artists modelled themselves on painters in the USSR who advocated socialist realism.

New styles such as colorful New Year pictures and picture stories received official support. In the seventies, peasant style painting became quite popular; its center is located in Huxian.

China's art today is influenced by two factors: first, by the great tradition of watercolor and woodcuts, and second, by the task of serving society. Artists are expected to paint an optimistic picture of society and to offer positive future perspectives. Since the fall of the Gang of Four, motifs such as idyllic landscapes, full of symbols, have again become popular; flowers and animals are also depicted. During the Cultural Revolution, traditional style painting was undesirable.

Among the younger artists, oil painting is also popular today. They have no models, within Chinese tradition, and must follow examples set by European works. Most of their pictures are in the post-impressionist style. Also interesting is photo-realistic painting which, since the Gang of Four's downfall, deals chiefly with political themes.

Calligraphy

The artistic and descriptive value of Chinese characters led to the development of its own art — calligraphy — which, like painting, enjoys great popularity in China.

Among the earliest examples of Chinese writing are the engraved characters on animal bones and tortoise shells from the Shang period. They were used in seeking the oracle's advice about military actions, natural phenomena and imperial undertakings, but also about personal business. In addition to this, inscriptions on clay vessels as well as those in bronze and stone were found. This early type of script, usually found in the inscriptions from the 11th to the 7th century BC, is known by the term *dazhuan,* big seal script. It is characterized by crude, powerful lines.

During the Period of the Warring States (475—221 BC), the big seal script developed in various ways in different regions. Numerous decorative types of writing and characters evolved and were used in individual states. After the unification of the empire in 221 BC under the Qin Dynasty, unification of writing also took place — big seal script was replaced by the so-called *xiaozhuan,* small seal script. The characters were rounder. Soon after this, at the beginning of the Han Dynasty, *lishu,* clerical script, prevailed — a type of writing which was preferred by officials as a kind of shorthand toward the end of the Qin Dynasty. Clerical script was supplemented by elements of small seal script, and this was standardized as *kaishu*, regular script. This type of writing has not changed until this day.

Further attempts to write even faster, in connection with striving to make handwriting more aesthetically pleasing, resulted in the semi-cursive script *xingshu*, running script, and in the fully cursive script *caoshu*, draft script, during the Han era: The latter is a type of shorthand which allows several strokes to be made in one. At the beginning, it was only used for hasty sketches. Thanks to its aesthetic attraction, more and more people began using it, and it is quite popular even today.

Until paper was discovered in 100 BC, strips of bamboo, wood and silk had served as writing materials. Brush and ink had been used for a long time.

Calligraphy as a form of art began to prevail in the class of officials from the 3rd century on, and soon a number of different styles developed. Among the greatest calligraphers of that time — and among the most famous of all — is Wang Xizhi (307—365). Also his son Wang Xianzhu (344—388) attained high standing. The legions of script masters and painter-calligraphers of later centuries looked to them as their models.

Many years of practice and study of the existing works of written art and theoretical literature were demanded of one in order to become a master of calligraphy. Great collections of calligraphies were begun; these served the students as materials for demonstration and instruction. A good calligrapher had to master all styles of writing and, in addition to this, develop his own style. The individual style can, as with handwriting in the West, disclose information about the character of the writer. Even today calligraphy is highly esteemed in the classes of educated Chinese, and it is taken as a personal mark of distinction if a poem in one's own calligraphy is given as a gift.

Stone Engravings and Woodcuts

During the Tang Dynasty — a cultural, economic and political heyday — a great demand arose for literature, making the mechanical reproduction of writing and illustrations necessary. Techniques already existed, for example stone engravings which were known as early as the Zhou era. Scenes from mythology and history as well as characters were cut into stone slabs as a negative relief. As early as the Han era, the change to a positive surface relief had been made. With the discovery of paper during this time, the technique took on great importance.

On the orders of Emperor Lingdi (2nd century) of the Han Dynasty, the Confucian classics were engraved in stone to give the teachings immortality (see page 56). One valuable side effect of this was that the texts could be made available to a large number of readers in the form of rubbings. Buddhists followed this example and also had their sutras engraved in stone. Making rubbings is relatively easy and has not changed over the centuries. A calligraphy or a picture cut in stone is covered with a thin damp piece of paper. The dampness gives the paper more elasticity. The paper is then brushed as long as it takes to fill in all the recesses of the relief and adhere tightly to the raised parts. As soon as the paper is dry, the raised parts are dabbed with a single color — usually black drawing ink. They are well set off from the white paper in the indentations and reproduce the stone engravings clearly. Most stone rubbings are made with black ink. Due to the contrast, these are the most impressive. There are, however, also monochrome red, blue, green and brown rubbings. Multi-colored ones are rare because this involves a more complicated process.

During the Tang Dynasty, stone cutting experienced a golden age. (Reliefs on steles and tombstones in Xi'an offer proof of this even today.) Art connoisseurs began to establish collections of beautiful calligraphies, including collections of rubbings from stone engravings. The choice of motif was no longer restricted to calligraphies, but took up themes from the world of flora and fauna. The works of great painters of that time were engraved in stone and, in this way some have been preserved until today. Picture series about agriculture and silk production are also still in existence today. From the 13th century on, the stages of manufacturing were engraved in stone, and entire series were made which served as directions for the inhabitants and as information for the emperor and officials. Even today, stone rubbings are produced in great quantities, which are either reproduction of old stone pictures or new ones, such as portraits of well-known people or modern poems.

Woodcut illustrations which were developed in the early 8th century along with wood block printing, were even more prevalent than stone engravings. Those who soon benefited from this invention included Buddhists and the representatives of religious Daoism who used it to propagate and circulate their teachings. The court also recognized this technique as a suitable means for strengthening the Confucian state doctrine.

Besides religious and ideologically-oriented texts, many publications were printed for general use, such as illustrated calendars and decks of cards; various instruction books, handbooks and fiction were in this category. Toward the end of the Tang Dynasty, collections of poems were among the most popular printed matter. Book and illustration printing reached its golden age during the Song Dynasty. The enthusiastic demand, especially for illustrated books for private libraries, caused the wood block printing business to flourish. Remarkable publications were created such as the eight-volume edition of a scholarly work from the Tang Dynasty: 'Great Plant Digest', the illustrations of which were of artistic merit, or the 'Book of Rewards and Punishments' and painting handbooks.

Various centers of printing arose which upheld the principle of division of labor. Soon such a high measure of artistry had been reached that their works were the examples that many artists followed over the centuries.

The printing process consisted of several operations. First, a picture was sketched by a painter and, in the form of an abstract, traced onto rice or silk paper. For each color that was to appear in the picture, one traced abstract design had to be made. The paper was then glued onto a 3—4 cm thick wooden block with the front side facing down. The next step was to rub the paper down to a thin layer until the drawing that was facing the woodblock became transparent. The block cutters could then carve the drawing in a relief-like fashion according to the outlines. The raised parts of the printing blocks could then be freed of the rest of the traced design and each could be given color. Now the actual printing process began. A piece of paper was laid on the printing block and pressed to the relief so that the ink came in contact with the paper and the drawing appeared right side up. Depending on the various colors and shadings of a picture, the whole process could include hundreds of steps.

The Ming Dynasty was the beginning of the epoch of the historical novelette, novel and musical drama and their rich illustrations. Among the most well-known works were Shuihu Zhuan, 'The Water Margin' and Xixiang Ji, 'The Story of the Western Pavilion'.

Up to this time, wood block prints had been used almost exclusively to illustrate texts. A change was about to take place. The first picture albums were made and became very popular, above all when color printing became known at the end of the Ming Dynasty. The 'Painting Manual of the Ten Bamboo Hall', an instruction book on painting, was one of the first works in which this technical innovation appeared. A Nanjing workshop's publication Jieziyuan Huazhuan, 'Painting Manual of the Mustard Seed Garden', published around the year 1700, also became famous.

At the beginning of the 20th century, black and white woodcut prints became more popular. The writer Lu Xun, who had composed several texts about traditional and modern woodcuts, considered this a means to awaken the masses and to educate them. He was influential in creating various wood block printing societies which found German, American and Russian woodcuts to be exemplary. Traditional style was totally forgotten and motifs and techniques were adopted from foreign works. They were basically pessimistic and showed mainly social class conflicts, exploitation and misery. Unlike traditional woodcuts, the new works were devoid of symbols and their message was distinctly clear to all.

Under the influence of Communist teachings, there was a tendency toward optimism among artists of the Yan'an period after 1936. They incorporated elements from the tradition of colorful New Year pictures in their work. Since the founding of the People's Republic of China, woodcuts have reached a zenith, especially during the Cultural Revolution, when they were again made an instrument of political discussion. The themes had changed greatly in the meantime. Artists chose their motifs from the areas of class struggle, agricultural and industrial production and technology. It was not the real present which was to be mirrored in the block prints, but rather the future for which one must strive. Optimistic messages encouraged the viewer to participate actively in the country's development.

New Year Pictures

The New Year's celebration, also called Spring Festival — the great family celebration in China — is the time of the colorful nianhua, New Year pictures, New Year door pictures and calendars.

New Year picture painting has a long tradition. It is estimated that its origins date back to the 3rd century. At first they were designed in the shape of protective and good luck symbols; later, patrons and good luck gods were portrayed. According to one legend, Tang emperor Taizong had the entrance to his room guarded by two generals because he believed himself to be followed by evil spirits. Later both of the generals were replaced by two pictures of generals, painted with frightening expressions. From that time on, they became frequent motifs for New Year door pictures which were attached to house gates to protect the families from harm. As early as the 11th century, hand-colored black and white prints appeared. The golden age of New Year pictures began with the development of colored woodcuts in the Ming era.

New Year pictures include a wide variety of themes. The spectrum ranges from depictions of certain protective gods such as the kitchen god, to depictions of scenes from peasant life and symbolic figures and characters promising good luck, in modern times. Spring motifs, landscapes, flowers and beautiful women are popular motifs. In addition, legends, novels and historical events are shown in series of pictures. Basically, New Year pictures mirror the wishes and desires of the people, their longing for happiness, peace, longevity, health, the blessings of children, justice and wealth.

Papercuttings

One of China's most popular folkarts is papercutting. Archaeological finds trace the tradition back to the 6th century; it is supposed that the beginnings of papercutting were even a few centuries earlier. Papercuttings are used for religious purposes, for decoration and as patterns.

As is still partly the case outside of China, various paper objects and figures used to be buried with the dead or were burned at the funeral ceremony. Papercuttings, which were usually of symbolic character, were part of this ritual. They also often served as decorations for sacrificial offerings to the ancestors and gods.

Today, papercuttings are chiefly used as decoration. They ornament walls, windows, doors, columns, mirrors, lamps and lanterns in homes and are also used for decoration on presents or are given as presents themselves.

They have special significance at festivals and on holidays. At the New Year's Festival for example, entrances are decorated with papercuttings which are supposed to bring good luck.

Papercuttings used to be used as patterns, especially for embroidery and lacquer work.

Papercuttings are not produced by machine, but by hand. There are two methods of manufacture: scissor cuttings and knife cuttings. As the name indicates, scissor cuttings are fashioned with scissors. Several pieces of paper — up to eight pieces — are fastened together. The motif is then cut with sharp, pointed scissors.

Knife cuttings are fashioned by putting several layers of paper on a relatively soft foundation consisting of a mixture of tallow and ashes. Following a pattern, the artist cuts the motif into the paper with a sharp knife which he usually holds vertically. The advantage of knife cuttings is that considerably more papercuttings can be made in one operation than with scissor cuttings.

In the countryside, papercuttings are usually made only by women and girls. This used to be one of the crafts that every girl was to master and that were often used to judge brides. Professional papercutting artists are, on the other hand, almost always men who have guaranteed incomes and work together in workshops.

Arts and Crafts Paintings

Arts and crafts paintings have increased in significance in China in the past years. A new branch in this field is shell pictures.

The technique of shell painting is based on experience with traditional mother-of-pearl inlay work. Shells are cut and polished and — according to their natural coloration, texture and shape — arranged in clever patterns into pictures. The subjects are usually borrowed from traditional painting. Depictions of birds, fruit, sea creatures, landscapes and scenes from popular folktales and ballads are preferred.

The same subjects are also captured in magnificently colorful feather pictures. Usually pheasant, swan and peacock feathers are used.

As with shell pictures, the color and grain of materials for bark pictures are also considered. Above all, subjects such as landscapes lend themselves to this type of painting. Bark is scraped from trees and glued together to form pictures. Bamboo paintings which are fashioned from the inner layer of bamboo also belong in this category.

Another branch of arts and crafts painting are pictures made from wheat stalks. They are often the material for pictures on notecards. Before beginning with the picture design, the stalks must first be flattened and dyed. Then they are cut to size and glued onto paper or silk to make a picture.

Other materials such as cork, braided straw and ox horn shavings are also used. Since this branch of Chinese art is relatively new, it is still in the experimental stage and looking for new natural materials.

Ceramics

The most famous of all Chinese arts is ceramics. Not only the Chinese love and appreciate them; they also receive great admiration and recognition abroad.

China's ceramics have a long tradition. The earliest evidence of Neolithic pottery was found in North China. Two great Neolithic cultures were named for the places where they were found: the Yangshao and the Longshan cultures (west of Henan and northern Shandong respectively). They date back to a time between 5,000—2,000 BC. The older of the two, Yangshao ceramics, were painted and consisted of impermeable red clay. They had been shaped by hand and fired at between 800—1,000°C.

During the end phase of the Longshan culture, ceramics which were almost black and often polished to a shine, were produced on a potter's wheel. In this phase, which was characterized by a high level of skilled craftsmanship, the basic shapes of Chinese ceramics were created. What was produced served as containers for the storage of food, as kettles for cooking over a fire or as funerary objects.

During the Shang Dynasty, clay had to yield to a new material, bronze, which was used for centuries for making ritual objects; clay was only used for the production of objects for daily use. When clay was 'rediscovered', the bronze shapes were retained at first.

Finds from the Zhou era offer evidence of the preference for black ceramics polished on a rotating potter's wheel, sometimes painted red or white and at times even lacquered.

The most important discovery of that time was a glaze containing feldspar which made porous clay objects impervious to dampness. Stoneware developed around 500 BC. Unlike earthenware, stoneware clay melts when fired at 1,200—1,400°C to an impervious homogenous substance.

During the Han Dynasty there was a great preference for vessels painted with cold (unfired) mineral pigments. Rich colors and expressive ornamentation decorated the vessels. The abandonment of human sacrifices at burials was a boon to the development of funerary ceramics. Figurines of wood and clay as well as vessels containing food and drink were buried with the deceased in the tomb. The clay figurines were usually made from molds and colorfully glazed or painted with unfired mineral colors. Hollow spaces and small openings prevented the objects from exploding while being fired. Among the most renowned examples of funerary ceramics were residential towers and figurines of warriors, riders and musicians.

Toward the end of the Han Dynasty, a type of ceramics for daily use with gray-green to olive green glaze was produced in what today is Shaoxing, Zhejiang. The so-called Yueyao ceramics became popular very quickly. Large bowls, wine vessels, round bottles, pitchers and vases were made. Especially popular were the utensils which were made for scholars' desks. A kind of ceramicware similar to Yueyao ceramics is celadon, which was already being produced during this period but did not flourish until the Song Dynasty. Celadon is stoneware with a white coating and green glaze.

Step by step, pure white, hard porcelain developed from stoneware. It is made of white kaolin, an unmeltable product of weathered feldspar, and an easily meltable feldspar material called 'bai dunzi' (small white cube) by the Chinese, and "petuntze" by the French. Feldspar material was delivered to the potters in small bricks. Kaolin is fired with the feldspar material at a temperature of 1,300—1,400°C so that the feldspar, a glasslike substance, holds the kaolin together.

At that time, the greenish Yueyao was still preferred and porcelain did not see its heyday until the Ming Dynasty.

During the Tang Dynasty, a golden age of politics and culture, many ceramics workshops acquired good reputations and renown, such as Xinzhou Yao in Hebei which became famous for white Tang porcelain, or Bushan Yao in Shandong with its yellow glazes and brown speckles. The products of the Yueyao potters in Shaoxing continued to be in demand.

Besides stoneware and porcelain, lead-glazed earthenware was also produced. San cai, three-color glaze (brown, green and red) was extremely popular. It marked the earthenware of the Tang era and was used mainly for funerary ceramics. The applied colors were either separated by engraved decorations or were allowed to flow together easily when fired. The figurines of funerary ceramics offer abundant information about the clothing, habits and daily life of that time.

During the Song Dynasty, ceramics reached a level of classic perfection; the search for harmony of form and glaze and limitation to the essential influenced the potters' creations. It was a time of creamy monochrome glazes (using feldspar colored with metallic oxide) which forced the decoration into the background. Stoneware was preferred to earthenware and porcelain.

The typical stoneware of the Song era is the greenish celadon, which was in great demand abroad and was exported mainly to Islamic areas in the Near East, but also to Japan and Korea.

One often encounters dull, thick glazes which decorate complexly-shaped objects. The color spectrum ranges from gray, green, blue, brown and yellow to sky blue. Brown and black glazes, manufactured in Fujian and Jiangxi, were enthusiastically received in Japan and were imitated again and again. They were called Temmoku ware, taken from the Tianmu Shan mountains near Hangzhou.

Decoration during this period was usually restricted to relief-like patterns or crackle. The latter was created by cracks in the glaze either during the firing — as a result of pressure which came from a bad ratio of glaze to vessel — or as a result of the object being cooled too quickly after firing.

In the meantime, ceramics increasingly became the central focus at the imperial court and in educated circles. During the Mongolian Yuan Dynasty at the start of the 14th century, porcelain became more significant and crowded other types of ceramics into the background. Shape was no longer the main focus, but rather decoration. Landscapes, people, animals and plants painted in vigorous, bright colors and sharp contrasts made for a pronounced sense of motion. At this time, products from the imperial workshops *Shifu Yao* became famous, making white porcelain with cobalt blue and copper red drawings under transparent glazes. Color was applied directly to the objects or to their white coatings.

The golden age of blue-and-white porcelain began at the beginning of the Ming era. A variety of shapes and decorative scenes from the world of plants characterize these ceramics. Popular motifs were flowers such as the lotus, the symbol for purity, and the chrysanthemum, the autumn flower.

Earlier there were different centers of ceramics production, but now centralization came about as a result of the increased manufacture of porcelain which demanded the extensive division of labor. Each vessel passed through the hands of almost 70 people. Jingdezhen Town in northeastern Jiangxi Province became the center of porcelain production. It was made the official imperial manufacturer at the beginning of the Ming Dynasty and remained the most important porcelain city until the fall of the Qing Dynasty in 1911. Jingdezhen had the important raw materials kaolin and petuntze in its immediate vicinity, and the convenience of the city's location in respect to transportation made it possible to transport the wares to Beijing quickly by water.

Besides the blue-and-white decor, there was also enamel paint decoration which very frequently featured pictures of animals. These vitrifiable colors were painted onto objects which were already glazed and, protected by muffles (saggers made of fireproof clay), combined indissolubly with the first glaze in a second firing at 700—800°C. The combination of underglaze and overglaze painting was popular, whereas cobalt blue decoration, which was applied before the object was fired, was supplemented and refined by various enamel colors and gold (gold leaf, powered gold) after firing. The peak of this overglaze painting was reached during the reign of Chenghua (1465—87).

As early as the Tang era, ceramics were sold abroad. Flourishing trade with Europe did not develop until the discovery of the sea route to East India by the Portuguese in 1516. Late Ming period porcelain, which gradually made its way to Europe, was enthusiastically received and gave rise to imitation. Above all, the cobalt blue underglaze painting was greatly admired and became the model for Delft Fayence.

The porcelain of the early Ming era was elegantly and gracefully decorated, but, with the start of the Jiajing period (1522—1566) in the late Ming era, it became more robust. Bright colors were preferred, and blue was applied to more surface area which made the decoration frequently appear flamboyant. Besides the outstanding products of the Jingdezhen manufactory, the products of other workshops also achieved a high reputation, for example the red-brown or yellowish stoneware from Yixing, Jiangsu or the high-quality pure white undecorated porcelain from Dehua in Fujian. Due to the high feldspar content, this relatively soft and translucent porcelain was suitable for the making of figurines.

Characteristic of the Ming period is the glazed pottery, which was especially used in making colored tiles and bricks for palace and temple buildings.

The porcelain city of Jingdezhen saw its golden age during the Qing Dynasty, during the reign of Kangxi from 1662—1722, of

Yongzheng from 1723—1735 and of Qianlong from 1736—1795. Blue-and-white porcelain continued to be produced, but characteristic of the Qing Dynasty is the revival of old forms and glazes from the Song era. There were also new developments in glazing techniques, decoration and color combinations. The so-called Oxblood glaze, a deep red coloring produced by copper oxide, became renowned. Imperial yellow was created with a yellow lead glaze; a mixture of cobalt and manganese with iron yielded a metallic, shiny black glaze. Painting with enamel color, using new shades of color such as pink violet, made possible the creation of delicate, impressionistic pictures. The method of foregoing glaze altogether and applying the enamel paint directly to the fired object was common. The profusely decorated object was then fired at 900°C anew, protected by muffles. In this way the colors attained a dull sheen.

No new high points in ceramics production occurred in the 19th century. In 1853, the center of porcelain manufacturing, Jingdezhen, was destroyed during the Taiping Rebellion. After reconstruction and after production was resumed, state subsidies ceased with the fall of the dynasty so that the manufactory again encountered financial trouble and was finally closed. With the founding of the People's Republic, Jingdezhen also experienced a new beginning. Today, the city is again considered to be the center of porcelain manufacturing. Also in Dehua, as during the Ming era, pure white, shining porcelain is produced on a large scale, following the tradition of plastic design. Other significant traditional places of production were also able to continue their work, for example the manufactory in Yixing which still produces red-brown and yellow stoneware. The manufactory in Tangshan was established only recently and produces primarily porcelain for daily use.

Bronze

Bronze casting is one of the oldest arts in China; it flourished from the early Shang to the Han Dynasty. During the Shang Dynasty, over 3,000 years ago, bronze casters reached an incomparable level of perfection in the production techniques, quality and decor of sacrificial vessels. By using clay molds which could be assembled, mainly ritual vessels, weapons, tools, implements, jewelry, mirrors and musical instruments were cast from an alloy made of copper and tin, but which could also contain additional metals. They had a gold-brown to silvery gray sheen.

Bronze casters were probably in the compulsory service of their employers, a small privileged class. Only they could afford the expense of bronze work. Workshops were located right in the neighborhood of palace grounds and administration buildings.

During the Shang Dynasty in the 2nd century BC, centers of the art of bronze work were in Zhengzhou and Anyang, in the present-day Province of Henan. Ancient Shang bronzes, usually ritual vessels, are characterized by a robust but perfectly detailed style. The containers were generally used for food, wine and water. After the ritual burial sacrifices were over, they were often placed in the grave with the deceased.

Geometric and animal motifs were preferred decorations on ritual bronzes. The magical countenance of an animal demon, Taotie, was especially common, but dragons, snakes, grasshoppers and birds were also chosen as motifs. These patterns were embossed on a background which often consisted of a finely-linked network of ring chains, raised ridges, spirals, whirls or meanders.

Besides a variety of perfected shapes, ritual vessels in the shape of animals also emerged in the late Shang period.

The style of Shang bronzes influenced bronze casting for centuries, but in the course of the Western Zhou period, a new style developed. Animal motifs slowly disappeared; abstract patterns and wide bands began to prevail.

Inscriptions on ritual vessels of the Shang Dynasty were still in hidden places. They were short and usually contained only the names of the contractor and the ancestor to whom the vessel was dedicated. Later the inscriptions became more extensive, also appearing on the outside of the vessel, and as decoration. They told of social and political events, of honorable deeds or rewards, such as on the occasion of a victory.

The bronze art from the Warring States was marked by a trend toward elegant shapes. Ritual vessels were no longer the focus of creativity, but rather implements of all kinds, such as axes, daggers, swords, mirrors, bells, belt hooks and metal fittings for horse and wagon. Variations in decor were afforded by gold, silver, copper, lacquered and precious stone inlay work that required a high measure of precision and skill. Realistic figure compositions, spirals and geometric patterns were also popular.

Significant examples of bronze musical instruments are chimes. The bronze bells had no clappers, but were rung with hammers. The greatest find of this kind was made in 1978 in Hubei Province: chimes with 65 bronze bells, the largest of which is 1.53 m high and weighs 203.6 kg, were recovered in their entirety and today are on display in the museum in Wuhan (see page 314).

In the following centuries, bronze had to yield to other materials. During the Han Dynasty, it gained renewed importance in the manufacture of mirrors. These were not only popular and useful objects, they also became indispensable funerary objects. The ability to ban evil spirits or to draw sunlight into the grave was attributed to their shining surfaces. The backs of the mirrors were richly decorated with the most diverse cast and multicolored decorations. The interest in ancient bronzes was not rekindled until the period of the Northern Song Dynasty; they became coveted collection pieces. At the start, this was mainly due to the inscriptions which had socio-historical value. From the 12th century on, they were a popular model for new bronze castings for centuries.

Jade

In Chinese, jade is called *yu,* including nephrite and jadeite.

Jadeite is lighter than nephrite and is either white or gray or green in color. Jadeite was probably first used in the Qing period. Nephrite has been known in China for more than three millenia. Almost all early jade artwork was made of nephrite. The color spectrum ranges from different shades of green to yellow, gray, brown and black-brown. Nephrite is sometimes translucent if thinly cut, but not transparent.

In traditional Chinese thinking, jade always symbolized the holy, honorable and immortal. It was the embodiment of heavenly powers. During the Shang and Zhou eras, ceremonial utensils and cosmic symbols were created from jade, such as replicas of weapons and heaven and earth symbols. Magical powers were also attributed to jade. Often, jade carvings used as funerary objects have been found in excavations, frequently in the shape of animals, such as grasshoppers. During the Han Dynasty, jade objects were manufactured for everyday use — plates, bowls, drinking cups. During the Ming and Qing eras, jade work increased in importance, and under the Qianlong Emperor (reigned from 1736—1795), it flourished.

Today, besides jade, other precious and semi-precious stones such as rose quartz, rock crystal, smoky topaz, coral, agate, lapis lazuli and turquoise are used to make ob'jets d'art and containers of various shapes for a wide range of purposes. Centers of jade and precious stone work are Beijing, Shanghai and Tianjin as well as Jiangsu, Guangdong, Liaoning and Henan Provinces. With much imagination and skill, objects are fashioned which are full of artistic expression. The variety of shapes ranges from plain to complicated to decoratively graceful. Especially popular are figurines from the world of flora and fauna.

Peking Opera

The Peking opera, whose roots go back to the Qing Dynasty, is a synthesis of music, dance, acrobatics, literature and the graphic arts — a successful cross between symbolism and realism. There are four main character types: *sheng, dan, jing* and *chou. Sheng* usually characterizes the positive, male protagonist: old men, recognizable by their beards, young men without beards, military figures of various ranks. *Dan* marks women's roles. *Jing* are heros, adventurers, bandits and scoundrels; they are always male. *Chou* also male roles, are clowns, if positive, and villains, if negative. The last two wear mask-like make-up, the color symbolism of which offers information about the character of the person portrayed. Red stands for courage, loyalty, uprightness; black for passion; white hints at cunning and malice; blue at cruelty. *Chou* performers can be recognized by their white-painted noses above which there is often a butterfly pattern. Rhythm makes it possible for the singers to express feelings. Monologues and dialogues are delivered in the Peking dialect. Performers do not use many props. Set gestures, familiar to the audience, symbolize horseback riding, climbing, rowing, the opening and closing of doors, etc. The crucial person at a performance is the drummer, who functions as director. The entire orchestra, consisting of percussion, string and wind instruments, and also the actors have to follow him. The fight scenes in Peking operas are exciting; they demand a high degree of acrobatic skill, and the audience can easily imagine what a long and rigorous training period the actors have to go through.

The Peking opera has a stock of more than 1,300 plays, many of which are based on classical ballads such as 'The Three Kingdoms' of 'Record of a Journey to the West' and on folktales and legends.

Part Two

Travel Information and Important Tips from A to Z

Airlines

Civil Aviation Administration of China

CAAC Booking Office
Beijing 117 Dongsi Xidajie
Domestic lines   tel. 55 04 97, 55 32 45
International lines   tel. 55 41 75, 55 06 26
                        tel. 55 67 20, 55 73 19
Shanghai 789 Yan'an Zhonglu
Domestic lines   tel. 53 59 53
International lines   tel. 53 22 55
Guangzhou 181 Huanshi Lu
Domestic lines   tel. 66 21 23 (ext. 904)
International lines   tel. 66 18 03
Hangzhou 160 Tiyuchang Lu
Domestic lines   tel. 2 42 59
International lines   tel. 7 25 75
Kunming 146 Dongfeng Donglu
All lines   tel. 2 42 70
Tianjin 242 Heping Lu
All lines   tel. 2 12 24, 2 58 88
Hong Kong Gloucester Tower, Pedder St.
tel. 5-21 64 16 (12 lines)

Further addresses are available at the end of the descriptions of the appropriate cities.

Most major international airlines have offices in Beijing.

Flight reservations and bookings can be made at international airline offices, but tickets are purchased at the offices of the national airline, CAAC.

International Airlines

In Beijing:
Aeroflot Soviet Airlines
5-53 Jianguomenwai, tel. 52 35 81
Air France
12-71 Jianguomenwai, tel. 52 38 94
British Airways
12-61 Jianguomenwai, tel. 52 37 68
Japan Air Lines
12-23 Jianguomenwai, tel. 52 34 57
JAT Yugoslav Airlines
2-2-162 Jianguomenwai, tel. 52 34 86
Lufthansa German Airlines
Great Wall Hotel, tel. 5 00 16 16
Pakistan International Airlines Corp.
12-43 Jianguomenwai, tel. 52 32 74
Pan American World Airways Inc.
Jianguo Hotel, Rm 135/137, tel. 59 52 61x135

Philippine Airlines
12-53 Jianguomenwai, tel. 52 39 92
Quantas
12-41 Jianguomenwai, tel. 52 31 95
Swissair
12-33 Jianguomenwai, tel.52 32 84
Tarom Romanian Airlines
Romanian Embassy Compound, Jianguomenwai, Tel. 52 35 52
Thai Airways International
12-31 Jianguomenwai, tel. 52 31 74
United Airlines
tel. 5 00-19 85
In Shanghai:
Cathay Pacific Airways
Jinjiang Hotel, North Wing Rm 123, tel. 58 25 82x123
Japan Air Lines
1202 Huaihai Zhong Lu Rm 102, tel. 37 84 67
Northwest Orient
tel. 37 73 87, 58 25 82 ext. 5 84 61
Pan American World Airways Inc
Jingan Guest House Rm 103, tel. 56 30 50x103

Airline offices are usually open from 9:00 a.m. to 12:00 p.m. and from 2:30 to 5:00 p.m..

Arrival and Departure

CAAC and major foreign airlines offer direct flights to Beijing from various international cities.

The trip to China can also be made by taking the Transsiberian Express, which is always a wonderful experience. It takes eight days to cover the distance of more than 9,000 km. Those who plan to take the Transsiberian Express only one way are urged to consider doing so on the return trip. There are many reasons for this. First of all, booked by the Lüxingshe in Beijing, it is cheaper to do so; secondly, one can get around the luggage limitations imposed by the airlines; and thirdly, it is simply much more relaxing to be able to adjust gradually to the changes in time and temperature on the way back home after the strenuous sightseeing tours and trips made within China.

The trip to China can be made by going from the West to Moscow, where one can spend the night and then continue the trip the next day with the Transsiberian Express. There are two routes: the first goes through Mongolia directly to Beijing, the second goes through the Northeast by way of Harbin.

Local travel agencies where reservations may be made can supply information about departure times and the cost for first and second class. There is also the possibility of making inquiries directly at a branch of the Soviet travel agency Intourist.

In order to make reservations, one must show a visa for China. Transit visas for Poland and the Soviet Union are handled by Intourist, whereas one for Mongolia can be applied for at the Mongolian Embassy.

Travelers can eat in the dining car, but it is also possible to buy various meals at the Russian train stations along the way. However, there is not a very large choice. Train-car axles are changed at the China border since the Soviet Union and Mongolia have wider train tracks than in China.

Arrival by Way of Hongkong

Specific information can be obtained from the China Travel Service (HK) Ltd. (see page 116).

By Plane

Flights connect Hongkong to various cities within China: Guangzhou, Guilin, Nanning, Kunming, Hangzhou, Shanghai, Nanjing, Tianjin and Beijing. Information can be obtained from the CAAC (see page 109) and Cathay Pacific.

By Train

Convenient express trains make the trip from Kowloon to Guangzhou in about three hours (daily departure at 8:15, 10:37, 12:55, 14:35). Officially, the traveler is only allowed the same amount of baggage as when traveling by plane, but this regulation is not strictly followed.

It is also possible to reach Guangzhou by local train. This is a less expensive way to travel, but it also entails getting out at the border and crossing the famous bridge there and then taking the next local train from the Chinese border station at Shenzhen to Guangzhou. The trip takes altogether about five and a half hours. More specific information is available from the China Travel Service (HK) Ltd..

By Ship

There are several ship connections to various Chinese ports, including Shanghai (a voyage that takes 60 hours with the passenger ships *Shanghai* or *Haixing*), Xiamen (17 hours with the *Gulangyu* or the *Jimei*) and Guangzhou (11 hours with the *Tianhu* or the *Xinghu* and only 2 ½ by hovercraft).

Departure

By Plane

Flights abroad can be booked through international airlines or through the national CAAC. An airport tax of 15 RMB in FEC is added to the cost of international flights. Cancellation fees range from 10 to 130 RMB.

With the Transsiberian Express

Reservations can be made through Lüxingshe. For proper planning, it should be kept in mind that it can take up to a week to procure a visa. For more about Transsiberian travel, see above.

The return trip can also be made by train or plane by way of Guangzhou and Hongkong. The same options exist here as under **Arrival.**

By Ship

Up-to-date information about prices and scheduling can be obtained from Lüxingshe in China and the China Travel Service (HK) Ltd..

Bank of China, Zhongguo Yinhang

Main office: 17, Xijiaominxiang, Beijing, tel. 33 85 21 Business hours: Mon.-Fri.: 9:00-12:00 and 1:00-4:00, Sat.: 9:00-12:00

The Bank of China has one or more branches in all major cities.

Bargaining

Prices in state-owned shops and department stores are fixed. It is customary to bargain in private shops and open markets.

Breakfast

In large hotels, western-style breakfast is served. Such fare is often rather monotonous, consisting of a combination of toast, an under- or overcooked egg, yogurt and coffee. A Chinese breakfast offers a much wider variety, although it might not suit the tastes of everyone. Tea, soup, such as rice or millet soup; steamed or fried noodles; salted, pickled vegetables and various other items are available.

Business Hours

As a rule, stores open between 8:00 and 9:00 a.m. and close between 7:00 and 9:00 p.m.. Open markets begin much earlier, usually around 6:00 a.m..

Chinese Cuisine and Beverages

Appreciation of good food has a long tradition in China. The proper preparation of various dishes was recorded long before the first millenium and over the centuries, the Chinese have developed into a people with gourmet tastes who can fix the most delicious meals using the ingredients of their respective regions. Three hot meals are usually served each day, in which rice serves as the main staple in the south, and steamed dumplings in the north. Different meat and vegetable dishes are served along with the rice and dumplings. There is great diversification in diet from region to region. Chinese cuisine can be divided roughly into four major groups:

North (Beijing and Shandong)

The Peking cuisine is noted particularly for its careful choice of ingredients and spices and the many different methods of preparation: frying, grilling, roasting, steaming, stewing, baking and braising. Peking duck is known all over the world, but Mongolian stew, Mongolian grill and cuisine from the emperor's palace are also among this region's specialities. In Shandong, mildness of flavor freshness, tenderness and aroma are particularly important. Swallow's nest soup is a frequent banquet entreé.

East (Shanghai, Jiangsu and Zhejiang)

In Shanghai, rich, colorful dishes prepared with freshly harvested vegetables are held in high esteem. Because Shanghai is so near the sea, there are also many seafood specialities. The cooks of Zhejiang and Jiangsu excel in preparing fish and fowl. Meats are often braised in their own juices to preserve their individual flavors.

West (Sichuan and Hunan)

Cuisine in this region is distinguished by its use of hot spices. All of the different flavors are within its range: sweet, sour, peppery, salty, bitter and hot. One of the specialities within this area is *Mapo Dofu,* a spicy bean-curd dish.

South (Guangdong)

The Cantonese cuisine makes use of all the many different types of vegetables that grow in this fertile region. A particularly short cooking time allows the dishes to retain their freshness, color and especially vitamins.

In general, the most preferred meats in China are duck and fish, followed by chicken and pork. Mongolians favor lamb.

Beverages include juices, soft drinks, beer (the most well-known beer, Qingdao Pijiu, is brewed according to a German recipe) and, for foreign currency, Coca Cola. Tea remains the favorite national beverage by far. Its quality depends upon the quality of the soil in which it was grown, when it was harvested and the type of water in which it is prepared. The most important types of tea are black tea (fermented), green tea (unfermented), blossom tea (green tea that has a special aroma resulting from flower petals, usually jasmine) and Wulong tea (half-fermented).

China also has a long tradition in the production of alcohol. The most well-known grain spirits are Wuliangyie and Daqu from Shanghai and Maotai Jiu from the small city of Maotai in Guizhou. Fenjiu comes from Fenyang district, Shanxi. It is brewed from sorghum and sweet green peas. The most important ingredients of Shaoxing Jiu are glutinous rice from Jiangsu Province and water from Jianghu lake. It is then produced in Shaoxing, Zhejiang. The most well-known herb spirits are Zhuyeqing and Wujiapi Jiu. Tonghua, China's most popular red wine, comes from Dongbei (Northeast China).

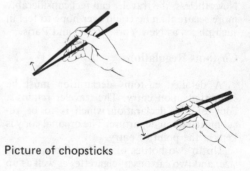

Picture of chopsticks

The art of eating with chopsticks often presents difficulties to the novice, but it is nevertheless easy to learn. The lower chopstick remains stable and is gripped between the tip of the ring finger and the hollow between thumb and index finger. The second, pivotal chopstick is held tightly by the thumb, pointer finger and index finger. In this way, the tips of the chopsticks can be spread apart or brought together to pick up a morsel. Should the technique still prove too complicated, most restaurants with foreign clientele also have silverware available.

Clothing

China covers a large territory, and the traveler should be prepared for various climatic conditions (see also page 1 and the climate chart on pages 4 - 5). In the transitional seasons, from the end of March to May and from September to October, it is wise to be prepared for both warm days and cold days. Especially at the end of October and in March, long underwear can often be a pleasant addition to the wardrobe. In winter, a warm, heavy coat, some type of headgear, and wool or leather clothing are advisable. Winters in the northern and central regions of China are dry and very cold. In the south, the temperatures are warmer, but the weather is moist and clammy. Clothing made from 100% cotton or silk is the most comfortable during the summer. A light raincoat and, most important of all, comfortable shoes are recommendable.

Most hotels provide laundry service, so there is no need to tote around heavy luggage.

Crime Rate

Due to juvenile unemployment, the crime rate in China has risen in the past few years. For this reason, one should not be careless when walking about with valuable possessions. Nevertheless, the traveler can feel considerably more secure than he could ever hope to feel in such places as New York, Rome and Paris.

Customs Regulations

A detailed customs declaration must be submitted upon entry. The traveler retains a copy of this declaration which is to be resubmitted upon departure. The original copy is kept at the point of entry.

Up to two bottles of alcohol (no specified size) and two cartons of cigarettes as well as up to 50 cigars may be brought along duty-free for personal use. Technical apparata, pocket calculators, radios, camera and movie equipment up to 8 mm (professional movie equipment requires a special permit) as well as personal valuables such as watches and jewelry may be taken into and out of China, but they are not to be sold or given away during the stay. Presents for people in China must be declared

as such and might be subject to duty. The amount of money that can be taken into and out of the country is not limited as long as it is duly noted in the customs declaration. (Keep track of receipts from the exchange of currency!) It is forbidden to bring wireless sets, weapons, ammunition, propaganda against the government, pornographic material, drugs, etc. into the country.

Upon departure, all of the items which were marked on the customs declaration must still be in the traveler's possession. Literature intended solely for *neibu* — use within China — may not be exported, nor the works of famous painters who are no longer living. Items of value which have been purchased in China may be taken out of the country if they are accompanied by proof of purchase. Antiques are included in this category, and one should obtain a receipt upon purchase so that it can later be presented at customs. RMB may not be exported.

Chinese customs officials may be very strict and examine everything in rigorous detail.

Discounts

Foreign tourists are required to pay considerably more for transportation and overnight lodging than Chinese citizens. Students can sometimes obtain discounts, though usually only if they are enrolled at a Chinese school or university. However, occasionally it is possible to get a reduction in price by presenting an international student identification card. Foreigners who are employed at Chinese institutions can also obtain price reductions by presenting proof of such employment.

Embassies

Embassies of the People's Republic of China:

Argentina:	Conesa 1964, Buenos Aires
Austria:	Metternichgasse 4,1030 Wien
Australia:	247 Federal Highway,Watson, Canberra, A.C.T. 2602
Belgium:	Boulevard Général Jacques No. 19, 1050 Brussels
Canada:	411-415 St. Andrews St., Ottawa, Ontario K1N 5H3
Colombia:	Carrera 15 80-25, Bogota
Denmark:	Oregaardsalle No. 25, 2900 Hellerup, Copenhagen
France:	11 Avenue George V, 75008 Paris
Federal Republic of Germany:	Kurfürstenallee 12, 5300

	Bonn 2 (Bad Godesberg)
Italy:	Via Giovanne, Paiseillo 39,
	Roma 00198
Japan:	15-30 Minami-Azabu,
	4-Chome, Minato-ku, Tokyo
Mexico:	Avenue San Jeronimo 217,
	Mexico City 20, DF
Netherlands:	Adriaan Goehooplaan 7,
	Den Haag
Norway:	111 Inkognitojaten, Oslo 12
Peru:	Jr. José Granda 150,
	San Isidoro, Lima
Sweden:	Bragevagen No. 4, Stockholm
Switzerland:	Kalcheggweg 10, Berne
United Kingdom:	31 Portland Place, London
	W1N 3AG
United States:	2300 Connecticut Ave., NW,
	Washington, DC 20008
Venezuela:	Quinta Mama, Calle Mohedne,
	Country Club, Caracas

Foreign Embassies in China:

Embassy of the Argentine Republic
Sanlitun Lu Dong Wu Jie, tel. 52 20 90

Embassy of the Commonwealth of Australia
Dongzhimen Dajie, tel. 52 23 31

Embassy of the Republic of Austria
Xiushui Nanjie, tel. 52 20 61, 52 15 05

Embassy of the Kingdom of Belgium
Sanlitun Lu, tel. 52 17 36, 52 27 82

Embassy of the Federative Republic of Brazil
Guanghua Lu, tel. 52 27 40, 52 28 81

Embassy of the People's Republic of Bulgaria
Xiushui Beijie, tel. 52 22 32, 52 19 46

Embassy of the Socialist Republic of the Union of Burma
Dongzhimenwai Dajie, tel. 52 14 25, 52 14 88

Embassy of Canada
Sanlitun Lu, tel. 52 14 75, 52 17 41

Embassy of the Republic of Chile
Sanlitun Dong Si Jie, tel. 52 20 74, 52 15 22

Embassy of the Republic of Cuba
Xiushui Nanjie, tel. 52 23 49, 52 17 14

Embassy of the Czechoslovak Socialist Republic
Ritan Lu, tel. 52 15 31, 52 15 37

Embassy of the Kingdom of Denmark
Sanlitun Dong Wu Jie, tel. 52 24 31

Embassy of the Arab Republic of Egypt
Ritan Dong Lu, tel. 52 18 80, 52 18 25

Embassy of the Republic of Finland
Guanghua Lu, tel. 52 17 53, 52 18 17

Embassy of the French Republic
Sanlitun Dong San Jie, tel. 52 13 31, 52 12 74

Embassy of the German Democratic Republic
Sanlitun Dong Si Jie, tel. 52 16 31

Embassy of the Federal Republic of Germany
Dongzhimenwai Dajie, tel. 52 21 61

Embassy of the Hellenic Republic
Guanghua Lu, tel. 52 13 91

Embassy of the Hungarian People's Republic
Dongzhimenwai Dajie, tel. 52 14 31, 52 12 73

Embassy of the Republic of India
Ritan Dong Lu, tel. 52 18 56, 52 19 08

Embassy of the Republic of Ireland
Ritan Dong Lu, tel. 52 26 91, 52 29 14

Embassy of the Italian Republic
Sanlitun Dong Er Jie, tel. 52 21 31, 52 14 21

Embassy of Japan
Ritan Lu, tel. 52 23 61

Embassy of the Democratic People's Republic of Korea
Ritan Beilu, tel. 52 11 89

Embassy of the State of Kuwait
Guanghua Lu, tel. 52 21 82, 52 23 74

Embassy of the Grand Duchy of Luxembourg
Neiwubu Jie, tel. 55 61 75

Embassy of Malaysia
Dongzhimenwai Dajie, tel. 52 25 31

Embassy of the United States of Mexico
Sanlitun Dong Wu Jie, tel. 52 25 74, 52 20 70

Embassy of the People's Republic of Mongolia
Xiushui Beijie, tel. 52 12 03

Embassy of the Kingdom of Morocco
Sanlitun Lu, tel. 52 17 96, 52 14 89

Embassy of the Kingdom of the Netherlands
Sanlitun Dong Si Jie, tel. 52 17 31

Embassy of New Zealand
Ritan Lu Dong Er Jie, tel. 52 27 31

Embassy of the Kingdom of Norway
Sanlitun Dong Yi Jie, tel. 52 22 61, 52 13 29

Embassy of the Islamic Republic of Pakistan
Dongzhimenwai Dajie, tel. 52 25 04, 52 26 95

Embassy of the Republic of Peru
Sanlitun, tel. 52 21 78, 52 29 13

Embassy of the Republic of the Philippines
Xiushui Beijie, tel. 52 27 94

Embassy of the Polish People's Republic
Ritan Lu, tel. 52 12 35

Embassy of the Portuguese Republic
Sanlitun, tel. 52 34 97

Embassy of the Socialist Republic of Romania
Ritan Lu Dong Er Jie, tel. 52 33 15, 52 34 42

Embassy of Spain
Sanlitun Lu, tel. 52 36 29, 52 35 20

Embassy of the Democratic Socialist Republic of Sri Lanka
Jianhua Lu, tel. 52 18 61, 52 18 62

Embassy of the Kingdom of Sweden
Dongzhimenwai Dajie, tel. 52 33 31, 52 33 33

Embassy of the Swiss Confederation
Sanlitun Dong Wu Jie, tel. 52 27 36, 52 27 38

Embassy of the Kingdom of Thailand
Guanghua Lu, tel. 52 19 03

Embassy of the Republic of Turkey
Sanlitun Dong Wu Jie, tel. 52 26 50, 52 21 84

Embassy of the United Kingdom of Great Britain & Northern Ireland
Guanghua Lu, tel. 52 19 61

Embassy of the United States of America
Xiushui Beijie, tel. 52 38 31

Embassy of the Union of Soviet Socialist Republics
Dongzhimenbei Zhong Jie, tel. 52 20 51

Embassy of the Republic of Venezuela
Sanlitun Lu, tel. 52 12 95, 52 26 94

Embassy of the Socialist Federal Republic of Yugoslavia

Sanlitun Dong Liu Jie, tel. 52 15 62, 52 16 93

Entry Regulations

To enter China it is necessary to have a passport with a valid visa and a customs declaration (see above). Visas for group tours are handled by the travel agency. Participants should submit their passports (which will not be at their disposal until the trip begins) to the agency approximately six weeks before the departure date so that a group visa can be applied for. Passports must be valid an additional six months beyond the intended date of return.

The group visa with a list of all participants is turned over to the travel guide.

Independent travelers need to have a valid visa issued by the Consular Department of the Chinese embassy or consulate-general. In order to obtain this type of visa, it is usually necessary to have an invitation from a Chinese resident or from a foreigner residing in China. Individual travel visas are more likely to be issued for the off-season (November – March).

Visa applications — available at the embassy or consulate-general – are to be filled out in duplicate and submitted to the Chinese embassy along with two passport photos and a valid passport. If the application is also accompanied by a written invitation, a visa is usually granted within a few days. If it is not possible to obtain such an invitation, the traveler may seek the help of a travel agent who has had experience in arranging trips to China and who can apply for an individual visa through the national Chinese travel agency. Since 1986 in exceptional cases independent travelers can get a visa valid for 1 month upon arrival at the airport of Beijing, Tianjin, Shanghai, Hangzhou, Fuzhou, Xiamen, Xi'an, Guilin and Kunming. A valid passport, one photo and an invitation are to be submitted.

It is often easier for an independent traveler to enter China by way of Hong Kong. Several of the travel agencies there offer short excursions with fixed itineraries. For some time now it has been possible to obtain an individual four-week visa through Hong Kong travel bureaus. The traveler is then responsible for planning his own trip and arranging his own accommodations. Visas may be extended in China. Applications for visas may be obtained at the following agencies:

China International Travel Service (H.K.) Ltd.,
Miramar Hotel, Room 2025, 134 Nathan Road, Kowloon.

CAAC Route Map

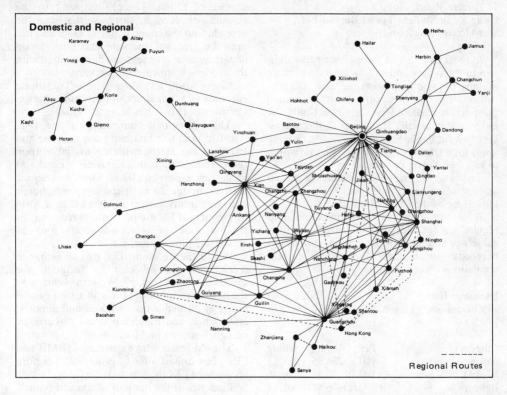

Domestic and Regional

Regional Routes

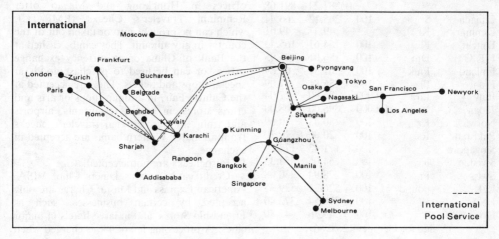

International

International
Pool Service

China Travel Service (H.K.) Ltd.,
77 Queens Road, Hong Kong.
Hong Kong Student Travel Bureau Ltd.,
Star House, Kowloon.

In most cases a visa can be obtained within two to three days and will be valid up to three months. For visa application one filled out application form, one passport photo and a valid passport are needed. Upon arrival in China, the independent traveler should go to the nearest Gong'an Ju, Public Security Bureau, in order to apply for a travel permit for the cities he wishes to visit (see **Travel Permit**).

Traveling on one's own requires a certain amount of courage, much patience and some knowledge of the Chinese language.

It is important to keep in mind that regulations for independent travel are often subject to change. For this reason, it is always necessary to inquire about the current regulations before planning a trip.

Exchange Rate
Official foreign exchange quotations rate in RMB *yuan*

Currency		Per	Buying	selling
Australia	$	100	236.95	238.13
Austria	Sch	100	26.31	26.45
Belgium	Fr	10000	(c)896.87	901.37
			(f)887.24	891.68
Canada	$	100	265.12	266.44
Denmark	Kr		49.37	49.61
Dutch	Fl	100	164.61	165.43
F.R.G.	Dm	100	186.01	186.95
Finland	Fmk	100	61.59	61.89
France	Fr	100	56.81	57.09
Italy	Lira	10000	26.90	27.04
Japan	Yen	100000	2396.00	2408.00
Norway	Kr	100	50.43	50.69
Pakistan	Rs	100	20.00	20.10
Singapore	$	100	171.43	172.29
Sweden	Kr	100	54.05	54.33
Swiss	Fr	100	228.94	230.08
U.K.	pound	100	526.71	529.35
USA	$	100	370.54	372.40
Hong Kong	$	100	47.56	47.80

(Value for October 12, 1986)

Source: *China Daily*

Forms of Payment
The basic denomination of Chinese currency, renminbi (RMB), is *yuan*, or, colloquially, *kuai*. A single *yuan* is divided into 10 *jiao/mao* or 100 *fen*. *Yuan* is printed in notes of one, two, five and ten, *jiao* in notes of one, two and five and *fen* in coins of one, two

and five. It is forbidden to bring renminbi into or out of China. There is no limit to the amount of foreign currency that can be brought into the country, but an exact account must be given of the sum and type. Upon departure this statement can be compared with the receipts from currency exchange.

Since April 1,1980, a type of substitute currency — *waihuiquan* — Foreign-Exchange-Certificates (FEC) has become available.

These come in denominations of one, five, ten, fifty and one hundred *yuan* and one and five *jiao* and are immediately available upon the exchange of cash or traveler's checks at banks and exchange offices. Many businesses, such as antique stores, friendship stores, hotels and restaurants, accept solely FEC as a form of payment. FEC are particularly required for the purchase of imported goods such as cigarettes, film, liquor, etc.

It is further recommended that all exchange receipts should be kept to facilitate the exchange back into Western currency. Exchange offices of the Bank of China can be found at all major train stations and airports, large hotels and friendship stores so currency exchange is not a problem.

The existence of two currencies (RMB and FEC) has caused a lot of problems, therefore abolition of FEC is expected soon.

Branches of the Bank of China and branch offices in Hongkong and Macao offer Renminbi Traveler's Checks (RMB/TC), which can be brought into or taken out of the country in any amount. They can be cashed at the Bank of China or at currency exchange offices or can be used to purchase goods at special shops and tickets. They are accepted at the Canton Fair, in antique shops or arts and crafts stores, in hotels, restaurants, airports and train stations. Foreign traveler's checks from all major Western banks are accepted in exchange.

Eurochecks are not accepted.

Credit cards such as Diners Club, VISA, American Express and Master Charge are only accepted by certain businesses, such as Friendship Stores, and in large hotels in major cities. A processing fee of 4% is charged when one pays by credit card.

Foreigners can open an account at the Bank of China where money from abroad can be transferred. It is possible to wire money from abroad. At the request of the recipient and with his passport number, money can be transferred from a Western bank to various branches of the Bank of China where a passport is required to pick up the money.

Gifts

Occasionally, the traveler may be in a situation where he wishes to present a small gift as an expression of appreciation. In the case of a temporary acquaintance, the gift should be no more than a small token. There are many possibilities within this range, including lighters, pens, musical cassettes, pocket knives, books one has finished reading for the interpreter, etc.

Hairdresser

Hairdressers are located in or near almost all large hotels. They are inexpensive and the employees do their best to meet the customers' demands. Chinese hairdressers are well-known for their relaxing scalp massages.

Health Tips

Any trip which involves a change of climate and diet can also lead to difficulty in physical adjustment at the beginning. For caution's sake, one should take along a few medicines, such as those for colds, diarrhea and constipation, as well as aspirin and vitamin-C

tablets. Those who take special medicine on a regular basis should be sure to carry an adequate supply with them.

In China, it is customary to boil water and avoid raw or under-cooked meat. Such customs are based on old hygiene rules.

Any foreign traveler who becomes seriously ill will be treated in the ward for foreigners in the city hospital. Most of the hospital equipment is out-of-date, but, as the authors know from personal experience, there are some outstanding doctors.

Medical treatment in China is usually very inexpensive. Immunization requirements for travelers are often subject to change, and it is advisable to make inquiries about the current regulations at one's travel agency, the public health department or an office of immunization well before the intended departure date (approximately six weeks in advance).

Holidays

Besides the new holidays celebrated according to the Western calendar, there are also traditional Chinese holidays celebrated according to the lunar calendar:

Gregorian Calendar	Lunar Calendar	Holiday	Vacation
January 1		New Year's Day	1 day
	1st day of the 1st month	Spring Festival	3 days
	15th day of the 1st month	Lantern Festival	
March 8		International Women's Day	½ day for women
	12th day of the 3rd month	Qingming Festival	
May 1		Labor Day	1 day
May 4		Youth Day (in memory of the May Fourth Movement of 1919)	
June 1		International Children's Day	1 day for children
	5th day of the 5th month	Dragon Boat Festival	
July 1		Founding of the Chinese Communist Party	
August 1		Founding of the National Liberation Army	
	15th day of the 8th month	Mid-autumn Festival	
October 1		National Day (in memory of the founding of the People's Republic of China in 1949)	2 days

Hotels

The Chinese travel agency usually looks after travelers in China and also takes care of accommodations. As a rule, hotel rooms are double rooms that are simply furnished, neat and clean. They are equipped with their own bathrooms with hot and cold running water. Ordinarily, everything needed to fix tea is placed in each room: a thermos with hot water, green tea and cups with lids. Other drinks can be ordered from the waiter on one's particular floor. Larger hotels normally have other services available, such as post office counters, places to exchange currency, hairdressers, laundry and ironing services and restaurants. Ping pong or billiard rooms are also available for leisure time activities. Addresses of the most frequented hotels are found at the end of city descriptions. Besides the larger hotels catering to foreign tourists and businessmen, there are also simple hotels for Chinese citizens and overseas Chinese that are considerably less expensive. However, these hotels are open to foreigners only when there are vacancies. The easiest way for the independent traveler who must arrange for his own accommodations to find inexpensive hotels is to seek aid from taxi-drivers.

Information

In addition to the traveler's own travel agency, the national Chinese travel agency Lüxingshe will also be of service to any foreigner who might have questions. A Lüxingshe agent can be contacted at most hotels. Moreover, almost every group tour is appointed a Chinese guide who has some knowledge of foreign languages.

Itinerary

After consulting Lüxingshe, individual travel agencies offer various itineraries from among which the interested party can then choose. Group trips are sometimes arranged according to the special interests of a particular group. The independent traveler can arrange his itinerary according to his own ideas as long as he obtains permission from the Public Security Bureau (see **Travel Permit**). It should be kept in mind that the traveler will frequently be covering long distances. This distance can be traveled by plane, which is time saving but relatively expensive, or by train, which is time-consuming but also interesting and inexpensive. Travelers who only have a limited amount of time should consider confining

themselves to a smaller area which they can then cover in greater detail.

Special interests can determine the choice of destination.

History of the Revolution: Guangzhou, Shaoshan, Wuhan, Chongqing, Yan'an, Shanghai, Beijing
History of the Taiping Rebellion: Nanjing
Archaeology: Xi'an
Buddhism: Wutai Shan, Emei Shan, Putuo Shan, Jiuhua Shan, Tian Shan
Daoism: Qingcheng Shan, Laoshan, Ruicheng, Wudang Shan
Silk Road: Kashi, Turfan Dunhuang, Liuyuan, Lanzhou, Xi'an
Confucianism: Qufu
Lamaism: Lhasa, Xigaze, Xining, Xiahe
Ming and Qing architecture: Beijing, Chengde
Park and garden landscaping: Suzhou, Hangzhou, Chengde, Beijing
Minorities: Yunnan, Xinjiang, Inner Mongolia, Xizang (Tibet), Qinghai, Guangxi
Attractive boat tours: Guilin, Lijiang; Sanxia, Changjiang; Wuyi Shan, Grand Canal
Swimming and relaxation: Beidaihe, Qingdao, Lushan, Putuo Shan
Universities: Beijing, Shanghai, Nanjing, Chengdu, Hangzhou, Xiamen
Ceramics: Yixing, Jingdezhen, Dehua, Foshan
Industry: Anshan, Daqing, Shanghai, Wuhan
Commerce: Beijing, Shanghai, Guangzhou (Canton Fair)
Hydroengineering: Yichang, Chengdu

Laundry

Laundry and dry-cleaning services are available at almost all hotels. The traveler turns in his clothes and they will be delivered approximately 24 hours later, so there is no need to pack extras which also entail extra weight. Payment is due when the clothes are picked up. Most hotels also provide a pressing service.

Mail

All large hotels and guest houses have post office counters where stamps, stationary and postcards are sold. A standard airmail letter abroad costs 1.10 *yuan*, aerograms and postcards 0.90 *yuan*. From Beijing a letter takes +-7 days to reach its destination abroad. Letters mailed from other cities can take two weeks.

Maps

Maps and atlases can be found at Chinese

bookstores and in the bookstalls at larger hotels. City maps are often offered to the traveler almost as soon as he has stepped off the train but can also be bought — assuming they are available — at hotels and bookstores.

Names

Chinese names have two or three syllables, and the surname is spoken first. Thus, the surnames of Zhou Enlai and Zhu De are Zhou and Zhu respectively. In accordance with the new Pinyin romanization system, first names with two syllables are written as one word.

Women keep their maiden names even if they are married. First names rarely reveal whether a person is male or female.

Newspapers, Periodicals and Books

Newspapers written in English are available only on a limited scale. The *China Daily* can be found almost everywhere. In Beijing, the major hotels carry *Time* and *Newsweek*. Books which have been translated into English are available at some bookstores and hotels. *China Reconstructs* and *Beijing Review* provide a picture of the land and the people. Those who can read Chinese naturally have a much larger selection of newspapers, periodicals and books to choose from.

Western periodicals and books may be brought into the country as long as they do not reflect a negative attitude towards the government and are not pornographic.

Packages

Travelers who have made too many purchases and are worried about exceeding their baggage allowance can send their things back home by mail. Packages must be taken to the post office before they are sealed and undergo a short inspection regarding the contents. In Beijing, packages can also be taken to the Friendship Store to be forwarded (see page 159).

Photos

Taking pictures in the vicinity of military posts or places where valuable cultural treasures are located — such as Qin Shihuang's underground army — is strictly forbidden. If it is discovered that someone has violated this regulation, the result can be both awkward and disagreeable.

One should abide by common courtesy when taking pictures of people. In East and West alike, many people do not like to have strangers take their pictures at close range.

Kodak and Fuji film can be bought at large hotels and Friendship Stores, and it can be developed in Beijing, Shanghai and Guangzhou. Camera accessories such as flash attachments and batteries should be brought along.

Punctuality

In China, punctuality is a quality that is highly valued.

It is not appreciated if individual members of a travel group are late for no reason. One is also expected to be on time for personal appointments.

Restaurants

The Chinese enjoy going out to eat and consider it a social occasion. For this reason, it is worthwhile to search out a simple restaurant at least once and observe the cheerful groups of people as they dine. Food orders are taken by the waiter, but the diner usually obtains his own drinks from the bar.

All larger hotels that host foreigners also have good restaurants. Speciality restaurants are usually expensive and are frequently booked up in advance. If a large group is planning to eat out, it would be wise to reserve a table in advance. One will have to indicate the number of people in the party and what the overall price per person should be.

As a rule, restaurants only accept cash. A few large restaurants in Beijing, Shanghai and Guangzhou make an exception and will also accept checks from the Bank of China and credit cards.

Well-known restaurants are listed at the end of the appropriate city descriptions.

Shopping

Tourists are given plenty of opportunities to go shopping. Tour groups are almost always led to the so-called Friendship Stores where there is a large array of Chinese export articles to choose from. Items range from canned fruits and vegetables and other like provisions, textiles, calligraphies and paintings to porcelain, toys and furniture. There is something in every price range. In these shops, the tourist has the advantage of being able to search for an article of interest undisturbed. Also, the store clerk serving the customers often has more than just an elementary knowledge of English. Normal shops and department stores are also open to the foreign traveler. Shopping in these stores can be more interesting, but in smaller cities the tourist should not be surprised to find himself surrounded by a group of curious but friendly local Chinese. Shopping under such circumstances can be rather trying, and it sometimes happens that the traveler ends up buying things that he normally never would have bought at all. Keep in mind that Chinese customers also carefully weigh the advantages and disadvantages before making a purchase, and taking a while to make up one's mind is nothing unusual. These kinds of stores do not usually have as wide a selection as the Friendship Stores. Antique shops are, for the most part, open just to foreigners with foreign currency.

Each city and region has its own specialities in the area of arts and crafts. A few are listed below:

Beijing: lacquerware, enamel-cloisonné, inlaid mother-of-pearl, carved ivory, polished precious stones, paintings, stone rubbings, prints, embroidery, carpets, silks, furniture, furs

Changsha: ceramics

Chengdu: bamboo and rattan articles, embroidery

Datong: bronze articles, rugs

Fuzhou: lacquerware

Guangzhou: carved ivory and jade, embroidery, ceramics, precious stone work

Guilin: scroll pictures, rocks for miniature landscapes

Hangzhou: silks, embroidery

Kunming: national minorities' embroidery and weavings

Lhasa: rugs

Nanjing: cloud brocade

Ningxia: woven rugs

Shanghai: inlaid mother-of-pearl, carved ivory, lacquerware, silver and precious stone work, silks, paintings

Shenyang: furs

Suzhou: embroidery, silk tapestries

Tianjin: inlaid mother-of-pearl, rugs

Wuxi: ceramics

Xinjiang: woven rugs, Uighur embroidery

Yangzhou: lacquerware, furniture, inlaid mother-of-pearl

Telephone, Telegram and Telex

Calls abroad can be placed through telecommunication centers or can be made from hotel rooms through the reception desk. A call to North America or Europe costs 9.60 *yuan* per minute with a three minute minimum which is considered to be the base fee. Calls are handled by the operator; there is no direct dialing, even between large cities in China. Local calls are free. Public telephones can be recognized by the sign 'gongyong dianhua'

Telegrams can be sent from post offices or the reception desks at large hotels. Telegrams abroad cost between 1.20 and 1.50 *yuan* per word.

At large hotels, main post offices and telecommunication centers, it is also possible to send messages by telex. The cost per minute to all overseas destinations, including Hong Kong, is approximately 8.40 *yuan* (three minute minimum).

Television

In larger hotels, rooms are usually furnished with TV sets. Chinese television has two channels. Programs are transmitted in color from 6:00 p.m. to about 10:00 p.m. naturally, in Chinese. The program selection consists of news broadcasts, including current world news, plays, documentaries and films, foreign language courses, etc.

Terminology

The official name of the country is either the 'People's Republic of China' or 'China'. The term 'Red China', which is still frequently heard in the West, is considered by the Chinese to be an insult.

If the subject of Taiwan comes up in conversation, it should be kept in mind that Taiwan is considered to be a province belonging to China, and such terms that signify it as an independent country, such as 'Formosa' or 'Republic of China', are not acceptable.

Time Differences

Time differences between Chinese and foreign cities:

Amsterdam	- 7	(hours)
Bangkok	- 1	
Berlin	- 7	
Chicago	- 14	
Dallas	- 14	
Hong Kong	+ - 0	
Honolulu	- 18	
London	- 7	
Los Angeles	- 16	
Montreal	- 13	
New York	- 13	
Paris	- 7	

Rio de Janeiro	-	11
Rome	-	7
San Francisco	-	16
Sydney	+	2
Tokyo	+	1
Vancouver	-	16
Zurich	-	7

At 12 noon in Beijing, the time in London is 5 AM, in New York 11 PM (of the preceding day).

Tipping

Tipping is not customary in China and one should not insist upon it. Occasionally, tips given discreetly are accepted.

Toilet Articles

Those who can not do without a certain brand of any particular article would do well to supply themselves adequately in advance. Local brands of cosmetics, soaps, toothpaste, etc. are available at all department stores. Many hotels and Friendship Stores offer Western products. Deodorants and sanitary napkins should be brought along. Tampons are still largely unheard of in China.

Transportation

Within China
Airplane: (see **Airlines**) The airline network of the Civil Aviation Association of China (CAAC) covers a distance of 90,000 km and connects more than 80 cities and regions. The booking and purchasing of tickets requires the submittal of a travel permit for the place of destination and a passport with a valid visa. For well-traveled routes, such as Beijing to Shanghai, early reservations are recommended. Such flights are frequently booked up two days in advance.

If payment is not made to the CAAC by the indicated deadline, any reservation is then forfeited. Cancellations and refunds can be made for a fee at the appropriate office up to two hours before flight departure time. If a cancellation is made with less than two hours notice, 20% of the ticket price is withheld as a cancellation charge.

If a traveler does not appear for his flight, his ticket is then forfeited.

Train: The train is the most important means of transportation for long distances. China's railway lines totalled a distance of about 50,000 km at the end of 1981. For foreigners, traveling by train is substantially cheaper than by airplane. Those who have a sufficient amont of time should make use of the train frequently, as the trip also provides an opportunity to get to know the land and the people. Traveling by night also saves additional hotel costs. Tickets can be purchased directly at the train station or through Lüxingshe. The traveler should note the date, the train number and the seat and compartment numbers which are printed on the ticket.

Tickets can be purchased for hard and soft class, namely *yingzuo*, 'hard seat', and *ruanzuo*, 'soft seat', as well as *yingwo*, 'hard sleeping berth', and *ruanwo*, 'soft sleeping berth', for longer distances. Foreigners are usually accommodated in soft class. The traveler is more comfortable and undisturbed, but also more isolated. Particularly for travelers who have some knowledge of the Chinese language, it is much more interesting to travel hard class because one comes into direct contact with Chinese travelers and can conduct stimulating conversations.

The train crew is responsible for cleanliness and looking after the passengers' well-being. They prepare hot water and in soft class pass out hot water thermoses so that the passengers can brew their own tea. Covered cups are also provided for this purpose. In addition, the train crew sells tickets which can be redeemed in the dining car for a tasty meal underway. Members of the crew go from compartment to compartment to take orders. Frequently, special orders will also be prepared if possible.

Bus: Members of group tours are provided with buses by the national travel agency to take them from one sight to another throughout their stay.

City buses are another story. During the rush hours they are hopelessly overcrowded, and customary politeness is often forgotten in the heat of the fray. Passengers inform the driver where they want to go and pay the appropiate fee. Foreigners who cannot speak the language should have the destination in writing and show it to the driver. The passenger will be informed when he has arrived. Traveling by bus is very inexpensive. Prices range from a few *fen* up to three *mao*.

Taxi: Taxi stands can be found in front of hotels, Friendship Stores and many large train stations and airports. A taxi can also be called from a hotel or Lüxingshe. By Chinese standards, the prices are relatively expensive, around ¥ 0.80 per km. The fare is fixed by the

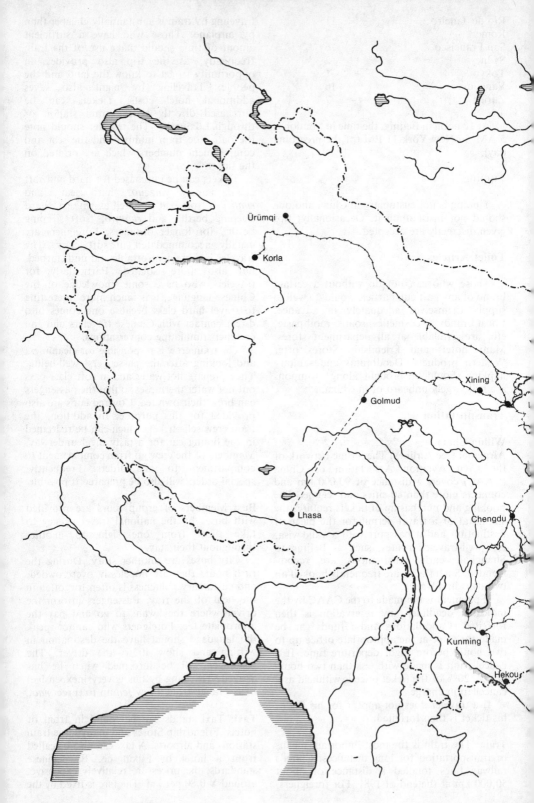

Ürümqi

Korla

Xining

Golmud

Lhasa

Chengdu

Kunming

Hekou

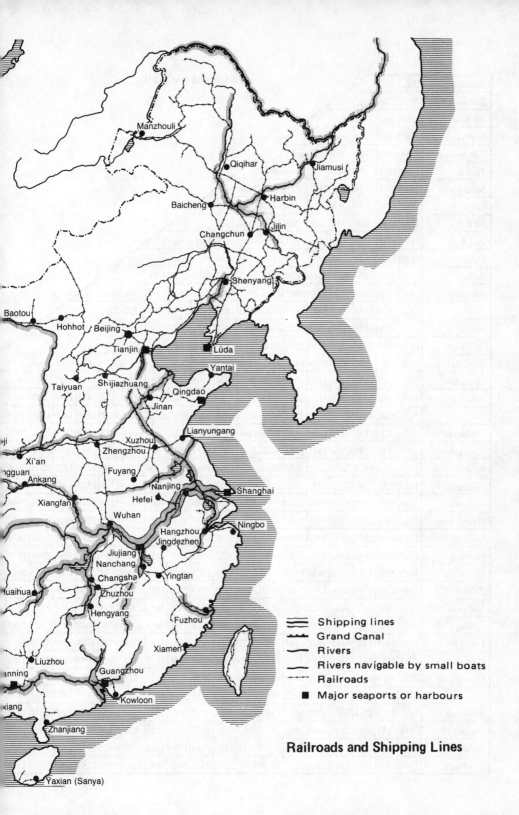

Manzhouli

Qiqihar

Jiamusi

Baicheng

Harbin

Jilin

Changchun

Shenyang

Baotou

Hohhot

Beijing

Tianjin

Lüda

Yantai

Taiyuan

Shijiazhuang

Qingdao

Jinan

Lianyungang

Xuzhou

Zhengzhou

Xi'an

ngguan

Ankang

Fuyang

Nanjing

Shanghai

Xiangfan

Hefei

Wuhan

Hangzhou

Ningbo

Jingdezhen

Jiujiang

Nanchang

Yingtan

uaihua

Changsha

Zhuzhou

Hengyang

Fuzhou

Liuzhou

Xiamen

anning

Guangzhou

xiang

Kowloon

Zhanjiang

Yaxian (Sanya)

```
≡≡≡   Shipping lines
⋯⋀⋯   Grand Canal
───   Rivers
───   Rivers navigable by small boats
⋯⋯⋯   Railroads
■     Major seaports or harbours
```

Railroads and Shipping Lines

Distances by Rail

	Beijing	Tianjin	Jinzhou	Shenyang	Changchun	Harbin	Manzhouli	Qiqihaer	Jilin	Dandong	Dalian	Jinan	Qingdao	Xuzhou	Hefei	Nanjing	Shanghai	Hangzhou
Beijing	Beijing																	
Tianjin	137	Tianjin																
Jinzhou	599	462	Jinzhou															
Shenyang	841	704	242	Shenyang														
Changchun	1146	1009	547	305	Changchun													
Harbin	1388	1251	789	547	242	Harbin												
Manzhouli	2323	2186	1724	1482	1177	935	Manzhouli											
Qiqihaer	1448	1311	849	760	530	288	693	Qiqihaer										
Jilin	1287	1150	688	446	128	275	1210	563	Jilin									
Dandong	1118	981	519	277	582	824	1759	1037	723	Dandong								
Dalian	1238	1101	639	397	702	944	1879	1157	843	674	Dalian							
Jinan	494	357	819	1061	1366	1608	2543	1668	1507	1338	1458	Jinan						
Qingdao	877	750	1212	1454	1759	2001	2936	2061	1900	1731	1851	393	Qingdao					
Xuzhou	811	674	1136	1378	1683	1925	2860	1985	1824	1655	1775	317	710	Xuzhou				
Hefei	1107	970	1432	1674	1979	2221	3156	2281	2120	1951	2071	613	1006	296	Hefei			
Nanjing	1157	1020	1482	1724	2029	2271	3206	2331	2170	2001	2121	663	1056	346	312	Nanjing		
Shanghai	1462	1325	1787	2029	2334	2576	3511	2636	2475	2306	2426	968	1361	651	617	305	Shanghai	
Hangzhou	1651	1514	1976	2218	2523	2765	3700	2825	2664	2495	2615	1157	1550	840	806	494	189	Hangz
Nanchang	2005	2142	2604	2846	3151	3393	4328	3453	3292	3123	2343	1793	2186	1476	1442	1130	825	636
Fuzhou	2623	2486	2948	3190	3495	3737	4672	3797	3636	3467	3587	2129	2522	1812	1778	1466	1161	972
Shijiazhuang	283	420	882	1124	1429	1671	2606	1731	1570	1401	1521	298	691	615	911	961	1266	1455
Zhengzhou	695	832	1294	1536	1841	2083	3018	2143	1982	1813	1933	666	1059	349	645	695	1000	1189
Wuhan	1229	1366	1828	2070	2375	2617	3552	2677	2516	2347	2467	1200	1593	883	1179	1229	1545	1356
Changsha	1587	1724	2186	2428	2733	2975	3910	3035	2874	2705	2825	1558	1951	1241	1537	1492	1187	998
Zhuzhou	1638	1775	2237	2479	2784	3026	3961	3086	2925	2756	2876	1609	2002	1292	1588	1441	1136	947
Guangzhou	2313	2450	2912	3154	3459	3701	3636	3761	3600	3431	3551	2284	2677	1967	2263	2116	1811	1622
Liuzhou	2310	2447	2909	3151	3456	3698	4633	3758	3597	3428	3548	2281	2674	1964	2260	2113	1808	1619
Nanning	2565	2702	3164	3406	3711	3953	4888	4013	3852	3683	3803	2536	2929	2219	2515	2368	2063	1874
Pingxiang	2785	2922	3384	3626	3931	4173	5108	4233	4072	3903	4023	2756	3149	2439	2735	2588	2283	2094
Xi'an	1165	1302	1764	2006	2311	2553	3488	2613	2452	2283	2403	1177	1570	860	1156	1206	1511	1700
Lanzhou	1813	1950	2412	2654	2959	3201	4136	3261	3100	2931	3051	1853	2246	1536	1832	1882	2187	2376
Xining	2098	2235	2697	2939	3244	3486	4421	3546	3385	3216	3336	2069	2462	1752	2048	2098	2403	2592
Ürümqi	3774	3911	4373	4615	4920	5162	3097	5222	5061	4892	5012	3745	4138	3428	3724	3774	4079	4268
Chengdu	2048	2185	2647	2889	3194	3436	4371	3496	3335	3166	3286	2019	2412	1702	1998	2048	2353	2542
Chongqing	2552	2689	3151	3393	3698	3940	4875	4000	3839	3670	3790	2523	2916	2206	2502	2552	2501	2312
Guiyang	2540	2677	3139	3381	3686	3928	4863	3988	3827	3658	3778	2511	2904	2194	2490	2343	2038	1849
Kunming	3179	3316	3738	4020	4325	4567	5502	4627	4466	4297	4417	3119	3512	2802	3098	2982	2677	2488
Taiyuan	514	651	1113	1355	1660	1902	2837	1962	1801	1632	1752	529	922	846	1142	1192	1497	1686
Hohhot	668	805	1267	1509	1814	2056	2991	2116	1955	1786	1906	1162	1555	1479	1775	1825	2130	2319
Yinchuan	1346	1483	1945	2187	2492	2734	3669	2794	2633	2464	2584	1840	2233	2003	2299	2349	2654	2813

Shijiazhuang	Zhengzhou	Wuhan	Changsha	Zhuzhou	Guangzhou	Liuzhou	Nanning	Pingxiang	Xi'an	Lanzhou	Xining	Ürümqi	Chengdu	Chongqing	Guiyang	Kunming	Taiyuan	Hohhot	Yinchuan
Shijiazhuang																			
412	Zhengzhou																		
946	534	Wuhan																	
1304	892	358	Changsha																
1355	943	409	51	Zhuzhou															
2030	1618	1084	726	675	Guangzhou														
2027	1615	1081	723	672	1079	Liuzhou													
2282	1870	1336	978	927	1334	255	Nanning												
2502	2090	1556	1198	1147	1554	475	220	Pingxiang											
923	511	1045	1403	1454	2129	2126	2381	2601	Xi'an										
1599	1187	1721	2079	2130	2805	2746	3001	3221	676	Lanzhou									
1815	1403	1937	2295	2346	3021	2962	3217	3437	892	216	Xining								
3491	3079	3613	3971	4022	4697	4638	4893	5113	2568	1892	2108	Ürümqi							
1765	1353	1887	1920	1869	2544	1574	1829	2049	842	1172	1388	3064	Chengdu						
2269	1857	1774	1416	1365	2040	1070	1325	1545	1346	1676	1892	3568	504	Chongqing					
2257	1845	1311	953	902	1577	607	862	1082	1809	2139	2355	4031	967	463	Guiyang				
2865	2453	1950	1592	1541	2216	1246	1501	1721	1942	2272	2488	4164	1100	1102	639	Kunming			
231	643	1177	1535	1586	2261	2258	2513	2733	651	1327	1543	3219	1493	1997	2460	2593	Taiyuan		
951	1363	1897	2255	2306	2981	2978	3233	3453	1292	1145	1361	3037	2134	2638	3101	3234	641	Hohhot	
1550	1654	2188	2546	2597	3272	3213	3468	3688	1143	467	683	2359	1639	2143	2606	2739	1319	678	Yinchuan

Land Communications in China

Tacheng

Yining

Ürümqi

Hami

Kashi

Korla

Yecheng

Qiemo

Ruoqiang

Jiayu Guan

Minfeng

Islamabad

Golmud

Xi

Shiquanhe

Yushu

Burang

Naggu

Qamdo

Ch

Lhasa

Xigaze

Nyingchi

Katmandu

Yadong

Xichang

Gongshan

Kunmin

Jinghong

state and determined by mileage and the type of car. The passenger is given a receipt for the fare.

It is also possible to rent a taxi for an all-day excursion. This is often a bargain for the independent traveler who can then visit a number of places of interest within a short time.

Bicycle: Anyone who buys or borrows a bicycle should keep in mind from the start that he cannot expect much consideration from cars, buses and trucks. Caution should be taken especially at all intersections. Chinese bicycles do not have back-pedaling brakes.

Ship: The voyage along the Changjiang and the sea voyage from Shanghai to Qingdao are among the most beautiful in the world. Questions about prices and schedules can be directed to Lüxingshe and to ship agencies.

Travel Agency — Lüxingshe

The national Chinese travel agency is divided into three departments. **Guoji Lüxingshe, China International Travel Service (CITS),** is primarily responsible for foreign independent travelers and tour groups. This is the most important department, to which the traveler can turn with problems and requests. Guoji Lüxingshe looks after the travelers' welfare, organizes transportation, board and lodging, arranges the agenda, provides guides for group tours, supplies interpreters, sets up cultural programs and much more.

The central office is located in Beijing. It has many departments arranged according to countries and language regions. Branch offices are located in all major tourist spots and at all entry points.

Available office addresses are listed at the end of the appropriate city descriptions.

Zhongguo Lüxingshe, China Travel Service, and **Huaqiao Lüxingshe, Overseas Chinese Travel Service,** are primarily for Chinese who come from Hongkong, Macao, Taiwan and abroad. Except for this distinction, these two agencies serve basically the same funtion as the CITS. The addresses of these offices are also listed at the end of the appropriate city descriptions.

The following addresses can serve as a starting point:

China International Travel Service
(central office, across from the Peking Hotel)
6, Dongchang'anjie, **Beijing**
tel. 55 05 83, 55 18 26, 55 10 31
For individual travelers they have an office in Chongwenmen Hotel, Rm. 1302, Beijing, tel. 75 71 81

China Travel Service (H.K.) Ltd.
77, Queen's Road, Central, **Hongkong**
tel. 5-25 91 21
or
75 Mody Road, Tsim Sha Tsui East, Kowloon, Hong Kong, tel. 3-72 15 31 7

Travel Permit

To visit any particular location, it is necessary to have a travel permit. For organized tours, this is taken care of by Lüxingshe. Any traveler who makes his own arrangements must go to the *Gong'an Ju,* Public Security Bureau, in the city where he arrives. There he can submit an appropriate application which lists all the cities he would like to visit. The granting of a travel permit can take several hours, a day or even several days. Requests to visit villages in border provinces, such as Xishuang Banna in Yunnan, could entail an even longer waiting period. The travel permit is an extremely important document which should be carried along at all times. Every city has its own Public Security Bureau, so those who fail to apply for permission to visit a particular city at the beginning can do so at a later date.

Many cities do not require a travel permit, including Beijing, Shanghai, Guangzhou, Tianjin and Taiyuan.

List of Places Open to Foreign Tourists (1986)

Group A: Travel Permit not required
Municipalities
Beijing, Shanghai, Tianjin.
Anhui Province
Hefei, Wuhu, Huangshan, Bengbu, Tunxi, Jiuhuashan.
Fujian Province
Fuzhou, Xiamen, Quanzhou, Zhangzhou, Chongan.
Gansu Province
Lanzhou.
Guangdong Province
Guangzhou, Foshan (Nanhai, Shunde), Zhaoqing, Shenzhen, Zhuhai, Shantou, Haikou, Zhanjiang, Zhongshan, Jiangmen, Shaoguan, Huizhou.
Guangxi Autonomous Region
Nanning, Guilin, Beihai, Liuzhou, Wuzhou.
Guizhou Province
Guiyang, Anshun.
Hebei Province
Shijiazhuang, Qinhuangdao, Chengde, Zhuoxian.
Heilongjiang Province
Harbin, Qiqihar, Daqing.

Henan Province
Zhengzhou, Kaifeng, Luoyang, Anyang.
Hubei Province
Wuhan, Yichang, Shashi, Xiantan, Jiangling.
Hunan Province
Xiangtan (Shaoshan), Hengshan, Zhuzhou.
Jiangsu Province
Nanjing, Suzhou, Wuxi, Lianyungang, Nantong, Changzhou, Yangzhou, Zhenjiang.
Jiangxi Province
Nanchang, Jiujiang (Lushan), Jingdezhen.
Jilin Province
Changchun, Jilin, Yanji.
Liaoning Province
Shenyang, Dalian,Dandong, Jinzhou, Anshan, Fushun.
Neimenggu (Inner Mongolia Autonomous Region)
Hohhot, Baotou, Manzhouli, Erlianhot.
Ningxia Autonomous Region
Yinchuan.
Qinghai Province
Xining, Huangzhong.
Shaanxi Province
Xi'an, Lintong, Xianyang, Yanan.
Shandong Province
Jinan, Qingdao, Yantai, Tai'an, Weifang, Zibe, Jining (Qufu, Yanzhou).
Shanxi Province
Taiyuan, Wutai, Fanshi.
Sichuan Province
Chongqing (Chengdu, Leshan, Emei).
Xinjiang Autonomous Region
Urumqi.
Yunnan Province
Kunming, Lunan (Stone Forest).
Zhejiang Province
Hangzhou, Ningpo, Wenzhou, Shaoxing.

Group B: Travel Permit Required
Anhui Province
Huainan, Huaibei, Tongling, Chuzhou, Chaohu, Shexian, Xiuning, Fengyang, Jingxian, Gansu, Anqing.
Gansu Province
Yongjing, Jiayuguan, Jiuquan, Tianshui, Linxia, Xiahe, Dunhuang.
Guangdong Province
Chaozhou, Maoming, Meixian, Xingning, Fengshun, Dapu, Huiyang, Belo, Huidong, Heyuan, Dongwan, Lufeng, Haifeng, Gaoyao, Xinxing, Yunfu, Sihui, Qiongshan, Wenchang, Anding, Qionghai, Wanning, Tunchang, Chengmai, Danxian, Lingao, Baoting, Baisha, Qiongzhong, Lingshui, Sanya, Ledong, Dongfang, Changjiang, Fengkai, Huaiji, Deqing, Loding.
Guangxi Autonomous Region
Wuming, Binyang, Guiping, Xingan, Luchuan,

Beiliu, Rongxian, Guixian.
Guizhou Province
Zunyi, Kaili, Liupanshui, Shibing, Qingzhen, Zhenyuan, Zhenning (Falls Huangguoshu).
Hebei Province
Baoding, Tangshan, Handan, Zunhua (Dongling).
Heilongjiang Province
Mudanjiang, Jiamusi, Yichun, Jixi Hegang, Wudalianchi, Qitaihe, Heihe, Suifenhe, Tongjiang.
Henan Province
Xinxiang, Xinyang (Jigongshan), Linxian, Gongxian, Nanyang, Puyang, Pingdingshan, Wenxian.
Hubei Province
Xianning, Danjiangkou, Huangshi, Jingmen, Suizhou, Shiyang, E'zhou.
Hunan Province
Xiangtan (Shaoshan), Hengshan, Zhushou.
Jiangsu Province
Xuzhou, Huaiyin, Changshu, Huai'an, Yixing, Yancheng.
Jiangxi Province
Ganzhou, Jinggangshan, Pengze (Longgongdong).
Jilin Province
Siping, Liaoyuan, Tonghua, Baicheng, Antu national park.
Liaoning Province
Yingkou, Liaoyang, Benxi, Fuxin, Tieling, Chaoyang.
Neimenggu (Inner Mongolia) Autonomous Region
Dalateqi (Xiangshawan), Hailaer, Dongsheng, Xilinhot, Zhalantun, Tongliao.
Qinghai Province
Taermu, Ledu, Gonghe, Lenghuzhen, Mangyazhen.
Shaanxi Province
Baoji, Hancheng.
Shandong Province
Kenli (Oil field Shengli).
Shanxi Province
Datong, Linfen, Yuncheng.
Sichuan Province
Wanxian, Xindu, Guanxian, Meishan, Zhongxian, Yunyang, Fengjie, Wushan.
Xinjiang Autonomous Region
Shihezi, Turpan, Kashi.
Xizang (Tibet) Autonomous Region
Lhasa, Xigaze, Nanshan.
Yunnan Province
Dali, Lijiangnaxi, Yuxi, Tonghai, Chuxiong, Jinghong, Menghai, Simao.
Zhejiang Province
Jiaxing, Huzhou, Deqing (Moganshan), Puto (Putoshan), Jinhua, Jiaojiang.

Voltage

220 V, 50 Hz current is found in all hotels. The British 3-prong flat plug or relatively narrow sockets can still be found in some areas. Adapters can usually be obtained at the reception desks of larger hotels. If in doubt, the traveler should bring along an adapter or change over to battery-operated appliances.

Weight, Measure and Temperature Equivalents

China has officially accepted the metric system, but the old system of weights and measures is still quite common.

Chinese system	Metric system	Amer./Brit. system/system
li	0.5 km	0.31 mile
gongli	1.0 km	0.62 mile
chi	0.33 m	1.09 ft.
mu	0.06 ha	0.16 acre
liang	50 g	1.75 oz.
jin	0.5 kg	1.1 lb.
gongjin	1.0 kg	2.2 lb.
sheng	1.0 l	1.06 qt./0.88qt.
dan	100 l	106 qt./88qt.

1 hectare = 2.47 acres

Centigrade	Fahrenheit
-10°	14°
0°	32°
10°	50°
20°	68°
30°	86°
40°	104°

When to Go, Climates and Seasons

The most pleasant times to travel are in the early summer (May—June) and in the fall (September—early October). During these months, the temperature is quite comfortable, and for this reason, it is also the main tourist season. Keep in mind that the Canton Fair takes place in Guangzhou in April and September, and during those times the hotels in Guangzhou and Hongkong are usually booked up as well as the transportation facilities.

Part Three

Description of Cities and Provinces

Beijing (Peking) 北京市
(Centrally administered municipality)

Area: 16,800 km² / Population: 9.2 million

Beijing, capital of the People's Republic of China, is the political, commercial and cultural center of the most highly populated country in the world. Together with Shanghai and Tianjin, it is the third centrally administered municipality and the seat of the central government. Party conventions take place here. The National People's Congress holds its sessions and the highest public authorities and ministries have their seat here. The fate of more than one billion people is determined in Beijing. As in a microcosm, this city represents the heritage of traditional China and the achievements of modern China. It would take several weeks to become acquainted with all the places of interest and the art treasures. The outstanding artistic skill of the Chinese architects, craftsmen and artists who have created the image of the city since the Jin and Yuan eras, will fill the Western visitor with amazement and enthusiasm. But especially in Beijing, he will inevitably be confronted with the infamous history of Western and Japanese imperialistic powers. Conflicts erupted here, caused by agressive foreign lust for power and the weakness of the instable Manchurian Qing Dynasty. Traces of this policy, the forcible opening of China, can still be seen today.

Location and Climate

Beijing is situated in the northwestern part of the North China Plain between the rivers Yongding He (Hunhe) to the southwest and Wenyu He to the northeast, at an elevation of 43.7 m above sea level. To the west, the northwest and the south, the city is surrounded by mountain ranges. Mountain passes in the northwest lead to the Mongolian Plateau, in the north, up into the northeastern mountains and in the east, along the coast into Manchuria. The Beijing Plain thus always worked as a natural link between China and her neighbors to the north.

The climate in Beijing is of the continental type, with cold and dry winters, due to the Siberian air masses that move southward across the Mongolian Plateau. The summers are hot owing to the warm and humid monsoon winds from the southeast bringing Beijing most of its annual precipitation.

January is the coldest month with an average temperature of -4°C, July the warmest with an average of 26°C.

Winter usually begins towards the end of October with cold, dry northwesterly winds. They sweep across Beijing until the end of March. Nasty sand storms, mostly towards the end of the winter, are not at all unusual. In all, there is frost for a period of approximately 80 days. Even in spring, April-May, Beijing is often visited by strong storms, but around that time of the year the temperatures climb to an average of 16°C. There usually is a rapid change from spring to summer. The summer months, June to August, are wet and hot with about 40% of the annual precipitation. Fall is a short season, starting in September. For the tourist especially, it is the most agreeable season of the year, with clear skies and pleasant temperatures.

History

The first settlements in the Beijing area existed as early as 500,000 BC. The skull of the so-called Peking man (Homo erectus pekinensis) was found on December 2, 1929, in Zhoukoudian, 48km from Beijing. An interesting exhibition in Zhoukoudian gives information about life in those days (see page 158).

Around 3,000 BC, neolithic communities settled in this area. Centuries later, the city of Ji, was established. It was situated very closely to the present city of Beijing, which is mentioned in ancient records as the seat of the Duke of Yan. During the Warring States Period, the kingdom of Yan was one of the seven hegemonic states.

Ji was destroyed by the troops of Qin Shihuang, the founder of the Qin Dynasty. In the year 206 BC, at the beginning of the Han Dynasty, a new town was built and known as Yan. Throughout the Han Dynasty and the following centuries, Yan's only significance was as a trading post and a strategic point in the struggle of the Han Chinese against the nomadic tribes of the Xiongnu from the north. The area was temporarily under the control of invading nomads.

In the 7th century under the Tang Dynasty, the city was called Youzhou. A canal that was built then offered a connection to the southern regions of the Huanghe and the Changjiang.

After the fall of the Tang Dynasty, Youzhou was destroyed by the Khitans, a steppe tribe. They established the Liao Dynasty and built one of their secondary capitals, called Nanjing (southern capital), on approximately the same site as the destroyed Youzhou.

In 1153, Nuzhen tartars invaded China, drove out the Liao and founded the Jin Dynasty with its capital Zhongdu, Central Capital, which the Liao had called Nanjing. The city was enlarged on a generous scale. Hundreds of thousands of workmen erected palaces and ramparts.

But in 1215, Zhongdu fell victim to a Mongol attack. The new regent and founder of the Mongolian Yuan Dynasty, Kublai Khan, determined to build a new capital, Dadu, Great Capital, on the site of the old Zhongdu in 1272. For the first time, present-day Beijing became the political center of the Chinese empire. Marco Polo described the brilliance and the splendor the city experienced throughout the following years in his travel logs. The White Dagoba in Beihai Park and Baita Si temple are still preserved from those days.

In 1368, Zhu Yuanzhang, leader of a peasant revolt, overthrew the Mongolian ruling class and established the Ming Dynasty. Jinling, from then on called Nanjing, Southern Capital, became the new capital. Dadu was called Beiping, Northern Peace, and was put under the rule of one of Zhu's sons. After Zhu's death, one of his grandsons took over, but his uncle contended with him for the throne and succeeded in establishing himself as emperor. He moved the seat of the government to Beiping, now called Beijing, Northern Capital, in 1403. Most of the palaces, temples, moats and city walls that remain today, were built during the following decades. Old Dadu was largely demolished. At the end of the Ming era, Li Zicheng led a peasant uprising against the Ming rulers and conquered Beijing. He was able to hold the city for 40 days before it was captured by invading Manchus.

The Qing Dynasty was founded by the victorious Manchus in 1644. Beijing remained its capital, its structure unaltered. Outside the city walls, several palaces, temples and pavilions were added, for example the old Summer Palace, Yuanming Yuan, in the 17th century and the new Summer Palace, Yihe Yuan, towards the end of the 19th century.

From 1860 onwards, Beijing was the scene of armed conflicts between the Imperial Court and foreign powers. English and French troops destroyed the old Summer Palace. Some of the ruins can still be seen today. The Imperial Court had to grant the foreigners the right of exterritoriality and to reserve them a legation quarter in the southeastern part of the Imperial City. In 1900, the situation worsened during the Boxer Rebellion (see page 148).

In 1911, the Qing Dynasty came to an end. Beijing became the political center of the Republic. A few years later in 1919, demonstration and protest meetings in connection with the Versailles Treaty were held, which went down in history as the May 4th Movement (see page 122).

In 1928, the government moved the capital to Nanjing. Beijing again was called Beiping, Northern Peace.

The Japanese occupied the city from 1937 — 1945.

On October 1, 1949, Mao Zedong announced the establishment of the People's Republic of China on Tian'anmen Square. Beiping became the capital again and was officially renamed Beijing, Northern Capital.

City Structure

Beijing actually consists of two cities, the northern Inner City and the southern Outer City. The square-shaped Inner City, in earlier times also called Tartar City, covers about the area of the former Mongolian city of Dadu. The rectangularly shaped Outer City arose during the Ming Dynasty. The old Imperial City, also laid out rectangularly, lay within the Inner City. Inside of it were the ministries, the Imperial Palace, also called the Forbidden City, surrounded by a red wall.

Beijing is laid out like a chessboard. One central axis leads from north to south and determined the sites of city walls, important gates, main streets and sacred buildings. Zhonglou, the Bell Tower, Gulou, the Drum Tower, Jingshan, Coal Hill, the Imperial Palace, Tian'anmen Square, Qianmen, the front gate, the Tianqiao quarter, Heavenly Bridge and Yongding Men, the Gate of Eternal Stability, are located on this axis from north to south.

The city was built symmetrically along the central axis in the east and the west. East of the axis, Taimiao, the Temple of the Imperial Ancestors, now the Working People's Cultural Park, was located in front of the Imperial Palace and west of the axis, the Altar of Earth and Grain, now Zhongshan Park. Dongdan, the eastern market, and Xidan, the western market, were situated farther away from the palaces.

Tiantan, the Temple of Heaven, and Ditan, the Altar of the Earth, are similarly situated on both sides of the axis in the Outer City.

Of the 16 gates constructed during the Ming era, two are directly on this axis. The main streets, laid out like a chessboard, linked the gates of the opposing walls and divided Beijing into rectangular quarters, through which a great number of narrow lanes ran. The main streets were laid out symmetrically around the centrally located Imperial Palace. Almost every unit was rectangularly shaped. During the Qing Dynasty most of the houses of the Inner City served as residences for civil servants and their families. Almost every building complex is surrounded by a high wall with an open courtyard in the center, flanked by houses on the eastern, western and northern sides.

Most of the structures have only one floor because they were not allowed to be higher than the Imperial Palace. Each important building faced south, mainly for climatic reasons, although the southern orientation is also a heritage from the past having to do with ancestral ceremonies and the worship of heaven and earth (for a more detailed description of the residential complex (see pages 74, 75).

Since 1949, the appearance of the city has changed considerably. Most of the city walls had to give way to new projects. Streets were widened and extended, for example, the Chang'anjie Boulevard extending 40km from east to west. Many tunnels and overpasses were built in recent years in the fringe areas. A subway runs along the city walls which have been torn down. Besides the extension of the road network, impressive public buildings and modern residential, industrial and university quarters were constructed. Inside of the former city walls, too, many old houses had to give way to modern apartment blocks. In the west, along the Xichang'anjie Boulevard and in the north, many government buildings arose. Near the Summer Palace to the northwest, the most important universities and research institutes are situated: Beijing University (Beida), Qinghua University, the People's University (Renda), the Institute for National Minorities and the Agricultural Academy.

Between 1953 and 1957, the period of the first five-year plan, new blocks of apartments were erected close to the newly-built government offices outside the Fuxing gate to the west. After 1958 big blocks of flats were built in the north between the Anding and Desheng gates. In contrast to the old houses, all the buildings are connected to the gas lines. In the east, outside the Jianguo gate, flats were built for the staff of the government offices nearby. This area was also declared the new legation quarter. It accommodates many foreign embassies and apartments for foreign diplomats and their families, furnished according to Western standard.

Suburbs in which various industries are located are also in the east.

Industry and Agriculture

Beijing has been very successful in the industrial sector. Ten years after the foundation of the People's Republic, the number of workers employed in Beijing factories rose from 70,000 in 1949 to 870,000 in 1958. At first, priority was given to the modernization, expansion or construction of the Mentougou coal mines and the Shijinshan iron and steel works respectively. Other important branches of industry are mechanical engineering and railroad car construction; in the field of light industry there are the textile, food production and chemical industries, electrical engineering and electronics.

In imperial times, Beijing handicrafts were already famous. Ivory carvings, objects made of jade, enamel-cloisonné, and glass and lacquerware are still highly appreciated today. Beijing silk, embroidery and, above all, its carpets are well known abroad, too.

The city is supplied with food by its neighboring communities. The plain southwest of Beijing is especially fertile. Reliable irrigation plants and favorable climatic conditions make two crops a year possible. Important crops are wheat, rice, corn, millet, sorghum and many different kinds of vegetables; mainly Chinese cabbage, egg plant, sweet potatoes, soy-beans, onions, tomatoes and spinach. Fruit grows well in Beijing, too: apples and pears, apricots, peaches, dates, nuts and melons. In some people's communes, pigs, fish and poultry are raised. They are especially known for their Peking ducks.

Culture and Places of Interest

There are good reasons why Beijing has the reputation of being the cultural center of the country. Thirty-five universities, institutes and institutions of higher learning have been enlarged or founded since 1949. Especially Beijing Daxue's—Peking University's—reputation is well-known abroad (see page 143). In 1949, Zhongguo Kexueyuan, the

Chinese Academy of Sciences, was founded. It has branches in various cities in China. The administration and most of its institutes, however, are based in Beijing. Zhongyang Minzu Xueyuan, the Central Institute for Minorities, is significant.

Beijing is visited by millions of guests from China and abroad every year. The city offers a bit of everything, no matter what line of interest the tourist chooses to follow. The most important sights are in the quarter around Tianámen Square with more recent buildings to the east, south and west and the Imperial Palace to the north. Visitors on a short trip should also visit the Summer Palace, Yihe Yuan. Equally attractive are the temple complexes, as for example the lama temple or the complexes in Xishan, the Western Hills. A must in every program is a trip to the Great Wall.

Tian'an Men Gate, Gate of Heavenly Peace
天安门

On the national coat of arms of the People's Republic of China, the Gate of Heavenly Peace is represented as the symbol of the revolutionary new China.

This is where Mao Zedong proclaimed the founding of the People's Republic of China on October 1, 1949. Tian'an Men is located north of Tian'anmen Square and leads to the Imperial Palace. It was built as early as 1417 and mentioned as the main gate of the former Imperial Palace, Chengtian Men. The wooden structure burned down in 1457 and was re-erected in 1651 and then called Tian'an Men. It is 34 m high, has red stone walls, a wooden roof and five entrances. A portrait of Mao Zedong hangs over the main entrance, which in earlier times only the emperor had the right to use; to the left are the signs 'Long live the People's Republic of China' and to the right: 'Long live the great union between the peoples of the world.' A grandstand for up to 20,000 guests is above those banners.

The gate is surrounded by a ring-moat, the Golden Water Spring, which was arranged to guard the Imperial Palace. Five white marble bridges, the Golden Water Bridges, lead to the five passages of the gate. Two stone pillars stand in front of the entire complex, symbols of heavenly peace and the emperor's authority. They show a relief of dragon motifs and stylized clouds. On top sits the mythical beast *Kong*. Next to each pillar stands an iron lion. The gate, as well as the square in front of it, were not accessible to the public in imperial times. Often religious and military ceremonies were held here, imperial decrees and the results of Mandarin tests announced, and death sentences carried out. The Tian'an Men gate was the stage of the last official act of the Qing Dynasty: on December 25, 1911, the emperor's mother Longyu had the official announcement made that her son Puyi, who had not even come of age, abandoned his claim to the throne.

Tian'anmen Guangchang, Tian'anmen Square
天安门广场

Tian'anmen Square was originally designed in 1651; it was cemented and quadrupled in size in 1958. Now it covers an area of 40.5 hectares and can hold up to one million people; thus, it is one of the largest public squares in the world. It is surrounded by several impressive structures. The oldest of these is the Tian'an Men gate to the north. To the east are the Museums of Chinese History and Revolution, to the west the Great Hall of the People and to the south the Chairman Mao Memorial Hall and the Qianmen gate.

In the middle of the square is the Monument to the People's Heroes. Tian'anmen Square has often been the scene of big demonstrations, mass meetings, parades and celebrations since it was built.

On May 4, 1919, more than 3,000 pupils and students of the Beijing schools and universities came here to demonstrate against imperialism and the rule of the military leaders. The event went down in the annals of Chinese history as the May 4th Movement. On October 1, 1949, hundreds of thousands of people crowded to this spot to witness the proclamation of the People's Republic of China. In recent days it was the scene of the so-called 'Tian'anmen Incident'. On the occasion of the Qingming Festival more than 200,000 people from Beijing had gathered spontaneously on the square on the 4th and 5th of April, 1976, to commemorate the death of the popular Prime Minister Zhou Enlai. The Monument to the People's Heroes in the center of the square was decorated with countless paper flowers and wreaths. At the same time it was a demonstration against the faction around Jiang Qing, later to become the 'Gang of Four' and in favor of Zhou Enlai's policy and his modernization program.

Renmin Dahuitang, Great Hall of the People
人民大会堂

On the western side of Tian'anmen Square is the Great Hall of the People. It is one of the ten splendid public buildings that were built before 1959. This building was completed within 10 months during 1958/1959 with the help of many cadre units, students and workers. This monumental structure, influenced by Western architecture, has a total surface area of 171,800 m², that is more than that the buildings of the Imperial Palace cover altogether. In front of the main gate there are 12 marble columns, each of them 25 m tall. The entrance gates are cast in bronze.

Besides the main meeting-hall (7,000 m²), with more than 10,000 seats, and a banquet hall for 5,000 people, this building also has various reception rooms and conference rooms. Each of these is named after a province or an autonomous region and furnished in its particular style.

The building contains many paintings. An enormous painting hangs opposite the main entrance that was produced by the best painters of the country in teamwork. It is called *Jiangshan ruci duo jiao,* 'The beauty of our country'.

The annual meetings of the National People's Congress, big party meetings and talks with foreign diplomats also take place here.

Zhongguo Geming Lishi Bowuguan
Museum of Chinese History and Revolution
中国革命历史博物馆

Open 8:30 to 5:00 pm, last tickets are sold at 3:30pm, closed on Sundays.

On the eastern side of Tian'anmen Square stands the gigantic museum complex which harbors the Museum of Chinese History and the Museum of the Chinese Revolution. The imposing structure with a total area of 65,000 m² was completed in 1959 and opened to the public in 1961. The main entrance, supported by eleven columns, leads to the reception hall which is the focus of the entire structure. It connects the left, or north, wing with the right, or south, wing. Each wing contains a hall with general information about the exhibitions and 17 exhibition rooms. In the left wing is the Museum of the Chinese Revolution which is devoted to Chinese History since 1919, the revolutionary movement and the historical development of the Chinese Communist Party. The museum was closed at the beginning of the Cultural Revolution in 1966, and remained so for the next twelve years. When it was again opened in 1978, the focal point was a photo-display depicting the life of Zhou Enlai. On October 1, 1979, the permanent exhibition — a retrospect of the historical development of the

Chinese Communist Party — was opened again. The Museum of Chinese History is located in the right wing. This museum was also closed for many years and reopened its doors for the first time in October of 1976. The exhibitions follow the course of Chinese history which is divided into epochs, covering the span of time from the beginnings of civilization to the 20th century: primitive societies (beginning 500,000 BC), slaveholding society (2100 — 475 BC), feudal society (475 BC — 1840 AD), semi-colonial and semi-feudal society. The history of the country up to the Sui Dynasty (581 — 618 AD) is depicted on the second floor and is illustrated by all types of archeological finds as well as reproductions of tools and inventions such as paper and the seismograph. The exhibitions on the third floor cover the period from the Tang Dynasty to 1919 and are largely devoted to ceramics and paintings.

Renmin Yingxiong Jinianbei
Monument to the People's Heroes
人民英雄纪念碑

The Monument to the People's Heroes stands at the center of Tian'anmen Square, a symbol of the Chinese revolution. Its corner stone was laid by Mao Zedong on September 30, 1949. It was unveiled on May 1, 1958. The monument consists of 17,000 pieces of granite and marble. It stands on a double terrace, decorated by marble balustrades. The obelisk, 38 m high, carries inscriptions of Mao Zedong on its north side and of Zhou Enlai on its south side. The inscriptions are in their original handwritings. Mao Zedong is quoted: 'The people's heroes are immortal.'

Zhou Enlai's inscription says: 'The heroes who have given their lives in the last three years for the people's fight for liberation and the revolution of the people, are immortal. The heroes who have given their lives in the last 30 years for liberation and the revolution of the people, are immortal. The heroes who, since 1840 have given their lives for the nation, its independence, for freedom and the happiness of the people, fighting against enemies from within and without, are immortal.'

This inscription is one of the few examples of his calligraphy accessible to the public.

Stairs lead up to the base of the obelisk where ten bas-relief carvings can be seen on which the highlights of the revolutionary movement are documented.

East side (start of the sequence)
Canton 1839: the patriotic and incorrupt-

ible Imperial Commissioner Lin Zexu ordered more than 20,000 crates of opium to be burned, which British merchants wanted to use to purchase their imports from China, such as tea, silk and porcelain.

The beginning of the Taiping Rebellion which arose in the small town of Jintian, Guangxi, in 1851.

South side

The uprising in Wuchang against Manchu rule on October 10, 1911. Demonstrations of Beijing students against the resolutions at the Versailles Peace conference on May 4, 1919, also called the May 4th Movement. The movement of May 30, 1925 in Shanghai, directed against England and Japan. Strike was the most efficient weapon in the struggle against imperialism.

West side

Nanchang military uprising on August 1, 1927; official founding date of the Red Army which has been called the People's Liberation Army since July 1946. — Scene from the guerilla war against the Japanese (1937-1945).

North side

Center: Victorious crossing of the Changjiang by the People's Liberation Army during their fight against the Kuomintang troops in 1949.

Right: Grain for the front.

Left: Long live the People's Liberation Army.

Altogether the 10 reliefs contain 170 figures. They were created by the best Chinese artists during a period of more than five years. The Monument to the People's Heroes was the center of the Tian'anmen Incident on April 5, 1976.

Mao Zhuxi Jiniantang
Mao Zedong Memorial Hall 毛主席纪念堂

The Mao Zedong Memorial Hall is situated between the Monument to the People's Heroes and Qianmen gate. On November 24, 1976, the Party Chairman at that time, Hua Guofeng, laid the foundation stone. It was completed on September 9, 1977, the first anniversary of Mao Zedong's death. The Memorial Hall forms a harmonious bridge between the Great Hall of the People and the Museum of Chinese History. It is 33 m high and covers an area of 20,000 m². The select building materials come from the different provinces and autonomous regions of the country. The eaves, made of yellow-gold glazed tiles are supported by 44

granite pillars; the base is made of red granite.

In the entrance hall is a white marble statue of Mao Zedong and in the background, a huge landscape painted by the artist Huang Yongyu. Inside the mausoleum the body of Mao Zedong lies in state, inside a crystal sarcophagus draped with the red flag of the Chinese Communist Party, watched over by an honor guard. In the southern hall hangs a huge marble scroll with one of Mao's poems on it in an enlargement of his own calligraphy. The Memorial Hall is not open to the public daily; please note the visiting hours.

Qianmen, Front Gate 前门

This gate was built during the reign of Yongle (1403-1424). It is one of the few city gates in the old wall around the Imperial city that still remains. For security reasons two gate buildings were erected, one behind the other. They were connected by a wall, thus forming an inner courtyard.

Gugong, Imperial Palace 故宫

Open 8:30 am to 5:00 pm, last tickets are sold at 4:30 pm.

The Imperial Palace, also called the Forbidden City, is one of the country's most important sights, for it is a symbol of traditional China and likewise the biggest and best preserved masterpiece of classical architecture. Every year millions of Chinese and foreigners throng to the huge palace grounds — about 10,000 everyday — to see the treasures and precious objects, power and splendor, abundance and extravagance of former emperors. The palace covers an area of 720,000 m². It is surrounded by a moat 50 m wide and a wall 10.4 m high with watch towers at each of the corners.

The entire palace grounds consist of two complexes, the outer and the inner courtyards. They contain six main halls and many smaller pavilions and buildings. In all, there are more than 9,000 rooms. The main building materials are wood and yellow-glazed tiles.

Its history dates back to the 13th century, when the Yuan imperial house established itself in Beijing and had a palace built. The Yongle Emperor of the Ming Dynasty, rejected Nanjing as a capital after he had come to power, and preferred Beijing. He had the Imperial Palace expanded to its present size; it was completed around 1420.

In the centuries to follow, it served as a residence to 24 Ming and Qing emperors until 1911.

After passing through Tian'an Men gate, one comes to Wumen, the Meridian Gate (1), the 38-m-high main gate of the palace. It has also been called the Five-Phoenix-Gate because of the five pavilions which tower over the structure on the central part and on both sides of the eastern and western wings of the gate. It was from here that the emperor annually announced the new calendar, presided over military ceremonies and confirmed or annulled death sentences.

Behind Wumen gate, five marble bridges, the inner Golden Water Bridges, span the 2,100-m-long inner Golden Water Spring. After crossing over the moat, a large courtyard with three gates at its northern end is reached. The gates lead into the next courtyard. The middle one, Taihe Men, Gate of Supreme Harmony (2), is the highest of the palace complex. It is 58 m wide and covers an area of 1,800 m². It is guarded by two bronze lions, symbols of power. At the beginning of the Ming Dynasty it was called Fengtian Men, Gate of the Veneration of Heaven, and served the emperor as a reception hall for ministers and generals.

In earlier times, the imperial stores were accommodated in the galleries east and west of the courtyard. Implements of all kinds, jewelry, fabrics, furs and furniture were sold here.

The following courtyard covers an area of more than 30,000 m². The 35-m-high Taihe Dian, Hall of Supreme Harmony (3), stands in the center, followed by Zhonghe Dian, the Hall of Central Harmony (4) and Baohe Dian, the Hall of Preserving Harmony (5), also named Golden Throne Hall or Golden Bell Hall. All three rise on a three-tiered 8.1-m-high marble terrace with a triple marble balustrade.

Taihe Dian, the Hall of Supreme Harmony, is the largest hall of the palace complex with an area of 2,400 m². It has 16 spacial units and 40 gilded doors. Three flights of stairs lead up to the hall; the two outer ones were meant for commoners, and the emperor, himself a 'dragon', sitting in his litter, was carried up the carved marble ramp decorated with a dragon on the central stairs. Eighteen bronze incense burners can be seen on the way to the hall, representing the 18 provinces of Imperial China. On the terrace to the left of the hall is a miniature temple where a grain measure, jialiang, was kept; to the right of the hall is a sundial. Both symbolize Imperial justice.

Inside the hall there are 24 columns, 12.7 m high and 1 m in diameter, supporting the richly decorated roof. Eighteen columns are painted red, the six surrounding the throne which stands on a 2-m-high platform, are gilded and covered with dragons. Above the throne is a magnificent coffered ceiling, decorated with dragons playing ball. The elaborately carved and painted golden throne can be reached via seven steps. A splendid screen stands behind it. During the Ming and Qing dynasties, ceremonies took place here marking great occasions such as ascensions to the throne, imperial weddings and birthday celebrations, official banquets, New Year's celebrations and the announcements of successful candidates in the imperial examinations. During an audience, the emperor's honor guard formed a lane from the hall to Wumen gate. In the order of their rank, civilian as well as military officials had to kneel three times before their emperor and touch the ground with their forehead nine times as a sign of their loyalty and reverence.

Zhonghe Dian, the Hall of Central Harmony (4), is directly behind Taihe Dian on the same terrace. It is the smallest of the three halls. Here the emperor made his final preparations before going to Taihe Dian, the Hall of Supreme Harmony, for high ceremonies and audiences. Some ceremonies took place in Zhonghe Dian, too, for example, the examination of seeds for the new planting or proofreading of the message that was to be read out in the Temple of the Ancestors.

The third of the three halls is Baohe Dian, the Hall of Preserving Harmony (5). It is a little smaller than Taihe Dian, but more spacious. Minor ceremonies and banquets took place here. The highest level examinations for government officials were also held here — starting with the reign of Qianlong, during the Qing Dynasty; they had previously been held in Taihe Dian. Today art objects are exhibited inside the anterooms to the left and right, including gifts that were presented to the Imperial Court, as well as objects from the imperial household and its treasures.

Behind Baohe Dian is the largest stone slab of the Imperial Palace. The marble dragon slab, 16.6 m long, 3 m wide, and 1.7 m thick is the center piece of the three flights of stairs leading from the terrace down into the courtyard.

Southeast of these halls is Wenhua Dian, Hall of Literary Glory (6) and southwest of them is Wuying Dian. Hall of the Martial Spirit (7). Wenhua Dian was the residence of the crown prince during the Ming Dynasty. At the time of the Qing Dynasty, the emperor and his scholars used it as a place to discuss questions of history and the Confucian classics. At the time of Qianlong's reign, the emperor had Wenhua Dian enlarged by the

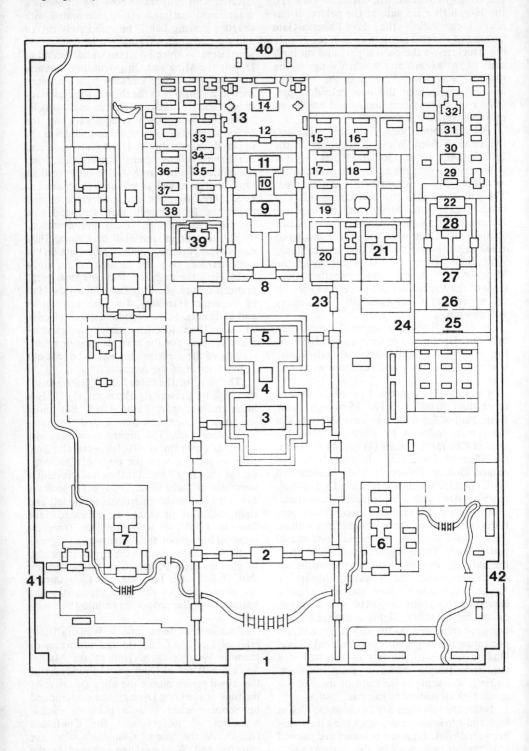

addition of Wenyuan pavilion, in which the imperial library, comprising 36,000 volumes, was accommodated.

Wuying Dian served the emperors of the early Ming era as a place where they could stay during fasts and where audiences could be held. When the Ming Dynasty was toppled by a peasant revolt in 1644, the leader of the rebels, Li Zicheng, led the short-lived Dashun Dynasty from here. A little later, his plans were defeated by the Qing troops that invaded Beijing. From then on, the prince regent Duoergun conducted his governmental business in Wuying Dian. During the Kangxi reign, the *Collected Works from the Past and the Present,* the *Kangxi Dictionary* and the *Peiwen Encyclopedia* were compiled in this hall.

One reaches the Inner Court through Qianqing Men, Gate of Heavenly Purity (8). Here the inner chambers of the imperial family are located. Thousands of women and eunuchs lived in this part of the palace; the only man who had access to it was the emperor. Gilded bronze water containers stand to both sides of the gate complex of Qianqing Men. During the Kangxi government period, day-to-day affairs of state were dealt with from here. Three palaces follow. They are also called the Rear Palaces and form the center of the Inner Court: Qianqing Gong, Palace of Heavenly Purity (9), is the first and largest of the three palaces. Built in 1420, it burned down several times. The present edifice dates from 1798. The emperors of the Ming Dynasty resided here; beginning with the Yongzhen period of reign during the Qing Dynasty, it was used as an audience chamber and banquet hall. When rebellious peasants under Li Zicheng's leadership occupied Beijing during the Ming era, the last Ming emperor killed his 15-year-old daughter and some concubines in this hall.

Then he hanged himself from a maple tree at Meishan, Coal Hill, today called Jingshan.

The interior of the Qianqing Palace dates from the Qing era.

In front of the palace are a sundial and a grain measure, symbols of imperial justice, bronze tortoises and cranes, symbols of longevity, and a small gilded bronze tower as well as tripods made of gilded bronze. Over the door of the palace hangs a tablet with the 'sincerity and openness', a calligraphy by the Sunzhi Emperor (1644-1661) which was engraved there under the Kangxi Emperor. Inside the palace is an ornate dragon screen behind the throne. In front of it are bronze cranes and blue cloisonné urns for burning sandalwood.

In the second palace, Jiaotai Dian, the Hall of Union (10), the emperor's birthday was celebrated. Twenty-five imperial seals from the Qianlong era, a bronze clepsydra and a chiming clock are kept here. The coffered ceiling is of exquisite beauty.

Kunning Gong, the Palace of Earthly Tranquility (11), served the empresses of the Ming era as a bedroom. Here Empress Zhou, wife of the last Ming emperor, hanged herself when the rebellious peasants took Beijing at the end of the Ming era.

According to Manchu rituals and customs, the Shunzi Emperor of the Qing Dynasty had the hall changed into a place of worship where a pig was offered to the gods every morning and evening. Today only a few *kangs* (heatable brick beds from North China) and large vats remain.

One room of Kunning Gong, Dongnuan Ge, Hall of Eastern Warmth, served as an imperial bridal chamber during the Qing Dynasty. The hall is covered with wood carvings. Everywhere, on the walls and lamps, the double character *Xi* appears, meaning joy and fertility. The predominant color red is a

Gugong, Imperial Palace

symbol for joy and marriage.

Leaving Kunning Gong through Kunning Men, the Gate of Earthly Tranquility (12), one enters Yuhua Yuan, the Imperial Flower Garden (13). It was laid out under the Ming, covers 12,000 m² and is an example of traditional Chinese horticultural art. Artificial rock formations, pavilions, ancient firs and cypresses, flowers and bamboo blend into a harmonious unit.

In the center of the garden stands Qin'an Dian, the Hall of Imperial Peace (14). East of it Yujing Ting, the Pavilion of Imperial Landscape, Chizao Tang, the Hall of Spirited Action, Fubi Ting, Pavilion of Floating Greenery, Wanchun Ting, Pavilion of 10,000 Springs, Jiangxue Xuan, House of Crimson Snow. West of Qin'an Dian, Yanhui Ge, the Pavilion of Lasting Glory, Chengrui Ting, the Pavilion of Sheer Happiness, Qianqin Ting, the Pavilion of Longevity, and Yangxing Zhai, the Studio of Virtuous Perfection, are located.

One leaves the imperial gardens through the plain Chengguang Men gate, which is flanked by two bronze elephants, and Shunzhen Men gate.

On both sides of the Rear Palaces are the magnificent Six Eastern Palaces, Dongliu Gong, and the Six Western Palaces, Xiliu Gong, built during the Ming era. During the Qing era, they were inhabited by the empresses and concubines. At the end of the Ming era, several thousand concubines are said to have lived here, guarded by even more eunuchs. Life for these women, with a few exceptions perhaps, was dreary. As soon as they entered the palace they were entirely cut off from the outside world. Some of them never set eyes on the emperor in their lives.

Each palace formed a separate unit. The northernmost of the Six Eastern Palaces are Zhongcui Gong (15) and Jingyang Gong (16), followed by Chengqian Gong (17) and Yonghe Gong (18) as well as Jingren Gong (19), and Yanxi Gong, which is closed. Museums of porcelain and bronze are housed in the other palaces. Zhaigong Palace (20) and Fengxian Dian hall (21) are part of the eastern building complex.

Zhaigong was built under the Yongzheng reign (1723-1735). Now it houses a museum for bronze objects. Fengxian Hall contained the memorial tablets of the imperial ancestors. Ningshou Gong (22) is close to the Six Eastern Palaces. On the way there, one passes Jingyun Men (23) and Xiqing Men (24). The palace was built at the beginning of the Qing Dynasty, but it was not magnificently furnished until the reign of the Qianlong Emperor. After he had

passed on governmental business to his successor in 1795, he spent the last four years of his life here. After his death, the palace was unoccupied for almost a century. At the end of the 19th century the Empress Dowager Cixi decided to live in these chambers. Today paintings and *objet d'art* made of jade, gold and silver are on exhibit in the palace.

The complex is divided into a southern and a northern part. Jiulong Bi, Nine Dragon Screen (25), 31 m long and 6m high, runs along Xiqing Men Gate. It was built of glazed tiles in 1773, during the reign of the Qianlong Emperor, and nine flying dragons are vividly depicted on it.

On the way to Ningshou Gong, one passes Huangji Men gate (26) to reach the courtyard of Ningshou palace. Ningshou Men gate (27) leads into the enclosure surrounded by galleries. In the center is Huangji Dian hall (28). In 1894, the Empress Dowager celebrated her 60th birthday in the palace. On her 70th birthday she received the embassadors of various Western nations and Japan. After her death, her coffin lay there for more than a year until the most propitious day for her funeral had come.

In Ningshou Gong, parts of the imperial collection of paintings can be seen. Yangxing Men gate (29) leads to the northern section of the grounds. Amidst winding covered ways, flower beds and picturesque stones are the private chambers of the Qianlong Emperor and the Empress Dowager Cixi.

One approaches Yangxing Dian, Hall of Character Cultivation (30) from Yangxing Men, then Leshou Tang, Hall of Delight and Longevity (31). Calligraphic stone engravings can be seen in its courtyard. Further north is Yihe Xuan, House of Relaxation (32). The Qianlong and Jiaqing Emperors are said to have written poetry here. In each of the three halls, parts of the Imperial treasures are on display (Imperial TREASURY).

Close to Yangxing Dian, the Hall of Mental Cultivation, is Concubine Zhen Fei's well. Zhen Fei was a favorite of the Guangxu Emperor. When the allied troops conquered Beijing in 1900, it is said that the Empress Dowager Cixi had the concubine Zhen pushed into the well shortly before she fled. Zhen had allegedly been a supporter of the 1898 reform movement.

Chuxiu Gong, Palace of Preserved Beauty (33), where the bedchamber of the Empress Dowager Cixi can still be seen is part of Xiliu Gong, the Six Western Palaces. Her 50th birthday was celebrated in this palace. On this occasion, she had the entire complex restored magnificently. Great paintings and carvings from those days can be seen in Chuxiu Gong palace, Tihe Dian, the Hall of Manifest Harmony (34), and Yikun Gong, Palace of Benevolence of the Earth (35). Bronze dragons and cranes can be seen in the courtyard.

Taiji Dian (38) contains magnificent wood carvings. A fan driven by a spiral spring, made towards the end of the Qing era, is an interesting feature.

Yangxin Dian, the Palace of the Culture of Mind (39), is also part of the Six Western Palaces. It was built during the Ming Dynasty and was the favorite residence of the Qing emperors. After the 1911 Revolution, Emperor Puyi lived here after having been dethroned, until he was driven away by general Feng Yuxiang's army in 1924. The buildings west of the Six Western Palaces were at the disposal of the empress and the concubines of the deceased emperor.

Shenwu Men, the Gate of Divine Prowess (40), is north of the palace. It was built in 1420 and restored during the Kangxi Emperor's reign.

Zhongshan Gongyuan, Sun Yatsen Park
中山公园

Sun Yatsen park lies northeast of Tian'-anmen square. Its northern part borders the moat of the Imperial Palace. During the reign of the Yongle Emperor, the Altar of Earth and Grain was moved here. From then on, the emperors made offerings to the gods of the fields and agriculture at this temple twice a year. After the fall of the empire, it became a public park in 1914. From 1928 on it was called Sun Yatsen Park after Dr. Sun Yatsen, the founder of the Chinese Republic.

Due to its central position and the large playground within the grounds, the park is very popular with the young and old and always well-frequented.

Xili Ting, Pavilion where ceremonies were practised (1), is reached via the south gate. It was controlled by the Ministry of Rites. Next to it is Tanghuawu, a hot-house, where flowers are exhibited (2) and Lanting Beiting, the Stele Pavilion (3). It houses a stele from the 18th century which, along with many other objects in this park, used to stand in Yuanming Yuan before it was destroyed. South of the hot-house is a small lake with a tiny island on which Siyi Pavilion (4) stands. Shuixie, the Waterside Pavilion (5), is on the southern shore of the lake. It used to be a meeting place for learned men and poets. In the western part of the park there are exhibition halls that are

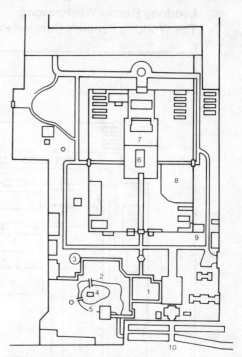

Zhongshan Gongyuan, Sun Yatsen Park

1. The Pavilion where ceremonies were practised
2. Flower Exhibition
3. Pavilion of Lanting Stele
4. Siyi Pavilion
5. Waterside Pavilion
6. Altar of Earth and Grain
7. Sun Yatsen Memorial Hall
8. Concert Hall
9. Teahouse
10. South Gate

frequently used.

In the center of the park is the square stone terrace of the Sheji Tan, Altar of Earth and Grain (6).

To the north stands the Hall of Prayer. It is more than 550 years old. In memory of Sun Yatsen it was renamed Zhongshan Tang, Sun Yatsen Memorial Hall (7), in 1928. This hall is the oldest well-preserved wooden structure in Beijing. It is an excellent example of early Ming architecture.

East of the Altar of Earth and Grain are a theater and a concert hall (8). Behind this hall, outside the altar complex, the cross-shaped Touhu pavilion is located.

In the north is a commemorative arch made

Laodong Remin Wenhuagong,
The Working People's Cultural Park

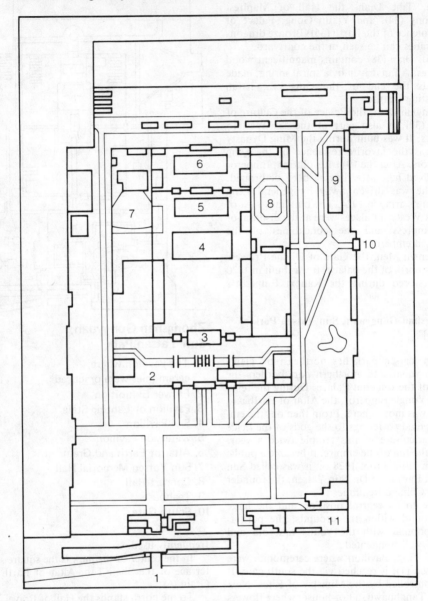

1. South Gate
2. Well Pavilion
3. Daji Men Gate
4. Taimiao Temple
5. Middle Hall
6. Rear Hall
7. Theater
8. Sportsgrounds
9. Cinema
10. East Gate
11. Library

of white marble, which was erected to pay homage to the German embassador, Baron Ketteler, who was killed by the Boxers in 1900. It originally stood at another location, but was moved here in 1918.

In the southeastern part of the park, is Laijinyuxuan teahouse (9) where the visitor may rest for a while.

Laodong Renmin Wenhuagong, The Working People's Cultural Park 劳动人民文化宫

The Working People's Cultural Park is situated northeast of Tian'anmen Square. It was built in 1420 under the Yongle Emperor's reign as a temple complex to honor the imperial ancestors. The buildings were restored after 1949 and the park was opened to the public for entertainment and cultural purposes. Today, people play table tennis and chess in the halls and courtyards, once sacred sites. There also is a basketball court, a theater, a cinema, a children's playground and exhibition rooms. In summer, open-air concerts are held and films are shown in the courtyard.

One walks from the south gate (1) past beautiful cypress trees to reach the southern wall of the temple. Three gates lead into the temple grounds. Daji Men gate (3) leads into the inner courtyard where three halls can be seen. The front one, Taimiao (4), was used for ceremonies honoring the ancestors. The genealogical tables of the emperors were kept in the middle hall, Zhongdian (5). They were moved to the front hall only for the ceremonies. The rear hall, Houdian (6), borders the temple complex to the north.

Jingshan Gongyuan Park 景山公园
(once called Meishan, Coal Hill)

Jingshan lies opposite Shenwu Men gate, the north gate of the Imperial Palace. Different versions exist about how this man-made mound — the highest in old Beijing — came into being. One has it, that it was made to serve as an observation hill at the time of the Yongle government while the Imperial Palace was being built, using the earth excavated in digging out the moat around the Imperial City. Another version claims that it was the earth from Beihai Lake, also man-made. One story tells of heaped up coal, from which the original names derives. In any case, Jingshan offered a welcome resort to the emperors of the Ming and Qing dynasties. The Qianlong Emperor had pavilions built on each of the five hills and had them planted with fruit trees. The park

was stocked with many small animals, for example hares. Towards the end of the Qing Dynasty, the park deteriorated. Not until recently, after it had been restored and replanted, has it become possible to imagine the former splendor and beauty of the grounds. Opposite the southern entrance of Jingshan park, Qiwang Lou, a beautiful watchtower, rises. A path leads to the middle hill, to Wanchun Ting, the Pavilion of 10,000 Springs, the largest of the five pavilions built under the Qianlong Emperor. It offers an excellent view of the center of Beijing, the Imperial Palace and the northern district with the drum and bell towers. On the eastern slope is the spot where the last Ming emperor is said to have taken his life. In the northern part of the complex stands Shouhuang Dian, the Hall of Imperial Longevity, also built under the Qianlong Emperor. Today, the Children's Palace is accommodated in it. Up to 1,000 Beijing children can take part in extra-curricular activities daily. There are, for example, groups for dancing, singing, wind and string instruments, theater, painting and sculpture as well as different sports. There are also opportunities to take part in courses covering technical fields.

Gulou, The Drum Tower 鼓楼

The Drum Tower was built under the Yongle Emperor in 1420. It marks off the northern end of the 13-km-long north-south axis along which the most important historical structures are to be found. The different drums placed here were beaten at night to mark the time and the changing of the night watches.

Zhonglou, The Bell Tower 钟楼

The Bell Tower is only a short distance north of the drum tower. This edifice was also built under the rule of the Yongle Emperor, but later burned down and was rebuilt under Qianlong. The bell struck the time of the day.

Beihai Gongyuan, North Lake Park 北海公园

Open 6:30 am to 8:30 pm in winter, 6:00 am to 9:00 pm in summer.

There are three lakes west of the Imperial Palace: Beihai, the North Lake, Zhonghai, the Central Lake, and Nanhai, the South Lake. Since the area around the Zhonghai and Nanhai lakes is today the seat of the State Council and the Central Committee of the

Chinese Communist Party and is therefore closed to the public, Beihai Park has become a favorite destination for many people from Beijing. Of Beihai Park's 680,000 m² are taken up by the lake.

The history of Beihai Park goes back more than 800 years. In the 10th century, during the Liao Dynasty, an imperial residence was built here. Although plans to establish an imperial amusement park already existed at that time, they were first realized by the rulers of the Jin Dynasty in the 12th century. They had a huge lake dug: Xihua Tan, Lake of the Western Flower. The excess earth was piled up to form hills and islands, like Qionghua Dao, Jade Flower Island. Pavilions and Guanghan Palace were also erected there.

When Beijing became the capital of the Yuan Dynasty, the first Yuan emperor, Kublai Khan, had the park splendidly designed. The large picturesque stones on the park grounds were brought here from the Imperial Garden of the Northern Song capital, Kaifeng. Marco Polo thought he was in paradise when he entered those grounds.

At the beginning of the Ming Dynasty in the 15th century, changes were again made in the park. The lake was divided into the present-day Beihai and Zhonghai. In 1651, the White Dagoba was built on the site of the ruins of Guanghan Palace which had been destroyed by an earthquake.

Under Qianlong, further extensive repairs and changes were undertaken. Many of the buildings that can still be seen today, mainly on the northern and eastern shores of the lake, date from those days. The park was opened to the public in 1915. In 1951, expensive restoration commenced: the lake was dug out, the marble bridge between Beihai and Zhonghai was built, lotus flowers and fish were bred, the buildings restored and newly painted, fruit trees and flowers planted. Today, Beihai is a popular amusement park. One can take out rowboats in the summer; in the winter the lake is turned into a giant skating rink.

The Beihai Park grounds are surrounded by a high wall. Three gates provide entrance to the park: the east, south and north gates.

In the southern section, right next to Beihai Bridge, Tuancheng, the Round City (2), is located. It is the center of the former capital of the Yuan Dynasty, Dadu. Originally it was part of the three islands, but after the division of the lake they all became part of the mainland again, except Qionghua Dao. A 5-m-high, early 15th century wall encircled the town. Right in front of Beihai Park's south gate there is a small gate leading into the Round City.

The halls and pavilions date from the Qianlong period of government. Most of the evergreens are supposedly even older. In the center of the courtyard is a small pavilion in which a globular jade basin is on display. It is 1.5 m in diameter, 0.6 m high and is decorated with dragons, sea horses and fish, playing in the rolling waves.

The basin supposedly dates from 1265 and was used by the Mongol emperor Kublai Khan as a wine container (3,000 l capacity). In those days it was kept in the Guanghan Palace. When that building was destroyed by an earthquake, the basin disappeared and fell into the hands of Daoist monks who used it as a storage vat. When Beihai Park was reconstructed under the Qianlong Emperor, the vat was rediscovered and placed in the center of the Round City.

The most important and interesting building of the Round City is Chengguang Dian, the Light-Receiving Hall (3). Due to its outstanding design, it is a unique example of Chinese architecture. All beams and pillars are richly painted. Inside the hall is a 1.5-m-high seated Buddha which was made from a single piece of white jade. Reportedly, this sculpture was imported from Burma at the time of the Guangxu period of reign (1875—1908).

Qionghua Dao island (7) is in the southern half of Beihai Lake. It is connected to the mainland by two bridges. The southern bridge, Yong'an Qiao, Bridge of Eternal Peace (4), dates from the Yuan Dynasty. In front of it is an ornamental gate, called Jicui. There is another one at the far end of the bridge, at the foot of Qiong Hua Shan hill, called Duiyun. Steps lead to Yong'an Si, the Temple of Eternal Peace (5), which was built in 1651 on the ruins of Guanghan Palace.

The first hall of the temple complex is Falun Dian (6). There are pavilions on both sides of this hall.

The small pavilion Shanyin Dian, Pavilion of the Benevolent Voice, is south of the dagoba. It has yellow and green glazed tiles and 455 niches in the walls, each containing representations of Buddha. This site offers a fantastic view: very close to it are the numerous halls and pavilions, picturesque stones and stone steles of Qionghua Hill. In the distance, Zhongnanhai, Central and South Lake, can be seen to the south, and to the east, the north-south axis of the city with its drum and bell towers, Jingshan Park, the Imperial Palace, Tian'anmen Square, the Monument to the People's Heroes, Chairman Mao Memorial Hall and Qianmen Gate.

Behind the pavilion, the 35.9-m-high Baita,

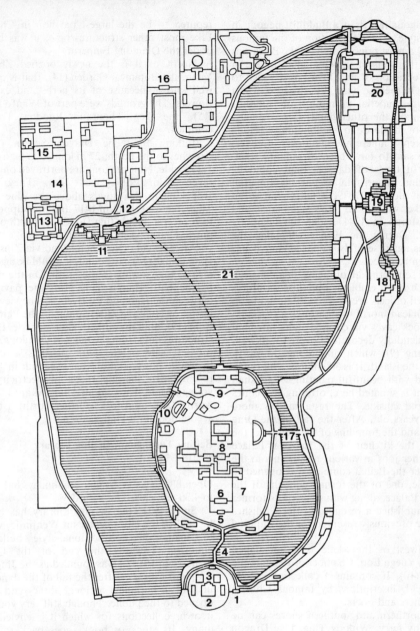

Beihai Gongyuan,
North Lake Park

White Pagoda (8), rises, a Buddhist pagoda in Tibetan style. At the suggestion of the famous Tibetan Lamaist priest Nomhan, the Baita was built on the ruins of the Guanghan palace in 1651 on occasion of the Dalai Lama's visit to Beijing. On the one hand, the structure was a sign of the imperial promotion of Buddhist teachings; on the other hand, it was an expression of the desire to maintain unity among the different Chinese nationalities. Moreover, it is also said to have been of military significance. In times of danger, flags could be hoisted and lanterns lit to put the Imperial troops on alert. In 1679, it fell victim to an earthquake, was rebuilt a few years later, and again restored in 1741 under the Qianlong Emperor. During the 1976 earthquake, the Baita was again severely damaged, but it has since been repaired.

In the southern wall of the pagoda there is a niche with a red emblem. Buddhist scriptures and sacred objects are supposedly stored here.

A path leads northward through artificially-shaped rock caves via covered stairs downhill to the splendidly decorated covered walkway, Yilan Tang (9), which runs along the north shore of the island. It is 300 m long and richly decorated with beautiful paintings. Fangshan restaurant is situated here, offering specialties of imperial cuisine. The restaurant is more than 50 years old. After the fall of the Qing Dynasty and the founding of the Republic, the chefs of the kitchen of the Imperial Palace found other jobs in various restaurants in the city. After the Beihai complex was opened to the public, one of the former eunuchs of the Imperial Palace, along with some of its former chefs, established a restaurant offering dishes that were previously reserved for the Imperial Palace.

Southwest of the island is a fan-shaped building, Yuegu Lou, Chamber of Reading the Classics (10). It contains a collection of 495 tablets with inscriptions by famous Chinese calligraphers and poets.

The northern and southern shores can be reached by ferry. Wulong Ting, Five Dragon Pavilion (11), is the first attraction there. It consists of five pavilions which seem to float on the water. They are linked by stone bridges. A temple used to stand to the north of it, where today a technical museum for children is located. Next to it, Zhenguan Hall rises with Tieying Bi, Iron Screen (12), on its south side. This wall consists of volcanic stones and dates back to the Yuan era. Reliefs depicting mythological beasts can be seen on both sides.

A little farther west is Xiaoxitian (13), Pavilion of the Miniature Western Heaven,

reputed to be the largest pavilion in China. Like most other structures here, it was built under the Qianlong Emperor.

North of it is the newly opened Zhiwu Yuan, the Botanical Garden (14), that is quite well known because of its herbs and exotic flowers. The grounds were part of Wanfo Lou (15), the Ten Thousand Buddha Tower complex.

Jiulong Bi, Nine Dragon Screen (16), stretches to the north, 27 m long, 5 m high and 1.2 m wide. Nine dragons are portrayed on it in seven colors of glazed tiles. They are frolicking in the clouds above the blue sea. The screen was built in 1417 and was supposed to protect a temple that stood just north of it, but has since been destroyed.

After leaving Qionghua island via Zhishan Qiao bridge (17) eastbound, it would be a good idea to take a walk to the north. On the right of the path Haopu Ting (18), the pavilion between the Hao and Pu rivers can be viewed, as well as Huafang Zhai, Studio on the Painted Boat (19), built in southern Chinese style. Both structures date from the reign of Qianlong. On the left side of the path there is a small hydraulic power station that was built in 1956 to emphasize the importance of electricity to young people. The Cantan Altar, Altar of Silkworms (20), used to be further north; it now accommodates a kindergarten.

Beijing Tushuguan, Beijing Library
北京图书馆

Open 8:00 am to 8:00 pm, on Sundays 8:00 am to 4:30 pm, closed on Saturdays.

Since 1931, the Beijing Library has been located in the city's center on Wenjinjie, west of Beihai in a traditional-style building complex. Towards the end of the Qing Dynasty in 1910, it was founded as the Jingshi (Capital) Library. After the fall of the dynasty in 1912, it became a national library and was opened to the public. Though still very young, it owns collections for which it is envied by many. Its stock of books goes back to the imperial libraries of the Southern Song, Ming and Qing dynasties, including the *Siku Quanshu,* a collection of classical works in 36,304 volumes. It was written by hand 200 years ago. Only 200 of the 11,095 volumes of the *Yongle Encyclopedia* of the Ming era survived the plunderings. In a special collection there are handwritings from the Song and Jin dynasties as well as printed books from the 10th—14th centuries, such as a collection of poems and writings bound by Wang Run in 1260, 'Flowers from the Literature Garden'.

Since the founding of the People's Republic, the library has been able to increase its stock of books considerably by buying used books and new publications, through exchange, donation and receipt of deposit copies from publishing companies. It now contains more than 9.8 million books. Although the area of the library was expanded from 8,000 m² in 1949 to 40,000 m², there is not sufficient space; a new building is under construction. Fifteen reading rooms are available to the 2,000 people who visit the library daily. Foreign visitors may use the public reading room. Taking out or copying books calls for a special permit which is most rapidly obtained by means of letters of recommendation from universities, institutes or Chinese authorities.

Baita, The White Dagoba 妙应寺白塔

The White Dagoba can be seen some distance away. It is north of Fuchengmennei Dajie street. With a height of 50.9 m, it is the tallest of its kind in China. It was built at the end of the 11th century under the Liao Emperors. In 1271, during the Yuan Dynasty of Kublai Khan, it was restored according to plans the renowned Nepalese architect Arniko helped to create. There was also a Lamaist temple built in front of the dagoba, but it burned down twelve years later. It was rebuilt during the Ming Dynasty and called Miaoying Si. Under the reign of the Kangxi and Qianlong emperors, this temple was restored. After the 1976 earthquake which damaged the White Dagoba, the inner wooden structure was inspected in 1978 as part of a general overhaul. Seven hundred and twenty-four scrolls of Tripitaka-sutras, more than 20 objects of worship, and the gown and cap of a monk were found in the spire. According to Buddhist custom, the 'Three Treasures', Buddha statues, sutras and monk's garments were enclosed in the walls in order to drive away evil spirits when a pagoda was built or repaired. According to the inscriptions, the treasures found in the White Dagoba date from the Qianlong period of government. Today they are on display in this temple.

Yonghe Gong, Lama Temple 雍和宫

Open 8:00 am to 5:00 pm, last tickets are sold at 4:00 pm, closed on Tuesdays and Thursdays.

Yonghe Gong, one of the best preserved temples in Beijing, is one of the most important attractions of the city. This complex, dating back to 1694, used to be the palace in which the son and successor of the

Kangxi Emperor lived. It became a temple and monastery compound after he had succeeded his father to the throne as the Yongzheng Emperor in 1723. According to an old tradition, the former residence of a successor to the throne could only be used as a temple. Actually, only one half was handed over to Lamaist monks from Tibet, the other half continued to serve the emperor as a residence. It burned down completely in 1725; only the temple remained. After that, the entire grounds were called Yonghe Gong. The lama temple, built on a north-south axis, has been preserved until today. Due to the efforts of Zhou Enlai, it survived the time of the Cultural Revolution undamaged. The entire furnishings remained intact. The temple still houses a small group of Lamaist monks, young and old, who also manage the complex. One enters the temple through the south gate. A garden path leads into the first courtyard where the Drum (2) and Bell (3) towers as well as two stele pavilions stand. To the north is the first of five important halls: Tianwang Dian, Hall of the Celestial Guardians (5). In the center of the hall is a statue of Maitreya, Buddha of the Future, with statues of the Four Celestial Guardians around it, holding symbolic objects in their hands: The celestial guardian of the east holds a pipa (a musical instrument), that of the south holds a sword, that of the west a snake, and the northern celestial guardian holds an umbrella. In the rear stands a statue of Weituo holding an iron bar in his hand, because he is the defender of the sacred Buddha. On leaving Tianwang Dian, the visitor passes a bronze tripod from 1757. It is decorated with two dragons playing with a pearl. Yubi Ting pavilion (6) is in the center of the courtyard. It contains a stele from 1792 with inscriptions in four languages (Han Chinese, Manchu, Tibetan and Mongolian) telling the history of Lamaism. Close by is a model of Xumi Shan, Sumeru (Paradise Mountain), cast in bronze. The lower part shows the sea; the four Celestial Guardians live on the slope and the palace of Sakyamuni stands on top. Then the main hall of the temple comes into sight, Yonghe Gong Dian (7). Three Buddha sculptures can be seen there: Sakyamuni, the Buddha of the Present, in the center; the Buddha of the Past to the west; and Maitreya, Sakyamuni's successor, the Buddha of the Future, to the east. Eighteen Luohan statues stand along the east and west walls. In the northeast corner of the hall one finds Dizang — Ksitigarbha who, according to the holy scriptures, rescues people from hell's tortures. In the northwest corner there is a

Yonghe Gong, Lama Temple

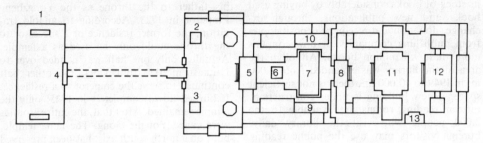

1. South Gate
2. Drum Tower
3. Bell Tower
4. Ornamental Gate
5. Hall of the Celestial Guardians
6. Yubi Ting Pavilion
7. Yonghe Gong Hall

8. Yongyou Dian Hall
9. Yaoshi Dian Hall
10. Hall of Mathematics
11. Falun Dian Hall
12. Wanfu Ge Hall
13. Zhaofo Lou Tower

characterization of Maitreya. The picture on the west side depicts Guanyin, the bodhisattva of charity, Avalokiteshvara, as a woman with 1,000 arms and eyes. Buddhist and Lamaist classics were studied in the eastern and western side halls of Yonghe Gong.

The third important hall is Yongyou Dian (8). The Buddha Amitabha is in its center; to his right is the Buddha of Medicine, Yaoshi Fo, and to his left the Buddha of the Lion's Roar, Shihou Fo (Sakyamuni's teachings shake the world like the roar of a lion, the king of beasts).

The adjoining hall to the east is called Medicine Hall, Yaoshi Dian (9), as medicine was taught here. There was a statue of Zongkaba (1357—1410) in this hall, a reformer of Lamaism and founder of the Yellow Sect. The Buddha of Medicine is south of it, the Buddha of Longevity to the north. The adjoining hall to the west is Shuxue Dian, Hall of Mathematics (10), where the sciences were studied. They were already familiar with astronomical instruments and globes then. Here, there is a statue of Zongkaba as well as two of his disciples. The four adjoining halls of Yonghe Gong and Yongyou Dian were called the Four Halls of Science.

The fourth hall is Falun Dian (11) with a 6.1-m-high bronze statue of Zongkaba, and murals telling of his importance. Books are kept along both sides of the walls: Buddhist writings in Tibetan, 108 volumes on the west wall and 207 volumes of the *Dazang Jing* on the east wall. The collection in this hall includes

two sacred books in the Tibetan language that were written in gold ink. Murals on the walls illustrate the life of the lecturing Sakyamuni. North of the Zongkaba statue is the mountain of the 500 Luohan, made of sandalwood; the Luohan statues are made of gold, silver, bronze, iron and tin. In the eastern side hall there are five Jingang patron statues. Some of the male and female gods have caused offence because of their tight embraces and were therefore covered up. Furthermore, the images of two wild bears carved from wood which were killed while the Qianlong Emperor was hunting, can be seen. Some weapons and hunting garments are also on display. The western side hall houses the Zhantan Buddha and two of his disciples, as well as some bodhisattva statues.

The fifth hall, Wanfu Ge (12), is the tallest building of the temple. It is linked to the two side halls by two 'heavenly bridges', hanging galleries. A statue of Maitreya is in Wanfu Ge hall. It is 18 m high, made of white Tibetan sandalwood, having been carved from a tree trunk 3 m in diameter. The statue is supposed to have been presented to the Qianlong Emperor in 1750 by the 7th Dalai Lama. Zhaofo Lou stands east of Wanfu Ge. It is a building containing a bronze Buddha resting on a pedestal of rare nanmu wood. The Qianlong Emperor's mother especially revered the statue, which was formerly decorated with a golden crown, a shining pearl and a golden umbrella. These treasures were stolen during the period of unrest before 1949.

Guozijian, The Imperial College 国子监
(Andingmen Dajie)

Open 8:30 am to 7:30 pm, on Saturdays and Sundays 8:30 am to 5:30 pm, closed on Mondays.

Guozijian Academy was built in 1287 according to plans for old imperial schools that existed during the Han Dynasty. During the Yuan Dynasty, Han Chinese studied Mongolian writing and the art of war, while Mongolian boys learned Han Chinese. During the Ming Dynasty, the school was further enlarged and improved. The most important subjects were the classics.

In 1784, the Qianlong Emperor had the entire complex totally restored and furnished like a palace. The roofs were covered with imperial-yellow glazed tiles. Today the school is part of the Beijing Municipal Library. It was restored in 1956.

The central building of the complex is Piyong pavilion which is situated on a small island in a pond; it dates from the Qianlong era. Here the emperor gave lectures on the classics to teachers, high officials and students. In the eastern and western galleries of the Guozijian more than 190 steles stood, in which Jiang Heng's classics were engraved within 12 years. The text consists of 63,000 characters. The following classics are included: *Zhouyi, Shangshu, Shijing, Zhouli, Yili, Liji, Chunqiu Zuozhuan, Chunqiu Gongyangzhuan, Chunqiu Guliangzhuan, Lunyu, Xiaojing, Erya, Mengzi*. These steles, also called Qianlong Steles, because they were made on his orders, are kept east of the Guozijian today.

North of Piyong pavilion stands Yilun Tang hall. It used to be a lecture room and library, but has been changed into a reading room today. In former times, the classics were on display in the adjoining halls. Behind Yilun Tang there is a courtyard and the Jingyi Ting pavilion where the administrative offices were formerly located. Since 1728, there have also been Russian students studying at this academy.

Kongmiao, Confucius Temple 孔庙
(east of Guozijian, on Andingmen Dajie)

Open 9:00 am to 5:00 pm, closed on Mondays.

Guozijian, the Imperial College and Kongmiao are linked by a covered walkway. This temple was erected during the Yuan Dynasty. Annual celebrations were held here on the birthday of the great sage.

Ancient pines grow in the courtyard. To the east and west there are pavilions where more than 190 steles were kept the names of scholars who passed the civil service examinations. In the center of the compound is Dacheng Dian hall, where the ceremonies were held and the spirit tablet of Confucius was kept. Congsheng Ci temple is behind Dacheng Dian. Confucius' ancestors were worshipped here. The most valuable object of the entire temple complex was a stone drum which was taken to Nanjing in 1933. A duplicate is on display today.

Minzu Wenhuagong, The Nationalities' Cultural Palace 民族文化宫
(Fuchengmennei Dajie)

Open 8:30 am to 4:30 pm, closed on Mondays.

On the 10th anniversary of the founding of the People's Republic, a cultural center for China's minorities was built. It is a white structure with a turquoise-glazed tile roof. The central building is 13 stories (67 m) high. The total area of the cultural palace measures 30,700 m². It consists of 18 exhibition halls, 20 apartment-guestrooms and a technical library with more than 300,000 volumes, in which magazines in the languages of the minorities are also available. The Library's collections include valuable old books like village chronicles and canonical scriptures of Lamaism.

In the restaurant, the visitor can enjoy dishes of the national minorities. The Mongolian dish *Shuan Yangrou*, a kind of fire pot, is especially recommendable. Very thin slices of mutton are put into boiling water for a short time and then dipped into a special sauce. The meat is from one-year-old sheep from Xinjiang Province or from Neimenggu, Inner Mongolia. Pretty textiles and objets d'art of the minorities can be purchased at a store next to the restaurant. In the east wing is an auditorium providing seating for 1,100 people. It is equipped with an ultrasonic simultaneous translation system for seven minority languages. Concerts are often held in this room.

A dance hall, a dining room, a Muslim kitchen and a club are in the west wing. Starting at 9.00 p.m., several activities such as dancing, billiards, archery or bowling are offered.

Lu Xun Bowuguan, Lu Xun Museum 鲁迅博物馆
(Fuchengmen Dajie)

Open 8:30 am to 11:00 am, 1:30 pm to 3:30 pm, closed on Mondays.

Zhou Shuren was born in Shaoxing, Zhejiang in 1881, started writing in 1918, using the pseudonym Lu Xun, and died in Shanghai in 1936. He is a pioneer of revolutionary literature in China. His works are among the most outstanding of the 20th century. Among his best-known works are the short stories *Diary of a Madman* and *The True Story of Ah Q*. He commented on the problems of his time in countless essays.

Lu Xun's works have been collected in the museum. One thousand and one hundred letters in all were collected as well as diaries from 1912 — 1936 (the 1922 volume was lost). The earliest works on display are from 1919. They are treatises on classical literature; the last writings he composed two days before his death. Most of the writings exhibited are from the estate which his wife Xu Guangping administered after his death during the civil war years. Others were made available by friends and acquaintances after 1949. Just recently, a letter from 1904, one he had written to a friend from Japan, appeared. It is one of the earliest samples of his handwriting.

The exhibit is divided into four sections; analogous to the dates of his life, the first section covers the period from 1881 — 1909: his childhood and education, as well as the first translations of foreign writings.

The second section deals with the period 1909 — 1927: his travels and first writings. In the third part, the period from 1927 — 1936 is covered: his stay and activities in Shanghai. The fourth section reports how the writer and his work influenced China. The first edition of his complete works is exhibited. The publication was financed after his death in 1938 by his friends. Today it is a rarity in China. Reportedly only three copies of it exist.

Lu Xun Guju, Lu Xun House 鲁迅故居

Just west of Lu Xun museum is the house where the author lived for two years after May 1942. It is a traditional-style private mansion. The furniture remained unchanged.

Zhongguo Renmin Geming Junshi Bowuguan, Military Museum of the Chinese People's Revolution 中国人民革命军事博物馆 (Fuxinglu)

Open 8:30 am to 4:30 pm, last tickets are sold at 3:30 pm, closed on Mondays.

The museum is one of the huge structures that were built in Beijing after 1949 within the shortest amount of time possible. In 1959, the building was opened. Its central part has seven stories; the side wings have four stories each. It documents the period from the founding of the Communist Party of China in 1921 up to the declaration of the People's Republic in 1949. Five thousand objects have been collected from their own side and the opposition's, which include photographs, plans, maps, documents, weapons and pieces of clothing such as those which belonged to the Canadian doctor Norman Bethune, who devotedly supported the revolutionaries. It further covers the time of the civil wars, the Sino-Japanese War 1937-1945, the defense of the Socialist revolution and Socialism.

Baiyun Guan, White Cloud Daoist Temple 白云观
(Baiyulu, south of Yanjing Hotel)

Open on Fridays and Sundays

Baiyun Guan, the chief temple of the Quanzhen Daoist Sect, was founded in the 8th century. The Tang Dynasty Emperor Xuanzong ordered its construction to house a stone statue of the seated figure of Laozi, the legendary founder of the Daoist school of thought. The temple burned down in 1202, the only thing that survived was the stone statue. It can still be seen in the exhibition hall. The Yuan Dynasty Emperor Genghis Khan had the temple rebuilt and invited, in 1224, the famous Daoist monk Qiu Changchun to live here. Qiu was the founder of the Longmen subsect under the Quanzhen sect. When Qiu died, his disciples buried his remains in the east of the temple.

Tiantan, Temple of Heaven 天坛

Open 6:30 am to 6:00 pm.

The Temple of Heaven is located in the southeastern part of Beijing. This compound is one of the largest parks in the city, covering 273 hectares. A bird's eye view shows that the park can be divided into a northern and a southern section. The northern, semi-circular section corresponds to the old Chinese image of a vault-shaped heaven. The southern, square section symbolizes earth. Three important structures, laid out on a north-south axis, can be viewed: to the north Qinian Dian, the Hall of Prayer for Good Harvests, south of it, Huangqiongyu, the Imperial Vault of Heaven and southernmost Huanqiu Tan, Circular Mound Altar. Each year the emperor came here at the time of the winter solstice in his capacity as the Son of Heaven to pray for a good harvest and to render homage to the heavens. This tradition was kept up until the fall of the dynasty in 1911. Yuan Shikai was the last one to hold a ceremony here in 1913.

The visitor enters the park through Xitian Men, the Western Heavenly Gate (1). A long

Temple of Heaven, Beijing

The Great Wall in Beijing

In the Palace Museum, Beijing

The Midair Temple, Shanxi

Carved Stones of Yungang, Shanxi

Yungang Grottoes, Shanxi

The Jin Ancestral Temple, Shanxi

The Temple of Five Pagodas in Hohhot, Neimenggu Autonomous Region

The Headless Stone Figures at Northern Imperial Tomb, Shenyang, Liaoning

Ice Lanterns of Harbin, Heilongjiang

Tiantan, Temple of Heaven

1. Western Heavenly Gate
2. Hall of Prayer for Good Harvests
3. Imperial Vault of Heaven
4. Echo Wall
5. Circular Mound Altar
6. Hall of Abstinence
7. East Gate

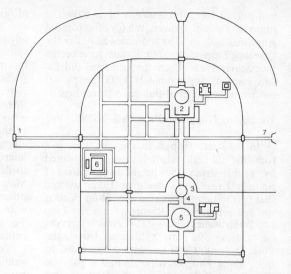

cypress grove leads east to the Qinian Dian, the Hall of Prayer for Good Harvests (2). It was built in 1420. After it was hit by lightning and burned down completely in 1889, it was re-erected according to the original plans. It is built on a three-tiered, round stone terrace; each level is encircled by a balustrade of white marble. The hall is a masterpiece of Chinese architecture. It is 38 m high and 30 m in diameter. It was entirely made of wood; not a single nail was used. The triple cone-shaped roof is made of 50,000 blue glazed tiles with a golden point and has neither spars nor beams. It is supported by 28 wooden pillars. The four central columns, called the Dragon Well Pillars, are 19.2 m high. It takes three people to embrace one of them. These four pillars represent the four seasons. Around them are two rings of 12 columns each. The inner one represents the 12 months of the year; the outer one symbolizes the 12 units of time of one day, according to the old Chinese calculation. All 28 of them were made from timber that was transported over thousands of kilometers from Yunnan Province in Southwest China. The brilliant painting of the ceiling vault is representative of Chinese color combinations. The walls of the hall are made of wooden lattice-work doors. In the middle of the floor lies a slab of marble: the Phoenix and Dragon Stone, Longfeng Shi. The imperial symbols can be recognized in its natural veining. The emperor used to pray to heaven for good harvests in this hall.

An elevated path leads south to Huang-qiongyu, the Imperial Vault of Heaven (3). It was built in 1530 and restored in 1752. It also sports a cone-shaped blue tiled roof with a golden point. It is brilliantly painted inside. The tablets used for ceremonies were kept here for the rest of the year and were only taken out for the ceremonies themselves.

At the surrounding brick wall, Huiyin Bi, the Echo Wall (4), one may experience an interesting acoustic phenomenon. If one stands facing the wall and whispers to another person at the opposite end of the wall, he can understand every word. Another curiosity is the Sanyin Shi, Triple Sound Stones, in front of the steps of the hall. When standing on the first stone, one hears a single echo, on the second, a double and on the third, a triple echo. The mystery behind this phenomenon lies in the varying distances of the slabs to the wall.

South of it lies Huanqiu Tan, Circular Mound Altar (5), a three-tiered stone terrace, enclosed by two walls; the inner one is round, the outer one square. The structure of the altar is based on the number nine. In former times, odd numbers used to be regarded as heavenly. As nine was the most powerful of them all, the altar was constructed with nine plus a multiple of nine stone slabs. The inner circle on the top tier consists of nine slabs, the second of 18, the third of 27, and so on. This order is continued in the central tier. The 27th and final ring of the lower tier consists of 243 stone slabs. When one stands in the center of the upper terrace, speaking in a normal tone of voice, one hears one's own voice considerably louder than the people around. That is due to the fact that the sound waves are reflected by the balustrades and the round wall back to the center of the terrace.

The emperor offered sacrifices to heaven

and prayed for good harvests here. Like the Imperial Vault of Heaven, the Circular Mound Altar was built in 1530 and renewed under the Qianlong Emperor in 1749. It must have been a spectacular event when the emperor and his entourage of approximately 1,000 people set out from the Imperial Palace to travel here.

Taoranting Gongyuan Park 陶然亭公园

In the southern part of the city there is a romantic old park, which is mostly frequented by people from the neighboring parts of Beijing. Excavations made in 1952, showed that first settlements existed here as far back as the 3rd century BC. Records from the Liao and Jin dynasties (10th—13th centuries) report the existence of a park in this area. During the Yuan Dynasty, Cibei monastery was built. In 1695, Jiang Zao, an official, had a pavilion erected next to the old monastery. It was called Taoran Ting, with reference to a poem that the Tang poet Bai Juyi had written about this place. Unlike other parks and gardens of the city which were reserved for the emperor and his family, this one was accessible to everybody. That is why the Taoran Pavilion above all became a popular meeting place for poets and literary men during the Qing Dynasty. With the decline of the dynasty, the park decayed, too. As the affluents and outlets were stopped up, the lakes soon turned into a filthy slough. In 1952, the complex was entirely redesigned. The lakes were dredged, seven small hills were formed, pavilions were built. Thus a charming park was created that offers possibilities for walks and boat trips, giving the public the chance for relaxation. The ancient Cibei An monastery and Taoran Ting pavilion are situated between the two lakes.

In the courtyard of the monastery, there are two Buddhist columns dating from 1099 and 1131, as well as a Guanyin stele from 1663. Southwest of the monastery there are two beautiful pavilions from the Qianlong era which were moved here in 1954. A Hall of culture that used to be the private property of a Qing official and an open air stage provide for cultural events.

Beijing Dongwu Yuan, Zoo 北京动物园

Open 7:30 am to 5:30 pm.

The Beijing zoo is situated next to the exhibition hall in the northwestern part of the city. During the Ming era, an imperial park was laid out here that was repeatedly redesigned by the Qing emperors. Around 1902 a zoo was opened: Wansheng Yuan, Park of 'Ten Thousand Animals'; a botanic garden was added in 1906. In 1908, the park was opened to the public. In the confusion of wartime, the zoo was completely neglected, so that the number of animals decreased rapidly. After the founding of the People's Republic in 1949, there were reportedly only 10 monkeys, three parrots and one emu left. Then the government supplied funds for the renovation of the zoo. Today it boasts more than 3,000 animals of almost 400 species. Of special interest are the Manchurian tigers, big marine turtles, yaks from Tibet, and gibbon apes. Most of the animals were caught in China, others are presents from friendly nations or were purchased in exchange for other animals. The main attraction for foreign visitors is, of course, the giant panda from Sichuan.

Today, panda bears are among those animals threatened by extinction. Attempts have been made to stop this development by introducing huge reservations. These bears are said to have inhabited all of South China half a million years ago. In those days they were omnivorous. Only in the course of the last centuries have they come to feed on bamboo as their staple diet. Today, there are only 1,000 surviving pandas. They live in the eastern foothills of the Himalaya in Sichuan, Gansu and Shaanxi Provinces. They prefer to live at an elevation between 2,800 and 3,200m and like a wet, cold climate. A fully-grown panda can weigh more than 400 kg and needs 20 kg of food per day. Its favorite meal consists of fresh, sweet bamboo shoots.

Zizhu Yuan, Purple Bamboo Park 紫竹院

The Purple Bamboo Park lies in the western part of the city and includes three lakes and two islands. During the Yuan Dynasty, the hydraulic engineer Guo Shoujing tried to regulate the flow of water from the northwestern Changping Xian district as well as from the Yuquan Shan mountain into these man-made lakes and re-direct it through the Changhe Canal to Beijing. Up to this day, this system has retained its importance in supplying the city with water.

At the end of the Qing Dynasty, the stream feeding the lakes became obstructed, causing them to dry up. In 1952, steps were taken to improve the general state of the system. The lakes were dredged, hills formed, bridges built, trees and flowers planted and pavilions erected. In 1958, the lakes were enlarged and bamboo and lotus flowers were planted.

Originally there was a large temple, called Wanshou Si, built in 1577, in Zizhu Yuan park. Zizhu Yuan, a small Lamaist temple, stood on the Wanshou Si temple grounds. Its remains can still be seen in the north-western part of the park.

Dazhong Si, Great Bell Temple 大钟寺

In Haidian district in western Beijing, Juesheng Si temple, also called the Great Bell Temple, is located. The temple would long ago have been forgotten, did it not house one of the biggest bells in the world, Huayan Zhong. It was cast in bronze during the Yongle reign (1403 — 1424), supervised by Yao Guangxiao. It is 6.75m high, 3.3m in diameter, and 18.5cm thick at the striking ring; it weighs 46.5 tons. To guarantee a good sound, Yao Guangxiao had it made in one piece by pouring liquid bronze from dozens of kilns into a huge clay mould. At each stroke of the bell, which can be heard 50km away, the sound echoes inside the hall for more than one minute.

Seventeen Buddhist sutras, totalling 220,000 Chinese characters, are inscribed on both sides of the bell. They were done by the famous calligrapher of the Ming era, Shen Du.

One hundred and seventy years after its completion, in 1577, the bell was transported to Wanshou Si, the Temple of Longevity. When Wanzhou Si was in danger of collapsing, the bell was placed in the tower of Juesheng Si temple compound, which was specially constructed for this purpose. But the transportation of the heavy bell posed a serious problem. A little story illustrates how a solution was found: The moving of the bell was delayed until the next cold winter set in. Water was then poured on all the roads, turning them into smooth slides. Thus, the bell could be pushed easily to Juesheng Si temple.

A staircase inside the tower leads to the upper story where visitors may take a close look at the bell. It remained undamaged, although it is more than 500 years old.

There are about 30 other bells on the temple grounds, which date back to the Song, Yuan, Ming and Qing dynasties.

Fayuan Si Temple 法源寺

Open 8:30 am to 11:30 am, 1:30 pm to 4:30 pm, closed on Wednesdays.

Fayuan Temple is on Fayuansi Houjie street in Xuanwuqu district. Its construction was ordered by the Zhengguang Emperor in 645. It was completed in 696 and the emperor called it Minzhong Si. In the course of the following dynasties, it was known by different names and was restored several times. Its present name goes back to 1734 (Yongzheng era).

Fayuan Si is a center of Buddhist doctrine and research. Its museum is a center of the arts. In 1956, the Buddhist Society established an academy here, dedicated to the teaching and investigation of Buddhism. It was closed during the Cultural Revolution and reopened in December 1980. Several of the country's monasteries send young monks, aged 18 to 30, to take up their studies at the academy. The course takes four to five years. Lectures are held in the mornings and afternoons. The subjects include history of Buddhism, the study of scriptures, classical Chinese, calligraphy, current and national politics and general sciences. English and Japanese are optional. The students live at the monastery. The academy pays all the expenses.

The first courtyard contains the bell and drum towers, on the left and right sides. In Tianwang Dian, Hall of the Celestial Guardians, there are statues of the four guardians, a Maitreya and a Weituo statue. In the second courtyard stands Daxiong Baodian, the main hall of the monastery, containing the statues of three generations of Buddhas — past, present and future — as well as 18 Luohan figures.

Dabianjue Tang hall houses statues made of various materials from different periods. One of the most valuable objects is a ceramic statue from the Eastern Han Dynasty (25 — 220).

Tanzhe Si Temple 潭柘寺

This imposing temple complex is in Mentougou district on Tanzhe Shan mountain. A visit is a must. First attempts to build a temple date back to 265—316. During the Tang Dynasty, this was a preferred spot to study the classics. The following dynasties undertook the restoration and expansion of the temple, each giving it a new name. Finally the name Tanzhe Si prevailed. Tan is a loan from *Longtan,* meaning Dragon's Pond and referring to the lake behind the temple grounds. *Zhe* comes from *Zheshu,* trees that used to grow on the hill in great numbers and provided nourishment for silkworms. The two syllables were put together and thus a new term emerged.

The complex is very large, yet very well organized. It consists of three parts which were seperately laid out on a north-south axis. A ceremonial arch, Pailou (1), forms the entrance. The way to Shanmen, the Mountain Gate (2), also called the main gate, is lined by many old pines, often likened to flying dragons. Behind the mountain gate are the

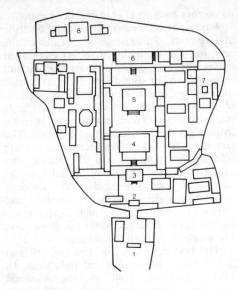

Tanzhe Si Temple

1. Ceremonial Arch
2. Mountain Gate
3. Hall of the Celestial Guardians
4. Treasure Hall of the Great Hero
5. Hall of Abstinence
6. Pavilion of Vairocana
7. Pavilion of the Floating Cups
8. Guanyin Dian Hall

following halls: Tianwang Dian (3), Daxiong Baodian (4), Zhaitang (5) and Pilu Ge, Pavilion of the Buddha Vairocana (6). On both sides of the roof of Daxiong Baodian there are two mythical beasts, sons of the dragon king. They guard the hall against fire. It is said that they date from the Yuan era. A monk supposedly saw them flying by one night during bad weather, caught them immediately and chained them to the roof.

A giant ginkgo tree stands north of Daxiong Baodian hall. It is said to have been planted during the Liao era (907—1125). The Qianlong Emperor of the Qing Dynasty called it Emperor's Tree. On the highest point of the grounds Pilu Ge pavilion stands. The eastern building complex covers the structures in which the Imperial family resided on their visits, as well as the abbot's rooms. An interesting feature of the courtyard is Liubei Ting, Pavilion of the Floating Cups (7). Its construction goes back to an old amusement of learned men: cups filled with wine were placed in the flowing water of small streams and

creeks. They followed them along the banks and sat down where they had landed, drank their wine, talked awhile and wrote poems. Later this custom was changed a little. On the third day of the third month according to the lunar calendar, people gathered here, placed filled cups in the stream and drank after they had drifted ashore. This procedure was supposed to keep bad luck away.

The western complex also includes a few interesting halls. The northernmost is called Guanyin Dian (8). It is reported that Miao Yan, the daughter of Kublai Khan, the first emperor of the Yuan Dynasty, entered the monastery to do penance for her father's sins. As she prayed in that hall from morning until evening every day, a small hollow can be seen on the stone on which she always knelt. Supposedly she was also buried within the temple compound.

Jietai Si Temple 戒台寺

Impressive Jietai Si is at the foot of Ma'an Shan mountain, 35km west of Beijing and 8km from Tanzhe Si temple. It was founded in 622. The monk Fachun lived here during the Liao Dynasty (907 — 1125). His ashes are still kept in an urn in one of the pagodas on the mountain slope. The two pagodas date back to 1091 and 1448. The temple was restored twice in 1441, during the Ming Dynasty, and again in 1685 under Emperor Kangxi. The Qianlong Emperor came here frequently. He left behind some poems, a few of which are engraved on tablets and have been preserved. Most of the buildings still existing date from the Qing Dynasty.

The main hall of the temple is the Daxiong Baodian. Behind it is the Ten Thousand Buddha Pavilion, a square-shaped building. Numerous small Buddha figures decorate the walls. Off to the side of the main path, between the two buildings an old 'trembling pine' grows. When you tug at one branch, the whole tree starts trembling. A three-tiered white stone terrace is another interesting feature. The monks' ordination used to take place here. This temple was an important ordination center for all of China. Among the oldest sights of the complex are the steles from the Liao and Yuan dynasties which stand in front of Mingwang Hall. They contain Buddhist inscriptions.

The temple complex is renowned for its old pines which are the subject of many songs. The lay-out of the complex with its many flowers, trees, courtyards, houses and pagodas conveys an air of South China.

Beijing Daxue (Beida), Beijing University
北京大学
Qinghua Daxue (Qinghua), Qinghua University
清华大学

Some travelers will certainly get the chance to visit one of Beijing's universities. The city's largest are Beijing Daxue (Beida) and Qinghua Daxue (Qinghua).

Today, Beijing Daxue is the biggest university for humanities in the country. It has a student body and staff of 20,000. It was established in 1898 with American assistance and was called Yanjing Daxue at that time. In those days, the campus was close to Jingshan. Yanjing University soon became the meeting place of progressive young people. Thoughts and ideas were developed here that students voiced in public during the May 4th Movement of 1919. New forces were constantly recruited from this university that advanced anti-Japanese resistance and the revolution. In 1953, the university was moved to the present campus grounds. This complex is the former private residence of an official favored by the Qianlong Emperor. In the meantime, many new buildings and dormitories have been added.

Chinese universities resemble small towns, where one lives, teaches and studies. Small stores supply teachers and students with all they need. During the Cultural Revolution, the university again became the center of confrontation with new thoughts.

There is a lake on campus. On its south shore lies the grave of Edgar Snow, an American journalist. Half of his ashes were buried here, the other half in Switzerland. Snow gained renown with his reports about scenes of the Chinese Revolution, his book *Red Star over China* and his friendly relations to Mao Zedong. In 1972, Mao Zedong authorized Snow to give the American President Richard Nixon a signal that China was willing to discuss meetings with the USA.

Qinghua Daxue is the biggest university for the natural sciences and technology. There are more than 10,000 professors and students in 13 departments.

At the time of the Cultural Revolution, conditions at both schools were chaotic. Many professors, lecturers and employees were attacked politically and persecuted. In fact, almost all classes had to be cancelled. After the fall of the Gang of Four, the governing body of the university was reorganized. Teachers who had been persecuted unjustly were rehabilitated and reinstated in their old positions.

Yihe Yuan, The Summer Palace 颐和园

Open 7:00 am to 6:00 pm.

The Summer Palace, Yihe Yuan, Garden of Harmonious Unity, lies in a northwestern suburb of Beijing. This is one of the largest and best preserved Imperial Chinese gardens; it is an outstanding example of classical Chinese garden landscaping. Man-made Kunming Lake, Longevity Hill, the man-made hills as well as halls, pavilions and temples blend harmoniously inspite of their individual styles. The method of 'borrowing', common to Chinese garden landscaping, was put into practice. The landscape that is not really part of the complex is also incorporated. Yuquan Shan, Jade Spring Mountain, to the west with its pagoda and Xishan, the Western Hills, seem to be part of the complex because they are reflected in Kunming Lake. This spot attracted the rulers for many centuries. The emperor of the Jin Dynasty laid the foundation stone in 1153 and he had Jinshui Yuan, Garden of the Golden Water, laid out. Under the emperors of the Yuan and Ming dynasties, the complex was extended further. During the Yuan era, the lake was again enlarged and deepened; during the Ming era, various pavilions were built. Under the Qianlong Emperor (1736—1795), large-scale work was done, and the park was made its present size of 290 hectares. Three-fourths of it are taken up by Kunming Lake. Since the Qianlong period, the garden has been called Qingyi Yuan, Garden of Clear Ripples. As the Imperial family spent most of the hot summer months here, the palace was soon called the Summer Palace.

In 1860, English and French intervention troops sacked the park. In 1888, the Empress Dowager Cixi had the Summer Palace rebuilt. The enormous costs were covered by funds that were appropriated for building a Chinese navy. She called it Yihe Yuan and made it her summer residence.

In 1900, the park was again sacked by foreign troops and went up in flames. Cixi did not hesitate to raise a large amount of money for yet another construction of the complex again in 1903. After the fall of the Qing Dynasty, the grounds were opened as a public park for the first time in 1924. Since 1949, large-scale restoration work has been carried out. Today the Summer Palace is a favorite destination for thousands of people.

The entire Yihe Yuan complex is surrounded by walls. There are three entrances: the west, north and east gates. Today the East Gate (1) serves as the main entrance. Between the two staircases in front of it, there is a huge stone

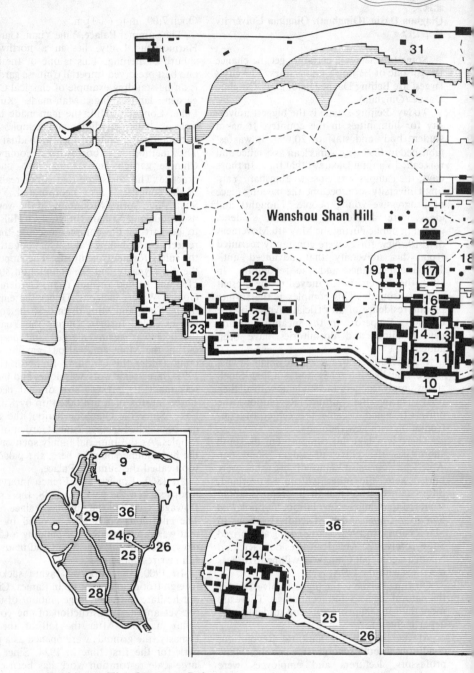

Yihe Yuan, The Summer Palace

1. Main Gate
2. Renshou Dian Hall
3. Dehe Yuan Garden
4. Yile Dian Hall
5. Yulan Tang Palace
6. Leshou Tang Hall
7. Yaoyue Men Gate
8. Changlang, Long Corridor
9. Wanshou Shan Hill
10. Paiyun Men Gate
11. Yuhua Dian Hall
12. Yunjin Dian Hall
13. Fanghui Dian Hall
14. Zixiao Dian Hall
15. Paiyun Dian Hall
16. Dehui Dian Hall
17. Foxiang Ge Pavilion
18. Zhuanlun Zang Comple

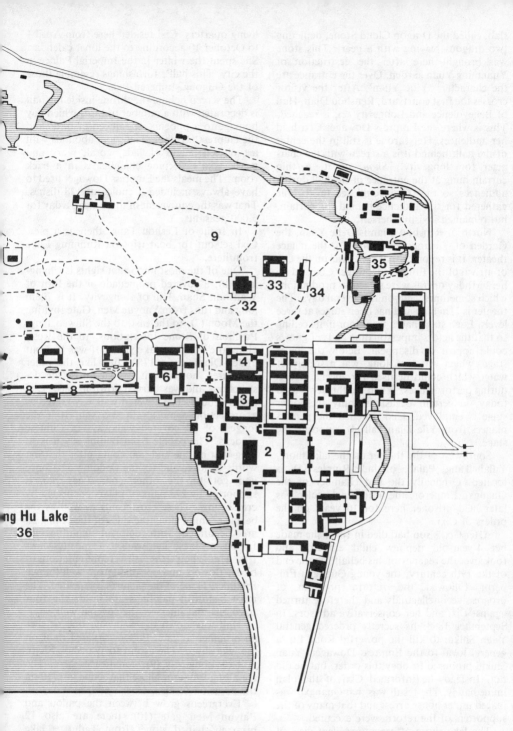

ng Hu Lake

36

9. Baoyun Ge Pavilion
0. Zhihuihai Hall
1. Tingli Guan Restaurant
2. Huazhongyou Pavilion
3. Shifang Marble Boat
4. Nanhu Dao Island

25. Shiqikong Qiao Bridge
26. Tongniu Bronze Ox
27. Longwang Miao Temple
28. Xidi West Dike
29. Yudai Qiao Bridge
30. Houhu Lake

31. Xumiling Jing Temple
32. Jingfu Ge Tower
33. Yishou Tang Pavilion
34. Lenong Xuan Pavilion
35. Xiequ Yuan Garden
36. Kunming Hu Lake

slab, called the Dragon Cloud Stone, depicting two dragons playing with a pearl. This stone was brought here after the destruction of Yuanming Yuan garden. Over the entrance are the characters 'Yihe Yuan'. After the visitor crosses the first courtyard, Renshou Dian, Hall of Benevolence and Longevity (2), is reached. This is where the Empress Dowager Cixi held her audiences. Her throne is still in the center of the hall; behind it is a screen with the character for 'longevity', Shou, on it. A thin curtain hung at the entrance of the hall during audiences so that Cixi could see the people gathered for the audience behind the curtain, but remained invisible herself.

North of Renshou Dian is Dehe Yuan, the Garden of Virtuous Harmony (3), the palace theater. It is reported that each year on the day of arrival of the Empress Dowager Cixi and on her birthday operas were staged — productions which sometimes went on for several days. The theater is 21m high and has open stages at three levels. Each stage had a trap-door in its ceiling so that the actors impersonating gods or ghosts could appear or disappear. Below the lower stage, which was 17m long, was a supply of water which could be used for special effects during performances. When the theater is used today on certain occasions, only the lower stage is employed. Cixi watched the performances from Yile Dian hall (4), opposite the stage.

Southwest of the theater on the lake shore, Yulan Tang, Palace of Jade Ripples (5), is located. Originally the bed chamber of the Guangxu Emperor, the unfortunate ruler was later held prisoner here for 10 years on the orders of Cixi.

After Cixi's son had died in 1874, she made her 4-year-old nephew child emperor and took over the regency on his behalf. At the end of the 19th century, the young Guangxu Emperor followed the reform program of progressive intellectuals and therefore turned against Cixi and her conservative advisors. In September 1898, he secretly ordered general Yuan Shikai to kill the powerful Rong Lu, a general loyal to the Empress Dowager. Yuan Shikai promised to obey this order, but he did not. Instead, he informed Cixi of the plan immediately. The result was that Guangxu was placed under house arrest and that many of the supporters of the reform were executed.

The lake shore offers an excellent view of the surroundings, including Jade Spring Hill and the Western Hills.

Further on towards the north Leshou Tang, Hall of Joy and Longevity (6), follows. This edifice was the main building of the entire living quarters. Cixi resided here from April 1 to October 10 according to the lunar calendar. She spent the winter in the Imperial Palace in the city. This hall's furnishings resemble those of the Gugong, Imperial Palace.

The screen behind the throne inside the hall is decorated with a number of birds which pay homage to a phoenix, the queen of birds and the empress' symbol. The room abounds with art objects made of jade, coral, ivory and pearl. Cixi's sleeping chamber is in a back room. The meals the Empress Dowager used to have always included a choice of 128 dishes. That was the equivalent of three meals a day for 5,000 peasants.

In front of Leshou Tang, there is a pier. Cixi set out for boat trips on Kunming Lake from here.

One of the most important sights is Changlang (8), a covered promenade at the foot of Wanshou Shan, Hill of Longevity. It is 728m long and runs from Yaoyue Men, Gate Inviting the Moon (7), to the east, to the Shiwen Ting, Pavilion of Stone Inscriptions, to the west, along the northern lake shore. It was laid out under Qianlong in 1750. Just like the other structures, however, it fell victim to the destructions and was burned down in 1860. Cixi had it rebuilt. The covered walkway served as a protection against rain and sun. It is the longest of all covered walkways in Chinese gardens. The people from Beijing say it is so long that at one end you could utter the first words of love, and fix the wedding date once you got to the other end. The roof is supported by 273 pairs of pillars connected by crossbeams. These crossbeams as well as the beams running along the sides of the ceiling all are decorated with colorful paintings of famous Chinese landscapes — mostly views from Hangzhou — as well as representations of birds, flowers and episodes from well-known folktales. None of the pictures is repeated. The most beautiful paintings are inside the four pavilions that intersect the covered walkway.

Half-way down the walkway, one reaches an ornamental gate, Pailou, situated right on the lake shore. The ascent to Wanshou Shan, Hill of Longevity (9), commences here. The Qianlong Emperor chose that name in 1750 on the occasion of his mother's 60th birthday.

Evergreens grow between the pailou and Paiyun Men gate (10); there are also 12 bizarrely-shaped stones from Taihu, a lake near Wuxi, representing the animals of the 12-year-cycle.

The Paiyun Men gate is flanked by two bronze lions. Yuhua Dian hall (11) is behind the gate on the east side. On the west side,

Yunjin Dian hall (12) is located. Through the second gate, Paiyun Dian, the Cloud-Dispelling Hall (15), is reached. Fanghui Dian (13) and Zixiao Dian (14) halls are on either side of it. Paiyun Dian stands on a terrace decorated with marble balustrades. It is accessible from three sides via flights of stairs. On her birthdays, the Empress Dowager received the congratulations of her officials in this hall. There is a portrait of her at the age of 69 which was done in oil by the Dutch painter Hubert Voß in 1903.

Two symmetrical corridors lead uphill to Dehui Dian, Hall of Virtuous Brilliance (16). From that point, steep stone steps lead up to Foxiang Ge, Pavilion of the Fragrance of Buddha (17). This massive complex is one of the most outstanding architectural features of the residence. A 41-m-high octagonal pavilion rests on a gigantic stone base. It is supported from the inside by four pillars made of so-called ironwood.

The terrace offers a magnificent view of the park. The Imperial relatives used to live in the buildings east of the mountain. Today they have been made into guest houses. East of the Foxiang Ge stands the Zhuanlun Zang, Revolving Library (18). In the middle of this complex, a stone stele rises bearing an inscription by the Qianlong Emperor: Wanshou Shan, Kunming Hu (Hill of Longevity, Kunming Lake); on the back of it is a report about the construction of the lake.

There is a pavilion on either side of the stele. Inside each of them is an octagonal pagoda made of wood — replicas of two pagodas in Fayun Temple in Hangzhou. West of Foxiang Ge is Baoyun Ge, Pavilion of Precious Clouds (19), made entirely of bronze, also called Tongting, Bronze Pavilion. The names of the craftsmen involved in building it are carved into a wall on its south side. North of the Foxiang Ge, on the summit of the Hill of Longevity, stands the rectangular structure Zhihuihai, Sea of Wisdom (20). It is decorated with yellow and green ceramic tiles. Buddhas are sitting in its niches. Many statues have been mutilated during the plunderings of the past few centuries. Inside the building, there is a gilded statue of a seated Buddha.

If one does not climb straight up the Wanshou Shan, but rather follows the covered walkway further west, one comes upon Tingli Guan (21) just before the end of the path. This complex houses the restaurant 'Listening to the Orioles Singing'. The Imperial family used to sit here and watch operas or listen to the songs of the orioles. A two-storied stage can be seen. Tables and chairs of a garden restaurant

are placed on its lower story today. The menu lists dishes of the Imperial cuisine. Fish dishes deserve special mention. Those with hearty appetites should have a fish dinner consisting of many courses. All fish are taken from Kunming Lake. The customer can pick his own fish from a pond stocked with carp. The fish of his choice is immediately netted and prepared for him. A further attraction is the possibility of having one's photo taken wearing old imperial robes. North of Tingli Guan restaurant, Huazhongyou (22), an octagonal pavilion, is located. A great view can be had from its upper story.

At the western end of the covered walkway, Shifang, the Marble Boat (23), stands. It is 36m Long with a base of marble and a superstructure of wood. Under the Qianlong Emperor, the marble base was erected as a pier and supplied with a wooden deck. Cixi had one more wooden story added and two stone wheels fixed on each side. The boat that originated in this way thus became an ironic symbol: the money, which had originally been intended for the construction of the badly needed Chinese navy, was used by Cixi to restore her private residence instead.

Nanhu Dao, South Lake Island (24), is in the southern part of Kunming Lake. It can be reached by a ferry that departs close to the Marble Boat or on foot from the southeast via Shiqikong Qiao, the Seventeen-arch Bridge (25), made of marble. This impressive bridge is 150m long. Its railings are decorated with 500 small columns topped by carved lions, each shaped individually. Just in front of the bridge, a bronze ox (26) lies on a stone base. According to an old tradition, an iron ox was placed at the site of each newly built hydraulic system to keep the water spirit in check. After the enormous enlargement of the lake, the Qianlong Emperor had this ox cast and placed at that location.

Longwang Miao, Dragon King Temple (27), and Hanxu Tang, Hall of Modesty, are on the island. To the south, Xiu'yi Qiao bridge spans the end of the lake. From there a canal leads to Beijing. West of the lake, Xidi, West Dike (28), is located, linking the northwestern part of the park to the southern one. The dike is a copy of Su Dongpo dike on Xihu, West Lake, at Hangzhou. The Qianlong Emperor and his mother were great admirers of the scenic beauty of Hangzhou. The six bridges which are part of the dike system are also replicas of the bridges in West Lake. The most beautiful of them is Yudai Qiao, Jade Belt Bridge (29), a single high arch with marble balustrades.

Most visitors to the Summer Palace crowd together in the gardens, pavilions and halls of Qianshan, the southern or front part of Wanshou Shan hill. Things are a lot more leisurely at the Houhu, Back Lake (30), also called Suzhou He, Suzhou River, that stretches along the northern foot of the Hill of Longevity. It is best reached by walking north from Dehe Yuan, Garden of Virtuous Harmony (3), or past the Marble Boat northward. It was once Suzhou street. A bridge led across to it and on to the north gate, previously the main gate of the Summer Palace. Suzhou street originally was a shopping street, lined with book and wine stores, antique shops and teahouses. It had been built under Qianlong — an attempt to imitate the lively activities on the canals of Suzhou. Obviously, ordinary people were not the ones who were permitted to run business inside the palace complex. They were eunuchs who, only on the occasions when the Imperial family was in residence, received permission to stage an amiable chaos. During the destructions, the street was burned down twice and never rebuilt again. South of former Suzhou street is the Buddhist temple Xumiling Jing (31), which was built under Qianlong. The 16-m-high octangular Duobao Ta, Pagoda of Many Treasures, decorated with yellow and green tiles, is also worth seeing. Small bells hang from its eaves and tinkle in a light breeze.

Farther east are *Jingfu Ge* (32), an observation tower, Yishou Tang, Pavilion of Longevity (33) and Lenong Xuan, Pavilion of Joy and Agriculture (34). To the east is the 'Garden within the Garden', as the Xiequ Yuan, Garden of Harmonious Interest (35), is affectionately called. Laid out in the southern Chinese style, it is the quietest and most harmonious unit of the Summer Palace. Four building complexes are grouped around a pond and linked by covered walkways. The pond, fed by Kunming Lake, is dotted with lotus flowers in summer. This complex, too, was built during Qianlong's reign and is the replica of a complex in South China, a garden at the foot of the Huishan mountain in Wuxi. In earlier times, it was therefore called Huishan garden. It was restored in 1893 after the devastation. Cixi then called it Xiequ Yuan. She used to have her tea and spent her lunchtime here. The furnishings of those days are still preserved.

Yuanming Yuan, the Ruins of the Old Imperial Palace Yuanming Yuan 圆明园遗址

When one describes the sights of Beijing, destruction by foreign powers has often been mentioned. In most cases the traces of destruction could be eliminated by restoration and reconstruction. The Yuanming Yuan, however, is today a reminder of foreign violence.

Yuanming Yuan lies on the northwestern outskirts of the city, north of Beida (Beijing University) and only 500m from the Summer Palace, Yihe Yuan. It was built during the Qing Dynasty over a period of 150 years (construction commenced in 1709) and included three gardens: Yuanming Yuan, Changchun Yuan and Qichun Yuan. They were laid out separately, yet in a way so that they complement each other harmoniously. The area covered about 340 hectares. The peaks of the Western hills formed the background; the hills and lakes were man-made. Countless springs flowed, feeding small canals winding their way through lovely valleys. White marble bridges spanned the water here and there. Palaces stood amidst emerald green woods; so did halls, pavilions and temples, some of them linked by covered walkways. Europeans took part in the designing, too, such as the Italian Jesuit F. Guiseppe Castiglione. Between 1747 and 1760, during Qianlong's reign, a complex of rococo palaces was built according to his plans.

In 1860, the grounds were completely destroyed within ten days. With utmost brutality, the French and British troops tried to intimidate the Imperial government and to gain new colonies and exterritoriality by force. After the most valuable treasures had been stolen, the whole complex was turned over to plundering soldiers. Finally, the British suggested setting fire to it, and the whole complex went up in flames. Only a few scattered ruins of the Xiyang Lou, the European-style Building, can be seen — a portal, a stone turtle, etc.

A small museum offers information about the lay-out and the destruction of Yuanming Yuan. A model conveys a vague idea of the former splendor and magnitude of the complex.

In comparison with other parks, Yuanming Yuan is frequented by few people from Beijing. A visit is worthwhile for Europeans, as it is a part of European colonial history that becomes visible here in a rather frightening way.

Xishan, Western Hills 西山

West of Beijing, lies an extended range of hills, called Western Hills. Its foothills descend slowly towards the city. Five interesting sights can be found in this area: Xiangshan Gong-yuan, Fragrant Hills Park; Wofo Si, the Temple of the Sleeping Buddha; Yingtao Gou, Cherry Vale; Biyun Si, the Temple of Azure Clouds; Badachu, the Eight Great Sites.

Unlike the man-made complexes of Beihai Park and the Summer Palace, the landscape of the Western Hills has been preserved in its originality, and the pavilions, temples and buildings have been designed to blend into the landscape.

By bus or taxi one heads west, past the Summer Palace. At a crossing just before Xiangshan Park, a road leads north to Wofo Si, the Temple of the Sleeping Buddha.

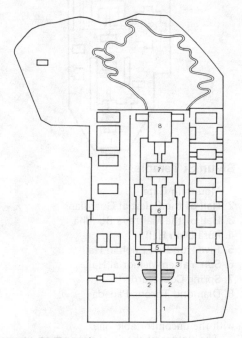

Wofo Si Temple

1. Ornamental Gate
2. Pond
3. Bell Tower
4. Drum Tower
5. Mountain Gate
6. Hall of the Celestial Guardians
7. Hall of the Three Saints
8. Hall of the Sleeping Buddha

Wofo Si, Temple of the Sleeping Buddha
卧佛寺

To the north, on Shou'an mountain, stands one of the oldest complexes of the Beijing area. A temple with a sleeping Buddha was first erected on this spot in the 7th century. Under the Yuan, Ming and Qing emperors, the complex was enlarged and improved. During the Ming era, it was called Yong'an Si, Temple of Eternal Peace. Since 1734, its official name has been Shifangpujue Si, Temple of Universal Spiritual Awakening; but because of its famous statue, it is commonly known as the Temple of the Sleeping Buddha, Wofo Si.

It is built into the mountainous countryside on a north-south axis. Ancient evergreens grow in front of the complex. The visitor enters by way of an 18th century ornamental gate. Three arches decorated with yellow and green glazed ceramic tiles rest on a white marble base. In the center of the first courtyard there is a small pond (2), spanned by a tiny bridge. To the left and right behind the pond, rise the bell (3) and drum (4) towers. The main gate, Shanmen (5), leads to the second courtyard where Tianwang Dian, the Hall of the Celestial Guardians (6), stands. It contains statues of Maitreya Buddha and the Four Celestial Guardians. Sansheng Dian hall (7) is in the third courtyard, built on a terrace. A Sakyamuni statue can be viewed here. His disciples flank him and the 18 Luohan stand along the walls. In the fourth and final hall, Wofo Dian (8), lies the Sleeping Buddha, 5m long, one arm resting on his body, the other one supporting his head. The statue is said to have been cast from 250 tons of copper during the Yuan Dynasty in 1321. Historical records report that thousands of workers were occupied with this task until 1331. The present statue, however, appears to be lighter and of more recent origin. Twelve sculptures of Sakyamuni's disciples surround the Sleeping Buddha.

Yingtaogou Yuan, Cherry Vale Garden
樱桃沟

Half a kilometer northwest of the temple are the Yingtao Gou, Cherry Vale, and Yingtaogou Yuan, Cherry Vale Garden, destination for many people tired of the city and for lovers. Summer and fall are the best seasons for a visit. From the temple area, a street leads northwest directly into the vale. Once many fruit trees, mainly cherry trees, grew here. A few hundred meters further is a small gate, the entrance to Cherry Vale Garden, from which little paths lead up the mountain. Close to it is a spring whose water is so clear that few people leave this place without drinking from it. The Rock of the White Deer rises opposite the spring; in its lower part is the

Cave of the White Deer. It is said that a god on a white deer once came to this point and, because he was so taken with the scenery, remained for a while.

Bantian Yunlin, Cloud Peak Half Way to Heaven is further uphill. It offers a beautiful view in all directions.

Biyun Si, Temple of the Azure Clouds
碧云寺

A poet of the Ming Dynasty once wrote: 'In the Western Hills there are hundreds of halls, pagodas and temples, but none of these places is as impressive, as solemn and as beautiful as Biyun Si.'

The temple is located northeast of Xiangshan park. Construction work commenced during the Yuan Dynasty in 1321 and was continued by several rich eunuchs during the Ming Dynasty. At the beginning of the 16th century, the imperial eunuch Yu Jing had the temple enlarged and a tomb built for himself. But he then lost the emperor's favor and was never buried there. In 1623, the eunuch Wei Zhongxian had the same desire. He also had the temple expanded and a tomb built. But his fate was the same as that of Yu Jing: in 1628 he lost the court's favor and hanged himself. In 1748, the Qianlong Emperor ordered the enlargement of the temple: the hall of the 500 Luohan was built as well as Jingangbaozuo Ta, the Diamond Throne Pagoda.

In front of the temple complex is a white stone bridge, guarded by two stone lions.

Behind the bridge stands the so-called Mountain Gate, Shanmen (1). Stairs lead up to it and on to Tianwang Dian, Hall of the Celestial Guardians (2), followed by Milefo Dian, Maitreya Buddha Hall (3), containing a Maitreya statue.

The second courtyard has a pond enclosed by a stone balustrade. Pusa Dian hall (4) is in the third courtyard. To the left is the 500 Luohan Hall (5). In all, there 508 statues in this complex — 500 of them are Luohan. Each of these gilded wooden statues is about 1.5m high and has its own character. Some seem to be friendly, others thoughtful or contemplative; some are young, others old men; a few stand, most of them are seated. Seven of the 508 statues represent gods and are displayed in the corridors. The visitor must search for another statue — it is happily sitting on a beam close to the gate and seems to be fanning fresh air. This is the monk Jigong. It is said that he was late again when the temple was being built, and as all seats were already taken, he had to make do

Biyun Si Temple

1. Mountain Gate
2. Hall of the Celestial Guardians
3. Hall of the Maitreya Buddha
4. Pusa Dian Hall
5. Five Hundred Luohan Hall
6. Sun Yatsen Memorial Hall
7. Spring Courtyard
8. Diamond Throne Pagoda

with the uncomfortable one.

The statues of the 500 Luohan Hall are an outstanding example of the Chinese art of sculpture.

Sun Yatsen Memorial Hall is on the other side. A bust of Sun Yatsen is in the center and next to it, a coffin which was a gift from the Soviet Union. The literary works and some of his handwritten papers are also on exhibit; his life and work are documented by photos in two side halls.

A little further west is Shuiquan Yuan, the Spring Courtyard (7), with many trees offering shade. It is said to be the ideal spot to avoid the heat of the summer, drink tea, enjoy the scenery and the fresh breeze.

Jinggangbaozuo Ta, the Diamond Throne Pagoda (8), built in 1748 under Emperor Qianlong, stands at the back part of the complex. The name Jinggangbaozuo Ta commemorates Bodh Gaya where Siddharta Gautama reached enlightenment. The pagoda is 37.4m high. Its two lower parts form a terrace; steep steps lead to a pavilion and its upper platform in the middle of which a white pagoda is situated, surrounded by four smaller pagodas and two dagobas. There are many stone reliefs. This spot offers a grand view of the entire grounds, Jade Spring Mountain and the northern outskirts of the city.

Sun Yatsen's body lay in state in Jinggangbaozuo Ta pagoda until taken to Nanjing. His clothes and hat were kept and buried in Beijing.

Xiangshan Gongyuan, Fragrant Hills Park
香山公园

The highest elevation in the neighboring vicinity of Beijing is Xiangshan, Fragrant Hill, at 557m. Two big stones lie on its peak. From a distance, they look like three-legged incense burners. As the summit is often covered by clouds, it looks as if smoke is rising from the burners. The hill was originally called Xianglu

Shan, Incense Burner Hill, shortened to Xiangshan, Fragrant Hill.

In 1186, a temple and a palace were built here. During the Yuan and Ming dynasties, the area became the imperial hunting grounds; the Qianlong Emperor had it made into a park. It became an imperial country estate, covering 1,600 hectares, surrounded by a wall. Hunting was prohibited. The emperor had pavilions, terraces and temples built, trees planted and the park stocked with rare animals. It was now called Garden of Clear Beauty. As many of the other palaces in Beijing, it was destroyed between 1860 and 1900. Everything except the pagoda burned down. During the years of the Republic, those in power had their summer residences built here. Nothing was left of the former splendor of the park. Only the results of restoration work done in the last ten years, reforestation and laying out of new paths offer the visitor a hint that this was once one of the most beautiful parks in China.

Late fall is the best time for a visit, when the leaves are a flaming red. Poets and learned men have always sung the praise of the red leaves of the Xiangshan. In spring and fall the

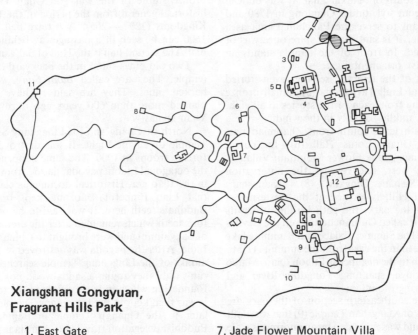

Xiangshan Gongyuan, Fragrant Hills Park

1. East Gate
2. Spectacles Lake
3. Pavilion of Introspection
4. Temple of Brilliance
5. Liuli Ta Pagoda
6. Lotus Hall
7. Jade Flower Mountain Villa
8. Xishan Qingxue Observation Point
9. Xiangshan Temple
10. Shuangqing Villa
11. Incense Burner Peak
12. Xiangshan Fandian Hotel

trees have rosy, feathery blossoms. Viewed from a distance, they look like fog tinted by the sun.

As the park is on a rather high elevation and fairly cool due to the trees, it is a popular destination for an outing, especially in summer.

The East Gate (1) is the main entrance; a lift takes one to Xiangshan's summit from the North Gate.

In the northern part of the park, Yanjing Hu, Spectacles Lake (2), is located. There are actually two lakes, connected in the middle by a bridge. In sunlight they look like a pair of glasses reflecting the light.

Jianxin Zhai, Pavilion of Introspection (3), stands southwest of Spectacles Lake; it was built in the Southern Chinese style in the 16th century and contains a large half-moon shaped pond fed by near by springs with a covered walkway around it. This courtyard is known for its echo, resounding from the eastern, southern and northern walls.

A few steps uphill is the Zhongning Tang hall — a quiet, peaceful spot, also known as Garden in the Park.

Zhaomiao, Temple of Brilliance (4), is situated south of Jianxin Zhai. It was built in the Tibetan style under Qianlong in 1780 and was meant to serve the Panchan Lama as a residence. It is said that its spire once was of pure gold. In front of the temple stands an impressive ornamental gate.

West of the temple rises the seven-storied octagonal Liuli Ta pagoda (5). Small bronze bells hang from each of the stories in all eight corners, tinkling quietly in the wind.

A path leads south from Zhaomiao past Furong Guan, Lotus Hall (6), to Yuhua Shanzhuang, Jade Flower Mountain Villa (7). Keeping west, one reaches the observation point Xishan Qingxue (8). Xiangshan, Fragrant Hill, is located at the westernmost point of the park; the path leading up to its summit is called Guijianchou, Even the Devil is Scared. The Summer Palace and Kunming lake can be seen in the east from the summit (11); to the south in the distance is Lugou Qiao, Marco Polo Bridge, spanning Yongding River and Jade Spring Mountain.

In the southeastern section of the park are the relics of Xiangshan Temple (9) that was built in 1186 and was expanded on an enormous scale in later dynasties. Five consecutive terraces were divided into hundreds of rooms. The complex was destroyed in 1860.

South of Xiangshan Temple, Shuangqing Villa (10) is situated. A quiet courtyard contains a lotus pool, fed by a small pool in the northern corner of the yard. This small pool is fed by two springs, so it is called Double Clean. According to tradition, more than 700 years ago the emperor visited Fragrant Hills Park and spent the night there. He dreamed that he had shot an arrow that landed in a spring. The next day he ordered his servants to inspect the place thoroughly, and they indeed found a spring. Since then it has been called Menggan Quan, Spring Found in a Dream.

A new attraction in the park is the first-class hotel Xiangshan Fandian.

Badachu, Eight Great Sites 八大处

Closed for foreigners (1986)

South of the Western Hills are two hills, Cuiwei Shan and Lushi Shan. Peace and relaxation are easily found here — one can amble quietly from one temple to another and enjoy the beautiful scenery amidst old pine, cypress, willow and gingko trees. The name Badachu, the Eight Great Sites, refers to eight temples which are situated in the Cuiwei Shan and Cushi Shan hills: Chang'an Si, Temple of Eternal Peace, is at the foot of Cuiwei Shan. It was built in 1502. In its first hall stands a bronze statue of the war god Guan Yu, an historical general from the period of the Three Kingdoms (220 — 265). A bronze bell from 1600 can be seen in a passageway behind the hall. The second hall is the Hall of Sakyamuni.

Two old pines stand in the backyard of the temple. They are called *Baipi Song*, white-barked pines. They are said to have been planted more than 600 years ago during the Yuan Dynasty.

North of Chang'an Si is Lingguang Si, the Temple of Divine Light. It was destroyed by foreign troops in 1900. The same happened to the octagonal Liaota pagoda, dating from 1071 in the Liao era. Historical documents claimed that Liao Emperor Daozong kept one of Buddha's teeth here. It was said to be one of four teeth which remained after the cremation of Sakyamuni and were brought to China from India. After the pagoda was destroyed in 1900, monks of the Lingguang Temple searched the ruins until they found a sandalwood box in its foundation which indeed contained the tooth. It was then kept in the Lingguang Temple and later in the Guangji Temple in Beijing. A Buddhist delegation traveled to Burma in 1955 to present it to their followers there. After it was returned to China, a new place was found for it in a pagoda built expressly for that purpose in 1956: the Foya Ta, Buddha's Tooth Pagoda. This pagoda stands in the courtyard of the Lingguang Si temple compound.

From Lingguang Si there is a path leading north to Sanshan An, Three Hills Monastery. It is situated among Cuiwei Shan, Lushi Shan and Pingbo Shan hills. Its construction date is unknown. It was restored under the Qianlong Emperor. The complex is relatively small.

There is a rectangular marble stone by the door to the main hall, the Water Cloud Stone, Shuiyun Shi, with a chiseled relief of a landscape. East of the main hall stands a pavilion offering a good view of the surroundings. The next destination is the Dabei Si, Temple of Great Pity, built during the Ming era in 1550. The 18 Luohan statues, attributed to the most famous sculptor of the Yuan era, Liu Yuan, make up this temple's main focus of interest. They are among the most beautiful statues of the Western Hills. Two gingko trees growing behind the main hall are said to be more than 800 years old.

Northwest of Dabei Si is Longwang Tang, Dragon King Hall, also known as Longquan An, Dragon Spring Nunnery. According to a saga, the Dragon King used to live here. The complex was built during the Qing Dynasty and is famous for its crystal-clear spring water. Not far from Longwang Tang, Xiangjie Si, Temple of the Fragrant World, comes into sight. Built during the Tang Dynasty, it was originally called Pingpo Si. It was restored in 1748 by Qianlong. It is the largest of the eight Badachu structures. Many steps lead up to the entrance. Two important edifices are situated here: a palace built under Qianlong and meant to be the emperor's residence, and a kind of library where Buddhist writings were kept. The library is the actual center of the temple. The bell and drum towers are on either side of the main hall. Three Buddha statues are inside the main hall — the Buddhas of the Past, Present and the Future — as well as 18 Luohan statues. The grounds are filled with flowers; when in blossom, the air is filled with their magnificent fragrance, specially that of magnolias. North of Xiangjie Si is Baozhu Dong, Precious Pearl Cave, on top of Cuiwei Hill. There are some pearl-shaped stones at the entrance, lending the cave its name. It is said that the monk Haiyou spent 40 years of his life here during the Qing Dynasty.

A path leads from the Baozhu Cave downhill to the opposite hill, Lushi Shan. From the foot of Lushi Shan, a path winds its way uphill. Hidden behind thick greenery, an old temple is visible — Zhengguo Si. It was built during the Tang Dynasty and later restored a number of times. There are some man-made hills on the grounds. A bronze bell from 1470 is in the first courtyard and

Tiaoyuan Ting pavilion further back. Mimo Yan, the Rock of the Mysterious Demon, can be seen to the north. It is a rock that has been so curiously shaped by nature that its lower end resembles the open mouth of a lion. Next to it is a cave, Lushi Dong, the Cave of Lushi. Legend has it that a monk named Lushi lived here during the Tang Dynasty. He had come to this place in a small boat, up the Yongding river from South China. Lushi had two students, the sons of the Dragon King. During a drought that lasted for many years, the people suffered terribly. With their master's permission, the two students turned into dragons and disappeared into the dried out springs. Three days later it started to rain. Since those days the hill has been called Lushi Shan and the cave Lushi Dong.

Fahai Si Temple 法海寺

The Buddhist temple Fahai Si is in a western suburb of Beijing, not far from Cuiwei Shan in the Western Hills. It is significant because of its murals. A stele on the temple grounds reports that it was built from 1439—1443. It originally included several halls, pavilions, a drum and a bell tower. Only Daxiong Baodian hall is of any interest today. Its inner walls are richly decorated with Ming murals.

These are partially damaged, but reveal a high level of artistry. The creators of these splendid murals would have remained unknown had not a pillar from 1444 been found which lists all the names of the painters and craftsmen involved. East of the big hall is a bronze bell, 2m high, decorated with Tibetan and Chinese characters. It is similar to the bell in Dazhong Si, Temple of the Great Bell.

Dajue Si Temple 大觉寺

Northwest of Beijing in the Western Hills stands an old Buddhist temple. In 1068 during the Liao Dynasty, it was built right into the mountain slope so that the spring water ran through the entire temple area. There are numerous small creeks, and the bubbling and splashing of water is heard everywhere, so that the temple was called Qingshui Yuan, Garden of Running Water. It was renewed in 1428 and renamed Dajue Si and was a popular destination for the Ming and Qing emperors. The temple is still well-known and popular because of its old magnolia trees.

The complex consists of nine halls. The three most important ones are: Tianwang Dian, Hall of the Celestial Kings,

Wuliangshoufo Dian, Hall of the Buddha of Longevity, and Longwang Dian, Hall of the Dragon King; all three date back to the Ming era. Most of the others were built in the Qing period. The bronze bells which can be seen inside the temple are also from the Qing period. A dagoba which is very similar to the White Dagoba in Beihai Park, stands in the upper part of the complex. A stele from the Liao Dynasty can still be seen. It documents the history of the construction of the temple. The writing can be read, but with difficulty. One can also admire an 800-year-old gingko tree. Its trunk has such a great diameter that it takes five people to embrace it.

Lugou Qiao, Marco Polo Bridge 芦沟桥

This bridge in the southwestern section of the city, spans the Yongding River. At first there was only a pontoon bridge here. In 1189, the Jin emperor Shizong ordered a stone bridge to be built which took three years to complete. In 1444 during the Ming era and later in 1698 under Kangxi's rule, it was restored after it had been partially destroyed by a flood.

Marco Polo passed this bridge in 1290. He described it so enthusiastically in his notes that from then on it was known in Europe as the Marco Polo Bridge. It is 235m long, 8m wide and made entirely of marble. Eleven arches support the structure. 280 parapets, each with a lion on top, decorate the balustrade.

Ming Shisan Ling, Thirteen Ming Tombs 明十三陵

On their trip to or from the Great Wall, most travelers take a side trip to the Ming Tombs.

The Ming Tombs are about 49km from the city's center in a 40km² basin-shaped valley, bounded by the Tianshou Shan hills to the east, west and north. The southern access to the valley is guarded by the Dragon and Tiger mountains. In earlier times, these mountains were connected by a wall so that the southern side was also closed. The only entrance was Dahong Men, the Great Red Gate.

In accordance with an old tradition, the emperors had their burial places prepared while they were still alive; that is why the third Ming emperor decided very early in his life to make this spot his last resting place. The site was chosen with the greatest of care and the assistance of geomancers. Local farmers were afforded no consideration; they were resettled. If they returned to their land, they were punished with death. This particular part of the country, one of the most beautiful around Beijing, with its lovely valley, hills, woods and many springs, met the expectations of the emperor and his officials.

The fact that the north was bounded by mountains was of special significance, for it held back the disastrous winds from the steppe as well as the bad spirits from the north.

Thirteen of the 16 Ming emperors and their wives and second wives are buried here. Unauthorized persons were not allowed to enter the grounds. A high wall linked to the Dahong Men, the Great Red Gate, sealed the area off towards the valley in the south; guards were posted on the hilltops. Those who were allowed to enter were not to come on horseback. Even the emperors had to dismount at the entrance. A great number of servants and thousands of workers took care of the entire complex.

Each burial site was divided into three parts:
1. the building where sacrifices were prepared and offered;
2. the stele tower where prayers were said;
3. the tumulus that covered the underground vault.

Two of the tombs have been partially restored:

Changling (10), tomb of the Yongle Emperor (reigned 1403 — 1424) and Dingling (4), tomb of the Wanli Emperor (reigned 1573 — 1620).

A tour of the tombs starts at the Shendao, Sacred Way (2). It leads for a distance of 6.4km from a marble gate in the south to the entrance of the Changling tomb. The marble gate with five arches dates from 1540. It is supported by six pillars and is 29m wide. The bas-relief carvings are of striking beauty. The next gate is some distance away: Dahong Men, the Great Red Gate, which is the proper entrance to the necropolis. Originally, there were doors in each of the three arches; the middle one was only opened when an emperor had to be carried to his final resting place. A stele pavilion follows with a 6.5-m-high marble stele from 1426 mounted on the back of a tortoise. The top of the stele is decorated with a dragon-relief. Its front side features an inscription of the Qianlong Emperor.

Next comes the Avenue of the Stone Sculptures. It has always been a custom to place stone sculptures outside imperial tombs. These sculptures date back to 1435. The formation of animals — some of them standing, others seated — is headed by one pillar on each side.

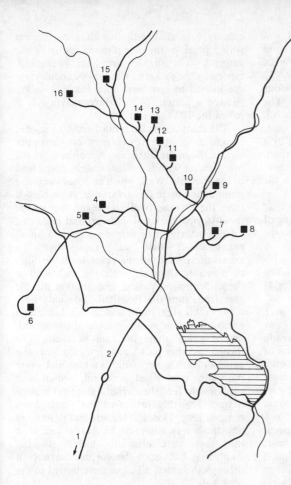

1. Road to Beijing
2. Sacred Way
3. Shisanling Reservoir
4. Dingling Tomb
5. Zhaoling Tomb
6. Siling Tomb
7. Yongling Tomb
8. Deling Tomb
9. Jingling Tomb
10. Changling Tomb
11. Xianling Tomb
12. Qingling Tomb
13. Yuling Tomb
14. Maoling Tomb
15. Tailing Tomb
16. Kangling Tomb

There are 12 pairs of animals: lions, camels, elephants and horses as well as the mythical beasts, *xiezhi* and *qilin*. Behind them are six pairs of statues of military and civilian dignitaries. At the end of the avenue, the triple-arched Longfeng Men, Dragon Phoenix Gate, is located. The Sacred Way leads to a bridge spanning the Shisanling Reservoir (3). It was built in 1958 to catch the huge amounts of water pouring down from the mountains after the summer rains. The dam, as part of the complex, was built within six months by 400,000 volunteers; among them were high-ranking military and party leaders, such as Mao Zedong, Zhou Enlai, Liu Shaoqi and Zhu De. The dam is 627m long, 29m high, 179m wide at the bottom and measures 7.5m at the top.

The reservoir is 20 times as big as Kunming Hu of the Summer Palace. It contributes to the water supply of the capital. Five big characters are written on the dam 'Shisanling Shuiku', Reservoir of the Thirteen Tombs. The characters were carved from marble modelled on a calligraphy of Mao Zedong.

Changling, the tomb of Emperor, Yongle lies further north. A path leads west toward the Dingling tomb. At that point, the entire complex becomes visible — the Tianshou hills and many evergreens, behind which the walls and the yellow-glazed tile roofs of the 13 tombs appear.

Changling, the tomb of the Yongle Emperor (10).

He reigned as the third emperor of the Ming Dynasty from 1403-1424. He was buried here with his wife, Empress Xu, who died in 1407. Archeological work has not been completed because the right access to the underground palace has not yet been found. The entire complex is enclosed by a wall. A big triple-arched gate leads into the first courtyard. To the right is a pavilion with a stele from the Qing Dynasty. On the other side stands Ling'en Men, Gate of Eminent Favors. Ling'en Dian, Hall of Eminent Favors, is in the next courtyard on a triple terrace made of white marble. Three flights of stairs lead up to it. The stairs in the middle are partitioned by a large stone slab with a phoenix and dragon motif on it. The magnificent roof, made of yellow-glazed tiles, is supported by 32 sandalwood columns from Yunnan. The four central columns are 1.17m in diameter. The ceiling inside the hall is especially beautiful. Another gate leads into the third courtyard. The opposite end of the yard is bordered by a square tower that is the base of a stele pavilion. The inscription on this stele reads: 'Tomb of the Emperor Chengzu' (a title given to the Yongle Emperor posthumously).

In front of the tower there is a marble altar with ritual objects on it. They are also made of marble. From this terrace one has access to the Precious Wall that encircles the tumulus.

Emperor Wanli, Empress Xiaoduan and his second wife Xiaojing are buried in the Dingling Tomb (4). The emperor ruled the empire for 48 years, from 1573-1620.

Empress Xiaoduan and the emperor both died in 1620. She had not given birth to any sons. His second wife, Xiaojing, had already died in 1612. She had two sons, the oldest of whom assumed the throne. He had his mother promoted to the rank of an Empress Dowager and laid her to rest in the Imperial tomb, too. She had originally been buried in the tomb reserved for imperial second wives.

In 1584, when he was only 22, Emperor Wanli had ordered the tombs built. Six years later they were completed. The costs amounted to 7.8 million ounces of silver.

The tomb was opened in 1956 and the secret of the Underground Palace disclosed. It is assumed that the lay out is typical for all Ming tombs. It was the first Imperial tomb that was officially opened in China.

Just behind the bridge over the reservoir, is a path leading west to the Dingling complex. Two more bridges follow. Behind the last one is a turtle bearing a stele on its back. It was once sheltered by a pavilion. The path leads past the stele to the entrance of the tomb. Like the Changling complex, it is encircled by a high wall. A big red gate leads into the first courtyard. On the other side there are flights of stairs leading on to a terrace that was once the site of a hall. The second courtyard is laid out in the same way: the terrace of the hall where sacrifices were formerly prepared and offered is still there. In the center of the third courtyard is Lingxing Gate, to the left and right are exhibition rooms where relics which were buried with the dead can be viewed. More than 3,000 artifacts made of gold, silver, jade and porcelain have been uncovered, including such precious objects as a golden filigree crown, decorated with two dragons playing with a pearl, or the blue phoenix crown of the empress. The dresses are also interesting, especially the jacket of Empress Xiaoduan: As she longed to give birth to a son, her jacket showed a pattern of little boys playing. It is called the 100-figure jacket.

The third courtyard is bordered by a square structure. A stele tower rises on its upper terrace. As in the Changling complex, there is a marble altar with five ritual vessels. Steps lead to the Precious Wall, which encloses the grave mound, and up to the stele tower. A path leads from the Precious Wall to the entrance of the three-storied vault, an underground palace of 1,100m². Steps take one down into a small ante-chamber that was built after the excavations. A triangular gate leads through the so-called Diamond Wall, the outer wall of the underground palace, and another marble gate leads into the first hall. No finds were made in this area. In the middle hall, behind an enclosure, stand three marble thrones with several small altars in front of them. The throne at the back was reserved for the emperor. At the very front is a blue and white porcelain vase filled with oil, which was supposed to feed the eternal flame, but lack of oxygen probably prevented the flame from burning long. Doors to the left and right open into the empty adjoining halls. It is reckoned that they were originally meant for the empresses, but since the coffins did not fit through the gates, all three were buried in the back hall.

The next door connects the middle hall with the third and last hall. Three coffins stand on a pedestal. The one in the middle is the biggest one and belongs to the emperor. To his left is the coffin of the first empress and to the right that of the emperor's second wife. Some of the 26 chests that once contained treasures, can be seen in the museums in the third courtyard.

Wanli Chang Cheng, The Wall of 10,000 Li (Great Wall) 万里长城

Most visitors to Beijing will get the chance to take a trip to the Great Wall. There are special daily tourist trains to Badaling, 85km north of Beijing. This pass was repaired in 1957. If one should get the chance to go by bus or by car, this is recommended, since one is not bound to a schedule and avoids the crowds which form on the wall after the train's arrival. The tour takes about two hours, no matter what means of transportation is used.

Juyong Pass is about 60km away. In former times it was of utmost strategic importance because it was a check point for the northern entrance to the capital. Today it is still renowned due to its 14th-century gate complex. Within the gates is Yuntai, the Cloud Terrace, a marble terrace from 1345. Originally, there were three towers on top of the terrace, but they were destroyed towards the end of the Yuan and the beginning of the Ming eras. Then the Tai'an temple was built, but it burned down in 1702; only its terrace survived. The semi-hexagonal arches, richly decorated with reliefs, are unusual. The gateway presents beautiful reliefs, for example a depiction of the Four Celestial Guardians and inscriptions in six different languages, including Mongolian, Uighurian, Tibetan and Sanskrit, which are proof of a strong Buddhist influence. Travelers arriving by train will discover a bronze statue of the railway engineer Zhan Tianyou (1860 — 1919) at Qinglongqiao station. After the Americans and Europeans had considered it unprofitable to build the Beijing-Baotou line through this steep mountain range, Zhan Tianyou realized this idea with the help of an ingenious plan. To express their appreciation, a monument was erected in his honor.

Once in Badaling, the right or the left part of the wall can be ascended; the left part is steeper and more difficult to traverse, but it is more attractive. Sturdy footwear is strongly recommended.

History of the Great Wall

The Wanli Chang Cheng, The Wall of 10,000 Li, is considered to be one of the most impressive structures in the world. It winds across deserts, valleys and mountains like a chain. But the Wall of 10,000 Li is not only 10,000 Li long (roughly 5,000km), it is in fact several hundred km longer. The section of the wall that can be visited today dates from the Ming Dynasty. The construction of walled defense systems, however, had been started long before. A vast number of walls exist in China, most of them severely damaged but still recognizable. Put together, they are about 50,000km long. Ruins can be found in all the northern provinces, as for example in Gansu, Ningxia, Shaanxi, Shanxi, Henan, Hebei and Liaoning. The building material used would suffice to build a road, 5m wide, that would reach around the world three times.

As early as the 7th century BC, construction on the wall began. After seven kingdoms had been created out of vassal states, armed conflicts occurred frequently; so it was necessary to fortify the national borders.

Single fortifications already existing, were linked and watch towers added. The first of these walls stretched out for a few 100km around the historical state of Chu in the south of present-day Henan Province.

In the 4th century BC, the northern kingdoms Yan, Zhao and Qin were often raided by nomadic tribes from the north. The kingdoms therefore saw the need for building a defense system on their northern border, the forerunner of the famous Great Wall. The King of Qin conquered all six states in 221 BC and unified China. He ordered his general Meng Tian and an army of 300,000 to drive the Huns from the area south of the Huanghe to the southwestern tip of today's Inner Mongolia. The emperor had the walls of the Yan, Zhao, and Qin kingdoms connected and extended. Thus the legendary Great Wall was created — as a fortification, not a border — to make the northern parts of the new empire secure.

All existing walls between the feudal states were torn down by order of the emperor to prevent separatist movements and another division of the empire into small states. Almost all of the following dynasties undertook repairs and improvements of the defense system. The most extensive work was carried out during the Han (206 BC — 220 AD) and the Ming (1368 — 1644) eras. During the Han Dynasty, the wall grew to a length of 10,000km, reaching from Liaoning to Xinjiang. During the Jin Dynasty (1115 — 1234), the rulers erected a 5,000-km-long wall as a protection against the Mongols. Ruins of that are still preserved in Heilongjiang and Inner Mongolia. The first emperor of the Ming Dynasty, Zhu Yuanzhang, ordered his marshal Xu Da to improve the fortifications and re-secure the passes. This project was more or less completed by 1500. The wall thus created, reached from the Yalu River in present-day Liaoning to the Qilian mountains in present-day Gansu, Qinghai, totalling 6,300km.

The pass at the eastern end was called Shanhai Guan, also know as First Pass on Earth, and at the western end, Jiayu Guan (1,773m above sea level). The entire complex was divided into nine commands, each subject to the Ministry of Defense and directly responsible to the emperor. Each command included several regions from which the terraces and fortresses were controlled. As soon as a garrison noticed hostile troop movements, it alarmed the nearest watch tower. The watch towers were either part of the wall or were placed as individual structures within sight of it.

During the day, alarm was raised by means of smoke signals, at night by fire. Smoke was produced by burning a mixture of wolf dung, sulfur and saltpeter. Shots were fired at the same time. The regulations of 1468 said that one column of smoke and one shot meant that the opposing army consisted of only 100 men, 2 columns and two shots meant 500 men, three columns and three shots, 1,000 men, and five columns and five shots stood for more than 5,000 men. Thus an alarm could be relayed over 500km within just a few hours.

The Great Wall varies in height and breadth due to the specific conditions of the terrain. On Badaling mountain, it is about 7 — 8m high and 6 — 7m wide. There are gateways built at intervals along its inside from which the walk on top of the wall, paved with a triple layer of bricks, can be reached. The wall is so wide that five horsemen or ten men can march along it abreast. Along the inner rim is a meter-high parapet. The battlements on the outside are double that size. Watch towers, two-storied buildings where the soldiers and arsenals were accommodated, are at intervals of 300 — 500 m with observation posts on top. Some of the towers had terraces from which the smoke and fire signals were given.

Soldiers and workmen, mainly peasants and prisoners who had to build the wall, came from all parts of China. Thousands of them lost their lives and were buried inside the wall. Dozens of legends and stories were told about the fate of the people banished to this place.

In those days, when the weapons used were mainly swords, spears, bows and arrows, the wall obviously represented a remarkably effective fortification that could hardly be conquered by the mobile nomadic tribes; the only way was to bribe single guards.

The wall was not only valuable as a defence system, it was also a significant thoroughfare. Great masses of people could cover long distances through rough areas comparatively fast and comfortably, whereas otherwise transportation would have caused considerable problems.

During the Qing Dynasty, the wall lost most of its significance. Due to the new political situation, the Manchu Emperor Kangxi (reigned 1662 — 1722) decided not to have the wall repaired and supplemented with new structures. The traditional confidence in fortifications was substituted by a policy that tried to gain control of the northern nomads by means of unification and appeasement. So the wall gradually fell victim to erosion by wind and water and to destruction by man, as it afforded enormous amounts of most-welcome building materials.

Zhoukoudian, Museum of Peking Man
周口店猿人遗址

On December 2, 1929, the Chinese anthropologist Pei Wenzhong and his excavation team discovered the skull bone of a man who had lived in this area 500,000 years ago. The find was made at Longgu Shan, Dragon Bone Hill, near the city of Zhoukoudian. Later, this species of man was called *Homo erectus pekinensis*, Peking man, for short.

In 1953, a museum was established at the Longgu Shan and a new exhibition hall was added in 1972. The museum complex consists of two parts, the exhibition hall and the remains of the cave of Peking man. The finds of Dragon Bone Hill as well as numerous other fossil finds from China are on display in the exhibition hall. The three departments are devoted to the following topics: origins of human life in general, life of the Peking man, and the development and achievements of paleoanthropology and vertebrate paleontology in China.

Longgu Shan, Dragon Bone Hill, is approximately 50km southwest of Beijing. The huge cave of Peking man lies at the northern foot of the mountain. It was filled with a layer of different sediments, 40m thick. Most informative were the four layers of ash, which indicate that fire was used in those times. The skull bone was found in the lowest layer of ash; in 1936, three others were discovered.

The thickest layer in the upper part of the sediments measured 6m. Several stone tools as well as fragments of bats and rats were found here.

Further uphill, the 18,000-year-old cave of a *Homo sapiens* was found. To date, the remains of eight people have been unearthed, among them, three complete skull bones. Fragments of a skeleton as well as bone and stone implements, jewelry and a 5-cm-long bone sewing needle were found in one grave. The needle seems to prove that the people made their clothes from animal skins.

The first to make those interesting finds in this area were workers in the limestone quarries. They occasionally came across fossils, which they called dragon bones, thus the name of the hill. In 1923, two human teeth were found and a permanent molar in 1927. Anthropologists think the latter comes from a species of man that has not yet been identified. Systematic excavations were begun in 1927.

From 1927 — 1937, numerous fossil finds were made, most of which, however, disappeared in Taiwan and the United States before 1949. After 1949, more extensive excavations were undertaken. In all, the remains of 40 persons have been discovered in the cave of Peking man.

Shopping

Youyi Shangdian — Friendship Store
(Jianguomenwai, extension of Chang'anjie in the eastern part of the city)

This is the largest Friendship store in China. Spacious sales departments on three floors offer a variety of goods, ranging from furniture, carpets, handicraft articles to tea and cigarettes. Fresh food is sold in a food department, and a small department offers flowers and plants.

The large selection of fabrics, especially silk, is quite attractive. The store's own tailoring is much valued by foreigners.

One of the Friendship Store's special services is the wrapping and sending of goods to foreign countries — even goods not bought in the store are shipped. This service is of particular interest to foreigners who are staying in Beijing for a longer period of time. It costs about RMB 300 *yuan* per m³.

The Friendship Store is open from 9:00 a.m. to 7:00 p.m. An exchange office and a taxi service are further convenient institutions.
Wangfujing, Beijing's main shopping street, leads north from Dongchang'anjie past the new wing of the Beijing Hotel. A shopping tour along this street can be very interesting, but also rather tiring, as it is always crowded.

Most shops are on the eastern side of the street. The most important ones are: the Xinhua bookstore, a handicraft department store and the large Dongfeng Shichang market, where many stores are accommodated under one roof. It cannot be seen from the street and is reached through a gateway. On the opposite side is the biggest department store in Beijing.
Chongwenmen Dajie and **Dongdan Shichang** market are between the Beijing Hotel and the train station.
Qianmen Dajie and its side streets is an interesting shopping area, south of Tian'anmen Square. In old days here was the district for theatres, story and fortune tellers and restaurants: a center of amusement for ordinary people. Today here are a variety of stores: at No. 80 is an antique store, at No. 149, a Jingdezhen porcelain store, at No. 208 a carpet

store. Some stores are more than 200 years old, for example the Liubiju store, whose pickled vegetables are considered to be a delicacy. It opened in 1530 as a bar. The Tongrentang drugstore in Dazhalan is known for its traditional Chinese drugs. It once supplied the Imperial drugstore. Medicinal herbs are mixed here according to old recipes. An information center gives advice on how to treat diseases. Foreigners and Chinese alike value the Neiliangsheng shoe store. Its specialty is hand-made cloth shoes. The butcher Yueshengzhai sells spiced, boiled mutton and beef that is very popular with the people of Beijing. Special attractions of this quarter are some department store facades from the Republican era.
Liulichangjie lane, the traditional center of the antique trade, lies in Xuanwu district in the southern section of the city. It crosses Nanxihuajie street and runs westward towards Xuanwumenwai Dajie and eastward towards Qianmen Dajie.

Originally, it was the site of the Imperial Ceramic Tiles Workshop. At the beginning of the Ming Dynasty, they produced Liuliwa, ceramic tiles, for the construction of palaces which gave the street its name. After the end of the Ming Dynasty, booksellers, calligraphers, printers and bookbinders gradually settled here. Printing shops and small stores were established. Everything a scholar needed could be found on this street: books, new and secondhand, ink, ink stones, brushes, paper and seals. A visit to Liulichang is an experience that should not be missed even today. Many prefer to do their shopping in the lane's small stores rather than in the big ones on Wangfujing. However, even here the old houses have to give way to new buildings, so that the charm of the old Liulichang has mostly been lost. Today antique stores predominate. The visitor can purchase porcelain, jewelry, stone rubbings, paintings mounted on scrolls, lanterns and secondhand books. A seal store and a printer's workshop are noteworthy. At No. 60 Liulichang, seals are made to order. The client can choose from a wide selection and have his name engraved in English or Chinese. Names are translated into Chinese here, too. The type of calligraphy must also be chosen. Cutting the seals takes about two days, but considering that the Beijing seal cutters have the best reputation of all, this is not a long wait.

The Rongbaozhai Studio at No. 19 is known in China and abroad. One can buy paintings, originals and reproductions, and can have paintings mounted on various materials. They sell artist's materials such as ink, ink and rubbing stones, brushes and paper. The walls of the sales rooms are decorated with the works of contemporary artists and reproductions. The actual workshop is in the courtyard. It looks back on a tradition of more than 200 years and specializes in wood-block prints.

At No. 24 there is an exchange office of the Bank of China which is open from 9:00 a.m. to 12:30 p.m. and from 2:30 p.m. to 6:30 p.m.

Hotels and Guest Houses

Hotels and guest houses of deluxe-level

Jianguo Fandian 建国饭店
Jianguomenwai Dajie, tel. 59 36 61, telex 2 24 39
At present, this hotel is one of the most modern and expensive in Beijing. It is situated near the Friendship Store and the legation quarter. It is a result of cooperation between foreign firms and the Chinese authorities. It has restaurants, a bar, a cafe, banquet halls, etc. as well as services and stores. The service is excellent. Management: Peninsula Group

Diaoyutai Binguan 钓鱼台宾馆
Sanlihelu, tel. 86 61 52
One of the most elegant and expensive hotels in the city; official and well-to-do guests stay here.

Zhuyuan Binguan 竹园宾馆
Xiaoshiqiao 24, Jiuguloulu, near the Drum Tower, tel 44 46 61
Zhuyuan Binguan, once the residence of a Qing Dynasty's high official, consists of a small complex of comfortable guesthouses with pleasant and quiet gardens.

Changcheng Fandian, Great Wall Hotel
长城饭店
Donghuanbeilu, Chaoyang district, near the Exhibition Hall of Agriculture, tel. 50 55 66, telex 2 00 45
One of the most modern and most expensive hotels in Beijing. It is located in the east of the city, in Chaoyang district, approximately thirty minutes by car from the center.

Jinglun (Beijing-Toronto) Hotel, 京伦饭店
Jianguomenwai Dajie 3 tel. 50 22 66, telex 21 00 11, 21 00 12

Xiangshan Fandian 香山饭店
Xiangshan Gongyuan, tel. 28 54 91
Situated in the lovely surroundings of the Western Hills; approximately 60 minutes by car from the center.

This hotel was designed by the Chinese-American architect I.M.Pei.

Expensive and moderately priced hotels and guest houses

Beijing Fandian 北京饭店
Dongchang'anjie,
tel. 55 83 31, 55 22 31, telex 2 24 27
Centrally located, near Wangfujing shopping street. The Beijing Fandian is one of the most popular and best-known hotels in Beijing. It consists of older west and middle wings and a modern east wing with 17 floors. There are various stores on the ground floor (liquor, tobacco, films, cosmetics, souvenirs, antiques, foreign newspapers and magazines, books, etc.) and services (bank, post office, barbershop). The hotel offers restaurants with excellent Chinese and Western cuisine. Two cafes on the ground floor are popular meeting places.

Lido Fandian 丽都饭店
Jichanglu, Jiangtailu, Dongjiao,
tel. 50 66 88, telex 2 26 18
Modern hotel near the airport.
Management: Holiday Inn

Yanjing Fandian 燕京饭店
Fuxingmen Dajie, tel. 86 87 21, telex 2 00 28
Modern hotel, built in 1981, with comfortably furnished rooms, several restaurants and the usual services.

Xiyuan Fandian 西苑饭店
Erligou, tel. 89 07 21, telex 2 28 35
Pleasant, quiet hotel in the western part of the city, near the Trade Center for Light Industry. It consists of an older complex and a new high-rise. Good meals; Xinjiang specialties.

Huadu Fandian 华都饭店
Xinlinanlu 8,
tel. 47 54 31, telex 2 20 28
Modern hotel, located in the northeast of the city, near the Great Wall Hotel. Regular services; stands and restaurants (Chinese and Western cuisine) are provided.

Qianmen Fandian 前门饭店
Yong'anlu, tel. 33 87 31, 33 87 33
Close to the street where antiques are sold, Liulichang, at the edge of the Old City, fairly old building.

Youyi Binguan 友谊宾馆
Xizhimenwai Baishiqiaolu, tel. 89 06 21
Hotel and guest house in the northwestern

section of the city; mainly for foreigners residing in Beijing for a longer period of time. Besides the regular services, recreation facilities such as tennis courts and a swimming pool deserve special mention.

Huaqiao Dasha 华侨大厦
Wangfujing Dajie 2, tel. 55 88 51
Mostly overseas Chinese stay at this hotel. A branch of the Lüxingshe travel agency is located here.

Xinqiao Fandian 新侨饭店
Dongjiaominxiang, tel. 55 77 31
Southeast of Tian'anmen; fairly central location; in former legation quarter. The Lüxingshe travel agency is opposite the hotel. Stands and restaurants (Chinese and Western cuisine) are provided.

Heping Binguan 和平宾馆
Dongsinan Dajie, Jinyuhutong 4, tel. 55 88 41
Centrally located, near Wangfujing shopping street. The hotel offers the usual services, stands and restaurants.

Dongfang Binguan 东方宾馆
Wanminglu 11, tel. 33 14 36
Pleasant small guest house for Chinese and Western visitors. Good restaurant.

Minzu Fandian 民族饭店
Fuxingmennei 51, tel. 66 85 41
Next to the Nationalities' Cultural Palace; central location. Restaurant with good Chinese cuisine.

Low-cost hotels and guest houses

Beiwei Fandian 北纬饭店
Xijinglu 13, tel. 33 86 31
Near Taoranting Gongyuan park grounds. A simple hotel that is among the most reasonable in Beijing.

Chongwenmen Fandian 崇文门饭店
Chongwenmenwai Dajie 2, tel. 75 71 81
houses the branch office of Lüxingshe

Xuanwumen Fandian 宣武门饭店
Xuanwumenwai Dajie, tel. 34 19 30
These two guest houses cater mainly to overseas Chinese and offer very reasonable lodging. Meals in their restaurants are very good and reasonably priced.

Guanghua Fandian 光华饭店
Donghuanbeilu, near the legation quarter and Friendship Store. This hotel is one of the cheapest in Beijing.

Yanxiang Fandian 燕翔饭店
Jiangtailu 2, Chaoyang district, tel. 47 11 31

Huaqiao Fandian 华侨饭店
Beixinqiao Ertiao, tel. 44 12 31
In Beijing demand for hotel rooms is still higher than supply. Therefore additional hotels are presently being planned and built.

Peking Specialty and Restaurants

Lovers of Chinese cuisine will be fully satisfied with their stay in Beijing. Situated in the north, the city offers Mongolian and Muslim specialties (lamb and mutton) as well as dishes from the former Imperial menu and cuisine from various provinces. In general, plenty of oil and fat are used for cooking in the dry north. The dishes are heavier than in the south. A specialty of the city are steamed, boiled or fried dumplings, with or without minced meat filling, such as *mantou*, *jiaozi*, *baozi*, *guotie* etc. Undoubtedly, the most famous dish is Beijing *Kaoya*, Peking duck, originally a specialty of the Mongolian cuisine. The special part of Peking duck is its skin. It is cut in slices and served as the main course. One or more pieces of the crisp skin are placed, together with leeks on a thin crepe, then coated with a thick soy paste and rolled up and eaten. Peking ducks are bred in the people's communes around Beijing. They are rather complicated to prepare properly and it takes an experienced chef to do it. The most important part of the procedure is inflating the duck with air in order to separate the skin from the meat. After a two-day drying process, the duck is roasted over an open fire. It is an old custom that the chef first presents the prepared duck to his guests and then carves it.

A big meal in a special Peking duck restaurant consists of a variety of duck dishes, including liver, tongue, heart, webs, broth, etc.

There are several hundred restaurants in Beijing, a few will be listed here. There is always a big run on them. It is advisable to make reservations one or two days in advance.

The restaurants are usually open from 10:30 a.m. to 1:30/2:00 p.m. and from 4:30/5:00 to 7:30/8:00 p.m.

Peking Duck Restaurants

Quanjude Kaoya Dian
Qianmenxi Dajie 24, tel. 75 13 79

Famous restaurant with large rooms.
Branch:
Shuaifuyuan 13, tel. 55 33 10

Beijing Kaoya Dian
Hepingmen, tel. 33 44 22, 33 80 31
This restaurant can accommodate 2,500. Meals are excellent but expensive.

Pianyi Fang
Chongwenmenwai Dajie 2, tel. 75 05 05
This restaurant is considered to be one of the best of its kind. In addition to the regular duck specialties, it offers dishes from Shandong Province and various other dishes.

Imperial Cuisine

Fangshan Fanzhuang
Beihai Gongyuan Park, tel. 44 25 73
The Fangshan is counted among the best restaurants in Beijing. Early reservations, several days in advance if possible, are advisable.

Tingli Guan Canting
Yihe Yuan (Summer Palace), tel. 28 39 55, 28 12 76
The Tingli Guan restaurant is located in the idyllic surroundings of the Summer Palace.

Other Specialty Restaurants

Beijing Sucai Canting, Beijing Vegetarian Restaurant
Xuanwumennei 74, tel. 33 42 96
Good vegetarian restaurant.

Duyichu Shaomai Guan
Qianmen Dajie 36, tel. 75 15 55
This restaurant was founded as early as 1738. It specializes in *shaomai*, dumplings filled with pork and steamed in bamboo racks.

Shaguo Ju Fanzhuang
Xisinan Dajie 60, tel. 66 11 26
Specialty: pork dishes

Shanxi Xiaomian Guan
Dong'anmen Dajie 16
This small, popular restaurant specializes in noodles.

Qingfeng Baozi Pu
Chang'anxi Dajie 122
Specialty of the house: steamed dumplings.

Beijing Fandian
Dongchang'anjie, tel. 50 77 66

One of the hotel's restaurants is located in the west wing, 7th floor. It offers northern specialties.

Hunan Cuisine

Xiangshu Canting
Wangfujing Dajie, Dongfeng Shichang, tel. 55 83 51, 55 47 54
A popular restaurant that is always crowded.

Jiangsu Cuisine

Jiangsu Canting
Dongsibei Dajie 172, tel. 44 26 10

Guangdong (Canton) Cuisine

Guangdong Canting
Xizhimenwai Dajie (south of the zoo), tel. 89 48 81
As in many other restaurants, there is a big dining room for Chinese guests. The meals are listed on boards on the wall. Quiet rooms are reserved for foreign visitors.

Mongolian and Muslim Specialties

Hongbin Lou Fanzhuang
Xichang'anjie 82, tel. 33 64 61
Lamb specialties of the Hui minority are offered. This restaurant looks back on a tradition of almost 100 years. Not only lamb specialties but also excellently prepared Peking duck are served.

Kaorou Ji
Shishaqianhai Dongyan 14, tel. 44 59 21
A small, excellent restaurant amidst old, narrow lanes north of Beihai Park. A specialty of the house is lamb on the spit, which the guest may grill himself on the first floor in the summer.

Minzu Wenhua Gong
Fuxingmennei Dajie, tel. 66 87 61
Restaurant in the Nationalities' Cultural Palace.
There is a wide range of tasty meals. The specialty of the house is a Mongolian fire pot.

Minzu Fanzhuang
Donghuamen 16, tel. 55 00 69
A reasonably-priced, popular restaurant, said to prepare the best Mongolian fire pot. A variety of other excellent dishes is also offered.

Donglaishun Fanzhuang
Wangfujing, Jingyuhutong Xikou 16, tel.

55 00 69

The specialty of the house is a Mongolian fire pot with finely-sliced mutton (on the second floor). Dumplings are served on the first floor.

Shandong Cuisine

Cuihua Lou Fanzhuang
Wangfujing Dajie 60, tel. 55 45 81

Fengze Yuan Fanzhuang
Zhushikouxi Dajie 83, tel. 33 28 28

The Fengze Yuan is one of the city's best-known restaurants. The fish dishes are excellent. Since it is always crowded, reservations are necessary.

Haidian Canting
Haidiannan Dajie, tel. 28 10 48

Tonghe Ju Fanzhuang
Xisinan Dajie 3, tel. 66 09 25

Shanghai Cuisine

Laozhengxing Canguan
Qianmen Dajie 46, tel. 75 26 86, 75 09 12

Songjiang Fanguan
Taijichanglu 10, tel. 55 52 22

Huaiyang Fanguan
Xidanbeilu 217, tel. 66 05 21

Zhenjiang Fanguan
Chang'anxi Dajie, tel. 66 21 15

Shanxi Cuisine

Jinyang
Zhushikouxi Dajie 241, tel. 33 16 69, 33 35 96

Among the specialties are chicken, duck, sea cucumber and prawns.

Sichuan Cuisine

Emei Jiujia
Yuetanbeijie, tel. 86 30 68

Meals are inexpensive and good. Drinks are available at the bar (self-service).

Sichuan Fandian
Rongxianhutong 51, tel. 33 63 56

The Sichuan Fandian was once considered the favorite restaurant of Deng Xiaoping and the best-known Sichuan restaurant in the North of China. The quality of the meals varies from time to time. The exterior is in-

teresting. The structure is a former villa of a Qing official. Reservations are necessary because it is always crowded.

Beijing Fandian
Dongchang'anjie

A large restaurant on the ground floor of the middle wing of Beijing Hotel offers a variety of excellent Sichuan specialties.

Lili Fanguan
Qianmen Dajie 30, tel. 75 23 10

One of the best Sichuan restaurants of the city.

Xinjiang Cuisine

Xiyuan Canting (in Xiyuan Hotel)
Erligou, tel. 89 41 95

Yunnan and Fujian Cuisine

Kangle Canting
Andingmennei Dajie 259, tel. 44 38 84

Good meals; noodles are one of the specialties.

Western Cuisine

Beijing Zhanlanguan Canting
Beijing Exhibition Hall Restaurant, Xizhimenwai Dajie, (near the zoo), tel. 89 37 13

The restaurant specializes in Russian cuisine. The exhibition hall was originally built and used by Russians.

Guoji Julebu
International Club, Jianguomenwai Dajie (next to the Friendship Store), tel. 52 21 88

Useful Addresses

Travel agency

Zhongguo Lüxingshe
Main office: Dongjiaominxiang 8, tel. 55 70 70, 55 27 01
Branch: Qianmendong Dajie 2, tel. 75 71 81-645
Chongwenmen Hotel

Huaqiao Lüxingshe (Overseas Chinese)
Main office: Dongjiaominxiang 8, tel. 55 60 61, 55 27 01
Branch: Qianmendong Dajie 2, tel. 55 48 79
Chongwenmen Hotel

Guoji Lüxingshe, CITS
Main office: Dongchang'anjie 6, (Opposite Beijing Hotel), tel. 55 10 31; European

Division tel. 55 31 21; American & Oceanic Division 55 77 58
Beijing branch: Qiandong Dajie 2, tel. 75 71 81, 75 52 72, Rm. 1302 Chongwenmen Hotel, Rm. 5102 Huadu Hotel

Gong'an Ju, Public Security Bureau
Beichizi Dajie 85, tel. 55 31 02

Police Emergency: tel. 110

Hospital (for foreigners): Shoudu Yiyuan
Wangfujing, tel. 55 37 31
Open 8:00 am to 11:30 am, 1:30 pm to 5:30 pm, closed on Saturday afternoons and Sundays.

Post and Communications:

Most of the tourist hotels have post offices. Parcels have to be taken to the
International Post Office, Yong'anlu 121, Tianqiao, tel. 33 77 17
Express Mail Service: International Post and Telecommunication Service, Dongdanbei Dajie 23, tel. 33 66 21
Post from abroad can be received at your hotel, your embassy or Poste Restante, Beijing, 121 Yong'anlu, International Post Office.
Telephone: Local and long distance calls can be made from your hotel room.
Information:　local calls: 114
　　　　　　　long distance calls (China): 113
　　　　　　　(international): 116, 33 74 31
Telegraph and telex: in your hotel or Xichang'anjie, tel. 66 49 00, 66 48 19

Bank of China, Zhongguo Yinhang:

Main office: Xijiaominxiang 17, tel. 33 85 21
Branch: Dong'anmen Dajie 19, tel. 55 62 14
　　　　Liulichangxijie, tel. 33 10 83
Open 9:00 to 12:00 am, 1:00 to 4:00 pm, closed on Saturday afternoons.

The Bank of China has exchange offices at the following places: Beijing Fandian (Peking Hotel), airport, Friendship Store, Minzu Fandian Hotel, Huaqiao Dasha, Qianmen Fandian, Xinqiao Fandian, Youyi Binguan, etc.

Airlines: (see page 97)

Airport: tel. 55 83 41, 52 29 31, 52 32 31.

Train station: Jianguomennei Dajie, tel. 55 48 66 (Ticket Office)
Ticket reservations at the CITS lüxıngshe: Qianmendong Dajie 2, tel. 75 52 72

Taxis

Main office: tel. 55 74 61, 86 36 61, 55 76 61
Beijing Fandian, tel. 55 62 62
Friendship Store, tel. 59 35 31-80
Import and Export Building, tel. Erligou 82 13 72
International Club, tel. 59 38 88, 59 27 82
Minzu Fandian, tel. 66 46 48, 66 85 41-486
Huaqiao Dasha, tel. 55 21 04
Heping Binguan, tel. 55 21 04
Qianmen Fandian, tel. 33 87 31-394
Sanlitun Diplomatic Quarter, tel. 52 10 92, 52 10 44
Xinqiao Fandian, tel. 55 00 61, 55 77 31-745
Youyi Binguan, tel. 89 06 21

Tianjin 天津市
(Centrally administered municipality)

Tianjin lies about 130 km southeast of Beijing (two hours by train). It is the largest trading and industrial center of the North. It is one of the three centrally administered municipalities, the others being Shanghai and Beijing. The province-level municipality covers an area of 11,300 km². It has a total population of 7.8 million; 4.8 million live in the inner city. Tianjin is the third largest city in China. Approximately 1.4 million of the inhabitants belong to minority groups, such as the Hui, Manchus, Mongols and Koreans.

Despite its proximity to the sea, Tianjin has a continental climate with dry, severe winters and hot summers, yielding 70% of the annual precipitation. The port of Tianjin is frozen over for about 80 days during the winter months.

Tianjin is an important railway and shipping center, for the city is the junction of various lines, for example Beijing-Shanghai; in addition, five navigable tributaries of the Haihe river meet here. The Haihe, along the banks of which the city stretches for more than 16 km, has frequently caused heavy flooding in the past. This danger has been overcome thanks to various dike construction projects. In 1952, a new port was completed north of the mouth of the Haihe. It is navigable for ships up to 10,000 gross registered tons. The port was further expanded in 1976.

Today the city has two well-known universities, Nankai and Beiyang.

The terrible earthquake of 1976 also hit Tianjin, though not as heavily as Tangshan. The city still carries some scars of this catastrophe.

History

Archeological finds indicate that first settlements in the Tianjin area must already have existed during the Warring States Period. Since the Jin and Yuan eras, Tianjin has been a garrison town. At that time it was called Zhigu. It rapidly developed into a commercial center and a port, a market for grain and other foodstuffs from Central and South China. The rulers of the Yuan Dynasty soon recognized the value of this port, established more warehouses and improved the harbor facilities. During the Ming Dynasty it was called Tianjin Wei.

In 1425, a mighty city wall was constructed. During the Qing Dynasty, Tianjin, favored by its location on the Grand Canal, achieved its position as the leading commercial center of North China. During the mid-19th century, trade declined slowly, because the European nations unremittingly pressed their demands for privileges. After two years of negotiations with the French and British governments, the Chinese government had no choice but to accept the Treaty of Tianjin in 1858, authorizing the establishment of British and French concessions. But the city rejected the conditions of the treaty. For this reason, in 1860, foreign governments saw themselves justified in shelling Tianjin and landing troops there. The Chinese government then declared Tianjin an open trading port: The city was now divided into concessions. This forced opening of trade relations by the foreign powers created much hatred. Ten years after the establishment of the first concession, heavy conflicts erupted. In 1900, in connection with the Boxer Rebellion, the French and the British occupied the city.

Nevertheless, Tianjin became China's second commercial center. The profitable export trade established firms and banks as a new force which influenced the country's policy. Many houses in the Western architectural style were built and gave the Chinese city an atypical appearance. This has remained so until today; sometimes the visitor will even forget that he is still in China. During the Sino-Japanese War (1937 — 45), Tianjin was occupied by the Japanese. After 1949, it grew into an industrial town, the most important one, next to Shanghai. Heavy industry dominates, but the light, textile, and chemical industries are also of importance.

Places of Interest

Shuishang Gongyuan, Park on the Water 水上公园

This nice park, the largest in Tianjin, is located in the southern part of the city. It features a zoo, a theater, pavilions and a swimming pool.

Qingzhen Dasi, Grand Mosque 清真大寺
Dafenglu

The Grand Mosque is the biggest and oldest mosque in Tianjin. It was built in 1644 in traditional Chinese style.

Zhongshan Park 中山公园

This park is the oldest one in Tianjin. It was built in 1905 and named Zhongshan Park in memory of Dr. Sun Yat-sen (Sun Zhongshan).

Dabei Yuan, Temple of Grand Mercy 大悲园
Tianweilu 26

Dabei Yuan is the biggest Buddhist temple in Tianjin. It was built in 1656.

Art Museum 艺术博物馆

The museum of art in 77 Jiefangbeilu was established in 1957. It contains an interesting collection of paintings from the Yuan to the Qing dynasty.

Tianjin boasts a long tradition of carpet production. Next to Beijing and the centers in West China, Tianjin today is considered one of the most important carpet producers of the country. In the *First Carpet Factory* through which foreign visitors are often led, 1,400 workers are employed. Most of Tianjin's carpets are exported.

Trip to the district capital Jixian, east of Beijing.

Dule Si Temple 蓟县独乐寺

Built during the Tang era, it was renewed in 984. It is one of the oldest wooden structures in China. The bracket systems, beams, roofs and chiweis (see page 67) are remarkable features. The most important structure in this temple is Guanyin Ge hall, 23 m high. Despite many earthquakes, it has remained undamaged. Inside the hall there is a Guanyin sculpture. This one, as well as the others, dates from the 10th century. The walls were painted during the Ming era.

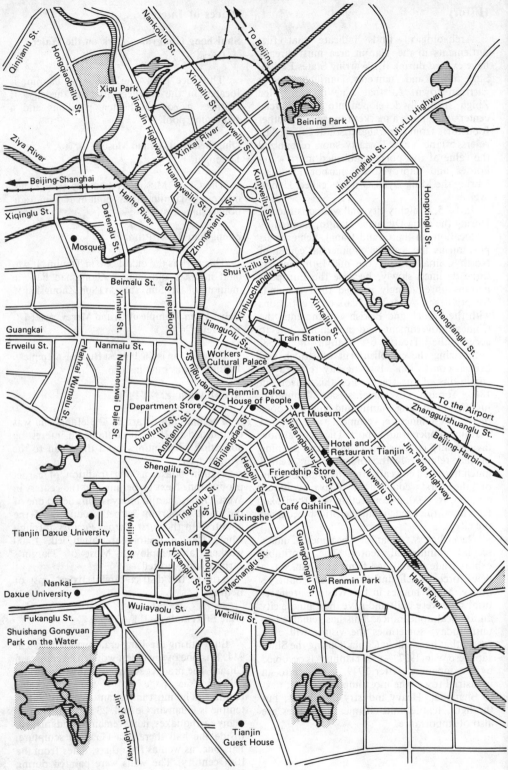

Map of Tianjin

Panshan Mountains 蓟县盘山

Situated 12 km northwest of Jixian, they can be reached by car directly from Beijing or Tianjin. The mountains can be divided into three sections. The upper part is renowned for its great pines, the middle one for its beautiful rocks, the lower one for its gorges, waterfalls and creeks. With its temples, pagodas and the five main peaks, the Panshan mountains offer many sights to see.

Since 1980, intensive efforts have been made to restore historically interesting complexes.

Inspired by the beauty of the scenery, the well-known general Li Jing of the Tang era supposedly forfeited his office to lead the life of a monk in Wansong Si monastery.

Hotels

Youyi Binguan, 友谊宾馆 Shenglilu, Hebeilukou, tel. 3 56 63, 3 56 03

Tianjin Fandian, 天津饭店 Jiefangbeilu 219, tel. 3 24 93, 3 43 25, 3 11 14

Tianjin Binguan, 天津宾馆 Youyilu, tel. 3 96 13

Yingbin Binguan, Machangdao 337, tel. 2 40 10

Tianjin Diyi Fandian, 天津第一饭店 Hotel No. 1, Jiefangbeilu 198, tel. 3 64 38

Restaurants

Qishilin Canting, Café Kiessling, Zhejianglu 33, tel. 3 20 20
Café Kiessling is a hangover from the German past. They usually stick to the recipes of the former bakers and chefs, and therefore offer a number of Western dishes and specialties.

Dengyinglou Canting, Binjiangdao 94, tel. 2 35 94, 2 37 57
Shandong cuisine

Dining-Hall at Friendship Club, Youyi Julebu Canting, Machang Dao 268, tel. 3 24 65
Local flavour

Hongqiao Fanzhuang, Beimenwai Dajie 62, tel. 3 20 20, 5 08 37

Kaoya Dian, Liaoninglu 144, tel. 2 33 35, 2 32 34
Peking duck restaurant

Hongye Fanguan, Huazhonglu, tel. 2 27 10

Cantonese cuisine

Tianheju Fanzhuang, Changchundao 189, tel. 2 51 42
Sichuan and Jiangsu cuisine

Tianjin Baozi Pu, Shandonglu 97, tel. 2 32 77
Baozi restaurant; Baozi are filled dumplings which are steam-cooked.

Yanchunlou Fanzhuang, Rongjijie 22, tel. 2 27 61
Muslim cuisine

Sucai Guan, Binjiangdao, tel. 2 51 42
Vegetarian restaurant

Shopping

Friendship Store, Zhangdedao 2

Quanye Bazaar, Hepinglu 353

Department store, Hepinglu 226

Arts and crafts shop, Hepinglu 234

Antique shop, Hepinglu 263

Yilinge Antiques shop, Liaoninglu 175

Travel agency

Guoji Lüxingshe CITS, Chongqingdao 55, tel. 3 48 81. For independent travelers there is a service desk at Youyi Binguan, tel. 3 72 44.

Zhongguo Lüxingshe and **Huaqiao Lüxingshe,** Jiefangbeilu 198, tel. 3 60 40, 3 64 38

Gong'an Ju, Public Security Bureau, Tangshandao 28, tel. 3 38 53

CAAC flight reservations, Hepinglu 290, tel. 2 40 45

Bank of China, Jiefangbeilu 80, tel. 3 15 59, 3 46 00

Post office, Binjiangdao 141, tel. 3 00 92. Jiefangbeilu 153, tel. 3 38 56

Hebei Province 河北省

Area: ca. 180,000 km²/Population: ca. 53 million, among those ca. 500,000 Hui and 10,000 Mongols/Capital: Shijiazhuang

Hebei, a province in North China, geographically consists of two almost equal sections: the eastern one is shaped by the northern part of the North China Plain, the western one by mountain ranges with an average elevation around 1,500 m, among which the Taihang Shan mountains are the most important.

Since ancient times, Hebei Province's main problem has been the regulation of the rivers, for the erosion of the western mountainous areas caused by the century-old destruction of wooded areas and the heavy rainfalls of the summer months wash enormous amounts of silt into the rivers of the Shanxi Plateau and the Taihang Shan. The silt is deposited in the Hebei Plain and is liable to cause big floods. Due to the climatic conditions there are severe dry winters and very hot summers with rainfall in July and August, which can, however, be very unreliable. The province often experienced disastrous periods of drought and floods. That is why from 1949 onward the government undertook gigantic projects for water control, for example the building of several reservoirs to regulate the Haihe river system and to irrigate the fields, as well as the construction of canals and dams. Thanks to these measures, agriculture experienced an enormous boom. Today Hebei is the supplier of more than a quarter of China's cotton.

Other important agricultural products are wheat, corn, millet, peanuts, sweet potatoes and soy beans.

Historically speaking, the only importance Hebei ever had from the Han Dynasty up to the 11th century was as a border region. Not before the foreign rule of the Liao, Jin and Yuan was the political center shifted to North China. The rulers of the Yuan Dynasty made Beijing the capital of the Chinese empire. During the Ming and Qing dynasties, too, Hebei remained the center of the empire.

After the rise in the political significance of the North, trade and crafts began to flourish in Hebei. With the second half of the 19th century, the establishment of industrial plants began. Today the centers of industry are in Shijiazhuang, Tangshan, Handan, and Qinhuangdao. Hebei possesses mineral wealth, such as coal and iron ore. Beside this, Hebei produces a quarter of China's salt, gained from the salt swamps at the coast of the gulf of Bohai.

Shijiazhuang 石家庄市

Shijiazhuang, the capital of Hebei, lies in the west of the province at the foot of the Taihang Shan mountains. Its population is about 900,000. Shijiazhuang is an important

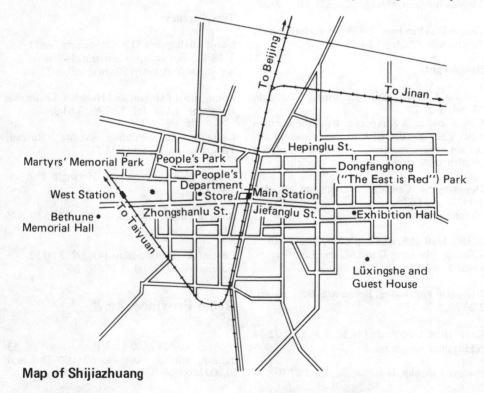

Map of Shijiazhuang

railway junction for the Beijing-Guangzhou and Taiyuan (Shanxi)-Dezhou (Shandong) lines.

Although the history of the settlement of the area can be traced back to the Western Han Dynasty, at the beginning of the century, Shijiazhuang was just a small village of 500-600 inhabitants. The completion of the Beijing-Hankou (Wuhan) railway line in 1905 changed the situation abruptly. Today Shijiazhuang is a rising industrial city, chiefly due to its textile industry. In the west of the city are coal and iron mines as well as lime and marble works.

Places of Interest

Anji Qiao Bridge

The oldest remaining segment arch bridge in the world, 40 km southeast of Shijiazhuang (see page 175), the 20 m high bronze Buddha at Longxing Temple in Zhengding, 10 km north of Shijiazhuang and Dafo Temple, 50 km away from Shijiazhuang.

International Bethune Peace Hospital of the People's Liberation Army
白求恩医院

The hospital, built in 1937, was named after the Canadian doctor, Dr. Norman Bethune, in 1940. Dr. Bethune had supported the medical care of the revolutionaries on the Communist side. Dr. Kotnis, an Indian, became the hospital's first director. Bethune Memorial Hall and Kotnis Memorial Hall can be visited inside the hospital.

Hotel

Hebei Binguan, 河北宾馆 Yucailu, tel. 63 51

Shopping

Friendship Store, Yuhualu

Renmin Baihuo Shangdian department store, Zhongshanlu

Travel agency

Guoji Lüxingshe CITS Weiminglu, tel. 89 62, 96 22

Zhongguo Lüxingshe, Weiminglu, tel. 96 39

Train station, ticket office, Gonglijie, tel. 22 27

Post office, Weiminglu, tel. 88 41

Bank of China, Hezuolu 7, tel. 91 05

Qinhuangdao 秦皇岛市

Qinhuangdao is an important port on the Bohai coast with a deep-sea port that is open to ships up to 10,000 gross registered tons. A railway line leads to the port, so that rapid shipment of the coal mined in Tangshan is possible.

In 1898, the Chinese government decided to open the port to foreign powers. In 1900, foreign troops landed during the Boxer Rebellion to take part in the events in Beijing. The South African Colonization Company had whole boat-loads of Chinese workers shipped to South African gold mines as cheap labor.

Qinhuangdao has some industrial plants, including a modern fiber glass factory.

From Qinhuangdao, it is not far to the best-known Chinese health and holiday resort Beidaihe. It is well worth visiting Shanhai Guan, the eastern end of the Great Wall.

Hotel

Qinhuangdao International Seaman's Club, Haibinlu 37, tel. 49 51, 41 86, bus no. 2 from train station.

Beidaihe, Holiday Resort 北戴河

Beidaihe, one of the best-known holiday and health resorts in China, is on the Bohai coast, 350 km east of Beijing. Chinese and foreigners alike, enjoy the 10-km-long beach, the soft sand and the clear water. Big sanitariums, various villas and rich gardens give the small place a special touch. The main season is from June until September.

The climate in Beidaihe is very favorable. Winters are mild, no wind in the spring, and the summers have an average temperature of 23°C.

At the beginning of the Tang Dynasty, Emperor Taizong marched through here with his troops and left a few stone inscriptions. At the time of the Ming Dynasty it gained some military importance as a guard post.

When the Tianjin-Shanhai Guan railway line was built at the end of the 19th century, the first foreigners came to Beidaihe and had their summer villas built there. By 1938, there were 590 private villas. After 1949, it was made a holiday resort for workers and employees. Sanitariums and guest houses were erected, and villas already in existence were opened to tourists; they number more than 3,000 today. The beach is divided into an eastern, a western and a central part.

The west beach is under the control of the International Travel Agency of China and accessible to foreign visitors.

As you walk along the beach eastward, you reach Yingjiao Mountain. On it stands a pavilion named after the mountain.

Lianhuashi Gongyuan, Lotus Blossom Stone Park 莲花石公园

Lianhuashi Gongyuan is on Donglian Feng mountain. Here there are many granite stones and rocks with diverse shapes as a result of weathering. Some stones resemble lotus blossoms, thus the park's name. A legend tells of a beautiful girl who, holding a lotus blossom in her hand, always saved the people from disaster during storms.

In the park stands a square bell pavilion with glazed tiles, dating back to the 16th century.

Hotels

Dongshan Binguan, 东山宾馆 Yingjiaolu, East Beach, tel. 25 28

Xishan Binguan, 西山宾馆 Xinjinglu West Beach, tel. 20 18, 26 78

Zhonghaitan Binguan, 中海滩宾馆 Xijinglu, Middle Beach, tel. 24 25, 23 98

Travel agency

Haibin Luyou Gongsi, In Xishan Binguan, tel. 29 48, 27 48

Antique Shop: in the Wenhua Gong (Cultural Palace)

Shanhai Guan Pass 山海关

Shanhai Guan pass is 30 km from Beidaihe and 310 km from Beijing on the border of Liaoning Province. It was the most important pass at the eastern end of the Great Wall, as for centuries it controlled the traffic between China's northern and northeastern regions. Many ancient structures give evidence of the strategical importance and the excellently constructed defense system of the Great Wall.

First settlements existed in the Shanhai Guan area as early as the 6th century B.C. In 618, a gate called Yuguan was erected at this location for the first time. In the centuries to follow, Han Chinese and invading northern tribes were engaged in heavy fighting in this area. The pass was built in 1381 as part of the extensive construction of the wall for an effective defensive complex.

The present structure dates back to 1639. After the fall of the Ming Dynasty, the Great Wall lost its significance because the Manchu rulers of the Qing Dynasty placed emphasis on a policy of harmony and appeasement towards the people of the steppe. Shanhai Guan became a rest stop for Qing rulers on their way to their ancestors' tombs in Shenyang. When the Boxer Rebellion erupted in 1900, the allied forces occupied Shanhai Guan. British, French, Italian and Japanese garrisons remained there until the 1920's.

Shanhai Guan city lies to the west inside the wall. Four gates lead to it. The northern gate has disappeared; the southern, western, and the eastern gate — the most beautiful one — still remain.

Tianxia diyiguan, First gate in the world, is the name of the east gate, which was restored in 1952. The entire pass owes its fame to it. A 10-m-high tower rises above the gate structure. On the uppermost ledge of the roof hangs the well-known inscription *Tianxia diyiguan* in the calligraphy of the scholar Xiao Xian from 1472. The 68 openings for archers can be clearly seen. In a small museum inside the tower, uniforms and weapons are exhibited.

North of the gate is a small park with the statue of a People's Liberation Army soldier who saved the life of a Korean child.

At Shanhai Guan the Great Wall is 10 m high and 5 m wide. The surrounding towers were used for signalling. Toward the east, the Great Wall leads to the sea where it is bounded by the 'Dragon's Head'. In earlier times, a stone dragon, looking out across the sea, had its place there.

About 10km east of Shanhai Guan stands the Jiangnu Miao, or Zhennü Ci temple. It is dedicated to Meng Jiang, the wife of Fan Xiliang who was sent to work on the Great Wall under the first emperor of the Qin in the third century BC. After a long separation, Meng Jiang began to look for him. She walked for hundreds of miles until she reached the section under construction at Shanhai Guan. There she was told that her husband had died long ago because of the hard work and the bad living conditions.

She cried so miserably for three days and three nights, that heaven, earth and all the gods and good spirits took pity on her, broke up the Great Wall and freed Fan Xiliang's corpse. Broken heartedly she carried him to the sea and threw herself and her husband's body into it. The stone from which she leaped is called Jiangnü Tomb.

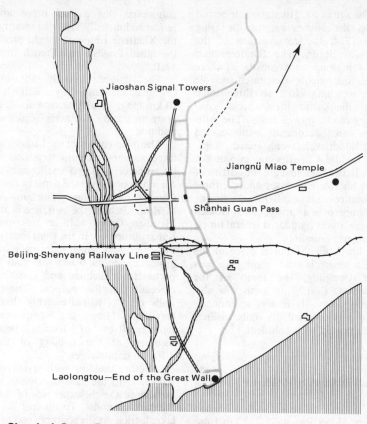

Shanhai Guan Pass and Surroundings

The temple houses a statue of Meng Jiang. On the walls are inscriptions of the emperors of the Qianlong, Jiaqing and Daoguang periods of government of the Qing Dynasty.

Yansai Lake

45 km long, is 6 km north of Shanhaiguan. It is a reservoir and a charming destination for an outing.

Zunhua District 遵化县

Dongling, Eastern Tombs (Qing Tombs) 清东陵

The Dongling complex, 125 km east of Beijing, contains the burial place of five emperors, 15 empresses, 100 imperial concubines and one princess of the Qing Dynasty (1644 — 1911). The founder of the Qing Dynasty, Emperor Shunzhi, had discovered the spot while hunting. The tombs were plundered at the beginning of this century and severely damaged. Not until 1949 did restoration begin.

Xiaoling, Mausoleum of the Shunzhi Emperor 孝陵

Xiaoling is the center of the entire complex. Inside the large stele hall stand two steles, each 6.7 m high. In Chinese and Manchu, their inscriptions praise the virtues and merits of the Shunzhi Emperor. The 'Sacred Way' is lined by stone sculptures as with the Ming tombs.

In earlier times annual ritual sacrifices took place in the magnificent ceremonial hall. Behind the hall there is a stele tower, followed by the grave mound. The mound covers the 'Underground Palace' where the emperor and the empress are buried.

Yuling, Mausoleum of the Qianlong Emperor 裕陵

West of Xiaoling is the grave of the Qianlong Emperor. Its 'Underground Palace' is one of the biggest and most beautiful of the Dongling complex.

The Qianlong Emperor was born in 1711

and died at the age of 88. His sixty-year period of reign was the golden age of the Qing Dynasty. In 1734, the construction of the mausoleum was begun. The 'Underground Palace' is 54 m long and consists of three rooms with four richly decorated double doors, each weighing close to three tons. Nevertheless, thanks to their special construction, they can be moved easily. The walls and ceilings are decorated with carved sculptures of Buddhas, heavenly guards, lions, flowers and Buddhist inscriptions in Sanskrit and Tibetan. In the back hall are the coffins of the emperor, his two empresses and the three most important concubines. Below the resting place of the emperor is a spring, called Golden Spring. The grave was plundered several times; only a few objects remain.

About 1 km from the burial place of the Qianlong Emperor is the most precious complex of Dongling, the tomb of the emperor's widow, Cixi. This tomb was also robbed several times. Its former splendor is evidenced by only one hall, its walls, ceilings and pillars decorated with gold leaf.

Chengde 承德市

Bishushanzhuang Summer Residence
避暑山庄

In northern Hebei Province, 250 km from Beijing, the Summer Residence of the emperors of the Qing Dynasty (1644 — 1911) was located. The city, formerly called Jehol, lies in a basin, 350 m above sea level, and is surrounded by mountains, forests and lakes. The Kangxi Emperor discovered this area while on an inspection tour and immediately ordered a summer residence to be built. Work commenced in 1703. The Qianlong Emperor had the complex expanded and added various buildings in the particular style of the nationalities, to express that he was trying to consolidate this country of many peoples and to strengthen the ties between the Manchurian ruling house and the foreign ethnic groups. In 1790, the 55th year of government of Qianlong, work was completed. The entire complex was one km² larger than the Imperial Palace and the Summer Palace in Beijing put together. As the emperors of the Qing Dynasty used to spend several months a year in Jehol, the residence became the second political center of country. Here, for the first time, Qianlong officially received the representatives of a Western government, a British legation. In the summer of 1820, the Jiaqing Emperor was struck by lightning and killed close to the palace. The Imperial Court considered this a bad omen and left the residence hurriedly, never to return again. Only the Xianfeng Emperor sought protection from the allied English and French troops here in 1860.

The palace grounds are in northern Chengde, surrounded by a wall which is about 10 km long. Its architecture unites elements of northern and southern Chinese building tradition.

The main entrance, the Lizheng gate (1), has three passages, a central large one, reserved for the emperor, and two smaller ones at the sides. An inscription gives the name of the gate in Han Chinese, Mongolian, Tibetan, Arabic and Manchu. Behind the entrance is the Wumen, Meridian Gate, with an inscription of the Kangxi Emperor. In the third courtyard follows the Zhenggong, main hall, made of the finest, aromatic *nanmu* wood that had been transported from Sichuan and Guizhou provinces especially for this purpose. The ceilings and walls of this hall are richly decorated with carvings. Here the emperors received representatives of foreign legations and members of the nobility of the empire's different nationalities.

Another building with seven rooms stands right next to the hall. It contains the imperial bedrooms. On the other side of the palace are the park grounds . To the east lies a beautiful lake district. At the southern end of this area, a stone bridge with three small Shuixin pavilions spans the Silver Lake and the Lower Lake. In early summer Silver Lake with its pink lotus blossoms is particularly attractive. Beyond the three pavilions in the northern part of the lake area is the Yanyu Lou, Fog and Rain House (9), the replica of a pavilion on the South Lake of Jiaxing in South China. This is where the emperors lingered when it rained and enjoyed the view of the far off mountains and the trees fading in the fog, a scenery resembling a traditional ink drawing. To the northwest in the Wenjin Ge (12) pavilion, a structure built in 1774,which contained part of the imperial library. Among the most famous works kept here was the *Gujin Tushu* (collection of works of ancient and modern times) and the *Siku Quanshu* (a collection of classical works in 36,304 volumes).

The western part of the Summer Residence, covering about 5/6 of the grounds, consists of mountains and valleys. Strange rock formations adorn the landscape, as for example the Heavenly Bridge Mountain and the Cockscomb Mountain. On the surrounding hills outside the Summer Residence to the north and south are eight groups of temple

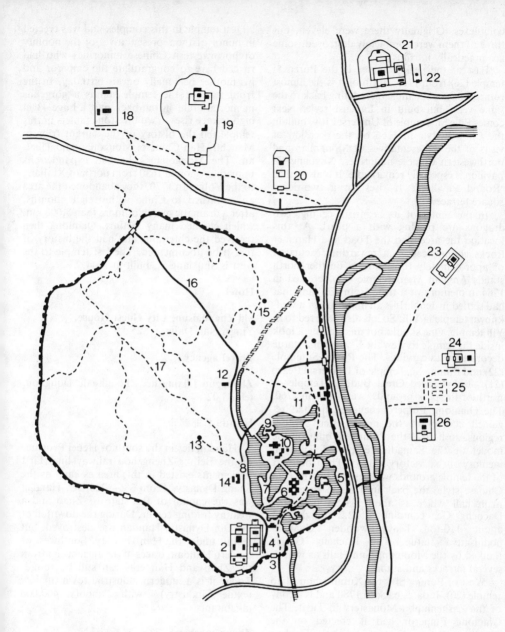

Summer Residence

1. Lizheng Men Gate	10. Ruyi Xie Pavilion	18. Shuxiang Si Temple
2. Zhenggong Palace	11. Wanshu Yuan Garden	19. Putuozongsheng Miao Temple
3. Dehui Men Gate	12. Wenjin Ge Pavilion	20. Xumifushou Miao Temple
4. Ruins of Donggong Palace	13. Songlin Yu Valley	21. Puning Si Temple
5. Silver Lake	14. Fangyuan Yu House	22. Puyou Si Temple
6. Lower Lake	15. Beizhen Shuangfeng	23. Anyuan Miao Temple
7. Upper Lake	Twin Peaks	24. Pule Si Temple
8. Ruyi Hu Lake	16. Songyun Xia Valley	25. Ruins of Pushan Si Temple
9. Yanyu Lou House	17. Lishu Yu Valley	26. Puren Si Temple

complexes. Originally there were eleven, but three of them were completely destroyed, some are practically in ruins.

East of the park complex is the Puren Si temple (26) from 1713; north of it is the almost ruined Pushan Si temple (25), dating back to the same year, but built in Lamaist style. Next comes Pule Si, Temple of Universal Joy, built in the Chinese style in 1766 on the occasion of visits of the representatives of Mongolian and northwestern Chinese minorities. Xuguang Ge pavilion is especially remarkable. It is also called 'Round Pavilion'. It rises on a two-tiered square terrace.

In the center of its beautiful ceiling, two dragons are playing with a pearl. At this location the ascent to the Toad and Hammer Rocks commences — a rewarding excursion of approximately three hours. Further north stands Anyuan Miao temple (23), erected in 1764 in memory of a tribe from Xinjiang that had settled in Jehol. It is an imitation of a well-known temple in Yili. So it is also referred to as Yili temple. One should not miss taking a look inside the temple to view the Ksitigarbha statue decorated with carvings. The Puyou Si temple (22) and Puning Si, Temple of Universal Peace (21) — also called Great Buddha Temple — north of the park grounds, were built in 1760. The Qianlong Emperor believed he had regained control of the northwestern border regions, so he had the Puning Si built on the model of the Samadhi temple in Tibet in memory of that victory in 1755. The front part of the temple grounds was designed in the Han Chinese style, the back in Tibetan style. The main hall which is about 37 m high, the Dacheng Ge, contains a 22.2-m-high and about 110-ton heavy wooden Guanyin bodhisattva statue. The Dacheng Ge is flanked by the Moon and Sun Halls as well as several terraces and stupas.

West of Puning Si is the Xumifushou Miao temple (20). It dates back to 1780 and is a copy of the Zashenlunbu Monastery in Tibet. The Qianlong Emperor had it erected on the occasion of the arrival of the sixth Panchan Lama. He had come to congratulate the emperor on his birthday. The roof of the main hall was covered with gilded copper tiles and decorated with eight gilded copper dragons. Each dragon is 5 m long and weighs more than one ton. Altogether, 1,500 kilograms of gold were used for the roof of the main hall and the dragons. The roof of the adjoining main hall to the west, Putuozongsheng Miao (19) was also gold plated. The temple is also called Little Potala, because it was designed in 1766 in the image of the Potala Palace in Lhasa. It is the largest temple in this complex and was erected in honor of the representatives of the nobility of northwestern Chinese minorities who had rushed here to congratulate the emperor and his mother personally on his birthday. In the front part of the temple stands a gorgeous memorial arch, in the back part a huge 43 m high terrace rises. Two big stone tablets in this temple tell the history of the Turgut tribe in Manchu, Han Chinese, Mongolian and Tibetan. The Mongolian tribe had expanded its nomadic region in 1630 from north of Xinjiang to the Volga. In 1770, they abandoned the area and returned to China within eight months, after a dramatic march of more than 5,000 km, which claimed many victims. Qianlong then received the chieftains and had the history of that tribe documented. The last temple to the west is Shuxiang Si, built in 1744.

Hotel

Shi Zhaodaisuo, City Guest House, Yingzi Nan Dajie, tel.25 51

Travel agency

Zhongguo Lüxingshe, Zhonghualu Dongkou, tel. 35 02

Handan 邯郸市

Handan lies in the south of Hebei Province on the Beijing-Zhengzhou railway line. First settlements existed in this area as early as the Shang Dynasty. From 386—228 BC, Handan was the capital of the state of Zhao and a wealthy trading center. During the downfall of the Qin Dynasty, Handan was destroyed, but rebuilt under the Han Dynasty. Southwest of modern Handan, traces of the ancient city from the Zhao and Han eras can still be found. Today it is a modern industrial town (mainly textile industry) with about 400,000 inhabitants.

Zhaowangcheng Yizhi 赵王城遗址

Remains of the ancient capital of the state of Zhao, relics of walls and foundations are located 4 km southwest of the present city center. The town of the Zhao era was divided into three districts, an eastern, a western and a northern one. The ruins still remaining belong to the western part. On the main axis of the district are still parts of the foundation of Longtai, Dragon Terrace, 285 m long, 265 m wide and 19 m high, where the main palace stood.

Congtai Platform 丛台

The platform is 26 m high and is situated in the northeastern corner of the ancient city. It was built during the rule of the Zhao king Wuling (325—299 BC). From this terrace the king is said to have supervised the training of his troops. He also supposedly used it as a place of leisure and entertainment. It must have been a park-like complex with bridges, caves, flower-gardens, towers and pavilions.

Lüzu Ci Temple (Lüweng Ci) 吕祖(翁)祠

The temple, 10 km north of Handan, was established during the Tang/Song eras. The present structure dates back to the Ming era. Of its three main halls, the back one, Lusheng Dian, is the most interesting. It tells of the life of the young Lu Sheng. He was an educated young man from a poor family who was striving for fame and fortune. One day he met the old Lü Weng who gave him a pillow which was supposed to grant the fulfillment of his desire. Lu Sheng put his head on the pillow and fell asleep, while next door millet gruel was being prepared. Lu Sheng had a wonderful dream. He was an honored man in an influential position, was married to a beautiful woman and had several sons, who all married women of wealthy families. Lu Sheng woke up even before the gruel was cooked. Yet everything came true. The term for wishful thinking and castles in the air has since then been *huangliang yimeng,* dream while millet is cooking.

The middle main hall is called Lüzu Dian. It houses a stone figure of Lü Weng.

Xiangtang Shiku, Echo Stone Grottos 响堂(山)石窟

These grottos are southwest of Handan on Shigu Shan mountain. They date from the 6th century; in the centuries to follow, they were enlarged and restored. In northern and southern sections they house about 3,000 sculptures. The southern section (seven caves) is situated at the southern base of the mountain on the bank of the Fuyang He river. The northern section (nine caves) is on the west side of the mountain approximately 15 km northwest of the southern grotto.

Travel agency

Zhongguo Lüxingshe, Zhonghualu, tel. 39 21

Anji Qiao Bridge 安济桥

The oldest remaining segment arch bridge in the world is 2.5 km south of the district capital Zhaoxian, 40 km southeast of Shijiazhuang. Under the direction of the builder Li Chun, it was constructed of stone from 605–616. Its total length is 50.8 m; it spans 37.3 m. The Europeans did not learn to build bridges such as this one until some centuries later.

Shanxi Province 山西省

Area: ca. 157,000 km^2 / Population : 25 million / Capital: Taiyuan

Shanxi, in the east part of the North Chinese Loess Plateau, borders on Shaanxi in the west and Henan in the south. The west and southwest borders are drawn by the curve of the Huanghe (Yellow River). The Taihang Shan mountains mark the borders in the southeast and east. In the north, the border runs along the Great Wall.

History

During the Western Zhou Dynasty (1100—711 BC), the fief of Qin was founded in the southwest along the Fenhe river. It quickly developed politically, economically and culturally into a regional center. During the Han Dynasty, Shanxi was a buffer state between the nomadic peoples of the north and west and the peasants who had settled in the fertile plains of what are today the Hebei and Henan provinces. The political status of the province varied according to the strength or weakness of the central government. From the end of the Han Dynasty until the reunion of the empire under the Sui Dynasty in 581, Shanxi was the seat of short-lived dynasties. Buddhism flourished in this province during the Northern Wei Dynasty. The Buddhist cave temples of Yungang, Datong, originated at this time. Shanxi Province was founded in the 14th century.

Two-thirds of the province consists of a plateau that lies about 300—1000 m above sea level. Due to the north-south alignment of the mountains, the province is influenced by the Mongolian climate. Dry northwest winds frequently cause periods of drought in the winter and spring, which often led to famines in the past — a danger that has been eliminated today by irrigation systems and central planning. About 70—80% of the yearly precipitation falls between June and September.

The average temperature varies 8°c in the winter and 3°c in the summer within the province.

The majority of the population is Han Chinese; a small minority is made up of Huis, Manchus and Mongols. About 85% of the population lives in rural areas. The most important crops are millet, sorghum, wheat and cotton. The fertile basins of Shanxi can be cultivated to a great extent due to the irrigation works.

Shanxi has extensive energy resources. The province has over 200 billion tons of coal reserves in the known coal fields, which comprise one-third of the entire minable Chinese coal reserves. Coal is mined in over 2,000 centrally and locally run mines in 80% of the districts of Shanxi. The mines of Datong are among the most important ones in the country.

Taiyuan 太原市

Taiyuan, the capital of Shanxi, lies on the Fenhe river in the heart of the province and in the northern part of the fruitful Taiyuan Basin. The city, with a population of more than 2.2 million, is one of the important industrial centers in China.

History

Taiyuan has always been a center of interest due to its mineral wealth, agricultural conditions and strategic position. It was the entry-way to the Shanxi plateaus, a favorite target of the northern tribes and an advantageous starting point for an occupation of the empire. Thus, Taiyuan was the scene of political and martial conflicts again and again.

After the foundation of the Zhou Dynasty, the fief of Tang arose, which was later called Jin. The city of Jinyang, present-day Taiyuan, was the capital. After the rulers of Qin had conquered the Jin area, in the meantime called Zhao, in 221 BC, Jinyang was renamed Taiyuan and made the seat of a frontier command post. Under the Han Dynasty, the city became a stronghold of great strategic importance due to the danger from the north.

The rulers of the short-lived Northern Qi Dynasty (550—577) built temples and palaces. After the foundation of the Sui Dynasty (581—618) and the reunion of the empire, Jinyang regained its importance as a frontier town.

The construction of new city fortifications

Map of Taiyuan

and palaces led to higher taxation that ended in a peasants' revolt and soon threatened the entire dynasty. The emperor sent a man called Li Yuan to Taiyuan to suppress the revolt. However, Li Yuan became the leader of the rebels, overthrew the dynasty and founded the Tang Dynasty in 618. Although Jinyang became a cultural and political center, it did not find peace due to the constant menace of the Turkic tribes. After the fall of the Tang Dynasty (in 907), the city's defenses were gradually enlarged. Taiyuan was in the hands of the Northern Han, a royal house that did not want to submit to the new Song rulers' reunion plans. After several futile attempts, the Song rulers were able to force the city to surrender in 979. In order to put an end to the endeavors for freedom, the city was burned to the ground and the waters of the Jin and Fe Rivers were redirected to wash away the ashes and thus remove the last remains of the city.

During the following years, the inhabitants of Jinyang settled in a nearby village. Slowly, a new city arose, a booming trade center with narrow streets and prosperous markets. Artisans and artists came; ceramic workshops were opened. After the mid-14th century, peasants' revolts, in which Taiyuan was not spared, again shook the land. Chaos and disaster decimated the population; almost all leading families are thought to have been ruined in those years.

During the Ming Dynasty, Taiyuan became the residence of the Viceroy of Shanxi Province.

The secret society White Lotus existed in Taiyuan as early as the 11th century. One branch of this organization, the Yihetuan, supported the movement against the increasing economic and financial power of the foreigners in Shanxi. Bloody clashes followed, contributing finally to the outbreak of the so-called Boxer Rebellion. After the revolution of 1911, the commander-in-chief, Yan Xishan, ruled as dictator of Shanxi from the seat of Taiyuan until 1948.

During the last 30 years, the city has developed into an important industrial center for heavy industry (iron and steel), coal mining, machine manufacturing, cement and chemicals.

Jinci, the Jin Ancestral Temple 晋祠

The Jinci temple complex is located about 25 km southwest of Taiyuan at the source of the Jinhe river and at the foot of Xuanweng Shan mountain. In the 11th century BC, Prince Shuyu ruled the fief of Tang. After his death, his son assumed power and renamed the fief Jin after the Jinhe river. In the 5th century AD, an ancestral temple, Jinci, was built in memory of Prince Shuyu. During the Northern Qi Dynasty (550 — 577) other halls, pavilions and gardens were added. The temple complex flourished during the rise of the city Jinyang. Li Yuan, who had not followed the Sui emperor's command to suppress a revolt in what today is called Shanxi, but rather made himself the leader of the rebels, supposedly made a sacrifice in the ancestral temple of Prince Shuyu of Tang and appealed for assistance.

After he had succeeded in overthrowing the dynasty and founded a new one in 618, he ostensibly named it 'Tang' out of gratitude.

Jinci was spared during the destruction of Taiyuan in 979. The entire temple complex was declared a national monument after 1949.

The former entrance gate Jingqing Men (2) is located on the south side; to the right of it is the new entrance (1). From this point, one directly approaches Shuijing Tai terrace (3), which served as a theater for earlier temple festivities. Not far from here, one can see Shengying Lou pavilion (4) on the left, the second story of which affords a good view of the entire temple complex. A small bridge, Huixian Qiao (5), over a branch of the Jinhe river, leads directly to Shengmu Dian, the Hall of the Blessed Mother. Jinren Tai (6) follows, a terrace in which iron statues from the 11th century stand in each of the four corners; they are deities represented as wild warriors. The path leads on through a gate to a hall from the 12th century, Xiandian (9), in which sacrifices were made to the Blessed Mother. On the other side of Xiandian is Feiliang bridge (10), the Flying Bridge.

This bridge, unique in Chinese antiquity, dates from the Song era and was built over the Yuzhao, the Fishpond Springs, in the shape of a cross supposed to symbolize a flying bird. The Yuzhao bubbles up under the Hall of the Blessed Mother and is one of the three sources of the Jinhe river. Shengmu Dian, the Hall of the Blessed Mother (11), also called Yijiang Hall, is the main hall of the temple complex and also the oldest wooden structure preserved in Taiyuan today. It was built between 1023 — 1031 to honor Prince Shuyu of Tang's mother. The hall harbors 44 unusual terra-cotta sculptures. A sculpture of Yijiang, the mother of Tang Shuyu, is situated in the center. She is surrounded by her maid servants, who are lined up along the walls of the hall. Each of these statues is a masterpiece. They vary in posture and expression. They seem to be

Jinci Temple

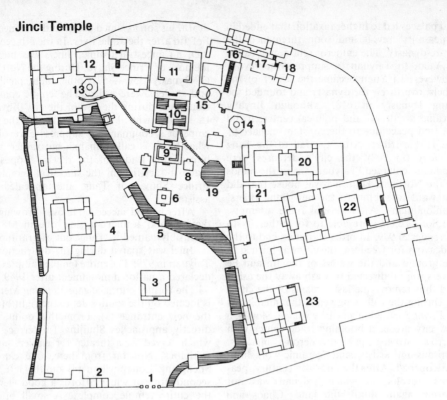

1. Entrance
2. Jingqing Men Gate
3. Shuijing Tai Terrace
4. Shengying Lou Pavilion
5. Huixian Qiao Bridge
6. Jinren Tai Terrace
7. Drum Tower
8. Bell Tower
9. Xiandian Hall
10. Feiliang Bridge
11. Shengmu Dian, Hall of the
   Blessed Mother

12. Shuimu Lou Temple
13. Nanlao Quan Spring
14. Shanli Quan Spring
15. Ancient cypress tree
16. Chaoyang Dong Cave
17. Yuntao Dong Cave
18. Daifeng Xuan
19. Lotus Pond
20. Tangshuyu Ci Temple
21. Tang Stele Pavilion
22. Guanyu Ci Temple
23. Wenchang Gong Palace

likenesses of real persons differing in age and appearance, some dreaming or amused, others about to ask questions or answer. Because they were created at the time of the Northern Song Dynasty, as was the hall, they provide information about the clothing and headdress of that time. Unfortunately, they were painted over in fairly glaring colors later on, which can hardly correspond to the taste in colors of the Song era.

West of Shengmu Dian hall, Shuimu Lou temple (12), dating from the mid-16th century, is located. It is dedicated to a young peasant woman who received a magic whip from an old man. Whenever she needed water, she only had to hit her water jug with the whip and water immediately bubbled up from the bottom of the jug. In this manner, she saved

herself the long way to the well, to which her evil mother-in-law sent her daily. However, her mother-in-law soon discovered her secret and tried to imitate her. The water kept on gushing up after she had hit the jug, so that the entire house was soon endangered. The horrified young woman ceased combing her long hair and sat on the jug, but the water continued to bubble up and finally became the source of the Jinhe river.

The temple has two stories. On both the ground and the second floors there are representations of the young, good-natured 'Water Mother' sitting with disordered hair on the source of the Jinhe.

There is an octagonal pavilion in front of Shuimu Lou and above Nanlao Quan, the Fountain of Youth (13). It was erected around

550 and later restored several times. Nanlao Quan is the most important of the Jinhe river's three sources. It provides 1.9 m³ of water per second; the flow of water remains constant even in drought or rainy seasons. The water temperature, 17°C, also does not change with the seasons. The third source, Shanli Quan (14), also springs up under an octagonal pavilion built around 550.

To the east of the Hall of the Blessed Mother is another sight worth seeing in the Jinci temple complex: an ancient cypress tree (15). To the north of Shanli Quan springs one can view some caves, Chaoyang Dong (16), which are dedicated to a deity possessing magic powers. Directly next to them, Yuntao Dong (17) is located, in which the Ming loyalist Fu Shan (1608 — 1684), a man of letters, calligrapher and doctor, lived for many years. The next building to the east, Daifeng Xuan (18), contains a small ceramics exhibit. A stairway leads to three more buildings. There is a good view of the temple complex and surrounding area from here.

Tang Shuyu Ci (20), the Temple of Prince Shuyu of Tang, is east of Shanli Quan springs. This was probably the location of the first ancestral temple. Next to it, one can see a pavilion containing a stele (21) dating from the Tang Dynasty. It shows an inscription with 1203 characters, an expression of gratitude composed by the second emperor of the Tang Dynasty in 646. He, like his father, felt very indebted to the Prince, because they believed that he helped them and brought them good luck in answer to their prayers. The emperor justifies his father's work, the overthrow of the Sui, and asks for protection for the Tang Dynasty.

The temple of Guan Yu (22) is located directly next to the stele pavilion. Guan Yu was a famous general during the period of the Three Kingdoms (220—265) who was later honored as a god of war.

Chongshan Si Temple 崇善寺

Chongshan Si, located on the eastern side of the city, was founded in the Tang era and enlarged by Zhu Gang, the third son of the first Ming emperor, in honor of his mother, Empress Gao, in 1381. In 1864, a fire destroyed the temple. The main gate, the bell tower, some adjacent halls and Dabei Dian hall were preserved. Statues of Guanyin, Wenshu bodhisattva and Puxian bodhisattva are on display in Dabei Dian. The hall and the statues are from the Ming era.

Shanxi Sheng Bowuguan, Shanxi Province Museum 山西省博物馆

This museum is worth a visit, for it offers copious illustrative material about the long history of Jinyang, present-day Taiyuan. The museum building itself is a temple complex from the Jin Dynasty (1115—1234), restored in 1881. In addition to findings from the Neolithic Age, bronze goblets from the Shang era, weapons, lacquered objects and bronze coins from the Period of Warring States as well as grave finds from later dynasties are among the objects on display. Further, one can see reproductions of calligraphies and paintings by the famous painter Gu Kaizhi (345 — 406).

Another, even more attractive part of the museum is located in the impressive former residence Chunyang Gong.

Shuangta Si, Two Pagodas Temple 双塔寺

This temple is located in the southeastern part of Taiyuan. It was built in the Ming Dynasty during the reign of Wanli (1573 — 1620). Its two 54-m-tall brick pagodas became the city's landmark.

Dou Daifu Ci Temple 窦大夫祠

Dou Daifu Ci is located approximately 20 km northwest of Taiyuan in the village Lancun. It was dedicated to Minister Dou Chou of the fief of Jin (in the second half of the Zhou Dynasty).

Dou Chou is especially credited for having the irrigation system in this area built. The buildings preserved up to the present originate from 1343. A spring arises next to the temple. Because its water is unusually cold, it is called *Hanquan*, Cold Spring.

Tianlongshan Shiku Grottos 天龙山石窟

About 40 km southwest of Taiyuan, Tianlong Shan mountain rises, containing eight grottos on the east summit and 13 grottos on the west summit. The oldest one was built between 535—549; most of the others originated in the Tang Dynasty. The greater part of their sculptures are damaged. An impressive Buddha statue in Grotto 9 is the best-preserved one.

Longshan Shiku Caves 龙山石窟

Some Daoist cave dwellings are located on Longshan mountain about 20 km southwest of Taiyuan. They were constructed by the Daoist monk Song Defang at the beginning of the Yuan Dynasty and contain more than 40 well-preserved sculptures. There are inscriptions from the Yuan era on the walls.

Dayun Si Temple 大云寺

Dayun Si, also called the Iron Buddha Temple, is located in the district capital Lingfen. It originates from 627 — 649 and contains the main gate, Xianting pavilion, Zhongdian hall, the Pavilion of Holy Writings and Fangta pagoda. The pagoda is 30 m tall and decorated with ceramic tiles. The so-called Iron Buddha is on the ground floor: a Buddha head cast in iron from the Tang era, 6 m tall and 5 m in diameter.

Guangsheng Si Temple 广胜寺

Guangsheng Si temple is situated at the foot of the south flank of Huoshan mountain, about 17 km northeast of the district of Hongdong. Surrounded by old pines, cypresses and springs, the temple was founded in 147. The temple complex is divided into an upper and lower temple district. In addition, a third temple, the Water Spirit Temple, is a part of the complex. The buildings of the upper district that have been preserved up to the present originate from the Ming Dynasty. However, they were designed in the Yuan Dynasty style. The main gate and front hall of the lower temple district are very impressive. The main gate is in keeping with the Yuan Dynasty style. The Buddha statues in the front hall are from the Yuan era. The murals that once decorated the inner walls were taken abroad in 1928; their remains can still be seen on the upper parts of the walls. Shuishen Miao, the Water Spirit Temple, on the western side was erected directly next to Huoquan spring on Huoshan mountain. Mingyingwang Hall from 1319 is noteworthy for its eleven representations of the water spirit Mingyingwang and his servants. The murals on the south wall are especially interesting. They provide information about common customs in the theater during the Yuan Dynasty; that is, about actors, make-up, costumes, music instruments and scenery.

Xuanzhong Si Temple 玄中寺

Xuanzhong Si, also called the Stone Wall Temple, is about 4 km southwest of the district capital Jiaocheng Xian, in the middle of an impassable, impressive mountainous area. There is a very good view of the main and adjacent halls from the entrance gate of the temple grounds. The temple was founded in 472. At the emperor's wish, Master Tan Luan studied and taught the *Jingtu* doctrine here, which found numerous followers, especially in Japan. Xuanzhong Si is considered a holy place by the *Jingtu* sect. The oldest building on the temple grounds is Tianwang Dian, the Hall of Celestial Kings, built in 1605. Stone steles and stone carvings from the 5th — 7th centuries have been preserved.

Hotels

Yingze Binguan, 迎泽宾馆 Yingze Dajie, tel. 2 32 11

Bingzhou Fandian, Yingze Dajie, tel. 4 59 24

Sanjing Dasha, Yingze Dajie, tel. 2 78 53

Jinci Binguan, 晋祠宾馆 Nanjiao, in the Jinci temple complex, tel. 2 99 41

Travel agencies

Guoji Lüxingshe, CITS, Yingze Dajie, in Yingze Binguan Guest House

Zhongguo Lüxingshe, Yingze Dajie, tel. 2 91 55

Shopping

Friendship Store, Wuyilu Nantou, tel. 2 81 80

Datong 大同市

Datong, with a population of more than 900,000, the largest city in the northern part of Shanxi Province, is about eight hours away from Beijing by train. It is situated south of the traditional fortifications of the Great Wall on a loess plateau more than 1,000 m above sea level and draws its water from the Sanggan He river.

History

During the Western Han Dynasty, this area was the main seat of the eastern frontier garrison for the Han armies, which were supposed to protect the land from the attacks of the nomadic Xiongnu. In the 4th century AD, the Toba, a central Asian tribe, invaded China. They founded the Northern Wei Dynasty and built their capital here in 398. Even after they had united the entire North under their rule, Datong remained the capital until the sixth emperor of the Wei Dynasty moved the capital to Luoyang in 494.

Datong was fortified in 421. The outer city

wall measured 16 km in circumference. The city gradually gained in greatness and magnificence and became the political, religious and cultural center of North China. In addition to palaces and official buildings, the imperial family had Buddhist cave temples built on the western outskirts of the city. After the seat of government was moved, Datong immediately lost in importance and was forgotten. During the Ming Dynasty, Datong again became one of the most important strategic points within the lines of defense against the Mongols.

After being connected up to the railway network, Datong developed into a modern city. Today, it is an important railway junction between Hebei and Shanxi Provinces and Mongolia and an important industrial center, known mainly for its coal mining and agricultural machine manufacturing. Although Datong is very interesting because of the Yungang rock temples, it is not one of the classic attractions. Shanhua Si and Huayan Si temples and the Nine Dragon Screen are among the sights of the city in addition to the Yungang rock temple, which can easily be reached by bus or taxi.

Vistors wishing to take something special with them from Datong should perhaps buy something in bronze, because Datong is known for its production of bronze objects, especially its richly decorated fire pots.

Jiulong Bi, the Nine Dragon Screen 九龙壁

The Nine Dragon Screen in the middle of Datong originates from the early Ming Dynasty. At one time, the residence of Zhu Gui was located here, the 13th son of the first Ming emperor. The entire complex burned down with the exception of the Nine Dragon Screen in 1644. Today, Jiulong Bi is one of the largest and oldest of its kind in China. In a very good representation made of colored ceramic tiles, nine dragons rise from the sea and fly towards the sun, the symbol of immortality. A small pool was laid out in front of the screen and the dragons are reflected in its water. When the surface of the water is disturbed by the wind, the dragons' reflections seem to dance.

Huayan Si Temple 华严寺

On top of the rise in the southwestern part of the city, Huayan Si is located. It belonged to the Buddhist school of Huayan, which was very widespread during the Liao Dynasty. The complex was built in the 11th century and soon burned down in 1122. However, the temple was quickly rebuilt; it was enlarged and divided into upper and lower temple districts between 1426 — 1456. At the beginning of the Qing Dynasty, it was destroyed once again, but the new emperors had it restored. The orientation of the main halls of Huayan Si to the east, which is an architectural peculiarity of the Liao master builders, is unusual.

The two main halls, Daxiong Baodian and Bojiajiao Cangdian, are the oldest buildings in the complex. Their original design from the Liao and Jin periods was preserved. The outer gate of Upper Huayan Si was built after the division of the complex during the Qing Dynasty. The main hall, Daxiong Baodian, is situated on a high terrace. The gateway and drum and bell towers are also on the terrace; however, they were not built until the reign of Wanli (1573 — 1620) during the Ming Dynasty. Daxiong Baodian hall dates from 1055 — 1064. In 1122, it burned down, but was rebuilt in 1140. It is one of the largest Buddhist halls from the Liao and Jin eras. Five gilded Buddha statues are in the middle of the hall. The three middle ones were made of wood in Beijing in 1427. The two on either side as well as the smaller figures were made of clay. Sculptures of gods line the walls, each one a work of art. The colorfully painted coffered ceiling is from the Qing Dynasty, as well as the splendid murals depicting Sakyamuni's life and those of other Buddhist holy men. The outer gate to Lower Huayan Si as well as the bell and stele pavilions are from the Ming and Qing eras respectively. The main hall, Bojiajiao Cangdian, was built in 1038 to store holy Buddhist scripts. Since the middle of the Liao Dynasty, 579 volumes of the *Dacang* scripts have been kept here. Parts of the collection were lost in the disturbances of the following centuries. During the Jin and Yuan dynasties, efforts were made to replenish the collection. Bojiajiao Cangdian faces east, like the main hall of the upper temples, and provides a typical example of Buddhist architecture in the Liao Dynasty. Inside the hall, three Buddha statues rest on a pedestal surrounded by several smaller statues, Buddha representations, bodhisattvas and boyish worshippers. They are clay statues that, with few exceptions, date from the Liao Dynasty. Some were later restored in their original form. They are supposed to represent the perfect harmony of the 'Buddhist world' and to impress believers with their dignity and solemnity. The bookcases, 38 in all, have been preserved in their original state and are spread over two stories.

Huayan Si Temple

1. Upper Huayan Si
2. Daxiong Baodian Hall
3. Lower Huayan Si
4. Bojiajiao Cangdian Hall

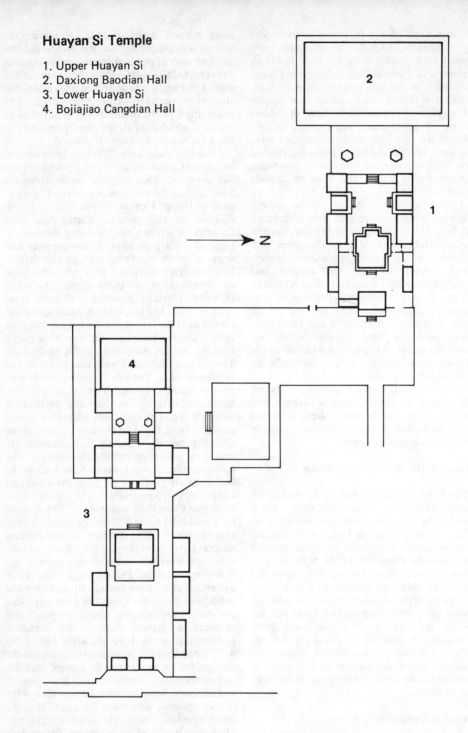

Shanhua Si Temple 善化寺

Shanhua Si temple complex, also called Nansi, the South Temple, is located in the southern part of Datong. It was built during the Tang Dynasty during Kaiyuan's reign (714 — 741). At that time, it was called Kaiyuan Si. It fell victim to the conflicts of war and burned down to the ground in 1122, but was rebuilt between 1128 — 1149 and restored during the Ming Dynasty.

The temple faces south. The front gate, Shanmen, and the middle hall, Sansheng Dian, are built in the Jin Dynasty style, whereas the rear main hall, Daxiong Baodian, is an example of Liao architecture. Shanhua Si and its main and side halls are among the best-preserved temple complexes from the Liao and Jin eras. Within the complex, more than 30 sculptures from this time are to be found.

The present main gate, Shanmen, is actually the Hall of Celestial Guardians, Tianwang Dian, built in the Song era style. Sansheng Dian, the Hall of the Three Saints, is considered to be a typical example of timber frame construction from the Jin Dynasty. The statues of the three saints stand on a pedestal inside the hall: Sakyamuni in the middle, the bodhisattva Wenshu to his left and the bodhisattva Puxian to his right. A stone stele from 1176 tells of the temple complex's construction. Puxian Ge pavilion follows to the left; its counterpart on the right has not been preserved.

The main hall of Shanhua Si is Daxiong Baodian, built during the Liao Dynasty and renovated from 1123 — 1149. Five Rulai Buddhas clothed in gold sit on their lotus thrones inside the hall. The material of their robes was formed so artistically that it seems to be real. The statues next to them have also been sculpted expressively. Statues of 24 gods are lined up on both sides of the hall. All of the figures here originate from the Liao and Jin dynasties. The murals were painted during the Qing Dynasty, although their style is that of the Yuan period.

Yungang Rock Temples 云岗石窟

The Yungang rock temples lie 16 km west of Datong in a valley on the south side of the Wuzhou sandstone mountains. They are an historical sight and extend westward along the mountain slopes for a distance of over 1 km. Most of them were built 1,500 years ago, from 460 — 494, at the time of the Northern Wei Dynasty (386 — 534), which had been founded by the central Asian Toba tribe. Chinese culture and art flourished at that time. Buddhism spread throughout China under the new rulers. Because Buddhism offered the non-Chinese rulers a welcome weapon against Chinese Daoism and Confucianism, they declared it a state religion. It is said that Emperor Taiwu (reigned from 424 — 452) was the first to be converted to Daoism. Numerous monasteries were then burned down, monks were relegated to lay status and, finally, Buddhism was forbidden. One day when the emperor became seriously ill, others convinced him that this was the penalty for his defamation of Buddhism. Buddhism flourished anew under his successor. In 460 the emperor commissioned the famous monk Tanyao to carve five huge Buddha statues into the sandstone of the Wuzhou mountains. Other works followed upon the completion of these first, monumental sculptures in caves 16 to 20; supposedly, 100,000 statues in all were produced. After the capital was moved to Luoyang in 494, the Yungang rock temples were gradually forgotten. In the 53 caves preserved today, there are 51,000 expressively carved sculptures. The largest is 17 m tall, the smallest only 2 cm. They are wonderful examples of Chinese sculpture in which Indian elements as well as Persian and Hellenistic influences can be recognized: the latter, coming from the west, left their mark in India.

Man and nature have greatly damaged the Yungang rock temples since their creation. At least 1,400 statues were stolen, especially at the beginning of the 20th century, or sold by irresponsible officials. Many of these statues are now on display in the museums of the western world. Since 1949, official attempts have been made to restore damaged figures and caves. One plan is to shield the sandstone from erosion with protective walls.

The rock temples are divided into three groups according to their location: the eastern caves 1 — 4, the middle 5 — 13 and the western 14 — 53. The most important ones are 5 — 6, 9 — 13 and 16 — 20.

A sort of several-storied pagoda has been preserved in cave 2. Cave 3 is the largest of the Yungang rock temples; it contains three statues: a sitting Buddha in the middle and a standing bodhisattva on each side. They are unique among the Yungang sculptures, for the expression and form of their clothing are characterized by special elegance and grace. They were presumably not carved until the time of the Sui or early Tang dynasties, as opposed to the other sculptures. Shifo Gusi, the Old Monastery of the Stone Buddhas, is on the other side of the eastern group of caves. It was built in 1651 and is the only one left of probably 10 monasteries once located at the Yunyang rock temples according to historical records.

Most visitors begin sightseeing at cave 5. It is well protected, thanks to the wooden monastery buildings. A 17-m-high Buddha sculpture rises at the entrance — the biggest one within the rock temples. One ear alone measures 3.1 m. The statue was restored during the Tang Dynasty. The walls and ceilings are richly decorated with reliefs, among them representations of the Bodhi tree, under which Buddha received his revelation. Caves 6 and 7 are the climax of the Yungang rock temples, although cave 6, also called Sakyamuni cave, is more interesting. It is dominated by a two-story, 16-m-high square pagoda, the upper part of which is decorated with nine-tiered pagodas on all four corners. Buddha figures were carved into all four sides of the lower story. Buddha and Luohan figures are depicted on the walls of the cave. The ceiling is decorated with 33 celestial guardians and animals. Scenes from the life of Sakyamuni have been carved into the east, south and west walls. In cave 7, six praying bodhisattvas and two lion sculptures are worthy of notice. Cave 8 is an example of the combination of various styles, namely, Chinese, Indian and Hellenistic (the representation of a guard with a trident is attributed to the Hellenistic influence). Caves 9-13 are also called the colorful caves. They are well-known for their brilliant coloring from the Qing era. In cave 11, an inscription on the east wall tells of the building history of caves 9-15. In addition to countless bodhisattva figures carved into the walls in small niches, the cave contains a total of 95 large stone carvings. Temple 12 provides valuable clues about music instruments of the 5th century among its representations. There is a 13-m-tall Maitreya statue in cave 13. Its raised head is supported by a second, four-armed figure standing on Maitreya's leg. Caves 14 and 15 are severely weathered. Thousands of tiny bodhisattva figurines are still in the niches and worth seeing. The next five caves are the oldest ones in Yungang. A colossal Buddha sculpture, 13 — 16 m tall, is in each of them. There is a Sakyamuni statue in cave 16 and a Maitreya statue in cave 17.

In the middle of cave 18, there is a Sakyamuni statue portraying him as vital and strong. Its stone robe is decorated with carvings showing innumerable small bodhisattvas. In cave 19, one can see a 16.7-m-tall sculpture of the seated Sakyamuni, the second-largest statue of Yungang. The 13.7-m-tall Buddha statue in cave 20 is probably the best-known, because it is easily photographed. It has become the symbol of Yungang. Originally, the statue was protected by a building that has since caved in. Temple 21 was not created until near the end of the Northern Wei Dynasty. It contains a five-tiered pagoda. Caves 22 — 53, as well as the other, unnumbered ones, originated mainly after 495.

Guest House

Datong Binguan, Geweihui'erlu, tel. 2 33 33

Travel agency

Guoji Lüxingshe, CITS, tel. 27 04 and Zhongguo Lüxingshe Xinjianlu

Hengshan Mountains 恒山

Hengshan is one of the five holy mountains in China. It rises in northern Shanxi and is famous for its Hanging Monastery located about 75 km from Datong. The monastery was originally built in the 6th century and reconstructed in the Jin, Ming and Qing Dynasties. Its forty small halls and pavilions were built along the contours of the cliff, a masterpiece of Chinese architectural art.

Wutai Shan Mountains 五台山

There are four sacred Buddhist mountains in China: Emei Shan in Sichuan, Jiuhua Shan in Anhui, Putuo Shan in Zhejiang and Wutai Shan in Shanxi. Wutai Shan, the Five Terraces Mountain, rises in eastern Shanxi on the border to Hebei. As the name implies, it consists of five terrace-like peaks, the highest of which is in the north and has an elevation of 3,058 m. The best time to see them is in June and July. In April, the snow is still melting and in September, the first snow falls. Wutai Shan can be easily reached by the overland bus from Taiyuan. The drive takes about nine hours and takes the visitor through breathtaking mountain scenery.

Wutai Shan is dedicated to Wenshu Pusa, the bodhisattva Manjusri, the god of wisdom. Wenshu Pusa is supposed to have lived and taught here at one time. The first monastery was erected during the Eastern Han Dynasty. Historical records show that more than 200 monasteries already existed here during the Northern Qi Dynasty (550 — 577). The richest of them had great power and considerable influence for a time. Pilgrims to the monasteries made wealthy donations, and the monasteries' silver mines, foundries and workshops yielded a high profit. However, their number decreased to 75 by the time of the Song Dynasty. Wutai Shan flourished anew in the Ming era, when there were over 300 monasteries in the region. Unrest, wars, total neglect and the raw climate were instrumental in reducing their number to a few dozen by 1949. Today, attempts are being made to restore the remaining monasteries.

A large, white dagoba is located in the middle of Wutai Shan. The temple surrounding it was added in the 15th century.

Xiantong Si, the oldest Eastern Han Dynasty temple, is behind this temple. The temple has been restored many times in the course of its long history, so that the buildings preserved until the present are in the Ming and Qing architectural styles. There is a total of 400 buildings on the grounds of Xiantong Si monastery, which covers an area of 8 hectares and is thus the largest complex on Wutai Shan. The most noteworthy of the halls in Xiantong Si is the Bronze Hall. Two 6-m-tall bronze pagodas stand in front of it.

The wealthy monasteries in the middle of Wutai Shan could afford frequent alterations, so that the remaining buildings are hardly more than 400 years old. The monasteries located close to the periphery were poorer and had to refrain from making many changes, which is why their buildings are much older. Pusa Ding lamasery is located on Linjiu Feng peak north of Xiantong Si temple. It is also called Wenshu Si temple because the bodhisattva Wenshu is supposed to have lived there at one time. The temple was founded as early as the Northern Wei era. Emperors Kangxi and Qianlong are supposed to have resided there several times and left behind some calligraphies.

Shuxiang Si temple was founded during the Tang era. The statues in Wehshu Ge pavilion dating from 1496 are interesting; one of them depicts the bodhisattva Wenshu Pusa riding a lion.

Foguang Si monastery is located in the southwest part of Wutai Shan. It faces west and is built on two levels. The monastery was founded at the end of the 5th century, but the main halls, murals, inscriptions and statues date from the Tang period.

Other important monasteries are: Bishan Si (from the Northern Wei Dynasty) containing Buddha of white jade, Nanshan Si convent (from the Yuan Dynasty), Nanchan Si with a Tang era hall, Longquan Si (from the Song Dynasty) with a white marble ornamental gate and Luohou Si (from the Tang Dynasty).

Ruicheng District 芮城

Yongle Gong Monastery 永乐宫

The Daoist monastery Yongle Gong, now located in north Ruicheng, was originally situated on the banks of the Huanghe in Yongle, a town bearing the same name as the monastery. When the government decided to build the Sanmenxia dike project in the fifties, it became necessary to move the monastery. It found a new home in Ruicheng at the

Yongle Gong Monastery

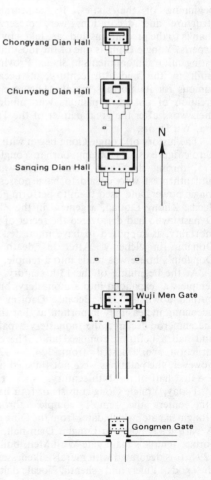

Chongyang Dian Hall

Chunyang Dian Hall

N

Sanqing Dian Hall

Wuji Men Gate

Gongmen Gate

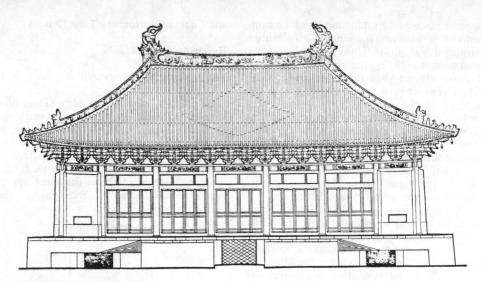

Sanqing Dian Hall

beginning of the sixties. Its appearance, structure and decorations were preserved, thanks to the precautions and care taken by the experts. Yongle Gong is one of the most interesting cultural monuments in Shanxi Province. Built in the mid-13th century, it became famous for its glorious murals. They are the creation of unknown painters who modeled their work after the great painter of the Tang era, Wu Daozi.

The history of Yongle Gong began with the heroic figure of Lü Dongbin, born in Yongle in 775, during the Tang Dynasty. He was a philanthropist who is said to have possessed magic powers and used them to perform good deeds. Zhong Liquan, a general in the Zhou Dynasty who had discovered the secret of immortality, is supposed to have interested Lü Dongbin in alchemy. After his death Lü Dongbin's house was made into a temple.

At the beginning of the 13th century, the temple was expanded into a monastery, but it burned down in 1231. Because Daoism was becoming increasingly important at that time, the emperor declared the monastery a palace and had a befitting complex built. The construction work lasted from 1247 — 1262; however, the paintings were not finished until the first half of the 14th century.

Today, Yongle Gong consists of four halls. One enters the temple complex through Gongmen gate, which dates from the Qing era. A path leads north to Longhu Dian hall, the former temple's main gate Wuji Men, built in 1294. It is decorated with murals, likenesses of the gods Yulei and shentu, local deities,

celestial warriors as well as celestial scribes and officials. Sanqing Dian, the largest of the four halls, is dedicated to the three highest deities of the Daoist Pantheon: Yuqing, Shangqing and Taiqing. A 94.68-m-long painting covers the walls. It was painted by Master Ma Junxiang from Luoyang in Henan from 1325 — 1358. Its theme: the immortals (286 in all) gather to honor the founders of Daoism. Chunyang Dian hall is dedicated to Lü Dongbin, also called Chun Yangzi. His life is pictured here in 52 episodes from his birth to his deification. The realistic portrayal of the people and their environment have made this painting an important source of information about life during the Yuan Dynasty. It was painted in 1358. The fourth hall, Chongyang Dian, is dedicated to the founder of the Daoist sect Quanzhen Jiao, Wang Chongyang (1112 — 1170). Episodes from his life and the lives of his disciples are shown in 49 pictures.

Neimenggu Autonomous Region (Inner Mongolia) 内蒙古自治区

Area: ca. 1,200,000 km²/Population: 19.2 million, including 16.5 million Han Chinese, 2.5 million Mongols, 145,000 Huis and 87,000 Manchus/Capital: Hohhot

Neimenggu is the third largest of China's provinces and autonomous regions. It stretches across the northern part of China and has an average elevation of 1,000 m above sea level. Geographically, it is a part of the North Chinese steppe plateau. A large part of it is desert and about half of its area can be used as grazing land. Only the area along both sides of the Huanghe, the Yellow River, which flows for hundreds of kilometers through Mongolia, is very fertile.

Neimenggu has a continental climate. Spring begins in May. The two hottest months of the year are July and August; in the capital, Hohhot, the average temperature in July is 25°C. Sixty percent of the annual precipitation falls in these two months. Winter begins at the end of September. It is bitterly cold and icy winds blow out of Siberia.

History

Tribes of the Xiongnu people lived in the area of what is now Mongolia as early as the 10th century BC. They started banding together around the 5th century BC and became a threat to the neighboring peoples, especially to the Chinese farmers settled in the adjacent southern areas. The latter protected themselves by building fortifications, finally creating the monumental Great Wall. Under the rule of Emperor Wudi during the Han Dynasty, the areas of present-day Gansu and Inner Mongolia were occupied to safeguard the trade routes to the west. In the 5th century AD, Turkic peoples invaded Mongolia and subordinated the country to their rule.

Mongolia was divided among several tribes during the 12th century. Finally, the Manghol tribe under the leadership of Genghis Khan succeeded in uniting the entire area under its rule. They conquered the Jin Empire in the 13th century and founded the Mongolian Yuan Dynasty with its capital in Beijing (Dadu). However, the last Yuan emperor had to flee to the Mongolian heartland in 1368. Struggles between the western, eastern and southern Mongols followed the fall of the dynasty until Dayan Khan managed to reunite the Mongolian tribes. In the 17th century, the Mongols recognized the danger the Manchus posed; however, the tribal leaders could not agree upon a common plan of action, as they were used to individual tribal autonomy. The Great Khan, Ligdan from the Tsachar tribe, was striving for a leading position, making him appear more dangerous to the individual tribal chiefs than the Manchus. Thus, the Manchus were able to force Ligdan to flee. The Inner Mongolian regions were annexed to the empire when the Manchurian Qing Dynasty was founded. In spite of a policy aimed at establishing a balance of power, the Manchus could not prevent numerous uprisings and independence movements. Emperors Kangxi and Qianlong were the only ones who were able to maintain their sovereignity over the Mongols. Even at the beginning of the second half of the 19th century, disturbances arose that were directed against Manchurian sovereignity and the masses of Chinese settlers on the one hand and against corrupt leaders on the other. Mongolian freedom fighters succeeded in separating Outer Mongolia from the empire in 1911 and declaring its independence with Russian support. In secret treaties, the Russians had promised Inner Mongolia to the Japanese, who invaded this area in increasing numbers during the thirties. The Mongols formed revolutionary secret societies which mostly joined the Communist movement. The leading figure in their struggle was Ulanfu (Wu Lanfu) who had joined the revolution at an early age and later became Chairman of Inner Mongolia. Even before the founding of the People's Republic of China, Inner Mongolia was declared an autonomous region on May 1, 1947. The region consisted of various former provinces to which others were added in 1954 — 55. Thus, Inner Mongolia soon comprised seven confederations (*meng*) covering an area of about 1.2 million km². The confederations were divided into cities, districts and banners (*qi*).

The policy of the central government towards Inner Mongolia changed with the advent of the Cultural Revolution. Action was taken out of fear of separatist movements and the revival of the old pan-Mongolian dream. The most decisive step was to separate large areas from Inner Mongolia and to annex them to other provinces in 1969, resulting in a reduction of area to about 450,000 km² consisting of only four confederations. The Chairman of Inner Mongolia, Ulanfu, fell into disgrace and was not rehabilitated until after the fall of the Gang of Four. Today, Mongolia's borders correspond to those before 1969.

Since the establishment of the People's Republic of China, the central government has tried to settle the nomads and expand agriculture. The population has been integrated into people's communes as far as possible. However, farming is only possible during the 110 — 160 days free of frost; therefore, two annual crops cannot be harvested. Frequent droughts also make farming difficult, though the construction of irrigation systems has made large desert areas arable. The most important crops are wheat, millet, corn and rice.

Inner Mongolia is one of China's most important stock-breeding areas; goats and sheep make up 70% of the livestock. Intensive industrial development began with the first five-year plan. Since then, Baotou especially has evolved into an industrial city. Coal and iron ore are mined near Baotou. Other mineral resources in addition to iron ore and coal are copper, chromium, aluminum, zinc and gold.

Hohhot, the capital, has chemical, machine, leather and wool industries.

The majority of Neimenggu's population is Han Chinese; only about 11% are Mongols. In addition, there are small minorities such as the Huis, Manchus and Koreans.

The typical dwelling of the nomadic Mongols is the yurt. It has a domed roof with a height of about 2.5 m and a circular wall with a diameter of 3 — 4 m. Wicker covered on the outside with a type of felt or leather is used as the building material. The yurt is held together with leather straps. It is set up on a foundation of earth and stones. Its interior is not partitioned: the stove is in the center, the stove-pipe runs outside through a hole in the

ceiling, and the beds are placed around the stove. Other pieces of furniture are placed against the wall. Large families have two or more yurts.

Agricultural expansion and irrigation have caused many Mongols to settle. Some yurts have given way to houses, and more modern building materials are frequently used for the remaining yurts today.

Hohhot 呼和浩特市

Hohhot, which means 'blue city' in Mongolian, is the capital of the Autonomous Region of Inner Mongolia with a population of 1.21 million. It is located south of Daqing Shan mountain on the edge of the traditional settled areas of China. In comparison to many other Chinese cities, it has a relatively short history; it was not founded until the Ming Dynasty by the famous tribal leader of the Tümed, Altan Khan.

He had been leader of the eastern Mongols since 1543 and led his forces close to Beijing in 1550, but was forced to retreat. Altan Khan tried to provide his country with an

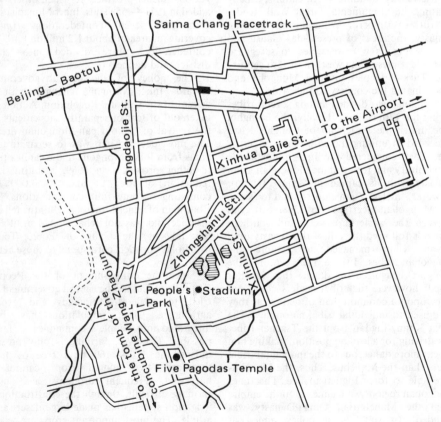

Map of Hohhot

administration modeled on the Han Chinese system. The new city, Kuku-Khoto (blue city) today called Hohhot, became the seat of government.

Towards the end of the Ming Dynasty, Chinese farmers settled in the fertile areas around Hohhot. During the Qing Dynasty, forces of the Kangxi Emperor entered parts of Mongolia to insure the supremacy of the Manchus, and soldiers were stationed about 4 km away from Mongolian Kuku-Khoto. A new, Chinese city arose. As time went by, both cities grew into one large one. The former Mongolian city developed into an important trade center for livestock and agricultural products and the new, Chinese city became the administrative and residential districts.

Hohhot was declared the capital of the newly-formed province Suiyuan in 1928. The region was controlled by the Japanese from 1937 — 1945 and the city has been the provincial capital of Neimenggu Autonomous Region since 1952. After the establishment of the People's Republic of China, Hohhot developed into quite an important manufacturing city with its chemical, textile, construction material as well as iron and steel industries.

Hohhot is not only the political, but also the cultural center of Inner Mongolia. In 1957, the first university of the region was established here.

There is a good view of the city and it surroundings from the drum tower in the New City: the mountains to the north, the fields to the south, the Old City to the west with the old drum tower and the mosque.

Many visitors to Hohhot consider the highlight of their stay to be the cultural entertainment, the demonstrations of Mongolian horsemanship and traditional boxing.

Renmin Gongyuan, People's Park 人民公园

The park has an area of 46.5 hectares. A lake covering 10.4 hectares offers enough room for boating in the spring and summer and ice-skating in the winter. Its attractions are a zoo and a flower garden. In addition, there is a martyrs' memorial tower on the grounds.

Wuta Si, the Temple of Five Pagodas 五塔寺

All that remains of the temple complex Wuta Si is the Diamond Pagoda. The rectangular, solid stone building dates from the reign of Yongzheng (1723 — 1735) in the Qing era. The lower part of the pagoda consists of seven narrow tiers decorated with reliefs. Texts taken from the *Jingang Jing* are

inscribed in Mongolian, Tibetan and Sanskrit. Five pagodas and a pavilion are located on the terrace of the lower part. The middle pagoda is the highest. The first floors of each of these pagodas are richly decorated with Buddha and bodhisattva figures.

Xilitu Zhao Lama Temple

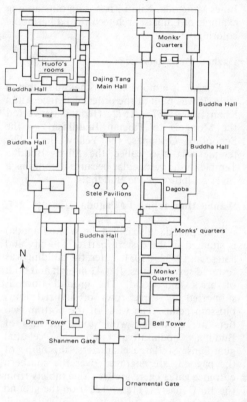

Qingzhen Dasi Mosque 清真大寺

The mosque is situated at the north gate of the Old City. It dates from the reign of Qianlong and faces west. The Holy Hall was restored in 1933 with the help of donations, and a minaret was also constructed. The mosque contains several valuable old editions of the Koran.

Xilitu Zhao Lama Temple 席力图召

Xilitu Zhao is located in Shitouxiang Lane in the Old City of Hohhot. During the Ming era, there was only a small temple here in which Huofo Xitituke lived. He was an honored person, for he was versed in the holy Buddhist writings and the Mongolian, Tibetan and Chinese languages. It is said that even the fourth Dalai Lama studied under his tutelage when he was young. At the beginning of the Qing era, the temple was expanded on a large scale and redesigned. The entire complex has five courtyards, from the ornamental gate in the south to its northern end. All of the halls were built in the Tibetan style. Southeast of the main hall Dajing Tang, there is a 15-m-tall dagoba said to be the most beautiful one in Inner Mongolia. Xilitu Zhao is an outstanding example of Lamaist architecture and harmonic coloring.

Dazhao Monastery 大召

Dazhao is a monastery in the Sino-Tibetan style. It was built at the order of Prince Altan Khan from 1567 – 1572. He had converted the Mongols to Tibetan Buddhism — the School of Gelugpas, the Yellow Sect. The temple was also called the Silver Buddha Temple in the vernacular because it contains a silver sculpture of the Buddha.

Wanbu Huayanjing Ta Pagoda 万部华严经塔

This pagoda (also called the White Pagoda) is situated in the eastern part of the city and dates from 983 — 1031. Later, the building was restored several times. It is 43 m high and built of brick and wood. The ground floor is supported by three rows of stylized lotus blossom petals. The walls of the bottom two tiers are decorated with stone carvings of Buddha, bodhisattvas and the celestial guardians. Six large characters, the name of the pagoda, are engraved over the southern entrance gate. There are six stone tablets from the Jin Dynasty (1115 — 1234) on the ground floor. On his way to the top, the visitor will discover various inscriptions made by pilgrims from all over China and from foreign countries on the walls. The oldest ones date from 1162.

Wang Zhaojun's Burial-place 昭君墓

Nine kilometers south of Hohhot, the tomb of Wang Zhaojun, the concubine of an emperor of the Western Han Dynasty, is located. She was married to Prince Han Xie Shanyu of the Xiongnu in 33 BC to establish peace between the two peoples. Supposedly, the Prince died after two years, upon which she became the wife of his successor, according to tribal custom. There are a great many stories and plays about the fate of Wang Zhaojun.

According to Mongolian tradition, Wang Zhaojun is respected for having been the wife of Han Xie Shanyu. After her death, she gradually became a part of myth as a goddess of fertility.

For the Han Chinese, she was a victim of war because she was given to the Prince of the Xiongnu. However, both sides consider her to be a symbol of peace, and therefore her tomb has always been considered to be of great significance. There is a pavilion in front of as well as on the hill. In a nearby exhibition hall, the story of Wang Zhaojun's life is told.

Hotels

Hohhot Binguan, 呼和浩特宾馆 Yingbinlu, tel. 2 28 38

Xincheng Binguan, 新城宾馆 Hulunnanlu, tel. 2 45 13

Minzu Lüshe, 民族旅社 Zhongshanxilu, tel. 2 53 67

Xilin Lüshe, 锡林旅社 Xilinbeilu, tel. 2 48 50

Bayantala Fandian, 巴彦塔拉饭店 Xilinbeilu, tel. 6 68 79

Travel agency

Zhongguo Lüxingshe, Xiuhuajie Yingbinlu, tel. 44 94

Baotou 包头市

Baotou, a city of 1.5 million, is the most important manufacturing center in Inner Mongolia. It is located at an elevation of 1,700 m above sea level on the Huanghe river. The young city has only a few cultural and historical attractions with the exception of the Buddhist monastic palace Wudang Zhao from the Qing Dynasty. The area around Baotou was inhabited as early as the Tang Dynasty, however, the village did not develop into a trading center until the Qing Dynasty. It was fortified in 1871. Baotou grew more quickly after completion of the railroad to Beijing in 1922 and became the most important commercial center of Mongolia and Northwest China. Wool, furs, grain, tea and clothing were the articles of trade. The city had over 300,000 inhabitants by 1932. The government built a railroad to Lanzhou in the fifties, thereby connecting Baotou to Sichuan in Central China and Xinjiang in Northwest China. An iron and steel integrated plant which relies on rich iron ore deposits in Bayan Obo to the north was a result of the first five-year plan (1953 — 57).

Wudang Zhao Monastery 五当召

Wudang Zhao (Guangjue Si) is called the Temple of the White Lotus in Tibetan and the Willow Temple in Mongolian. Located 70 km northeast of Baotou on Huluntu Mountain, it is the best-preserved Lama temple in Inner Mongolia. It was erected during the reign of Kangxi and restored in 1749. At one time, 1,000 — 1,200 monks lived here. The largest hall of the complex is the impressively furnished Suguxin Dugong, in which monks gathered for study and prayer on the ground floor. Dong Ko'er Dugong hall is the oldest and because of its sculptures, the most important hall in the monastery.

Genghis Khan Mausoleum 成吉思汗墓

The mausoleum is beautifully situated about 15 km southeast of the town of Atengxilian in Yijin Horo Qi banner. Genghis Khan himself supposedly chose this as his last resting-place. He died a natural death during a campaign against the Western Xia in 1227. This region has been called Yijin Horo, Grave of the Leader, since his burial. Genghis Khan lies in the back part of the main hall with his three wives; his fourth son and his son's wife lie in the east hall. The prince's weapons are on display in the west hall.

Nadamu, the Autumn Festival 那达慕大会

The famous Mongolian Nadamu festival originally was held to honor the gods of the mountains and roads. Nowadays, however, the religious background of this merry national festival is hardly discernible. Many competitions take place, for example in riding, boxing and archery. Musical and theatrical performances are offered and a small market is held.

Hotels

Baotou Binguan, 包头市宾馆 Gangtie Dajie, tel. 2 66 12

Qingshan Binguan, 青山宾馆 Wenhualu, tel. 3 36 08

Donghe Binguan, 东河宾馆 Hongguang Dajie, tel. 4 34 86

Gangcheng Fandian, 钢城饭店 Gangtie Dajie, tel. 2 59 73

Travel agency

Zhongguo Lüxingshe, Baotou Hotel, tel. 2 46 15

Liaoning Province 辽宁省

Area: ca. 145,000 km²/Population: 35.7 million/Capital: Shenyang

Liaoning Province is the southernmost of the three provinces of Northeast China, formerly called Manchuria. Owing to its industry, it is among the most important provinces in the country. Forty percent of China's steel is produced in Liaoning and one quarter of the entire output of heavy industry is manufactured here. The reasons for this are the government's heavy investments in industry since 1949 and the build-up of industry starting as early as the end of the last century. In addition, the province is also rich in natural resources, especially iron ore, hard coal, bituminous slate, bauxite, lead and salt.

Liaoning extends around the Gulf of Bohai. The capital, Shenyang, is located on the Liaohe river lowlands, which cover about a third of Liaoning's entire area. Mountains border them to the east and west. The climate is substantially milder than in the other northern provinces owing to its proximity to the sea.

The average temperature near the coast is -5°C in January and 25°C in July; in Shenyang, it is -13°C in January and, in July, also 25°C. Three-quarters of the annual precipitation falls between June and September.

The population is comprised of 95% Han Chinese; the 5% minority of 70% Manchus and 30% Mongols, Huis and Koreans. Over 40% of the population lives in urban areas, which is reflected by the high degree of Liaoning's industrialization.

History

Northeast China was settled early, though only sparsely. Chinese peasants settled early in the Liaohe river lowlands and it was chiefly Manchus and Mongols who carried on woodworking, grazing, mining and fishing in the outlying areas. In the course of its long history, Liaoning became increasingly important as an immigration area for the Han Chinese. The Manchurian rulers tried to stop this development during the Qing Dynasty. In the 19th century, Northeast China became increasingly interesting for foreign powers and Liaoning, rich in mineral resources, was especially affected. The Russians built the Northeast China Railroad between 1896 — 1903, which linked up the port city Dalian to Changchun, Jilin and Harbin, Heilongjiang before continuing on to Vladivostock. In this way, they secured their access to the ice-free port Lüshun (present-day Lüda). In 1907, the Russians lost their influence in South Manchuria after the Russian-Japanese War. Japan considered Liaoning's mineral resources a welcome addition to its own industry. Thus, they tried to gain control over the economy and, by way of investments, to use the industrial sector, especially heavy industry and mining, to further their own interests. Liaoning was a part of the 'independent' Japanese-run state 'Manzhouguo' from 1932 — 1945, headed by the former Qing emperor Puyi. Some of the province's manufacturing plants suffered heavy damages during the Russian-Japanese and Civil Wars; a large part was dismantled by the Russians and thus lost. Therefore, industrial reconstruction and expansion was one of the declared goals of the new government after 1949. Heavy industry was especially favored. One of the most important projects was the iron and steel integrated plant in Anshan. Today, the cities of Shenyang, Lüda, Anshan, Fushun, Benxi, Fuxin and Beipiao represent the largest industrial centers of Liaoning.

Liaoning's most important agricultural products are: corn, soybeans, sorghum (Gaoliang), rice (especially in the Liaohe lowlands), raw silk, peanuts and sweet potatoes.

Shenyang 沈阳市

Shenyang, the capital of Liaoning, is called Mukden in Manchurian. It is 841 km from Beijing and one of the largest cities in China with a population of five million. It is located on the Hunhe, a tributary of the Liaohe, on a fertile plain. The center of Shenyang is the Chinese Old City, where the Manchurian Imperial Palace is also located. The imperial tombs, Beiling, are north of the Old City. The wide boulevards are typical of Japanese construction in the western part of this city after 1905 and 1932.

History

The Shenyang area has been a settlement area for Chinese immigrants from Shandong and Hebei since the Han Dynasty.

The rulers of the Khitan tribe in North China set up the Liao Dynasty and made Shenyang into an important military base in the 10th century. The Liao rulers were followed by the Jin, who were in turn succeeded by the rulers of the Mongolian Yuan Dynasty. In the 13th century, the settlement was named Shenyang. In the 17th century, the groups of Tungusic Sushis, later called Manchus, living in eastern and southeastern Manchuria united under the leadership of Nurhachi (1559 — 1626) and brought the region of Manchuria under their control. In 1625, they made Shenyang their capital and renamed it Mukden. Using the city as a starting point, they conquered the rest of China during the following years. In 1636, Abukai, one of Nurhachi's sons, founded the Qing Dynasty in Shenyang. The Manchus succeeded in gaining control of the Chinese empire in 1644. Beijing became the new capital, but Shenyang was still honored as the old capital and as the seat of ancestral temples.

During the past 100 years, the fate of the city has largely been determined by foreign powers. After receiving the concession to build the railroad, Russia made Shenyang its base. After The Battle of Mukden (2/19-3/10/1905) during the Russian-Japanese War, Russia had to give up its rights to southern Manchurian ground to the Japanese. Mukden then became the most important Japanese base for their exploitation of Manchurian mineral resources. After World War I, Japan tolerated Zhang Zuolin as ruler of the northern provinces in Mukden. However, he was assassinated by a bomb in 1928. In September 1931, the Mukden Incident followed the murder of a Japanese captain: the Japanese attacked Mukden and occupied all of Manchuria. The 'independent' state of Manzhouguo was founded in 1932 with its capital in Changchun. Russia declared war on Japan at the beginning of August 1945 and Mukden was captured shortly thereafter. It was during this time that the Russians dismantled the manufacturing plants. In the spring of 1946, the city was occupied by Chinese Nationalist troops. On October 30, 1948, the Communist troops succeeded in taking the city. Shenyang was the capital of Dongbei, the northeast region, from 1949 — 1954, Dongbei being one of the six large administrative regions into which China was divided at that time. The development of Northeast China took a dramatic turn in the direction of an autonomous region under the rule of Gao Gang, who was, however, removed from power in 1954.

The region was divided into three provinces and Shenyang became the capital of Liaoning Province.

Map of Shenyang

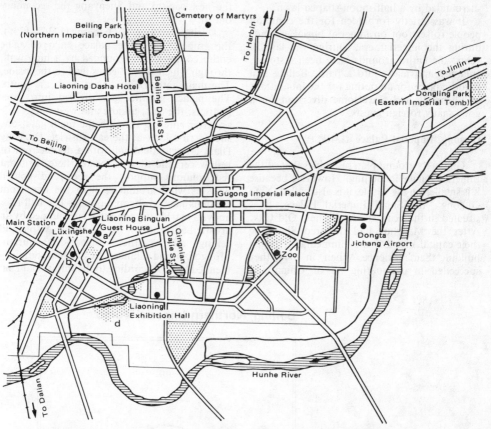

a. Zhonghua Theater   b. Cultural Palace   c. Zhongshan Park   d. South Lake Park   e. Qingnian Park

Shenyang and its neighboring cities Fushun, Anshan and Benxi form the most important industrial area in China today. The largest machine manufacturing center is located here, as well as such branches of industry as the electric, metal, chemical, textile and food-processing industries. Shenyang is not only the industrial center of North China, but also its cultural one. Various technical institutes, academies and the University of Liaoning are of significance.

The best time to travel is in August and September.

Beiling, Northern Imperial Tomb 北陵 (昭陵)

The Beiling tomb, also called Zhaoling, is located in the northern part of the city and is the largest of the three Manchurian imperial tombs. The founder of the Qing Dynasty, Taizong (Abukai), who died in 1643, lies there with his first wife and some of his secondary wives. Later Qing emperors frequently came here and offered sacrifices to their ancestors.

Beiling was constructed on an area of 450 hectares between 1643 — 1651. The entire complex is surrounded by a gigantic wall. The entrance gate, Zhenghong Men, is on the southern end of the north-south axis; it is a red building with a yellow ceramic tile roof. In the outermost courtyard of the complex, stone columns and animal sculptures line both sides of the path. Among the animal sculptures are two white horses called Great White, Dabai, and Little White, Xiaobai, portrayals of the emperor's two favorite horses. The path leads northward to the so-called Sacred Virtue Stele and to the 'Rectangular City', which is surrounded by a high wall. A tower rises above the southern entrance gate, Long'en Men. A large hall, Long'en Dian, is in the middle of the inner courtyard. Minglou tower is located north of it with a stele bearing the inscription 'Tomb of Emperor Taizong'. From the tower terrace, one can see the grave-mound surrounded by a half-moon-shaped lawn.

It was strictly forbidden for the common people to set foot on imperial burial grounds during the imperial era. During the last 30 years, the entire grounds have been restored, enlarged and made into a park. Beiling is a favorite place for an outing for the inhabitants of Shenyang and a welcome diversion for a good many foreign guests.

Gugong, Imperial Palace 沈阳故宫

Gugong's ground plan resembles that of the Imperial Palace in Beijing. However, because it is smaller on the whole, it is also called 'Xiao Gugong', the Small Imperial Palace. It is situated in the heart of the Chinese Old City. After the Manchus had declared Shenyang their capital in 1625, they immediately began building their residence. When, in 1644, they succeeded in conquering all of China and

entered into the Ming heritage, Beijing became the new capital and Shenyang the secondary one.

During the reign of Qianlong (1736—1795), the emperor had the palace enlarged. The entire complex is surrounded by a high wall, through which several gates lead to the inside. The main gate, Daqing Men, is in the south. The palace grounds are divided into three districts: the east, middle and west ones.

After entering through the main gate, one should first look at the east district. Dazheng Dian, an octagonal hall with a double roof of yellow ceramic tiles, is located here. Brilliant red columns support the roof and golden dragons wind around each of the two front columns next to the main door. The hall rises above a marble terrace and is surrounded by an artistic balustrade of carved stone. A splendid ceiling adorns the inside. Manchurian, Mongolian and Chinese art are harmoniously blended here. According to the traditional Han

Beiling, Northern Imperial Tomb

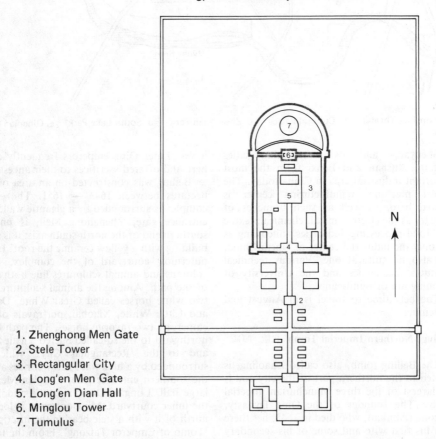

1. Zhenghong Men Gate
2. Stele Tower
3. Rectangular City
4. Long'en Men Gate
5. Long'en Dian Hall
6. Minglou Tower
7. Tumulus

Gugong, Imperial Palace

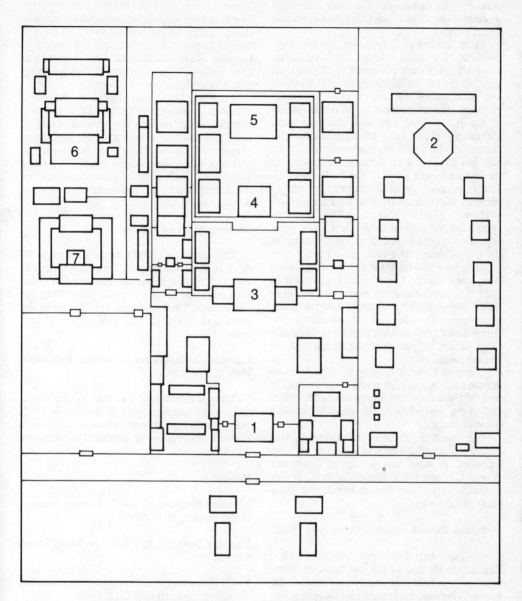

1. Daqing Men Gate
2. Dazheng Dian Hall
3. Congzheng Dian Hall
4. Fenghuang Lou Tower
5. Qingning Gong Palace
6. Wensu Ge Library
7. Theater

Chinese style, the hall has no outer walls; instead, it has lattice-work doors. The Manchurian ruler carried out the most important ceremonies and announced his plan to conquer China here.

There is a row of five smaller, square kings' pavilions. On each side of Dazheng Dian. Formerly, they were presented to the imperial generals for successful battles; today, weapons and garments of war are on exhibit in these pavilions. If one proceeds to the center district of the palace, one first sees the main hall, Congzheng Dian. Like Dazheng Dian, it is decorated with a yellow ceramic tile roof. Two columns adorned with dragons are located on the left and right sides of the hall's interior. The gorgeous imperial throne is placed between the columns in front of a screen with engraved golden dragons. The emperor conducted his official duties here. The great ceremony on the occasion of the founding of the Qing Dynasty also took place here.

The next building to the north is Fenghuang Lou, the Phoenix Tower, which was built in 1627. The tower has three stories and was used by the emperor for conferences and banquets. Fenghuang Lou was also the entrance to the 'Inner Chambers' and led directly to Qingning Gong palace, the northernmost building on the central palace axis.

Qingning Gong, erected in 1625, rests on an approximately 4-m-high terrace. In the eastern part of the palace is the imperial bedchamber and in the western part, the imperial couple's place of sacrifice.

The western district of Gugong was completed in 1782 and was used for cultural activities. A stage was set up in front and Wensu Ge library was housed in back. It was originally used for the collection of Siku Quanshu's works.

Dongling, Eastern Imperial Tomb 东陵 (福陵)

Dongling burial grounds, officially called Fuling, are located 11 km northeast of Shenyang on the banks of the Hunhe and at the foot of Tianzhu Shan mountain. Dongling was constructed for Nurhachi and his wife on an area of 194,800 m² from 1629 — 1651. Nurhachi whose posthumous title was Taizu, had united the groups of Tungusic Sushis (later called Manchus) under his rule and made Northeast China his dominion. He was the father of Abukai, the founder of the Qing Dynasty, who is buried in the Beiling burial grounds.

The arrangement of Dongling coincides with that of Beiling burial grounds. The

entrance gate, Zhenghong Men, is on the southern end of the north-south central axis. There is a row of stone sculptures to its north. The path then leads uphill over 108 steps and a stone bridge to the stele tower, where the Sacred Virtue Stele containing a calligraphy of Emperor Kangxi is located. The 'Rectangular City' follows, just as in the Beiling complex, and is surrounded by a high wall.

Long'en Dian, the Hall of Ancestral Worship, is situated in the middle of the city. Minglou tower rises to the north of Long'en Dian and contains a stele with the inscription 'Tomb of Emperor Taizu'. The grave-mound within a half-moon shaped border is behind Minglou. Dongling burial grounds are one of the special sights of Shenyang due to their natural surroundings.

Shisheng Si Lama Temple 实胜寺

This temple was built on an area of 5,500 m² in 1638. Shanmen gate, Tianwang Dian, the Hall of Celestial Kings and Dadian, the Great Hall, are lined up one after the other along the central axis. These buildings are flanked by the drum and bell towers as well as several side halls.

Liaoning Zhanlanguan, Liaoning Exhibition Hall 辽宁展览馆

The exhibition hall was built in the Soviet style in the southern part of the city in 1959. Here, visitors can inform themselves about the latest state of industrial products in Shenyang and its environs.

Hotels

Liaoning Binguan, 辽宁宾馆 Hongqi Guang-chang Square, tel. 3 26 41

Liaoning Dasha, 辽宁大厦 Huanghe Dajie, tel. 6 25 46

Youyi Binguan, 友谊宾馆 in the western part of Beiling Park, tel 6 28 22, 6 13 98

Huaqiao Fandian, Zhongshanlu 3, tel. 3 42 14, CTS has an office in this hotel.

Restaurants

Laobian Jiaozi Guan,
Beishichang, tel.2 18 19. Jiaozi are small filled pastries, either boiled or fried.

Shenhe Fandian,

Zhongjie, tel. 4 40 20

Lumingchun,
Zhonghualu, tel. 2 51 27, local specialties.

Shopping

Friendship Store, Youyi Shangdian,
Zhongshanlu
In Taiyuanjie Street there is a book, antique
and art shop.

Travel agency

Guoji Lüxingshe, CITS,
Nanzhan, South Train Station, tel. 3 46 53

Zhongguo Lüxingshe,
Nanzhan, South Train Station, tel. 3 46 53

CAAC ticket sales,
Zhonghualu, tel. 3 37 05

Train station,
Ticket sales, tel. 3 35 25, 2 01 61
Information, tel. 20 41 93, 20 30 03

Taxis,
North of the train station, tel. 3 43 64, 3 49 78

Bank of China,
Zhonghualu, tel. 3 29 19

Post office,
Taiyuanjie, tel. 3 27 27

University,
Liaoning Daxue, tel. 6 25 41
Foreign students, tel. 6 33 56

Telephone,
Long distance calls 03
Information 06

Fushun 抚顺市

Fushun, one of the coal centers of China, is
situated about 40 km east of Shenyang on the
Hunhe river. Fushun has very large bituminous
and oleiferous coal reserves estimated at one
billion metric tons, some of which is mined in
open pits. Annual production is said to be 15
million tons. In addition to the coal mines, the
city has other industries such as chemical,
aluminum and cement manufacturing,
petroleum fields, iron and steel works and
electric power plants.

Wheat, cotton and tobacco are among the
most important agricultural products.

Dahuofang Reservoir and Surroundings
大伙房水库

Dahuofang, one of the largest reservoirs in
China, lies in a beautiful area on the upper and
middle courses of the Hunhe, about 15 km
from Fushun. It was erected on an area of 110
km^2 from 1954 — 1958 and provides for the
irrigation of about 120,000 hectares. In
addition, 50 million kilowatts of electric
current are produced annually. The reservoir
and its surroundings make a charming
destination for an outing.

Yuanshuailin Tomb 元帅林

Yuanshuailin was originally built as a burial
place for the warlord Zhang Zuolin in 1929.
When the Japanese won control of this area in
1931, Yuanshuailin could no longer be used for
its designated purpose. The burial place,
located directly on the reservoir, abounds in
stone carvings and sculptures; there are 260
marble representations that used to be in the
Long'en Si temple in Beijing and date from the
Ming and Qing dynasties.

Sa'erhu Shan Hill 萨尔浒山

Sa'erhu Shan is 70 m high and located
southeast of the reservoir. It was of great
strategic importance in past centuries. The
Qing emperor had a stone stele erected in 1776
that bears an inscription commemorating the
victory of the Qing over the Ming at this place.

Travel agency

Guoji Lüxingshe, CITS, is located in Fushun
Binguan guest house, tel. 65 50, 65 60

Xinbin District 新宾县

Yongling Imperial Family Tomb 永陵

Yongling burial place northwest of the
small city of Yongling in Xinbin district is one
of the three imperial burial grounds of the
Qing Dynasty that are open to visitors in
Liaoning. Nurhachi's relatives lie here.
Yongling was built on 11,880 m^2 in 1598. Its
design is similar to that of the tombs at
Shenyang.

Anshan 鞍山市

The steel center of China is situated about
90 km southwest of Shenyang at the foot of the
Qianshan mountains in Anshan, a city of over

one million inhabitants. Other branches of industry in Anshan are the chemical, textile and electric industries, farm machinery manufacturing, ceramics and repair shops. Wide streets lined by trees and flowers and the many green areas are an attempt to spare Anshan the grayness of a typical manufacturing city.

History

Anshan was officially established in 1387 and fortified as a part of the expansion of defences against the Manchus during the Ming Dynasty. The city burned down to the ground during the Boxer Rebellion and suffered heavy damages for the second time during the Russian-Japanese War (1904 — 1905). A new Anshan arose 10 km north of the old city. In 1909, rich iron ore deposits were found in and around Anshan and the first iron-works opened in 1918, the first steelworks in 1935.

Anshan was heavily bombed towards the end of the war. Large parts of the remaining plants were dismantled and removed by the Russians, and the Civil War resulted in further destruction. After the founding of the People's Republic in 1949, the build-up of heavy industry was one of the declared goals of the new government. The reconstruction and expansion of the iron and steel industries in Anshan was begun right away under the first five-year plan.

Today, Anshan is one of the most important manufacturing cities besides Shanghai, Tianjin and Wuhan.

Tanggangzi Springs 汤岗子温泉

Tanggangzi springs are located about 10 km southeast of Anshan in the middle of a lovely park. They are hot springs and their water is crystal-clear and rich in minerals. Especially people who suffer from rheumatism expect a great healing effect from the water.

All visitors, also foreign ones, can bathe here in private rooms provided for this purpose.

Qianshan Mountains 千山

Qianshan, the Thousand Mountains, are located 20 km east of Anshan and are one of the three best-known mountain ranges in Northeast China. Their average height is 700 m. The 990 peaks gave the mountain range its name.

Qianshan is a very beautiful region, abounding in canyons, springs, pine trees, pavilions and temples. The sights mentioned below are only the most important of various attractions. Xianrentai in the southeastern Qianshan is the highest peak with an elevation of 708 m. There is a 20-m-high rock on its peak that is often compared to the head of a goose.

Longquan Si temple, Dragon Springs Temple, in the northern part of the Qianshan mountains is the region's largest. From time immemorial, the Dragon Springs, Longquan, have bubbled up here. Longquan Si was built during the Ming era in 1558.

The Daoist monastery Wuliang Guan in the northeastern Qianshan was founded by Daoist monks in 1677. Several main halls have been preserved.

Wufo Ding, the Five Buddhas Peak, is the second highest mountain and is located in the northwest.

Pu'an Guan monastery is located about 3 km west of Longquan Si at the foot of Wufo Ding. It is the highest of the many monasteries and temples in the Qianshan. A climb up the mountain eastwards from the monastery leads to the top of Wufo Ding, which affords an excellent view.

Travel agency: in Anshan Hotel.

Lüda (Lüshun-Dalian) 旅大市

Lüda, the consolidation of the cities of Lüshun and Dalian, is on the south end of Liaodong peninsula. Lüda has 4.7 million inhabitants and is an important port and industry town. In addition, the pretty surroundings, mild climate and many sand beaches make this area a favorite vacation spot.

Lüshun, better known to westerners as Port Arthur, lies in a strategically important place, for the entrance to the Gulf of Bohai, the seaway to Northeast China and Tianjin, is controlled from here. The city's harbor is very deep and, therefore, suited for large ships. Moreover, it remains open during the entire winter.

During the Qing Dynasty, the main base of the coastal defenses was located here. In 1878, Lüshun was chosen to be the home port of the Beiyang fleet, China's first modern naval force. Lüshun was involved in the Japanese-Russian conflicts at the end of the 19th century. Russia needed the ice-free port to insure itself an entry-way to the Pacific, whereas Japan wanted to hold open its way into Manchuria. In 1903, the Russians completed the railway to Lüshun and built up an important naval base that they had to relinquish to the Japanese after the Russian-Japanese War (1904 — 1905). After 1949, Lüshun again developed into an important Chinese naval base.

Dalian's fate is closely bound to Lüshun's. Under Russian influence, the town developed into a commercial city, and shipyards and wharfages arose. Dalian was conceded to the Japanese with Lüshun. They sped up the development of Dalian into a modern port for their own interests. The harbor basin was expanded and warehouses and shipyards were constructed. In 1931, Dalian was one of the country's most important ports. Industry developed at the same speed. Locomotive and railroad-car factories were built in connection with the new Northeast China Railway. They were followed by machine manufacturing, textile and cement factories as well as more shipyards during the next years. Since 1949, heavy investments have been made to expand the harbor and industrial complexes. A new oil port accessible for tankers with a capacity up to 100,000 gross registered tons was erected in 1976. It was also possible to improve agriculture in Lüda. Today, the area is called the home of the apple. Apples, daily fare in Europe, are in great demand in China and preferred to other fruits. Of course, there is also seafood here. The port of Lüda is one of the most important fishing ports in China.

Dalian's Museum of Natural History 大连自然博物馆

The Museum of National History lies north of Shengli Bridge and is one of the largest of its kind in Northeast China. A total of 40,000 objects are exhibited in an area of 2,470 m², including extinct mammals and marine animals, rare plants and minerals.

Dalian offers three pretty parks: Laodong Gongyuan 劳动公园 with a small lake and pavilions east of Stalin Square; Laohutan Gongyuan 老虎滩公园 and Xinghai Gongyuan 星海公园 both situated directly in the ocean.

Lüshun Museum 旅顺博物馆

Lüshun Museum is on Xinshijie Street in Lüshun district. Included in its exhibits are historical documents, bronze objects, ceramics, paintings and carvings displayed on an area of 1,700 m² since 1954.

Yingchengzi Tomb 营城子壁画墓

Yingchengzi lies south of the village Shagang in Ganjingzi district. The special feature of this tomb are the murals, which afford interesting insights into the life of the Chinese upper class and the high level of artistry of the Eastern Han era.

Hotels

Bangchuidao Binguan, beach hotel 棒锤岛宾馆 Bangchui Dao (Ginseng Island), tel. 2 57 44

Dalian Binguan, 大连宾馆 Zhongshan Guangchang, center of the city, tel. 2 31 11, 2 43 63

Dalian Fandian, 大连饭店 Tianjinjie, tel. 2 31 71, 2 39 41

Youyi Binguan, 友谊宾馆 Stalin Lu 137, tel. 2 38 90

Yunshan Binguan, 云杉宾馆 Zhongshan Guangchang, tel. 2 51 63, 2 67 19

Nanshan Binguan, Fenglinjie 56, tel. 2 51 03 CITS office in the hotel.

Travel agency

Guoji Lüxingshe, CITS, Zhongguo Lüxingshe, Huaqiao Lüxingshe Fenglinjie 56, tel. 2 51 03

CAAC Office, Dagongjie 12, tel. 3 58 84, 3 54 83

Train station, ticket sales, Qingniwaqiao, tel. 20 33 31

Taxis, Qingniwaqiao, tel. 3 59 55, 3 52 45

Jilin Province 吉林省

Area: 187,000 km² / Population: 22.6 million / Capital: Changchun

Jilin occupies the center of Dongbei, the northeastern part of China. The province can be divided into three geographical regions: the heavily forested, mountainous east, the central hilly area and the western plains. Three important rivers have their sources in the eastern Changbai Shan mountains: the Yalu, the Tumen and the Songhua Jiang (Sungari). The latter is the most important river in Jilin.

The population is comprised of 92.9% Han Chinese. The majority of the remaining 7.1% are Koreans (1.05 million) and Manchus (318,000); the Huis and the Mongols (71,000)

make up smaller groups. Climatically, Jilin lies between raw Heilongjiang and milder Liaoning. Thus, Jilin's winters are long and cold and the rivers are frozen over for up to five months, but the summers are hot. Eighty-three percent of the annual precipitation falls from May to September. The greatest amount of precipitation falls in the eastern, mountainous area; it decreases considerably farther west.

History

The province was not founded until 1907. After the Japanese occupied it, Jilin belonged to the puppet state Manzhouguo from 1932 — 1945. During the first half of 1945, Russian troops invaded Jilin. After they had left, the Chinese Nationalists came, who were, in their turn, driven away by Communist troops in 1948.

Forestry is one of Jilin's most important branches of industry, as about 27% of the province is covered by woods.

Soy beans, corn, rice, sugar beets, sorghum (Gaoliang) and millet are the most important crops.

Stock-raising (horses, cattle and sheep) is carried out especially by Mongols. Also important are deer-raising and ermine fur farming. East Jilin is famous and valued for its medicinal herbs. Ninety percent of the Chinese ginseng production comes from this area.

Changchun 长春市

Changchun, the capital of Jilin since 1954, is the center of the Chinese auto industry. Because it is such a new city, it has no noteworthy historical sights. In 1933, the Japanese declared the city the capital of Manzhouguo, the country they had created,

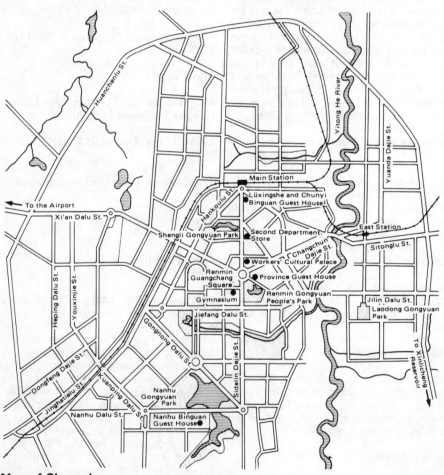

Map of Changchun

and named it Xinjing.

Changchun lies on the banks of the Yitong He river and has 1.5 million inhabitants. Since the establishment of China's first auto factory here in 1953, it has been the motor city of China. The factory's models include the Jiefang truck, Liberation; and the well-known Hongqi sedan, Red Flag. Buses, tractors, locomotives and railroad cars have also been manufactured in Changchun since 1957.

Changchun's universities and research institutes are also of importance. The former administration and government buildings of the Japanese occupation powers have now become centers of university life. Changchun's movie studios are known throughout the entire country.

The countryside about 20 km from Changchun on the upper course of the Yitong He river is especially lovely. The noted Xinlicheng reservoir is located there.

Imperial Palace 伪满洲国皇宫

The former residence of the last Qing emperor, Puyi, northeast of Changchun is open to visitors.

After Japan occupied Manchuria in 1931, they tried to separate it from China by establishing a so-called 'independent state'. Puyi, the last emperor of the Qing Dynasty, was brought to Changchun on March 9, 1932, and declared emperor of Manzhouguo, a hereditary 'empire', in 1934. The power over this empire was in the hands of the Prime Minister, a Japanese government official.

The palace is divided into two districts. The 'emperor' carried out his official duties in the outer area and the private chambers were in the inner area.

Hotels

Chunyi Binguan, Sidalin (Stalin) Dajie 2, tel. 3 84 95

Nanhu Binguan, 南湖宾馆 Nanhu, tel. 5 35 51

Changchun Binguan, 长春宾馆 Changchun Dajie 128, tel. 2 67 72

Travel agency

Guoji Lüxingshe, CITS, in Chunyi Binguan guest house, tel. 3 85 95, 3 84 95
and Xinminjie 12, tel. 5 24 01

Shopping

Friendship Store, Youyi Shangdian, Xinfalu 1, tel. 2 32 52

Arts and crafts store, Damalu 13, tel. 3 82 85

Antiques, Xi'an Dalu 7, tel. 2 25 37

Jilin 吉林市

The young city Jilin lies in the middle of the province of the same name on the banks of the Songhua Jiang river. It is surrounded by the Changbai Shan mountains. Jilin is one of the largest cities in the province with about one million inhabitants. It was the provincial capital until 1954.

The city has made great progress in industry and agriculture since 1949. The wood, food, chemical and electrical branches are among the most important industries. Jilin is famous for its production of ginseng, antlers and ermine furs.

The two most important sights of the city are Songhua Hu lake and Beishan Park with its temples and pavilions.

Songhua Hu 松花湖

Songhua Hu lake is 24 km southeast of Jilin. It is a man-made lake covering an area of 480 km². It is fed by the Songhua Jiang river and provides for the irrigation of the surrounding 33,000 hectares of farming land in addition to being used by fish hatcheries. The lake is also a favorite recreation area.

Beishan Hills 北山

Beishan hills are west of Jilin. Their highest point is 270 m. There are several Qing Dynasty (1644 — 1911) buildings, including Guandi Miao, a temple dedicated to the war god Guandi, near the East Hill.

The largest temple complex in the Beishan hills is Yuhuang Ge, completed in 1725.

A 10-m-high pavilion, Kuangguan Ting, tops the peak of the West Hill. The entire city can be seen from this pavilion.

Two man-made lakes lined by pavilions and walkways lie at the foot of the West Hill. The Beishan area is also frequented in winter because one can ski and ice-skate here.

Hotels

Xiguan Binguan, 西关宾馆 Songjianglu 661, tel. 56 45

Dongguan Binguan, 东关宾馆 Songjianglu 223, tel. 35 55

Travel agency

Guoji Lüxingshe, CITS, Songjianglu 223, tel. 35 55

Tianchi, Lake of Heaven 天池

The Changbai Shan mountains lie in eastern Jilin Province. Their highest elevation is Baitou Shan mountain, 2,744 m high, directly on the Korean border. The 16 'Miracle Peaks' of Baitou Shan surround a volcanic crater in which Tianchi Lake spreads out over 9.2 km² at an altitude of 2,155 above sea level. It is frozen half of the year and the water temperature rises only a few degrees above freezing during the rest of the year. The few tourists who come up this high are rewarded by the wonderful scenery.

There is an outlet, the so-called Damen gate, on the lake's northern shore. Water flows from there down to an altitude of 1,250 m, where it then plunges down 68 m as a waterfall. This is the source of the Songhua Jiang river.

Heilongjiang Province 黑龙江省

Area: 469,000 km² / Population: 32.6 million, including 1.4 million Manchus, Mongols, Koreans and Huis / Capital: Harbin
Heilongjiang is the northernmost of China's northeast provinces. The border to the Soviet Union runs along the Heilongjiang (Amur) and Wusuli Jiang(Ussuri) rivers in the north and east; the province is bounded in the northwest and southeast by sub-alpine mountains. Wide plains extend over the central and extreme northeastern regions. The province's longest river is the Heilongjiang, which is frozen over about 180 days of the year. Hard winters lasting five to eight months and short, very warm summers are characteristic of Heilongjiang's climate. The average temperature in January is -20°C on the plains and -30°C in the mountains; the average temperature in July is 23°C.

History

The Heilongjiang area was a steppe and forest area where horse and pig raising and, along the coast and rivers, fishing was carried out right up into the 19th century. Urbanization did not begin until the construction of the rail-way from 1896—1903 and industrialization increased. Russian troops occupied Heilongjiang from 1900—1905, after which time the area was more or less under Chinese control until the Japanese occupation in 1931. After that, it experienced the same fate as Jilin. Since 1949, the population has increased greatly. Heilongjiang is one of China's most important development areas. The wide plains have been cultivated, soy beans, corn, summer wheat and sugar beets planted and the forests exploited. Heilongjiang has become one of China's most important timber suppliers (birch, fir and larch). The mineral resources are also immensely important, especially oil and coke.

Harbin 哈尔滨市

Harbin, the capital of Heilongjiang Province, lies on the Songhua River in the middle of a fertile plain. A hundred years ago, Harbin was still only a small market-town. Today, it is a manufacturing city with 2.5 million inhabitants and an important railway junction.

History

This area was settled by the ancestors of the Manchus a thousand years ago. They founded the village of Arjin, from which the name Harbin derives. The town did not start expanding until the construction of the railroad in 1896. The Russians chose Harbin as the starting-point for the line after having been awarded the concession for building a railroad inside Manchuria. They named the Harbin train station Songhuajiang. The new line was linked up to the Trans-Siberian Railroad. During the Russian-Japanese War (1904 — 1905), Harbin was Russia's most important base.

Ten years after Japan's victory and the withdrawal of the Russian troops, many Russians again came to Harbin as refugees from the Russian Revolution of 1917. Harbin was the largest Russian city outside of Russia for a time. Even today, about 30 churches bear witness to the former Russian presence. However, the Russians were not the only group of foreigners for long. Increasing numbers of Japanese, British, French, Germans, Italians and Americans came and built their consulates, banks, hotels and villas here. Thus, Harbin still strikes one as being western rather than Chinese.

After 1946, most of the Russian refugees accepted Stalin's offer of amnesty and returned to the Soviet Union.

Map of Harbin

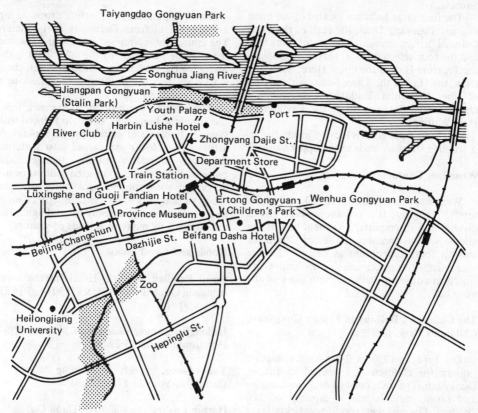

Taiyangdao Gongyuan Park

Songhua Jiang River

Jiangpan Gongyuan
(Stalin Park)

Youth Palace

Harbin Lüshe Hotel

River Club

Port

Zhongyang Dajie St.

Department Store

Train Station

Lüxingshe and Guoji Fandian Hotel

Province Museum

Ertong Gongyuan (Children's Park)

Wenhua Gongyuan Park

Beijing-Changchun

Dazhijie St.

Beifang Dasha Hotel

Zoo

Heilongjiang
University

Hepinglu St.

During the last three and a half decades, Harbin has developed into an important manufacturing center. Furthermore, the city is the province's cultural center. It has several noteworthy universities and institutes; the Polytechnic School of Harbin is known throughout China. During the cold season, Harbin becomes the most important winter sports resort in the northeast. The favorite sports are skating, ice-yachting and hockey.

The winter is long in Harbin; it lasts about six months with an average temperature of -19°C.

Specialties of the Harbinese cuisine are bears' paws, moose, hazel-hens and a special type of fungus called 'monkey-head mushroom'.

Jiangpan Gongyuan Park 江畔公园

The Songhua Jiang river winds its way eastward through the city. Jiangpan Gongyuan extends along its south bank. It is one of the favorite recreation areas for the people of Harbin in their free time because it offers

numerous attractions such as a Youth Palace, an aquatic sports center, the Riverbank Restaurant and the 'River Club'. In the middle of the park, there is a monument to the flood of 1957, during which the Songhua Jiang reached a water level of 46.5 m. The water was 3 m deep in the streets. Volunteers helped build a 50-km-long dam, thus preventing an even greater catastrophe.

Taiyang Dao Gongyuan 太阳岛公园

Sun Island Park, lies north of Jiangpan Gongyuan on the other side of the river. It is Harbin's vacation center and has 14 sanatoriums and hotels. The island's natural beach invites young and old to swim and sunbathe. Entire families often come to the park to enjoy a picnic in midsummer.

Jile Si Temple 极乐寺

Jile Si, Heilongjiang's largest temple, is located at Dazhijie Street 5 in the Nangang district of Harbin. It dates from 1924, covers an area of 26,000 m² and is divided into three districts.

The four large halls are located in the main district: Tianwang Dian, the Hall of the Four Celestial Kings, housing statues of Maitreya and the four celestial kings; Daxiong Baodian, the Treasure Hall of the Great Hero; Sansheng Dian, the Hall of the Three Saints with statues of the Amitabha Buddha, Guanyin and Dasizhi; and Cangjing Lou, the Pavilion of Holy Writings.

Qiji Futu Ta pagoda is located inside Jile Si. A wooden stairway leads to the upper stories.

Wenmiao, Confucius Temple 文庙

Wenmiao is situated on Dongdazhijie Street, Nangang. It was built in 1926 and is divided into three parts. The main hall of the middle section contains statues of Confucius and his four companions as well as 12 other wise men. Remembrances of his pupils are stored in adjoining halls on both sides of the main hall.

The Children's Railway in Ertong Gongyuan, Children's Park 儿童铁路

On June 1, 1956, a 2-km-long miniature railway for children was opened in Ertong Gongyuan. The train consists of a diesel engine and seven cars. It has a capacity of 200 children. The engineer, conductor, ticket-taker — the entire train staff — even the railway police, are played by elementary and middle-school pupils under 13 years of age. They take turns running and managing the railroad. The train has traveled over 750,000 km and carried 3.4 million passengers up to the present.

Zoo 动物园

The zoo is located in the southwestern part of the city. It has about 140 species of animals. The Northeast China tigers are especially interesting.

Heilongjiang Province Museum 黑龙江省博物馆

The Heilongjiang Province Museum is on Hongjunjie Street. It owns over 130,000 exhibition articles, including many objects indicating the historical development of the province. In addition, representations of extinct animals are on display. A highlight is the fossil of a mammoth excavated in Zhaoyang district in 1974.

Ice Lanterns 冰灯

The temperature in Harbin drops to an average -25°C from December to February. The entire city is wrapped in ice and snow and seems to be paralyzed by the cold. That is the season of the ice lanterns. In some cases, these works are real ice sculptures that attest to a high artistic level.

Blocks of ice are brought to the park from the Songhua Jiang river and then worked with saws, hammers and chisels by the ice-lantern artists. The blocks are carved into lanterns, pagodas, animals, flowers, temples and palaces. Finally, the completed sculptures are decorated with colored light bulbs or neon tubes so that they shine enchantingly at night in the reflection of the many colored lights and are admired by many thousands of visitors.

Hotels and Guest Houses

Guoji Fandian, 国际饭店 Hotel International, Nangang Qu, Dazhijie 124, tel. 3 30 01, 3 14 31, telex 8 00 81

Heilongjiang Sheng Zhaodaisuo, 黑龙江省招待所 Hongjunlu 52, tel. 3 29 50

Youyi Gong, 友谊宫 Friendship Palace, Daoli Qu, Youyilu 57, tel. 4 61 46

Harbin Lüshe, 哈尔滨旅社 Daoli Qu, Zhongyang Dajie 129, tel. 4 58 46

Beifang Dasha, 北方大厦 Nangang Qu, Huayuanjie 115, tel. 3 30 61

Hepingcun Binguan, 和平村宾馆 Nangang Qu, Zhongshanlu 109, tel. 3 20 93

Tian'e Hotel, tel. 5 10 06, telex 8 00 80

Restaurants

Beilaishun Fandian, Daoli Qu, Shangzhi Dajie 113, tel. 4 56 73, 4 90 27. Moslem cuisine.

Huamei Canting, Daoli Qu, Zhongyang Dajie 142, tel. 4 73 68. Western cuisine.

Jiangbin Fandian, Daoli Qu, Xishisandaojie 15, tel. 4 47 21

Jiangnanchun Fandian, Nangang Qu, Fendoulu 316, tel. 3 43 98, 3 48 60

Shopping

Friendship Store, Youyi Shangdian,
Nangang Qu, Dazhijie 93

Arts and crafts, Nangang Qu, Dachengjie 2,
tel. 3 43 36

Wenwu Shangdian, antiques,
Nangang Qu, Hongjunjie 50, tel. 3 50 82

First Department Store,
Daoli Qu, Diduanjie 146

Fur store,
Daoli Qu, Zhongyang Dajie 88, tel. 4 96 83

Travel agency

**Guoji Lüxingshe, CITS, Zhongguo Lüxingshe,
Huaqiao Lüxingshe**
Nangang Qu, Dazhijie 124, tel. 3 30 01, 3 14 41

**Gong'an Ju, Public Security Bureau of
Harbin,**
Daoli Qu, Zhongyang Dajie 44, tel. 4 62 26

Gong'an Ju, Public Security Bureau of
Heilongjiang Province,
Nangang Qu, Zhongshanlu 95, tel. 3 21 32

CAAC ticket office,
Nangang Qu, Zhongshanlu 85, tel. 5 18 68, 5
23 34

Taxis,
Daowai Qu, Nankanjie 24, tel. 4 27 28

Ning'an Xian District 宁安县

Xinglong Si Temple 兴隆寺

This temple, built during the Qing period, is
located south-west of the town of Bohai in
Ning'an Xian district. The following halls have
been preserved: Guandi Dian, the Hall of the
God of War, Guandi; Tianwang Dian, the
Hall of the Celestial Kings; Daxiong Baodian,
the Treasure Hall of the Great Hero; and
Sansheng Dian, the Hall of the Three Saints.
There is a large stone Buddha in Sansheng
Dian. The Stone Lamp Pagoda, Shideng Ta, is
located between Daxiong Baodian and Sansheng Dian. It dates from the Tang era (618 —
907) and is one of the most important stone
structures in China.

Daqing 大庆市

Daqing, a center of Chinese oil production,
lies about 1,400 km northeast of Beijing
between the cities of Harbin and Qiqihar. It
arose from nowhere and developed into a
model petro-chemical complex within two
decades. The spirit of Daqing, the enthusiasm
and discipline of its workers is held up as an
example for all of Chinese industry.

The first drillings were made with technical
assistance from the Russians in 1958. After the
departure of the Russian experts the following
year, the Chinese carried out the drilling alone.
The great technical and scientific difficulties
were mastered by the workers and engineers
with courage, enthusiasm and self-sacrifice.
Some workers went down in the history of
Daqing as heroes, for example, the 'Iron Man'
Wang Jingxi. On September 26, 1959,
the workers struck oil, a triumph for the
Chinese people. Apartments were not erected
until the oil production began. Housing was
intended to reflect the city-country character:
detached, city-quality housing units were built
in rural surroundings. Agriculture was
expanded at the same time as the petroleum
industry. The families of the oil workers are
occupied in that sector, thus closely linking
agriculture to industry in Daqing.

Shanghai 上海市
(Centrally administered municipality)

Area: 6,185 km², the city itself covers 145
km² / Population: 11.8 million

Shanghai is a special city in every respect.
Only 50 years ago, it was still considered one of
the most important metropolises of the world,
as the trading and banking center of Asia, as a
city of extremes, an El Dorado for
adventurers.

Foreigners lent Shanghai its appearance,
making it more Western than Chinese.
Twenty-story-high buildings reach skyward;
there are vast hotel complexes, villas and
palaces that a visitor from the West can more
easily identify than a temple, for they were
built according to Western architectural style
by former business and military men.

The colonialists have gone, but their
buildings remain, and the bustling life and
activities of a large Chinese city prevail around
them. A special kind of people lives here. The
people of Shanghai are feared by some and
loved by others, for they are especially brisk,
smart, flexible and ingenious and make more

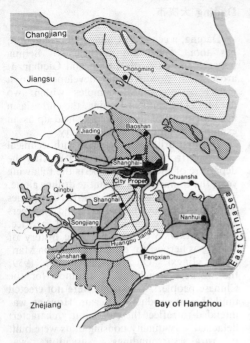

Changjiang

Jiangsu

Chongming

Jiading

Baoshan

Shanghai

City Proper

Chuansha

Qingbu

Shanghai

Songjiang

Nanhui

East China Sea

Huangpu Jiang

Qinshan

Fengxian

Zhejiang

Bay of Hangzhou

Shanghai Municipality

of their appearance than other Chinese. In Shanghai, one is always ahead of the times — trends are set here. It was in Shanghai that make-up was first used and permanents worn, that the people risked wearing fashionable Western clothes. Things that leave people in speechless amazement elsewhere in China are often already old hat in Shanghai.

The people of Shanghai are talented merchants and clever politicians, many of them are invested with high positions in the government, economy and administration. Shanghai also has its own special political tradition. In 1925, students and workers joined together in protest demonstrations against feudalism, capitalism and poor government. In March 1927, the city experienced an uprising of 800,000 workers.

The city has made great social and economic progress since 1949. The Shanghai of the past had unsolvable economic problems, a dreaded underworld, masses of unemployed, beggars and homeless, thousands of prostitutes and pimps. Today, it presents itself as an orderly large city where everyone has enough to live on and no ragged coolies and beggars loiter about. Shanghai is the largest city in China and a trade and manufacturing center. Almost one-half of all national and international trade is transacted in Shanghai,

which has trade relations with 115 countries. Shanghai is also China's most important port. There are 275 different shipping connections with foreign ports. Inland shipping is conducted on the Changjiang to the interior as far as Sichuan. The four airports have inland and foreign connections.

History

The area around Shanghai was settled fairly early; however, the settlement remained little more than a fishing village for centuries. By the 13th century, Shanghai had become known under its present name as a trading town. Shanghai's natural advantages, its location on the Huangpu and Wusong Rivers, its proximity to the sea and a deep natural harbor led to flourishing coastal and inland shipping. During the Ming era, the first industrial manufacturing plants were built. About 70% of the agricultural production around Shanghai was used to supply the city's cotton and silk spinning mills. The development of its political and commercial importance began in the 19th century with the arrival of the foreigners. They, too, recognized the advantages of its location and forced Shanghai to open up to foreign trade. At the end of the Opium War, the Treaty of Nanking was signed by the victorious foreigners and the imperial government on August 29, 1842. This was the first of the Unequal Treaties extorted from China by force of arms. It bound China to open five ports, including Shanghai, to overseas trade. Furthermore, the foreigners were granted special rights and privileges. The international colony and the French concession arose next to the Chinese city, thus dividing the town in three districts. The international colony developed out of the integration of the British and American settlements. Modern buildings in the European style were built, soon giving the city a Western appearance.

Increasing numbers of foreigners were drawn to Shanghai. Banks, import and export companies, factories, shops, parks and a race-track were built. After the Qing government was overthrown in 1911, the foreigners took over the entire administration. They even controlled the Chinese customs office. In 1935, the city had more than 3.7 million inhabitants in its three districts, including over 57,000 foreigners. Even today, many Chinese are very unwilling to think back on this time, when the foreigners erected signs forbidding the Chinese and dogs from walking on lawns or armed Indian Sikh police guarded the entrances to banks and other buildings. The Chinese people's resistance to foreign rule in China thus found many supporters in Shanghai. This can be seen in various political events: the growth of the revolutionary movement, the boycott of foreign goods and the protest demonstrations of students and workers against feudalism, capitalism and the official silence towards imperialist foreign enterprises.

The alliance of students and workers supported the Nationalists under Chiang Kai-shek at that time, and yet, the Nationalists were the ones who violently and bloodily suppressed this alliance in 1927. The Communist Party was founded in Shanghai in 1921. After war broke out between Japan and the United States, the Japanese occupied the foreign concessions and took over the administration. The food situation became increasingly difficult and inflation, corruption and smuggling flourished. Even after Japan's capitulation, the living conditions did not improve very much. The economic problems seemed insolvable until Communist troops reached the city in May 1949 and put an end to the chaos.

Shanghai has changed radically since that time. Various cultural institutions have come into being: museums and parks have been built. The population has increased drastically. The construction of entire housing settlements is an attempt to master the general housing shortage. The heart of the city is already hopelessly overcrowded, yet it still exerts a powerful magnetism. Many people would prefer to give up better living conditions in the country and move to bustling Shanghai.

Today, Shanghai is the most important center of heavy and light industrial manufacturing and supplies all parts of China with industrial goods.

Shanghai is also very important in the cultural and scientific sectors. Opera, ballet and circus companies known in China as well as abroad are based in Shanghai. One hundred and ninety research institutes, universities and technical schools have made Shanghai into a center for the sciences.

Shanghai lies on the west bank of the Huangpu Jiang river, which flows into the Changjiang (Yangtze) 28 km farther upstream. The northern part of Shanghai is separated from the rest of the city by the Wusong Jiang river. Zhongshanlu street begins at the confluence of the Wusong Jiang and the Huangpu Jiang. Its famous riverside avenue (formerly called the Bund), with its park-like green areas and tall buildings, is Shanghai's landmark. Here, the visitor stands in front of

magnificent buildings in the art nouveau style that once housed the clubs, banks, companies and hotels of the foreign rulers. Today, the Sailors' Club and the managements of several state institutions have been installed there. The eastern side of Zhongshanlu borders directly on the Huangpu Jiang river. A broad view of the river can be had from there. The people of Shanghai like to go to the parks to relax for an hour in the evening or for morning exercises. Very many people gather in the morning for shadow-boxing, *Taijiquan*, across from the Friendship Store. Everyone can join in, even the guest from abroad.

Nanjinglu street leads westward from Zhongshanlu past the Peace Hotel to the People's Park. Nanjinglu is Shanghai's main business street, where there are shops of all sorts as well as cinemas and restaurants.

Yan'anlu street is parallel to Nanjinglu. The Shanghai Industrial Exhibition Hall and the Children's Palace are located on its eastern side. Yan'anlu used to mark the border between the international and French concessions. Further south, Huaihailu street runs parallel to Yan'anlu. It is also an important shopping street and was formerly the main business street of the French concession.

The Port and Mouth of the Huangpu river

A small passenger steamer departs daily from the landing in Huangpu Park (Zhongshanlu) and heads for the port and mouth of the Huangpu river. The steamer travels past sailing junks, many large freighters, passenger ships from the whole world and the Shanghai shipyards. The trip lasts about three and a half hours.

Most important sights: Riverside avenue (Bund), Yuto Si Temple, Old Town, and Yuyuan Garden

The Museum of Art and History
艺术历史博物馆

The interesting Museum of Art and History, well worth a visit, is located at Henannanlu street 16 in a former bank building. The objects on display range from Neolithic ceramics to bronze objects dating from the Shang and Western Zhou eras, terra-cotta figures from the grave of Qin Shihuang in Xi'an all the way to Buddhist statues from the 5th to the 9th centuries, porcelain from the Tang, Song, Yuan and Ming eras and valuable paintings from many epochs.

Map of Shanghai

Zhennanlu St.

Beijing-Shanghai

Cao'anlu St.

Yanglu St.

Cao

Wusonglu St.

Hutailu St.

Gonghexinlu St.

Zhongshanbeilu St.

Tianmulu St.

Changshoulu St.

Yufo Si Temple

Guoji Fandian Hotel

First

Wusong Jiang River

Zhongshan Park

Wanhangdulu St.

Beijinglu St.

Renmin Gongyuan Park

Renmin Guangchang Square

Changninglu St.

Shanghai Zoo

Hongqiaolu St.

Zhongshanxilu St.

Jing'an Si Temple

Shanghai Industrial Exhibition Hall

Nanjinglu St.

Shimenlu St.

Jinjiang Fandian Hotel

Hongqiao Airport

Yan'anlu St.

Huashanlu St.

Huaihailu St.

Henshanlu St.

Fuxing

Site of the National C of the CCP

Fuxing Gongyuan Park

Fuxinglu St.

Caoxilu St.

Former Residence of Dr. Sun Yatsen

Wenhua Guangchang Square

Ruijinlu St.

Lubanlu St.

Lu

Zhaojiabanglu St.

Shanghai Gymnasium

Zhongshannanlu St.

Huangpu Jiang River

Huminlu St.

Shanghai-Hangzhou

Longhuasi Ta Pagoda

Yaohualu St.

Shanghai Industrial Exhibition Hall
工业展览馆

This exhibition facility was built in the Soviet style in the fifties and called the 'China-Russia Friendship Building' at that time. About 5,000 products from Shanghai's light industry as well as from the handicrafts and industrial arts are on display here and can be bought.

Shaonian Gong, Children's Palace 少年宫

The Children's Palace offers talented children between seven and fourteen various courses, for example in music, ballet, painting, mathematics or technology in which the children can specialize according to their aptitudes.

The building in which the Children's Palace is located used to belong to a rich family. The creation of Children's Palaces, of which there are 11 in Shanghai alone, is due to the initiative of Song Qingling, the widow of Sun Yatsen.

Renmin Gongyuan, People's Park 人民公园

Renmin Gongyuan is south of Nanjing-zhonglu and west of Xizangzhonglu streets. During colonial times, there was a race-track here. In 1952, the new government had the northern part of the area made into People's Park and the southern part into People's Square. The Shanghai Library is now housed in the former starting and finishing building of the race-track. A small museum displays a collection of historical art objects, among them are bronzes and ceramics.

Yufo Si, Jade Buddha Monastery 玉佛寺

The Chan (Zen) Buddhist Yufo Si monastery is located in Anyuanlu street in western Shanghai. It dates from 1918 and is well worth a visit, not only for its two well-known, valuable jade Buddha statues. The monastery is still inhabited by monks. Visitors who understand Chinese should ask one of the friendly monks for a guided tour.

Huigeng, a monk, made a pilgrimage from the Buddhist mountain Putuo Shan to Burma around 1880. He was given five valuable statues of Sakyamuni Buddha there. After his return, he presented two of them to the Shanghai Jiangwan Temple. Between 1918 and 1928, a new temple, Yufo Si, was erected especially for the two statues. Each of these Buddha statues is carved out of a single piece of white jade.

The temple consists of three main halls and two courtyards. There are statues of the four celestial kings (see page 83 for their importance and meaning) in Tianwang Dian hall. Gilded statues of Maitreya Buddha and Weituo are also located there. Daxiong Baodian, the Treasure Hall of the Great Hero, contains three large, gilded Buddha statues: the Buddhas of the past, present and future. There are 18 gilded Luohan statues to their left and right.

One of the two jade Buddhas, a 1.9-m-tall portrayal of the real Buddha sitting at the moment of his enlightenment, stands on the second floor of Wentang Hall together with a collection of valuable Buddhist writings. The second Buddha statue, located in a hall on the western part of the temple grounds, portrays the reposing Sakyamuni during his passage into nirvana, 96 cm long.

In addition to these two main attractions, Yufo Si also has a collection of interesting sculptures, the oldest of which date from the 5th century, as well as a collection of 7,000 Buddhist classics. Some of them date as far back as the Tang era (618 — 907).

Shanghai Zoo (Xijiao Gongyuan, Western District Park) 上海动物园（西郊公园）

Xijiao Gongyuan is on Hongqiaolu street in the city's western district. It has an area of 70 hectares. The foreigners' golf links used to be located here, but they were redesigned into a park and zoological garden in 1954. About 340 different species of animals live there. Among the most interesting are the panda bears, the Manchurian tigers, the Yunnan leopards, white-lipped deer and the Yangtze crocodile, a 200-million-year-old species. Many small lakes, pavilions, beautiful trees, lawns and flowers entice the visitor to take restful walks.

Old Town

The Old Town is situated in the southeast part of the city center and is surrounded by Renminlu street. Formerly a neglected neighborhood where hardly any foreigners dared set foot, it now is a cosy, interesting area that no visitor should miss, because its many narrow alleys and streets are full of a cheerful hustle and bustle. There are many restaurants and stands offering delicious foods, including many Shanghai specialities. Most of the restaurants are simple, quite small and, above all, crowded. However, that does not bother the people of Shanghai, for they are gourmets and know how well they can eat here. In

Yuyuan Garden in 1784

addition to the numerous small restaurants, there are various shops where it is possible to buy tea, porcelain, books, beautiful silks and many other things.

Chenghuang Miao Temple 城隍庙

The Temple of the Town Deity is located south of Yuyuan Garden. There used to be a temple to the local deity, which the inhabitants believed would protect them, in every city. The city deities were frequently real persons to whom the town owed something. Today, an arts and crafts store is in the temple.

Yuyuan Garden 豫园

Yuyuan Garden is northeast of the Old Town. A high official had it designed in the Suzhou style as a private garden and built from 1559 — 1577. Later, it was restored several times. In spite of its relatively small area of two hectares, it seems considerably larger due to the skillful arrangement of 30 different landscape scenes.

The garden consists of an inner and an outer section. The inner garden, Neiyuan, is in the southern part and substantially smaller than the outer one, but then, it is more impressive and romantic, if it is possible to

visit it in the early morning hours in order to enjoy it alone. An excellent calligrapher displays his work in one of the halls.

The outer part is in the north and contains numerous halls, pavilions and lakes. In 1853, the Pavilion of Spring in the northeast was the seat of the *Xiaodao Hui*, the Society of Little Swords, who led an uprising against Qing rule and occupied Shanghai for 17 months. Today, weapons and coins made by the Xiaodao Hui society, among other objects, are exhibited in this hall.

A man-made, 11-m-high hill bounds the garden in the northwest. Huxin Ting teahouse is a favorite with the citizens of Shanghai. It is in the southwest, outside of the garden grounds, a two-story building resting on posts in the middle of a pond and connected to the shore by a 'Zigzag Bridge'.

Botanic Gardens 上海植物园

The Botanic Gardens, laid out in 1954, are on Longwulu street in Longhua district in south Shanghai.
A collection of miniature gardens and bonsai trees provides an interesting view of the development of the Chinese tradition of reproducing landscapes in miniature.

Fuxing Gongyuan Park 复兴公园

Fuxing Park is south of Huaihailu street inside the former French concession. It comprises an area of 8.8 hectares and dates from 1909. Many densely foliated shade trees grow in the park, which many old people visit during the day to accompany their grandchildren to play or to play chess under the trees.

Former Residence of Dr. Sun Yatsen 孙中山故居

Sun Yatsen's small house is at Xiangshanlu street 7 near Fuxing Park. He was the first president of the Republic of China and lived and worked in this house after 1920. Most of the pieces of furniture are his own.

Site of the First National Congress of the CCP 中共第一次全国代表大会会址

The first congress of the Chinese Communist Party took place at Xingyelu street 76 — at that time Wangzhilu 106 — in the former French concession. In July 1921, 13 representatives of the 53 Chinese Communists took part in the congress. The meeting had to be interrupted because of the danger of the French police making a raid. The participants in the congress had received a notice to that effect in time. Those present decided to continue their conference on a small boat in the district capital Jiaxing in Zhejiang Province. The formation of the Chinese Communist Party was announced at this congress.

Former Residence of the Author Lu Xun 鲁迅故居

Lu Xun's house is at Dalu Xinxun lane 9 on Shanyinlu street. He was the best-known Chinese author of the 20th century and lived in this house from April 11, 1933 until his death on October 19, 1936. He wrote his last works, such as *Huabian Wenxue* and *Qiejieting Zawen*, at his desk in the study on the second floor. He also translated Gogol's *Dead Souls* here.

The author and former Communist Party leader Qu Qiubai temporarily lived in the back room on the third floor.

Lu Xun's Tomb (Hongkou Gongyuan Park) 虹口公园|〈鲁迅墓〉

Lu Xun's burial place is located in Hongkou Gongyuan park. After his death, he was first buried in Wanguo Gongmu cemetery. In 1956, the grave in Hongkou Gongyuan was laid out on the occasion of the 20th anniversary of his death. A bronze statue of the author stands in front of the complex.

Lu Xun Exhibition Hall 鲁迅纪念馆

This hall is also located in Hongkou Gongyuan. It is a building in the Shaoxing style. (Shaoxing was Lu Xun's hometown.) The exhibit contains manuscripts, publications, objects from Lu Xun's daily life and a collection of pictures and documents about his life and work.

Catholic Church 徐家汇天主堂

There is a large Catholic church in Caoxibeilu street in Xujiahui district in southwest Shanghai. It was built in 1906. Its two bell towers are over 50 m tall.

Song Qingling's Grave 宋庆龄墓

Wanguo Gongmu cemetery, Hongqiaolu street. Song Qingling, the wife of Sun Yatsen, was buried in the Song family grave, which dates from 1932.

Song Qingling was one of the first Chinese women to receive a modern, western education and to be allowed to study abroad. She studied at Wesleyan College in Macon, Georgia, USA, for five years, starting in 1908, and ended her studies with a Bachelor of Arts degree. She married Sun Yatsen in October 1915 and supported his work. After his death, she continued to work for his goals. She was renowned and honored as a patriotic and democratic fighter and was Honorable Chairwoman of the People's Republic of China and Vice-Chairwoman of the Standing Committee of the National People's Congress. She died at the age of 88 on May 29, 1981.

Longhua Si Ta Pagoda and Longhua Si Temple 龙华寺龙华塔

Longhua Si is on the west bank of the Huangpu Jiang river in Longhua district in southern Shanghai. Its 40-m-high pagoda makes it an important sight.

Historic documents indicate that a pagoda was built here as early as the 3rd century. The present pagoda dates from 977. It was restored several times in later centuries and is built of wood and bricks.

Longhua Si temple dates from the same

period.

A bronze bell from 1382 said to weigh 1,500 kg is a feature of interest. In 1954, the entire complex was restored and a park added. It is especially pretty here in the springtime when the peach trees are in bloom.

Xingshengjiaosi Ta Pagoda 松江兴圣教寺塔

This 48.5-m-high pagoda, also called the 'Rectangular Pagoda', is in the eastern part of the district capital Songjiang, a suburb southwest of Shanghai. It is one of the most important sights in the Shanghai area and was built from 1068—1094 and restored from 1975 — 1977. It has elements of the Tang era architectural style.

Huzhu Ta Pagoda 松江护珠塔

Huzhu Ta pagoda, which tilts to the west, is on Tianma Shan mountain in Songjiang district and was built in 1079. In 1788, important wooden parts were destroyed by fire, upon which old money was discovered between the bricks. In the hope of finding even greater treasures, the people tore more bricks out of the western side. Owing to this, the pagoda tilted several degrees and has threatened to collapse for the last 200 years. It has become famous because it still stands in spite of all fears.

Universities, Daxue

Fudan Daxue 复旦大学
Jiangwan, Handanlu 22

Patriotic professors, instructors and students left the French Catholic University, Zhendan Xueyuan, in 1905 and founded Fudan Gongxue, which was changed to Fudan Daxue university in 1917. During the Sino-Japanese War, the University first moved to Lushan, Guiyang, and then to Chongqing. After the end of the war, it returned to Shanghai. It has been a general university where the humanities and natural sciences are taught in addition to technical subjects since 1952.

Jiaotong Daxue 交通大学
Huashanlu 1945

Jiaotong Daxue began in 1897 as Nanyang Gongxue. It developed from a technically oriented school into an engineering school, Gongye Zhuanmen Xuexiao. In 1921, the Tangshan engineering school and the Mail and Communications School of Beijing were incorporated, after which time it was called Jiaotong Daxue.

Tongji Daxue 同济大学

Tongji University specializes in architecture, construction and technical science. It was founded in 1907 as a German-language medical school to which a school of engineering was later added.

It has been a technical college since 1949.

Jiading District Capital 嘉定

(near Shanghai)

Confucius Temple 孔庙

The Confucius Temple was built in 1219 during the Southern Song Dynasty and restored and expanded several times during the Yuan, Ming and Qing dynasties. It is one of the largest temple complexes south of the Changjiang. A rice-processing factory moved into the temple buildings during the period of the civil wars and chaos. In 1958, the government had the temple remodeled into a museum, in which historic documents and paintings are displayed, among other objects.

Qiuxia Pu Garden 嘉定秋霞圃

Qiuxia Pu is also in the town of Jiading in Jiading district. It was laid out during the Ming period and belonged to a high official.

Nanxiang Village 嘉定南翔

(near Shanghai)

Guyi Yuan Garden 古猗园

Guyi Yuan is located in Nanxiang in Jiading district northwest of Shanghai. It was laid out in the 16th century, and the grounds are an excellent example of traditional garden landscaping.

Hotels

Jinjiang Fandian, 锦江饭店 Maomingnanlu 59, tel. 53 42 42
Jinjiang Fandian is one of the largest and most comfortable hotels in Shanghai. It consists of five building complexes and a shopping street. Services, shops of all sorts, four restaurants and banquet halls are available. It was built by the French at the turn of the century.

Shanghai Binguan 上海宾馆 Wulumuqi beilu 505, tel. 31 23 12
A new first class hotel, opened in May 1983.

Heping Fandian, 和平饭店 Nanjingdonglu 20, tel. 21 12 44
The Heping, the Peace Hotel, is a luxurious building built by the English in 1906. It is located on Zhongshanlu and affords its guests an excellent view of the Huangpu River. This hotel offers services of all kinds. The central office of the CITS Lüxingshe is located on its ground floor.

Dahua Binguan, 大华宾馆 Yan'anxilu 914, tel. 52 30 79

Hengshan Binguan, 衡山宾馆 Hengshanlu 534, tel. 37 70 50

Jing'an Binguan, 静安宾馆 Huashanlu 370, tel. 56 30 50

Guoji Fandian, 国际饭店 Nanjingxilu 170, tel. 22 52 25

Shanghai Dasha, 上海大厦 Beisuzhoulu 20, tel. 24 62 60
This 20-story-high hotel was built by the English. There is a wonderful view of the Huangpu and its park grounds from its top floor.

Xijiao Binguan,
1921 Hongqiaolu, tel. 37 96 43
Luxurious hotels in Shanghai's western district.

Low-cost Hotels and Guest House

Pujiang Fandian, 浦江饭店 Hankoulu 740, tel. 22 51 15

Huaqiao Fandian, 华侨饭店 Nanjingxilu 104, tel. 22 62 26
This hotel is used mainly by overseas Chinese guests.

Restaurants

The Shanghai cuisine is one of the best in China and is characterized by its many and varied ingredients and spices. Shanghai's location of the rivers and the sea has made its inhabitants enthusiastic fish-eaters. Shrimp, eel, crab and many sorts of fish often unknown in the west are specialties. Foods are often very hot in Shanghai. This is necessary to prevent the cooking oil from affecting the taste of the foods as it is cooling.

Shanghai Lao Fandian, Old Shanghai,
Fuyoulu 242, tel. 28 27 82
This restaurant was opened in 1862. It serves the best Shanghai specialties and is, therefore, always full. Reservations are necessary!

Yangzhou Fandian,
Nanjingdonglu 308, tel. 22 58 26
The Yangzhou Fandian is one of the best-known restaurants in the city. Reservations should be made several days in advance.

Renmin Fandian,
Nanjingxilu 226, tel. 53 73 51
This restaurant serves specialties of the Shanghai and Suzhou cuisines.

Chengdu Fandian,
Huaihaizhonglu 795, tel. 37 64 12
Sichuan cuisine.

Luyangcun Jiujia,
Nanjingxilu 763, tel.53 97 87
Sichuan cuisine.

Sichuan Fandian,
Nanjingdonglu 457, tel.22 22 46

Meixin Jiujia,
Shanxinanlu 314, tel. 37 39 91
Cantonese cuisine.

Xinghua Lou,
Fuzhoulu 343, tel. 28 27 47
Cantonese cuisine, snake specialties.

Xinya Yuecai Guan,
Nanjingdonglu 719, tel. 22 36 36
Cantonese cuisine.

Gongdelin Sucai Guan,
Vegetarian Restaurant, Huanghelu 43, tel. 53 13 13
This restaurant was opened by Buddhists in 1922.

Meilongzhen Jiujia,
Nanjingxilu 1081, Nong 22, tel. 53 25 61
This restaurant is proud of the fact that Zhou Enlai once ate here.

Qingzhen Fandian,
Moslem Restaurant, Fuzhoulu 710, tel. 22 42 73

Yanyun Lou,
Nanjingdonglu 755, tel. 22 61 74

Hongfangzi Xicai Guan,
Shaanxinanlu 37, tel. 56 57 48
French cuisine.

Deda Xicai He,
Sichuanzhonglu 359, tel. 21 38 10
German cuisine.

Shopping

Nanjinglu is the main shopping street. Antique and arts and crafts stores, as well as department stores, are located there.

Arts and crafts, Nanjingxilu 190, open from 9 a.m. to 9 p.m.

Antiques, rarities, souvenirs, Nanjingxilu 694, tel. 53 80 92, 53 09 75, largest store of this type in Shanghai.

First Department Store, Nanjingdonglu 830

Tenth Department Store, Nanjingdonglu 635

Duoyunxuan, paintings and calligraphies, Nanjingdonglu 422, tel. 22 34 10

Silk shop, Nanjingdonglu 592

Porcelain store, Nanjingdonglu 550

Chinese musical instruments, Nanjingdonglu 114

Shanghai Antiques, Guangdonglu 192 — 226

Friendship Store, Zhongshandongyilu 33, open from 9 a.m. to 11 p.m.
One of the largest Friendship Stores in China with generously laid out sales departments.
Another interesting shopping area is Huaihailu.

Second Department Store, Huaihaizhonglu 889 — 909

Yuyuan Bazaar, Yuyuanlu 119

Travel agency

Guoji Lüxingshe, CITS, Xiangganglu 59. tel. 21 72 00, telex 3 30 01, Service desk at Heping Hotel.

Zhongguo Lüxingshe, Huaqiao Lüxingshe, Nanjingxilu 104, tel. 22 66 06, 22 66 53

Gong'an Ju, Public Security Bureau, tel. 21 53 80

CAAC, Yan'anzhonglu 789, bookings tel. 53 22 55, domestic 53 59 53, international 53 22 55

Huangpu Tours, Beijingdonglu, tel. 21 10 98

Train station, Tianmudonglu, reservations tel. 24 22 99

Taxis: 56 44 44

Bank of China, Zhongshandongyilu 23, tel. 21 74 66

Telephone office for international calls, Sichuanbeilu 1761, tel. 66 04 10

Clubs

International Club,
Shanghai, Yan'anxilu 65, tel. 53 84 55

International Sailors' Club,
Zhongshandongyilu 33, tel. 21 62 26

Jinjiang Club,
Maomingnanlu 58, tel. 37 01 15, acrosss from the Jinjiang Hotel

Sailors' Club,
Huangpulu 20, tel. 24 46 80

Universities

Fudan Daxue,
Handanlu 220, tel. 6 18 15 - 1 09

Tongji Daxue,
Jiangwan, tel. 45 52 90

Foreign Language Institute,
Xitiyuhuilu 119, tel. 66 02 31

Lodgings of the foreign experts,
tel. 66 31 68

Chinese Academy of Sciences,
tel. 37 96 50

Jiangsu Province 江苏省

Area: 107,000 km² / Population 60.5 million / Capital: Nanjing Jiangsu Province is situated on the east coast of China. It was established in 1667 during the reign of

Emperor Kangxi of the Qing Dynasty. The name derives from the two important prefectures, Jiangning and Suzhou, which were situated within this area.

Two big rivers run through the province: the Huaihe in the north and the Changjiang in the south. They have carried so much mud with them, that throughout the course of millennia the coast has moved several kilometers seaward; thus, large lakes were formed. Some of the largest are the famous Taihu in the south, the Gaoyou Hu in the central region and the Hongze Hu in the north. Throughout its long history, Jiangsu has continually been plagued by tidal waves and floods. As early as the 7th century, people began protecting themselves by building dikes. The danger of high tides and flooding has meanwhile been kept in check due to numerous projects to redirect the course of the river that were carried out in the 1950's. So today, the Huaihe river does not flow straight into the East China Sea anymore, but first into Hongzhe Hu lake, from there southward into the Gaoyou Hu lake and then into the Changjiang. It flows northward from Hongze Hu lake through two canals into the East China Sea.

The delta of the Changjiang river divides the province into a northern and a southern part. The south is densely populated and industrialized. Its skilled craft products and silks are well known in China as well as abroad. Suzhou, Nanjing, Wuxi and the municipal city of Shanghai are situated in this area. The north is located in the area of the floodplains of the Huanghe river; its delta was here until 1853.

The climate in this province varies considerably. The central and the southern parts of Jiangsu have a humid, temperate climate. The northern region is part of North China, as far as climate goes. Therefore it is cooler and subject to many temperature changes. The annual precipitation decreases from south to north. Only after extensive irrigation works had been built did the cultivation of rice become possible in the north, while rice has always been intensively cultivated in the south. Silkworm-raising is also of great importance in this region. The coast of Jiangsu is frequently stricken by typhoons in late summer and fall.

History

With the exception of its northern part, the area of the present-day Jiangsu Province belonged to the state of Wu until the 6th century BC. In the centuries to follow, various parts of the province were allotted to different administrative units. During the Song Dynasty, the Mongols conquered North China. In the 12th century, the rulers of the Song Dynasty fled south, so that southern Jiangsu developed into an economical, cultural and political center. Not until 1667 did the present-day borders of Jiangsu Province evolve. From 1839—1842, the English attacked the Changjiang delta region. During the Sino — Japanese war, the Japanese occupied Jiangsu. In those years the province suffered severe damage.

Nanjing (Nanking) 南京市

Nanjing, the capital of Jiangsu, is the political, economical and cultural center of the province. It is an important port on the river Changjiang. The administrative district of the city covers an area of 4,500 km^2 and the population numbers 3.74 million. The Zijin Shan mountains rise to the east — the people from Nanjing say they look like a coiled dragon; to the west cowers a tiger, the ancient Stone City. Nanjing is one of the oldest cities in China. Between the 3rd and 15th centuries, it was the capital of eight different dynasties. The name Nanjing was not used until 1421, when the city was made the 'Southern Capital' during the Ming Dynasty.

History

The history of the city dates back to the Eastern Zhou period (8th — 3rd centuries BC) and it subsequently was part of the states of Wu, Yue and Chu. The place was first mentioned in the annals of the Spring and Autumn Periods. At the time of the Three Kingdoms, Nanjing developed into the political and cultural center of Southeast China. Under the name of Jianye it became the capital of the Eastern Wu Kingdom. A mighty city wall was erected during the following years. As legend has it, the famous advisor, Zhuge Liang, discussed political and strategic problems with Sun Quan, King of Wu, on top of this wall.

From 317 to 420 Nanjing, at that time called Jiankang, was the capital of the Eastern Jin Dynasty. The rulers of the Jin and many North Chinese families came here seeking protection against the foreign invaders from the north. Until 589 Jiankang remained the capital of four other dynasties: the Song from 420 — 479, the Qi from 479 — 502, the Liang from 502 — 557, and the Chen Dynasty from 557 — 589. During these politically troubled times, the city grew into a flourishing center for trade, craftsmanship, arts and culture. The tea and silk industries became important; excellent poets, philosophers and painters set new standards. It was a period of extraordinary intellectual creativity. From 581 (beginning of the Sui Dynasty) until 1368, Nanjing was a prefectural city. For that reason, it indeed lost some of its political importance, but it still remained one of the most important economic and political centers of the country. From 937 — 975 it was the seat of the Southern Tang Dynasty. From 1126—1279, Yue Fei used it as the center of resistance against the foreign peoples moving in from the north.

In 1368, Zhu Yuanzhang made the city the capital of his new empire, the Ming Dynasty. He named it Yingtian. A mighty city wall and a huge imperial palace were constructed. Only a few ruins of that epoch can still be seen today. In 1421, his son moved the capital to Beijing. Yingtian, renamed Nanjing 'Southern Capital', remained the secondary capital.

Trade and industry made the city wealthy during the following years. Shipbuilding, textiles and ceramics were among the most important branches of industry. The ships for the famous expeditions undertaken by the eunuch Zheng He were built in the shipyards in the northwestern part of the city. The Imperial Academy, Guozi Jian, attracted up to 9,000 students; 2,000 of them came from abroad. Here, work was done on the great Yongle encyclopedia. During the Qing Dynasty, Nanjing became the residence of the viceroy of Jiangnan who ruled over the provinces of Jiangsu, Jiangxi and Anhui.

After the Opium War, the first of a series of unequal treaties was signed in 1842. This opened the doors to foreign powers (mainly England, France and the USA) for unrestricted trade in various Chinese cities and accelerated China's development into a semi-colony. The policy of the foreign powers, corruption and the incompetence of the Qing government had caused indignation and despair among the people, which resulted in a powerful peasant revolt in 1851 based on a religious and revolutionary ideology. The troops of the Taiping Rebellion occupied Nanjing in 1853 and made it the residence of the Taiping Tianguo, the 'Heavenly Kingdom of Great Peace', for 11 years. After the failure of the Taiping Rebellion in 1864, Nanjing was also destroyed; it took many years to rebuild it.

After the 1911 revolution, its leaders made Nanjing the seat of the provisional government of the Republic of China. Yuan Shikai moved the capital back to Beijing. In 1928, the Kuomintang again declared Nanjing the capital of the country and had modern boulevards and new government buildings erected. In 1937, the city fell to the Japanese who took the lives of 40,000 in a massacre. It remained under Japanese supremacy until 1945. From 1946—1949, Nanjing was again the capital of the Kuomintang government, until Communist troops crossed the Changjiang river on April 23, 1949 and took possession of the city which became the capital of Jiangsu Province in 1952.

Throughout the centuries, Nanjing has been renowned mainly for the production of brocade, velvet and silk, ceramic goods, paper and ink stones. Since 1949, it has developed into the industrial center of the province for other areas of industry, too.

Important agricultural products of the city's environs are rice, wheat, vegetables, fruit, tea and peanuts. Today, Nanjing is also an important university town. Nanjing Daxue, Nanjing University, is not only well-known within China, but also outside of it. In addition, the city has 14 institutions of higher education.

Changjiang Daqiao, Bridge over the Changjiang 长江大桥

The bridge was built between 1960 and 1968. It is the pride of Nanjing and the whole country because it was constructed during difficult times without any foreign help. Economically, too, it is extremely important because it connects the regions north and south of the Changjiang.

The Changjiang Daqiao Bridge is a so-called double-decker bridge. Its upper part is used by pedestrians, cyclists and motorists, while the lower part carries train traffic in both directions. The bridge spans the river for 1,557 m; its traffic lanes total 4,589 m and its railroad tracks, 6,720 m. Nine supports, each 80 m high, were rammed into the riverbed, 160 m apart. Stairs lead up to the bridge administration building. From here, one has a wonderful view of the bridge and Nanjing.

Monument to the Memory of the Crossing of the Changjiang

(on the south bank of the Changjiang, at the Yijiang Men gate)

In 1949, the People's Liberation Army crossed the Changjiang and took the capital of the Kuomintang government.

On the 30th anniversary of this event in 1979, a monument was erected on the southern

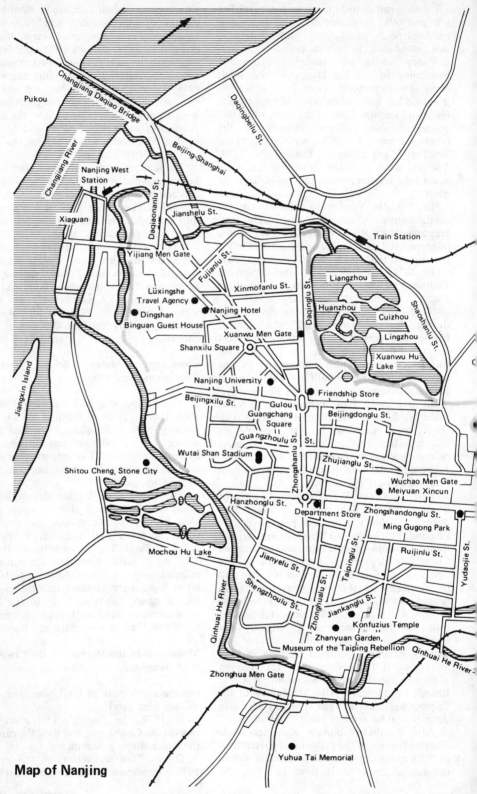

Map of Nanjing

Pukou

Changjiang Daqiao Bridge

Changjiang River

Nanjing West Station

Xiaguan

Beijing-Shanghai

Daqingbelu St.

Daqiaonanlu St.

Jianshelu St.

Yijiang Men Gate

Fujianlu St.

Xinmofanlu St.

Lüxingshe Travel Agency

Dingshan

Nanjing Hotel

Binguan Guest House

Xuanwu Men Gate

Shanxilu Square

Nanjing University

Beijingxilu St.

Gulou

Guangchang Square

Guangzhoulu St.

Wutai Shan Stadium

Shitou Cheng, Stone City

Hanzhonglu St.

Department Store

Mochou Hu Lake

Jianyelu St.

Qinhuai He River

Shengzhoulu St.

Zhonghualu St.

Jiankanglu St.

Zhonghua Men Gate

Train Station

Liangzhou

Daqinglu St.

Huanzhou

Cuizhou

Lingzhou

Shaoshanlu St.

Xuanwu Hu Lake

Friendship Store

Beijingdonglu St.

Zhongshanlu St.

Zhujianglu St.

Wuchao Men Gate

Meiyuan Xincun

Zhongshandonglu St.

Ming Gugong Park

Taipinglu St.

Ruijinlu St.

Yudaojie St.

Konfuzius Temple

Zhanyuan Garden, Museum of the Taiping Rebellion

Qinhuai He River

Yuhua Tai Memorial

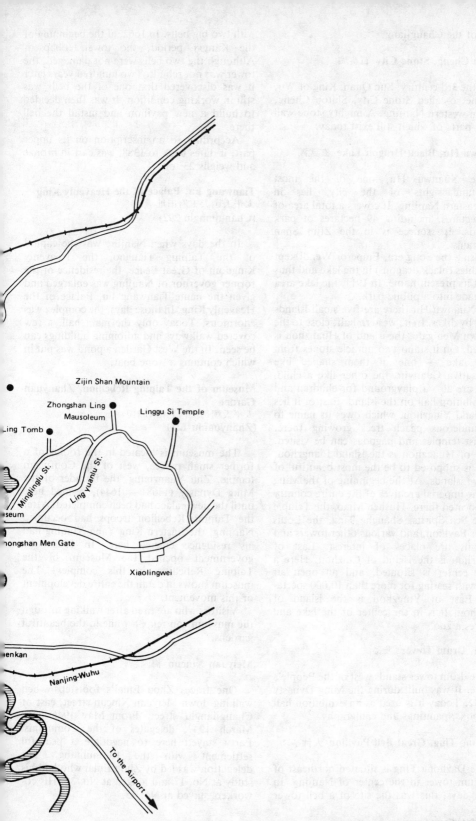

Zijin Shan Mountain

Zhongshan Ling
Mausoleum

Linggu Si Temple

Ling Tomb

Minglinglu St.

Ling yuanlu St.

Museum

Zhongshan Men Gate

Xiaolingwei

enkan

Nanjing-Wuhu

To the Airport

bank of the Changjiang.

Shitou Cheng, Stone City 石头城

In the 3rd century, Sun Quan, King of Wu, had the so-called Stone City, Shitou Cheng, built in western Nanjing. A mighty stone wall arose, parts of which still exist today.

Xuanwu Hu, Black Dragon Lake 玄武湖

The Xuanwu Hu, one of the most important sights of the city, lies in northeastern Nanjing. It covers a total area of 444 hectares, including 49 hectares of park grounds. Its source is in the Zijin Shan mountains.

During the Song era, Emperor Wendi kept crocodiles (black dragons) in the lake and thus gave it its present name. In 1911, the lake area was made into a public park.

In Xuanwu Hu there are five small islands linked by dikes. In its western half, close to the Xuanwu Men gate, the island of Huanzhou is situated. On it stand two miracle stones from Taihu lake — one of them shaped like bodhisattva Guanyin, the other like a child. There are also a playground for children and an exhibition hall on the island. East of it lies the island Yingzhou, which owes its name to the numerous peach trees growing there. Lamaist temples and pagodas can be visited. North of Huanzhou is the island Liangzhou, which is supposed to be the most beautiful of the five islands. At the beginning of the Ming era, the imperial archives of the entire country were located there. Hushen Miao, the Temple of the Sea Spirits, Shanghe Ting, the Lotus Flower Pavilion, and various other towers and pavilions are places of interest. East of Liangzhou is the island of Cuizhou. Here a youth center is situated, and an open air stage with seating for more than 10,000 spectators. East of Yingzhou is the island of Lingzhou. It is in the center of the lake and features a zoo.

Gulou, Drum Tower 鼓楼

The drum tower stands west of the People's Square. It was built during the Ming Dynasty in 1832. Today it is used as an exhibition hall for books, paintings and calligraphy.

Dazhong Ting, Great Bell Pavilion 大钟亭

The Dazhong Ting is situated northeast of the drum tower in the center of Nanjing. In earlier days, this was the site of a bell tower with two big bells. In 1662, at the beginning of the Kangxi period, the tower collapsed. Although the two bells were not damaged, the tower was not rebuilt. Two hundred years later it was discovered that one of the bells was still in working condition. It was then decided to build a new pavilion and install the bell there.

According to an inscription on its upper part, it dates back to 1388, was cast in bronze and weighs 23 tons.

Tianwang Fu, Palace of the Heavenly King 太平天国天王府旧址 (Changjianglu 292)

In the days when Nanjing was the capital of the Taiping Tianguo, the Heavenly Kingdom of Great Peace, the residence of the former governor of Nanjing was enlarged and given the name Tianwang Fu, Palace of the Heavenly King. In those days, the complex was enormous. Today only the main hall, a few covered walkways and adjoining buildings can be seen. In the West Garden a pond was put in which contains a stone boat.

Museum of the Taiping Rebellion, Zhanyuan Garden 太平天国历史博物馆（瞻园） (Zhanyuanlu 128)

The museum is located in the rooms of a former small palace, west of the Confucian temple. Zhu Yuanzhang, the founder of the Ming Dynasty (1368 — 1644), resided here until the new palace had been completed. After the Taiping Rebellion troops had occupied Nanjing, the Eastern King Yang Xiuqing had his residence erected here. In 1958, the government opened the Museum of the Taiping Rebellion in this complex. The museum shows in detail the entire development of this movement.

Visitors who are tired after walking through the museum can relax a while in the beautiful gardens.

Meiyuan Xincun 梅园新村

One traces Zhou Enlai's footsteps when walking down Meiyuan Xincun street, east of Changjianglu street. From May 1946 until March 1947, delegates of the Communist Party stayed here to negotiate a peaceful settlement with the Kuomintang. The delegation was led by Zhou Enlai who had his study at No. 17 and lodged at No. 30. His co-workers stayed at No. 35.

Wumen Gongyuan Park, (Ming Gugong)
午门公园（明故宫遗址）

In eastern Nanjing are the ruins of the first Imperial Palace of the Ming Dynasty.

Construction of a huge Imperial palace commenced in 1369. It was completed after more than ten years. When Zhu Yuanzhang died in 1398, his grandson, son of the late crown prince, came into power. His right to the throne was disputed by his uncles, the sons of Zhu Yuanzhang. One of them, the king of Yan who resided in Beijing, succeeded in making himself emperor by force.

After the new emperor had moved the capital to Beijing, the palace slowly went to ruin. The war of the following centuries ensured its total destruction. Now only a few ruins give the visitor a faint idea of its former splendor and beauty.

Today, the visitor enters the complex from the north. The ruins of the main gate, Wumen, still give an impression of the size of the palace's buildings. Outside the main gate, the Five Dragon Bridge can be seen, as well as the remains of the Fengtian Dian, one of the main halls.

Nanjing Bowuyuan, Nanjing Museum (Jiangsu Provincial Museum)
南京博物馆

(Zhongshandonglu 321)

The idea to make this a museum came from the well-known educator Cai Yuanpei (1863 – 1940).

The front part of the main hall was designed in the wooden framework style of the Liao era (907–1125). In an area of 90,000 m², about 5,000 years of Chinese history from its beginnings are presented. In addition to a well summarized history of Jiangsu Province, countless exhibition objects, for example bronzes, ceramics, tools, *objets d'art*, calligraphies and paintings make the museum well worth a visit.

Zhongshan Men Gate 中山门
(Zhongshan, Sun Zhongshan, Sun Yatsen)

The road leads through Zhongshan Men gate to the sights of the eastern part of the city. At the beginning of the Ming era, this was the site of Chaoyang Men gate, the east gate of the Imperial Palace. During the construction of the Zhongshan Ling Mausoleum in 1927, Chaoyang Men was torn down and Zhongshan Men gate erected in its place.

Xiao Jiuhua Shan, Jiuhua Shan Small Mountain 小九华山

Xiao Jiuhua Shan is approximately 100 m high. During the time of the North and South dynasties (420 – 589), it was of great military significance. In later years that area was turned into an amusement park for the nobility. The temples and pavilions, once numerous, were destroyed during the course of many wars. Only the stone pagoda Sancang Ta still remains. It is said to hold relics of the famous monk Xuanzang (Sancang). The pagoda was named after him.

Zijin Shan Mountains 紫金山

The 448-m-high Zijin Shan mountains are east of Nanjing. The beautiful scenery they offer, makes them one of the most popular holiday resorts of the people from Nanjing.

They afford various sights: an observatory, the Sun Yatsen mausoleum, the tomb of the first Ming emperor and Linggu Gongyuan park with its Linggu Si temple

Zijinshan Tianwentai, Zijin Shan Observatory
紫金山天文台

On the western peak of Zijin Shan, a road leads up to one of China's major observatories. It was formally opened in 1934 and restored and modernized after 1949. A few interesting antique astronomical instruments as well as a collection of valuable documents still exist today. A guided tour of the area, including a look at instruments, should best be arranged in advance with an agent of the official travel agency, Lüxingshe.

Mingxiao Ling Tomb 明孝陵

The tomb is located at the foot of the Zijin Shan mountains. It is the final resting place of the first emperor of the Ming Dynasty, Zhu Yuanzhang. He had it built from 1381 – 1383. Besides the emperor, who died in 1398, the emperor's wife (died 1382) and several concubines as well as number of female servants are buried here.

The tomb complex is divided into a front and a back section. The front section begins at Dahong Men, the Great Red Gate. The Sacred Way, 800 m long, is lined by stone statues, arranged in pairs, of animals, columns and military as well as civilian dignitaries; it leads toward the back section which starts at the front main gate. From here the path leads to a stele pavilion. Another gateway, the

Rectangular City, and the grave mound follow. Several parts of this grave complex have been heavily damaged or destroyed over the years. Nevertheless, the entire Mingxiao Ling complex is one of China's biggest and most solemn emperor's tombs.

Zhongshan Ling Mausoleum 中山陵

This is the mausoleum of the first president of the provisional government of the Republic, Dr. Sun Yatsen, also called Sun Zhongshan. Sun Yatsen, born on November 12, 1866, in Xiangshan (today Zhongshan) district, Guangdong Province, totally devoted 40 years of activity to the revolution. He died in Beijing on March 12, 1925.

In accordance with his will, he was buried in Nanjing. The mausoleum is situated on the southern slope of the Zijin Shan mountains. It was designed by the architect Lü Yanzhi and built from 1926—1929. The building materials were granite from Suzhou and blue ceramic tiles. On June 1, 1929, the coffin with Sun Yatsen's remains was transported in state from Biyun Si temple in Beijing to this mausoleum.

By climbing a few steps, one reaches a memorial arch which carries the inscription *Bo Ai*, 'Universal Love'. A wide, wooded area stretches out in front of one's eyes. In its center, the individual buildings are arranged along a north-south axis.

The inscription over the middle arch of the main gate that follows reads: *Tianxia Wei Gong*, 'The world belongs to everyone', done according to a calligraphy by Sun Yatsen. Behind the main gate is a stele pavilion, inside of which a granite stele with an inscription can be seen, telling that Sun Yatsen, leader of the Chinese Kuomintang party, is buried here. From here, a long flight of 299 steps, in eight sections, leads uphill to the memorial hall, 700 m away. It is a white granite edifice built in palacial style and contains a marble statue of Sun Yatsen. The four sides of the pedestal are decorated with reliefs documenting some of his most important deeds. This is the work of the French artist Paul Landowski. On the walls, engraved in golden script on black marble, is the program for national development in Sun Yatsen's own writing. To the north, a door leads to the crypt, where a recumbent marble statue of Sun Yatsen lies. His remains are buried 5 m beneath this statue.

Linggu Si Temple 灵谷寺

Linggu Si is east of the Sun Yatsen mausoleum in a large public park. It was built during the Liang era under the reign of Emperor Wudi in 514. Originally the temple was situated on the spot where the first Ming emperor's tomb complex now stands. But, as the emperor had chosen just that spot for the building of his tomb, the temple had to be moved and was re-erected further east in 1381.

The temple's surroundings are considered to be the most beautiful within the Zijin Shan mountains. In 1381 this temple must have been huge. The distance from the main gate to the main hall alone measured 2.5 km. Around 1850, a large proportion of the temple was destroyed. The most interesting remaining and restored building is Wuliang Dian hall, an edifice that is 600 years old, made entirely of stone and brick, without any wood.

The Linggu Ta pagoda, 60 m tall, within the temple district, was built in 1929 in memory of the victims of the Northern Expedition (1924 — 1927).

Inside the pagoda, a staircase leads up to the top floor. From there one has a broad view of the surroundings.

Mochou Hu Lake 莫愁湖

In southwestern Nanjing, outside the Shuixi Men gate, the charming complex of the Mochou Hu is situated.

According to legend, a young girl named Mo Chou from Luoyang was made to marry someone from this area during the Southern Qi era (around 480). It is said that she often came here, sad and homesick.

An interesting feature of the park is Shengqi Lou building, dating from the early Ming era. Emperor Zhu Yuanzhang is said to have played chess here with the powerful general Xu Da. Supposedly he let the general win and gave him the entire Mochou Lake grounds as a sign of his appreciation to ensure his loyalty.

In 1929, the park area was made accessible to the public. Large-scale expansions were made in 1953.

Yuhua Tai Terrace 雨花台

Yuhua terrace is in the southern part of the city outside the Zhonghua Men gate on a 100-m-high hill. A legend tells the story of a Buddhist monk who, in the 4th century, held such a moving sermon that it rained flowers from the sky. Many colorful pebbles, called *Yuhua Shi*, can still be found in this area. Their colors are showed off to their best advantage if the stones are put into a glass of water.

During the years 1927 — 1949, Yuhua Tai was an execution ground for revolutionaries. Altogether, more than 100,000 people are said to have been executed here on the orders of Chiang Kai-shek and the Kuomintang party. A stele was erected in memory of these 100,000 people after the revolution. The inscription reads: 'Eternal life to the martyrs of the revolution.'

Niushou Shan Mountain 牛首山

South of Nanjing is Niushou Shan. After 1949, two graves from the Southern Tang Dynasty (937 — 975) were uncovered here. They are the burial places of the first emperor, Li Sheng, and his son and successor to the throne, Li Jing. The burial grounds are divided into three parts, which are subdivided into 13 rooms. Interesting reliefs and murals have been preserved.

Yanzi Ji, Swallow's Rock 燕子矶

The rock is situated on top of one of the Yanshan mountain's cliffs, north of the city. The mountain is right on the Changjiang; it towers out over the cliff, resembling a flying swallow. On the tip of the rock stands a pavilion where a stone stele with a calligraphy by Emperor Qianliong stands: 'Yanzi Ji'. On the back of the rock, there is a poem about this area written by the emperor.

Temples, pavilions and caves are not far away. Of the twelve original caves, only three are still in existence: Toutai Dong, Ertai Dong and Santai Dong. Santai Dong is the most remarkable cave.

Qixia Shan Mountain 栖霞山

About 22 km northeast of Nanjing rises the 440-m-high Qixia Shan mountain with its three peaks.

The following sights in this area are especially worth mentioning:

Qixia Si temple, at the western foot of the central peak. Originating from a private estate in 483, the temple fell victim to fire in 1855 and was then re-erected. Today only the main gate, the halls Tianwang Dian, Pilu Dian and Canjing Lou, the Tower of the Holy Books, remain. A stone statue from around 400, stone pagodas from the Wudai era, stone steles from the Tang era as well as the Sheli Ta pagoda are still found on the temple grounds.

The Sheli Ta pagoda, 15 m tall, supposedly dates back to 601, but the Buddhist figures chiseled into seven walls lead to the conclusion that it originated in the 10th century.

Qianfo Yan, Thousand Buddhas Rock, lies east of Sheli Ta pagoda. Tradition has it that the head of the district during the Nanxi era (478 — 502), Zhong Zhang, had two Buddhas chiseled into the rock. Later on, more and more figures were added. Today there are more than 299 niches, containing 515 Buddhist sculptures.

Next to this rock stands the Buddhist Wuliang Dian hall. It is said to have been erected originally in 484. The outer walls and the arched gate are made of stone.

Special local products

Yunjin Brocade from Nanjing

The famous Nanjing brocade, also called cloud brocade, is one of the three best kinds of brocade from China. It is distinguished by its beautiful colors and patterns.

Since the 3rd century, Nanjing has been an important silk producing city. From 420 — 589 there was an official brocade office in Nanjing. At that time, the exportation of silk to foreign countries began. Cloud brocade was manufactured mainly for Imperial families, high-ranking civil servants and merchants. Today, all parts of China are supplied and it is also exported.

Hotels

Jinling Fandian, 金陵饭店 Xinjiekou Guangchang, tel. 4 41 41, telex 3 41 10

Nanjing Fandian, 南京饭店 Zhongshanbeilu 259, tel. 3 41 21

Shuangmenlou Binguan, 双门楼宾馆 Zhongshanbeilu, Shuangmenlou 38, tel. 8 55 35, 8 59 31, 5 93 13

Low-cost Hotels

Dingshan Binguan, 丁山宾馆 Chaha'erlu 90, tel. 8 59 31

Shengli Fandian, 胜利饭店 Zhongshanlu 75, tel. 4 22 17

Restaurants

Jiangsu Jiujia, Jiankanglu 126, tel. 2 36 98

Sichuan Jiujia, Taipingnanlu 171, tel. 4 22 43, 4 36 51

Tongqinglou Caiguan, Zhongshannanlu 10, tel. 4 28 85

Beijing Lamb Restaurant, Zhongshandonglu 94, tel. 4 25 85

Dasanyuan Caiguan, Zhongshanlu 38, tel. 4 10 27

Shopping

The most important shopping street is Zhongshanlu. The **Friendship Store,** Youyi Shangdian, is located at Daqinglu street 3-9. An antique shop can be found at Hanzhonglu 7-11.

Travel agency

Guoji Lüxingshe, CITS, Zhongguo Lüxingshe, Huaqiao Lüxingshe, Zhongshanbeilu 313, tel. 8 51 53

CAAC office, Zhongshandonglu 76, tel. 4 33 78

Train station, Nanjing Huochezhan, Shaoshanlu, tel. 3 42 72

Taxis, Beijingxilukou, tel. 3 38 90

Telephone, long distance calls in China 113; international calls 4 15 00, 4 28 13; information 116

Post office, Zhongshanlu 25, tel. 4 23 38, 4 23 14

Bank of China, Zhongshandonglu 2, tel. 4 23 38, 4 23 14

University, Nanjing Daxue, Mankoulu 11, tel. 3 46 51-3, foreign students' dormitory: tel. 3 46 51-6 63

The Grand Canal 大运河

The Grand Canal is the longest and oldest man-made waterway in the world. The first part of it was dug 2400 years ago, from the Changjiang river via the city of Yangzhou to Huai'an. It enabled the Wu Kingdom (present-day Jiangsu province) to transport its soldiers to fight against the Qi Kingdom in the north (present-day Shandong province). At the end of the 6th century the Sui dynasty Emperor Yangdi ordered the connection of many small canals and rivers to form one waterway. Thereby all the rivers flowing west-east such as Haihe, Huanghe, Huaihe, Changjiang and Qian-

tangjiang were linked by the Great Canal which flowed north-south. The new capital of Luoyang had now a connection with the old capital Xi'an in the west, the city of Yangzhou, where Emperor Yangdi built his residence, and Hangzhou. From that time rice could be transported within a short time from the fertile areas in the south to the north. Food supplies for the Emperor's troops were secure. The cities along this canal such as Hangzhou, Suzhou and many others flourished. In the 13th century, during the reign of the Mongolian Emperor Kublai Khan, the canal was straightened and directly extended to Beijing. The old part of the canal in the west silted. The new canal stretched 1794 km in length, it guaranteed supply for the capital. Rice, important tributes and taxes were transported from the south to the north, as well as building materials for the palaces and residences.

Following the development of the railways in China, many parts of the canal have fallen into decay and have become dilapidated. The floods of the Huanghe river caused heavy damage. At present the southern half of the canal is still used intensively for transportation.

Some years ago, the CITS 'discovered' the Grand Canal and started to organise different tours on this magnificent waterway.

Zhenjiang 镇江市

Zhenjiang is about a four-hour train ride from Shanghai in the direction of Nanjing. It is located in a beautiful area.

Its favorable location on the south bank of the Changjiang, which is intersected by the Grand Canal at this point, helped Zhenjiang to become an important port and trade center in the course of its long history. Today, Zhenjiang is an industrial town with an inland port and a population of 300,000.

The places of interest in Zhenjiang center around the three mountains, Beigu Shan, Jiaoshan and Jinshan. But the Zhenjiang Museum (collection of classical books, paintings, bronzes and porcelain) and the Shaozong Library (Boxian Park) are also of interest. The library has a collection of 80,000 volumes, which includes books from the former library of the Jinshan monastery and the old Shaozong library. Of importance is the 100-volume work Baikongliutie (written from the 7th — 11th centuries), a dictionary of old sayings and proverbs.

Beigu Shan Hill 北固山

Beigu Shan is 48 m high and lies northeast

of the town on the banks of the Changjiang.

The sights worth seeing are at the back part of Beigu Shan, which is closely related to the history of the Three Kingdoms.

In those days, the founder of the state of Wu, Sun Quan, ruled over the central and the lower regions of the Changjiang. His opponent, the Emperor of Shu, Liu Bei, married his sister, Sun Shangxiang. In this area, where today Ganlu monastery stands, Liu Bei is said to have been introduced to Sun Quan's mother. Ganlu Si dates back to the year 265, but has been destroyed and rebuilt a number of times over the years.

The marriage between Liu Bei and Sun Quan's sister could not resolve the conflicts between the two states. Liu Bei was defeated during a war and died in Baidicheng, on the upper Changjiang. His wife made offerings to him in the Lingyun Ting pavilion. It is said that she could not get over her husband's death and threw herself to her own from here.

Next to the temple there is an iron pagoda, Ganlusi Tieta.

This is the place where Liu Bei was said to have married Sun Shangxiang. The iron pagoda was built during the years 825 — 826. Seven stories high in former years, the pagoda fell victim to an earthquake, leading to the destruction of all but the two lower stories. After 1949 it was restored.

On the top of the mountain is the Duojing Lou, a two storied building. Here, Liu Bei's wife is supposed to have dressed and made herself up. In past centuries, Duojing Lou used to be the preferred meeting place of many scholars, poets and painters. The great poet of the Tang era, Li Bai, composed a poem about Beigu Shan here.

Jiaoshan Hill 焦山

Jiaoshan lies northeast of the town in the middle of the Changjiang. It resembles a piece of green jade floating on the tide of the river. It is approximately 150 m high and covered with old trees dating back to the Song and Ming eras.

The sights described in the following passages are all well worth a visit:

The Buddhist Dinghui Si monastery dates from the Eastern Han Dynasty. The halls that still remain are from the Qing Dynasty.

Xijiang Lou, a building on top of Jiaoshan, part of Biefeng An temple, has large windows on all four sides which offer a broad view of the Changjiang.

On Jiaoshan there are 263 stone tablets, among them are a few from the Southern

dynasties. Today the tablets are stored in the Baomo Dian hall. The famous stone inscription *Yiheming* by the great calligrapher Wang Xizhi of the Yin Dynasty, stands in a pavilion of its own. Wang Xizhi loved cranes.

It is reported that he watched a pair of cranes die on Jiaoshan and then documented his sadness in a poem. The poem was chiseled into the rock on the banks of the river, but part of it was lost when sections of the hill fell into the river. Not until the Qing Dynasty was the precious rock rescued and placed in its present spot.

Former fortifications stand on the east side of the hill. They were used during the Opium War on July 15th, 1842, when the attempt was made to drive British battleships away with cannons.

Jinshan, Golden Hill 金山

The name Jinshan derives from gold finds which were made in this area during the Tang Dynasty.

The hill, 60 m high, used to be an island in the Changjiang which was praised by the poet Zhang Ku of the Tang Dynasty. During the Qing Dynasty the hill was connected to the mainland.

Here there are several pavilions and solemn looking halls. The temple Jinshan Si dates from the Eastern Jin Dynasty. It consists of several main and secondary halls, which were built into the slope and fit harmoniously into the landscape. While it flourished, more than 3,000 monks lived here. Today, the monastery is still inhabited by monks.

The Cishou Ta pagoda is situated on top of the hill. Tradition has it that it was first erected during the Tang Dynasty. By the early Ming Dynasty it had fallen into ruin and was rebuilt in 1900.

A spiral staircase offers access to the individual floors.

Hotels

Jinshan Fandian, Jinshan Xilu, tel. 2 49 62

Yiquan Fandian, Yiquanlu, tel. 2 34 22

Lüyou Fandian, Jiefanglu, tel. 2 36 71

Renfang Fandian, Fengcheshan, tel. 2 29 66

Travel agency

Zhongguo Lüxingshe, Zhongshanlu 407, tel 2 32 81.

Changzhou 常州市

Changzhou is on the Shanghai-Nanjing railway line between Wuxi and Zhenjiang. After the completion of the southern part of the Grand Canal in 609, Changzhou developed into an important grain market. Since the beginning of the 20th century, the main emphasis has been on building up the textile industry. During the last 30 years, food producing and machine manufacturing factories have been built.

Jinyuan Garden 近园

Jinyuan, where the guest house of the city of Changzhou is located, was laid out between 1668 — 1672. Its arrangement corresponds to the style of the Ming Dynasty.

Tianning Si Temple 天宁寺

All that can still be visited of this temple, constructed on a large scale from 901 — 904, are the Daxiong Baodian, Jingang Dian, Wenshu Dian, Puxian Dian, Guanyin Dian halls and the Hall of the 500 Luohan. All of them were restored according to old plans during the Qing Dynasty.

Hongmei Gongyuan Park 红梅公园

In the park, there is a 17 m high pavilion, the imposing structure of which has made the complex a special attraction. It dates from the Qing Dynasty. It is not only the pavilion that made this park well-known, but above all its red-flowering ornamental trees. Visitors spending time here during March or April should not miss seeing them in bloom in Hongmei Gongyuan.

Hotels

Changzhou Fandian, Dongdajie, tel. 2 37 37

Dongfanghong Lüguan, Dongdajie, tel. 2 20 65

Lüyang Fandian, Dongdajie, tel. 2 28 05

Travel agency

Zhongguo Lüxingshe, Dongdajie 101, tel. 48 86

Yixing 宜兴市

Yixing, not far from Taihu lake in the southern part of Jiangsu Province, has been well known in China and abroad since the 12th century for its ceramic production. Even today ceramics are still of great importance. They are mostly unglazed, in various shades from brown to brownish violet and yellow. These vessels are often decorated with engraved plant or animal motifs or designs. Some objects are shaped like fruit, blossoms or pieces of bamboo. The products from Yixing are mostly designed for daily use, for example tea pots, tea cups, plates, soup bowls, bowls and flower pots.

Former Residence of King Fuwang of the Taiping Tianguo 太平天国辅王府

The former residence of one of the Taiping kings is located on Hepingjie street. In earlier times, a high official of the Qing Dynasty lived here. When the Taiping troops occupied the town, King Fuwang (Yang Fuqing) made the estate his residence. Even today, murals from the Taiping Tianguo era can be seen here.

Zhanggong Dong Caves 张公洞

The Zhanggong Dong Caves are 22 km southeast of the district capital Yixing at the foot of Yufeng Shan. In earlier times, the famous Daoist Zhang Daoling (Zhang Gong) is said to have lived here. Thus, the caves were named after him.

They are divided into a front and a back complex and have a total area of 3,000 m².

The front cave is very large and can hold several thousand people. Through an opening surrounded by trees, one can look up into the sky. Many steps make the path, leading 1 km through the 72 caves, passable. The colorful illuminated 'halls' with their bizarre shapes and the music that sometimes can be heard in the background are a delight to the visitor.

Linggu Dong Caves 灵谷洞

The Linggu Dong Caves are situated 30 km southwest of Yixing at the southern foot of Shiniu Shan mountain, 6 km from the Zhanggong Dong caves. Their total area amounts to 2,413 m². They are divided into five so-called stone halls. Using all his imagination, the visitor can recognize numerous interesting figures and landscapes and even a huge stone waterfall, which falls from a height of 17 m.

Shanjuan Dong Caves 善卷洞

The Shanjuan Caves are 25 km southwest of Yixing in Luoyan Shan mountain. They are three stories high and have a total area of 5,000 m². The path through them is 800 m long. A peculiarity of its upper part is that all year round the temperature remains constant at 23°C. The most beautiful and amazing cave is in the lower part, where a waterfall tumbles down. One can take a boat trip on the river to the end of the cave, 120 m away.

Hotel

Yixing Binguan, 宜兴宾馆 Renminnanlu, tel. 21 79

Suzhou 苏州市

Suzhou, with a population of 670,000, is in the southwestern region of Jiangsu Province, south of the Changjiang Delta, on the southern part of the Grand Canal in one of China's most fertile regions. The city is called the Venice of the East, because it is surrounded and divided by many small canals. Suzhou is well known because of its landscaped gardens, in which nature and architecture blend harmoniously. So Suzhou today is a main tourist attraction. Several million people, from China and abroad, visit the city annually.

History

The history of Suzhou can be traced back to the year 484 BC, when the city was the capital of the state of Wu for a short period of time. With the construction of the Grand Canal, Suzhou developed into an important administration and trade center. The city flourished during the Ming and early Qing dynasties. Innumerable families of wealthy landowners, high-ranking officials and merchants settled here. During this period, most of the gardens were laid out. Suzhou was a center of finance and banking, of arts and scholarship; the silk industry and the art of embroidery made the city wealthy. From 1860 — 1863 it was occupied by the troops of the Taiping Rebellion and badly damaged. After the failure of the Taiping movement, attempts were made to obliterate the traces of this period and to rebuild the economy, but in the meantime, the city had already relinquished its leading position as a trade center to Shanghai. Today Suzhou is a center of the silk and cotton industries.

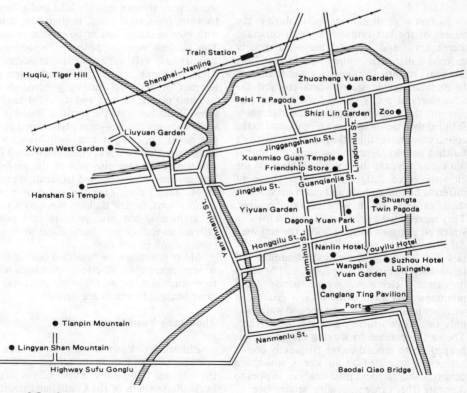

Map of Suzhou

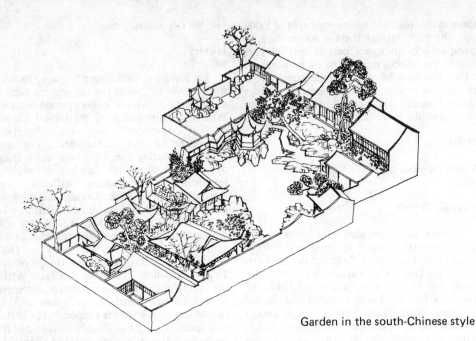

Garden in the south-Chinese style

Suzhou's Gardens

Suzhou's gardens were built during the course of the last centuries by rich officials, merchants and landowners. Formerly successful dignitaries retired here to spend the last years of their lives in peace and harmony. In Suzhou, great estate-owners enjoyed the advantages of a city but still did not have to give up the country atmosphere. Merchants fulfilled their desire to own a plot of land in the country and were still within reach of the city's bustling activity. Historical sources reveal that during its heyday, the notable gardens of the city numbered 200. Villas in the shape of different buildings, halls and pavilions stood in these gardens, which were of varying sizes. They represented a small world of their own, in which all elements existing under the sun were supposed to be present. The builders had the task of creating a maximum number of landscapes within a limited space. The most important elements were ponds and mountains. As Suzhou lies on low ground, it was easy to install ponds: the ground water was only one to two meters beneath the surface. The earth obtained by digging the ponds was heaped up to mounds. One frequently comes across the so-called Taihu stones which are bizarrely shaped rocks used singly or in piles to decorate the gardens. Taihu stones are of porous limestone, which usually comes from

West Mountain Island in Taihu lake. The stones were thrown into the lake and exposed to water for several years. In that way, stones with bizarre shapes full of holes were created. The gardens were supposed to reproduce a country as well as an urban atmosphere. Thus, pavilions, terraces, halls and towers are all part of a typical Suzhou garden, as are bamboo plants, flowers and different kind of trees. Walls surround the gardens. In the inner walls there are moon — and vase-shaped gates, polygonal openings and windows with imaginative lattice-work. Animals, mainly fish and song-birds, are also part of the gardens. The gardens were supposed to create a poetic mood. Often they were the scene of poets' competitions. So the builders not only had to be architects, but also painters and poets. Often, several people were engaged in the construction of one garden.

Many grounds were neglected during times of war. Since 1949, all efforts have been made to restore them. In the following passages, the most beautiful gardens are described.

Zhuozheng Yuan Garden 拙政园

Zhuozheng Yuan covers 4 hectares in northeast Suzhou. It is the largest garden of the city and a typical example of the art of horticulture south of the Changjiang river.

It was laid out in 1513 by the censor Wang

Xiancheng after his retirement from political life. After his death, his son gambled away the gardens.

When Taiping troops occupied Suzhou in 1860, King Zhongwang picked this one and the neighbouring buildings of the present Historical Museum as a residence and center for his political activities.

Three-fifths of its area is covered by magnificent ponds. All of the buildings are right next to the ponds, so that the garden seems to be floating on the water. The entire grounds can be divided into three parts: an eastern, a central and a western part. The central one is especially worth a visit. It centers around Yuanxiang Tang pavilion. Two artificial islands linked to each other in the lotus pond north of the pavilion are densely overgrown with bamboo plants and trees. In the western part, Sanshiliu Yuanyang Guan hall, the Hall of the Thirty-Six Mandarin Ducks, will attract the visitors' special interest. On the adjoining lake, one used to be able to see mandarin ducks, symbol of marital faithfulness. Today, some swim in a fenced-off part of the lake.

West of the garden there is a noteworthy *bonsai* exhibition and a teahouse.

The Exhibits of the Historical Museum 历史博物馆

Next to Zhuozheng Yuan garden, the exhibits of the Historical Museum include a description of the province, emphasizing political, economic and cultural aspects.

Beisi Ta Pagoda 北寺塔

Beisi Ta is in the northern part of ancient Suzhou. It dates from 450 and is relatively well-preserved. The top floor offers a fine view. If the weather is good, bird lovers bring their pets along to meet in the teahouse behind the pagoda.

Shizi Lin Garden 狮子林

Shizi Lin is on Yuanlinlu street in northeastern Suzhou. It is one of the most famous old gardens of the city. From 1341—1367, during the Yuan Dynasty, a monk named

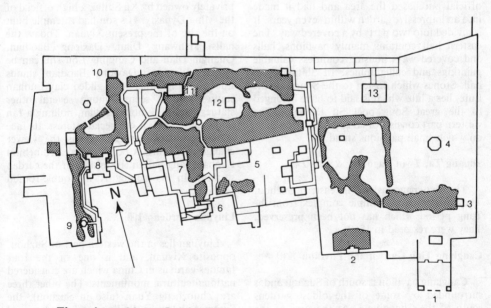

Zhuozheng Yuan Garden

1. Damen, Entrance
2. Hanqing Ge Pavilion
3. Furong Xie Pavilion
4. Tianquan Ting Pavilion
5. Yuanxiang Tang Pavilion
6. Xiao Canglang Pavilion
7. Xiangzhou Pavilion

8. Hall of the Thirty-Six Mandarin Ducks
9. Taying Ting Pavilion
10. Daoying Lou Tower
11. Jianshan Lou Tower
12. Xuexiangyunwei Ting Pavilion
13. Tea House

Tianru had a Buddhist temple built on this spot as a memorial to his master Zhongfeng. The present garden is at the rear of the grounds. Shizi Lin's special feature is the abundance of Taihu stones. Some resemble flowers, others animals, but most of them are supposed to bear a similarity to lions, thus the name Shizi Lin (Lion's Grove).

Xuanmiao Guan Daoist Temple 玄妙观

Xuanmiao Guan is on Guanqianjie street. It is assumed to have been founded in 270. The temple originally consisted of 31 halls. Today only the main gate, Shanmen, and Sanxing Dian hall remain. Sanxing Dian hall was rebuilt in 1179 and is among the oldest Daoist temple halls in China. There are three gilded statues of Daoist saints, Sanxing Xiang, made of clay.

Yiyuan Garden 怡园

Yiyuan is on Renminlu street. This is where the villa of Minister Wu Kuan (1435 — 1504) originally stood. In 1876, a high-ranking official purchased the area and had it made into an impressive garden within seven years. It is divided into two parts by a covered way. The eastern half contains mainly pavilions, halls and covered ways housing countless valuable paintings and calligraphies. In Shitingqinshi hall, Stones which Listen to the Sound of the Lute, lies a lute which is said to have belonged to the great Song poet Su Dongpo. The western part consists of lakes and artificial hills on which small pavilions stand.

Shuang Ta, Twin Pagodas 双塔寺双塔

The two pagodas are in eastern Suzhou. They are part of a temple complex from the Tang period which has not been preserved. They were restored in 1860.

Canglang Ting Garden and Pavilion 沧浪亭

Canglang pavilion is south of Suzhou and is surrounded by some of the oldest gardens south of the Changjiang. At the time of the Five Dynasties, the heart of the grounds was the villa of a high-ranking official, bought in 1041 by the poet Su Shenqing and expanded by adding a garden with pavilions and halls. In 1954, it was restored and opened to the public.

Today, the garden covers an area of one hectare. A bridge leads to the entrance gate. From there, a covered way leads to the western part of the garden past an artificial hill, the center of Canglang Ting. On top of the hill is the small Canglang Ting pavilion.

Wangshi Yuan Garden 网师园

The Wangshi Yuan (Garden of the Master of Nets) is in southern Suzhou, very close to Suzhou Hotel on Shiquanjie street. In 1140, a high official, Shi Zhengzhi, had his residence built here. Because he enjoyed the company of intelligent and educated men, the garden was intended as a 'net' to catch them. Completely restored during the Ming era, Wangshi Yuan is well known because it contains a large number of cleverly laid out buildings and landscapes in an extremely limited space. The living quarters are in the eastern part. Dianchunyi hall, built in the Ming style, stands in the western part in a small yard. It is considered a typical example of Suzhou garden halls.

Xiyuan Garden 西园

Xiyuan is on Liuyuanlu street in the western part of the city, opposite Liuyuan garden. Originally, they formed one garden, which was privately owned by Xu Shitai, a high official of the Ming Dynasty. His son had a temple built on the site of the present Xiyuan. Today, the halls Tianwang Dian, Daxiong Baodian, Guanyin Dian and Cangjing Lou still can be visited. West of Daxiong Baodian stands Luohan Tang, where 500 gilded clay Luohan statues can be seen. Among several other statues, one of a monk, Jidian, holding a fan in his right hand, is of special interest. Its face seems to change expressions as the viewer changes positions. A pond was created behind Luohan Tang hall in the middle of the garden section. In its center is a double-roofed pavilion.

Liuyuan Garden 留园

Liuyuan lies in the western part of Suzhou, opposite Xiyuan, and is one of the four famous gardens in China which are considered national cultural monuments. The other three are Zhuozheng Yuan (also in Suzhou), the Summer Palace in Beijing, and the Imperial Residence in Chengde, Hebei. Liuyuan and Xiyuan originally made up one complex owned by Xu Shitai, a high-ranking official. In 1800, the Liu family bought this part of the gardens and had it redesigned. At the beginning of the 20th century, the garden was growing wild, but finally fully restored and then opened to the public. On an area of three hectares, various courtyards were created by building walls and

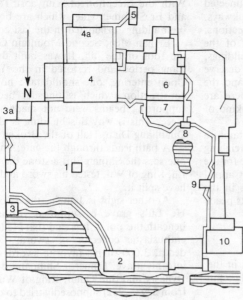

Canglang Ting
Garden and Pavilion

1. Canglang Ting Pavilion
2. Mianshui Xuan
3. Guanyu Chu
3a. Wenmiao Xiangshi
4. Mingdao Tang Hall
4a. Yaohua Jingjie
5. Kanshan Lou Pavilion
6. Hall of the 500 Sages
7. Qingxiang Guan Hall
8. Buqi Ting Pavilion
9. Yubei Ting Pavilion
10. Ouxiang Shuixie Pavilion

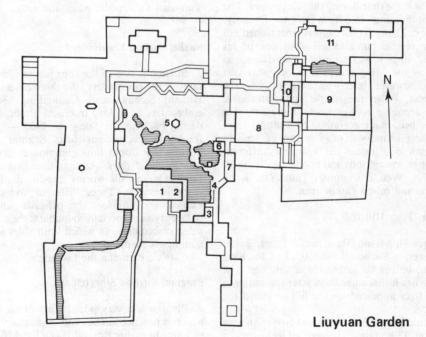

Liuyuan Garden

1. Hanbi Shanfang Hall
2. Mingse Lou Hall
3. Gumu Jiaoke Courtyard
4. Haopu Ting Pavilion
5. Keting Pavilion
6. Qingfeng Chiguan Hall

7. Quxi Lou Hall
8. Wufengxian Guan Hall (Nanmu Ting)
9. Yuanyang Ting Hall
10. Huanwodushu Chu Courtyard
11. Guanyun Ting Pavilion

artificial hills. These courtyards are connected to each other by 700 m of covered walkways. The garden can be divided into four sections. A pond and rocks are in the center of the garden. In the eastern part are buildings, pavilions and halls, two of which deserve special mention: the Yuanyang Ting and the Wufengxian Guan halls, in which there are beautiful carvings of *nanmu* wood, a kind of cedar from South China.

The northeastern courtyard contains a curiosity: a 6.5 m high Taihu stone weighing five tons, which has been standing there for the last 400 years and is called the Cloud-Capped Peak. There are mostly artificial hills in the western part. The northern part with its peach trees is noteworthy.

Hanshan Si Temple 寒山寺

The Buddhist temple Hanshan Si is in the village of Fengqiao Zhen, approximately 5 km west of Suzhou.

Hanshan Si was founded in 503—508 during the Liang era and later named after the famous Buddhist monk Hanshan, who lived here for some time during the 7th century. The present buildings date from the Qing Dynasty. The poet Zhang Ji (8th century) mentioned not only a temple but also a bell in one of his poems. Since it was no longer in existence as early as the Ming era, a new one was cast which, however, later was taken away by the Japanese. When the temple was restored in 1905, Japanese monks made a present of a bronze bell, made according to a model from the Tang Dynasty. Today it can be seen in Hanshan Si. Inside the temple's different buildings, inscriptions and poems by Zhang Ji, Yue Fei, Wen Zhengming, Tang Yin, Kang Youwei and others can be seen.

Huqiu, Tiger Hill 虎丘

Tiger Hill is on Shantangjie street, 3 km northwest of Suzhou. In 480 BC, Fu Cha, King of Wu, buried his father He at this site. The legend has it that three days after the burial, a white tiger appeared on the hill to guard the grave.

Huqiu is only 30 m high and covers an area of about 13 hectares. Throughout its history, it has been a very popular place to visit, because of its temples and pagodas, waterfalls, rocks and trees. A famous poet, Bai Juyi (772 — 846), wrote about it: 'To visit the place 12 times a year is not little, but it is not too much either.' In the course of time these grounds have been destroyed and restored seven times.

With the exception of Yunyansi Ta pagoda and Er Shanmen gate, which are both older, the buildings originated in the last century.

Ershan Men, Second Mountain Gate, is at the foot of the hill. It was built during the Tang period and restored in the Yuan era. Upon entering, one should take note of the construction, which is unusual because the supporting beams were not made from one piece. This is why this building is also called Duanliang Dian, Hall of the Broken Beams.

A path leads through the gate; on the right one sees the Shijian Shi, a stone on which He Lü, King of Wu, tested his sword and is said to have split it.

Another sight is Jianchi, the Sword Pond. He Lü's grave is supposed to have been beneath this pond. It is said that He Lü was an enthusiastic collector of swords. After his death, 3,000 of his favorite swords were put into his grave. Emperor Shihuang of the Qin Dynasty and Sun Quan, King of Wu (reigned from 229 — 252) supposedly tried to dig up the swords. They had deep pits dug for this purpose. Water gathered in these pits, so that a pond was formed. On top of Tiger Hill is Yunyansi Ta pagoda, which dates back to 959 — 961.

Suxiu, Suzhou Embroidery

Suzhou is one of the four places which are famous for embroidery, the three others being Hunan, Sichuan and Guangdong. Suzhou embroidery has a long tradition. Embroideries dating back to the Song era (960 — 1279), found in excavations near Suzhou, offer information about how common embroidery was in those days. At that time, almost all families raised silk-worms, produced silk and embroidered it. Three different styles were known: the popular, the officials' and the palace styles. Especially valuable is the double-sided embroidery, in which both sides appear completely identical.

Cats were among the favorite motifs.

Pingtan, Suzhou Storytelling

Pingtan is a very popular art of recitation which is practiced in Suzhou, Shanghai and its vicinity. In earlier times it was a local form of acting which today is wide-spread in China. In Pingtan the actors tell stories or play an instrument and accompany it by singing some kind of a ballad. Voice imitations can also be part of it. Equipped only with props such as fans or wooden percussion instruments, the artists succeed in brilliantly entertaining their

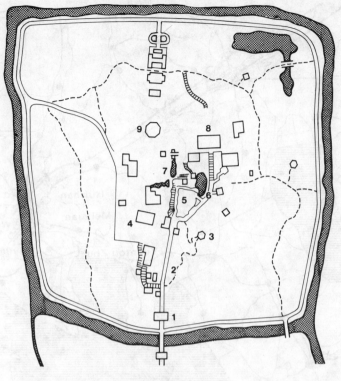

Huqiu, Tiger Hill

1. Second Mountain Gate
2. Shijian Shi
3. Sunwuzi Ting Pavilion
4. Lengxiang Ge Pavilion
5. Qianren Shi (Stone of One Thousand Men)
6. Diantou Shi (Stone of Agreement)
7. Sword Pond
8. Yunyan Si Temple
9. Yunyansi Ta Pagoda

audience for three hours or more. Suzhou Pingtan originated during the last years of the Qing Dynasty and evolved from two types of entertainment of the Tang era: Pinghua, narrated love-stories, and Tanci, short stories and novels which were sung.

Hotels

Gusu Fandian, 姑苏饭店 Youyilu 115, tel. 46 46

Suzhou Fandian, 苏州饭店 Youyilu 115, tel. 59 31, 48 52

Nanlin Fandian, 南林饭店 Gunxiufang 20, tel. 44 41

Lexiang Fandian, 东乡饭店 Dajingxiang 18, tel. 28 15

Nanyuan Binguan, 南园宾馆 Youyilu, tel. 46 41

Restaurants

Dongting Fandian, Dongshan Zhen, Renminjie, tel. 53

Songhe Lou, Guanqianjie 141, tel. 20 66

This restaurant can look back on a tradition of almost 300 years.

Xinjufeng Caiguan, Renminlu 657, tel. 37 94

Shopping

The main shopping street is Guanqianjie. At No. 28 is a shop for paintings and calligraphies. Antiques can be purchased at Renminlu 433. The Friendship Store is located at No. 604. The shops in Xuanmiao Guan are worth a visit.

Travel agency

Guoji Lüxingshe, CITS, Zhongguo Lüxingshe, Huaqiao Lüxingshe, Youyilu 115, tel. 59 31, 25 93, 46 46, telex 36 30 2

Gong'an Ju, Public Security Bureau, Dashiqiaoxiang 7, tel. 40 94

Train station, reservations: tel. 36 28-3 26

Bank of China, Guanqianjie 50, tel. 63 09

Post office, Cayuanchang, tel. 34 80

Taxis, Youyilu 271, tel. 29 40, 46 41

Huishan

Meiyuan

Yuantou Zhu

Wuxi

Liyuan

Gu

Taihu Lake

Dongting Xishan

Sanshan

Taihu Lake and Surroundings

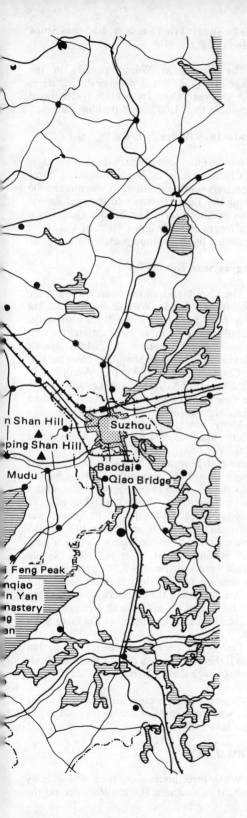

Taihu Lake and Surroundings 太湖

Taihu Lake, the third largest lake in China, lies between the provinces of Zhejiang and Jiangsu. Its average depth is two meters and it covers an area of 2,420 m², including 48 islands which vary in size. There are numerous places of interest in its vicinity.

Dongting Xishan 洞庭西山

Lake Taihu's largest island is a mountain, 336 m high, which is frequently visited because of its lovely scenery. It has inspired poets for centuries.

Dongting Dongshan Peninsula 洞庭东山

This peninsula is southeast of Dongting Xishan. It is a mountain, on the western slope of which Zijin Yan monastery from the Tang Dynasty is situated. It features 16 Buddhist Luohan statues. They are supposedly the creation of the famous sculptor Lei Chao and his wife, both from Hangzhou.

Moli Feng, 293 m high, is the highest elevation on the peninsula.

Longtou Shan Mountain 龙头山

Longtou Shan is in the village of Jianqiao Cun on Dongting Dongshan peninsula. From its peak, a 5-km-wide lotus flower field can be seen. It is an old custom of the people of this region to gather at this location on the 24th day of the 6th month according to the Chinese lunar calendar to enjoy the sight of the lotus blossoms.

Southwest of Dongting Dongshan mountain is the mountainous island Sanshan with its three peaks. These peaks are said to have been owned by three sisters, the concubines of the king of Wu. Sanshan is well known for its charming scenery and its curiously shaped stones.

Guangfo Ta Pagoda 吴县光佛塔

Guangfo Ta, in the small town of Guangfo in the Wuxian district, was built in the 6th century. The present structure originates from the Qing era and is in ruins today. But, as it is situated on the peak of a mountain, it can be seen from a great distance and is therefore well known in the surrounding areas. The view of Taihu lake from here is praiseworthy.

Wanfo Shita, 'Ten Thousand' Buddhas Stone Pagoda 吴县万佛石塔

The rectangular Wanfo pagoda in the village of Xijing Cun in Wuxian district dates from the year 1306. Its interior is decorated with more than 1,000 small Buddha statues.

Baodai Qiao Bridge 吴县宝带桥

Baodai Qiao, one of the best known bridges in China, stands in Wuxian district, three kilometers south of Suzhou. It was built in 806 during the Tang Dynasty and restored several times in later years. The Baodai Qiao has a total length of 317 m and a width of 4 m and is supported by three stone piles.

Lingyan Shan Hill 灵岩山

The 82-m-high Lingyan Shan rises near the small town of Mudu, Wuxian district, 12.5 km away from Suzhou. Viewed from a distance, the hill appears to be an elephant and for that reason is called Elephant Hill. Many legends center around Lingyan Shan; one dates back to the Chunqiu era (770 — 476 BC). According to it, the beautiful Xi Shi was given as a present to the King of Wu by the King of Yue. He had a palace erected for her on Lingyan Shan.

Many poets and writers from different epochs, like Li Bai, Bai Juyi, Li Shangyin and Tang Yin, have praised this hill. On the summit of Lingyan Shan stands the Buddhist temple Lingyan Si, also known as Congbao Si. With the exception of the pagoda, the complex was rebuilt from 1919—1932. Duobao Ta pagoda dates from 1147. Its roof was destroyed by lightning in 1600; in 1977 repairs were made. Next to the temple there is a park with Wanhua Pond. It is said that Xi Shi played here with flowers 2,500 years ago. At the western foot of the hill is the tomb of a famous general of the Southern Song era, Han Shizhong, and his wife, Liang Hongyu.

North of Lingyan Shan lies **Tianping Shan hill.** 天平山

One of the special places of interest in that area is the Yixiantian, a narrow path that leads through high cliffs. It is also called Dragon Gate.

Tianping Shan is especially beautiful in the fall, when the leaves of the century-old maple trees turn red.

Wuxi 无锡市

Wuxi, three hours away from Shanghai by train, is in southern Jiangsu Province on the

Map of Wuxi

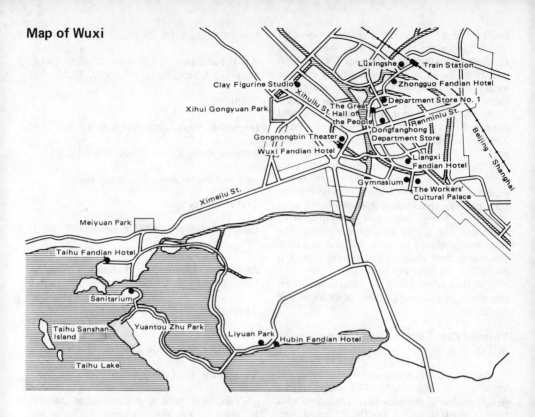

northern shore of Taihu lake in the middle of a fertile region.

Wuxi is one of the oldest cities in the Changjiang delta. During the Zhou and Qin eras, tin was found here, and it is said that the city was then called Youxi, which in Chinese means 'has tin'. But as early as the beginning of the Han Dynasty, the tin deposits were exhausted, and it was thereafter called Wuxi, 'without tin'.

After the completion of the Grand Canal in the 13th century, Wuxi developed into a shipping center for grain destined for the capital. Wuxi grew into one of the largest grain markets in China and became the seat of wealthy merchants. Due to the construction of railroad lines at the beginning of the 20th century, Wuxi maintained its position, in spite of the decay of the Grand Canal.

Wuxi can look back on a long tradition of silk and cotton mills. After 1949, the textile industry was modernized and expanded; so were other branches of light industry. Today, Wuxi is a city with a population of more than 800,000. It is a well-known holiday resort. Several sanitariums dot the area around beautiful Taihu lake. Most of the city's sights are situated on the lake shore.

The culinary specialities of Wuxi are known throughout China, for example, spiced fried ribs, *Xiaopaigu*, as well as fish, mainly fried eel, *Shanyu*, and crabs from Taihu lake.

Meiyuan Garden 梅园

Meiyuan is southwest of the town on Hushan mountain. Originally this was the private garden of a high-ranking official of the late Qing period. In 1911, the richest family of the city, the Rong family, purchased Meiyuan. Many ornamental trees grow here. It is most beautiful when the plum trees blossom in the spring, but also at other times of the year it is pleasant to take a walk and enjoy the pavilions, halls, man-made caves, and plants. Nianqu Ta pagoda was erected in 1930. Its top floor offers a splendid view of the garden and Taihu lake.

Xihui Gongyuan Park 锡惠公园

Xihui Gongyuan is in the western suburb of the town. *Xi* and *Hui* are the names of two mountains. Xishan, Tin Mountain, is actually only a small hill (74.8 m high) next to the higher Huishan Mountain. The name 'tin mountain' derives from the tin that was mined here from the 4th—2nd centuries BC. A well known spring, *Tianxia Dierquan*, Second Spring Under the Heavens, originates here at Huishan mountain. It is famous for the high quality of its water. During the Song era, the local government paid part of its tribute to the Imperial Court with the water of this spring.

At the eastern foot of the mountain, old temples and pavilions can be seen. In 1958, Xishan and Huishan were connected by Xihui park.

Clay figurines from Huishan Mountain are well known. The clay figurines from Wuxi, especially those from Huishan, have a tradition that dates back more than 400 years.

Today there are two manufacturing methods: one works with plaster casts. The figurines produced by using this method have plain and clear shapes. The other method is modelling the figurines by hand.

The figures presented are often heroes from the world of Chinese theater, or children and peasants.

Yuantou Zhu, Turtle's Head Peninsula 黿头渚

Yuantou Zhu peninsula is southwest of Wuxi city in Taihu lake. The shape of the peninsula has commonly been compared to a turtle's head, so that it was finally called that. In 1918, a garden was laid out here, which was later extended into a park.

Pavilions, halls, man-made mountains and many small teahouses make the park a popular place to visit.

Liyuan Garden 蠡园

Liyuan is southwest of the city at Wuli Hu lake. Originally it consisted of two gardens which were laid out in 1927 and 1930, respectively. In the fifties they were connected by a covered way. Especially in the spring, during peach blossom time, Liyuan is well worth a visit.

Hotels

Taihu Fandian, 太湖饭店 Meiyuan, Houwanshan, tel. 39 31, 23, 98

Hubin Fandian, 湖滨饭店 next to Liyuan park, tel. 29 41, 58 24

Shuixiu Fandian, 水秀饭店 east of Hubin Fandian, tel. 29 85, 35 47

Restaurants

Liangxi Fandian, 梁溪饭店 Zhongshanlu,

Shixinxiangkou, tel. 29 51, 37 98

Wuxi Fandian, 无锡饭店 Ximen, Gongnongbing Guangchang, tel. 26 97, 38 50

Shopping

Friendship Store, Zhongshannanlu 8, tel. 25 13

Antique shop, Zhongshanlu 466, tel. 25 12

Arts and crafts shop, Renminlu 192

Travel agency

Guoji Lüxingshe, CITS, Xinshenglu 7, tel. 54 69

Zhongguo Lüxingshe, Huaqiao Lüxingshe, Chezhanlu 53, tel. 30 24

Train station, Information , tel. 20 12 , tickets, tel. 59 26-2 54

Post office, Renminlu 230, tel. 44 48

Yangzhou 扬州市

Yangzhou, with a population of 300,000, is situated on the northern bank of the Changjiang river.

History

The history of the city can be traced back to the 4th century BC when it was part of the state of Wu. In 605, Yangzhou became the Southern Capital of the Sui Dynasty. With the completion of the Grand Canal, which flows through the center of the city into the Changjiang, Yangzhou became a hub of transportation between South and North China and an important port for foreign trade.

During the Ming and Qing eras, Yangzhou was the center of the salt trade. The salt merchants accumulated incredible wealth and, between the 16th and 18th centuries, acted as patrons, so that Yangzhou developed into a cultural center. In 1853, Taiping troops invaded the city. During heavy fighting, many historically significant buildings were destroyed. The Grand Canal floods in 1855 were a large-scale catastrophe which resulted in the shipping of all Beijing-bound grain by sea from Shanghai to Tianjin.

After 1949, Yangzhou became an important land and water traffic junction in the northern part of the province. Arts and crafts are of special significance in Yangzhou.

Among these are the traditional lacquerware, jade carvings, silhouttes, embroidery and printing. The lacquered works of Yangzhou have a tradition of more than 2,000 years. The golden age of this trade was as early as the Han Dynasty. The art of jade carving does not go back that far; in Yangzhou it did not reach its peak until the Tang era.

The people of Yangzhou are known in China as the 'masters of three knives', mainly for their skills as cooks, barbers and pedicurists.

Shou Xihu Lake 瘦西湖

Shou Xihu lake, Yangzhou's most important place of interest, is in a western suburb. The people of Yangzhou are very proud of the beauty of this lake and love to compare it to the famous Xihu lake in Hangzhou.

It actually is a widening of the Baozhang river and various buildings are situated along about 5 km of its banks. It was the poet Wang Hang who called the Shou Xihu river Narrow Western Lake in a poem written during the Qing era.

The following places are worth a visit:

Xiyuan Garden was laid out in 1751 in the traditional style.

Dahong Qiao Bridge, Great Rainbow Bridge, was built at the end of the Ming Dynasty and was originally made only of wood. Because of its red coat of paint, it was called Dahong Qiao, Great Red Bridge. During the Qianlong era, the wooden structure was torn down and replaced by an arched bridge made of stone. Since then it has been called the Great Rainbow Bridge. It is well known all over the country and has been praised by many poets.

Xiao Jinshan is a small, interesting hill in the middle of the lake on which several buildings stand.

Diaoyu Tai pavilion, west of Xiao Jinshan island, is square-shaped and has a 'flying' double roof. This was said to have been the

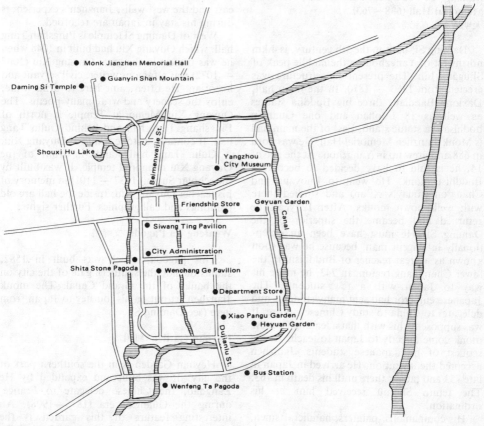

Map of Yangzhou

Qianlong Emperor's fishing spot. Three walls of the pavilion have so-called moon gates and offer an unobstructed view of the water. The fourth side is completely open, decorated only with lattice-work. White Lianxingsi dagoba dates from the Qianlong era and bears a resemblance to the one in Beijing's Beihai park. When the Qianlong Emperor went fishing at Diaoyu Tai pavilion, he reportedly regretted that there was no white dagoba like the one in Beihai park in Beijing. Upon hearing this, a rich salt merchant reportedly had a dagoba of white salt heaped up overnight.

Wuting Qiao bridge was built in 1757 by salt merchants to welcome the emperor. It is 55 m long, has 15 arches and stands next to the dagoba. There are five pavilions on the bridge.

Fuzhuang Island lies southeast of Wuting Qiao bridge and north of the dagoba. A zig-zag bridge connects it to the mainland. On the island, there are some beautiful pavilions and covered ways surrounded by trees.

Daming Si Temple, and Monk Jianzhen Memorial Hall (688—763)
大明寺（鉴真纪念堂）

Daming Si, built in the 5th century, is 4 km northwest of Yangzhou on the middle peak of Shugang hill. The present-day structure was erected from 1860 — 1870. In the main hall, Daxiong Baodian, three big Buddha statues as well as 18 Luohan and one Guanyin bodhisattva statue stand. East of the main hall is Monk Jianzhen Memorial Hall. He was born in 688 and grew up in Yangzhou. At the age of 14, he is said to have decided to become a Buddhist monk. He went to Luoyang and Chang'an (today's Xi'an) and studied there with well-known monks. After 12 years he returned and became the superior of the Daming Si. He must have been an exceptionally intelligent man, because he was soon known as a great teacher of Buddhism in the lower Changjiang region. In 743, he made his way to Japan with a few students. The Japanese emperor had sent many students and delegates to China to study Chinese culture. It was supposedly his wish that a leading Chinese monk come directly to Japan to teach. At the request of his Japanese students, Jianzhen accepted the invitation. He arrived in Japan in late 753 and taught there until his death in 763. The tenno Shomu received him at his ordination.

His companions: painters, handicraftsmen, wood-carvers and embroiderers, passed their knowledge on to the Japanese population.

Jianzhen's students had finished a statue of him shortly before he died. Today it is kept in Nara (Japan) in the Toshodai temple. In 1980, a Japanese delegation took the statue to China for 40 days. It was shown in Daming Si, among other places. On this occasion, the abbot of the Toshodai temple in Nara made a gift of a stone lantern to the Jianzhen Memorial Hall.

Jianzhen Memorial Hall was completed in 1973. It is a replica of the 'Golden Hall' of the Toshodai temple in Nara. In 1963, on the 1,200th anniversary of Jianzhen's death, the Japanese and Chinese held a joint festive ceremony in Daming Si and made the decision to build this memorial hall. The hall was divided into a front and a back part. In the front there is a stone tablet measuring 2.1 m in height and 3 m in width, displaying an inscription of the historian and writer Guo Moruo, who died in 1979. On the back of it is a calligraphy of the well-known leading Buddhist, Zhao Puchu, relating the biography of Jianzhen. In the center of the back part of the hall stands a reproduction of Nara's statue of Jianzhen, made of *nanmu* wood. On the east and the west walls, Jianzhen's experiences during his stay in Japan are recorded.

West of Daming Si temple is Pingshan Tang hall, which Ouyang Xiu had built in 1048 when he was prefect in the area. Ouyang Xiu (1007 — 1072) was a famous writer, civil servant and historian. He often came here to drink wine, enjoy the scenery and write many poems. The Ouyang Xiu Memorial Temple is north of Pingshang Tang hall and behind Gulin Tang hall. It contains a stone statue of Ouyang Xiu.

Gulin Tang hall stands in front of the Ouyang Xiu memorial temple. It was built by the scholar Su Shi (1037 — 1101) in memory of his teacher Ouyang Xiu. Inside the hall are old paintings and calligraphies. Further sights:

Wenfeng Ta Pagoda 文峰塔

This pagoda, which was built in 1582, stands outside the southern gate of the city on the banks of the Grand Canal. The monk Jianzhen set out on his journey to Japan from here (see Daming Si).

Heyuan Garden 何园

Heyuan Garden is in the southern part of the city. It was built and expanded by He Zangdao, the Chinese delegate to France, during the Guangxu era (1875—1908). An interesting feature of this garden is the 430-m-long covered walkway, which winds its way through the entire complex connecting the individual buildings. A pavilion, which could be used as a stage, is the focal point of a small pond.

Xiaopangu Garden 小盘谷

This garden, situated in Dashuxiang lane, dates from the Qianlong era (1736—1795). The focus of the classically laid out garden is a man-made mountain range, that, when viewed from a distance, strikes one as curious. Many say it resembles a group of nine romping lions. A few are sitting or standing, some are sleeping, others jumping. This is why the mountain is also called the Nine Lions Mountain.

Wenchang Ge Pavilion 文昌阁

Wenchang Ge is in the western section of the city. It was originally built in 1585. The present structure, however, is from the late Qing era.

Gumulanyuan Shita Stone Pagoda
古木兰院石塔

This stone pagoda from the Qing era stands close to Wenchang Ge Pavilion.

Siwang Ting Pavilion 四望亭

Siwang Ting, on Ximenjie street, dates back to 1559.

Geyuan Garden 个园

Geyuan garden is located on Dongguanjie street. Its former owner was the painter Shi Tao (1642 — 1718). In this garden, an attempt was made to create an impression of elements from northern and southern Chinese landscape painting. Groups of varicolored stones and flowers have been used to reproduce landscapes in the four seasons, for example Xianshan, Summer Mountain, laid out in light grey stones with lotus flowers and small streams as symbols of summer.

Yangzhou City Museum and Shigong Ci Temple 扬州市博物馆

The museum is outside Guanshu Men gate. Its exhibits include lacquered work and jewelry and objects of daily use made of jade and embroidery. Inside the museum complex is the kenotaph of the famous Ming loyalist Shi Kefa (died in 1645). He had resisted the authority of the new ruling house of the Qing and was

killed by Qing soldiers. His body was never found. In his honor, a temple was erected next to the kenotaph in 1772.

Tianning Si Temple 天宁寺

Tianning Si is north of Yangzhou. In the 3rd century, the villa of Xie Ao, a high-ranking official, stood here. There was a temple in the rear courtyard of the estate in which a monk from Nepal translated the famous Buddhist work Huayan Jing into Chinese in 418. When the Qianlong Emperor traveled south in 1757, he also visited Tianning Si. Today the main gate, the Hall of Celestial Guardians and Daxiong Baodian hall, among others, still remain.

Hotel

Xiyuan Fandian, Fengleshangjie 1, tel. 2 42 02

Travel agency

Zhongguo Lüxingshe, Fengleshanlu 1, tel. 2 48 04
In Xiyuan Fandian Hotel

Arts and crafts shop, Dukoulu 240

Xuzhou 徐州市

Xuzhou, in northwest Jiangsu, has earned the reputation of a transportation center in the course of its history. It has remained so to this day.

The city has always been of utmost strategic importance. During the Sino-Japanese war, the area around Xuzhou was the scene of a desperate battle. From 1945—1949 Communist and Nationalist troops opposed each other.

Today, Xuzhou has developed into a thriving industrial city.

In this area, there are many archaeological treasures to be found. They are the witness of the wars in the past. The most sensational find is the terracotta army in a Han-dynasty grave unearthed on December 2, 1984. This army consists of figurines of horses, officials and warriors, more than three thousand in all. The difference between the figurines at Xi'an and here at Xuzhou is that the latter are much smaller in size, with a horse figurine measuring about 70 cm in length and a warrior 40 cm in height.

In the north surroundings of Xuzhou you will find some Han-period graves with wonderful stone figure paintings.

Xuzhou City Museum 徐州市博物馆

The buildings of the present city museum at Hepinglu 44 form a complex arranged in the traditional style, a former residence of the Qianlong Emperor.

Among other things, the exhibition features a number of interesting stone engravings.

Huaxiang Shimu Stone Tomb 汉画像石墓

Huaxiang Shimu is at the western foot of Fenghuan Shan mountain, about 13 km north of the city. It dates from the Eastern Han era and was not discovered until February 1952.

The inside of the tomb is decorated with 21 stone tablets in which circus and acrobatic scenes, as well as those of banquets, parades, pavilions and animals, are engraved.

Yunlong Shan Mountain 云龙山

Yunlong Shan is in the southern suburb of Xuzhou. It is one of the city's main attractions, although it only rises to a height of 130 m.

At the eastern foot of the mountain is Xinghua Si temple complex, containing both large and small Buddhist sculptures, scriptures, and landscape scenes carved into the rock wall. The earliest of them are from the 5th century.

At the western foot of Yunlong Shan is a stone statue of the bodhisattva Guanyin.

From the top of the mountain, one has a beautiful view of the city to the north, and across the former bed of the Huanghe river to the east.

Hotel

Nanjiao Binguan, Hepinglu 20, tel. 36 11

Travel agency

Guoji Lüxingshe, CITS, Hepinglu 20, tel. 48 42.

Lianyungang 连云港

The city of Lianyungang is in northern Jiangsu Province. Since the 7th century, it has been a center of salt production.

In 1905 it was opened to the western powers as a trading post. As a result, it developed into a market for agricultural products, which were shipped from there to Qingdao and Shanghai. After 1949, the port facilities were expanded.

Yuntai Shan Mountain 云台山

The people of Lianyungang enjoy making excursions to Yuntai Shan. Formerly, it was a small island in the sea near the coast, but it was connected to the mainland around 1700. The mountain is renowned for its curiously shaped rocks.

Huaguo Shan Mountain 花果山

This mountain, also called Cangwu Shan, lies 15 km southeast of the city. It has an elevation of 625 m, making it the highest mountain in Jiangsu Province. It is the scene of many episodes from the novel *Xiyou Ji, The Journey to the West.* Since the Tang era, almost all dynasties have built their temples on Huaguo Shan. The 1,300 year old Sanyuan Gong temple stands here at an altitude of about 400 m.

Shuilian Dong Cave, Water Bead Curtain Cave, is at the top of the mountain. From inside looking out toward the entrance, one can see beads of water fall from the rocks like a curtain of pearls. This is the cave where the famous monkey-king Sun Wukong from the novel *Xiyou Ji,* is supposed to have lived.

Moya Stone Cutting from the Han Era

Two km south of Lianyungang on Kongwang Shan mountain is a valuable picture cut in stone, called Moya. It is 15.6 m long and 9.7 m high and depicts 108 Buddhists.

Hotel

Lianyun Fandian, Zhongshanlu, tel. 24 92 62

District Capital Huai'an 淮安县

Huai'an is the birthplace of the late Prime Minister Zhou Enlai. It is situated in a valley between the Huanghe and the Huaihe on the Grand Canal, which flows west of the city from Hangzhou to Beijing. Thanks to its location on the waterways, the town had developed to an important center for the transport of grain by the time of the Yuan and Ming dynasties. Even when, by the middle of the 19th century, the Grand Canal was deteriorating, it still maintained its important position. There have always been famous people who were born in Huai'an, for example Wu Cheng'en, the author of the well known novel from the Ming era *Xiyou Ji, The Journey to the West.*

Zhou Enlai's Birthplace　周恩来故居

The house where Zhou Enlai was born is 300 m northwest of the drum tower in the center of Huai'an at the junction of the Quxiang and Hongguang xixiang lanes.

The structure is divided into two courtyards. Between them is a fountain. Zhou Enlai was born on March 5, 1898, in the eastern part; his uncle's family lived in the Western part. This is where Zhou Enlai spent his childhood until he left Huai'an at the age of 12. After his death, the district administration decided to renovate his birthplace and make it accessible to the public.

Zhenhuai Lou Tower　镇淮楼

Zhenhuai Lou forms the center of Huai'an. During the Song era, it was the location of a big restaurant. During the Ming era, it was made into a bell tower. The present structure is a replica from 1881, where, among other things, historic documents are on display.

Wentong Ta Pagoda　文通塔

Wentong Ta stone pagoda is located northeast of Huai'an. It dates back to 984 and is 44 m tall.

Hotel

Huai'an Binguan, Beiyouyilu, tel. 27 59

Zhejiang Province　浙江省

Area: 101,800 km² / Population: 38.88 million / Capital: Hangzhou

The coastal province of Zhejiang is one of the most densely populated areas in China. For a number of centuries it was the cultural center of the empire. From ancient times, Zhejiang has been considered the home of rice, tea and silk.

History

The history of Zhejiang can be traced back to the 8th century BC. In those days, the western part of the area belonged to the state of Wu. The eastern part was inhabited by the Yue tribes. During the 6th century BC the Kingdoms of Wu and Yue, which originated from the two parts of Zhejiang, became rivals. This finally led to the conquest of Wu by Yue. Thus, Yue became one of the most dominant feudal states of the Zhou era. In 334 BC, however, the Yue area was conquered by the kingdom of Chu and in 223 BC by the kingdom of Qin. In the 3rd century AD it belonged to the kingdom of Wu. During the Tang and Song eras, present-day Zhejiang was divided into a western and an eastern part, Zhexi and Zhedong. The province experienced an immense period of prosperity, mainly in cultural respect, when the Song imperial family fled south because of invading tribes from the north and continued its reign in present Hangzhou. The prosperous period that started at that time came to an abrupt halt with the Taiping Rebellion. During World War II, Zhejiang was occupied by the Japanese.

The north of Zhejiang is an extension of the fertile Changjiang Delta. Its largest part stretches south of Hangzhou Bay and consists mainly of mountainous terrain. About 18,000 small islands lie off the rocky and jagged coast. Zhoushanqundao, an archipelago consisting of 400 islands, is in Hangzhou Bay. Putuo Shan, one of the sacred mountains of Buddhism, rises in the midst of this group.

The most important river in Zhejiang is the Qiantang Jiang, also called the Zhejiang. The Qiantang Jiang flows from west to northeast and empties into the East China Sea at Hangzhou. Innumerable streams and rivers cross the north of the province, supplemented by a dense canal system, thus enabling the population to transport wares and passengers with ease.

Zhejiang has a subtropical climate. Especially in the winter, there are differences in temperature between north and south, the coastal and inland regions, the highlands and the lowlands. In the late summer and early fall, the coastal area is frequently plagued by devastating typhoons. About 15% of the population of Zhejiang lives in the cities. The biggest city is Hangzhou, followed by the port cities of Ningbo and Wenzhou. 40% of the population lives in the fertile North Plain, an important rice-growing area. Only 20% of the total area of Zhejiang is arable land, two-thirds of which are used for the cultivation of rice, wheat, barley, corn and sweet potatoes. Zhejiang accounts for about 20% of China's annual tea production. The famous Longjing tea is grown in the Hangzhou region.

Zhejiang has a long tradition in breeding silkworms. The province provides about 36% of China's annual cocoon output.

Traditional handicrafts are still of great importance, such as wood and stone carving, embroideries, tapestry-work, and the production of silk umbrellas.

Zhejiang possesses very little mineral wealth. In the field of energy production, a number of hydroelectric power plants have been constructed during the last few years. One of the most important ones is the Xin'an Jiang Shuidianzhan on the northern source of the Qiantang Jiang. Mechanical engineering and chemical industry are of importance in the industrial sector.

Hangzhou 杭州市

Hangzhou, the capital of Zhejiang, is one of the old Imperial Cities in China; the others are Xi'an, Luoyang, Kaifeng, Nanjing and Beijing.

Marco Polo called Hangzhou the most distinguished and beautiful city in the world. The widely-traveled Venetian was fascinated with the splendor of the huge edifices, the wide paved streets and the magnificient grounds along the shores of the Xihu, West Lake. He admired the people's friendliness, hospitality and peaceableness, their silken clothing and the women's valuable jewelry. In those days, Hangzhou had an estimated population of 1.6 million, and the city was a flourishing trade center.

In fact, Hangzhou is still one of the most beautiful destinations of a trip through China; and, like Marco Polo, the visitor will be pleasantly surprised at the friendliness of the people of Hangzhou. It can be easily reached by train from Shanghai, but it is also possible to get there by plane from Beijing, Nanjing, Guangzhou and Hongkong.

Hangzhou lies in northern Zhejiang at the southern end of the Grand Canal. The city is linked to Central China by an extensive network of canals.
Population: 5.28 million.

History

Although the first settlements were established in ancient days, Hangzhou did not develop into a local trade center until the completion of the Grand Canal in the 7th century. Its golden age started in the 12th century when the Song rulers fled south and made Hangzhou the capital of the Southern Song Dynasty. Artists and scholars accompanied them, and a cultural center arose that maintained its leading position for a considerable time, even after the downfall of the Song Dynasty. During the Ming and Qing dynasties, too, Hangzhou was an immensely wealthy city. It was positioned in the center of a fertile rice-growing area and owned the most important silk industries in the country.

During the years of the Taiping Rebellion, Hangzhou fell to the rebels and suffered severe damages. The city recovered fairly rapidly from the catastrophe, but never regained the importance it had had before.

Today, Hangzhou presents itself as a modern center for industry and agriculture. The city has a remarkable number of factories in light and heavy industries.

The most important sight in Hangzhou is Xihu, West Lake, and its surroundings. Travelers on a one-day visit are urged to take a trip to the islands and the shores of Xihu, Baoshi Shan mountain and Lingyin Si and Yuemiao temples.

The visitor who can spend two or three days here should not miss the teahouse at Hupao Quan, the Running Tiger Spring, and have a cup of the famous Longjing tea. Those who know tea are likely to enjoy a visit to the Longjing plantations. On the way there (see Jiuqi Shibajian, page 248), one encounters farmers selling their tea. The Qiantang Jiang river basin and Liuhe Ta pagoda are also of interest. Anybody who is in Hangzhou around the 18th day of the eight month according to the Chinese lunar calendar should not miss the Qiantang Jiang's spring tide.

It is possible to make excursions from Hangzhou by train to the east, for example to Shaoxing and Ningbo; to the west; to the Mogan Shan; to the south to the Yandang Shan; or to Xin'an Jiang. It is also possible to go by bus to Huangshan mountain in Anhui Province. This trip is organized by *CITS*.

Xihu, West Lake 西湖

Xihu is in the western section of the city.

The lake covers an area of 566 km^2, its circumference is 15 km, its average depth 1.5 m. Two dikes, Baidi and Sudi, divide the lake and make it possible to cross it. There are four small islands in West Lake: Gushan, Xiao Yingzhou, Hushan Tang and Ruangong Dun. There are 40 sights of interest in the Xihu vicinity. Three sides of the lake are surrounded by hills up to 400 m high, the fourth is bordered by the city.

The famous poet Su Dongpo, who was prefect of Hangzhou during the Northern Song Dynasty, described the charming scenery of the Xihu in many of his poems.

During the Southern Song Dynasty, the West Lake area was part of the Imperial residence. The emperors of the Qing Dynasty took pleasure in the Xihu and its grounds. Replicas of buildings and garden complexes can be found in Yihe Yuan, the Summer Palace, in Beijing and in the park of the Imperial Residence in Chengde.

Liulang Wenying Park 柳浪闻莺

The park is next to the southeastern bank of the Xihu and the sight closest to the city center. During the Southern Song Dynasty, this was the site of the Imperial Garden.

Duanqiao Bridge, Baidi Dike 断桥残雪，白堤

Those who come from the city wishing to visit Baidi dike pass by *Duanqiao* bridge on the way.

This bridge plays an important part in a classical Chinese love story. The White Snake Spirit turns into a charming, beautiful girl and meets a young man named Xu Xian at the bridge. They fall in love and get married. Fahai, a monk, objects to this marriage and succeeds in separating them and trapping the Snake Spirit underneath Leifeng pagoda on the Xihu's southern shore. In 1924, the pagoda collapsed.

The Baidi dike was originally called Baisha Di, White Sand Dike. While in office in Hangzhou, the poet Bai Juyi wrote a poem about this dike, which was later named for the famous poet.

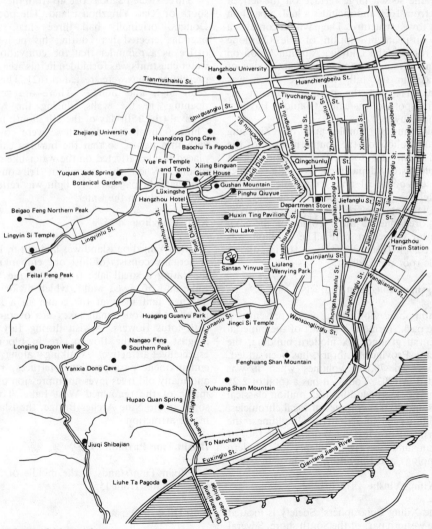

Map of Hangzhou

Gushan Island 孤山

Gushan, a 38-m-high hill covering an area of 19 hectares, constitutes the largest island in West Lake. The island can be reached coming from the northeast by crossing Baidi dike, from the northwest by crossing a bridge. Between the 12th and the 17th centuries, rulers favored this spot for imperial residences. The residence of the Qianlong Emperor once stood on the south shore, but was destroyed during the Taiping Rebellion. The Zhejiang Museum, Wenlan Ge library, Zhongshan park and the Zhejiang Provincial Library are situated on this site today.

If one crosses over to the island via Baidi dike, one sees a large terrace on the left; it dates from 1699 and includes a hall, a pavilion and a tower structure. The pavilion contains a stele with an inscription of the Qianlong Emperor: Pinghu Qiuyue, Autumn Moon on the Calm Lake. The emperor loved the view of the lake in the fall, when the moon was shining. He had the pavilion built at his favorite spot, so it is called Qianlong Pavilion Pinghu Qiuyue.

Shengyin Si temple and the Zhejiang Museum follow on the southern shore of the island from east to west. The latter has a sizeable history department as well as smaller botanic, zoological and geographic sections. Wenlan Ge pavilion is part of the museum. The Qianlong Emperor had it laid out in 1782 and stored one of the 7 copies of the Siku Quanshu collection here. The pavilion was renewed in 1880, when two stories and a double roof were added.

Zhongshan Gongyuan 中山公园

Zhongshan Gongyuan park, presently a public park, formerly was part of the imperial residential grounds. A modern building, the Zhejiang Provincial Library, has been added. It possessed 70,000 volumes when it was founded in 1903. Today, it has a total of 2.25 million books, including 1.25 million classical works and 30,000 volumes of local chronicles. The library is housed in two buildings: the Department of Classical Works at the foot of Gushan and the Departments of Modern Technology and Literature on Daxuelu street.

The Xiling Yinshe 西泠印社

The Xiling Epigraphers' Society is located on the western part of the South shore. Several beautiful pavilions can be visited here; among them, Zhuge, the Bamboo Pavilion, designed by Bai Juyi. The Stone House of the Three Gentlemen from the Han Dynasty contains a stele from the Eastern Han Dynasty. It is the oldest stele in the province.

From the top of Gushan one has a good view of the surrounding area. The grave of Lin Hejing, a poet of the Northern Song Dynasty, is in the northern section of the island, as well as Fanghe Ting pavilion, which was erected during the Yuan era to commemorate him. Utterly disgusted by corrupt officials, Lin Hejing retreated from the public eye and led a life of contemplation here.

Santan Yinyue 三潭印月

Three stone pagodas rise up from the water south of Xiao Yingzhou island. The poet Su Dongpo originally had three small stone pagodas erected here during his period of office as a reminder that the cultivation of water chestnuts was forbidden in this area. The present pagodas were erected in 1621. They are 2 m high and hollow. There are several openings in the walls; during the Moon Festival (the 15th day of the 8th month in the Chinese lunar calendar) these were covered with thin paper, so that the burning candles placed inside reflected on the water like small moons. When the moonlight fell on the artificially lit pagodas, the light was reflected enchantingly on the water.

Xiao Yingzhou 小瀛洲

Xiao Yingzhou island was laid out in 1607. It actually consists of just one embankment separating a small lake from the large West Lake and of paved walks, which divide it in quarters and meet at the center in a small island. The four small lakes are overgrown with lotus flowers. A visit during July and August when the flowers are in bloom is especially attractive. Walking along the embankment past pavilions, terraces, rocks and many old trees gives an impression of the magic of the renowned West Lake. To the south is the Nine Arches Bridge, the island's major attraction.

Huxin Ting Pavilion 湖心亭

Huxin Ting stands in the middle of Xihu lake. It dates from 1552.

Sudi Dike 苏堤春晓

Sudi dike is in the western part of Xihu and connects the north and the south shores. It was named after the poet Su Dongpo, who worked in Hangzhou in 1071 and in 1089; he had the dike with six stone bridges built then.

Huagang Guanyu Park, Viewing Fish at Flower Harbor 花港观鱼

Huagang Guanyu is southwest of Xihu lake. The eastern side adjoins Sudi dike. Small creeks and rivers cross through the park. Peonies, pavilions, bridges and fish-ponds are a pleasure to the eye.

Baochu Ta Pagoda (Baoshu Ta) 保俶塔

Baochu Ta is situated on top of 200-m-high Baoshi Shan, the Treasure Mountain, north of Xihu lake. In earlier times, jade was reportedly found here and the mountain was named accordingly.

Baochu Ta was erected from 969 — 976 and was damaged and destroyed several times, but always rebuilt. The present structure is 45.3 m high and made of bricks. It was restored in 1933. The narrow pagoda belongs to the typical panorama of West Lake. It can be seen from afar and is a landmark of Hangzhou.

Huanglong Dong, Yellow Dragon Cave 黄龙洞

Huanglong Dong is north of Xihu at the northern foot of Qixia Ling mountain. The remarkable feature of this cave is a dragon's head with water bubbling forth from its mouth. A story has it that a monk, Huikai, tried to build a temple on this site during the Song era. It is said that suddenly a rock burst open inside the cave and laid open a spring. Later, the dragon's head was shaped and the spring directed in such a way that the water came running out of the dragon's mouth. The cave's surroundings are very impressive. Close by, a small gate leads through a white wall into a bamboo grove.

Yuemiao, Yue Fei Temple 岳庙

General Yue Fei (1103 — 1142), of the Southern Song era, went down in Chinese history as a great patriot. Several times, he succeeded in driving back the troops of the Jin empire which were advancing southward. But shortly after his success he fell victim to a plot at the age of 39. In the opinion of the jealous general Zhang Jun and Qin Hui, the chancellor of the Southern Song Dynasty who held secret contacts to the Jin rulers, Yue Fei had become too powerful and dangerous. They had him thrown in jail on false accusations and executed shortly thereafter. The death of Yue Fei caused anger and sadness among the people. His merits were never forgotten. Twenty years later, Emperor Xiaozong (1127 — 1194) considered it an opportune time to rehabilitate Yue Fei and order an official burial. In 1221, a temple was erected in his honor. This man's fate and merits are still remembered today. Yue Fei even now is a symbol of loyalty.

In 1979, the temple was restored.

A statue of the general is in the main hall. Above the statue there are four characters in Yue Fei's handwriting: 'Recover our lost territories!' The ceiling is decorated with 373 cranes, symbols of immortality and steadfastness. Yue Fei's grave is situated northwest of the main hall.

Stone statues: tigers, sheep, and horses as well as three pairs of officials, flank the way there. The tomb's stele bears the inscription: 'Grave of the Prince of the Song Dynasty.' Next to Yue Fei's tomb is that of his adopted son, Yue Yun (1120 — 1142), who shared his father's fate by his side. Four kneeling iron statues are in front of the grave and stone statues, images of those who were responsible for Yue Fei's death. They are chancellor Qin Hui, and his wife as well as the head of the prison and the jealous general Zhang Jun.

Lingyin Si Monastery 灵隐寺

This monastery, also known as Yunlinchan Si, is one of the ten famous Buddhist sacred sites in China. It is west of Xihu lake at the foot of Lingyin Shan mountain.

In front of Lingyin Si, Feilai Feng, Peak which Flew here from Afar, can be seen. According to a legend, the Indian monk Huili climbed this mountain in 326. He believed that he had found part of a sacred Indian mountain which had miraculously flown here. Thus the mountain received its name. It is 168 m high, covered by tall, ancient trees and strangely shaped rocks. The forms of the rocks easily lend themselves to comparisons with plants and animals; some are called Flying Dragon, Running Elephant, Squatting Tiger or Timid Monkey. Feilai Feng is renowned because of its many caves, reliefs and sculptures. It is located on the way to Lingyin Si monastery. There are said to be more than 380 Buddhist Sculptures in the rock, among them depictions of Mituo, Guanyin and Dashi. The oldest were made in the 10th century. The sculpture of the Maitreya Buddha, dating back to the Song era (around 1100), can be seen from afar. He sits in one of the large niches, laughing and playing with a string of pearls.

Cuiwei Ting pavilion was erected around 1170 by general Han Shizong. It is dedicated to the famous general Yue Fei.

A temple was first built on the side of the mountain on the initiative of the monk Huili. It received the name Lingyin, Hidden Saints, because the monk believed that holy gods were hidden here. In later centuries, the temple was enlarged. It then counted more than nine towers, 18 pavilions and 270 halls. More than 3,000 monks lived there. The present complex was built in the 19th century after the ravages of the Taiping Rebellion.

The entrance gates are followed by two stone pillars from the 10th century decorated with Buddhists texts, and Tianwang Dian hall, the Hall of the Celestial Kings. The laughing Buddha Maitreya can be seen in the center of the hall in a magnificently decorated niche. The sandle-wood statue of Weituo from the Southern Song era is at the back: The four celestial kings are placed alongside both sides of this hall.

Daxiong Baodian, a large Treasure Hall of the Great Hero, is behind it. It is 33.6 m high. Two octangular nine-tiered stone pagodas from the 10th century stand in front of the hall and contain Buddhist texts and figures in relief. In the center of the hall, there is a gilded statue of the seated Buddha Sakyamuni made of camphor wood; behind the partition a statue of the bodhisattva Guanyin can be seen.

Excursions through the area around the temple lead past deep gaps, springs and forests.

Beigao Feng Mountain 北高峰

Beigao Feng lies north of Lingyin Si temple. Several hundred steps lead via 36 bends up the 314 m high mountain. From the top, one has a brilliant view across West Lake and the surrounding area.

Yanxia Dong Cave 烟霞洞

Yanxia Dong is situated at the foot of Nangao Feng mountain. There are two other caves besides Yanxia Dong in the area: Shiwu Dong and Shuiyue Dong. Yanxia Dong, 60 m deep, is the oldest of the three caves. It was discovered in 944 and decorated with Buddhist sculptures.

Longjing, Dragon Well 龙井

The Dragon Well is southwest of Xihu at the edge of the village bearing the same name

on Fenghuang Ling mountain. Longjing village is renowned for its excellent tea. It is situated in the middle of beautiful scenery, surrounded by lush tea plantations.

Longjing tea is available in different grades of quality. Shifeng Longjing is the best. People often enjoy drinking it on hot summer afternoons because it has a cooling and refreshing effect.

The Dragon's Well is an underground spring, which was discovered at the time of the Three Kingdoms. A peculiar feature about the spring's water is that when it is touched, the rings that are formed do not seem to move away from each other but rather toward each other.

Hupao Quan, Running Tiger Spring 虎跑泉

Hupao Quan is one of the country's most famous springs. According to a story, the spring rose up after two tigers had run by this spot. Its water is excellent for the preparation of Longjing tea. Dinghui Si temple, originating from the Tang Dynasty, is close to the spring. A teahouse is located inside. The water's high surface tension is interesting, which can be tested out for oneself by asking for a bowl of water and then carefully placing a few coins in the water. Some people manage to make them float on the surface, whereby the level of the water soon rises 3—4 mm above the rim.

Jiuqi Shibajian, Region of the Nine Brooks and Eighteen Bends 九溪十八涧

The region of the nine brooks and the 18 bends is south of Longjing, approximately 10 km from Xihu lake. The creeks flow from the village of Longjing through 18 valleys and on into Qiantang Jiang river. This area is a popular destination for short trips. A walk past the lush tea plantations, ancient trees, creeks and mountains accompanied by the singing of the birds and the gurgling of the water can be very relaxing and interesting.

Those who have plenty of time should hike from Jiuqi Shibajian to Longjing, about a one-and-a-half-hour walk. There is a bus connection from Longjing to downtown Hangzhou. Tea lovers have the unique possibility of buying the highest quality of fresh Longjing tea directly from the farmers. If one is lucky enough to be able to buy the best quality, one may have to pay up to 55 *yuan* per pound.

Liuhe Ta Pagoda 六和塔

Liuhe Ta is southeast of the city on the bank

of the Qiantang Jiang river on Yuelun Shan mountain. It was built on the orders of the Wu Yue king in 970 to protect the city against floods and serve as a light house at the same time. The present edifice, 60 m high, originates from 1899 and has seven stories, but several false stories that were built into the facade makes it look as if there were thirteen. The building materials used were bricks and wood. A staircase leads up to the upper stories. On the way up, one can step out onto the balconies and enjoy the view across the river and the surroundings.

Qiantangjiang Daqiao Bridge 钱塘江大桥

Spanning the Qiantang Jiang river Qian-tangjiang Daqiao Bridge is near Liuhe Ta pagoda. It is a street and railway bridge and of decisive importance for railway transportation between Shanghai and the southern provinces. Built in 1937 according to a design by the bridge-building engineer Mao Yisheng, it was the first double-decker bridge in China. The bridge has a length of 1,322 m.

Wuyun Shan Mountain 五云山

This mountain is situated southwest of Xihu lake on the banks of the Qiantang Jiang river. It is 344 m high. A path with more than 1,000 stone steps, including 72 bends, leads to the summit.

Yuhuang Shan Mountain 玉皇山

Yuhuang Shan, 237 m high, lies between West Lake and Qiantang Jiang river. At the foot of this mountain, there are Buddhist sculptures dating back to the period of the Five Dynasties (907—960) carved into the rock. It is possible to drive up the mountain, but walking is far more beautiful. There used to be a Daoist temple, Fuxing Guan, on its top. Today, those premises house a vegetarian restaurant that is frequently visited by the locals. From the top, one has a view of a Bagua Tian, a land distribution according to the ancient 'well field' system.

Botanical Garden 杭州植物园

The botanical garden, west of the Xihu, is considered to be one of the best in China. It covers an area of 230 hectares and contains 4,000 species of plants. Of the six large sections, in which the garden is divided, those for herbs, ornamental plants and the different species of bamboo attract special attention.

On the grounds of the botanical garden there is, among other things, a goldfish pond. It is fed by The Jade Spring, yuquan. Not far away on a hill is the Shanwaishan restaurant, where one can eat a good meal.

The Qiantang Jiang Spring Tide 钱塘潮

(Excursion to the community of Yanguan, Haining district) The spring tide of the Qiantang Jiang river occurs during the three days after the 15th day of the 8th month of the lunar calendar. In ancient China it was regarded as a miracle and is still considered breathtaking today.

Due to the moon's gravity, the sea water is dammed up in the estuary of the river, which is shaped like a funnel. The closer the thundering waters of the Qiantang Jiang get to the mouth of the river, the higher they rise, finally forming a huge wave. Local youngsters wait on the banks for the most convenient moment and then enjoy diving into the floods. Others greet this natural phenomenon by hitting gongs and drums, making a deafening noise.

The spring tide can best be viewed from Yanguan, approximately a two hour bus ride northeast of Hangzhou.

Hotels and Guest Houses

Hangzhou Fandian, 杭州饭店 Huan-hubeilu, Yuefenjie 2, tel. 2 29 21, 2 58 28

Huaqiao Fandian, 华侨饭店 Hubinlu 92, tel. 2 34 01, 2 31 00

Wanghulou, 望湖楼 Zhongshannanlu 50, tel. 61 61

Xiling Binguan, 西泠宾馆 Huanhubeilu, tel. 2 29 21

Xihu Binguan, 西湖宾馆 Huanhuxilu, tel. 2 17 28

Xizi Binguan, 西子宾馆 Huanhunanlu, tel. 2 17 28

Huagang Fandian, 花港饭店 Xishanlu, Huanhuxilu, tel. 2 40 01

Huajiashan Binguan, 花家山宾馆 Faxiang-xiang, tel. 2 64 50

Liulang Binguan, 柳浪宾馆 Qingbomen Xueshiqiao 1, tel. 2 17 28

Liutang Fandian, 柳塘饭店 Faxiangxiang,

tel. 2 63 54

Xinxin Fandian, 新新饭店 Beishanjie 78, tel 2 69 71

Zhejiang Binguan, 浙江宾馆 Santaishan, tel. 2 44 83

Restaurants

Louwailou Caiguan, Waixihu 2, tel. 2 16 54, 2 32 55
One of the best-known restaurants in Hangzhou. Specialties of the house are: Xihucuyu — sweet-sour West Lake fish; Longjingxiaren — shrimp garnished with Longjing tea leaves; and a soup with West Lake water shield — a rare aquatic vegetable.

Hangzhou Jiujia, Yan'anlu 132, tel. 2 34 77
Good restaurant; Hangzhou specialties.

Kueiyuan Guan, Jiefangjie, Guanxiangkou, tel. 2 59 21
Renowned for its noodle dishes.

Shanwaishan Caiguan, Yuquan, tel. 2 66 21
Excellent restaurant.

Tianwaitian Caiguan, Lingyinlu, tel. 2 24 29
This restaurant is close to Lingyin temple; it is well known for its good meals.

Tianxianglou Caiguan, Jiefangjie 676, tel. 2 20 38
A reasonably priced restaurant; Hangzhou specialties.

Suchunzhai, vegetarian restaurant, Yan'anlu 68, tel. 2 32 35

Yan'an Caiguan, Youdianlu 94, tel. 2 27 20
One specialty of the house is snake dishes.

Yuehu Lou, Yuefenjie, tel. 2 54 13

Shopping

Two of the main shopping streets in Hangzhou are Hubinlu and Jiefangjie. On Hubinlu, one can purchase antiques, calligraphies, paintings, silk and satin. Department stores can be found on Jiefangjie. The Friendship Store is at Tiyuchanglu 302.

Travel agency

Guoji Lüxingshe, CITS, Yuefenjie 2, Hangzhou Hotel, tel. 2 29 21

Zhongguo Lüxingshe, Huaqiao Lüxingshe, Hubinlu 92, tel. 2 34 01

Gong'an Ju, Public Security Bureau, tel. 2 24 01

CAAC ticket office, Tiyuchanglu 160, tel. 2 42 59, 7 25 75

Train station: Chezhan, tel. 2 69 18

Taxis: Longxiangqiao, tel. 2 48 63

Boat trips on Xihu, West lake:
ticket office Hubin Gongyuan park, tel. 2 20 ticket office Zhongshan Gongyuan park, tel. 2 23 36
ticket office Huagang Gongyuan park, tel. 2 55 86

Shaoxing 绍兴市

Enchanting and peaceful, Shaoxing is about 60 km southeast of Hangzhou on the Ningbo railway line. It is one of the oldest cities in Zhejiang and, to the Western visitor, one of China's friendliest. Shaoxing was mentioned as the capital of the state of Yue as early as the 7th century BC. Today, Shaoxing is associated with the names of prominent people. Lu Xun (1881—1936), the most important modern Chinese writer, is a native of Shaoxing. Qiu Jin (1875—1907), the unforgotten poetess, revolutionary and at the same time a pioneer of the Chinese women's movement, was also born in Shaoxing. The famous calligrapher Wang Xizhi (321—379) spent a long time in this city. Lu You (1125—1210), a poet of the Southern Song era, was also born in Shaoxing.

Shaoxing is situated amidst picturesque scenery between Mirror Lake and Kuaiji Shan mountain. A network of small canals runs through the city; small boats with black roofs, arched bridges, whitewashed houses with black tiled roofs, narrow paved streets leave their mark on the city's atmosphere, thanks to extensive irrigation.

Shaoxing had already become the center of flourishing rice and silk trade long ago. The surrounding rice fields yield two crops a year. Tea plantations have been located in the hills south of the city since ancient times. The city's wine, Shaoxing Jiu, is one of China's most famous wines.

Dashansi Ta Pagoda 大善寺塔

The pagoda is situated in the center of

Shaoxing. It is a 40-m-high brick building that was first erected in 504. The pagoda had to be rebuilt and restored many times.

Qiu Jin Guju (Qiu Jin's Former Residence)
秋瑾故居、纪念碑

Qiu Jin (1875 — 1907) was a remarkable poet and revolutionary. She spent the years between the age of 15 — 20 with her parents in the house at Hechangtang 23. After a two year stay in Japan, she returned in 1906. One of her main concerns was the emancipation of Chinese women. At the end of 1906, she founded the *Zhongguo Nübao, Magazine for the Chinese Woman*. In 1907, while working as the director of two schools in Shaoxing, she organized an uprising together with friends, which had as its goal the occupation of the provincial capital Hangzhou by revolutionary troops. The plan failed and ended with Qiu Jin's arrest and public execution.

Numerous items which she used on a daily basis and her literary works, as well as photos, are shown in her parents' house.

Qiu Jin Jinianbei, Qiu Jin Memorial Stele

Her memorial stele is placed on Jie-fangbeilu, where she was executed.

Lu Xun's Birthplace 鲁迅故居、纪念馆

In Dongchangfang street 208, today called Luxunlu, stands the house in which the writer Lu Xun was born in 1881. He spent his childhood here. He left Shaoxing at the age of 12 to take up his studies in Nanjing and, from 1902 onwards, in Japan. In 1910, he returned to Shaoxing and taught at the middle school, Shaoxingfu Zhongxuetang, and at the teachers' college, Shanhui Shifan. Some of his earlier works were written during this period. Two years later, he left Shaoxing. In 1919, he returned for the last time for just 20 days.

Today, numerous articles of his daily use can be seen at the house where he was born. East of the house, on the other side of the street, is Sanwei Shuwu, Three Aroma Studio, where Lu Xun pursued his studies from 1892 — 1897. The original furnishings have been reinstalled.

Lu Xun Jinianguan, Lu Xun Exhibition Hall

Lu Xun Exhibition Hall is just east of the house where he was born. Among other items, letters, calligraphies, photos and his works are on display here. Barely 100 m west of Lu Xun's birthplace, the famous wine tavern Xianheng Jiudian is located, where the well-known Shaoxing wine is served. Lu Xun drank wine here and described the tavern in his work. Since then, however, it has been renovated and no longer corresponds to the one of his time.

Dashun Miao Temple 大舜庙

Dashun Miao is on Shunwang Shan mountain on the Shuangjiang Xi river. It was built from 1851—1861, during the Qing Dynasty.

Donghu, East Lake 东湖

Donghu lake is 3 km east of the city. Narrow dikes and stone bridges lead across the lake.

Some pavilions that fit harmoniously into the landscape were erected at the end of the Qing Dynasty.

It takes about half an hour to walk around the lake. It is also possible to take a short boat ride or to climb the cliffs.

Yuling Tomb 禹陵

Four km southeast of Shaoxing is a grave, allegedly that of Yu, the ruler of the Xia Dynasty. It is surrounded by the Kuaiji Shan and Tingshan mountains.

According to legends, Yu is the tamer of waves. He saved the population from disastrous flooding by having canals that diverted the water into the sea built throughout the country.

In 1979, the local government had a memorial pavilion erected. It houses a stone stele on which three large characters can be seen: 'Da Yu Ling', Tomb of the Great Yu.

Yumiao Temple 禹庙

Yumiao was originally erected in the 6th century in honor of the Great Yu. Some of the present-day halls are from the Qing era, the main hall, from 1935. It is 24 m high. Inside the hall is a statue of Yu. Directly after the entrance gate and in front of Wumen gate, there is a memorial pavilion with a stele dating from 1541, which corresponds in its design to the style of the Xia era.

Lanting, Orchid Pavilion 兰亭

Fourteen km southwest of the city is the famous Lanting pavilion, the construction of which is documented by the calligrapher Wang Xizhi (321 — 379) in his work *Lanting Jixu*.

The present complex was built in 1548.

In the charmingly situated main hall hangs a fan-shaped painting depicting Wang Xizhi and his 41 friends. The friends met for a game at the stream in front of the complex. The poets sat on the banks, filled cups with wine and set them afloat on lotus leaves. The poet in front of whom a cup landed was required to immediately compose a poem. If he was not able to do so, he had to drink the wine. In the right-hand side of the picture lies a poet who looks rather unsuccessful.

Liuchang Ting pavilion makes up part of the complex, where inscriptions and calligraphies of the Kangxi and Qianlong Emperors, among others, can be seen.

Shifo Si, Stone Buddha Temple 石佛寺

The stone Maitreya Buddha, dating back to the Sui era (581 — 618), is located in the village of Xiafangqiao Zhen, approximately 20 km northwest of Shaoxing. An additional temple was built during the Tang Dynasty.

Hotels

Huaqiao Fandian, 华侨饭店 Shangdalu, tel. 23 23

Chaoyang Luguan, 朝阳旅馆 Jiefangbeilu, tel. 29 30

Shaoxing Fandian, 绍兴饭店 Longshanlu, tel. 32 54

Travel agency

Guoji Lüxingshe, CITS, Zhongguo Lüxingshe, Huojie 57, tel. 32 52

Ningbo 宁波市

Ningbo, an old port city with 400,000 inhabitants, is in the eastern part of Zhejiang where the Yongjiang and the Yaojiang meet, about 25 km from the mouth of the river at the East China Sea. The city can be reached by bus or train from Hangzhou or by boat from Shanghai.

History

During and after the Tang era (618 — 907), Ningbo became a center of overseas and coastal trade. During the Southern Song Dynasty, the city experienced a period of immense prosperity due to the transfer of the Imperial Court to Hangzhou. The trade between the coastal provinces and the capital was organized via Ningbo. However, with the beginning of the Ming Dynasty, trade experienced a setback. Overseas and coastal trade were extensively limited by the government.

With the arrival of Portuguese, Dutch and British merchants at the end of the 16th century, Ningbo once again began to expand its trade. Coastal trade was intensified and reached from Manchuria to Guangzhou; connections with Taiwan and the Phillipines could also be established. Ningbo's successful merchants played an important role for China in the area of economy and trade during the 17th and 18th centuries. In 1843, Ningbo had to be opened to foreign trade from the West as a treaty port. But it soon lost its important position to Shanghai. Today, Ningbo is a junction for coastal, canal and highway traffic and a market for agricultural products, wood, textiles and consumer goods. Industry has been expanded since 1949; mostly in the fields of textile production and food processing and machine and ship building.

Tianyi Ge Pavilion, one of the Oldest Private Libraries in China 天一阁

The library is in the western section of the city. It once was the private library of the high-ranking military official Fan Qin of the Ming era. He bought a remarkable collection that had been started in the 11th century from a family, and expanded it considerably. From 1561 — 1566, he had Tianyi Ge pavilion laid out to store his books. The collection which Fan Qin left to his heirs numbered 70,000 volumes, including many local manuscripts from the Ming era, rare editions of classics and literary documents. During the Qing era, the Qianlong Emperor had various works from this library brought to Beijing, where they were included in the *Siku Quanshu*. A large part of the collection was lost during times of war. It is said that only 13,000 volumes still remained in the 1950's. A commission especially founded for that purpose succeeded in tracing 3,000 of the missing volumes. Today, the library contains tens of thousands of volumes, including many that were donated from private libraries.

Tianfeng Ta Pagoda 天封塔

Tianfeng Ta is in the southern part of the city. It was made in 1330, and its staircase leads up to the upper story from where the entire city can be viewed.

Baoguo Si Monastery 保国寺

Baoguo Si is north of Hongtang district on the slope of Lingshan mountain about 15 km from Ningbo. The monastery includes several halls. The main hall, Daxiong Baodian, Treasure Hall of the Great Hero, was built in 1013. Today it represents the oldest wooden structure still remaining in Zhejiang Province.

Tiantong Si Monastery 天童寺

Tiantong Si, an imposing place and beautifully situated on the slope of the Taibai Shan, 34 km east of Ningbo, was founded during the Jin era (265—420). It was destroyed and rebuilt repeatedly. Several large halls have been preserved. Inside, rare, sacred Buddhist sutras and paintings are stored. The monastery exerted great influence on the Buddhists of South East Asia. During the 13th century, a group of Japanese, led by the monk Dogen, studied here and founded the Sotoshu sect, which still is an important religious belief in Japan today. Approximately 100 monks live in this monastery today. Lodging is available in the monastery itself or in the guest house across from it.

Ayuwang Si Temple 阿育王寺

The 5th-century Ayuwang temple stands on Yuwang Shan mountain, close to Tiantong Si. A stupa that supposedly contains a relic of the Sakyamuni Buddha (a chip of the parietal bone) can be seen here. Within the temple, calligraphies of the Song emperors attract special interest. A two-day trip to Putuo Shan Island (see page 254) can be highly recommended. It is a five-hour boat ride from Ningbo harbor.

Tiantai Shan Mountains 天台山

Tiantai Shan is quite far from the tourist area. You can get there by bus from Hangzhou, Shaoxing, Ningbo or Wenzhou.

Tiantai Shan was an important center of Mahayana Buddhism. During the 6th century the monk Chi Yi founded here a monastery and the famous Tiantai school, which was based on an interpretation of the Lotus-Sutra. In monasteries of the Tiantai school you will often find the Vairocana Buddha as the only sculpture in the halls.

Travel agency

Guoji Lüxingshe, CITS, Liudingjie 106, tel. 31 75

Zhongguo Lüxingshe, Liudingjie 100, tel. 21 81

Hotels

Ningbo Fandian, Mayuanlu 65, tel. 24 51, 25 98

Huaqiao Fandian, Liaodingjie 100, tel 31 75, 31 88

Mogan Shan Mountains 莫干山

Mogan Shan lies about 60 km southeast of Hangzhou and 200 km from Shanghai Direct bus service is available from both places.

Along with Beidaihe and Lushan, Mogan Shan is considered one of the best holiday resorts in China. The climate is particularly pleasant; the summer temperatures are lower than in Shanghai and Hangzhou. The highest mountain is 758 m, the entire area extends more than 30 km from west to east, more than 20 km from north to south. Thick bamboo groves, springs, rivers and waterfalls mark the landscape. After the Opium War, foreign missionaries and business men settled here; later on, Chinese, rich city dwellers and functionaries of the Kuomintang party followed. Today, sanitariums are housed in their former villas. There also are hotels, restaurants, a department store and a post office (Yinshanjie street).

Mogan Shan offers many beautiful sights, such as the impressive three storied Jianchi waterfall which tumbles down with a deafening roar from 100 m above. To the left of the waterfall, a path leads to the eastern side of Yinshan mountain and Guanbao Ting pavilion, which offers a good view. From this pavilion a bamboo-lined path leads to Tianqiao, Heavenly Bridge.

Inside the beautiful Luhuadang park grounds there are attractive buildings, some of which provide lodging for tourists. A path leads to Guanri Tai terrace, a good spot to view the sunrise.

Putuo Shan Mountains and Island 普陀山

The Putuo Shan mountain range forms a 12.5-km² island, which is part of the Zhoushanqundao islands and may be reached by boat from Ningbo. The trip takes five hours.

The Putuo Shan is one of the four sacred mountains of Buddhism (the others are Jiuhua Shan, Wutai Shan, Emei Shan). It is dedicated to the bodhisattva Guanyin. He is said to have meditated and held sermons here for years. Finally he reached the preliminary stage in becoming a Buddha. More than 300 temples and monasteries of all sizes were built here during the course of the years and at one time accommodated 3,000 monks. Puji Si, Fayu Si and Huiji Si are among the biggest ones today.

Putuo Shan has much to offer: interesting, beautifully-situated monasteries; magnificent beaches for sunbathers and clear, warm water for swimmers; the hustle and bustle in the small village lanes. A walk from the harbor to the village takes about 20 minutes. Lodging in one of the guest houses can be arranged in advance by CITS.

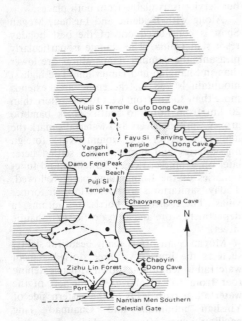

Putuo Shan Mountains

Puji Si Monastery 普济寺

The main and the oldest monastery, is located in the southern part of the island. It was founded as early as 1080 and continually expanded throughout the years. In former times, more than 1,000 monks lived here; today they number less than 100. The Puji Si halls appear very solemn. The main hall, Dayuantong Dian with its gigantic Guanyin statue, is especially imposing. One attraction in front of this hall is a bronze tripod which is more than 2 m high.

Fayu Si Monastery 法雨寺

The second largest on the island, it is situated on the southern slope of Foding Shan.

Yangzhi convent, southwest of Fayu Si, contains a remarkable stone slab, 2 m high, with an engraved representation of Guanyin from 1608.

It is about 5 km from the port to Huiji Si monastery on top of the 291 m high Foding Shan mountain; the ascent is difficult in parts. Duota stone pagoda from 1334 is passed on the way.

Most people probably visit the island because of its Buddhist sights, but nevertheless, it should be mentioned that there are a few other curiosities, such as two big stones on the western side of the island above Guanyin Gudong convent, which are shaped like turtles. One 'turtle' seems to be stretching out its head.

At the southern end of the island is Chaoyin Dong grotto; as sea water enters the grotto it creates a loud roar. An opening on top of the rock, called Heavenly Window, offers a view down into the grotto.

In the summer, the beach and ocean on the eastern shore are an open invitation for swimming.

Jinhua 金华市

Jinhua lies in the center of Zhejiang Province. It is accessible by bus and train from all directions.

Since ancient times, Jinhua has been a flourishing trade center in the middle of a wealthy rice-growing area and a trading post for wood and agricultural products.

The city's best known sights are the three Jinhua caves, Shuanglong Dong, Binghu Dong and Chaozhen Dong. Boats can pass through Shuanglong cave. A tumbling waterfall can be seen inside Binghu Dong. Jinhua still shows traces of the Taiping Rebellion. The former residence of the Taiping general Li Shixian is open to visitors. Murals can be seen there. Bayong Lou tower stands in the city center. From its top, the southern part of the city and its surroundings can be viewed. The tower dates from the Southern Xi era. Famous poets such as Li Bai, Cui Hao and Li Qingzhao are said to have written poems here. A bus tour to Fangyan mountain, 60 km away, is interesting. The mountain is 400 m high and rises up like a pillar. A single path leads up the mountainside; Buyun Ting pavilion is located at the halfway point. After one reaches the top, Guangci Si temple can be visited. There are quite a few other sights in the vicinity, for instance, caves. The same path leads back to Buyun Ting pavilion. If one veers to the right at this point, steps lead the way to Wufeng Shuyuan, the

Five Peaks School: cave dwellings where the philosophers Zhu Xi and Chen Liang are said to have taught.

Yandang Shan Mountains 雁荡山

The Yandang Shan mountains, a breathtaking area with high peaks, bold rock formations, roaring waterfalls and rocky cliffs, lie northeast of Leqing district in the southern part of Zhejiang Province.

The Yandang Shan mountains can be reached by taking the boat from Shanghai to Haimen and then proceeding by bus and train, which is also possible from Ningbo and Wenzhou. The area offers innumerable sights: temples, pavilions, caves, waterfalls, peaks, etc., can be visited, not to mention the many gorges, rock formations and passes. The highest mountain of the Yandang Shan range is 1,150 m high. The entire massif covers an area of 400 km².

One turns off the Wenzhou-Huangyan highway at Baixi to reach Lingfeng monastery at the foot of Lingfen mountain. Lingfeng is 270 m high and is one of the most important attractions of the Yandang Mountains. In the near vicinity, there are many waterfalls, caves and impressive rock formations. Lingfeng Si monastery was erected in 1023 and now contains a guest house that offers overnight lodging and meals. Beidou Dong cave is about 500 m northwest of Lingfeng Si; calligraphies by Zhu Xi and Dong Qichang are on display here. Southwest of Lingfeng Si is 40-m-deep Guanyin Dong cave, which is the biggest cave in the Yandang Shan. It used to be a destination for Buddhist pilgrimages.

There is another temple north of Lingfeng Si — Zhenji Si. A three-level waterfall, Sanzhe Bao, is situated southwest of Lingfeng Si next to Lanhua Tai terrace. The second largest terrace of the 18 ancient temple complexes on Yandang Shan is Lingyan Si. It is said that a monk led 300 students from Sichuan here during the Jin era (265 — 420) and reached enlightenment in front of the Dalongqiu Pubu waterfall. The temple was erected in his honor in 979. During the Ming and Qing eras, the complex was renovated several times. Lingyan rock rises behind Lingyan Si temple and is frequently compared to a screen shielding the temple.

Not far from Lingyan Si there are two peaks: Tianzhu Feng and Zhanqi Feng. The Southern Heavenly Gate, Nantian Men, is between them.

Tianzhu Feng peak seems to reach up to the sky, so it is called Pillar of Heaven.

Dalongqiu Pubu waterfall is 4 km west of Ma'an Ling peak. It is one of the largest waterfalls in China.

In its vicinity, numerous gorges, caves and Buddha sculptures can be seen. One can climb up to the Dragon's Back, Longqiu Bei. From there, one has a view of all the peaks in the Yandang Shan range. Nengren Si temple, on the banks of Jinxi creek, was laid out in 999. It is the largest temple on Yandang Shan. An iron vessel more than 800 years old is the most interesting item inside the temple.

Not far from Nengren Si is Jinzhu Gorge. It is known for its 18 ponds. Another pond, Yanhu, is located on the second highest peak of the Yandang Shan, at a height of about 1,000 m, its banks overgrown by lush grasses. In literary works, it has been described as the home of the wild geese, because they return to this area every year. Yanhu offers a fantastic view of the surrounding mountains. The sunset is famous for its outstanding beauty. Xianren Qiao bridge is on Hexian Ting mountain in the northern part of the Yandang Shan. It is about 100 m long and has a curvature similar to a turtle shell.

Wenzhou 温州市

Wenzhou is situated on the south bank of the Oujiang, about 30 km from its mouth at the East China Sea. Wenzhou's history can be traced back to the 2nd century BC, when this area was the kingdom of Dong'ou. Since 1949, Wenzhou has become an important port and the most important trade center of southeast Zhejiang. Export items include primarily tea, jute, timber, paper, alum, bricks and tiles. The city's two main industries are food processing and paper manufacturing. Machine-building factories and the traditional handicraft workshops are also of importance.

Jiangxin Yu Island 江心屿

Jiangxin Yu is in the northern section of the city in the Oujiang river. Originally there were two islands; these were connected during the Song era at the initiative of a monk, Qingliao; there is a pagoda on both of the island's two hills. The eastern pagoda was built in 869, the western one in 969. Two temples can be visited, the Temple of Wen Tianxiang and Jiangxin Si; also a Maitreya hall and a museum of the history of the southern part of Zhejiang Province. Jiangxin Si temple was built from 861 — 874. The Temple of Wen Tianxiang was first erected in 1482; the present structure dates from the Qing era. Wen Tianxiang was a patriotic general of the Southern Song era who was executed by the Mongols in Beijing in 1279.

Hotels

Jingshan Binguan
Huaqiao Fandian Xinhejie 17, tel. 39 11

Travel agency

Zhongguo Lüxingshe, Xinhejie 17, tel. 24 04

Jiaxing 嘉兴市

Jiaxing lies by the side of the Grand Canal, northeast of Hangzhou in the middle of a fertile rice growing area. For centuries, the city has been an important market for rice and silk. Textile production and food processing as well as papermaking constitute the main industries.

Nanhu, South Lake 南湖

The lake is divided into an eastern and a western section. Its area totals 35 hectares. Two small islands, Huxin Dao and Xiaozhou, rise up in the middle of the lake. A Memorial Hall to the Revolution and Yanyu Lou hall, Mist and Rain pavilion dated 1549, are located on Huxin Dao.

Site of the 1st Party Congress of the Chinese Communist Party 中共第一次全国代表大会

The First Congress of the CCP took place on a small boat on Nanhu lake. The members were forced to leave their original meeting place in Shanghai because of impending house raids by the French police. The foundation of the party was announced, the party program passed and the executive committee was elected aboard this boat. Today, a replica of the boat lies just off the southern bank of Huxin Dao island. The boat is 16 m long and 3 m wide. The conference room inside the boat has been reproduced.

Anhui Province 安徽省

Area: 139,000 km² / Population: 49.66 million / Capital: Hefei

The eastern Chinese province of Anhui has experienced an enormous increase in prosperity since the establishment of the People's Republic of China. Until 1949, it was considered the most underdeveloped province in eastern China. In the meantime, it has become an important center of heavy (iron and steel) industry. The biggest cities are Hefei, Bengbu, Huainan and Wuhu.

Two big rivers, the Huaihe and the Changjiang, flow through the province from west to east. The Huaihe forms the natural border to North China. The northern part of Anhui is part of the North China Plain. Mostly wheat, barley, corn and sorghum are cultivated there. More than ten tributaries of the Huaihe cross this part of the country, and in past centuries, they were the cause of catastrophic flooding time and time again. After 1949, vast irrigation schemes succeeded in averting this danger. Between the Huaihe and Changjiang rivers, the Dabie Shan mountain range extends into the province from the West. Part of the Changjiang Plain is the traditional area of glutinous rice cultivation. Accordingly, this part of Anhui is densely populated. Southern Anhui is mountainous. Here lies the province's main attraction, the granite massif Huangshan. For many generations, it has been an inexhaustible theme for Chinese poets and painters.

The summers in Anhui are hot and wet, the winters are cold and dry. The precipitation in the southern part of the province is evenly distributed. Towards the north, its variability rises, whereas the amount of precipitation decreases, so that the northernmost part of the province often suffers from droughts.

History

During the Warring States Period, Anhui was part of the state of Chu. After the unification of the empire under the Qin, a great southward migration began. Thus, Anhui became the first part of South China to be settled by Han Chinese. After the fall of the Han Dynasty, the migration from the north to the south increased. Anhui became the connecting link between North and Central China, and as such held great importance in the geographic and military respect. Anhui experienced difficulties whenever the empire was divided and power struggles were taking place. Unrest and rebellions shook the area when the Huanghe changed its course in the early 1850's and the amount of water entering the Huaihe Basin decreased, causing great distress to the farmers of North Anhui.

In 1938, the Huanghe was diverted south of Shandong by the Nationalist Government led by Chiang Kai-shek, so that the dikes in Henan broke, the land was flooded, and the advance of the Japanese troops was stopped. This

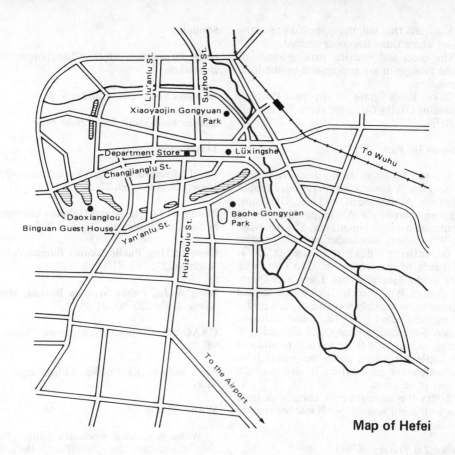

Map of Hefei

operation led to heavy flooding that reached as far as Anhui and cost more than 1,000,000 lives. During World War II, most of Anhui was occupied by Japanese forces. From 1946 — 1949, Anhui was controlled by Nationalist troops. After the establishment of the People's Republic of China, intensive attempts were made to exploit the mineral resources. Anhui has rich coal and iron-ore deposits. The main center of coal mining is Datong, the center of iron and steel production is Ma'anshan. Throughout the province, new industrial plants and workshops were built.

Hefei 合肥市

Hefei, the capital since 1949, is the natural center of Anhui. The city is a junction for land and water traffic.

Ancient Hefei was located further north than the modern city. At the time of the Three Kingdoms (220—265 AD), Hefei was a military mainstay of the Wei empire. The greatly outnumbered troops of the legendary Cao Cao beat the troops of Sun Quan thanks to an ingenious strategy. During the Sui and Tang dynasties, Hefei became part of the Lu prefecture and was called Luzhou. During the Southern Song era, it became the center of defence against the Jin invaders. From an economic point of view, Hefei always was a trade town, a market place for agricultural products and a center of the handicraft industries.

Today, Hefei is an aspiring industrial city with various plants in both light and heavy industry; light industry holds the leading position. It amounts to about two-thirds of the gross production value.

Baogong Ci, Temple of Duke Bao 包公祠

Duke Bao Zheng was from Luzhou. During the Northern Song era, he was prefect of Kaifeng. He fought against corruption and for justice, so he was very popular with the people. Today he is still regarded as an example of an incorruptible official.

The temple, laid out in the Ming era, is located in the beautiful Baohe Gongyuan park on Xianghua Dun hill, the supposed site of the school where Duke Bao once studied.

The quiet and relaxing park grounds of Baohe Gongyuan are appreciated by the local population.

Duke Bao's grave is in the People's Commune Daxing Gongshe, about 7.5 km east of Hefei.

Xiaoyao Jin Park 逍遥津

Xiaoyao Jin lies in the northeastern section of the town. A famous battle was once fought at this site. At the time of the Three Kingdoms, Hefei was part of the Wei empire and was of the utmost strategic importance. The troops of the Wu empire, outnumbering their enemies by far, suffered a disastrous defeat in 215 at the hands of the soldiers of Cao Cao, who were led by general Zhang Liao. Sun Quan, the king of Wu, tried to flee, which seemed impossible, as the only way to escape, a bridge across the Feishui river, had been destroyed earlier. Nevertheless, Sun Quan succeeded in fleeing on back of a flying horse. The story of this battle was passed on by the people from one generation to another. It also was the subject of an opera.

Today the beautiful park contains a large lake with small islands, pavilions, many trees and flowers.

Jiaonu Tai Terrace 教弩台

Jiaonu Terrace, where park grounds are now located, is east of Huaihelu street. According to a local chronicle, Cao Cao had it laid out as a defence against Sun Quan's troops. In those days, it was 50 m from the Feishui and 100 m from the Jingshui rivers — close enough for the troops armed with bows and arrows to drive back Sun Quan's soldiers approaching from the water. Five hundred archers were stationed there. A temple was erected on this site for the first time in the era of the Southern Dynasties on orders of Emperor Liang Wudi (reigned 503—519). The present temple, Mingjiao Si, dates back to the Qing Dynasty. In the eastern part of the park grounds is a meeting place for young people, a children's playground, a zoo, a flower garden, covered walkways and a teahouse. There is a restaurant in the western part.

Hotels

Daoxianglou Binguan, 稻香楼宾馆 tel. 47 91

Jianghuai Lüshe, 江淮旅舍 Changjianglu 68, tel. 22 21, 22 27

Shopping

Hefei Department Store, Changjanglu, Huizhoulukou

Antiques and crafts, Huizhoulu 45

Xinhua book store, Huizhoulu 39

Travel agency

Guoji Lüxingshe, CITS, Changjianglu 68, in Jianghuai Hotel, tel. 22 21, 22 27

Zhongguo Lüxingshe and Huaqiao Lüxingshe, in Jianghuai Hotel, tel. 22 21, 22 27

Gong'an Ting, Public Security Bureau, Anhui, Anqinglu 272, tel. 41 81

Gong'an Ju, Public Security Bureau, Hefei, Xiangyanglu 220, tel. 31 38

CAAC ticket office, Changjianglu 73, tel. 37 98

Train station, ticket office, Mingguanglu, tel. 34 81

Wuhu 芜湖市

Wuhu is situated where the Qingyi Jiang river flows into the Changjiang, the city's history dates back more than 2,000 years. During the Zhou Dynasty it was known by the name of Jiujiang; its present name was given the city during the Han Dynasty.

In earlier times, Wuhu was a city of trade. Today, it is a center of light industry.

Wuhu is located amidst beautiful scenery. Rivers, lakes, hills and mountains, within as well as outside the city limits, give it a charming appearance.

Above all else, Wuhu is known abroad for its arts and crafts products. Wrought-iron silhouettes, carved lacquer Ware and feather pictures are among the typical products.

Zheshan Hill 赭山

Zheshan, 86 m high, is in the city. It was developed into a beautiful garden complex; a zoo and an exhibition hall are located there. A pavilion, dating from 1522 — 1566, stands on top of Zheshan.

Guangji Si temple 广济寺

Situated at the southern foot of Zheshan,

Guangji Si temple was established in the 9th century. The present structure dates from the Qing Dynasty. It consists of several halls, which were built into the slope, one after the other. The visitors who used to go on a pilgrimage to the sacred mountain Jiuhua Shan usually lingered for a while inside the temple.

Jinghu, Mirror Lake 镜湖

Jinghu lake is directly in the city's center. Restaurants and guest houses were built along its shores. In the middle of the lake there is an island with an exhibition hall and a library.

Hotels

Tieshan Binguan, tel. 45 30, 39 20

Wuhu Fandian, Renminlu, tel. 30 60, 26, 76, 28 45

Jiuhua Shan Mountains 九华山

The Jiuhua Shan mountains rise in the southern part of Anhui Province about 20 km from the district capital Qingyang Xian. If traveling by bus to the foot of the Jiuhua Shan, one can either leave from here or from Anqing Xian district. The mountain range, one of the most famous in China, is an ideal holiday resort during the hot summers. Its scenic charm, its peaks, creeks, stone caves, waterfalls and trees will fascinate any visitor. Of all the 99 summits of Jiuhua Shan, Shiwang Feng, at an elevation of 1,431 m, is the highest. The highest mountain accessible to tourists is the Tiantai Shan, 1,323 m above sea level. Nine of Jiuhua Shan's peaks are especially attractive. Li Bai, the famous poet of the Tang Dynasty, compared them to lotus blossoms in one of his poems. Since then, the mountains have been called Nine Blossom Mountains, Jiuhua Shan. It is of special significance in Buddhism. Along with Wutai Shan, Emei Shan and Putuo Shan, it is one of the four sacred Buddhist mountains and dedicated to the bodhisattva Dizang. During its golden age, the area of Jiuhua Shan was the location of more than 200 temples where more than 5,000 monks lived. About 50 temples are still well preserved. Jiuhuajie street, 1 km long, is the usual route to the mountains. Along this road there are stores, hotels, restaurants and the famous temples Huacheng Si, Zhiyuan Si, Zhantanlin and Roushen Baodian. Huacheng Si was established in the 8th century. With the exception of Cangjing Lou, built from 1426 — 1434, other remaining buildings are from the Qing era. Several historically valuable documents and sutras remain in the temple's possession.

The 200 — year — old Zhantanlin temple is located opposite Huacheng Si. Daxiong Baodian hall stands in the center of the complex. It contains a gilded Sakyamuni sculpture, flanked by the bodhisattvas Guanyin and Dizang. Besides Daxiong Baodian, there are further halls, towers and pavilions.

West of Huacheng Si temple is Roushen Baodian complex, established in 794. The present complex was built between 1862 — 1878. Stairs lead up to the temple. There is an exhibition of Buddhist items as well as calligraphies and sacred books from the Song, Yuan and Ming dynasties.

Zhiyuan Si, east of Huacheng Si, the largest temple in the Jiuhua mountain range, was built during the Jiajing period of government (1522 — 1566) of the Ming Dynasty. Three large, gilded Buddha statues stand in the Daxiong Dian main hall.

Baisui Gong, the Hundred-Year-Old-Palace, is northeast of Jiuhuajie on Mokang Ling Mountain. The gilded mummy of the Monk Haiyu, also called Wuxia, is worth seeing in this temple. Haiyu lived here during the Wanli period of the Ming Dynasty. He died at the age of 120. There are differing accounts of his death and the mummification.

On the way to the summit of the Tiantai Feng, one passes the village of Minyuan, also called Zhong Minyuan. Outside this village is a large bamboo grove, called Zhuhai, Bamboo Sea. There are tea plantations in the vicinity. Chinese visitors do not miss the opportunity to take a cup of tea in Minyuan. The way up to the Tiantai Feng peak is very impressive. The scenery changes at each bend: high mountains are followed by valleys; one passes monasteries, temples and terraces. Dizang Chanlin Temple stands on top of the peak.

Tiantai Feng is 1,323 m high. To the east rises Longtou Feng peak, to the west, Longzhu Feng. From Tiantai Feng, it is possible to see the entire Jiuhua Shan mountain range. Huangshan can be seen to the south, the Changjiang river to the north.

The 1,002-m-high peak Tianzhu Feng is 3.5 km north of Tiantai Feng. It is frequently compared to a turtle lifting its head.

Hotel

Jiuhuashan Dongya Binguan, Jiuhuajie.

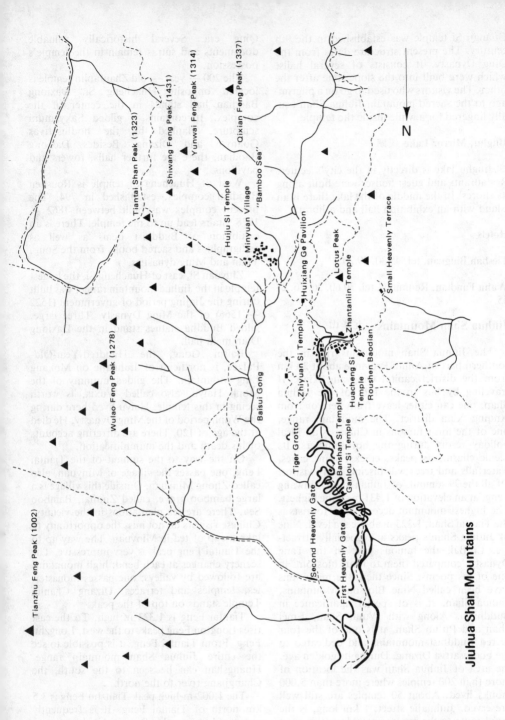

Jiuhua Shan Mountains

Anqing 安庆市

Anqing, also referred to as Huaining, is situated on the north bank of the Changjiang in southwest Anhui. The city is an important commercial and cultural center for the plains north of the Changjiang. At the beginning of the Qing Dynasty, it became the capital of Anhui Province and retained that status until 1949. During the Taiping Rebellion, Anqing played an extremely important role as one of the major bases of the rebel forces.

Yingjiang Si Temple 迎江寺

Yingjiang Si is one of the most famous temples along the Changjiang river basin. It dates back to 974 and consists of several halls. Here is Zhenfeng Ta pagoda, built in 1570. Inside, 600 Buddhist figures and several stone inscriptions can be found. Steps lead to the upper stories. From the top, one has a good view of the whole town and the Changjiang.

Chen Duxiu's Tomb 陈独秀墓

Chen Duxiu's tomb is outside the northern gate of Anqing. Chen Duxiu, editor of the progressive journal *Xin Qingnian, New Youth*, and co-founder of the Communist Party of China, was born in Anqing on October 8, 1879. He died in Jiangjing, west of Chongjing, in 1942. In 1947, his grave was moved to this site.

Huangshan Mountains 黄山

The Huangshan Mountains in southern Anhui have some of the most fascinating scenery in China. It is often called China's most magnificent mountain range. Huangshan offers everything that pleases a Chinese heart: steep peaks and bizarrely-shaped rock formations, drifting clouds which often only let the very tops of the summits peek through, gnarled pines which grow from cracks in the rocks and steep gaps — sometimes vertically, sometimes horizontally — and hot springs. Many poets and painters devoted their attention to these mountains in their works. The region, barely touched by man, is the home of many rare birds and plants.

There is a cable car system running from Yungu monastery, the eastern reception center, up to Bai'e Feng on the Beihai, a distance of 2.7 km in eight minutes.

Within the last few years, various guest houses, sanitariums and streets have been built. Today one can go part way up by car.

The Huangshan mountain massif covers an area of 154 km². It can be reached by bus and car:

— from Hangzhou by car or bus straight to Wenquan, the Hot Springs (about eight hours),

— from the south by train to Jingdezhen (Jiangxi), by bus or by car to Tunxi,

— from Nanjing by car via Wuhu and Nanling or by train via Tongling, from there by car via Jingyang to Taiping,

— from Hefei by train to Yusikou, after crossing the Changjiang,

— from Wuhu by train or car, or by plane to Tunxi and then on by car.

Huangshan's highest mountains reach elevations of over 1,800 m. For that reason, suitable clothing should be brought along. It is cool in the mornings and evenings. The average temperatures at 1,800m are as follows:

January:	- 3.2°C	July:	17.7°C
February:	- 1.8°C	August:	17.3°C
March:	4.7°C	September:	13.7°C
April:	7.9°C	October:	8.9°C
May:	11.7°C	November:	3.9°C
June:	14.8°C	December:	- 0.7°C

Information and services: Zongfuwuzhan, Huangshan Binguan guest house, tel. 44.

One or two days are not sufficient to visit all

Distances in Km

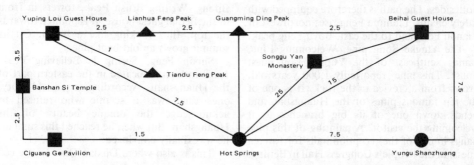

Yuping Lou Guest House — 2.5 — Lianhua Feng Peak — 2.5 — Guangming Ding Peak — 2.5 — Beihai Guest House
3.5
1
Banshan Si Temple — Tiandu Feng Peak
Songgu Yan Monastery
2.5
7.5 — 2.5 — 1.5
7.5
Ciguang Ge Pavilion — 1.5 — Hot Springs — 7.5 — Yungu Shanzhuang

the sights that the Huangshan has to offer. There are various possibilities for overnight lodging, such as:

south: Wenquan Binguan guest house
              Taoyuan Binguan guest house
center: Beihai Binguan, Yuping Lou
east: Yungu Si temple
north: Songgu Yan monastery

The Wenquan Binguan guest house is in an enchanting location, close to Ziyun Feng, Purple Cloud Peak. Visitors who are not pressed for time, are urged to enjoy the hot springs. They are renowned all over the country. Water temperature remains a constant 42°C throughout the year. 48,000 l of water flow from the springs per hour. The water contains various minerals, such as silicon, magnesium, potassium and sodium oxide. It is extremely well-suited to the treatment of rheumatism, diseases of the skin and nerves, as well as diseases of the digestive tract. One can drink the water — small drinking fountains are provided for that purpose — or take a mineral bath in the bathhouse or the swimming pool. Taohua Feng, Peach Blossom Peak, rises southwest of the guest house.

Guanpu Lou waterfall can be seen from an observation pavilion at the foot of the mountain.

Heading northward, one passes Renzi Pu waterfall. As the water tumbles down, it is diverted along two paths by projections in the rock, so that the Chinese character for *ren*, person, is formed. Ciguang Ge pavilion is reached a little farther north. It is a quiet place that is surrounded by mountains and bamboo groves. In earlier times, it was part of a monastery. Emperor Wanli (reigned 1573 — 1620) had a special regard for the monastery and made generous donations. Today, only part of the complex is preserved. It houses a restaurant.

Tiandu Feng, 1,810 m high, is one of the three main peaks of the Huangshan and also the steepest. On the way up, one crosses Jiyu Bei, Fishback, a cliff that drops off steeply on both sides. The path is therefore equipped with safety chains. Lianhua Feng rises northwest of Tiandu Feng and to the east, Boyu Feng peak.

The Yingke Song pine, Welcoming Pine, stands southeast of the Yuping Lou guest house. This pine, reportedly 1,000 years old, grows from a crevice in the rock. It is one of the ten famous pines of the Huangshan and bends down one of its big branches as if welcoming the visitor. A painting of this pine hangs in one of the reception halls for foreign guests in the People's Congress Hall in Beijing.

It is a symbol of friendship between China and other countries.

Yuping Lou guest house stands between the two highest peaks of the Huangshan, Tiandu Feng and Lianhua Feng, at an elevation of 1,680 m. Wenshu (Bodhisattva) terrace is located in front of the building. Originally, Yuping Lou was a Buddhist temple. In 1952, it fell victim to a fire and three years later, a guest house was built there.

Walking towards Yuping Feng peak, one reaches a spot at which the path winds its way between two rocks standing very close to each other. This stretch is called Yixian Tian, a Strip of Heaven.

With an elevation of 1,860 m, Lianhua Feng is the highest of the three main peaks. It is surrounded by a few small summits and together they form the shape of a lotus blossom. In 1268, a party of three climbed this mountain within three days. This was the first ascent mentioned in a local source. Today stone steps make the task considerably easier.

Aoyu Feng peak is 1,780 m high. The locals like to compare its shape to a tortoise snapping for food. Inside of the mountain, stairs lead through a cave up to the top.

Guangming Ding peak, 1,840 m high, is Huangshan's second highest peak. The Huangshan weather station is located on its top. On top of Feilai Feng summit, there is a rock about 10 m high. It is called Feilai Shi, the Rock Flown from Afar, as if it had once flown here.

Paiyun Ting pavilion, in the western part of the Huangshan range, is surrounded by a group of sharp peaks, called Xihai Qunfeng. This is one of the most beautiful sections of the mountains.

Shizi Feng, Lion Peak, 1,690 m high, is already a part of the northern Huangshan. Its shape resembles that of a reclining lion. The surrounding landscape is especially rugged. One comes across old pines, cypresses, a spring, and also pavilions, temples and terraces. Qingliang Tai terrace is situated on Shizi Feng. It falls off steeply on three sides. Bifeng, Writing Brush Peak, towers in front of the Beihai guest house. It is pointed towards the top, thus looking like a brush. On its summit grows an old bent pine.

Shixin Feng, Seeing Is Believing Peak, 1,668 m high is located in the eastern part of the Huangshan. According to an old story, once there was a sceptic who refused to acknowledge the unique beauty of the Huangshan. But when he reached this summit, he was finally convinced.

This is also where Duxian Qiao bridge can

▲ Songgu Yan Monastery

● Gufu Si Temple

● Cuiwei Si Temple

Qingliang Tai Terrace ●

Lion Peak ▲
Beihai Guest House ●

▲ "Seeing is Believing" Peak
Flower Grown out of a Writing Brush Peak

▲ Paiyun Ting Pavilion

▲ Feilai Feng Peak

▲ Aoyu Feng Peak

● Diaoqiao Yan Monastery

Guangming Ding Peak

▲ Lianhua Feng Lotus Peak

▲ Yuping Feng Peak
Yuping Lou Guest House ● Welcoming Pine

Tiandu Feng Peak

Boyu Feng Peak

Banshan Si Temple ●

● Yungu Si Temple

Ciguang Ge Pavilion ●

Xianglu Feng Peak ▲

Purple Cloud Peak ▲
‖‖ Nine Dragon Waterfall

Bus station ●
Guanpu Lou Observation Pavilion ●
Renzi Pu Waterfall
‖‖ Thousand Foot Waterfall
Wenquan Binguan Guest House
● Guanpu Ting Pavilion

Taoyuan Binguan Guest House

N

Peach Blossom Peak ▲

Huangshan Damen Gate

Tangkou ●

─── Street
───── Path
‖‖ Waterfall

Huangshan Mountains

be found. It is said that this bridge leads to heaven. Next to the bridge grows an old pine, Duxian Song, that bows to those crossing the bridge as if in greeting. In the old days, many writers came to the summit to write poetry and to play music. That is the reason why it is also called Terrace of Musical Instruments.

Songgu Yan monastery is in the northern section of the Huangshan range at the foot of Diezhang Feng peak. The Daoist monk Zhang Yipu once lived here. From this monastery, one has a view of a beautiful bamboo grove. Jiulong Pu waterfall, the Nine Dragon Waterfall, is close to Xianglu Feng peak. It is the most beautiful waterfall in the Huangshan and drops down via nine cascades. A pond has formed at each level. This waterfall is all the more impressive after heavy rainfalls.

Between the Qingtan Feng and Ziyun Feng peaks, the water of the Baizhang Pu, Thousand Foot Waterfall, tumbles down from a height of 1,000 m. It appears as if a thousand small silk figures were dancing through the air. A terrace on which Guangpu Ting pavilion was erected, is nearby. It offers the best view of the waterfall.

Fujian Province 福建省

Area: ca. 120,000 km² / Population: 25.9 million, including about 200,000 She, Huis, Gaoshan and Manchus / Capital: Fuzhou

Fujian lies opposite the island of Taiwan on the southeast coast of China. Due to this location, the province remained under-developed economically for a great many years; hardly any investments were made due to unsolved political conflicts and the potential threat of war. The political situation has since calmed down, and the city of Xiamen has been declared a special economic area. Thus, in many places one hears that Fujian has just come alive and will now grow economically. Along with this development, it is hoped that tourism will also flourish. Up to the present, only a few Western visitors have discovered the charm of this area or made excursions through old Quanzhou, to the wonderful Wuyi Shan mountains or to the unique nature preserve.

There is a good ship connection from Hong Kong to Xiamen. The trip lasts about 13 — 14 hours; departure is from Tai Kok Tsui port in Kowloon on the *MV Jimei* or the *MV Gulang Yu* on Tuesdays and Fridays.

About 95% of the province is covered by mountains up to 2,300 m high. The Wuyi Shan mountains form Fujian's border to Jiangxi Province in the northwest and constitute one of the most beautiful regions in the province.

Fujian's many rivers have always been of great importance for, in the past, they were the only transportation routes. The coast is rocky and fissured, with a large number of islands, peninsulas, bays and natural harbors.

The climate is subtropical — very hot in the summer and cool in the winter. The year is divided into three periods according to temperature: the warm period from March to May, the hot period from June to October and the cool period from November to February. Fujian is often designated one of the most beautiful areas of Asia with its wooded mountains, streams, fruit orchards, tea plantations and rice fields.

History

During the Chunqiu period (770 — 476 BC), the region belonged to the Kingdom of Yue. After Yue had been conquered by the Kingdom of Chu during the Period of Warring States (475 — 221 BC), a son of one of the king's of Yue fled to the area near Fuzhou and founded the Kingdom of Min Yue. The region was annexed to the empire under Qin Shihuang, but did not regain its status as a kingdom until the first period of the subsequent Han Dynasty. It did not lose its autonomy again until the period of Han Wudi (140 — 87 BC). A second Kingdom of Min was established at the beginning of the 10th century AD, although it only lasted from 909 — 944.

Foreign trade has always been of special significance for Fujian. As early as the 11th century, foreign trade prospered, making the city of Quanzhou, above all, incredibly rich. As foreign trade increased, many people left Fujian for Southern Asia — about 3/8 of all overseas Chinese originally come from this area. The settlement of Taiwan by immigrants from Fujian began with the expulsion of Dutch troops by a general loyal to the Ming, Zheng Chenggong, in 1662. The Taiwan dialect is based on one from southern Fujian.

In 1842, Fuzhou and Xiamen were opened to foreign trade as treaty ports. Export trade from Fujian became less important after 1949, because coastal traffic had to be limited due to the Taiwan issue and the presence of American marines on Taiwan. Jinmen Dao and Mazu Dao, two islands off the coast near Xiamen and Fuzhou, are still under Taiwanese control.

Fujian's economy is now chiefly based on agriculture, fishing and industry. The most important crop is rice, which yields two crops annually.

An important foundation for industrial development was first created with the building of the railroads. Thanks to the large forest stands, wood and paper products are among the most important manufactured goods. Arts and crafts also have a long tradition. Blanc de Chine ceramics from Dehua and lacquerware from Fuzhou are known all over the world.

The most important mineral resources in Fujian are coal, iron, copper, gold and kaolin.

Fuzhou 福州市

Fuzhou lies on the north bank of the Minjiang river. An exceptional feature of the city are its hot springs. Some of their water is directed right into the hotels and their rooms and has a special curative effect on skin diseases, but is not potable.

History

The Fuzhou area was settled as early as the 2nd century BC. At that time, Dongye, the capital of the Kingdom of Yue, was located here.

Fuzhou was already the capital of the Kingdom of Min from 909 — 944 and since then has remained the center of Fujian.

Fujian increasingly developed its foreign trade during the Song Dynasty (960 — 1279), and between the 16th and 19th centuries, the city flourished economically. In 1842, the port was forced to open up to English-Chinese trade. The most important export item was tea.

The city was occupied by the Japanese from 1940 — 1945.

Fuzhou has grown since 1949, and its population now numbers about 1.66 million. Much has changed economically. It was possible to expand the Minjiang to Nanping to accommodate medium-sized ships, and the city was connected to the main lines of the railway network in 1956. Emphasis was placed on industrial development, especially of the paper, textile and food-product industries and machine manufacturing.

The most important sights of the city are: Gushan, Drum Mountain; Xihu, West Lake; and Xichan Si temple, which was being restored in 1984. A trip by train and bus or by ship from Fuzhou to the Wuyi Shan mountains is recommended (see page 276).

Yushan Hill 于山

This 58-m-high hill is located in the middle of Fuzhou. It is often compared to a huge turtle by the inhabitants.

Baita, the White Pagoda, also called Dingguang Ta, is at the foot of the hill to the west. The city's landmark is a 41-m-high building dating from 904 (Tang Dynasty) and was originally made of brick covered by wood. Lightning set fire to the pagoda in 1534, and the wood covering as well as much of the brick frame burned. In 1548, the destroyed parts were replaced by new bricks, and the entire pagoda was painted white, giving it its name. A small temple hall, Baita Si, is located south of the pagoda. It was first built in 905, but renovated during the Qing Dynasty. Today, it houses Yushan Library. North of this hall stands another hall which was formerly a school of navigation. The well-known translator Yan Fu is supposed to have studied here in 1866.

To the east lies Qigong Ci temple complex. A high-ranking general of the Ming Dynasty, Qi Jiguang (1528 — 1587) was sent to Fujian in 1562 to fight the Japanese pirates. He was able to win three large battles, and when he returned to the capital, a stone inscription was dedicated to him out of gratitude. Later, the Qigong Ci memorial temple was built next to the inscription. The present-day temple was built in 1918 and contains a bust of the general.

Visitors will come across many stone inscriptions on their excursions through the Yushan area, the oldest of which dates from the Song era. Some of them are very valuable as a source of documentation. When almost at the top of the hill, one passes the former Daoist temple Fenglai Ge. Today, it houses calligraphies and stone inscriptions. The peak of Yushan is a favorite meeting-spot for Fuzhou's older men in the summer. They like to enjoy the pleasantly cool evening breezes here. This is also where the television tower stands.

On the way back, one comes upon Dashi Dian hall, also called Guanyin Ge. The commanders of the revolutionary army established their base in this hall in 1911. They fired a cannon shot at dawn on November 9, 1911 — the signal to join the uprising against the Qing Dynasty.

Wushi Shan Hill 乌石山

Wushi Hill, also called Wushan, is located downtown across from Yushan. The highest point of elevation is 86-m-high Xianglu Feng. This hill was a favorite spot for outings as early as the Tang era. The Moya stone tablets, scattered over the entire area, are especially

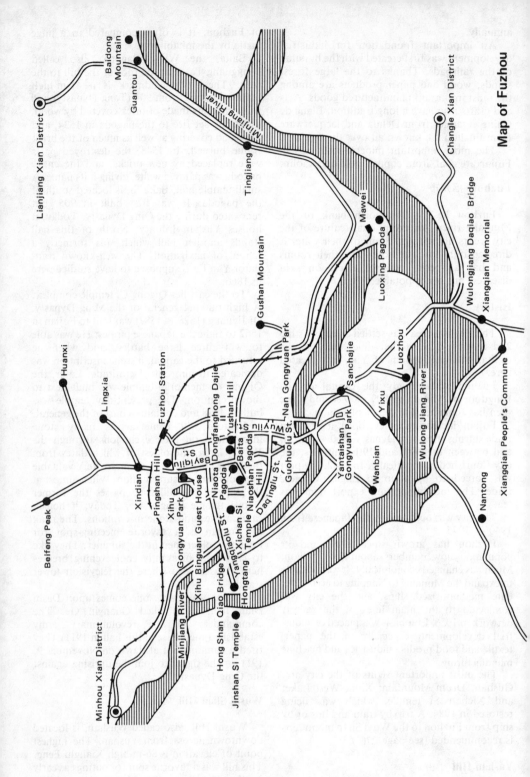

Map of Fuzhou

Lianjiang Xian District

Baidong Mountain

Guantou

Minjiang River

Changle Xian District

Tingjiang

Mawei

Wulongjiang Daqiao Bridge

Xiangqian Memorial

Luoxing Pagoda

Gushan Mountain

Huanxi

Lingxia

Fuzhou Station

Nan Gongyuan Park

Sanchajie

Luozhou

Xiangqian People's Commune

Beifeng Peak

Xindian

Pingshan Hill

Xihu

Xihu Gongyuan Park

Dongfanghong Dajie

Yushan Hill

Wuyilu St.

Baita Pagoda

Niaota Pagoda

Guohoulu St.

Yantaishan Gongyuan Park

Yixu

Wulong Jiang River

Wanbian

Nantong

Niaoshan Temple

Daqinglu St.

Minjiang River

Xihu Binguan Guest House

Yangqiaolu St.

Xichan Si

Hongtang Temple

Hong Shan Qiao Bridge

Jinshan Si Temple

Minhou Xian District

Shanghai

Mochou Hu Lake, Nanjing, Jiangsu

Suzhou, the Chinese Venice, Jiangsu

Bridges in Suzhou, Jiangsu

Xiao Yingzhou, Hangzhou, Zhejiang

Baochu Ta Pagoda in Hangzhou, Zhejiang

"The Monkey Looking at the Sea of Clouds", Huangshan Mountains, Anhui

Pearl Cultivating Enclosure on Taihu Lake, Jiangsu

Gulang Yu Island, Xiamen, Fujian

Sunrise Watching Stone on Mt. Taishan, Shandong

A Catholic Church, Qingdao, Shangdong

A Beach in Qingdao, Shandong

Longmen Grottoes in Luoyang, Henan

Dengfeng Observatory, Henan

Sun Yat-san Memorial Hall, Guangzhou, Guangdong

worth seeing. They include a tablet written in the *lishu* style by calligrapher Li Yangbing from 772.

On the eastern part of Wushan, Wuta pagoda is located, also called Wushi Ta. It is considered to be the complement of the White Pagoda at the foot of Yushan and is therefore also often called the Black Pagoda. Wuta, 35 m high, dates from 941.

Xihu Lake 西湖

Xihu is located in northwestern Fuzhou. It was named after the famous lake in Hangzhou.

In 282, Prefect Yan Gao had the water from various mountains streams diverted into a lake here for the purpose of irrigating the surrounding fields. Later, the lake and the attractive facilities on its shores became a favorite recreation area. After 1949, the city administration had the lake and lakeshore area enlarged and expanded several times. Banyan trees and weeping willows dominate the shores. Pavilions, terraces, small dams and bridges are reflected in the water and ensure an interesting walk. The Province Museum is also located here at the Jadeband Bridge. Numerous historical objects from various dynasties are displayed there. A wooden coffin shaped like a ship is especially interesting. It is supposed to be several thousand years old and to have come from the Wuyi Shan mountain area. It used to be the custom there to lay the dead in such coffins and place them in the highest cliffs. Tomb figures from the 10th century are also important. There is a pretty view of the lake from 40-m-high Dameng Shan hill. In 1957, a zoo was opened here and on the adjoining grounds.

Pingshan Hill 屏山

Pingshan Hill is in northern Fuzhou. An old temple dating from 965, Hualin Si, is located at the foot of the hill to the south. The main hall, Daxiong Baodian, is the only one of the Song-era, South-Chinese style buildings remaining; the other buildings preserved up to the present, date from the Qing era. Mostly public administration offices are now located in the Pingshan area.

Linyang Si Temple 林阳寺

Linyang Temple, which is located 19 km from Fuzhou on Beifeng Shan mountain, was founded in 931. The remaining buildings date from the Guangxu period of the Qing Dynasty.

Chongfu Si Temple / Lingxia 崇福寺

Chongfu Temple, at the foot of Mount Beiling, 8 km from Fuzhou, dates from 977. It was expanded at the end of the Ming and beginning of the Qing eras. It was one of the five largest temples in Fuzhou at the end of the Qing Dynasty. The present buildings were all built during the Guangxu period (1875—1908)

Lin Zexu Memorial 林则徐纪念馆

The complex was built in 1905.

The imperial government sent Lin Zexu as Chief Commissioner to Canton in 1839 to cut off the opium trade. Lin was an able, incorruptible official who carried out his task systematically. He managed to confiscate and burn 20,000 cases of opium that had been loaded onto English ships outside the harbor area of Canton and were intended to be smuggled in and sold. The success of this action, which was also sanctioned by the imperial government, resulted in English warships being sent to China. Lin had assumed that his activities were also in the interests of the British court, as it had officially forbidden the opium trade. However, opium was actually the most important article of trade, which enabled the British merchants to balance the import of Chinese goods, such as tea, silk and porcelain. Thus, the English employed their warships in an attempt to force China to buy opium. Lin Zexu's energetic measures almost brought the trade between the two countries to a standstill. In the summer of 1840, British troops occupied parts of the Chinese coastal areas and forced further ports to open to trade. The Qing government felt its authority threatened by the English and therefore made concessions. Lin Zexu was held responsible for the reactions of the English and was removed from the offices he held. Opium trade could continue. Lin was banned to Xinjiang, yet rehabilitated a few years later and made governor of Yunnan and Guizhou provinces.

Tomb of Lin Zexu (1785 — 1850) 林则徐墓

Lin Zexu's tomb is in the northern suburb of Fuzhou. Lin was buried in his home town after his death in 1850; his wife, brother and sister-in-law were also laid to rest here.

Gushan Mountain, Drum Mountain 鼓山

Gushan lies on the banks of the Minjiang east of the city and is called the Drum Mountain because a huge, flat stone in this

Gushan, Drum Mountain

1. Yangzhi Ting Pavilion
2. Waterfall Observation Pavilion
3. Seven-Buddha Pavilion, Qifo Ting
4. Banshan Ting Pavilion
5. Tea Pavilion
6. Gengyi Ting Pavilion
7. Xiaoluohan Tai Terrace
8. Orchid Garden
9. Huilong Ge Pavilion
10. Heshui Yan Cliff
11. Longtou Quan Spring
12. Stone Boat, Shichuan
13. Stone Gate, Shimen
14. Shuiyun Ting Pavilion
15. Baiyun Ting Pavilion
16. Songting Pavilion
17. Dalushan Tai Terrace
18. Lüxian Yan Cliff

19. Qianfo Yan Monastery
20. Jinchan Dong Cave
21. Xianglong Dong Cave
22. Fulong Dong Cave
23. Fahua Yan Cliff
24. Pantao Lin Forest
25. Gexian Ju Square
26. Tianwang Dian Hall
27. Daxiong Baodian Hall
28. Shengjian Tang Hall
29. Mingyue Lou Tower
30. Cangjing Dian Hall
31. Restaurant
32. Lushan Quan Spring
A. Bus Station
B. Yongquan Si Temple
C. Service Hall
D. Floorplan of Yongquan Si Temple

area supposedly gives off drum-like sounds during storms and showers. The 669-m-high mountain boasts numerous sights and historical monuments, including Yongquan Si temple from 908 at an elevation of 455 m. Today, 25 large and small halls are still in existence. It is one of the largest temples in the city. Its 7,500 volumes of holy writings and the white-jade statue of a reclining Buddha are especially valuable.

The two ceramic pagodas Qianfo Taota, the Thousand-Buddhas Ceramic Pagodas, stand in front of Tianwang Dian hall. They date from 1082 (Northern Song era) and were located in Longrui Si temple on Nantai Dao island at that time. In 1972, they were brought here. A total of 1,078 Buddhist figures and bells are fastened to the pagodas, which are almost 7m high. The individual tiers were separately finished and then placed one on top of the other. This type of ceramic pagoda is very rare in China, and thus these two are considered to be valuable examples of Song-era skilled craftsmanship.

Two bronze statues of children catch one's eye in Daxiong Baodian hall. A childless couple had made sacrifices here to Sakyamuni Buddha and asked for children. When their wish was granted soon after, they donated these figures. Women begging to be blessed with children still go to this hall, light incense sticks and touch the statues.

A beautiful bronze sculpture of Guanyin is located in the following hall, Fatang.

The temple kitchen has a so-called '1,000-man-pot', a bronze vessel in which rice soup was cooked for the temple congregation. Today, over 100 monks again live in the temple. To the east of the temple, the visitor will find more than 400 stone inscriptions of various calligraphies. They are scattered over the area of the Eighteen Sights of Gushan Mountain, Gushan Shiba Jing. The center of the stone inscriptions is near Heshui Yan cliff, about five minutes from Yongquan Si temple.

Luoxing Ta Pagoda and Mawei Gang Harbor 罗星塔和马尾港

Luoxing Ta pagoda is located on Luoxing Shan mountain in Mawei Gang harbor, 21 km southeast of Fuzhou. According to a legend, a rich man who lived during the Song Dynasty (960 — 1279) desired beautiful Liu Qiniang. However, she was married, so the rich man falsely accused her husband of a serious crime. He was then sentenced to death. After the death sentence was carried out, Liu Qiniang sold all her belongings and had this pagoda built for her husband. The present stone pagoda was restored from 1621 — 1627. It is 31.5 m high and can be seen from afar by sailors due to its elevated position. There is an excellent view of the surroundings from the top of the pagoda. The International Sailors' Club is located below it.

Xichan Si Temple 西禅寺

Xichan Temple is located on Yishan mountain in a suburb 3 km west of Fuzhou. It is one of the most important sights of the city; most of the complex dates from 1875 — 1908. During the Cultural Revolution, it was largely destroyed. Departments of the university and individual factories moved into many of the temple's buildings and are only moving out very slowly. Each hall is being completely restored. A community of monks, living mostly on donations from overseas Chinese, has been in existence here again since 1979.

Hotels

Wenquan Binguan, 温泉宾馆 Wusilu

Xihu Binguan, 西湖宾馆 Hubinlu 20, tel. 3 22 27

Wuyi Fandian, 武夷饭店 Wuyizhonglu, tel. 3 26 46

Huaqiao Dasha, 华侨大厦 Wusilu, tel. 3 13 86

Fuzhou Fandian, 福州饭店 Dongdalu, tel. 3 30 57

Minjiang Fandian, 闽江饭店 Wusilu, tel. 5 78 95

The visitor should take note of the fresh spring water from Fuzhou's hot springs, which is directed right into the hotels.

Travel agency

Guoji Lüxingshe CITS, Wusilu 4, tel. 3 39 62 at Huaqiao Dasha Hotel

Zhongguo Lüxingshe, Wusilu 4, tel. 3 39 62

Restaurants and shopping

Bayiqilu is Fuzhou's main business street; here there are several restaurants and interesting shops. A specialty of the city's arts and crafts is lacquerware — a great variety is sold in the shops and hotels.

Juchunyan Canting Restaurant, Bayiqibeilu 130, tel. 3 23 38. Fujian cuisine. Their specialty is *fotiaoqiang*.

Huafu Lou Restaurant, Bayiqizhonglu 795. Fujian cuisine.

Quanzhou and Surroundings 泉州市

Quanzhou has not yet been connected up to the railroad network and therefore can only be reached by car, bus or ship.

By Chinese standards, Quanzhou is only a small town with its 140,000 inhabitants, but despite this, it has the atmosphere of a lively big city. The shops have a good selection of goods and the open-air markets are an experience. Hundreds of farmers stream into the city daily to sell their produce.

The city has not yet lost its old structure. Many narrow streets, lanes and a total of 127 bridges invite the visitor to go exploring. One is constantly made aware of the age and former importance of the city. Many a traveler will come to love Quanzhou and its hospitable inhabitants.

History

Quanzhou is a city with a great past. It used to be one of the most important port and trade cities of the world. Long before its foundation in 700, the people of this area had conducted foreign trade. Towards the end of the Tang

Dynasty (618 — 907), Quanzhou was already one of China's four major seaports and competed especially with Canton. Quanzhou was a center of foreign trade and shipbuilding. Its inhabitants numbered 500,000 during the Song Dynasty (960 — 1279). At that time, coral trees were planted all over the city, but only a few still remain. When Marco Polo came to Quanzhou in the 13th century, he was of the opinion that the city had the second-largest trading port in the world after Alexandria. Quanzhou had trade relations with over 100 foreign and Chinese cities, mostly in Asia and Africa. The most important export items were porcelain, silk and tea, as well as bronze and iron articles; the major import items were spices, perfumes and precious gems.

Quanzhou started declining economically at the beginning of the 15th century. The Ming Dynasty government had no great interest in far-reaching trade relations between Quanzhou and foreign countries. Raids by Japanese pirates also caused unrest. The silting-up of the harbor had catastrophic consequences. During the 17th century, Xiamen (Amoy) and Fuzhou competed with Quanzhou, finally reducing the city to a second-rate trading port. Quanzhou's only important remaining trading partner was the island of Taiwan.

The economic decline let to large parts of the population being deprived of their means of livelihood. Many people went abroad, especially to the countries of Southeast Asia. According to statistics, 2.2 million overseas Chinese come from this region.

Since 1949, efforts have been made to revive Quanzhou's economy. The city now has over 250 new factories. The porcelain and textile factories are especially important, as are wood-carving workshops. The harbor was expanded so that large commercial ships can now put into it.

Kaiyuan Si Temple 开元寺

Kaiyuan Si, on Xijie street, dates from 686. During the Song and Yuan dynasties, it was expanded. More than 1,000 monks are said to have lived here, but today there are only about 30. Despite having been repeatedly destroyed, it was rebuilt over and over again. Even today, its area of about 70,000 m^2 makes it one of the largest temples in China. The main buildings are all located on the middle axis. In Tianwang Dian hall, only two celestial kings can still be seen. The small stone pagodas on the left and right of the following courtyard date from the

Ming era, the two larger ones in front of Daxiong Baodian, from the Song period. A special feature of the next hall are the 'flying fairies' in the bracket system. There are 24, symbolizing the 24 seasons of the traditional lunar calendar. Two stone columns rise behind Daxiong Baodian hall and their reliefs tell a story from Indian Buddhism. Both the relief on the terrace in front of the hall as well as the two stone columns are remnants of the Indian Brahmana temple that stood here between the Song and Yuan eras. Ganlu Jietan follows, the terrace where monks were ordained. It dates from 1019 and is dominated by a three-story, square terrace. One sees Pilo on the top floor, Sakyamuni on the second and Amitabha on the ground floor. The terrace is watched over by two guardian sculptures on each side; the sculptures reflect a strong Indian influence. Cangjing Ge, the Pavilion of Holy Books, is the last building on the middle axis. Over 10,000 volumes of holy writings are housed here.

The Twin Pagodas, Shuangta, are a special feature of the temple. The eastern one is called Zhenguo Ta and dates from the end of the Tang Dynasty. It is 48 m high. The western pagoda is 44 m high and called Renshou Ta. It dates from the Wudai era (907 — 960). Both structures were formerly made of wood. Not until the years between 1228 — 1250 were they rebuilt as stone pagodas. They are often considered to be the landmarks of Quanzhou.

Qingjing Si Mosque 清净寺

This mosque, one of the oldest in China, is located on Tumenjie street. It is supposed to be an imitation of a mosque in Damascus and is made of black and white granite. It was built in 1009 during the Northern Song Dynasty by foreign Moslems. Many foreigners, including Arabs, Persians and Syrians came to Quanzhou after the 7th century to conduct trade, to travel and to act as missionaries. They usually lived in the southern part of the city. The construction of the mosque was made possible by donations. Although the mosque has partially deteriorated in the course of time, it is still very impressive. The main gate is the best-preserved structure. Originally there was a spire on top of the gate tower, but it was destroyed in the Qing era. Zhusheng Ting pavilion used to stand to the east of the passageway; today, a few steps are all that remain of it. The stone walls and main gate of the former main hall, west of the gate, have been preserved. The hall faces west, towards Mecca.

Haiwai Jiaotongshi Bowuguan, the Museum of the History of Foreign Trade
海外交通史博物馆

The museum was opened in 1959 and documents the history of Fujian's foreign relations. In the first section, a sailing ship is displayed that was excavated from a depth of 2 m under the sea-bottom of the Bay of Quanzhou in 1974. It was intended for overseas voyages and is assumed to date from the 11th century. The upper part of the ship has not been preserved.

Li Zhi's Home 李贽故居

Li Zhi (1527 — 1602) was one of the 16th century's progressive philosophers. He wrote works like *Fenshu* and *Cangshu* in which he criticized the conditions of his time. When he was 76 years old, he was arrested, and he died in the Tongzhou district prison. Tongzhou is now administered by Beijing. Li Zhi's works influenced later reformists.

His home is located at Wanshoulu street 159. Until 1862, it was a matter of controversy whether or not Li Zhi had actually lived in this house. However, two of Li Zhi's stone seals were found during restoration work, which took place from 1862 — 1874, thus providing proof of his residence.

Qingyuan Shan Mountain 清源山

Mount Qingyuan, also called Beishan, the North Mountain, is 3 km north of the city. It is 490m high, and its three peaks, caves, pavilions, ancient trees, canyons, springs, waterfalls and Moya stone inscriptions entice the visitor to take an interesting walk. Laojun Yan, the cliff of Laozi is located on the right-hand peak of Qingyuan Shan. (Laozi is considered to be the founder of Daoism.) Some Song era artists had created the image of an old man from a huge piece of rock. In their work, they also paid attention to such details as eyebrows, the hair of his beard, the folds of his clothing, etc. The carving is an interesting example of Song era sculpture. There used to be many Daoist monasteries in this area. The Laojun rock sculpture was originally located in such a monastery, but nothing remains of the buildings.

South of Laojun Yan, a path leads to Qianshou Yan and Mituo Yan cliffs. There is a newly built teahouse which serves the famous Wulong tea, brewed in fresh spring water near Qianshou Yan. Another path goes up the mountain from the teahouse to a memorial pavilion dedicated to a monk, Li Shutong. It continues on to Mituo Yan cliff where a building is located that houses a tall Yuan era statue of Buddha Amitabha. Many visitors try to throw coins into the Buddha's hands, for this is supposed to bring them wealth. A convent stood here before the Cultural Revolution.

Halfway up the left-hand peak of Qingyuan Shan is Ruixiang Yan cliff. A stone temple built during the Ming era stands there. It was erected to house a tall statue of the Sakyamuni Buddha dating from 1087.

Ci'en Yan Temple is situated farther up the mountain and consists of several halls. In Fodian hall is a stone sculpture of the bodhisattva Guanyin made in the Northern Song era.

A steep path leads from behind Ci'en Yan Temple to Wutai Ding peak.

Luoyang Qiao Bridge 洛阳桥

Luoyang Bridge is located at the mouth of the Luoyang Jiang, 10km northeast of Quanzhou. If one takes the highway from Fuzhou to Xiamen, one passes over this bridge. The Luoyang Jiang river was formerly an important transportation route between Guangdong and Fujian provinces.

The bridge dates from 1053 — 1059. Today, it measures 834 m. It consists of stone slabs supported by 47 posts. Because the current at the mouth of the river is so strong, construction of the bridge was very difficult. Even laying the foundations proved to be extremely complicated. A method was finally developed of first pushing large pieces of rock into the river. Oysters were thrown into the spaces between the rocks to secure them, for the oysters grew very quickly and supposedly held them together. The bridge was built on this foundation.

There is a view of the broad river area and of cliffs and stones on which the inhabitants grow oysters.

Hui'an village is located on the other side of the bridge. Here, one can tour a granite-processing factory in which interesting granite pictures are produced, among other things. Most of the products are exported to Japan and the USA.

Jiuri Shan Mountain 九日山

Mount Jiuri rises from the north bank of the Jinjiang river in the western suburb of Quanzhou.

It is said that many people migrated south

to Fujian during the Jin ear (265 — 420). Each year on September 9, they came to Jiuri Shan to look homeward; thus, the mountain was called Jiuri Shan, the Ninth-Day Mountain. This mountain has been considered a great attraction since ancient times. Many poets and writers came here to be inspired. Numerous inscriptions in the cliffs provide evidence of their work today, some are by such famous poets as Zhu Xi, Cai Xiang and Su Shunzhi of the Song era. One could almost call these cliffs a museum of calligraphy. The *Qifeng* inscriptions from the Northern Song era, the Prayers to the Wind, are especially worth mentioning. At that time, ceremonies were held twice a year that were supposed to make the winds favorable for shipping. This custom existed for over 200 years. The ceremonial rites as well as the participation of important personages were recorded on the rock walls.

Yisilanjiao Shengmu, the Holy Islamic Burial Grounds 伊斯兰教圣墓

The burial grounds lie at the southern base of Lingshan mountain, east of the city. Shortly before arriving at the complex, one passes two huge rocks on the right, piled one on top of the other. The top one tips a bit if one pushes it with all one's might.

In the middle of the burial grounds is a stone pavilion that contains two stone sarcophagi. It is said that four followers of Mohammed came to China in 618 — 626. Two of them went to Canton and Yangzhou, the other two came to Quanzhou and died there. There is an old Arabian inscription dating from 1327 in back of the two tombs.

Other stone sarcophagi from the Song, Yuan and Ming dynasties are located in this area. Many foreigners were interred here.

Stone Bamboo Shoot 石笋

Half a kilometer outside of Xinmen gate is a turtle-shaped hill, Guishan, the Turtle Mountain. The stone bamboo shoot rises from this hill; five large granite stones sit on top of each other to a height of 3 m. They taper off at the top.

Quanzhou Fuxue, the Quanzhou Confucian School 泉州府学

This school is located in Sanjiaopu village. It was originally a Confucian temple to which a school was added in 982. The complex was restored several times and completely rebuilt in 1761 under Qianlong. The buildings have

remained in relatively good shape up to the present.

Hotel

Huaqiao Dasha, 华侨大厦 Baiyuanqingchi, tel. 21 92, 23 66

On the rooftop terrace is a bar which is well-frequented by the hotel guests as well as the inhabitants in the evening.

Travel agency

Guoji Lüxingshe, CITS, Baiyuanqingchi, tel. 8 65

Zhongguo Lüxingshe, Baiyuanqingchi, tel. 8 61

Anhai 安海市

The small city of Anhai is the homeland of many overseas Chinese. Local chronicles from as far back as the Song and Yuan periods tell of the large numbers of people who went abroad as a result of the soaring overseas trade. Because Anhai was located 30 km from the Quanzhou harbor and could be easily reached by large ships, the city used to be a prosperous center of trade.

The neighboring town of Shitou, important to Anhai, could be reached by boat. During sudden storms, treacherous currents sometimes led to a disastrous end for ship travelers. Ships capsized, and many people drowned. Thus the plan to build a bridge was formed. Quanzhou's local chronicles indicate that the first attempts to carry out this plan were made in 1138 but were not successful. In 1151, Prefect Zhao Linjin made a further attempt which was successfully concluded after a period of 13 years. The resulting Anping Qiao is now a national monument. It is 2,070 m long and 3 — 3.6 m wide and is made up of 7 — 10 m long stone blocks placed together and supported by 331 piers. A pavilion from the Qing era is located in the middle of the bridge; originally, 5 pavilions stood here.

In the course of the centuries, the bridge was repaired many times. Today, since the coast has filled in with sand, the bridge is no longer so important.

Longshan Si Temple 龙山寺

Longshan Temple stands in northwest Anhai. The building dates back to the Sui Dynasty (581 — 618) and contains a 2.2-m-high bodhisattva statue. An eye in the palm of each hand represents the versatility of his divine powers. According to one story, during the Eastern Han Dynasty a monk by the name of Yi Lisha discovered a fig tree here in which he suspected a holy spirit was present. He ordered craftsmen to come and bade them to carve a 'thousand-handed' bodhisattva statue. A temple was built in the years 618 — 619 to commemorate this incident. The present temple was built during the Qing Dynasty.

Nantian Si Temple 南天寺

Nantian Temple, erected in 1216 and rebuilt in 1773, is located at the foot of Daishan mountain about 5 km from Anhai.

Three tall stone statues stand in its main hall. The middle one represents the Buddha Amitabha and is flanked by the bodhisattvas Guanyin and Dashi Zhi.

Cao'an Manijiao Yizhi, Traces of the Manichaean Monastery 草庵

This monastery is located approximately half an hour from Quanzhou at the foot of Huabiaoshan mountain in Luoshan village.

In the third century, the Persian Mani (216 — 276) founded the religion of Manichaeism, which is a mixture of Christianity, Parseeism and Buddhism. It is said that Mani had already spread the thesis of his doctrine by the time he was 25 years old. He was banished from the country and subsequently travelled to East Asia. He returned to his homeland in 270 and was reputedly executed by Bahram I in 276. His doctrine, however, continued to live on. From the 7th century onward, this religious orientation gained followers in China. The Chinese Manichees also referred to their religion as Mingjiao. Emperor Taizu of the Ming Dynasty took offence at the 'misuse' of the term Ming and ordered the demolition of all Manichaean monasteries and the banishment of the Manichaeans. From that time on, it was no longer possible to practice Manichaeism. The sole existing remains of any of the Manichaean monasteries are here at the foot of Huabiaoshan. Manichaeism spread from this point. The present building is a replica built in 1922. It contains a stone representation of Mani.

The Tomb of Zheng Chenggong 郑成功墓

This tomb lies on Fuchuanshan mountain in Kangdian village in the district of Nan'an. General Zheng Chenggong (1624 — 1662) led his troops to Taiwan in February of 1662 to drive the Dutch away from the island. He died later that same year on Taiwan. His tomb was moved from Taiwan to Fuchuanshan mountain on May 22, 1699. His son, wife and parents are also buried here.

Zheng Chenggong Jinianguan Memorial Hall 郑成功纪念馆

In 1962, on the 300th anniversary of the liberation of Taiwan, the government ordered the erection of a hall next to Zheng's tomb. Besides biographical records, the hall also contains certain objects which were once owned by Zheng, such as weapons and presents from the emperor.

Chongwu, Ancient City Walls 崇武城

The ruins of this city are located on a peninsula 35 km south of Hui'an district. In 1079, during the Northern Song Dynasty, the government stationed a military observation post here. During the Ming period, in 1387, a small settlement was established. It was built from stones and was surrounded by a city wall that was 2,455 m long and 7 m high. Numerous wars took place in this region, and today only a few sections of the wall are still left intact.

Anxi County 安溪县

Wenmiao, Confucian Temple 安溪文庙

The palatial Anxi Wenmiao, south of the district capital Anxi, dates from the Guangxu period of the Qing era. The compound contains many halls and has a number of beautiful stone and wood carvings. Originally, only a single Confucian school, founded in 1001, stood here.

Qingshui Yan Temple 安溪清水岩

This temple stands on Pengshan mountain in Penglai village on the upper course of the Jinjiang river. A Buddhist monk ordered its construction in 1083, and it was later restored in the 16th century.

Dehua Yaoci, Dehua Porcelain Factories 德化窑瓷厂

Visitors to Quanzhou should take the time to see the Dehua factories. Porcelain was manufactured for export here as far back as the Song era. In the West, this porcelain was known as Blanc de Chine. The characteristic features are an ivory-colored or a milk-white glaze and a lack of paint. The shapes of the vessels are frequently based upon ancient patterns. In the course of its long tradition, Dehua distinguished itself above all else for the shape of its porcelain works. Buddhist and Daoist sculptures and animal and genre figures were favorite themes.

Today, porcelain is still manufactured in Dehua in the traditional style. In the meantime, many new models, motifs and techniques have also become part of the accepted program. The district has 2 state porcelain factories and 43 communal production concerns.

Xiamen (Amoy) 厦门市

The port city of Xiamen, called Amoy in the Fujian dialect, is situated on an island off the southeast coast of China, 2,800 miles from Beijing.

The city is one of the economic special zones of China where the economy is guided with the aid of capitalistic principles. Xiamen is easily reached from Hongkong (from Tai Kok Tsui port, Kowloon, on the MV 'Jimei' or the MV 'Gulang Yu' on Tuesdays and Fridays; the crossing takes 13 to 14 hours) or by train from Fuzhou and Nanping, by bus from Quanzhou or by plane from Shanghai and Beijing, among other cities. The island is frequently referred to as 'Egret Island' by its inhabitants, because so many egrets used to live here. Towards the end of the Ming Dynasty, General Zheng Chenggong (1624 — 1662) set up his marine base in Xiamen.

As a result of the Opium War, Xiamen and four other cities were opened up as treaty ports to oversea trade. Xiamen has a favorably located natural harbor where ships up to 10,000 registered tons can dock. After 1949, 2 dams were built to connect the island to the mainland. The first was a 2,212-m-long dam built from Gaoqi to Jimei in 1953; in 1956, a 2,820 m long dam was built to connect Jimei to Xinglin, Xiamen. Railway lines, a street and foot-paths cross over the dams.

After 1949, Xiamen slowly developed into an industrial city. Most of the factories were set up in the outlying suburbs and consist mainly of textile, agricultural and chemical industries, as well as machine manufacturing.

There are three important bus routes in Xiamen:

No. 1: University-train station
No. 2: University-ferry landing
No. 3: Train station-ferry landing

Gulang Yu Island 鼓浪屿

The enchanting island of Gulang Yu is located west of Xiamen. After Xiamen's harbor was opened to overseas trade, Gulang Yu became a residential area for foreigners.

The island, which is only 1.64 km², seems substantially larger because of its mountains. Longtou Shan, Dragon Head Mountain, is the highest elevation on the island. Hutou Shan, Tiger Head Mountain, rises up loftily across from Longtou Shan in Xiamen. For this reason, the native Chinese say that a dragon and a tiger guard over Xiamen.

Ascending Longtou Shan, one passes the so-called Dragon Caves, huge rocks and many inscriptions. Riguang Yan cliff forms the tip of Longtou Shan and offers a fantastic view. The Zheng Chenggong memorial stands to the north of Riguang Yan cliff. It was built in 1962 for the 300th anniversary of the recapture of Taiwan. Zheng Chenggong (1624 – 1662) maintained his military headquarters on the islands of Xiamen and Gulang Yu and trained marine troops there. He remained faithful to the overthrown Ming Dynasty and refused to submit to the Qing Dynasty rule. In 1659, he and General Zhang Huangyan attempted to capture Nanjing. His defeat forced him to return to Xiamen. In 1661, he led his troops to Taiwan, which was then occupied by Dutch troops. A year later, following an eight-month struggle, the Dutch governor capitulated. Since that time, Zheng Chenggong has been exalted as a national hero. This memorial hall has seven exhibition rooms in which the life and deeds of Zheng Chenggong are portrayed.

A 300-m-long sandy beach stretches out south of Riguang Yan cliff (dressing rooms are available). This is the location of Shuzhuang Park. The founder of the park grounds was a wealthy Taiwanese businessman. After the Japanese occupied Taiwan, he fled with his family to Gulang Yu island in 1895. In 1913, he arranged to have the lovely park laid out. A bridge with 44 twists and turns is particularly striking — it was built by the former owner when he was 44. After 1949, the park was opened to the public.

Wanshi Yan, 'Ten Thousand Rocks' Park 万石岩

The Wanshi Rocks are located in Shishan, the Lion Mountains, in the northeastern part of Xiamen. Some tourists will prefer an excursion to this area to a boat trip to Gulang Yu island.

In the early morning hours, when the entire

area is still shrouded in heavy mist, the atmosphere becomes particularly alluring.

Many pavilions and temples stand here amidst bizarre rocks and tropical and subtropical plants. The Wanshi Reservoir is located in the vicinity.

Tianjie Si temple, built during the Qianlong period (1736 — 1795), stands west of the park. Changxiao Dong, a cave with poems thought to date from the Ming period engraved into its walls, is located behind the temple.

The Taiping Yan cliff is the highest elevation in the Shishan mountains. The special feature about this boulder is the view that it offers of the pointed stone peaks and stone caves in the area.

Nanputuo Si Temple 南普陀寺

Nanputuo Si, the largest monastery in Xiamen, is located at the foot of Wulao Shan mountain in the southeastern part of the city.

Today, more than 60 monks live in this compound. In the foremost hall, Qiandian, there are statues of the Maitreya Buddha and the four celestial kings. The drum and bell towers are behind Qiandian to the left and right. Daxiong Baodian hall is next with its three magnificent Buddha statues: Sakyamuni, the historical Buddha, in the center; Yaoshi Fo, the Master of the Art of Healing, to his left; and Amitabha, the Ruler of the Western Paradise, to his right. In front of Sakyamuni, there is a wooden sculpture of the thousand-handed bodhisattva Guanyin. Octagonal Dabei Tang hall, restored in 1962, is worth mentioning for its statues of the bodhisattva Guanyin and its fine coffered ceiling. Directly north of Dabei Tang is Cangjing Ge hall, where the monks' daily instruction takes place. The library of the monastery is located on the second floor of this hall. Its exhibits include two books written in blood, one dating from 1644 and the other from 1646. A bronze bell from the Song Dynasty and a bronze pagoda, about 2 m high, are also of interest. Behind this hall rise the rock walls that are so characteristic of this area. A huge red character, 'Fo' for Buddhism, can be seen.

Xiamen Daxue University 厦门大学

In 1921, this university was donated by patriotic Chen Jiageng. At that time, it consisted of five departments. Today, it includes 10 departments with 30 different disciplines of study. A memorial to the famous writer Lu Xun is located within the university. He taught here from September 4, 1926, to

January 16, 1927.

Bailu Dong Cave 白鹿洞

This cave is located northeast of the city on the southern side of Yuping Shan mountain. The mountain has numerous caves and precipices. Bailu Lou, White Stag Tower, was erected in Bailu Dong cave in honor of the famous writer Zhu Xi, who founded the Bailu Shuyu school in Jiangxi Province. Several Buddhist pavilions and temples where sacrifices were made to the writer are located in the area.

Jimei 集美

Beyond Xiamen island lies the birthplace of Chen Jiageng (1874 — 1961), who left his home and became extremely wealthy as an entrepreneur in Singapore. He shared his success with Jimei and funded the establishment of various institutions, including an elementary and a middle school, a teachers' college, several technical schools (among them, one for navigation), an institute for tropical plants, a museum and a library. Today, Jimei is called the 'School City' and has a student population of about one million. Meanwhile the schools are financed by the state, but they are also supported by alumni who now work overseas.

Dragon Pond, where boat races take place in the fall as part of the Dragon Boat Festival, is located outside the 'School City'.

One of Jimei's important sights is Aoyuan, the Turtle Garden, including Chen Jiageng's tomb. The first part of the complex resembles a long tunnel. Information about the life of Chen Jiageng is displayed on its walls; above the information, stone carvings depict China's history.

The adjoining square is surrounded by a wall with stone carvings illustrating the development of animals, plants and human life and work. The square is largely dominated by a tall monument to the liberation of 1949. Chen Jiageng's tomb, which is located behind it, was built in round, which is typical for Fujian.

Guilai Tang hall, which Chen Jiageng had built for his descendants, and his former home, situated behind the hall, are also attractions in Jimei.

Hotels

Gulangyu Binguan, 鼓浪屿宾馆 Riguangyanlu 25, Gulangyu, tel. 20 52

Lujiang Dasha, 鹭江大厦 Lujiangdao 54, tel. 22 12

Huaqiao Dasha, 华侨大厦 Zhongshanlu 444, tel. 27 29

Xiamen Binguan, 厦门宾馆 Huyuanlu 16, tel. 24 46, 28 90

Xiaxi Lüshe, 霞溪旅社 Xiaxilu 30, tel. 45 74

Travel agency

Guoji Lüxingshe CITS and Zhongguo Lüxingshe, Zhongshanlu 444, tel. 42 86, 27 29

Gong'an Ju, Bureau of Public Security, Xinhualu 51, tel. 23 29

Ferry Xiamen, tel. 34 93

Ferry Gulang Yu, tel. 34 94

Train station, information, tel. 28 12

Bank of China, Zhongshanlu 8, tel. 30 07 (exchange)

Antique store, Zhongshanlu 211, tel. 33 63

Wuyi Shan Mountains 武夷山

The fascinating Wuyi Shan mountains are in the northern part of Fujian Province, on the Jiangxi Province border, south of Chong'an district. They are in one of the most beautiful areas in China and are famous for the wide variety of flora and fauna, delicious tea — a particular type of Wulong tea — and the many medicinal herbs which are found there.

An easy way to reach the area is by train from Fuzhou along the Minjiang river to Nanping and then by bus straight to Wuyi Shanzhuang Guesthouse (such excursions are arranged by the Fuzhou branch of the Lüxingshe travel agency). It is also possible to make the trip by boat. Wuyi Shanzhuang Guesthouse is so centrally located that one can set out on excursions in all directions from there. It takes about two days to visit the major sights, but one can easily spend a week or more there. Its extremely enchanting scenery and the pleasant and interestingly furnished Wuyi Shanzhuang hotel will tempt many travelers to spend an entire holiday there. One part of the Wuyi Shan mountains has been designated as a nature preserve by the government because of the natural wealth and rarities located in its pine and deciduous forests,

including 700-year-old gingko trees, nut and beech trees and more than 140 types of birds as well as reptiles and amphibians. Native and foreign researchers alike refer to Wuyi Shan as an amphibian and reptile paradise. There are more than 50 species of snakes here, including many poisonous ones.

One of the great advantages that the Wuyi Mountains offer is the possibility of traveling comfortably by boat down a small river that winds its way through a 7-km-long gorge in the mountains. A three hours' journey lets the tourist become familiar with the scenery along this water route. The river goes around a total of nine bends within the gorge; for this reason, the area is called Jiuqu Xi, Nine Bend Gorge. Behind every bend, a completely different landscape is revealed. Most boat trips are undertaken downstream from bend 9 to 2, taking about 90 minutes. The same trip upstream takes approximately three hours, but is not as exciting. One can rent a boat for a full day and stop along the way to take short inland trips.

First bend: The 400-m-high Dawang Feng, Peak of the Great King, stretches toward the sky here. The mountain slopes steeply on all sides and looks as if it would be impossible to climb. However, on the south side, there is a narrow cleft in the walls of stone in which wooden steps were built and man-made footholds formed that lead to the top of the peak.

Second bend: Yunü Feng, Peak of the Fairy, the most famous mountain of Wuyishan and its symbol. Local people claim that it resembles a beautiful girl. It is located directly across from Dawang Feng peak. One legend tells about the Celestial Emperor's daughter and a young peasant who fell in love. When a devil informed the Celestial Emperor of this, he became furious and ordered the devil to bring his daughter back to heaven. The daughter refused to go, and the devil changed both her and her lover into cliffs. To separate the two forever, he then placed himself as a sentry between them. An ugly blue rock, the devil, rises up in the gorge between the two lovers, the peaks of Dawang Feng and Yunü Feng.

Third bend: A wall of rock which looks as though it had been cut by a knife, Xiaocang Feng, towers above the gorge on the west bank. High above, two wooden boats, Jiahe Chuan, hang in a cleft in the wall. They are coffins, and there are many more in the cliffs in this region. They are formed from hollowed-out tree trunks, and the dead are placed inside along with a few offerings. This burial method was a custom of the Guyue minority more than 2,000 years ago. It is surmised that the purpose was to protect the bodies from wild animals.

Fourth bend: Here a large cliff and huge caves that are too high up to be reached can be seen. The water between the fourth and fifth bends is quite calm and is suitable for swimming.

Fifth bend: After the fifth bend, a bamboo grove and a deciduous forest come into view. Zhu Xi's house used to stand on this spot, and he gave lectures about philosophy here well into his old age. Zhu Xi (1130 — 1200) was a famous philosopher and writer from the Southern Song Dynasty. After he was removed from his official position, he founded an art school here in 1183, Wuyi Jingshe, where such scholars as Cai Yuanding and Huang Gan studied.

Sixth bend: This is the shortest bend, but it also reveals the most beautiful peak, Tianyou Feng. The poet Qian Bingdeng wrote about this peak during the Ming period: 'Once one has seen the peak of Tianyou Feng, there is no need to search any longer; a more beautiful sight cannot be found.' This peak is the highlight of the nine bends. From the top of Tianyou Feng, there is a splendid view of the river and the other peaks. The ascent is rather strenuous, but it is well worth it. Some of the red inscriptions that can be seen from the boat are by Zhu Xi.

Seventh bend: The three peaks of Sanyang Feng mountain can be seen. This mountain is the highest within the Wuyi Mountains.

Eighth bend: The current at this bend is extremely strong, which is rather exciting when going downstream.

Ninth bend: After passing a tea factory, one reaches the end of the gorge and Xingcun village. Interesting excursions into · the mountains can be made from Wuyi Gong. Sturdy footwear is a must! A ride through the nature preserve is fascinating. A great variety of wildlife still exists in its woods, mountains and valleys — a landscape which is still largely undisturbed by human beings. Traveling in the direction of Shaowu, one passes Tangtou Cun village where a nationally known poisonous snake research institute is located. The restaurant which is part of the institute offers various snake dishes — snake soup can be recommended.

Hotel

Wuyi Shanzhuang Guest House, 武夷山庄 Chong'an County, tel. 53
The hotel was designed and furnished in the local style by architects from Nanjing University.

Jiangxi Province 江西省

Area: 166,600 km². Population: 33.18 million, approximately 10,000 members of minorities such as Miao, Yao, Hui and She. Capital: Nanchang. Jiangxi is surrounded by Anhui and Hubei in the north, Hunan in the west, Guangdong in the south and Fujian and Zhejiang in the east.

History

The present area of Jiangxi was part of the Kingdom of Chu during the Zhou Dynasty. It was inhabited predominately by people other than Han Chinese. The colonization of the area by the Han Chinese occurred in the 3rd through the 6th centuries as multitudes of people fled to the south from the invading tribes from the north. Many settled down in Jiangxi. The present provincial boundaries were established during the Ming Dynasty. Many famous philosophers and poets came from Jiangxi, including Tao Yuanming, a poet from the Jin era, Zhu Xi, a philosopher from the Song era, and Wang Yangming, a philosopher from the Ming era. During the 20th century, the province moved into the center of interest. In 1927, China's most important soviet area was set up in the Jinggangshan mountains, headed by Mao Zedong and Zhu De. The revolutionaries' first large power base developed here.

The Ganjiang crosses the province from south to north. For ages, it has been one of the main transportation routes for trade, the military and emigration. In the north, it flows into the Poyang Hu, the largest fresh water lake in China, and empties into the Changjiang near Jiujiang. The valleys along the Ganjiang and Shushui rivers as well as the plains around the Poyang Hu are among the most important areas for growing rice in China. Like the Dongting Hu region, the wet growing area around Poyang Hu produces one of the country's largest rice surpluses. The growing season in Jiangxi ranges from 10 to 11 months, which makes it possible to harvest two rice crops a year. Seventy percent of the arable land here is used to grow rice. Heavy rains fall regularly; in comparison with the north of China, the rainfall variability is slight. When the weather is cooler, such dry-field crops as barley, wheat, sesame and rape are cultivated.

The low-lying plains are surrounded by hills and mountains. The soil in the hills is not very rich and is therefore not suited to rice cultivation. Here, the primary crops are sweet potatoes and corn. In the mountains, tea is grown. The centers for tea production are Ji'an, Wuning and Xiushui. The mountains along the border provide wood for commercial purposes. Approximately 10% of the province is covered by lush forests. Some of the most-sought-after woods are cedar, camphor, maple and pine. The trunks are bound together to form rafts and then driven down the Ganjiang river.

Jiangxi is one of China's most important fruit growing areas. Besides watermelons, pears, persimmons and apples, oranges — grown in central and southern Jiangxi — are also an important crop. The seedless mandarine oranges from Nanfeng are well-known throughout the country.

Up to 1949, industry played no significant role. Since the founding of the present government, great strides have been made in both light and heavy industry. Large deposits of coal are located in Pingxiang and Fengcheng. The huge deposits of tungsten in the Dayu Ling Mountains, supposedly the largest in the world, are of extreme importance. The supplies of Kaolin and petuntse on the east bank of the Poyang Hu Lake and in the Changjiang valley gave rise to Jingdezhen's important porcelain factories. These workshops, established during the Song period, have produced excellent porcelain for centuries.

Nanchang 南昌市

The capital city of Nanchang lies on the east bank of the Ganjiang. It is a junction for land and river traffic.

Nanchang was founded as early as the 2nd century BC. It was always a center of administration and a market for agricultural goods. Up to 1949, industry existed only on a very limited basis. During the past 30 years, Nanchang has developed into a rising industrial city with a population of almost 2.5 million.

Nanchang has a revolutionary past. On August 1, 1927, a rebellion led by Zhou Enlai, among others, took place here. Chiang Kaishek's troops were defeated, and the city was held for three days. August 1, 1927, is considered to be the official date for the founding of the Red Army, whose name was changed to the People's Liberation Army in July 1946.

Many of the places of interest in Nanchang celebrate the city's revolutionary past.

Bayi Gongyuan Park,
August The First Park 八一公园

This park is located on Changzhenglu street. It was laid out in 1932 and covers an area of 26 hectares. During the Nanchang Uprising, violent battles took place here.

Jiangxi Lishi Bowuguan Museum,
The Historical Museum of Jiangxi Province
江西省历史博物馆

The historical museum in the city's center south of Bayi Guangchang Square was established and organized from 1953 — 1958. Some of the topics that it covers are as follows: archeological finds, the technical development of agriculture in ancient China, ancient calligraphies from the Ming and Qing eras and the Guixi Yamu cliff graves

Bayi Nanchang Qiyi Jinianta,
Memorial Pagoda of the Nanchang Uprising
八一起义纪念馆

This pagoda, in the south part of Bayi Guangchang square, was erected on the 50th anniversary of the Nanchang Uprising of August 1, 1927. It is 45.5 m high and is made of concrete covered with marble and granite. There are nine golden characters on the front side of the pagoda: Bayi Nanchang Qiyi Jinianta. Below the nine characters, a brief account of the events surrounding the Uprising is given. The events of the Uprising itself are depicted on the remaining three sides of the pagoda.

Geming Lieshi Jiniantang,
Martyrs Memorial 革命烈士纪念堂

In 1953, this memorial was built on Bayidadao street. Its exhibits are dedicated to the 10 major battles of the civil war and the lives of 300 martyrs.

Bayi Qiyi Jinianguan,
Former Stronghold of the Leaders of the
Nanchang Uprising of August 1, 1927
八一南昌起义纪念馆

This former stronghold can be found on Zhongshanlu street. In July of 1927, Zhou Enlai set up a command center here. On August 1, 1927, Zhou Enlai, He Long and Ye Ting raised the cry for the Nanchang Uprising.

A museum is now located in the rooms that

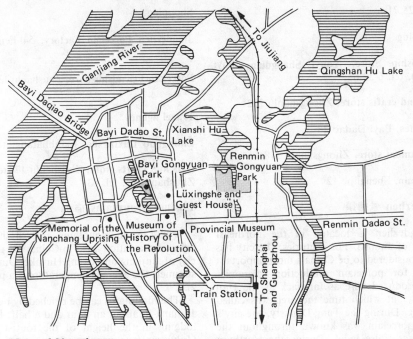

Map of Nanchang

once housed this command post.

Da'an Si Temple 大安寺

Da'an Si, built during the 4th century, is located on Yuzhanghoujie street. Inside the temple, there is a large iron vessel from the time of the Three Kingdoms.

Youminsi Tongzhong, Bronze Bell 佑民寺铜钟

A bronze bell dating back to 967 can be seen at 29 Huanhulu street. It was made at the bidding of General Lin Renzhao during the Southern Tang Dynasty. It reputedly weighs 5,032 kg and is about 2 m tall. In 1929, a bell tower was erected next to Youmin Si temple.

Sancun Taohua Yuan, Peach Orchard 三村桃花园

A well-known peach orchard is located in Shangtaohua Cun village. For the native Chinese, this orchard is a favorite destination for outings, especially in the spring when the peach trees blossom.

Qingyunpu Temple 青云浦

Qingyunpu is in Nanchang's southern suburb. The rooms of the temple house a museum which contains the works of Bada-shanren and his pupils. Badashanren lived in the 17th century. He was not willing to recognize the Qing Dynasty, which began its rule in 1644. In 1661, at 37 years of age, he was said to have moved to Qingyunpu temple and lived there for the next 26 years. The temple has three main halls. The foremost hall is dedicated to the god of war, Guandi, the middle hall to one of the eight holy figures of Daoism, Lü Chunyang (Lü Dongbin), and the last hall to Xu Xun, who, according to legend, managed to stop a flood by killing the creature responsible, an evil dragon.

Hotels

Nanchang Fandian, 南昌饭店 Zhanqianlu, tel. 6 35 93

Jiangxi Fandian, 江西饭店 Changzhenglu, tel. 6 36 24

Jiangxi Binguan, 江西宾馆 Bayi Dadao 64, tel. 6 48 61

Travel agency

Guoji Lüxingshe, CITS and **Zhongguo Lüxingshe,** in Jiangxi Binguan, Bayi Dadao, tel. 6 25 71

Friendship Store, Youyi Shangdian, Bayi Dadao, tel. 6 32 68

Arts and crafts store, Zhongshanlu 222

Antiques, Bayi Dadao 28

Department store, Zhongshanlu 318

Porcelain, Shenglijie 12

Jingdezhen 景德镇

Jingdezhen is located in the northeast section of Jiangxi. For centuries, the city has been considered to be China's most important center for porcelain production. Ceramics were produced here as far back as the Han Dynasty, at which time the area was called Xinping. During the Tang Dynasty, the city's white porcelain was known throughout the empire as 'false jade'. During the Northern Song Dynasty under the reign of Jingde (1004 — 1007), an edict from the emperor made Jingdezhen the production center for imperial porcelain, and the mark 'made in the Jingde period' was printed on the bottom of each item. Later, the city was named 'Jingdezhen' after this period of reign. In the Yuan, Ming and Qing periods, the city continued to be the hub of porcelain manufacturing. Jingdezhen's porcelain was described as being as white as jade, as clear as a mirror and as thin as paper, with a sound as clear as a bell.

Today, Jingdezhen has 250,000 inhabitants. The most important ingredient for porcelain, kaolin, comes from Gaoling, a village 50 km away that has produced the world's best porcelain clay since ancient times. The clay was named after the village. High quality glazes come from the neighboring areas. There are more than 14 large state porcelain factories in Jingdezhen. The most famous types of porcelain from Jingdezhen are the blue and white porcelain, which has been produced since the Yuan Dynasty, and the rice-patterned porcelain that was introduced during the Song era.

Items on display in the city museum illustrate the development of porcelain manufacturing in full.

Hotel

Jingdezhen Binguan, Lianhuatang, tel. 927

Jingdezhen Porcelain Factory, 54 Fengjinglu, tel. 498

Porcelain-Friendshipstore, Zhushanlu 13, tel. 22 31

Travel agency

Zhongguo Lüxingshe, Lianhuatang, tel. 293

Arts and crafts store, Zhushanlu 17, tel. 63 Zhushanlu 17, tel. 63

Lushan Mountains 庐山

The Lushan mountains, one of the most beloved recreation areas in China, are near the city of Jiujiang on Poyang Hu lake. During the summer, the average temperature is a pleasant 22.6°C.

The mountains can be reached by bus from Jiujiang in about an hour and a half. Finding lodging in the height of the tourist season (July) can be a problem. It is a good idea to make reservations in advance through CITS in Jiujiang or to seek the help of CITS in Lushan in finding a room. Even in ancient times, Lushan's peaks, veiled in clouds and mist, were well-known and lovely.

During the Eastern Han Dynasty, a Buddhist center arose here. Famous poets and political figures, such as Tao Yuanming, Li Bai, Du Fu, Bai Juyi, Su She, Yue Fei, Wen Tianxiang and Li Shizhen left their writings behind here. Lushan's highest peak is 1,474 m. Guling, a summer health resort, is located in the central Lushan at an elevation of 1,167 m. There are also hotels, guest houses, department stores, restaurants, a movie theater and a library here.

There are more than 200 interesting sights in the Lushan mountains, including numerous peaks and rock formations, ponds, springs waterfalls, pavilions and temples. Only a few are mentioned in the following paragraphs.

Xianren Dong, Cave of the Immortals, is located northwest of Guling. The Daoist monk Lü Dongbin is supposed to have once meditated here.

Yubei Ting, Imperial Stele Pavilion, stands northwest of Xianren Dong on Jinxiu Feng peak. It houses a tall stele, the inscription of which was composed by the first Ming emperor, Zhu Yuanzhang.

Datian Chi pond can be found on Tianchi Shan mountain, west of Yubei Ting pavilion. Supposedly, the pond has never dried up, even in times of draught.

Longshou Ya, Dragon's Head Cliff, is several hundred meters away from the above-mentioned pond. It appears as if two large boulders had been laid down, one on top of the other. The bottom section towers up vertically, while the upper section is horizontal. The view from there is highly praised.

The Lulin Daqiao dam provides a link between Guling Peak and Hanpo Kou mountain. It was built in 1955, and one of its results was the Lulin Hu reservoir that can hold more than two million cubic meters of water. Three unusually tall trees can be seen west of Lulin Daqiao. They are called San Baoshu and include two conifers and a gingko tree. Each of the evergreens is 40 m tall, and it takes four adults to embrace one of the trunks.

The Botanical Garden in the southern part of the Lushan is, at an elevation of 1,200 m, one of the highest-lying gardens in China. More than 3,400 different types of plants grow there. Over 200 research institutes from 53 countries have contributed to it and are continuing their scientific exchange. From the southwest towards Xianren Dong cave, the 'Path of 99 Bends' leads by the sides of cliffs in which calligraphies were once carved. These were cut during the Song, Yuan, Ming and Qing periods.

The Wulao Feng peaks are located 1 km away from Wansongping village in the southeastern Lushan. From far away, the peaks resemble five old men who are sitting close together. Bailudong Shuyuan, White Stag Caves School, is located in the valley below the Wulao Feng Peaks, 7 km from the district capital, Xingzi Xian. From 785 — 805, two scholars are said to have spent their time raising deer as well as pursuing their studies. One of them later became the prefect of Jiujiang and had the complex enlarged.

Many writers sought refuge here at the end of the Tang period; a school developed which later was considered to be one of the most famous in imperial China. At the beginning of the Song Dynasty, this school was said to be the world's fourth largest.

In 1179, the famous official Zhu Xi who taught here, made way for the construction of additional halls. Most of the buildings, which can be visited today, were built during the Qing Dynasty in the Daoguang period of reign (1821 — 1850). The main hall was restored in 1982. Those who can read Chinese script will be interested in viewing the valuable stone inscriptions in the western and eastern parts of the complex.

Qinglian Si temple is on the other side of Wulao Feng. It is said that the famous poet Li Bai, also called Qing Lian, lived here for a while.

Sandie Quan waterfall, Spring with Three Folds, flows in Lushan's eastern valley. The water cascades over three levels down into the valley.

Guanshan hill, directly across from the waterfall, is a good observation point.

Dongling Si temple stands at Lushan's northwest foot. It is believed that the Buddhist school of thought Jingtu Zong (Lianzong) was started here.

The temple was built during the Eastern Jin period in 384, at the bidding of the famous monk Huiyuan. At that time, he also founded the Lianshe society (Bailian She). Later, he was described as the founder of the Jingtu Zong school of thought. Particularly during the Tang Dynasty, many Buddhist monks came here from foreign countries to study these Buddhist teachings.

The temple consists of several halls. The main hall, Shenyun Baodian, contains numerous statues, including ones of Sakyamuni, Wenshu, Puxian and Gaye.

Xilin Ta pagoda stands in the distance to the west of Dongling Si temple. It dates from the Tang Dynasty, the Kaiyuan period of reign (714 — 741).

Xiaotian Chi pond lies 1 km northeast of Guling on top of a pine-covered mountain. Wangjiang Ting pavilion stands to the west of the pond. From there, one can look out over a deep ravine and see the faraway village of Guling.

Hanyang Feng peak rises up in Lushan's southeast. At 1474 m, it is the highest elevation in these mountains. The peak is shrouded in clouds almost the entire year.

Lushan Wenquan hot springs have their source at the foot of the Lushan across from Hanyang Feng peak and 41 km from Guling Peak. The water's average temperature is 62.6°C. After 1949, a sanatorium with 300 beds was set up here. Cases of skin disease, rheumatism and gynic illnesses are handled.

Haihu Si temple is located at the southern foot of the Lushan. It was erected in 1618, and since then it has been restored several times. Numerous books are kept on the premises, including the 81 holy volumes of Huayan Jing.

Xiufeng peak is in the southern Lushan. The Xiufeng Si temple, to which the mountain owes its fame, used to stand here, but today not much remains of it.

A stone stele, more than 1,200 years old, stands next to Shanmen, Mountain Gate. It contains an engraved representation of the bodhisattva — Guanyin. There are also a number of other steles with engravings from famous calligraphers and writers. Even the Kangxi and Yongzheng Emperors from the Qing Dynasty left their handwriting behind.

Qingyu Xu waterfall is located in Xingzi Xian district at the southern foot of Lushan. The waterfall rushes down between Shuang-jian and Wenshu Peaks. A second waterfall makes its way down between Heming and Xingbao Peaks. The two falls then meet in the canyon to form a single stream which is one of the most beautiful spots in the Lushan mountains.

Hotels

Lulin Fandian, 芦林饭店 Lulin, tel. 24 24

Lushan Binguan, 庐山宾馆 Hedonglu 446, tel. 22 75

Yunzhong Binguan, 云中宾馆 Henanlu 528, tel. 25 47

Travel agency

Guoji Lüxingshe, CITS, and Zhongguo Lüx-ingshe, Hedonglu 443, tel. 24 97

Ganjiang River 赣江

The 760-km-long Ganjiang offers many places worth seeing. Those who make the trip to Ganzhou by boat have an opportunity not only to enjoy beautiful scenery, but also to study a bit of revolutionary history. During the second civil war, many important bases were established here.

Ganzhou 赣州

Ganzhou is the largest city on the upper course of the Ganjiang and an important junction for traffic between Guangdong and Fujian. A number of older interesting sights are located in the city, for example, the three-level terrace, Yugu Tai, from the Tang era. It is in the northwest section of the city on the peak of Huolan Shan mountain. The entire city of Ganzhou can be seen from there. Downstream from Ganzhou is Ji'an, the most important city in the Jinggang Shan region. The scenery in this area is particularly fascinating. The neighboring Qingcheng Shan mountains are Ji'an's greatest attraction. There one can see a Buddhist temple from the Tang period, Qingyuan Si, and Qihe Ta pagoda.

The Jinggang Shan mountains are part of the Luoxiao Shan mountain range along Hunan's border. Most of Jinggang Shan's major peaks are over 1,000 m high. The mountains resemble a great fortress, and from a military standpoint, they were quite secure. In order to reach Ciping village, one must first cross over various small and large passes. The crossing of five large passes by the Red Army has not been forgotten even today. When Mao Zedong led his forces into this region in 1927, Ciping became the Red Army's headquarters. The founding of the first peasants' and workers' government took place here. In 1934, the Red Army left the Jinggang Shan mountains and began its legendary Long March.

Travel agency

Zhongguo Lüxingshe, Ciping, tel. 5 04

Poyang Hu Lake 鄱阳湖

Poyang Hu is the largest fresh water lake in China. It has an area of 5,000 km².

The region surrounding Poyang Hu is among the wealthiest in Jiangxi. The famous mountains Lushan and Shizhong Shan rise up from its shores. Several scenic islands are located in the lake. One of these is Xieshan, Shoe Mountain. As the story goes, a heavenly goddess once washed her feet in Poyang Hu, but as she did so, one of her shoes fell into the water. The shoe reached the middle of the lake and finally formed this island.

Shizhong Shan is on the southern bank of the Changjiang, on Poyang Hu. This mountain was considered to be worth seeing as far back as the Han era. From a military viewpoint, it played an important role in the wars of ancient China. Many famous poets, calligraphers and political figures left their works behind here. Several pavilions decorate the landscape, including Yilan Ting, which is located on the cliffs by the Changjiang and serves as a good observation point.

Jiujiang and Surroundings 九江市

Jiujiang lies on the shores of the Changjiang, north of the Lushan mountains. It can be reached by train from Nanchang.

Jiujiang is an important port. Throughout the course of centuries, it has played a significant role, both strategically and commercially. The city was among the most important centers of tea trade, and the trading of porcelain from Jingdezhen was also considerable. Jiujiang was opened to foreign trade in 1862. After the building of the railway which connected Nanchang to the coast (1936 — 1937), Jiujiang lost its influence in inter-regional trade and remained significant only as a center for local trade. Since 1949, various branches of industry have developed here, including the textile and food industries as well as brickworks and machine factories. From Jiujiang, one can go by car or bus for an outing to Jingdezhen, the city famous for its porcelain, or to Lushan Mountains.

Gantang Hu Lake 甘棠湖

Gantang Hu is located in the center of the city. A pavilion complex was built on a small island in the middle of the lake from 1816 — 1818, which was later restored in 1972. From Gantang Hu, Dasheng Ta pagoda, part of the Nengren Si temple, can be seen in the distance.

Nengren Si Temple 能仁寺

Nengren Si, which used to be called Chengtian Yuan, is in the eastern part of the city. It was founded during the 6th century. The present compound dates back to 1870. The temple complex contains the imposing main hall, Daxiong Baodian, as well as the halls, Jingang Dian, Tiefo Dian and Cangjing Lou. Dasheng Ta pagoda stands southeast of Daxiong Baodian hall. It is 42 m tall and was built during the Eastern Jin period. Later it was destroyed and then rebuilt in the 8th century during the Tang era.

Suojianglou Baota Pagoda 锁江楼宝塔

This pagoda stands on a hill by the shores of the Changjiang in the northeastern part of the city. According to local chronicles, it was built in 1585. The pagoda in 35 m tall, and to seamen who travel along the Changjiang, it is a landmark of the city of Jiujiang.

Tianhua Gong Temple 天花宫

In the vernacular, this complex on the shores of Gantang Hu lake is called Niang-niang Miao, Mother's Temple or Temple of the Distinguished Lady. According to one chronicle, the complex dates back to 1870. Niangniang Ting pavilion is especially worth seeing.

The Temple and Grave of Tao Yuanming 陶渊明祠墓

The famous poet Tao Yuanming (365 —

427) lived during the Jin Dynasty and was the district supervisor of Pengze. Because he was dissatisfied with the local government of the times, he resigned from his post at 41 years of age. From then on, he devoted his time solely to poetry and literature. The temple and his grave are located in Mahuiling village in Jiujiang district. The date of construction is unknown.

Longgong Dong Stalactic Cave 龙宫洞

Longgong Dong, Palace of the Dragon King Cave, is 36 km southwest of the district capital, Pengze. It was discovered only recently. With its enormous size (2,700 m in length), it is easily comparable to the largest cave in China (Qixing Yan) in Guilin. As in the fantastic descriptions of dragon palaces in ancient legends, the cave is divided into an eastern, a western and a central palace. The central palace is located 1,100 m into the cave's interior. A hall that is 80 m long, 70 m wide and 60 m high is situated there.

Hotel

Nanhu Binguan, 南湖宾馆 Nansilu 77, tel. 22 72

Travel agency

Guoji Lüxingshe (CITS) in the Nanhu Binguan hotel, Nansilu 77, tel. 40 15

Shandong Province 山东省

Area: 150,000 km² / Population: 74.4 million / Capital: Jinan

Shandong can be divided into two areas: an inland zone which borders on the provinces of Hebei, Henan, Anhui and Jiangsu, and the peninsula which is surrounded by the Bohai and Huanghai seas. Within the inland area, there is a mountainous region which stretches from the northeast to the southwest. The highest elevation is Taishan with a height of 1,545 m. This mountain is one of China's five sacred mountains. Shandong's lowlands are part of the North China Plain, and geologically they are made up of loess-rich alluvial land from the Huanghe River. The region is very fertile, and consequently it is used down to the last plot for agricultural purposes. Winter wheat, barley, millet, sorghum, beans and soy beans are among the most important. Shandong has always been one of the most densely populated regions in China. Due to the deforesting of land and the ecological consequences of it, the amount of land available for agricultural purposes has decreased through the course of history. Therefore, millions of people have made their way across the sea to Manchuria in the past centuries to earn their living there as farmers. The economy on the Jiaodong peninsula is based on fishing and mining.

Shandong can also be divided into two climatic zones. The inland area falls under the continental climate zone with hot, dry summers and cold winters. A considerably milder climate with relatively high humidity is prevalent in the peninsular region.

History

Shandong did not become the province with its present dimensions until the 15th century, but it was one of the earliest populated regions in China. In 1928, archeologists came across the traces of a culture in the Longshan region, which had experienced its most prosperous times around 2800 BC. The small state of Lu, the home of the famous philosophers Kongzi (Confucius) and Mengzi, developed in the southern part of the province during the Chunqiu period. As far back as the 4th century AD, the area of present-day Shandong held the position of a leading navigation center. Goods were shipped to Shandong from the southern regions where Guangdong and Fujian are now located. From Shandong, they could be transported further north and to the interior of the country. During the 19th century, Shandong was subject to heavy flooding and natural catastrophes. The Huanghe River, which from 1194 to around 1850 used to flow towards the ocean along the border between Shandong and Jiangsu, changed its course after dramatic floods. Its present course is maintained with the aid of extensive dike constructions. Emigration to the northeast reached its peak during these catastrophic years.

At the end of the 19th century, the province increasingly came under the influence of British, Japanese and German power politics. The area was briefly occupied by the Japanese from 1894 — 1895. In 1897, German troops landed and declared the Jiaozhou Bay area to be part of their sphere of influence. In the treaty of 1898, the weakened Chinese government was forced to agree to a 99-year lease and to grant permission for the building of a railway and a marine port in Qingdao. Up to 1914, the Germans controlled Shandong's trade, constructed a railroad line to Jinan and enlarged the coal mines. After the start of World War I and Japan's declaration of war against Germany, the area came under Japanese control following the blockade of Qingdao. The Japanese claimed the right to former German privileges until the Washington Conference in 1922. During the Sino-Japanese War from 1937 — 1945, the Japanese occupied the region once more.

Since 1949, the province has been able to develop economically especially in the areas of light and heavy industry. The provincial capital, Jinan, and Shandong's largest port, Qingdao, are the main centers of heavy industry, followed by Yantai.

Jinan 济南市

Jinan is not only the capital of the province, but with a population of 3.3 million, it is also its political, economic and cultural center. The city lies between the Huanghe River in the north and the famous Taishan mountain in the south. When Shandong Province was formed in the Ming Dynasty, Jinan received the status of provincial capital.

The modern development of Jinan did not begin until 1852, when the Huanghe changed its course towards the north, and the city obtained access to the waterways of north Shandong and south Hebei. As the 20th century began, a significant center of trade for important agricultural products such as grains, peanuts, cotton and tobacco sprang up in Jinan. This development was due in large part to the construction of the railroads. In 1904, a railway line to Qingdao was established, and in 1912, was connected to the line between Tianjin and Pukou.

Industry developed parallel to trade. Excluding Qingdao, Jinan soon became the province's most important industrial center. Jinan is the city of springs. During the Jin Dynasty (1127 — 1224), 72 springs were counted, and their names were chiseled into a stone tablet. Within the city's present boundaries, however, there are more than 100 springs. The water bubbles up from the ground — sometimes sparingly — and maintains a constant temperature of 18°C. Most of the springs are located in the older section of Jinan. Parks were built around the most famous ones.

Baotu Quan Spring 趵突泉

Baotu Quan is located south of the Ximen Qiao bridge within Baotuquan Park.

A memorial dedicated to the poet Li

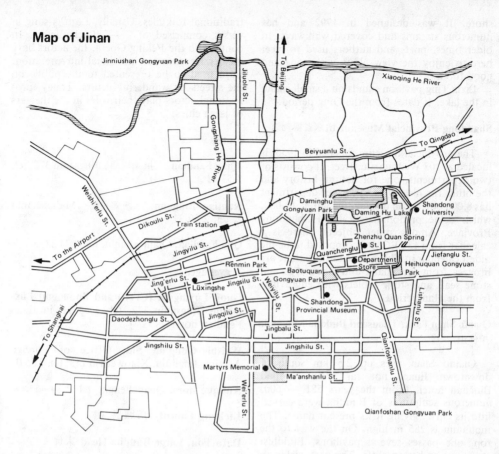

Map of Jinan

Jinniushan Gongyuan Park

Jiluolu St.

To Beijing

Xiaoqing He River

To Qingdao

Gongshang He River

Weishi'erlu St.

Beiyuanlu St.

Dikoulu St.

Train station

To the Airport

Daminghu Gongyuan Park

Daming Hu Lake

Shandong University

Jingyilu St.

Zhenzhu Quan Spring

Quanchenglu St.

Jiefanglu St.

Rénmin Park

Department Store

Heihuquan Gongyuan Park

Jing'erlu St.

Baotuquan Gongyuan Park

Jingsilu St.

Lüxingshe

Weiyilu St.

To Shanghai

Daodezhonglu St.

Jingqilu St.

Shandong Provincial Museum

Lishanlu St.

Jingbalu St.

Jingshilu St.

Jingshilu St.

Qianfoshanlu St.

Wei'erlu St.

Martyrs Memorial

Ma'anshanlu St.

Qianfoshan Gongyuan Park

Qingzhao (1084 — ca. 1151) stands east of the spring. Li Qingzhao was born in Jinan. She wrote many well-known poems and was also a noteworthy artist. She is supposed to have lived by Suyu Quan spring, which is also in Baotuquan Park. The memorial was built in 1956 and restored in 1980. A portrait of the artist as well as several of her works are here on display.

Zhenzhu Quan Spring 珍珠泉

Zhenzhu Quan, Pearl Spring, is north of Quanchenglu street. The water shoots up from the ground and then falls down in tiny droplets. For this reason, it was named the Pearl Spring.

Heihu Quan Spring 黑虎泉

Heihu Quan, Black Tiger Spring, is located on Heihuquandonglu street. Its waters flow into a pond through the jaws of stone tigers. In the surrounding area one encounters man-made mountains, covered walkways and winding paths.

Wulong Tan Pond 五龙潭

Wulong Tan is located outside Ximen gate, half a kilometer south of Baotu Quan spring. The waters from five springs, coming from different directions, meet here to form a deep pond. Since it used to be thought that dragons lived in the deep water, the pond was given the name 'Five Dragons Pond'.

Daming Hu Lake 大明湖

In the northern part of the old city, waters from several springs unite in the Daming Hu and flow towards the Gulf of Bohai. Around the lake there are pavilions, paths and many beautiful trees. Xiayuan garden was laid out to the south of the lake in 1909. Beiji Ge Daoist temple, built during the Yuan Dynasty, is north of the garden. The temple provides a broad view of the lake and its beautiful surroundings.

Tingyuan garden is located on the northern

shore. It was designed in 1792 and has numerous streams and covered walkways. In older times, poets and authors used to meet here to enjoy the view along with wine and good food.

Lixia Ting pavilion stands on a small island in the lake. It dates from the Qing period.

Shandong Provincial Museum 山东省博物馆

The provincial museum, opened in 1956, is located at 103 Wenhuaxilu street. It consists of two departments, one for natural history and the other for history. The former department has 8,000 objects on display, the latter, 13,000, which come predominately from Shandong Province. Among other objects, there is a calendar from 134 BC. It is supposed to be the oldest calendar in China. In addition, there are bronzes from the Shang and Zhou eras and stone seals and stone tablets with engravings from the Han period.

Qianfo Shan Park, Thousand Buddha Mountain 千佛山

Qianfo Shan rises up 2.5 km south of downtown Jinan, not far from Nanjiao Binguan hotel. From the years 581 — 600, numerous sculptures of Buddha were carved into its cliffs, giving it its present name. The mountain is 285 m high. On the way to the top, one passes several pavilions, Buddhist structures and steep cliffs. The park yields an extensive view of Jinan and the Huanghe.

Local Arts and Crafts

Yumaohua, Feather pictures: feather art is well-known in the Jinan area. All types of feathers are used, but peacock feathers are preferred. The feathers are combined together to create pictures with widely varying themes. Caobian, Wickerwork: excavations have determined that this type of handcraft has been practiced for over 5,000 years. A wide variety of materials are used, such as straw, willow twigs, lianas and corn husks. Wonderful baskets, boxes, bowls, purses, chairs, screens, etc. are made with great skill. The articles are practical and a real buy and therefore they are in great demand both at home and abroad.

Lüju Local Opera

Lüju is a local opera from Shandong Province. At present, it is enjoying great popularity. This art evolved from Shandong's traditional folktales. Usually, Lüju is sung in verses comprised of 7 — 10 characters. In contrast to the Peking Opera, the actors have greater freedom for individual interpretation. Lüju used to be presented to the public on the streets by wandering actors. Today, professional actors play their roles in the theaters of large cities.

Hotels

Jinan Fandian, 济南饭店 Jingsanlu 372, tel. 3 53 51

Nanjiao Binguan, 南郊宾馆 Ma'anshanlu 2, tel. 2 39 31

Qilu Fandian, Qianfoshanlu, tel. 4 34 23

Travel agency

Guoji Lüxingshe (CITS) and Zhongguo Lüxingshe, Jingsanlu 372, tel. 3 53 51, in Jinan Fandian hotel

Waishi Gong'an Shi, Office of Foreign Affairs, Jingliulu, Xiaoweierlu 233, tel. 3 55 01

Antique store, Quanchenglu, tel. 2 34 46

Licheng County 历城县

Dafo Tou, Large Buddha Head 大佛头

3.5 km north of Jinan, there is a large Buddha head carved in stone on the north side of Fohuishan mountain. It is 7 m tall and was created in 1035 — 36.

Longdong Shan, Dragon Caves Mountain 龙洞山

Longdongshan lies in the southeastern part of Licheng district. A cave leads 500 m into the western side of the mountain. At its highest it measures 8m, and numerous figures are carved into its walls. People used to come here to ask the dragon king for rain, as it was thought that the cave belonged to the dragon king who ruled over water, rivers and seas. Some of the carvings come from the Eastern Wei period (534 — 550) as well as the Sui and Tang eras.

Jiuding Ta, Nine Point Pagoda 九顶塔

Jiuding Ta, on Lingjishan mountain, was built during the Tang period. The peculiar feature about this 13-m-high pagoda is that an additional nine small pagodas stand on its roof.

Simen Ta, Four Door Pagoda 四门塔

The famous Simen Ta is on Qinglongshan mountain in Licheng district where a Buddhist center was once located. It was erected in 611 and rebuilt in the 14th century. It is one of the oldest stone pagodas in China that is still in good condition. It is a square structure, each side measuring 7.4 m in length and 15 m in height. The pagoda's name derives from its doors, one in each side. The doors are rainbow-shaped and 1.8 m wide.

Longhu Ta Pagoda, Pagoda of the Dragon and the Tiger 龙虎塔

Longhu Ta is approximately 10 m tall and is located northwest of Simen Ta pagoda. Its name was taken from the dragon and tiger chiseled into the building. It is uncertain when the pagoda was built, but its style suggests the Tang or Song period. The adjacent forest of stupas and Tang period terrace are also of interest.

Qianfo Ya Cliff, Thousand Buddha Cliff 千佛崖

Impressive Qianfo Ya, west of Longhu Ta pagoda, has more than 100 niches containing over 200 Buddhist sculptures. Most of them date back to the early Tang era.

Changqing County 长清县

Lingyan Si Temple 灵岩寺

Lingyan Si is 78 km from Jinan near Taishan on Fangshan mountain. The temple was constructed during the Northern Wei period and took on a greater importance during the Tang and Song dynasties. At that time it consisted of more than 40 halls and over 500 rooms.

Today, the following buildings can be visited:

Qianfo Dian, Thousand Buddha Hall, is the temple's main hall. It was first built during the Tang Dynasty, but the present building comes from the Ming period. Its ceiling is painted in rich colors. In the center of the hall there are three terracotta statues of Buddha: Pilu, Maitreya and Yaoshi. The 40 Luohan statues which line the walls are famous for their realistic form. The politician and scholar from the late Qing period, Liang Qichao (1873

— 1929), thought them to be the best he had ever encountered.

Other buildings include Daxiong Baodian, Treasure Hall of the Great Hero, Zhonglou and Gulou, bell and drum towers, pavilions, pagodas and stone steles and columns, all of which are of great historical and artistic value.

Pizhi Ta pagoda is 56 m tall and was built at the beginning of the 11th century. Chiseled representations of the torments of hell can be seen on its eight walls.

In the western section of the temple complex there are 167 pagodas which make up Muta Lin, Forest of Stupas, which were built in honor of leading monks who had died. The oldest pagoda was built during the Tang period and is called Huizong Ta. It is 5.3 m tall, made of stone, and it was built to honor the monk Huizong. Huizong had been active in the monastery from 742 — 756. The pagoda was built after his death, presumably in the year 760.

Chengzi Ya Cliff with Traces of the Longshan Culture 城子崖遗址

In 1928, as he was carrying out excavations in the vicinity of Longshan, the Chinese archeologist Wu Jinding came across evidence of a prehistoric culture. He named it Longshan after the place of discovery. Stone tools, bones and especially ceramics — an almost black, often polished pottery — were brought to light. This society most likely flourished around 3000 BC, and its range of influence reached from Hebei in the north to Zhejiang in the south. At that time, Longshan ceramics were already formed on a potter's wheel. They are relatively thin and exhibit patterns and shapes that were later further developed by casters of bronze.

Other than black ceramics, white and red ceramics were also produced, but not in such large quantities. The excavation area covers 60 — 70,000 m^2.

Qingdao 青岛市

Qingdao is located on the picturesque coast of the Yellow Sea, Huanghai, in the eastern part of Shandong Province. The city's importance is attributed to its harbor, which remains ice-free throughout the year and is deep enough for large ships. Qingdao has 4.26 million inhabitants and is a young city.

History

The rulers of the Qing Dynasty were the

Map of Qingdao

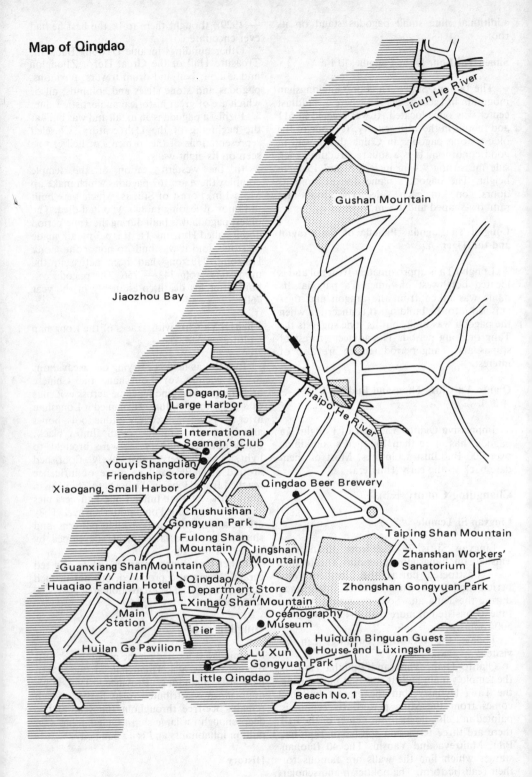

Licun He River

Gushan Mountain

Jiaozhou Bay

Dagang, Large Harbor

International Seamen's Club

Youyi Shangdian Friendship Store

Xiaogang, Small Harbor

Haipo He River

Qingdao Beer Brewery

Chushuishan Gongyuan Park

Fulong Shan Mountain

Jingshan Mountain

Taiping Shan Mountain

Zhanshan Workers' Sanatorium

Guanxiang Shan Mountain

Huaqiao Fandian Hotel

Qingdao Department Store

Xinhao Shan Mountain

Zhongshan Gongyuan Park

Main Station

Pier

Oceanography Museum

Huilan Ge Pavilion

Lu Xun Gongyuan Park

Huiquan Binguan Guest House and Lüxingshe

Little Qingdao

Beach No. 1

first to recognize the city's favorable location. A small naval station was established in Qingdao and fortifications built in conjunction with the build-up of the Beiyang fleet. After the Germans succeeded in obtaining a 99 year-lease on Jiaozhou Bay and the surrounding lands, Qingdao developed much in the style of a European city, and that impression still remains today.

After 1949, Qingdao was able to build up its already existing industry on a large scale. Furthermore, the original economic base, fishing, was modernized and intensified. Today, Qingdao has a large fishing harbor.

Thanks to the city's mild climate and convenient, picturesque location, Qingdao has become a bathing and holiday resort. Thousands of visitors come here each year to enjoy the natural bays, the clear water and the long stretch of beach. Most of the sanatoriums are located in southeast Qingdao, on the beach and bays and in the mountains.

The city has few cultural memorials. Nevertheless, it is worthwhile to visit Qingdao, to stroll through beautiful parks and be captivated by Laoshan mountain and its Daoist temples.

Zhongshan Gongyuan, Sun Yatsen Park 中山公园

Zhongshan Gongyuan is a favorite place for outings because of its beautiful grounds and plant life.

Lu Xun Gongyuan Park 鲁迅公园

This park, named after the writer Lu Xun, lies directly on the sea coast in south Qingdao. It is filled with pine trees, flowers and cliffs. Narrow paths wind through the park along the rocky coast up to the Oceanography Museum.

Haichan Bowuguan, Oceanography Museum 海产博物馆

The Oceanography Museum is divided into two sections. The first deals with details of the historical development of ocean plants and animals. The aquarium makes up the second section.

Xiao Qingdao, Little Qingdao 小青岛

The small island Xiao Qingdao is located off the coast south of the city. A pier connects it to the mainland. A 15.5-m-tall white lighthouse stands on the island's highest point. It has become Qingdao's landmark for sailors.

Qianhai Zhanqiao Pier 前海栈桥

This pier is in the southern section of the city and extends the main street, Zhongshanlu, into Qingdao Wan bay. It was built in 1891 and expanded in 1931. At present, it is 440 m long and 10 m wide. An octagonal pavilion, Huilan Ge, stands at the end of the pier.

Zhanshan Si Temple 湛山寺

This Buddhist temple in the eastern part of the city was built in 1934. It consists of the main halls, Daxiong Baodian, Treasure Hall of the Great Hero, Sansheng Dian, Hall of the Three Saints, Tianwang Dian, Hall of the Celestial Kings, and Cangjing Lou. An octagonal stone pavilion stands in the eastern part of the complex. The temple complex is enclosed on three sides by the mountains Fushan, Zhanshan and Taiping Shan.

Laoshan Mountain 崂山

Laoshan is located east of the city. It is 1,333 m high, and its attraction lies in its tall, bizarre peaks, bamboo trees, springs, deep caves, wonderfully shaped rocks and beautiful waterfalls. Together, they provide a great richness in changing scenery. The mountain slopes steeply towards the east down to Laoshan Wan bay, in the west it slopes down to the plains, and in the south it is bordered by the sea.

Laoshan has many places of interest. A few of these are described in the following paragraphs.

Taiqing Gong Daoist Temple

An excellent view of the sea can be had from Taiqing Temple in southeast Laoshan. The temple was founded by the monk Huagai during the Song era. It was later enlarged. The halls Sanguan Dian, Sanqing Dian and Sanhuang Dian can still be visited.

Huayan Si Temple

The Buddhist temple on the mountain's east side, Huayan Si, was built from 1628 — 1644. During times of war, it later burned down. Afterwards, it was rebuilt, and at the beginning of the Qing period, the temple was restored. A path with stone steps leads from the sea up to the temple's main gate. A nine-story stone pagoda stands outside the gate.

Taiping Gong Temple

This temple was built on the initiative of the Daoist monk Huagai during the Song era.

Hualong Gong Temple

Hualong Gong is located on the north side of Laoshan mountain and dates back to 1325. It was built at the suggestion of the Daoist monk Liu Zhijian. It is made up of the halls Laoyuan Dian, Yuhuang Dian and Guandi Dian.

Laoding (Ju Feng) Peak

With a height of 1,333 m, Laoding is the massif's highest peak. The view from the top is splendid.

Shangqing Gong Temple

Shangqing Gong, on the southeast side of the mountain, northwest of Taiqing Gong temple, was built in the 14th century. Daoists are supposed to have lived there as far back as the Han period.

Longtanpu Waterfall

This waterfall, approximately 1 km north of Shangqing Gong temple, tumbles down the steep stone sides of the Dragon Abyss from a height of 20 m.

Hotels

Badaguan Binguan, Shanhaiguanlu, tel. 2 68 00

Huiquan Binguan, 惠泉宾馆 Nanhailu 9, tel. 2 52 16

Zhanqiao Binguan, 栈桥宾馆 Taipinglu 31, tel. 2 74 02

Huaqiao Fandian, 华侨饭店 Hunanlu 72, tel. 2 77 38

Donglou Hotel of Qingdao Restaurant, Qufulu, tel. 2 67 47

Youyi Binguan, Xinjianglu 12, tel. 2 77 78

Restaurants

Qingdao Fandian, 青岛饭店 Zhongshanlu 53, tel. 2 72 92

Chunhe Lou, 春河楼 Zhongshanlu, 2 73 71

Haibin Fandian, Guangxilu, tel. 2 44 47

Shopping

The main business streets are Zhongshanlu and Xinjianglu. The Friendship Store is located at Xinjianglu 12.

Travel agency

Gouji Lüxingshe, CITS, Nanhailu 9, tel. 2 88 77

Zhongguo Lüxingshe, Longjianglu 34, tel. 2 58 66

Huaqiao Lüxingshe, Longjianglu 34, tel. 2 85 43

Gong'an Ju, Bureau of Public Security, Hubeilu 29, tel. 2 62 31

CAAC ticket agency, Zhongshanlu 29, tel. 2 60 47

Train station, Tai'anlu 2, tel. 2 79 71

Taxi, Huangxianlu 1, tel. 2 74 39

Qingdao Harbor, Dagang, ship passage reservations Xinjianglu 6, tel. 2 50 01

Bank of China, Zhongshanlu 62, tel. 2 61 09

Post office and **telegraph office,** Guangxilu 21, tel. 2 66 78

Yantai 烟台

Yantai, called Chefoo (Zhifu) in former times, is situated in the north of the Jiaodong Peninsula. It is a bustling port and important because of the fishery and the ice-free harbor.

Two hundred years ago this city was still a small fishing village with a signal tower, which stood on Yantai hill. It played an important role as coast guard. The name 'Yantai' means 'Smoking Terrace'. When danger threatened this area, people burned the dung of wolves. Its smoke could be clearly seen from far away.

In 1862 this area was opened for foreign trade. Yantai has now 330,000 inhabitants. There are a· lot of fruit plantations in the surrounding area.

Yantai Museum, Yulanjie 2

Yuhuang Ding, The Mountain of the Jade Emperor

In the southern part of this city is a mountain,

on which stands a Daoist temple from the 13th century. It is dedicated to the Jade Emperor.

Bathing beaches are located in the east suburb of Yantai.

Hotels

Zhifu Binguan, East suburb of Yantai, tel. 69 89

Yantaishan Binguan and **Huaqiao Fandian** near the center and CITS.

CITS Shuntaijie, tel. 56 26, 36 15

Restaurant

Huibinlou, Shenglilu 268, tel. 33 32

Qufu County 曲阜县

Qufu, 15 km east of Yanzhou, is where Confucius (551 — 479 BC) was born and died (Trains stop at Yanzhou. From there, one can travel to Qufu by bus.)

Like no other, Confucius influenced China's culture for over 2,000 years. He was not particularly successful during his lifetime; it was his disciples who first managed to create a Confucian doctrine and build an ideology around him. Confucius spent his last years in Qufu with the companionship of his pupils. For a time, Qufu was the Mecca of China. A year after his death, Duke Ai of Lu ordered the philosopher's home to be turned into a temple.

After the Han Dynasty, the temple was rebuilt repeatedly by imperial order and enlarged many times over. Today, the temple complex covers an area of 22 hectares and is divided along a 1-km north-south axis. Dacheng Dian hall is the center point of the complex. The empire provided Confucius's descendants with living quarters which came to include 463 buildings.

Qufu is a city that lives from the Confucian legacy and ideology. Since the temple buildings and grounds were restored a few years ago, it is possible to imagine the complex's former splendor and selectivity, and one has an idea of the important position that the Confucian ideology held in imperial China.

In addition to the places worth visiting for their connection to Confucius (Temple of Confucius, the Residence of Confucius' Descendants and Confucius' Forest), there are also other attractions in Qufu's surrounding areas: the Temple of the Duke of Zhou (11th century BC), brother of King Wu, founder of the Zhou Dynasty; the ruins of the Halo Palace, which was once the center of the capital of Lu; and the Tomb of Shao Hao, one of the five legendary emperors. The city's many stone gates are also interesting. It should be kept in mind that these sights generally close around 4:00 p.m.

Kongmiao Temple 孔庙

The temple's main gate, Lingxing Men, was built in 1754. It leads to the first courtyard and its ornamental gate dating from the Ming era. Shengshi Men, the second entrance gate, also constructed during the Ming era, is located on the middle axis towards the north. Three arched passageways lead to the second courtyard. A small brook, Yudai He, crosses the yard from east to west, with three bridges leading from one side to the other. Two stone statues, former tomb figures, stand in front of the bridges to the left. They are more than 2 m high, were made during the Han period and placed here in 1953. After the third gate, Hongdao Men, yet another gate follows, Dazhong Men. Up to the Song period, the latter was the temple's main entrance. Two towers dating back to 1331, rise to the east and west of the gate.

The fifth gate is Tongwen Men. Architecturally, it differs from the other gates as it stands in the middle of a courtyard and does not make up part of a wall. Many inscribed steles are located in the courtyard. A number of the steles are supported by so-called Bixi animals (Bixi is the Dragon King's son). To the left and the right of the yard, there are two small separate courtyards in which preparations for sacrificial ceremonies were made. The small eastern one was supposedly used by the Kangxi and Qianlong Emperors. Kuiwen Ge pavilion, behind the Tongwen Men gate, is about 23 m tall. It was built in 1018 and partially restored in 1191 and 1500. The pavilion survived the earthquake of 1504. It is an excellent example of traditional Chinese timber frame architecture. Original calligraphies as well as the sacrificial documents of various emperors used to be kept here. Unfortunately, a large number of these are missing.

In the next courtyard are the Thirteen Pavilions of the Imperial Steles, Shisan Yubei Ting. These pavilions date from the Jin (1115 — 1234), Yuan (1271 — 1368) and Qing (1644 — 1911) eras. They were supposed to protect the 53 stone steles of emperors from various dynasties. All of the steles bear inscriptions in the calligraphy of the emperor of the time. The oldest stele is from 668, the largest from 1668, which exhibits a calligraphy by the Kangxi Emperor. Another stele bears an inscription from 1307, created by Emperor Chengzong of the Yuan Dynasty. It is written in Mongolian and also contains a Chinese translation.

Dacheng Men, the seventh gate, was constructed in the Ming period. It used to be opened only on great ceremonious occasions, and at all other times, the two small side entrances were used. Xingtan, Ginkgo Pavilion, is located in the next courtyard. It is said that Confucius instructed his pupils here in the shade of the gingko trees, thus the pavilion's name. Before the Song period, the temple's main hall stood here. In 1024, it was torn down and rebuilt farther north. A terrace was built in its place and ginkgo trees planted. The trees have not survived. During the Ming Dynasty, the terrace was restored, and a rectangular pavilion was erected on it. The pavilion has two roofs made of yellow-glazed ceramic tiles. Yellow, which appeared gold in the sunlight, was the color reserved for the emperor. Thus, by the color alone, it can be seen in what high honor Confucius was held. The ceiling inside the pavilion is decorated with splendid colors. Two stone steles are stored here, one of which bears a calligraphy by the Qianlong Emperor who visited this temple eight times. Dacheng Dian hall is the center of the complex. Sacrifices to Confucius were made here. The hall was constructed in the 11th century and restored in 1499 and 1724. It stands on a terrace more than 2 m tall and covers an area of 1,836 m². The roof is made of yellow-glazed tiles and is supported by stone columns which originated in 1500. Dragons are carved in the columns, and those in bas-relief on the front 10 columns are especially graphic. Inside the hall, the objects, musical instruments, etc. needed for the sacrifices are on display. In the adjoining east and west rooms, there are reliefs and stone steles.

Qindian hall follows Dacheng Dian. It is one of the largest halls in the complex. It was built in 1018; renovations took place in 1500 and 1730. Here, sacrifices were made to Confucius' wife.

Shengji Dian hall is the last hall on the middle axis. It dates from 1592. Inside, there are 120 scenes carved in stone depicting Confucius' life. Unfortunately, some of these are severely damaged.

The place where Confucius is said to have spent his childhood is located in the complex's eastern section. An ancient well stands at this spot, surrounded by an ornamental balustrade. Ostensibly, it used to be the Kong's family well. Next to it there is a small temple

called Wudai Si, Temple of Five Generations. Sacrifices to Confucius' ancestors were made here. Shili Tang, Hall of Poetry and Rites, stands in front of the well. It was built as a rememberance of two Confucian sayings, 'Without learning the Classic of Songs, it is impossible to express oneself,' and, 'Without studying the rites, it is impossible to strengthen one's character.'

Lubi wall is in back of the well. When Emperor Qin Shihuang had books burned, Confucius' descendant of the ninth generation, Kong Fu, is supposed to have hidden the Confucian works *Lunyu, Xiaojin* and *Shujing* in a wall. During the Han Dynasty, under the rule of Emperor Jingdi (156 — 141 BC), the Prince of Lu ordered the enlargement of Confucius' family house. When one of the walls was torn down, the books which had been hidden inside were discovered. Lubi wall was erected in honor of this event.

Jinsi Tang hall, in the temple's western courtyard, was built during the Jin period (1127 — 1279). Old musical instruments are kept here. Music was an important element of Confucian ceremonies. Another hall, Qisheng Dian, is in back of Jinsi Tang. It was erected during the Yuan Dynasty (1271 — 1368) in honor of Confucius' parents.

Kongfu, Residence of the Kong Family 孔府

The rulers of the Han Dynasty soon recognized the advantages of Confucian teachings. They provided a good base for state order and helped to secure the rule of the imperial family.

The veneration of Confucius and his family followed the revaluation of Confucian ideology. By the Han Dynasty, Confucius' descendants were raised to the nobility. Further titles were bestowed in later dynasties. Under Song rule, male descendants of the main line received the title Yanshenggong, Sacred Duke of Yan, which they kept up to the end. They were ranked directly below the imperial house and managed the temple and its properties. At times, the family had more than 64,000 hectares of land in five different provinces at its disposal. Furthermore, the family was supposed to oversee the temple rites and ceremonies and manage the archives. The power of the Kong family reached its high point during the Ming Dynasty. The first emperor of the Ming Dynasty had a residence built for Confucius' descendants near Kongmiao. Previously, they had lived outside of the area of present-day Qufu. The new residence was restored and enlarged time and time again. It includes 463 rooms and nine courtyards and coveres approximately 16 hectares. The compound is divided into an eastern, a western and a central area. The family temple and a hall which was used to receive important officials and delegates from the emperor are located in the eastern section. The western section was used primarily as a place for learning. The central section is the main area, and it is divided into an outer part and an inner, private one. The private garden is located behind this area. Visiting this residence, in which Confucius' direct descendants lived up to 1937, provides excellent insight into the traditional Chinese style of living, which, as it was maintained into the thirties, included certain Western articles such as clocks and sofas.

One of the greatest treasures at Kongfu is the Kong family archives, which contain records from 1534—1948. They are subdivided into such categories as the Kong family history, relatives, records of acquired degrees and titles, descriptions of the temple and residence along with inventory lists, property management records, lists pertaining to leases, official positions, finances, legal procedings, sacrificial ceremonies, etc. The archives give precise information about the life of an elite family within the traditional social structure, and as such, they are unique in all of China.

The main gate, Damen, was built in the Ming period and leads to the residence's central section. It bears the inscription Sheng Fu, Sacred Residence. Chongguang Men gate is located in front of Datang, Great Hall. It dates back to 1503. The gate was opened with a 13-gun salute only for important ceremonious occasions, a visit from the emperor or other significant events. Various administrative offices were housed in the wings.

The next hall, Datang, was used for ceremonial engagements and the receiving of high officials. The chair covered with leopard skin on which Confucius supposedly sat, is located in the middle section of the hall along with a red table with a large seal, a pennant and other requisites of a high official position. Two secretariats are located east and west of the hall. Ertang hall follows immediately to the north. The Sacred Dukes of Yan carried out their office here. They gave orders, taught ceremonial procedures, read the sacred books and imposed penalties. Santang hall stands behind Ertang. A calligraphy by the Qianlong Emperor is kept in the hall's central section. This hall was used to receive the highest dignitaries or for private gatherings. Family matters were discussed here and rules and instructions for the family were decided upon. The hall's eastern section was the general reception room, the western section was a secretariat. Letters to the emperor were written here.

Neizhai Men gate comes after Santang hall. It leads to the inner chambers (the women's chambers), where the entrance of strangers was prohibited under threat of severe punishment. The guards' and servants' quarters were located on either side of the gate. In the wall, there is a stone basin. It was the servants' job to fill it up with fresh water every morning. The water flowed from the basin to the compound's interior, where it could then be drawn by the female servants in the inner chambers.

After passing through Neizhai Men, one is then in the first courtyard. The luxuriously decorated main hall, Qianshangfang, is located there. Originally, it was a reception hall for close relatives, but banquets and ceremonies in connection with weddings and funerals also took place there. It is said that such banquets included 196 courses. The archives' household records note that on August 24, 1852, the birthday of the wife of the Sacred Duke of Yan was celebrated with a feast that lasted for six days.

The next sight to follow is Tanglou, a hall complex. The grounds can be divided into a front and a back complex. Two-story halls are located in the east and west sections. The rear east hall used to house the servants' quarters. All of the other rooms were living quarters and bedrooms for members of the Kong family.

Houwu Jian, Five Rooms Hall, used to be a study for the direct descendants of Confucius and is now a very interesting museum which houses a gilded Thousand Buddha pagoda.

Tieshan Yuan garden adjoins the compound in the north. The man-made mountains were created from accumulations of iron-ore and led to the garden's name, Tieshan Yuan, Iron Mountains Garden. Kongfu's western section, Xixueyuan, was intended for the purpose of learning. Scholars met there to converse. The main halls from south to north are Hong'e Xuan, Zhongshu Tang and Anhuai Tang. These three halls were put at the disposal of the Sacred Duke of Yan for study and composition. Guests were received in the so-called north and south flower halls. A secretariat was located in the south flower hall. Today, there is a hotel in this section of the residence.

Mu'en Tang is one of the most important halls in Kongfu's eastern section. The hall was used for sacrifices to Kong Xianpei, a descendant of Confucius from the 72nd generation, and his wife, Yu Shi. Yu Shi was the daughter of the Qianlong Emperor. He wanted his daughter to marry one of Confucius' descendants, but the law prohibited marriages between Manchus and Han Chinese. So, the emperor devised a strategy and allowed his daughter to be adopted by the official Yu Minzhong, who was a Han Chinese. There was no longer anything standing in the way of a marriage with Kong Xianpei. To show their gratitude to the emperor, this hall was built by later descendants.

Konglin Forest 孔林

Most of Confucius' descendants and perhaps Confucius himself were buried in Konglin, Confucius Forest, also known as Shenglin, Sacred Forest. The forest is 1.5 km north of Qufu, and it is still the place of burial for local members of the Kong family. The best way to see it is to hire a bicycle-taxi so that one may get a better impression of the whole area.

The ornamental gate Wangu Changchun Fang is also called Wumen Paifang, Gate with Five Entrances. It is located on the route to Konglin and dates from 1594.

Zhishenglin Fang gate, also called Dalin Men, is the front entrance to Konglin forest. It was built during the Kangxi period of reign (1662 — 1722).

Kongzi Mu tomb, Confucius' tomb 孔子墓

It lies in the northwest section among the graves dating from the Eastern Zhou period. There are two steles in front of the grave, the larger one dates from the Qing period and the smaller from the Song period. It is not certain if Confucius is actually buried here. The tomb of Confucius' son, Kong Li, is located east of this grave site, and the tomb of his grandson, Kong Ji, is to the south. Three pavilions to the southeast were erected in honor of the emperors from the Zhenzong period (998 — 1022, Yuan Dynasty), and the Kangxi and Qianlong periods (Qing Dynasty). They serve as reminders of the imperial visits to this spot.

Kaiting pavilion stands further to the south, next to a withered tree. The tree was supposedly planted by Zi Gong, one of Confucius' pupils. After the great sage's death, Confucius' students gathered here, lived in huts and mourned for three years. Zi Gong remained here an additional three years.

In 1523, a high official had the pavilion built in his honor.

Yanmiao Temple 颜庙

Yanmiao temple, with its quiet, contemplative atmosphere, is located on Louxiangjie street in the northwestern section of Qufu. It was built in honor of Confucius' favorite pupil, Yan Hui. Yan Hui had modest origins, but his aptitude and his thirst for knowledge were extraordinary. It was a tragic blow for Confucius when Yan Hui died at the age of 32.

Allegedly, the Han emperor Gaozu (period of reign 206 — 194 BC) came to Qufu to make a sacrifice to Confucius and then donated the temple. The complex was renovated and enlarged during the Ming and Qing dynasties. Numerous halls, pavilions, gates and stone steles are within the temple complex. The main hall, Fusheng Dian, is located behind Yangsheng Men gate. It is 16 m high, and its roof is made of green ceramic tiles. The four front stone columns are embellished with chiseled dragons.

Luguo Gucheng, the Ancient Capital of the State of Lu 鲁国古城

Luguo Gucheng is located northwest of the present district capital, Qufu. At the beginning of the Western Zhou era, King Wu of Zhou leased the area of Lu to his brother, the Duke of Zhou. The duke, however, remained at the imperial court and sent his son, Bo Qin, to manage the region in his stead. Consequently, Qufu became the capital of the newly established State of Lu. Many generations followed the Duke of Zhou and resided in this city up to 249 BC.

Ancient Qufu was laid out in the form of a rectangle measuring 3.5 x 2.5 km and had 11 city gates. Seven streets ran from east to west and six from north to south. The widest street was 15 m, the others were about 10 m broad. Palace grounds were located north of the city's center, and workshops and a residential area were located in the vicinity of the grounds. In the city's western section, archeologists uncovered tombs and valuable funerary objects.

Hotel

There is a charming guesthouse at the Residence of the Kong Family.

Travel agency

Zhongguo Lüxingshe, Donghuamen Dajie 1, tel. 3 74

A service desk is in the guesthouse at Kongfu residence.

Antique sales and the **Bank of China** at Kongfu, Residence of the Kong Family.

Zibo 淄博市

The area around Zibo, on the train route from Jinan to Qingdao, offers only three particularly interesting sights: the double tomb of the Dukes of Qi, Minister Guan Zhong's grave and the family house of the poet Pu Songling.

Erwang Zhong Tomb 二王冢

The 'Tomb of Two Kings' is on Ding-zushan mountain in Zhenjiagou district. Duke Huan of Qi, who governed from 685 — 643 BC, is supposedly buried here. Under his rule, the city of Qi became increasingly more influential. Jinggong (547 — 490 BC), who was also Duke of Qi and Duke Huan's successor, is buried next to the grave of Duke Huan. The earth covering the two graves is of different shades. This presumably reflects the fact that dukes throughout the country used to bring soil from their homeland with them to be used later for burial purpose. There are many old graves in the area. Several can be seen even from the train.

Guan Zhong's Tomb 管仲墓

Guan Zhong's tomb is located at the northern foot of Niushan mountain in the city of Lingzi. Guan Zhong (died in 645 BC) was a high ranking public official and one of the most important political figures of the Chunqiu period. He was also the founder of the state doctrine of Legalism, which he practiced in the State of Qi. The entire land was divided into administrative areas, and the inhabitants were assigned to individual units. The best and the most capable ones were chosen with the help of tests and certain selection procedures and placed in the Duke's service. Everyone was subject to the laws that he created. Under his new tax system, taxes were determined by the nature and the quality of the land. Due to Guan Zhong's wise policies, Qi became the strongest and most important state of that era.

The Family House of the Poet Pu Songling
浦松龄故居

The house stands in Pujia Zhuang village in Zichuan district. Pu Songling (1640 — 1715) wrote a famous collection of short stories, *Liaozhai Zhiyi,* and as a consequence, he is also known by the name 'Sage Liaozhai'. This house, where Pu Songling lived until he died, can be visited today. The main building to the north is where the poet was born and consists of three rooms. Later, Pu Songling moved his study rooms here. There is a portrait of the poet at 74. Some of the articles that he used still exist. Not long ago, a display room was built west of the courtyard which exhibits the poet's original works as well as their translations.

Travel agency

Guoji Lüxingshe, CITS, Zhangdian Qu, Zhongxinlu, tel. 2 21 38

Taishan Mountain 泰山

Taishan is one of the five most famous mountains in China. (The other four are Huashan in Shaanxi, Hengshan in Hunan, Songshan in Henan and Hengshan in Shanxi.)

Taishan rises up in the middle of Shandong's mountainous region, bordered by Tai'an, Licheng and Changqing districts, and can be reached by train or bus from Jinan.

The main peak is north of the district capital Tai'an. It is 1,545 m high and is considered to be a symbol of sublimity and dignity. Taishan has been worshipped as a sacred mountain since ancient times. Numerous temples, halls and pavilions, stone steles and inscriptions were created. Kings came here as far back as the 1st century BC to make sacrifices to the mountain. The most expensive and lavish ceremonies were Fengshan, sacrifices which paid homage to the earth and the heavens. Later, emperors often came to Taishan at the height of their power to thank the heavens and the earth for their benevolence. The sacrificial ceremony to the earth took place in Daimiao temple at the foot of the mountain; sacrifices to the heavens took place at the top of Taishan. The last sacrificial ceremony of this type was held in 1008, but due to the magnificence and extravagence of this tradition, it has never been forgotten.

Today, there is still much in good condition that can be visited. The best months to go to Taishan are May and October. It is advisable to wear sturdy shoes. The path leading from the foot of the mountain to its peak is almost 9 km long.

Those who don't want to walk can take a minibus from Tai'an train station to Zhongtian

Tourist Attractions on Taishan

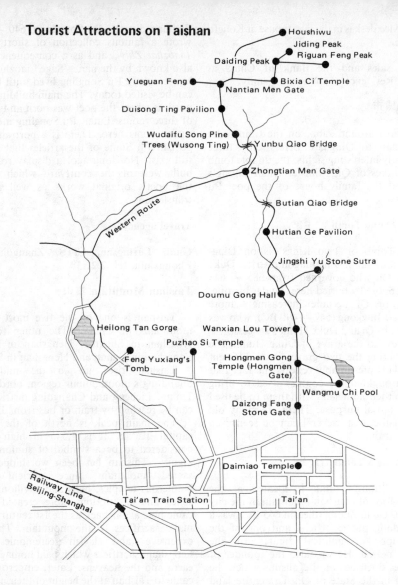

Houshiwu

Jiding Peak

Riguan Feng Peak

Daiding Peak

Bixia Ci Temple

Yueguan Feng

Nantian Men Gate

Duisong Ting Pavilion

Wudaifu Song Pine Trees (Wusong Ting)

Yunbu Qiao Bridge

Zhongtian Men Gate

Western Route

Butian Qiao Bridge

Hutian Ge Pavilion

Jingshi Yu Stone Sutra

Doumu Gong Hall

Heilong Tan Gorge

Wanxian Lou Tower

Puzhao Si Temple

Feng Yuxiang's Tomb

Hongmen Gong Temple (Hongmen Gate)

Wangmu Chi Pool

Daizong Fang Stone Gate

Daimiao Temple

Railway Line Beijing-Shanghai

Tai'an Train Station

Tai'an

Men. (departure every morning at 7:30, 8:30 and 9:30). From Zhongtian Men there is a cable car system running to the top of Yueguan Feng.

Daimiao Temple 岱庙

The Daoist Daimiao is located at the southern foot of Taishan mountain in the district capital Tai'an and is the starting point for the ascent up Taishan. When the temple was built is unknown, but it was enlarged as far back as the Qin and Han periods. Large-scale building and expansion followed during the Tang and Song eras. Records from the year 1122 indicate that at that time, the temple complex consisted of several hundred halls, pavilions and towers.

Today, only a few buildings remain.

The temple's focus is the main hall, Tiankuang Dian, which was built in 1009 and restored in 1956. Tiankuang Dian is an excellent example of traditional Chinese architecture. It stands on a terrace and is surrounded by a white stone balustrade. The red columns and the red doors with their ornamental carvings stand out against the magnificently decorated bracket system. The double roof with its yellow-glazed tiles indicates that this is a holy site. A splendid mural inside the hall is sure to astonish visitors. It depicts a procession of the god of Taishan. He was responsible for guarding and maintaining control over the mountain. The style of the painting suggests that it probably was created during the Song era.

There are a total of 157 stone steles, Daimiao Beike, from various dynasties within the temple complex. The oldest is from 209 BC. It is engraved with a calligraphy by Chancellor Li Si containing 222 characters. One hundred and forty-six of the characters are still recognizable today. This stele is one of the oldest in China.

The building Dongyu Zuo is located east of Peitian Men gate and served as an intermediate stop for the emperor when he traveled. Numerous sacrificial objects are on display in the main complex. Three of these are of particular value: a lion made from aloeswood (Aquilaria malaccensis), a jade scepter and a porcelain hulu (a gourd). They are called the temple's three treasures.

Hanbai Yuan, a pine yard from the Han period, is in the temple's southeast section. Five ancient pine trees stand here.

Tongting, Bronze Pavilion, stands in the eastern part of the rear courtyard. It was built in 1615 and originally stood on Taishan's peak. It was brought down from the summit during the Qing era and finally re-erected in this complex in 1972.

Tieta, Iron Pagoda, is located next to the Bronze Pavilion. It was made of iron, tier by tier, in 1533. The pagoda is hexagonal, and at one time, it had 13 stories. Today, only three of these still remain.

The eastern route is generally preferable for the ascent up the mountain as there are more sights than along the western route. The first object of interest is the gray, stone gate, Daizong Fang. It is located north of Daimiao temple and was constructed from 1567 — 1572. The three roofs are quite striking. Wangmu Chi, Celestial Queen Pool, is located in a courtyard farther north of Daizong Fang gate.

Beyond the pool, steps lead up to Wangmu Dian, Hall of the Celestial Queen. Sacrifices to the celestial queen were made here. During the summer, this spot is a welcome and cool place to rest. A reservoir, Hushan Shuiku, can be seen north of the courtyard.

The incline begins here. Going northwest from Wangmu Chi pool, one reaches Hongmen Gong temple. It is not known when the temple was built, but it was restored in 1626.

The next stop is the building Wanxian Lou. It was built in 1620 and restored in 1954. A sacrificial hall for the celestial queen used to be located here. Today, stone engravings from the Ming era can still be seen.

The former Daoist convent, Doumu Gong, is to the north of Wanxian Lou.

Jingshi Yu, Valley of the Stone Sutra, stretches out to the northeast. It leads to a huge rock in which the text of the Diamond Sutra, Jingang Jing, is carved. The work consists of 1043 characters. It is estimated that the inscription was made around 550. Not far away, there is a small pavilion that affords a beautiful view. Northward along this route, Hutian Ge pavilion is the next place of interest. It was erected during the Ming era. Yuanjun Dian hall is located to the north, and Yishan Ting pavilion to the west. From this pavilion, one can look down upon a forest of conifers.

From this point on, the climb to the top becomes more and more arduous. Zhongtian Men gate is located half-way up the mountain and is the intersection between the eastern and western routes. It is possible to spend the night in a guest house here. Nantian Men, Southern Celestial Gate, can already be seen from here. Several thousand steps connect the two gates.

North of Zhongtian Men gate, there is an impressive stone bridge, Yunbu Qiao, Bridge Over the Clouds. It leads across a deep gorge through which clouds often float. A waterfall, Yunqiaofei Pu, can be seen to the north.

One soon reaches three pine trees, Wudaifu Song, which were planted in 1730. They are named after the tree which was given the title Wudaifu by Emperor Qin Shihuang (period of reign 221 — 210 BC) because it had provided him with shelter during a storm.

Duisong Ting pavilion is the next stop to the north. From here, one can see two pine-covered mountains facing each other. Shiba Pan, Stairway of Eighteen Bends, demands an all-out effort. It has more than a thousand steps.

After a short time, one stands before Shengxian Fang gate. The following steps are steeper and lead directly up to Nantian Men gate. A glance into the depths below leads easily to the impression that the world of mortals has been left behind. After conquering the many steps, one finally reaches Nantian Men gate which is at the ascent's end. Peaks rise up on either side of the gate, Feilong Yan and Xiangfeng Ling. The gate was built in 1264. On the other side of the gate, there is a hall from a more recent date (1956).

The temple Bixia Ci stands slightly to the east of Nantian Men. It was constructed from 1008 — 1016. The temple's roof is covered with bronze and iron tiles to make it invulnerable to storms. The roof of the main hall is ornamented with bells and animal figures which are supposed to provide protection. A bronze figure representing the goddess of Taishan, Bixiayuanjun, is located inside the hall. In the eastern and western adjoining halls, there are additional bronze statues depicting gods.

On top of Daiding peak, there is a 13-m-high and 5-m-wide cliff in which numerous characters have been carved. On the right-hand part there is an inscription with 996 characters from the year 726, which was composed by the Tang emperor Xuanzong. A guest-house is located here. Riguan Feng, Sunrise Peak, rises southeast of Jiding. It is an ideal location to watch the sun rise. The sunrises which can be seen from Taishan are famous throughout China.

At 1545 m, Jiding, also called Yuhuang Ding, is the mountain's highest peak. Yuhuang Dian temple stands on the summit and includes a sacrificial hall for the celestial emperor. Wanghe Ting pavilion is located to the west, and it is from there that the sunset can best be observed.

Houshiwu, the mountain's rear section, is about 2 km from Beitian Men gate. Those with energy to spare should seek it out without hesitation. Just to visit Zhangren Feng peak, Daxian Dong cave and Yunüshan mountain makes the excursion worthwhile. The wonderful rock formations and the old pine and cypress trees are especially beautiful.

Heilong Tan, Black Dragon Gorge, is located along the mountain's western route. Here one can see a waterfall tumbling over the cliffs into the gorge below. A 23-m-long bridge leads over the waterfall.

Feng Yuxiang's Tomb 冯玉祥墓

Feng Yuxiang (1882 — 1948) was originally from Anhui Province. He was a warlord who entered the Sino-Japanese War with his troops after Manchuria was occupied in 1931. Later, he was elected chairman of the Revolutionary Committee of the Kuomintang National Party.

Hotel

Taishan Fandian, Daizongfang, Tai'an, 31 15

Zhongtianmen Binguan, half-way up the mountain

Daiding Binguan, on top of Taishan

Travel agency

Zhongguo Lüxingshe, Hongmenlu, tel. 32 59, Tai'an, in Taishan Hotel

Henan Province 河南省

Area: 167,000 km² / Population: 74.4 million / Capital: Zhengzhou

The North China province of Henan is located on the lower course of the Huanghe and is surrounded by Anhui, Hubei, Shaanxi, Shanxi, Hebei and Shandong. The name of the province means 'south of the Huanghe'.

History

Henan's history can be traced back to prehistoric times. Neolithic relics were uncovered in Yangshao Cun village. Painted ceramics were included among the finds. The Yangshao culture was named after the place of discovery. The people were farmers who lived at the confluence of the Huanghe, Weihe and Fenhe rivers. This area is considered to be the cradle of Chinese civilization. The Shang Dynasty reached its greatest prosperity in the northern and western regions of the province. Highly informative excavations were carried out in the vicinity of Anyang and Zhengzhou. It is believed that the Shang capital had been located near Anyang since 1384 BC. Luoyang was the capital of the Zhou beginning in the 8th century BC. During the Zhou period, the region was called Yuzhou, and *Yu* is still the classical name for Henan today. Not until the Sui era was the name changed to Henan for the first time. Up into the 10th century AD, the capital alternated time and time again between Chang'an (present-day Xi'an) and Luoyang. Kaifeng was the capital during the period of the Five Dynasties and the Northern Song Dynasty.

Henan can be divided into two topographical areas. The first area consists of the loess covered hill lands in the west, and the second area makes up part of the North China Plain in the east. Mountains tower above the hills along the northwestern and southern borders with peaks extending up to 2,400 m. The Nanyang Basin is located in southwest Henan, encircled by the Funiu Shan and Dabie Shan mountains. The province has three river systems: the Huanghe, which flows from west to east through the northern part of the province, the Huaihe in the southeast and the Tanghe and the Taohe in the southwest.

Each year the Huanghe carries away approximately 1.6 billion metric tons of sediment from the loess plateau of Shaanxi and Shanxi. As soon as the river reaches the plains, the sediment settles and leads to flooding. Extensive dike construction projects have been carried out in the region from time immemorial. Meanwhile, the river bed has become higher than the surrounding land, and the dikes must be raised constantly. Breaches in the dikes lead to catastrophic floods; the water flows over the farm lands, and when the flood-level recedes, it can no longer make its way back to the high river bed. In 1938, the national government ordered the destruction of the dikes near Zhengzhou in an attempt to stop the Japanese army from advancing. Since the population had not been forewarned, more than a million people lost their lives in the resulting floods.

In 1960, the huge Sanmenxia reservoir was constructed. When the Huanghe is high, the reservoir brings it under control as it enters the province. The Huaihe and some of its most important tributaries originate in the mountains in the western part of Henan and flow towards Anhui.

Henan has hot, damp summers and cold winters. However, the winters are not as cold as in the rest of North China; the mountain chains in the west provide considerable protection. In January, the average temperature is -2°C in the north and -2°C in the south. In July, the average temperature on the plains is 28°C, and it is correspondingly colder in the mountains. About 50% of the annual precipitation (approximately 600 — 700 mm) falls during July and August.

The amount of precipitation within the province decreases from southeast to northwest, whereas the variability increases in the same direction. During the dry winter and spring months, irrigation is extremely important. 60 — 70% of the cultivated farm lands lie in the plains region in the eastern part of the province. The most important crop is wheat; Henan is China's largest wheat producer. In the summer, the land is used for the cultivation of gaoliang (sorghum) and soy beans. Thanks to constant improvements in the irrigation system, rice cultivation is also on the increase. Rice is planted in the Huaihe and the Huanghe regions and in the Nanyang Basin. Cotton and tobacco are cultivated as commercial crops. In addition, Henan is an important producer of sesame, walnuts and tea. These products are exported in large quantities. Henan also has a long tradition in silk production which reaches back to the Han Dynasty.

Luoyang, Zhengzhou, Anyang, Kaifeng and Xinxiang are the leading industrial cities in Henan. Anyang is the center of heavy industry. China's first tractor factory was built in Luoyang in 1955. Zhengzhou is located in the cotton growing region and has become the center of the textile industry. Kaifeng is a center of trade and crafts.

In the province's northern section, there are significant deposits of coal at the foot of Taihang Shan.

With Zhengzhou as its capital, Henan is a junction of China's most important transportation routes. The railway lines from the north-south route, Beijing — Wuhan — Guangzhou, and the east-west route, Lianyungang — Lanzhou and then to Qinghai and Xinjiang, meet here.

Besides Zhengzhou, the ancient imperial city Kaifeng is regarded as one of Henan's centers of culture and education.

Zhengzhou 郑州市

Zhengzhou is a modern industrial city that has been the capital since 1954. It is located south of the Huanghe. It's population numbers 1.58 million, and as mentioned above, the city is a junction of the main transportation routes from Beijing to Guangzhou and Lianyungang to Xinjiang.

History

Zhengzhou is one of the oldest cities in China. Relics from the Shang Dynasty prove that the city had been a significant cultural center in ancient times and can look back on a history of more than 3,500 years. Between 1956 and 1973, archaeologists succeeded in partially uncovering the city wall from the Shang period. The wall has a total length of 7,195 m, and even today it reaches a height of 9 m and is 36 m wide at the base. In 1974, two *fangding*, rectangular bronze kettles with four legs, were discovered in the immediate area. They are among the most important finds from the Zhengzhou period (16th — 14th century BC).

In 605, during the Sui Dynasty, the city was named Zhengzhou for the first time. At the beginning of the 20th century, its importance increased significantly once again. In 1903, the Beijing — Hankou railway line reached Zhengzhou and was later extended to Guangzhou. Zhengzhou was connected to Luoyang and Kaifeng in 1909. That was the beginning of the famous Longhai line, which today goes from Lianyungang in the east to Xinjiang in the west. Thus, the city became one of the most important railway junctions in the empire, and as a result, also a center of trade and administration. In 1923, Zhengzhou was the focal point for the Beijing — Hankou

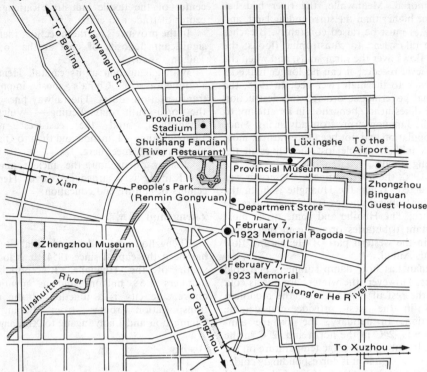

railway workers' strike which went down in history as the 'February 7th Strike'.

Since 1949, Zhengzhou has developed into a modern industrial city; it became the center of Henan's textile industry. Furthermore, there are also metal working, chemical and food processing plants and tobacco and cigarette factories, as well as machine manufacturing.

Erqi Jinianta Memorial Pagoda 二七纪念塔

Erqi Jinianta is located in the center of the city on Erqi Guangchang square. It was built in commemoration of the February 7th Strike of 1923. On February 1, 1923, the railway workers from the Beijing — Hankou line formed their own union, which the warlord Wu Peifu attempted to prevent by force. The union called for a general strike on February 4th. On February 7th, Wu Peifu put a savage end to the strike. The most serious conflicts were concentrated in Zhengzhou, Jiang'an in Hubei and Changxindian in Beijing. The leaders of the strike, Lin Xiangqian and Shi Yang, were executed. Likewise, the local leaders from Zhengzhou, Wang Shengyou and Si Wende, were not spared from this fate; they were executed at the spot where Erqi

Guangchang square is now located. Today, this memorial pagoda stands there. It was built in 1971, is 63 m high and consists of two star-shaped pagodas built next to each other. For this reason, it is also called Double Pagoda.

Henansheng Lishi Bowuguan, Henan Provincial Museum of History
河南省历史博物馆

Those who wish to acquire information about Henan's cultural and historical development should not pass up the chance to visit the provincial museum. The oldest items date back to neolithic times and come from the Yangshao and Longshan cultures. The exhibitions are divided into two sections: Ancient History and History of the Revolution, beginning with the railway workers' strike of 1923.

Renmin Gongyuan, People's Park 人民公园

The People's Park is located in the middle of the city between the old and new sections and is a favorite destination for young and old alike. The city's turmoil is forgotten among the evergreen trees, impressive pavilions, bridges and walkways. The Jinshui He river flows through the park grounds and is an open invitation to boating parties.

Dahuting Hanmu, Han Tombs of Dahuting
密县打虎亭汉墓

Two Han period tombs are located southwest of Zhengzhou in Dahuting Village, Mixian district. A bus travels there daily from Zhengzhou.

The two tombs are only 30 m apart. The first tomb is decorated with stone engravings, and according to ancient texts, it is the last resting place of Prefect Zhang Boya from the Eastern Han Dynasty. The second tomb is ornamented with murals, and a relative of the prefect is supposedly buried here. Both tombs are still in relatively good condition. Zhang Boya's tomb is divided into three main chambers and various adjoining chambers. The coffin stands in the back chamber. Engravings on the walls and doors cover a total area of approximately 200 m ^{2}. They portray scenes from the life of the deceased. The tomb of Zhang Boya's relative is somewhat smaller. The colorful murals take up an area of about 100 m^2. Here too, scenes from the life of the deceased are portrayed.

Hotel

Zhongzhou Binguan, 中州宾馆 Jinshuihelu, tel. 49 38

Zhongyuan Dasha, 中原大厦 opposite the train station

Guoji Fandian, Jinshuihelu, tel. 2 34 13

Travel agency

Guoji Lüxingshe, CITS, Jinshuihelu 8, tel. 55 78

Zhongguo Lüxingshe, Jinshuihelu 8, tel. 27 01

CAAC, Bei'erqilu, tel. 2 43 39

Shopping

Friendship Store, Bei'erqilu

Arts and Crafts Store, Jiefangxilu 21

Kaifeng 开封市

Kaifeng, one of the six old capitals in China, is in eastern Henan, a few kilometers south of the Huanghe river.

Population: 600,000

History

During the Warring States period, Kaifeng was the capital of the State of Wei. It was destroyed by Qin troops in the 3rd century BC. As a market place, Kaifeng was significant only at the local level up until the 5th century. After the Sui Dynasty, the city's importance increased enormously. The construction of the Grand Canal made it possible to conduct trade with important parts of the country. During the Five Dynasties, Kaifeng was successively the capital of the late Jing, Han and Zhou. Kaifeng was also the capital of the Northern Song Dynasty. At that time, the city was a metropolis with around one million inhabitants and the most important Far East trade center. The building of the canal system led to further economic wealth. The city underwent a time of great prosperity. The city was divided into an outer city surrounded by a 25 km long wall, an inner city and a palatial city within the inner city. The famous picture *Qing ming shanghe tu* from the Northern Song era portrays the bustling life in the streets, on the canals and at the markets of Kaifeng. Today, it is on display at the Palace Museum in Beijing. With all likelihood, Jewish teachings made their way to Kaifeng in the 12th century. For centuries, the city had a Jewish community whose history was exemplarily recorded down through the years.

When the Northern Song Dynasty fell, Kaifeng also suffered destruction and gradually lost its significance. It remained an important center of regional government, but it never managed to regain the important position that it had held during the Northern Song period. In 1644, a disastrous flood in Kaifeng claimed more than 300,000 lives. Ming loyalists had opened the dikes of the Huanghe as resistance against the advancing Manchurian troops. Even in times of peace, the danger of flooding was always present. Consistent dike maintenance was therefore extremely important in deciding the city's fate. Until 1954, Kaifeng was the capital of Henan Province. Today, as previously, it is a center of trade and crafts. Industries are also located here, including manufacturing concerns for agricultural machinery and fertilizer factories. Kaifeng's silk and embrodiery handwork is also well-known.

Xiangguo Si Temple 相国寺

Xiangguo Si, located in the southern part of

the city's older section, is one of the most famous temples in China. During the period of Warring States, Prince Xinling Jun of Wei lived here. In 555, during the Northern Qing Dynasty, Xiangguo Si was erected on the same site. It acquired fame as a Buddhist temple, especially during the Tang and Song periods. At the end of the Ming Dynasty, the temple was destroyed by floods. The buildings existing today were built in 1766. Daxiong Baodian hall and Cangjing Ge pavilion have beautiful roofs of yellow and green ceramic tiles. The bell tower contains a large Qing-period bell which is said to weigh more than 5,000 kg. The

octagonal hall Bajiao Liuli Dian is particularly striking. A gilded wooden statue of the Bodhisattva Guanyin stands inside the hall.

Longting, Dragon Pavilion 龙亭

Longting stands in the northwest of the old section of the city. The rear gardens of the Imperial Palace were originally located here during the Northern Song Dynasty. As decreed by the Kangxi Emperor, the pavilion was erected on Meishan hill in 1692. The emperor gave it the name Dragon Pavilion. Approximately 70 steps lead up to the pavilion; a

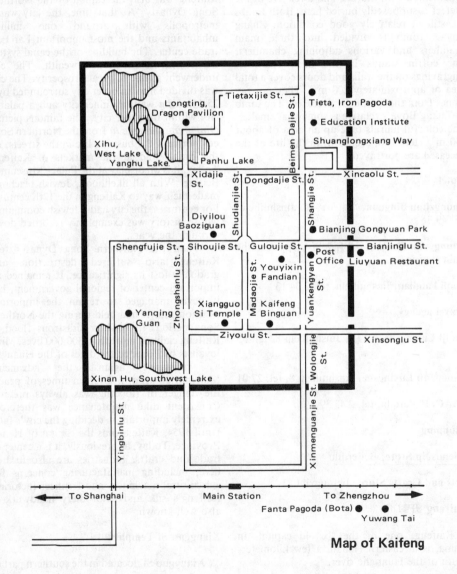

Map of Kaifeng

dragon carved in black stone winds its way between the steps. In 1929, a bronze statue of Sun Yatsen was placed in front of the pavilion.

Tieta, Iron Pagoda 铁塔

Tieta is also called Yougousi Ta, as it once belonged to the Yougou Si temple. Today, this temple is no longer in existance. The pagoda, in the northeastern part of the old city, was built in 1048. It is a 13-story octagonal structure with a height of 54.66m. The outside walls are made of iron-colored ceramic tiles. Thus, the name reflects the color of the pagoda rather than the material that it is made of.

Tiexiniu, Iron Rhinoceros 铁犀牛

The iron rhinoceros can be found 2 km outside of Beimen, North Gate, in a pavilion which is part of Huilong Miao temple. The rhinoceros is approximately 2 m high and was cast in iron in 1466, on the orders of the high official Yu Qian of the Ming Dynasty. In accordance with ancient belief, such iron animals were made to provide protection against floods. Nevertheless, the temple was destroyed by a great flood at the end of the Ming Dynasty, and the rhinoceros sank into the morass. It was unearthed in 1691, and a new temple was erected.

Guchui Tai Platform and Yuwang Tai 古吹台（禹王台）

Guchui Tai is in Yuwangtai Gongyuan park in the city's southeastern suburb. It is said that the musician Shi Kuang of the State of Jin played upon this platform during the Chunqiu period. In the Ming period, Yuwang Miao temple was erected here in honor of the mythical Emperor Yu. The temple complex contains an eastern and a western courtyard. Sanxian Ci hall, dedicated to the famous poets Li Bai, Du Fu and Gao Shi, stands in the eastern courtyard. These poets used to frequently drink wine and write poetry here.

Fanta Pagoda (Bota) 繁塔

Fanta was built to the west of Yuwang Tai in 977. It was part of the Tianqing Si temple complex which no longer exists today. The hexagonal brick building is 31.67 m high. Originally, it had nine stories and was about 66 m high. The pagoda was partially destroyed, presumably in 1368, and at present only three stories remain. Along with the Large Wild Goose pagoda in Xi'an, this is one of the most immense tower constructions in China.

Hotel

Kaifeng Binguan, 开封宾馆 Ziyoulu

Restaurants

Diyilou Baozi Guan,
Sihoujie, specialized in dumpling dishes.

Youyixin Fandian, Guloujie

Travel agency

Guoji Lüxingshe, CITS and Zhongguo Lüxingshe,
Ziyoulu 102, tel. 37 37

Luoyang 洛阳市

Luoyang, one of the six old capitals in China, is a modern industrial city and a center of agriculture and trade. It has a population of about 980,000. The city lies south of the Huanghe river, 112 km from Zhengzhou on the banks of the Luohe, the river after which the city was named.

History

Luoyang is one of the oldest cities in China and has a history that goes back more than 3,000 years. For 960 years, Luoyang was the capital of the empire and consequently the country's political, economic, cultural and military center.

Finds from the first settlements in the Luoyang vicinity date back to the Neolithic era and come from the Yangshao and Longshan cultures. In 770 BC, the Zhou Dynastial rulers made Luoyang their official capital. Two fortified residences were established: Wangcheng on the west bank of the Chanshui River (Wangcheng Gongyuan park still serves as a reminder of its existence), and Chengzhou on the Chanshui's east bank, east of Baima Si temple. During the Eastern Han Dynasty (25 — 220), Luoyang was made the official capital once more. The city must have expanded immensely at the time, and done its reputation as a cultural center justice. Historians reported about the great imperial academy which consisted of several hundred buildings and which was attended by approximately 30,000 students from all over the country. The imperial library is also supposed to have been huge. During this period, Luoyang was a meeting place for scholars and artists. The invention of paper by the legendary eunuch Cai Lun occurred during this time span, as well as the arrival of Buddhist teachings.

During the following centuries, Luoyang continued to be a significant place for cultural and political life. During the era of the Three Kingdoms, Luoyang was the capital of the Wei empire and immediately afterwards, the seat of government for the rulers of the Western Jin Dynasty (265 — 316). During the short-lived Northern Wei Dynasty, Luoyang also attained capital status. The Northern Wei rulers were important patrons of Buddhism. At the time, there were 1,367 Buddhist temples in the city. Luoyang was completely destroyed at the end of the Northern Wei Dynasty. Emperor Yangdi had the city re-built west of the Baima Si temple during the Sui Dynasty. During the Tang Dynasty, Luoyang was the eastern capital along with Chang'an, and at times, it served as the seat of the imperial family. The notorious Empress Wu Zetian (684 — 705) especially liked the city. Luoyang became a center of literature, and famous poets such as Du Fu, Bai Juyi and Li Bai lived and worked here. During the Five Dynasties period (907 — 960), Luoyang was intermittantly the capital of the Liang and Tang dynasties. After a brief period, the Jin rulers relocated the capital to Kaifeng. From then on, the city lost much of its importance. Only during the last decades has the city been able to regain a certain reputation as a rising industrial city. In 1955, China's first tractor factory was built here, and in 1959, one of the most important ball-bearing factories was established.

Luoyang is the City of Peonies; more than 150 varieties bloom here. Peonies have been grown in Luoyang for over 1,000 years. The Tang poet Baj Juyi and the writer Ouyang Xiu from the Northern Song era admired the magnificance of the flowers in bloom.

Wangcheng Gongyuan Park 王城公园

Wangcheng Gongyuan was laid out in the area of the Zhou period capital, Wangcheng. Two Han period tombs in the park are of cultural and historical interest. They were discovered in 1957, northeast of the old section of town, and restored and moved to this park. One of the tombs dates back to the 1st century BC. It contains the oldest known brush murals, which, in spite of their age, are still in good condition. The second tomb dates back to the Eastern Han Dynasty. It has ornamentally carved stone doors. (The first tomb is opened only upon special request.)

The local Chinese love this park because of its many peonies. In April, when the flowers are in bloom, people come from far and wide to enjoy the sight. During the New Year's festivals, a lantern exhibition takes place. The production of lanterns has a century-long tradition in Luoyang.

Mangshan Mountain 邙山

Mangshan rises in the northern part of the city and is a favorite destination for the inhabitants. A splendid view of the city can be enjoyed from its peak.

The Old City 元明清老城

The old section of the city reflects Luoyang as it was during the Yuan, Ming and Qing periods. It is well worth a visit. Besides century-old houses and streets, there are also interesting, small shops where local crafts are sold.

Luoyang City Museum 洛阳市博物馆

This museum has been in existence since 1958. It is located within the Ming - era Guandi Miao temple in the southern part of the city. Archaeological finds are on display which were discovered in the fifties as fields were being terraced. These finds include neolithic earthenware and bronze articles, ceramics, weapons and tomb figures from the Shang and Zhou eras.

Hanwei Luoyang Gucheng, The Old City of Luoyang from the Han — Wei Dynasties 汉魏洛阳古城

The Zhou era capital – Chengzhou – is located 12 km east of present-day Luoyang. The first emperor of the Eastern Han Dynasty decided to make it his capital, as did the rulers of the Western Jin and the Northern Wei Dynasty. The western, northern and eastern sections of the city wall can still be seen today. Eight large streets traversed the city.

Baima Si, White Horse Temple 白马寺

Baima Si is located 10 km east of the city. It was designed during the Eastern Han Dynasty in 68, and it is one of China's first Buddhist temples. A legend tells of two Indian monks who rode upon white horses and brought Buddhist teachings and scripts to Luoyang. Baima Si, White Horse temple, was erected at the spot where the horses came to a halt. The complex has been restored and renovated

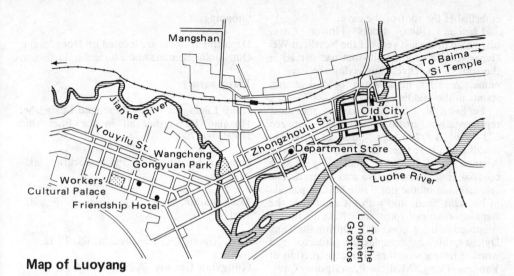

Map of Luoyang

numerous times. The buildings still existing today were built during the Ming period and include Tianwang Dian, Dafo Dian, Daxiong Dian and Pilu Ge halls as well as two tombs inside the gates in which the remains of the two Indian monks supposedly lie. Qiyun Ta pagoda, built in 1175, stands in the temple's eastern section.

Longmen Shiku, Longmen Caves 龙门石窟

Approximately 12 km south of Luoyang, the Yihe river flows northwards through Longmen, Dragon Gate. According to an ancient legend, a mountain once stood here. Behind the mountain, a dragon lived in a huge body of water and wreaked great havoc and chaos. The mythical Emperor Yu put an end to this activity by splitting open the mountain and providing the dragon with a passage towards the sea.

Longmen Shan, also called Xishan, West Mountain, rises up on the west bank of the Yihe. Xiangshan is located on the east bank and is also called Dongshan, East Mountain. Caves and grottos were cut into the sides of the mountains, and wonderful Buddhist sculptures were carved. The Longmen Caves are among the most important cave temples in China, along with the Datong and Dunhuang caves. The oldest caves date back to the Northern Wei Dynasty (386—534). The Northern Wei rulers were patrons of Buddhist teachings and had already ordered the construction of cave temples in their first capital, Datong. When the capital was moved to Luoyang in 494, similar projects were begun

here. The work continued during the following dynasties. Most of the caves were made during the Tang Dynasty from 713 — 741.

Today, there are 1,352 caves, 750 niches, 39 pagodas, 97,000 sculptures and 3,680 inscriptions to be seen on the slopes of East and West mountains. Unfortunately, man has destroyed much during the last centuries. A number of sculptures are on display in European, Japanese and North American museums. Erosion has also damaged the grottos, although to a lesser extent.

The most important caves on Longmen Shan are, from north to south Qianxi Si, Binyang Dong, Jingshan Si, Wanfo Dong, Lianhua Dong, Weizi Dong, Tangzi Dong, Fengxian Si, Yaofang Dong, Guyang Dong, Huoshao Dong, Shiku Si and Ludong. Several of these are described in more detail in the following text.

Qianxi Si was made at the beginning of the Tang Dynasty and contains a sculpture of Amitabha with a disciple on each side. Two bodhisattvas and two celestial guardians can be seen on the walls.

Binyang Dong is a cave complex consisting of a northern, central and southern section. It was built upon the orders of the Xuanwu Emperor from the Northern Wei Dynasty in honor of his parents. The middle section alone took 24 years to build. It contains 11 large statues of Buddha, and musicians and dancers are depicted on the roof of the cave.

Wanfo Dong, Cave of Ten Thousand Buddhas, dates back to the year 680. More than 15,000 figures of Buddha are carved in the cave's walls. A huge lotus blossom embellishes the roof of the cave.

Lianhua Dong, Lotus Flower Cave, originated in the last years of the Northern Wei Dynasty. A large lotus blossom was carved in the roof of the cave, thus giving the cave its name. A 5.1-m-high statue of Sakyamuni stands in the middle of the cave.

Fengxian Si, Longmen's largest and most representative grotto, originated between 672—676. A 17-m-high statue of a seated Buddha is in the center. The disciples Jiaye and Ananda stand to either side, as well as a celestial king, a bodhisattva and a guard. The celestial king on the north side holds a pagoda in his right hand, and with his right foot, he steps upon an evil spirit. Touching his foot is supposed to bring good luck. During the Tang Dynasty, this huge complex was protected by a wooden temple structure. The construction of Yaofang Dong, Medical Prescription Cave, was begun during the Northern Wei Dynasty but was not completed until the Tang era. This cave's special feature is the 140 prescritions for various illnesses that are chiseled here in stone, a treasure chest for researchers in traditional medicine.

Guyang Dong, the oldest of the Longmen grottos, was created in 495. The inscriptions, most of which were carved during the Northern Wei era, are significant.

The most important caves on Xiangshan are called Kanjing Si. They were built during the regency of Empress Wu Zetian at the end of the 7th century. Their roofs contain chiseled lotus blossoms, as well as figures playing music and dancing. There are 29 Luohan figures on the walls

The tomb of the famous poet Bai Juyi who died in Luoyang in 846, is also located on Xiangshan on Pipa Peak. A stone stele in front of the grave bears the inscription: *Tang shaofu bai gong mu,* Tomb of the honorable Shaofu (title for public servants) Bai of Tang (see also Bai Juyi, page 51).

Hotels

Youyi Binguan, 友谊宾馆
Friendship Guest House, Jianxi Qu, Taiyuanlu, tel. 21 39

Guoji Lüshe 国际旅社
Nanlou, Hotel International, Xigong Qu, Zhongzhoulu, tel. 71 55

Restaurant

Guangzhou Jiujia,
Jianxi Qu, Dongfenglu, tel. 21 70

Shopping

Department stores are located on Dongfenglu, Qingdaolu, Beidajie and Zhongzhoulu streets.

Travel agency

Guoji Lüxingshe CITS, Zhongguo Lüxingshe, Huaqiao Lüxingshe, all in the Friendship Hotel, tel. 7006 x 701

Gong'an Ju, Bureau of Public Security, tel. 74 23

Train Station, Xigong Qu, Jinguyuanlu, tel. 72 01

Taxi, Xigong Qu, Bolichanglu, tel. 70 32

Gongxian County 巩县

Gongxian is located along the railway line Zhengzhou-Luoyang.

Shiku Si, Temple of the Caves 石窟寺

Temple of the Caves is located 8 km northeast of the district capital Gongxian at the foot of Dali Shan mountain. Work on the temple began in 517, but it was not completed until the Northern Song Dynasty. Altogether, there are a total of five caves, 256 niches and 7,743 sculptures.

Du Fu's Family House 杜甫故里

The famous Tang poet Du Fu (712 — 770) was born by Bijia Shan mountain, approximately 1km east of the district capital Gongxian. The dwelling is actually a cave which was finished with brick. The poet spent many years of his life here.

Songling, Tombs of the Song Emperors 宋陵

Eight Song-period tombs are located in Gongxian district — in the vicinity of Xicun, Zhitian, Xiaoyi and Huiguo. The father of the dynasty's founder and seven Song emperors were buried here. The tombs are similar in form and construction. The burial area is enclosed by a wall; each of the four sides has a gate and each corner, a tower. A path lined with stone figures of civil and military officials and animals leads from the southern gate. During the Song period, it was the custom not to begin construction of the imperial tomb until after the emperor had died. Since the deceased had to be buried within seven months, the tombs from this period are very modest in proportion and adornment in comparison with those from other dynasties. Two of the eight tombs can be visited by the public, namely Yongzhao Ling, Tomb of the Renzong Emperor, and Yonghou Ling, Tomb of the Yingzong Emperor.

Songshan Mountains 嵩山

The Songshan mountains stretch out over 60 km north of the district capital Dengfeng The 72 peaks were given their names long ago and are divided into an eastern and a western mountain range. The eastern range is called Taishi Shan and reaches up to a height of 1,440 m. The western range is Shaoshi Shan, and its peaks have elevations up to 1,405m. The distance between the two ranges is 10 km. The Songshan massif belongs to the five holy mountains in China. It is often called a 'treasure chest of cultural memorials'; countless temples, pagodas, monasteries, stone steles, can be seen in the mountains. Even in ancient times, this area was known for its monasteries and schools.

Shaolin Si Monastery 少林寺

The Zen-Buddhist Shaolin Si lies at the northern foot of Shaoshi Shan, about 80 km southwest of Zhengzhou and 15 km northwest of the district capital Dengfeng. This temple is renowned both at home and abroad because one of the most famous styles of *wushu* (Kungfu), the traditional Chinese art of fighting, was developed by the monks here – namely, Shaolin Quan, Shaolin Boxing. The temple was built during the Northern Wei era in 495. It is said that the Indian monk Tuoba came to China during this period to spread Buddhism, and the Xiao Wen Emperor made this monastery available to him. Later, the legendary Indian monk Bodhidharma, Damo in Chinese, came to this

monastery. Bodhidharma is given the credit for founding the large Buddhist sect Chanzong. Because he practiced Chan Buddhism (Zen Buddhism) for so many years at Shaolin Si, today the temple is regarded as the starting point for this branch of Buddhism. Bodhidharma is also considered to be the founder of the famous Shaolin Quan, as he developed 'methods of physical training' for his pupils which were a prototype of the Shaolin fighting style.

During the Tang period, the temple attained great importance. The monks had helped Li Shimin, the first emperor of the Tang Dynasty, in the struggle against his enemy, Wang Shichong; and the emperor showed his gratitude in later years by donating large amounts of money and land to the temple. Shaolin Si experienced a time of prosperity; at times, it provided lodging for up to 1,000 monks.

Shaolin Si was destroyed several times and then rebuilt. Qianfo Dian, Thousand Buddha Hall, is the main hall within the temple complex. It dates back to the Ming era and contains colorful murals depicting the 500 Luohans. Two rows of depressions can be seen in the brick floor. These were caused by the many generations of monks who practiced their fighting styles here. Baiyi Dian also contains an interesting mural: a depiction of 30 monks practicing Shaolin Quan. Bodhidharma Pavilion was erected in honor of the loyal disciple of and successor to Bodhidharma, Huike (487 — 593).

Talin, Forest of Stupas 塔林

The largest forest of stupas in China is located half a kilometer west of Shaolin Si. For centuries, famous abbots and monks have found their last resting place here in this cemetery. Approximately 220 pagodas from various epochs can be seen.

Songshan Mountains

Chuzu An, Temple of the First Ancestor
初祖庵

Chuzu An is located northwest of Shaolin Si, halfway up the mountain. The temple was originally built during the Northern Wei period, but it was restored in 1125. The temple contains a mural portraying 28 abbots from Shaolin Si.

Songyue Ta Pagoda 嵩岳寺塔

The brick pagoda Songyue Ta, located 5 km northwest of the district capital Dengfeng on the southern part of Taishi Shan within the Songyue Si temple complex, was built in 520. It is 40m tall and 12-sided and is the oldest pagoda of this type in China.

Songyue Si temple stands next to the pagoda. At one time, it was the residence of the Xuanwu and Xiaoming Emperors of the Northern Wei Dynasty.

Zhongyue Miao Temple 中岳庙

Zhongyue Miao is located 4km from Dengfeng beneath Huangtai Feng peak at the spot where Taishi Si (built during the Han Dynasty) once stood. It was the religious center of the holy Songshan mountains, where emperors made sacrifices to thank heavens and earth for their benevolence. The present complex was designed during the Qing era and is the largest temple complex in Henan. The middle axis is 650 m long. The complex is divided into 11 courtyards containing numerous gates and halls. Four iron men with angry expressions are an interesting sight northeast of Chongshen Men gate. They were cast in 1064.

Songyang Shuyuan, Songyang Academy
嵩阳书院

The Songyang Academy is about 5 km west of Zhongyue Miao. Songyang Temple of the Northern Wei period was originally located here, but it was converted into an imperial academy in 1035 and went down in history as one of the eight largest academies of the Song Dynasty. The famous brothers and Neo-confucians Cheng Hao and Cheng Yi taught here.

Dengfeng Guanxing Tai, Dengfeng Observatory 登封观星台

This observatory, 15 km southeast of Dengfeng within the Zhougong Miao temple complex, is the oldest surviving observatory in China. An observatory was located here as far back as the Zhou era.

The astronomer Guo Shoujing (1231 — 1314) designed this particular observatory in 1276, at the beginning of the Yuan period. The building is an angular construction made of brick and stone and stands 9.46 m high. A 31.9-m-long stone rod stretches out in front of the building and is used to measure the sun's shadow. Based upon his own diagrams and with the aid of information collected by other observatories, Guo Shoujing worked out a calendar which corresponds to the present-day Gregorian calendar. A calculation that he made of the amount of time that it takes the earth to revolve around the sun was off by only 26 seconds.

A small covered building, 3.16 m high, was set up on the observatory platform during the Ming Dynasty.

Anyang 安阳市

Anyang, located in the northern part of the province, can be reached by train from Luoyang, Zhengzhou or Beijing.

Yin, the Shang Dynasty capital, was once located in the area where Anyang is now situated. Anyang is a center for regional trade and agriculture and has a population totalling about 500,000. The city's industry has been able to advance considerably since the founding of the People's Republic of China. Skilled crafts, especially the carving of jade, have a long tradition here.

The discovery of the capital of the Shang Dynasty, Yin, was the result of a happy coincidence. In 1889, the scholar Liu Er (1857 — 1909) visited his ailing friend Wang Yirong (1845 — 1900) in Beijing. The latter was in the process of preparing his medicine as his friend arrived. One of the medicine's ingredients was old tortoise shells upon which the friends found scratched symbols. Being immediately convinced that it must be an ancient form of Chinese writing, they tried to find out more about the tortoise shells which were sold in pharmacies for medicinal purposes. It was ascertained that the shells came from Xiaotun village near Anyang and had been found by farmers while plowing the fields. The farmers called them dragon bones as it was thought that dragons shed their bones as they grew. People believed that dragons brought luck, and their bones were thought to contain supernatural healing powers. Thus, they were collected and sold to pharmacies.

Actually, tortoise shells and the shoulder blades of oxen were used during the Shang

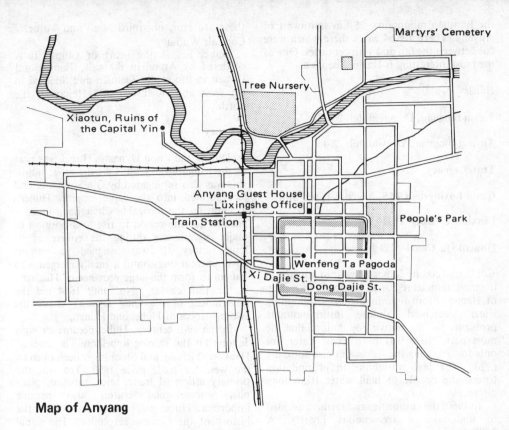

Map of Anyang

Dynasty in consulting the oracle. Questions pertaining to military and civil affairs, sacrificial rites, astronomical phenomena or agricultural problems were scratched into the shells and bones. These were then thrown into the fire, and the answers to the questions were interpreted according to the cracks resulting from the fire's heat. They supply present-day science with unforeseen information about the most diverse aspects of the Shang era.

The discovery of the oracle bones of Xiaotun called attention to the Han historian Sima Qian whose descriptions stated that Yin, the capital of the Shang rulers, was once located in this region. It was founded about 1380 BC but was destroyed by Zhou troops in 1111 BC. Excavations in the Xiaotun area did not begin until 1928, and they are now being continued in the Wuguan and Houjiazhuang areas. The ruins of the former capital Yin were actually discovered. They covered an area of 24 km² and were divided into four zones: the king's palatial complex, the imperial tombs, the artisans' quarter and the residential area. Among other things, pit tombs in the form of crosses and the foundations of the palace complex were exposed, and a number of

bronze, ceramic, ivory, marble and jade articles were found. Many of these are now on display at the Historical Museum in Beijing.

Wenfeng Ta Pagoda (Tianningsi Ta)
天宁寺塔（文峰塔）

The stone pagoda Wenfeng Ta stands in the western part of the city within the Tianning Si temple complex. Its base, which is smaller than the upper part of the pagoda, was given the shape of a lotus blossom. The second story windows, doors and outer walls display Buddhist ornamentation and dragon designs. The pagoda's unusual feature is its 10-m-high dagoba spire. The pagoda was built in 952, but the second story decorations appear to have been added during the Ming period.

Renmin Gongyuan, People's Park 人民公园

People's Park is a favorite excursion place for the Anyang inhabitants. It is located in the east part of the city.

Cave temples are also located in Anyang's surrounding areas. These are the Lingquansi Shiku caves 灵泉寺石窟 which are located in the Baoshan mountains, 25 km southwest of Anyang. There are 64 caves there which were cut between the 6th and 11th centuries. One of the most interesting is Dazhu Shengku.

Hotels

Taixin Binguan, Dengtalu, tel. 20 12

Anyang Binguan, Youyilu, tel. 22 44

Travel agency

Guoji Lüxingshe CITS, Youyilu 1, tel. 21 45

Linxian County 林县

Hongqi Qu Canal 红旗渠

Linxian county is located west of Anyang in the mountainous region in the northern section of Henan. From time immemorial, obtaining water presented almost insurmountable problems for the native population. For the most part, there was insufficient water not only for irrigating the fields, but also for daily needs. The high variability in precipitation forced the people to haul water from long distances.

In 1960, the authorities and farmers decided to undertake a tremendous project. A 2,000-km-long canal system was to be dug through the mountains to conduct the water from the Zhanghe in Pingshun district, Shanxi Province to Linxian. The project took a total of nine years. Besides the actual canal system, pumping stations, dams, bridges, dikes and aquaducts also needed to be built. The lack of machinery was made up for by hand labor. After 10 years, the people celebrated the completion of the Red Flag Canal. It was an extensive canal system which consisted of a 70-km-long, 4.3-m-deep and 8-m-wide main canal, three secondary canals with lengths of 41.5, 48 and 4 km and 1,690 subsidiary canals. In addition, there were 338 middle-sized and small reservoirs and 52 small hydro-electric power stations. The Red Flag Canal solved Linxian's water supply problems. It provides for the irrigation of 40,000 hectares of farmland.

Hubei Province 湖北省

Area: ca. 180,000 km² / Population: 47.8 million. Only about 40,000 inhabitants are members of minority groups, two-thirds of these are Hui, one-third Miao and Tujue. / Capital: Wuhan

Hubei lies in the heart of China. It is bordered by Anhui in the east, Jiangxi and Hunan in the south, Sichuan and Shaanxi in the west and northwest and Henan in the north.

History

During the Zhou Dynasty, Hubei was part of the Kingdom of Chu. Like the other states, this was also subjugated by Qin Shihuang and incorporated into the large empire. Hubei's location on the navigable Changjiang made it possible for the region to rise to a position of major significance during the course of its long history. It was assigned to various governmental units, until it finally merged with Hunan to form the large province of Huguang in the 13th century. Not until 1664 did the government of the Qing Dynasty create the two provinces of Hubei and Hunan.

In the 19th century, Hubei became strongly involved in the Taiping Rebellion. The cities of Hankou, Yichang and Shashi had been open to the west for trade since 1860. Tea was the primary article of trade; later, tobacco, plant oils, sesame and cotton also became important. Hubei played a special role in the history of the Chinese revolution. The signal for the revolution of 1911 which led to the overthrow of the Manchurian Qing Dynasty came from Wuchang.

Most of the province lies north of the Changjiang. Here are the low-lying lands which are bordered by the foothills of the Daba Shan and the Fangdou Shan mountains in the west and the Dabie Shan and the Tongbai Shan mountains and the foothills of the Qinling Shan in the north. From Sichuan, the Changjiang makes its way into the province through small ravines. Due to the gradual incline, it flows leisurely from Yichang through the Hubei plains. Numerous lakes and scattered mountains characterize the plains — a landscape of depressions and elevations.

Hubei's winters are short and often very cold. Due to monsoons, the summers are hot and humid. Wuhan's summers are known to be unbearable throughout China. The average temperature in January is 4°C, in July, 29.7°C. The amount of precipitation increases from the northwest to the southeast and is approximately 600 — 700 mm per year. The month with the most rain is June, and that with the least, December. Cyclones, which move through the Changjiang Valley eastward can be dangerous. They bring much-needed rain for the cultivation of rice in the early summer, but if they remain in the valley too long, the result is rainfall for days on end which leads to dangerous flooding of the Changjiang. In 1931 and 1954, this resulted in catastrophic floods. Extensive dike construction projects, such as those which have been carried out in Shashi and Yichang in the last decades, have diminished the danger of inundation considerably. The variation in the water-level between summer and winter amounts to about 13 m. During the winter, the Changjiang flows along lazily, and the water-level sinks to 2 m. Only the flat river steamers can make their way up the river to Wuhan. With the spring and summer rains, the river changes into a mighty torrent. During the summer months, ships up to 15,000 gross registered tons can pull into port at Wuhan.

Only 11% of Hubei's population lives in the cities. The largest of these are Wuhan, Huangshi, Shashi, Yichang and Xiangfan. Hubei lies between the wheat-growing regions of the north and the rice-growing regions of the south. In the south and southeast sections of Hubei, sufficient rainfall and precipitation falls so that 40 — 60% of the farmland can be used to cultivate rice. This area and the northern section of Hunan are part of China's rice-basket. When Hubei and Hunan were joined together as Huguang Province during the Ming period, one saying went: If the harvest was good in Huguang, then the empire is in good shape. It is possible to harvest crops two times a year. In the cooler seasons, barley, wheat, sorghum, rape, beans and sesame are planted. Wheat-growing predominates in the north as the amount of precipitation is less and the variability greater. Cotton is also a frequent crop; Hubei is one of China's most important cotton producers.

The province is rich in iron-ore, which is mined in Daye in the southeast. Large iron and steel integrated plants are located in Wuhan and Huangshi. Hubei also has copper and coal deposits.

Wuhan 武汉市

Wuhan was created in 1927, when three previously independent cities — Wuchang, Hankou and Hanyang — were merged into one. The name combines the *Wu* of Wuchang and the *han* of Hankou and Hanyang. The three cities are located at the confluence of the Hanshi and the Changjiang and are linked together by bridges. Hankou and Hanyang on the Changjiang's west bank are separated from one another by the Hanjiang river: Hankou in the north and Hanyang in the south. Wuchang stretches out on the Changjiang's east bank. Wuhan has a total population of 4.18 million. It is the most important center of trade in Central China, a reflection of the fact that all the important roads and railway lines meet here, as well as the ship traffic along the Changjiang. In addition, Wuhan is an important industrial city.

The area was settled as far back as the Han era. At the time of the Three Kingdoms, the capital of the state of Wu was located here.

Wuchang 武昌

Wuchang is the oldest of the three cities. It was the capital of Huguang Province and plays an important role in modern revolutionary history. On October 10, 1911, soldiers from the New Army revolted in Wuchang. By the next day, the city was already in the hands of the rebels. Hankou and Hanyang were captured during the coming days. The rebellion's positive outcome encouraged revolutionary forces in other provinces to join the revolt against Qing Dynasty rule. Today, Wuchang is the political and cultural center of Wuhan. The areas around Donghu, East Lake, and Sheshan, Snake Mountain, offer many interesting sights. The Hubei Museum and the university are also located in this section of the city.

Up to the beginning of the 19th century, Hankou was only a small fishing village. After 1858, trade concessions to western countries, particularly to Great Britain, had to be granted, and Hankou developed into a leading center of trade.

The building of the railway line from Beijing to Hankou favored the city's industrial development, which, however, also gave rise to the proletariat. This would later play an important role in the revolutionary movement. After the revolt of October 10, 1911, the revolutionaries waged the first successful battle against imperial troops on October 17th, in the vicinity of Hankou. The success served as an impetus to the revolution. In 1923, Hankou was one of the centers of the railroad workers' strike of February 7th. A monument dedicated to the heroes of this strike stands in the northern section of the city. At present, Hankou is Wuhan's most modern area. The large hotels and the business district are located here.

Hanyang 汉阳

Hanyang was founded during the Sui era

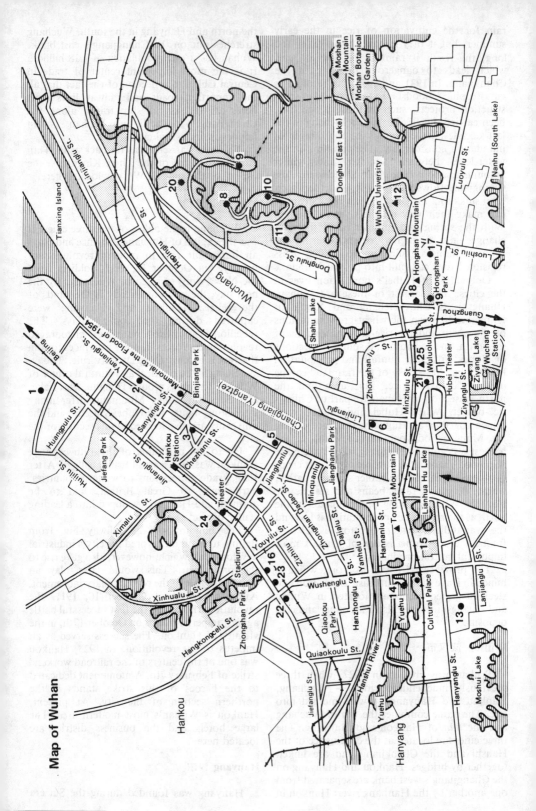

Map of Wuhan

Tianxing Island

Linjiang St.

Beijing

Huangpulu St.

Jiefang Park

Ximalu St.

Huilu St.

Xinhualu St.

Hankou

Hangkongcelu St.

Zhongshan Park

Stadium

Qiaokou Park

Qiaokoulu St.

Jiefanglu St.

Yuehu

Hanshui River

Hanyang

Moshui Lake

Hanyanglu St.

Lanjianglu St.

Cultural Palace

Yuehu

Wushenglu St.

Hanzhonglu St.

Yanhelu St.

Hannanlu St.

Tortoise Mountain

Lianhua Hu Lake

Daijialu St.

Jianghanlu Park

Minquanlu

Zhongshan Dadao St.

Youyilu St.

Zizhilu

Theater

Chezhanlu St.

Hankou Station

Jiefanglu St.

Sanyanglu St.

Memorial to the Flood of 1954

Nanjianglu St.

Binjiang Park

Changjiang (Yangtze)

Linjianglu

Zhongshan lu St.

Minzhulu St.

Wuluolu St.

Hubei Theater

Ziyanglu St.

Ziyang Lake

Wuchang Station

Guangzhou

Luoshilu St.

Luoyulu St.

Nanhu (South Lake)

Hongshan Park

Hongshan Mountain

Wuhan University

Donghu (East Lake)

Moshan Botanical Garden

Moshan Mountain

Heping lu

St.

Donghulu St.

Wuchang

Shahu Lake

Linjiang St.

2
1
3
4
5
6
7
8
9
10
11
12
13
14
15
16
17
18
19
20
21
22
23
24
25

and is the smallest of the three cities. It used to be a favorite retirement place for members of the upper class and the military. In 1894, China's first modern iron and steel works went into operation in Hanyang. Today, light industry predominates.

Taken as a whole, heavy industry prevails in Wuhan. The region's rich iron-ore deposits made it possible to build the large steel integrated plant which was set into operation in 1958.

Tourist Attractions in Wuchang

Changjiang Daqiao, Changjiang Bridge
长江大桥

Changjiang Bridge was the first bridge to be built across the Changjiang. It connects Guishan mountain in Hanyang to Sheshan mountain in Wuchang. The bridge took two years to build, from September 1, 1955, to October 13, 1957, and has a total length of 1,670 m and a height of 80 m. The upper section was designed for street traffic while trains travel across the lower section.

The bridge is economically important, not only for Wuhan, but also for all of Central China as it joins China's northern and southern regions. Formerly, the only way to cross the Changjiang was by ferry.

Sheshan, Snake Mountain 蛇山

Sheshan actually does snake its way through the old section of Wuchang. The 'head' is by the Changjiang, and the 'tail' is in the city's east. Directly across from the mountain on the other side of the river, Guishan, Tortoise Mountain, rises above the surrounding landscape. In ancient times, both of these mountains were strategically important. Sheshan was also culturally well-known. It was referred to time and time again in the works of historians and poets.

Huanghe Lou, Yellow Crane Tower, is the most important attraction. Although it burned down in 1884, its memory was still alive in the hearts of the native population, therefore the city authorities decided upon the tower's reconstruction.

The following legend is told about Yellow Crane Tower: Once upon a time, there was a small wine tavern located at the foot of Sheshan that was often frequented by an immortal. The host was always friendly and polite when he served this guest. One day, after the immortal had partaken of several glasses of wine, he took an orange-peel, painted a yellow crane on the wall and then left the tavern and the city. The crane, however, would sometimes fly down from the wall and dance in front of the guests. This attracted so many customers that the tavern soon became a large, prosperous wine restaurant, Yellow Crane Tower. The immortal returned years later, only to disappear once more — this time carried away on the wings of the crane. Huanghe Lou supposedly stood here as far back as the 4th century.

Shenxiang Baota Dagoba 胜象宝塔

This stone dagoba originally stood on the west side of the mountain. It was moved to the east side in 1957 to make way for the Changjiang Bridge. The pagoda was built in 1343 and is 9.36 m tall. Various patterns and inscriptions were carved into the base.

The former headquarters for the military government of the Wuchang uprising of 1911 were located at the foot of the mountain.

Map of Wuhan

1. Monument to the Martyrs of February 7, 1923
2. Shengli Fandian Hotel
3. Jianghan Fandian
4. Lüxingshe
5. Wuhan Guan Harbor
6. Former Location of the Peasant Movement Institute
7. Changjiang Bridge
8. Changtian Lou Pavilion
9. Huguang Ge Pavilion
10. Xingyin Ge Pavilion
11. Hubei Museum
12. Luojia Shan Mountain
13. Guiyuan Si Temple
14. Guqin Tai Terrace
15. Hanyang Park
16. Wuhan Exhibition Hall
17. Baotong Si Temple
18. Xingfusi Ta Pagoda
19. Shi Yang's Tomb
20. Jiunü Dun Memorial
21. Former Offices of the Insurgent Military Government in Wuhan
22. Wuhan Fandian Hotel
23. Wuhan Department Store
24. Children and Youth Palace
25. Snake Mountain

Hongshan Mountain 洪山

Hongshan used to be called Dongshan. East Mountain. It is located outside of Dadong Men, Great East Gate. It is a favorite destination for outings as its cliffs, caves, ancient trees, springs and brooks offer variety for young and old. Baotong Si temple, Fajie Gong temple. Lingji Ta pagoda, Xingfusi Ta pagoda, Huayan Dong cave, Bailong Quan spring and the stone engravings are all well worth seeing.

Baotong Si Temple 宝通禅寺

Baotong Si, located on the southern part of Hongshan, was originally built during the Southern Song Dynasty and once stood in Suixian district. It was later moved here. The halls which can still be visited today, Daxiong Baodian and Zushi Dian, the east and west side halls, were built from 1865 — 1879.

Lingji Ta Pagoda 灵济塔

The stone pagoda in back of Baotong Si temple, Lingji Ta, was first erected during the Tang era. The present 43-m-high construction was built in 1865.

Xingfusi Ta Pagoda 兴福寺塔

The stone pagoda Xingfusi Ta, located on the southwest slope of the mountain, was erected in 1702. It is 11 m high and has a base decorated with extensive carvings.

Shi Yang's Tomb 施洋墓

The attorney Shi Yang (1889 — 1923) was a leader of the railroad workers' strike of February 7, 1923. He was arrested on the same day and executed on February 17th. In 1953, his tomb was officially moved to this spot, and a memorial stele was erected.

Luojia Shan Mountain — Wuhan University 珞珈山——武汉大学

Luojia Shan is located in the eastern part of Wuchang on the south bank of East Lake. Wuhan University was built in the midst of its beautiful scenery. It evolved from the Wuchang Teachers' College in 1925 and today it has more than 20 departments in all areas of the social and natural sciences, excluding technology.

Donghu, East Lake 东湖

Donghu, located in eastern Wuchang, is known throughout China. It covers an area of 33 km², and its wooded east bank offers visitors an opportunity to relax and recuperate at the sanatorium located there. A fishing village is located on the north shore. There are numerous places of interest on the west shore, which have all come into being during the last three decades. Some of these are expounded in greater detail.

Hubei Museum 湖北省博物馆

The Hubei Museum is divided into two areas: Hubei from its beginnings up to the Opium War and the revolutionary history of the province. The display concerning the tomb of Marquis Yi of Zeng is particularly interesting. The tomb was excavated in May 1978, about 2.5 km northwest of the district capital Suixian. The marquis was presumably a great music lover. When he died in 433 BC, assorted valuable musical instruments were buried along with him, including a *bianzhong (chimes made of bronze bells), a bianqing (a set of 32 stone chimes), a jiangu (a large drum) and a sheng* (a mouth organ). The most impressive is the bianzhong with 19 small and 46 middle-sized and large bronze bells. The largest bell is 153 cm high and weighs 203 kg. The bells hang in rows from wooden beams on an L-shaped stand. Their total weight is 2,500 kg. The instrument's sound has been recorded, and the tape is played at the request of the visitor.

Besides the musical instruments, a large number of religious objects were also found, including bronze mugs and wine vessels as well as weapons, jewelry and sculptures of people and animals.

Tingtao Xuan Hall

Tingtao Xuan is an imposing brick and wood construction. A teahouse and a restaurant are located here.

Xingyin Ge Pavilion 行吟阁

Xingyin Ge, located on a small island, can be reached from the west bank by crossing the Hefeng Qiao bridge. It is 22.5 m high and has three stories. The three roofs are covered with green ceramic tiles. A statue of the famous poet Qu Yuan (ca. 332 — 295 BC) from the state of Chu (see page 48) stands in front of the pavilion.

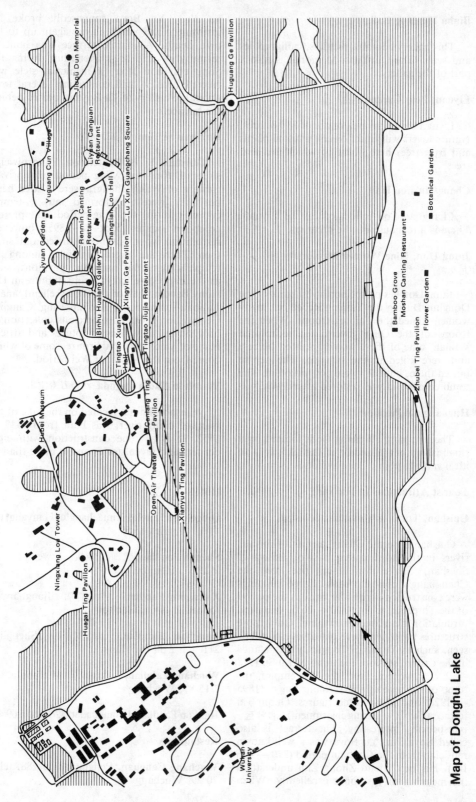

Jiaqü Dun Memorial

Huguang Ge Pavilion

Yuguang Cun Village
Liuyan Canguan Restaurant
Renmin Canting Restaurant
Changtian Lou Hall
Lu Xun Guangchang Square
Liyuan Garden
Binhu Hualang Gallery
Xingyin Ge Pavilion
Tingtao Xuan Hall
Tingtao Jiujia Restaurant

Botanical Garden

Bamboo Grove
Moshan Canting Restaurant
Flower Garden
Zhubei Ting Pavilion

Hubei Museum

Centang Ting Pavilion
Open-Air Theater

Xianyue Ting Pavilion

Ningxiang Lou Tower
Huagai Ting Pavilion

N

Wuhan University

Map of Donghu Lake

Binhu Hualang Gallery

This gallery contains pictures, calligraphies and seals. The Qu Yuan Memorial is also a part of the gallery.

Liyuan, Pear Garden 梨园

Liyuan covers an area of about 33 hectares. Nature lovers will find flowers, unusual plants and fruit trees here, most of which are pear trees.

Changtian Lou Hall

Changtian Lou is located east of Liyuan. There is a teahouse on the premises.

Jiunü Dun, Nine Women Memorial 九女墩

Jiunü Dun lies on the northwest bank of the Donghu. During the Taiping Rebellion, many women joined the Taiping troops. When the troops of the Qing government recaptured Wuhan, nine of these women resisted fiercely and were killed in the struggle. The people buried them, but they were not forgotten. The tomb compound was restored after 1949.

Huguang Ge Pavilion

The imposing Huguang Ge is located on a small island in the middle of the lake. It is an ideal vantage point. The pavilion is 19 m high.

Tourist Attractions in Hanyang

Guishan, Tortoise Mountain 汉阳龟山

Guishan is on the Changjiang and Hanshui rivers in the northeastern part of Hanyang. Sheshan, Snake Mountain, rises on the Changjiang's opposite bank. Large buildings were constructed here as far back as the period of the Three Kingdoms (220 — 265). Wars and turbulation destroyed everything. Only those structures built in more recent times can still be seen, such as Yugongji Temple, which stands in the eastern section, the tomb of Lu Su (172 — 217), a general from the Wu empire, the tomb of the revolutionary Xiang Jingyu (1895 — 1928) and Moya tomb figures. Guqin Tai terrace (*Guqin* = string instrument) 古琴台 is especially interesting. The terrace is also called Boya Tai. Yu Boya was a well-known musician from the Chunqiu period (770 — 476 BC). His best friend Zhong Ziqi understood the meaning of his songs excellently. When he died, Yu Boya supposedly broke his instrument and never played again up to his own death. A marble terrace was built in memory of this deep friendship during the Song era, and later, a memorial stele was erected here. A hall containing several texts about the history of Yu Boya is located behind the terrace.

Guiyuan Si Temple 归元寺

Guiyuan Si is located on Yangcuiweijie street. During the Ming period, the private gardens of Wang Zhangfu were located here, but they were transformed into a temple complex during the Qing period. The present compound dates back to 1895; however, restoration work has been carried out since then. There are several highlights among the temple's numerous halls and pavilions, such as the impressive Sakyamuni sculpture in Daxiong Baodian hall or the 500 excellently made Luohan sculptures in Luohan Tang. Cangjing Ge pavilion contains a precious collection of holy sutras, as well as sculptures and articles made of jade, ivory and bronze, some of which come from the Northern Wei period.

Wanshou Baota Pagoda 沙市万寿宝塔

Wanshou Baota, located on the dike of the Nanjing Jiang river, was built from 1548 — 1552. It is a stone construction with eight corners and seven stories and is more than 40 m tall.

Hotels

Qingchuan Hotel, 1 Ximachanglu, Hanyang, tel. 44 11 41, telex 85 50

Shengli Fandian, 晴川饭店 Siweilu 11, tel. 2 25 31, Hankou

Xuangong Fandian, 璇宫饭店 Jianghanyilu 45, tel. 2 44 04, Hankou

Jianghan Fandian, 江汉饭店 Shenglijie 211, tel. 2 39 98, Hankou

Wuchang Fandian, 武昌饭店 Jiefanglu, tel. 7 15 87, Wuchang

Hankou Fandian, Jiefangdadao 326, tel. 5 69 41

Restaurants

Wuchang Canguan, Pengliuyanglu 188, tel. 7 20 29, Wuchang

Guiyuan Si Temple

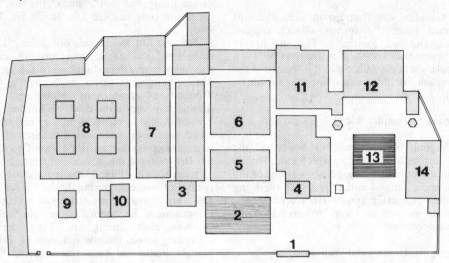

1. Shanmen (Main Gate)
2. Lotus Pond
3. Gulou Drum Tower
4. Zhonglou Bell Tower
5. Weituo Dian Hall
6. Daxiong Baodian Hall
7. Vegetarian Restaurant

8. Luohan Tang Hall
9. Tianwang Dian Hall
10. Dizang Dian Hall
11. Dashi Ge Pavilion
12. Cangjing Ge Pavilion
13. Cuiwei Guchi Pond
14. Nianfo Tang Hall

Guangdong Canguan, Jianghanlu 115, tel. 2 35 75, Hankou (Cantonese Cuisine)

Reganmian Canguan, Pasta restaurant, Zhongshan Dalu 844, tel. 2 47 69, Hankou

Laotongcheng Canguan, Dazhilu 1, tel. 2 15 62, Hankou (local specialities)

Sijimei Canguan, Zhongshan Dadao 888, tel. 2 28 42, Hankou (specialized in dumplings)

Shopping

The main business streets are located in Hankou, namely Zhongshan Dadao, Jiefang Dadao and Jianghanlu.

Friendship Store, Jiefang Dadao

Department Store, Jianghanlu 139 and Jiefang Dadao 208

Arts and Crafts Store, Zhongshan Dadao, Minshenglu

Antiques, Zhongshan Dadao 1039

Travel agency

Zhongshan Dadao 1395, Hankou:

Guoji Lüxingshe, CITS, tel. 2 50 18

Zhongguo Lüxingshe, tel. 2 16 66

Huaqiao Lüxingshe, tel. 2 35 05
service desk at Xuangong Hotel

Gong'an Ju, Public Security Bureau, Shenglijie 206, tel. 2 51 29, Hankou

CAAC flight reservations, Lijibeilu 209, tel. 5 12 48, Hankou

Changjiang Steamship Line, Yanjiang Dadao 80, Hankou
Reservations, tel. 5 32 07
Information, tel. 5 38 75

Bank of China, Zhongshan Dadao 1061, tel. 2 22 22, Hankou

Post office, Zhongshan Dadao 1051, Hankou, tel. 2 18 79

Xiangfan 襄樊市

Xiangfan was founded in 1950 and was formed from the former district capitals Xiangyang and Fancheng. The city lies in northwest Hubei on the Hanshui river and has a population of 680,000. Since it is located at the intersection of three railway lines, the city can be easily reached by train.

Migong Si Temple 米公祠

Migong Si was built in honor of the calligrapher Mi Shi. Along with Su Shi, Huang Tingjian and Cai Xiang, Mi Shi was one of the four most famous calligraphers of the Song period. His calligraphies are stored in the temple, as well as those by several of his contemporaries.

Lüying Bi, Ornamental Wall 绿影壁

This ornamental wall in the southern part of the city is made of greenish stone. King Xiang had his palace built here in 1436, which was completely destroyed in 1641. This large wall was the only thing to remain. It is decorated with an impressive carving: Dragons Playing with a Pearl. The border is embellished with 99 small dragons.

Guangde Si Temple 广德寺

Guangde Si is located 13 km west of where Xiangyang was formerly located. Its special feature is the impressive Duobao Fuota pagoda that was built in 1496. The pagoda is 17 m tall. Five small pagodas stand on its octogonal base. The middle one is a lama pagoda; the other four are hexagonal and are built in the style of pavilions. Those who are interested in the period of the Three Kingdoms will find Xiangfan to be of special interest. Zhuge Liang (181 — 234), the famous political figure and military advisor of the state of Shu, lived here for many years.

Longzhong 古隆中

The former home of Zhuge Liang is located on Longzhong Mountain, approximately 10 km west of Xiangfan. It can be reached from Xiangfan by bus. Zhuge Liang, also called Zhuge Kongming, came originally from Shandong Province. When he was 17 years old, he moved to Xiangyang (present-day Xiangfan) with his uncle, Zhuge Xuan. It is said that Liu Bei, later Emperor of Shu, hurried here three times in 207 to offer Zhuge Liang the post of military advisor. Allegedly, Zhuge Liang was 'not at home' the first two times and only received Liu Bei on his third visit.

He and Liu Bei supposedly discussed the realm's political situation in a straw hut, and it was then that Zhuge Liang gave the advice which later went down in history as the 'Council of Longzhong Mountain': the strategically important cities of Jinzhou and Yizhou should be seized as military bases, and a pact should be made with Sun Quan of Wu to unite against the superior enemy Cao Cao. Liu Bei followed this advice and triumphed.

Even today, Zhuge Liang is regarded as a symbol of wisdom. During the Jin era (265 — 420), an incised stone stele was set up in Longzhong in his honor. The temple Wuhou Ci was built during the Tang period. According to old records and legends, Zhuge Liang's home has been reconstructed. The scenery in the area is very attractive, and the region is well worth a visit for that reason alone.

Travel agency

Zhongguo Lüxingshe, Youyilu 13, tel. 83 33

Wudang Shan Mountains 武当山

The Wudang Shan massif, also called Taihe Shan, Mountain of Supreme Harmony, is located in Junxian district in the northwestern part of the province. The railway line from Xiangfan to Chongqing passes by the northern slopes. The Wudang Shan massif stretches out for more than 400 km. Tianzhu Feng peak is the highest elevation at 1612 m. This peak rises loftily towards the sky and was named Pillar to the Sky by the local inhabitants. It is surrounded by 71 neighboring peaks.

Wudang Shan is one of the sacred mountains of Daoism. Consequently, there are many Daoist attractions that can still be seen there today. Many temples and monasteries sprang up during the Song and Tang eras, but most of them were destroyed at the end of the Yuan period. In 1412, the Yongle Emperor allocated 300,000 workers to his master builders and ordered them to carry out a tremendous construction project on Wudang Shan. Within six years, 46 temples and halls, 72 grottoes, 39 bridges and 12 pavilions and terraces had been completed. Still more buildings were erected from 1552 — 1554. Many are still in good condition today.

The travelers' target is the Heavenly Column, Tianzhu Feng, with its Golden Summit, on

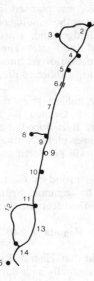

Wudang Shan Mountains

1. –
2. Yuanhe Guan Temple
3. Yuxu Gong Temple
4. Huilong Guan Temple
5. Fuzhen Guan Temple (Taizi Po)
6. Jianhe Qiao Bridge
7. Zixiao Gong Temple
8. Nanyan Cliff Monastery
9. Qixing Shu Tree
10. Huanglong Dong Cave
11. Chaotian Gong Temple
12. Old Route
13. New Route
14. Taihe Gong Temple
15. Jinding, Golden Summit

which stands the Golden Hall. From the middle part of the mountain, at the end of the road, up to the peak, you have to climb up hundreds of steps passing many streams, waterfalls and bridges. It takes about three hours. The way to the top is not dangerous at all, but exhausting. A pair of comfortable shoes for that way is necessary.

Xuanyue Men gate stands at the foot of Wudang Shan. The stone construction was made in 1552, is 20 m high and is embellished with five roofs. Its beautiful carvings are remarkable.

Yuzhen Gong Temple is located at the northern foot of the mountain, about 1 km from Xuanyue Men gate. It was built in 1417 in honor of the Daoist monk Zhang Sanfeng. A bronze statue of the monk, located in Zhenxian Dian, Sacred Hall, is the temple's main attraction. Besides visiting the main hall, visitors can also look at Shanmen, Mountain Gate, and minor halls or else wander down the various walkways.

Constructed in 1413, Yuxu Gong Temple with its two thousand rooms was the largest complex on Wudang Shan. The Red Gate, Red Wall, colorful ceramic models and a stele pavilion still remain. It is not much, but it suffices to give an impression of the former size and splendor.

Yuanhe Guan Temple was laid out in 1413. Interesting bronze statues are located within the complex.

Fuzhen Guan Temple was built into the mountainside in 1419. Taizi Dian hall is located at the highest point. The temple complex fits in well with the natural scenery. A path winds its way among the individual buildings, Longhu

Dian hall, Dragon Tiger Hall, Zhengdian, Main Hall, Houdian, Rear Hall, and the minor halls to the left and the right.

Zixiao Gong Temple is located northeast of Tianzhu Feng peak, directly beneath Zhanqi Feng and 7.5 km from Fuzhen Guan. It was built in 1413 and is one of the best preserved complexes on Wudang Shan. The temple has numerous main and subsidiary halls. The visitor should first turn his attention to the main hall Zixiao Dian; its roof, walls, bracket system, ceilings and sacred sculptures are highly impressive.

Nanyan Cliff Monastery is located 2.5 km west of Zixiao Gong on the steep slope just below the main peak. During the Yuan and Ming periods, it consisted of more than 640 rooms, but unfortunately, almost all of these were destroyed. However, there are still interesting sights that have survived, including the Southern Celestial Gate from the Ming period, stone figures and steles, as well as stone halls from the Yuan period which were carved out of matching stones and put together in the style of a timber frame construction. The scenery is stupendous, but the climb requires a certain amount of fortitude.

Taihe Gong Temple half-way up the main peak Tianzhu Feng, was built in 1416. Bell and drum towers are located left and right of the main hall. A bronze bell from 1416 still hangs in the bell tower. A small bronze hall dating back to 1307 can be found inside Zhuanzhan Dian hall on a small hill across from the main hall.

Behind Taihe Gong, a path leads to Zijin

Cheng wall's southern gate and is the only route to the top of Tianzhu Feng.

Jinding, Golden Summit is Tianzhu Feng's highest point and a point of orientation for the visitor. A bronze hall, the so-called Golden Hall, was erected here in 1416. It is 5.54 m high and 4.4 m wide. It was built in the style of a timber frame construction and is the only one of its kind in China of this magnitude. The hall, which rests upon a granite base, contains several bronze sculptures embellished with gold. One of these represents the Daoist deity Zhen Wu. The symbol for it and Wudang Shan is tortoise and snake.

From Golden Summit, one can see the entire surrounding area, both near and far.

Wulong Gong Temple once stood north of the main peak Tianzhu Feng, about 15 km southwest of Yuxu Gong. The lay-out dates from 1286 but has been almost entirely destroyed. The only sections that can still be seen are the main gate, the Red Wall, a stele pavilion and an old well.

Yichang 宜昌市

Yichang, an old port city on the northern bank of the Changjiang, lies directly before the Changjiang gorges. The steamboats used to make their way this far from the lower course of the river, but they could not risk passing through the gorges. Throughout the city's long history, there were repeated struggles for control of Yichang as the city was the gateway to the rich regions of Sichuan. In the years 1937 — 45, Yichang was largely destroyed by the Japanese, who were also trying to force their way from Hankou to Sichuan.

Today, Yichang is still an important port city, though it no longer represents the only route to Sichuan. Because of the huge hydraulic engineering project that was carried out in the vicinity, the largest one of its kind in China, the city has often been a topic of interest in recent years.

Gezhou Ba Dam 葛洲坝

The key project of the Chinese electric industry, Gezhou Ba, is located about 5 km west of the city. This dam makes it possible to regulate the Changjiang to a considerable extent. It blocks the upper course of the Changjiang, thus making it easier to navigate, controls catastrophic flooding and supplies electricity.

At Yichang, the Changjiang divides into three branches at the point where two islands rise up from the water. The dam's engineers

took advantage of this natural division, and construction was planned in two stages. The first stage was the building of two ship locks, a sluice to dredge sand, a hydro-electric power station and flood-gates. The second phase was the construction of yet another hydro-electric power plant, a sluice to dredge sand and ship locks.

Twenty million gross registered tons can pass through Gezhou Ba in each direction every year. It is hoped that the two hydro-electric power plants with a total capacity of 2.715 GW will put forth an annual supply of 13.8 GWh.

China is proud of Gezhou Ba, especially because the gigantic hydraulic engineering project resulted from its own national efforts.

Tianran Ta Pagoda 天然塔

It is said that Tianran Ta, 7 km east of the city, was originally built during the Jin period and later renovated during the Qing period in 1792. The stone building is octagonal and 42 m high. From the uppermost story, there is a good view of the Changjiang and the mountains.

Travel agency

Zhongguo Lüxingshe, tel. 31 03

Hunan Province 湖南省

Area: 210,000 km^2 / Population: 54 million, 10% of which are Miao, also including Zhuang, Yao, Dong, Tujia / Capital: Changsha. The South China province Hunan is surrounded by Jiangxi in the east, Guangdong and Guangxi in the south, Guizhou and Sichuan in the west and Hubei in the north. The name Hunan means 'south of the lake', namely, south of Dongting Hu.

History

During the Warring States period, the area of present-day Hunan was part of the southernmost region of the Kingdom of Chu. At the time, the area was only sparsely populated by Miao and Yao. From the 3rd to 4th centuries, Han Chinese began coming from the north to settle the land. The native population was forced to resettle in the western and southwestern areas of the province. Migrations from the north would occur again in later dynasties when the north was conquered by other peoples, such as the Mongols and Manchus. During the Yuan and Ming dynasties, the present-day provinces of Hunan and Hubei were joined together to form Huguang Province. Huguang played a key role in the realm during this period with respect to supplying rice as it was one of the most significant agricultural regions. Most of the crops were delivered to the north. The common saying, 'If the harvest was good in Huguang, then the empire is in good shape!' suggests how important the region was from an economical point of view. The rulers of the Qing Dynasty divided Huguang into Hunan and Hubei provinces. In the 20th century, Hunan was the center of the revolutionary movement. Mao Zedong, born in Shaoshan on December 26, 1893, is the most well-known of Hunan's sons. He organized the revolutionary peasant movement in the province from 1926 — 27 and led the Autumn Harvest Uprising of 1927.

In the eastern, southern and western sections of Hunan, there are mountains and hills. Dongting Hu, the second largest freshwater lake in China, spreads out in the northeast. The center of the province is also mountainous. The famous Hengshan mountains which are up to 1,290 m high are located there.

The province's most important river is the Xiangjiang, which flows through the province from south to north and empties into Dongting Hu. Hunan's climate is characterized by damp, hot summers and short, relatively cool winters. The average temperature in Changsha is 30°C in July and 6°C in January. The greatest amount of precipitation occurs during the summer, but the winters are also relatively damp. The variability in precipitation is significantly less than in North China.

Hunan is one of the most important rice-producing regions, because it yields a surplus. The richest area is located along Dongting Hu. Glutinous rice is cultivated here during the summer. However, due to the cool winter months, only one rice crop is possible each year. Dry land farming is resorted to in order to bring in a second harvest, yielding such crops as corn, winter wheat, barley, sweet potatoes, soy beans and sorghum. Only about one-fifth of the province's land can be put to agricultural use; one-half of that is used for rice cultivation. In the mountainous regions, tea crops take precedence.

Approximately 22% of the province is covered with forests and is put to use by the wood industry. Pine, maple, bamboo, cedar and spruce are among the most important types of wood. Hunan is also interesting as a supplier of mineral resources. The province has what is probably the world's largest supply of antimony. Furthermore, there are also deposits of tin, lead, zinc, tungsten, copper and coal.

Since 1949, light and heavy industries have had the opportunity to develop. Iron and steel works have sprung up in the cities of Changsha, Xiangtan and Zhuzhou.

Changsha 长沙市

Changsha is located on the Xiangjiang's east bank. With a population of 2.4 million, it is the political, economic and cultural center of the province.

History

In the 1st century BC, the center of the Kingdom of Chu was located here. Even then, the people who resided here were greatly skilled in metal and lacquer work and embroidery. More than a thousand graves have been uncovered in the area during the last decades, some of which date back to the Zhou and Han dynasties. They contained cult objects, jewelry and silk and lacquer work, the unusual beauty of which is likely to astonish the beholder. Therefore, it is advisable to take advantage of a chance to visit the Hunan Provincial Museum and see the funerary objects uncovered in the Mawangdui grave. The city was given the name Changsha in 589. In the following centuries it became one of China's leading rice markets and a large trading center. It was fortified at the beginning of the Ming era, and nine city gates were built. In 1644, after the division of Huguang Province, Changsha became the capital of Hunan. Rebel troops besieged the city during the Taiping Rebellion but never succeeded in capturing it. To the contrary, Changsha played the major role in putting down the rebellion. Zeng Guofan, born in Changsha, was the high official and commanding officer of the provincial army that dealt the Taiping Rebellion its final blow.

In 1904, the city was opened up to foreign trade. Europeans and Americans settled down in Changsha. The construction of the railway line connecting Changsha with Hankou and Beijing in 1908 sped up the development of light industry. The city suffered serious damages during the Sino-Japanese War. After the founding of the People's Republic, Changsha was able to build up its position as an important hub of trade, especially for rice,

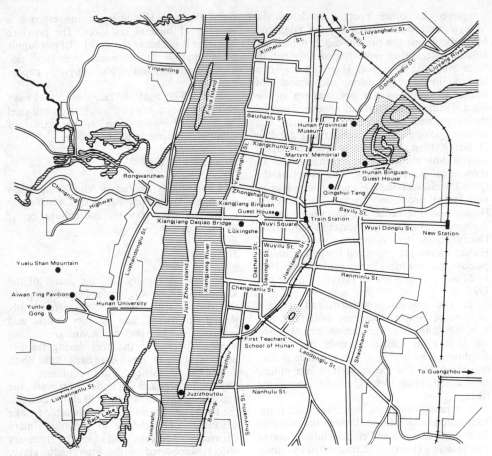

Map of Changsha

cotton and wood. Changsha's location on the Xiangjiang favors this role. Its harbor is the largest one along the Xiangjiang. Meanwhile, Changsha has become a modern industrial city. Light industry and the aluminum industry predominate.

Schools and academies have been located here for quite a long time. As far back as the Song Dynasty, an excellent academy was located here where the philosopher Zhu Xi occasionally taught.

The visitor is frequently confronted with historic sites connected with Mao Zedong. Mao lived in Changsha from 1911 to 1923. He worked and studied here.

Yuelu Shan Mountain 岳麓山

Yuelu Shan lies on the Xiangjiang's west bank. It attains a height of 297 m. The mountain is not only interesting for its scenery, but also because it can be considered the

province's cultural center. Hunan University, a teacher's college, and polytechnic and research institutes are all located here. A park opened in 1975 contains the following places of interest:

Yuelu Shuyuan, Yuelu Academy 岳麓书院

Yuelu Academy is located at the eastern foot of Yuelu Shan. It was built in 976 and was one of the four largest academies during the Song Dynasty. The philosopher Zhu Xi (1130 — 1200) taught here occasionally.

The academy was changed to a university in 1903. Hunan University has been located here since 1925.

Aiwan Ting Pavilion 爱晚亭

Aiwan Ting was built in a maple wood on a small hill behind the old Yuelu Academy in 1792.

Lushan Si Temple 麓山寺

Lushan Si is located halfway up Yuelu Shan. It was founded in 268 and has been renovated several times. It is one of the oldest temples in Hunan.

The main gate and the pavilion Cangjing Ge can still be visited today. Not far away, there is a stone tablet from 730, with an inscription by the famous Tang calligrapher Li Yong (678 — 747). The inscription contains more than 1,400 characters and reports of the building of the temple and the Buddhist ceremonies that were held there. This tablet is one of the most precious ones in China.

Yuwang Bei Stone Stele 禹王碑

This stele, located on the mountain peak, has an inscription consisting of 77 characters. It is supposed to be from the official He Zhi of the Southern Song period. It describes the battle led against floods by the mythical Emperor Yu.

Juzi Zhou, Orange Island 橘子洲

Orange Island is located in the middle of the Xiangjiang, and it stretches out more than 5 km from north to south with a width of only 45 — 145 m. The island was named for the many orange trees that grow here. In the south, a beautiful pavilion stands in a public park. The view across the river is especially good from the southern end of the island.

Hunan Diyi Shifan Xuexiao, The First Teachers' School of Hunan 湖南第一师范学校

The first Teachers' School where Mao Zedong studied from 1913 — 1918 and worked from 1920 — 1921 is located in the southern part of the city. During this period, Mao organized a students' union and one of the first night schools for workers. In addition, he founded the research group *New People, Xinmin Xuehui*, and a Marxist students' committee. The school was destroyed by fire in 1938 and rebuilt following the original plans after 1949.

Qingshui Tang 清水塘

Qingshui Tang, Clear Water Pond, is the name of the building where the first few meetings of the Hunan Party Committee took place. The rooms where the meetings were held and the living quarters of Mao Zedong and other leading party members can still be visited

today.

Lieshi Jinianta, Martyrs' Memorial Pagoda 湖南烈士公园纪念塔

Lieshi Jinianta, located in Lieshi Gongyuan park, Martyrs' Park, was erected in 1955 in honor of the martyrs of the struggle for liberation. The memorial pagoda is 36.8 m high. An exhibition hall is located within the pagoda's base.

Hunan Sheng Bowuguan, Hunan Provincial Museum 湖南省博物馆

The Provincial Museum, in the northeast part of the city not far from Martyrs' Memorial Pagoda, contains an extremely interesting display of archeological finds that were obtained when a more than 2000-year-old grave was uncovered. In 1972, grave sites from the Western Han period (206 BC — 8 AD) were excavated by archeologists in Mawangdui, northeast of Changsha. One of these contained the corpse of a 50-year-old woman, the consort of a high official who probably lived from 190—140 BC. Surprisingly, the corpse was still completely preserved. Medical investigations revealed details about the woman's eating habits and her medical history. The grave cavity was located 20 m below the ground. All of the artifacts placed in the grave, the magnificently formed outer and inner caskets, as well as the corpse itself, can be seen at the museum. The body laid wrapped in more than 20 layers of silk and linen inside an inner casket upon which a banner for the soul, a T-shaped silk picture, had been placed. The picture, which is still in good condition, is one of the most exciting finds from the grave site. It describes the voyage of the dead to the next world and shows the living creatures and plants which belong to that world. The painting techniques and colors are of the highest quality. The other funerary objects, particularly the lacquer work, demonstrate a surprising artistic skill for craftsmen of that time.

Kaifu Si Temple 开福寺

Kaifu Si, located on Xiangchunjie street, dates back to the year 907, but it had to be constantly rebuilt and restored after the repeated destruction that it suffered during the Song, Ming and Qing periods. The present-day complex still contains the halls Sansheng Dian, Daxiong Baodian and Pilu Dian, as well as part of the main gate. Daxiong Baodian hall was built in 1923.

Hotels

Xiangjiang Binguan, 湘江宾馆 Zhongshan-donglu, 267 tel. 2 62 61, all services available. The Friendship Store, Youyi Shangdian, is also located at this hotel.

Furong Fandian, 芙蓉饭店 Wuyilu, tel. 2 53 10, newly established modern hotel.

Hunan Binguan, 湖南宾馆 Yingbinlu 9, tel. 2 63 31, (only for Chinese guests)

Rongyuan Binguan, at Nianjia Lake, tel. 26 74 00

Restaurants

Changsha Fandian, Wuyidonglu 116, tel. 2 50 29

Youyicun Fandian, Zhongshanlu 116, tel. 2 42 57

Shopping

Friendship Store, Xiangjiang Binguan, see above

Antiques Store, in Hunan Provincial Museum, Dongfenglu, tel. 2 52 77

Arts and Crafts Store, Wuyi Guangchang, Wuyilu 92

Zhongshanlu Baihuo Shangdian Department Store, Zhongshanlu 213

The main business streets are Zhongshan and Huangxinglu.

Travel agency

Guoji Lüxingshe, CITS, and **Zhongguo Lüxingshe** and **Huaqiao Lüxingshe,** Wuyixilu, Sanxingjie 130, tel. 2 22 50 at Furong Hotel
Gong'an Ju, Public Security Bureau, Daqinglu, Simenkou, tel. 2 48 98

CAAC ticket agency, Wuyidonglu 5, tel. 2 38 20

Train station, Wuyidonglu, tel. 2 63 26

Yueyang 岳阳市

Yueyang is located on the railway line Beijing — Guangzhou on the east bank of Dongting Hu Lake in the northern part of the province. It is about 8 km from the place where Dongting Hu flows into the Changjiang river.

Yueyang was a fortified town as far back as the Han Dynasty. In 589, the city was given the name Yuezhou by the Sui rulers. During the Song Dynasty, it became the headquarters of the military prefecture Yueyang.

Above all else, Yueyang specializes in trade and is a redistribution point for cotton, grains, and particularly wood. The wood is rafted along various waterways towards Yueyang, and from there it is transferred to further points by train or down the Changjiang.

The city's most well-known tourist attraction is Yueyang Tower 岳阳楼 on the shores of Dongting Hu. It is one of the three largest tower constructions south of the Changjiang. It was originally set up on the south side of Tianyue Shan mountain in 716, but was a victim of destruction in later centuries and had to be restored several times. After it had been rebuilt once more in 1867, it was turned into the city's west gate.

The tower has three stories and is 19.7 m high. It was built entirely of wood; four main columns made of *nanmu* wood form the building's core, which is finished off by 24 outer and 12 interior columns. Many famous poets have praised this tower in the past, including Du Fu, Li Bai, Bai Juyi and Han Yu. The most famous lines were written by Fan Zhongyan (989 — 1052) in 1045 after the tower was rebuilt once again. 'From the dawn's first glimmer to the glow of dusk, the tower is blessed with a thousand changing faces.'

Dongting Hu Lake 洞庭湖

Dongting Hu is south of the Changjiang and is joined with the latter by several canals, thus making it a significant factor in regulating the mighty river. About 40% of the river's water flows into the lake, which is also fed by the four rivers of Xiangjiang, Zishui, Yuanjiang and Lishui. At Yueyang, water from Dongting Hu flows once more into the Changjiang. During the dry season from October to April, more water flows from Dongting Hu into the Changjiang than flows into the lake from the Changjiang in the west, and the water level falls considerably. For this reason, the size of the lake also varies. In normal times the area is ca. 3,700 km^2, but it increases up to 4,900 km^2 during the yearly high water periods from June to October.

Many poets dedicated their works to Dongting Hu. One of the first was Qu Yuan (ca. 332 — 295 BC). Those who travel by boat from Yueyang's harbor to Dongting Hu are rewarded by a magnificent view of Yueyang, Yueyang Tower and Junshan Island.

Junshan Island 君山

Junshan is located in Dongting Hu, approximately 15 km southwest of the city. It has an area of 100 hectares and consists of small hills, ravines, woods, terraced tea plantations and small canals. It can be compared to a botanical garden which, above all else, excels in different bamboo varieties. The island's tea is excellent. It used to be delivered as tribute to the emperor.

Xiangtan 湘潭市

Xiangtan lies at the confluence of the Xiangjiang and the Lianshui about 35 km southwest of Changsha. Since 1957, the city has been connected to the railway line from Zhuzhou to Huaihua. Xiangtan has become considerably more important as a port city and a trading center for rice and other agricultural products from the southern part of Hunan in the last decades. It used to be a medicinal herbs center. Since 1949, various industries have been opened, including textile factories (Xiangtan is an important location for cotton finishing) and a large iron and steel integrated plant. The present population is estimated at 400,000.

Guansheng Dian Temple 关圣殿

Guansheng Dian, located on Pingzhenglu street, was built in the first years of the Qing Dynasty and dedicated to Guan Yu, a general of the state of Shu during the period of the Three Kingdoms. He became famous for his bravery. After his death, he was declared a war god. The present complex consists of the main hall, *Dadian, Chunqiu Ge* pavilion and a drum and a bell tower.

Shaoshan Village, The Birthplace of Mao Zedong 韶山村

Shaoshan, the village where Mao Zedong was born, lies in a valley surrounded by hills ca. 100 km from Changsha and 45 km west of Xiangtan. Even today, many of the inhabitants are numbered among the Mao clan.

The House where Mao Zedong was Born
毛泽东故居

Mao came into the world in a farmhouse built in the typical Hunan style on December 26, 1893. The house is quite spacious. Mao's father was among the relatively well-off peasants who owned a piece of land for themselves. The house was originally divided into two sections, but today it is divided into three. The reception hall for visitors is located in the right wing. The living quarters — consisting of three bedrooms, a dining room, kitchen and bathroom — border on the inner courtyard from where one can reach a small guest room and various storage rooms. A lotus pond in which Mao is supposed to have bathed as a small boy is located in front of the house. He once labored in the surrounding rice fields. Time permitting, a stroll through the immediate neighborhood can be very pleasant.

Mao left his parents' home in 1910 and did not return until 1925, when he came to organize the peasant movement. One result of this work was the report 'Investigation of the Peasant Movement in Hunan' from February, 1927.

Mao Zedong Museum

Mao Zedong's childhood and revolutionary works are documented by the pictures and writings on display in this museum. Shaoshan Guest House offers its visitors board and lodging. Those who are only passing by can also try a meal here prepared in the typical Hunan style.

Hengshan Mountains 衡山

Hengshan, also called Nanyue, South Mountain, or Goulou Shan, is one of China's five sacred mountains. The other four are Taishan in Shandong, Huashan in Shaanxi, Songshan in Henan and Hengshan in Shanxi. (The names of the two Hengshan mountains correspond to each other only in the way they are pronounced and not in the way they are written.)

The Hengshan massif rises up south of Changsha and north of Hengyang in Hengshan district. If one takes the Beijing — Guangzhou train from Changsha traveling southwards, it is possible to get out at Hengshan and take a bus at the train station direct to the Nanyue Zhen community at the foot of Hengshan.

Hengshan is not only known for its magnificent scenery, 72 peaks and the many ancient trees, but also for its cultural sites. Ancient texts tell of mythical emperors who made sacrifices to the mountain. In the course of centuries, Daoist and Buddhist temples were established here. The rulers of the Qing Dynasty proved to be generous and had many

1. Bus Station
2. Nanyue Zhen Community
3. Nanyue Miao Temple
4. Zhusheng Si Temple
5. Jiahe Feng Peak
6. Huangting Guan Monastery
7. Zhonglie Ci Temple
8. Nantai Si Temple
9. Fuyan Si Temple
10. Mojing Tai Terrace
11. Banshan Ting Pavilion
12. Fangguang Si Temple
13. Tianzhu Feng Peak
14. Magu Qiao Bridge
15. Tiefo Si Temple
16. Wuyue Dian Hall
17. Shuzhuang Tai Terrace
18. Cangjing Dian Hall
19. Yanxia Feng Peak
20. Furong Feng Peak
21. Southern Celestial Gate, Nantian Men
22. Shizi Yan Stone
23. Guangji Si Temple
24. Shangfeng Si Temple
25. Wangri Tai Platform
26. Zhurong Feng Peak

Hengshan Mountains

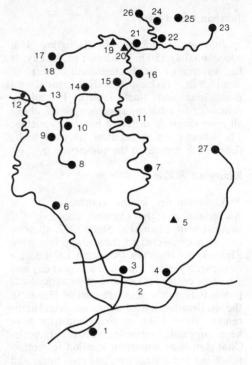

of the temples restored. Poets and writers expressed their admiration of Hengshan. Many of their words and sayings were chiseled in stone and can still be seen on the mountains today.

Zhusheng Si Temple founded in the Tang era, is located several hundred meters east of Nanyue Miao temple. The present buildings date back to 1714. Among the separated halls, Luohan Hall is especially interesting.

Nanyue Miao, South Mountain Temple is located north of the Nanyue Zhen community. It is the largest temple on any of the five sacred mountains and also one of the three most famous temples in China. (The other two are Daimiao in Tai'an, Shandong, at the foot of Taishan and Zhongyue Miao in Dengfeng district, Henan.) The temple was built during the Tang period in 725. During the following centuries, it had to be restored several times and later, entirely rebuilt. The complex which can be visited today dates from 1882. The main hall, Zhengdian, is a magnificent example of a timber frame construction. Its double roof is supported by 72 columns, representing Hengshan's 72 peaks. The hall stands upon a terrace surrounded by an artistically carved balustrade.

Behind the temple, a path leading to the top

of Zhurong Peak passes by Luosi Tan pond and the Nanyue Reservoir, Nanyue Shuiku, across Yuban Qiao bridge. It then leads to Zhonglie Ci, the ceremonious memorial complex which was built in 1942 in memory of those who fell during the Sino - Japanese War. A memorial tablet records the Japanese attack of July 7, 1937. The path then leads to Banshan Ting, a pavilion located half-way up the mountain which was built in 1878. Those who have the time and interest can diverge towards the west from here. One crosses Magu Qiao bridge and arrives at Mojing Tai terrace.

The 6th century temple complex Fuyan Si is located about half a kilometer south of Mojing Tai. The present complex was built in 1870 and consists of several halls, South of Fuyan Si and about 4 km from Nanyue Miao stands Nantai Si temple. It originally dated from 561 — 565. The present buildings were built from 1902 — 1906. A path leading northwest from Mojing Tai takes one to the ancient temple Fangguang Si from 503, which was restored at the beginning of the Qing era. There is a wonderful view of the mountains from this spot.

From Banshan Ting, the steep, zigzag path leads by four small compounds, Yehou

Shuyuan school, Tiefo Si temple, Wuyue Dian hall and Xiangnan Si temple. It finally reaches Nantian Men, Southern Celestial Gate, about 10 km from the Nanyue Zhen community. If one looks out from Nanyue Zhen, Nantian Men appears to be located at the mountain's highest point, but this is deceptive. Three paths lead away from Nantian Men in different directions. The first path leads east towards Guangji Si temple, and a second one leads west towards Cangjing Dian hall where sacred Buddhist texts, a present from the first Ming emperor, Zhu Yuanzhang, used to be stored. The present hall was built in 1931. The view of the surrounding area is beautiful. If one takes the path from Nantian Men leading towards the north, one reaches Zhurong Feng, which, at 1,290 m, is the highest of Hengshan's 72 peaks. Zhurong Dian hall, built at the end of the 16th century and restored in 1751, stands here. Reconstruction followed in 1881. Zhurong Feng offers a splendid view of the surrounding peaks and the far-off landscape.

Travel agency

Zhongguo Lüxingshe Hengyang, Jiangdong Qu, Guangdonglu, tel. 33 14

Guangdong Province 广东省

Area: 212,000 km² / Population: 59.299 million / Capital: Guangzhou

Guangdong is the southernmost of China's 21 provinces and autonomous regions. Hainan, China's largest island excluding Taiwan, with an area of 34,000 km², is also part of Guangdong Province. The province borders on Guangxi, Hunan, Jiangxi and Fujian and on the South China Sea. Guangdong has the longest coast of all of China's coastal provinces.

History

Parts of present-day Guangdong were subjugated under Emperor Qin Shihuang (period of reign 221 — 210 BC) and annexed to the empire. At that time, Guangdong was populated by non-Han-Chinese ethnic groups. Presumably, Miao, Li and Yao were the area's first inhabitants. The most important group to be added to this list by the 3rd century was the Zhuang minority, whose descendants were later called Yue.

Under Han Wudi (period of reign 140 — 86 BC), the Chinese empire was expanded to include Hainan Island. The area of present-day Guangdong was officially already part of the empire, but few Han Chinese lived there. The situation did not change until the 6th century. The areas now known as Guangdong and Guangxi were joined together to form the independent state of Nanhan from 909 — 971. By the 12th century, Guangzhou city had developed into a center for foreign trade with a population of several hundred thousand inhabitants. The large migrations of Han Chinese towards the south and consequently towards Guangdong began in the 12th century when the Song Dynasty rulers were driven south by the invading Jin from the north. A second large wave of migration began in the 13th century. At that time, it was the Mongols who made their way into China from the north. With the enormous increase in population caused by those who had fled from the north, Guangdong's economy and culture underwent a period of rapid development. Even in the 17th and following centuries, people continued to stream southwards towards Guangdong, Guangxi, Sichuan and Taiwan. Later, many people from Guangdong made their way to Southeast Asia and North America, and they soon played an important role in spreading foreign trade and establishing world wide relations.

Foreign influence left its traces in Guangdong as far back as the Tang Dynasty (618 — 907). Muslim travelers brought their religion with them and built one of the first mosques in Guangzhou (Canton). During the 16th century, Europeans began to gain influence. In 1553, Macao fell under the administrative authority of Portugal, Hongkong under British authority in 1841—1842 and in 1898, Guangzhou Bay under French authority.

Guangdong has produced famous political figures and philosophers such as Kang Youwei, Liang Qichao and Sun Yatsen. Guangdong is separated from the Changjiang by the Nanling massif. More than 70% of the province's area is mountainous or hilly, and there are a total of 1,343 streams and rivers. Thanks to a high annual precipitation, Guangdong's rivers have large quantities of water and are well situated as transportation routes. The largest rivers are the Hanjiang and the Zhujiang river system (Pearl River), whose three most important rivers are the Xijiang (West), Beijiang (North) and Dongjiang (East) rivers. The Xijiang's lower course is named Zhujiang on the far side of the confluence of the three rivers.

Guangdong's climate ranges from sub-tropic to tropic. The average temperature is 28

— 30°C in July and 13 — 16°C in January. The summer season lasts 10 months in Hainan and six months in the northern part of the province, where, in winter, there is even frost at times.

The annual precipitation ranges from 1,500 — 2,500 mm. The rainy season begins in mid-May and lasts until mid-October. Approximately half of the annual precipitation falls between June and August. Typhoons plague the region from July to September and can cause catastrophic damage with the heavy rainfall.

Only about 15% of the total land area can be put to agricultural use, a fact which makes intensive farming unavoidable. About two-thirds of the farmland is used for the cultivation of glutinous rice. Two rice crops are feasible each year; in some areas a third crop, using dry land farming, is also harvested. Irrigation is extremely important in rice cultivation. Great strides have been made in this area since 1949. The construction of numerous reservoirs, canals and pumping stations has not only guaranteed a smooth-running irrigation and drainage system, but has also dispelled the dangers of flooding. Agricultural products other than rice include sugar-cane, sweet potatoes and peanuts. As a producer of fruit, Guangdong is also important nation-wide. Oranges, litchis, pineapples and bananas are among the most coveted fruits.

A number of industrial crops are grown, such as sisal, hemp, coffee, black pepper and rubber. The fishing industry should also be mentioned. Guangdong supplies about one-fourth of China's fish requirements.

Guangdong has various mineral resources. Among these, the deposits of manganese are particularly important and account for about 60% of China's total supply. Furthermore, there are also deposits of coal, tungsten, antimony, lead and iron. Light industry plays an important role; it accounts for approximately 3/4 of industrial production. The food-processing and textile industries are its most essential branches. Metal finishing and machinery and ship building are the most important branches in the heavy industry sector.

About 2% of the population are members of minorities. Among these are Li, who make up the largest group and live mostly in the mountainous regions on Hainan Island. Yao are the next largest group, followed by Miao and Zhuang.

There are many dialects in Guangdong. Cantonese is by far the most prominent of these, and it is especially spoken in the western and center regions of the province. The Hakka dialect can be heard in the north and northeast, and the Fujian dialect, primarily in the eastern coastal regions.

Guangzhou (Canton) 广州市

With a population of 5.61 million, Guangzhou is the largest city in South China. It lies on the fertile plains along the banks of the Zhujiang, 50 km from Humen, Tiger Gate, the entrance to the sea, and 180 km from Hongkong. Guangzhou is a significant industrial center and concurrently, one of China's most important locations for foreign trade, which is favored by the harbors and the close vicinity to Hongkong.

History

The symbol of Guangzhou is goats. A legend tells of five gods who came riding down from heaven on goats. Each goat carried a stalk of rice in its mouth. The gods gave the rice to the people of the Zhujiang plains and called, 'May you always be free from hunger!' With that, the gods disappeared. Only the goats remained and turned into stone statues.

The first settlement in this region was founded by the troops of Qin Shihuang in the 3rd century BC. Beginning in the Tang Dynasty, Guangzhou developed into a center of foreign trade. The foreign influence left its mark, and a large Islamic community came into being. During the Song Dynasty, the city experienced prosperous times. Production works developed, including, above all, shipyards in addition to ceramic workshops. Guangzhou became the first city to fall under the influence of the western power struggle. In 1517, the Portuguese landed in Canton, then came the Spaniards and the Dutch, who would later be followed by the British, French and Americans. The British, who did not manage to set up trade in Canton until the end of the 17th century, became the leading foreign power by the 19th century. Guangzhou was one of the first five harbors that were forced open to foreign trade under the conditions of the Unequal Treaties of Nanjing. The French and British concessions were founded on Shamian Island in 1858. After 1880, foreign businesses built large administration buildings on the new streets along the shores. Nationalism, a willingness for reform and the desire for revolution came about early as a result of the confrontation with foreigners and foreign influence. In the middle of the 19th

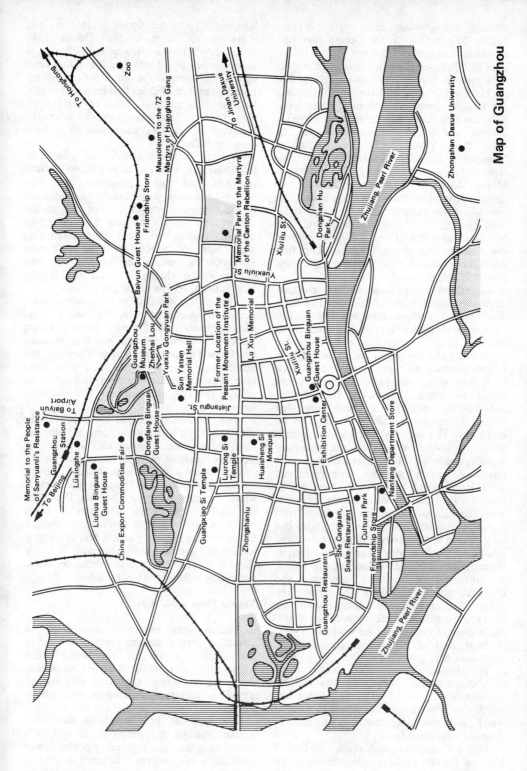

Map of Guangzhou

Zoo

To Hongkong

Mausoleum to the 72 Martyrs of Huanghua Gang

To Jinan Daxue University

Memorial Park to the Martyrs of the Canton Rebellion

Zhongshan Daxue University

Zhujiang, Pearl River

Dongshan Hu Park

Xiuliu St.

Yuexiu St.

Baiyun Guest House

Friendship Store

Guangzhou Museum

Zhenhai Lou

Yuexiu Gongyuan Park

Sun Yatsen Memorial Hall

Former Location of the Peasant Movement Institute

Lu Xun Memorial

Guangzhou Binguan Guest House

Xiuliu St.

To Baiyun Airport

Guangzhou Station

Memorial to the People of Sanyuanli's Resistance

To Beijing

Lüxingshe

Dongfang Binguan Guest House

Jietangu St.

Exhibition Center

Liuhua Binguan Guest House

China Export Commodities Fair

Liurong Si Temple

Huaisheng Si Mosque

Guangxiao Si Temple

Zhongshanlu

She Canguan, Snake Restaurant

Cultural Park

Nanfang Department Store

Guangzhou Restaurant

Friendship Store

Zhujiang, Pearl River

century, revolutionary ideas were put into action. The prelude to the Opium War, the courageous actions of Lin Zexu who had more than 20,000 cases of British opium destroyed, took place in Guangzhou (see page 267). The people's indignation and their revolt against the English threat resulted in the Sanyuanli Rebellion (see page 334). Guangzhou played a decisive role in the Revolution of 1911. In 1923, Sun Yatsen, who was born in Guangzhou himself, founded the Kuomintang, the National Party, here. The Whampoa Military Academy was opened in 1924; one of its most famous students was Zhou Enlai. The city was a revolutionary center up to 1927. Mao Zedong, Zhou Enlai, Lu Xun and Guo Moruo taught here at the first cadre school, the Peasant Movement Institute. The first attempt to create an urban commune also took place in Guangzhou.

Guangzhou's appearance has changed drastically since the first revolution. The city's much-needed modernization was begun after 1918 under the direction of Sun Yatsen. Streets had to be built, since up to this time, except for the streets along the shores and in the English-French concessions, there was only a network of narrow alleys and paths which were not suited for cars and streetcars. Hundreds of huts were torn down, filthy canals were filled in and streets and arcades were built in all directions. The old city wall had to be torn down in order to procure the necessary building materials. The measures that were introduced by Sun Yatsen have been continued to a large extent since 1949. New public facilities such as schools, hospitals, parks, sport facilities and museums have been built. People who lived on boats, such as today can only be seen in Aberdeen, Hongkong, received new living quarters. More than 3,000 industrial concerns arose, including steel manufacturers, machine and ship-building concerns, and chemical, textile and food industries. The famous Canton Fair, which takes place in the spring and autumn, attracts more than 30,000 businessmen from all over the world each year. A large part of China's foreign trade is conducted here.

The People's Communes in the areas around Guangzhou supply the city with an abundance of food of all kinds. Hongkong, which also depends on Guangzhou to meet its water and electricity needs, can also be supplied with fresh food.

Today, Guangzhou is also called the City of Flowers. Flowers make their impression on the street scenery everywhere; they can be seen at the markets, in houses, on window sills and balconies. There are flower exhibitions, and every spring there is the Flower Fair. Guangzhou's love of flowers is partly due to economic reasons. More than a hundred years ago, Guangzhou was a center for tea export. Large quantities of dried flowers were brought here to scent the teas. Most of the flowers came from the land around the city where the breeding of flowers had meanwhile been commercialized.

Guangzhou is not only a trade and industrial city, but also an important cultural center in South China. Zhongshan Daxue, Sun Yatsen University, is also famous abroad. Fans of the Chinese opera should not pass up the opportunity to visit the local Yue and Chao operas. Guangzhou has many interesting sights. Some of the most beautiful are Yuexiu Park, Qixing Yan, Seven Star Cliff, located 118 km west of Guangzhou, and the Conghua Hot Springs, 80 km to the north.

The city is divided by two main transportation axes. Jiefanglu, the central axis, runs vertically from the north past the China Export Commodities Fair, Dongfang Binguan hotel and Yuexiu Gongyuan park towards the Exhibition Center in the south. Zhongshanlu (Sun Yatsen Street) intersects Jiefanglu and divides the city into northern and southern halves.

The Cantonese cuisine should also be mentioned as it is famous not only at home but also abroad. Since Guangdong is a coastal province, seafood plays an important role.

No matter how full your program is, try anyhow to pay a visit to Qingping free market, which stretches along the Qingping Road. To the southern end of this street you will see a bridge, which leads you to the north part of Shamian Island. Here you will find everything for eating, not necessarily palatable to every Cantonese. There are also herbs, ceramics, porcelains and other things for sale.

Yuexiu Shan Park 越秀山

Yuexiu Shan mountain, considered an attraction even in ancient times, is located in the north. Several of the stone stairs supposedly date from the Western Han period. After the revolution, the entire area around Yuexiu Mountain was converted into a huge public park.

The park has three man-made lakes with islands, bridges and pavilions, as well as a sports complex, two swimming pools, flower exhibitions and gardens. The city's landmark, the monument of the five goats, can also be seen here.

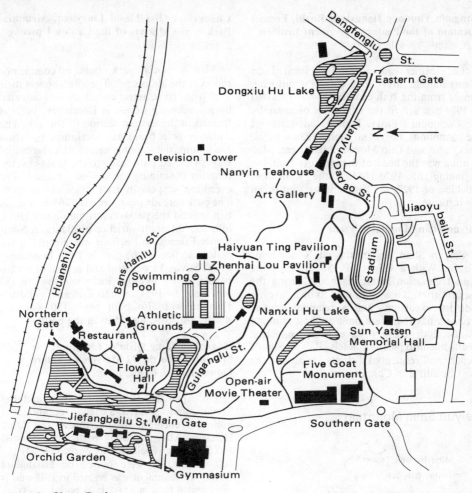

Yuexiu Shan Park

The park's most impressive building is Zhenhai Lou, Sea View Pavilion. It was originally constructed in 1380 and rebuilt after a fire in 1686. At that time, it was a watch tower to guard against foreign and local pirates.

Zhenhai Lou is 28 m high and has five stories. The dark red building has housed the Guangzhou Museum, Guangzhou Bowuguan, since 1953. Prehistoric times and the first dynasties are dealt with on the ground floor. Archeological finds, such as funerary objects, tools and bronze and lacquer items can be seen in the exhibitions. The Sui — Yuan dynasties are the theme of the next floor, followed by the Ming era. The 19th century from the Opium War up to the Revolution of 1911 and Sun Yatsen are handled on the fourth floor. The last floor contains displays describing, among

other things, the communist movement in Guangzhou.

A memorial to Sun Yatsen, Zhongshan Jinianbei, built from granite in 1929, is located on the mountain peak. It is 27 m high. Sun Yatsen's testament can be read on the front side of the stele. Steps lead away from the memorial up to Zhongshan Jiniantang, Sun Yatsen Memorial Hall. When Sun Yatsen died in 1925, this hall was erected to commemorate his revolutionary works. The building was built from 1929 — 1931, following the plans of the architect Lü Yanzhi. The hall has palatial dimensions. The roof was covered with ceramic tiles. The inner rooms can accommodate 4,700 people for meetings or cultural events. A display in the adjacent hall to the west gives information about the life and works of Sun Yatsen.

Nongmin Yundong Jiangxisuo Jiuzhi, Former Location of the Peasant Movement Institute 农民运动讲习所旧址

The former cadre school is located on Zhongshansilu street in a former Confucian temple from the 16th century. It was founded in 1924 and served the education of cadre by the Communist Party. Famous advocates of the communist movement such as Zhou Enlai, Qu Qiubai and Guo Moruo taught here. Mao Zedong was the head of the institute from the beginning of 1926. After the Cantonese rebellion of 1927, the Kuomintang shut down the institute.

Baiyun Shan Mountain 白云山

Baiyun Shan lies in the city's northeast suburb. With a height of 382 m, it is the highest elevation in Guangzhou. During the last centuries, it has continued to be a favorite spot for excursions and a religious center. Private villas that were built at the beginning of the 20th century have been converted meanwhile into pleasant hotels. Baiyun Shan's scenery and residential districts are among the most beautiful in China today.

Baiyun Shan Mountain

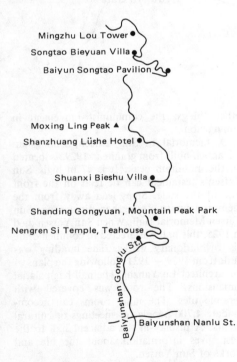

Mingzhu Lou Tower
Songtao Bieyuan Villa
Baiyun Songtao Pavilion

Moxing Ling Peak ▲
Shanzhuang Lüshe Hotel

Shuanxi Bieshu Villa

Shanding Gongyuan, Mountain Peak Park
Nengren Si Temple, Teahouse

Baiyunshan Gonglu St.

Baiyunshan Nanlu St.

Guangzhou Qiyi Lieshi Lingyuan, Memorial Park to the Martyrs of the Canton Uprising 广州起义烈士陵园

This memorial park, built in commemoration of the almost 5,700 people who lost their lives when the Canton commune was defeated by Kuomintang troops in December, 1927, is located in the eastern section of the city. The entrance gate bears an inscription by Zhou Enlai and the monogram of this memorial spot. A paved path leads to the grass-covered tumulus containing the victims' remains. The execution supposedly took place at this spot. The park spreads out more than 26 hectares. A trip around the park reveals man-made lakes, hills and different varieties of plants. A Sino-Soviet Friendship Pavilion was erected in the eastern section of the park in 1957, in memory of the Soviet Vice-consul and several of his co-workers who likewise lost their lives in the rebellion. In 1964, a Sino-Korean Friendship Pavilion was also built here. 150 Koreans, mostly students, also died in the battle.

Huanghua Gang Qishi'er Lieshimu, Mausoleum to the 72 Martyrs of Yellow Flower Hill 黄花岗七十二烈士墓

On April 27, 1911, Sun Yatsen and the Tongmenhui, United League, organized a military rebellion to overthrow the Qing Dynasty. After a bloody battle that claimed 100 lives, the rebellion was put down. Of the 100 victims, 72 were buried on Huanghua Gang. A monument was erected in 1918 and is surrounded by a huge park. A path leads from the entrance directly to the grave site where a pavilion-like stone building and an obelisk stand. A decorative building rises up in the background which is exceeded in turn by a pyramid-shaped wall. The wall consists of 72 stones, symbolizing the 72 victims.

Lu Xun Jinianguan, Lu Xun Memorial 鲁迅纪念馆

Lu Xun Memorial is located on Yan'anerlu street on the premises of the old Guangzhou University. The first congress of the Kuomintang, the National Party, met here in 1924 under the leadership of Sun Yatsen. Guangdong University, founded by Sun Yatsen in 1924, was re-named Zhongshan University after his death. The leading champion of modern literature, Lu Xun, lived and taught here in 1927. His living quarters and the rooms where he taught can still be visited. A display tells about the writer's life

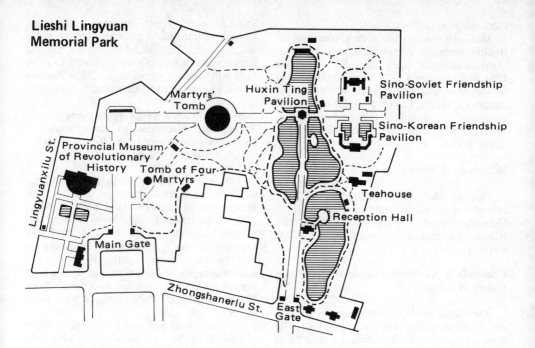

Lieshi Lingyuan Memorial Park

Martyrs' Tomb

Huxin Ting Pavilion

Sino-Soviet Friendship Pavilion

Sino-Korean Friendship Pavilion

Provincial Museum of Revolutionary History

Tomb of Four Martyrs

Teahouse

Reception Hall

Main Gate

Lingyuanxilu St.

Zhongshanerlu St.

East Gate

and works.

In 1931, the University moved to the southern part of the city, where it is still located today.

Zhonghua Quanguo Zonggonghui Jiuzhi, Former Office of the All-China Federation of Trade Unions 中华全国总工会旧址

This historical site is south of Lu Xun Memorial at Yuexiunanlu street 93. The All-China Union was founded during the second national meeting of workers in May 1925. The central administration office was set up here in the same year and moved to Hankou in 1927. The building was converted into a memorial in 1958.

Liuhua Park 流花公园

Liuhua Park lies west of Dongfang Guest House. A stroll through the park alongside the man-made lake, across bridges and past pavilions is a pleasant way to relax. In the early morning hours, many of the locals do shadow boxing here.

Guangxiao Si Temple 光孝寺

Guangxiao Si, located on Hongshubeilu street, is one of the city's oldest edifices. Huineng is supposed to have undergone his

initiation as a monk here in 676. Many Indian monks have come to this temple. The temple has been restored and rebuilt numerous times. It received its present name in 1511.

The halls Daxiong Baodian, Liuzu Dian, Jialan Dian and Tianwang Dian are located at Guangxiao Si along with pavilions and pagodas. Two iron pagodas are very interesting. Dongtie Ta, East Iron Pagoda, dates from 967. It is 6 m tall and contains more than 900 niches with small Buddha sculptures.

Xitie Ta, West Iron Pagoda, was built in 963 and originally looked very much like the East Pagoda. Today, there are only three stories left standing. Both pagodas are among the oldest iron pagodas in the country.

Liurong Si, Temple of the Six Banyan Trees 六榕寺

The ancient Buddhist temple Liurong Si is located on Chaoyangbeilu street. It was erected in 537. In 1099, the famous poet Su Dongpo came to this temple and discovered six magnificent banyan trees in the temple courtyard. Filled with awe, he composed a calligraphy with the characters *liu rong,* six banyan trees. The temple has been called Liurong Si since the Ming era in remembrance of Su Dongpo and the six banyan trees, which, however, are no longer there. Liuzu Tang hall contains a bronze statue of the monk Huineng from the Song period.

Monk Huineng is the sixth predecessor of Bodhidharma, the presumed founder of Chan (Zen) Buddhism (see page 57). Guanyin Dian hall contains a tall Guanyin statue. One of the most interesting sights in the temple complex is Huata, Flower Pagoda. It was first erected in 537, rebuilt in 1097 and restored in 1980. It is 57 m high and a stairway leads to the upper stories.

Huaisheng Si Mosque 怀圣寺

One of the oldest mosques in China, Huaisheng Si, stands south of Liurong Si on Guangtalu street. It dates back to 627. The Islamic community is estimated at 4,000 members.

Chenjia Ci, Ancestral Temple of the Chen Family 陈家祠

The Chen family ancestral temple, located on Zhongshanbalu, was built in 1890. The complex is very large; it contains six courtyards and nine halls. Both inside the buildings and outside, one comes across numerous wood, stone, ceramic and iron sculptures. The figures on the roofs are especially beautiful.

Shengxin Dajiaotang, Roman Catholic Cathedral 圣心大教堂

This cathedral, one of the largest churches in China, can be seen on Yidelu street. It dates from 1888 and was erected according to the sketches of the French architect Guillemin. The church steeple is 58 m tall.

Regular worship services are held here.

Wenhua Gongyuan, Cultural Park 文化公园

The 8-hectare-large Cultural Park is located in the southern section of the city near the large business street Renminlu and offers a variety of entertainment for young and old. Exhibition halls, an opera, concert halls, open-air theaters, ping-pong courts, etc. are all located here. The evening hours are usually the busiest.

Shamian Island 沙面

Shamian, an island in the Zhujiang, is 900 m long and up to 300 m wide. During the Opium War, it was an important military base. From 1861 on, the island was a concession territory belonging to the British and French. The consulates of the two countries were located here, as well as banks, churches, administration buildings, tennis courts and a sailing club. The island was part of the territory which Chinese were allowed to enter only with special permission. China did not regain its control of Shamian until 1949.

Sanyuanli Renmin Kangyingdouzheng Jinianguan, Memorial to the People of Sanyuanli's Resistance to the British Attack 三元里人民抗英斗争纪念馆

This hall is located in Sanyuanli village, today a northern suburb of Canton. An ancient temple used to stand here. In May, 1841, as the British troops shelled Canton and burned Sanyuanli village to the ground, the vegetable farmer Wei Shaoguang raised the cry for resistance. People gathered in the old temple complex and swore to take up the fight against the British. Together with people from 103 other villages, they managed to achieve victory.

The memorial hall was erected in memory of this battle. A stone stele that tells about the resistance of Sanyuanli in full is located not too far from the memorial. Yiyong Ci temple, honoring the victims of Sanyuanli, has stood near Shijing Qiao bridge since 1981.

Luogang Hill 萝岗洞

Luogang Hill, well-known and treasured for its magnificent plum blossoms, is about 30 km northwest of Guangzhou. It is part of Luofeng Shan mountain. Luofeng Si temple, built during the 13th century, also stands here. It contains inscriptions, calligraphies and paintings by Han Yu, Wen Tianxiang, Hai Rui, Zheng Banqiao and others.

Zoo 动物园

Guangzhou's zoo lies in the far eastern section of the city. It is one of the largest zoos in China and would be well worth a visit if only to see its beautiful grounds. The panda bears are among the best-loved animals.

Huanan Zhiwuyuan, Botanical Garden 华南植物园

Guangzhou's botanical garden is one of the four largest in China. It is located in the northeastern suburbs and contains 3,200 different varieties of plants, most of which are rare. Above all else, the garden is famous for its orchids.

Sites around Guangzhou (see page 337)

Hotels and Guest Houses (a selection from about 60 hotels)

Zhongguo Dajiudian, China Great Hotel, Liuhualu, tel. 6 68 88, telex 4 41 88, 4 48 88

Huayuan Jiudian, Garden Hotel, Huanshidonglu 368, tel. 7 33 88, telex 4 47 88, Management: The Peninsula Group

Dongfang Binguan, 东方宾馆 Xicungonglu, tel. 6 99 00
This large hotel, located in the northern section of the city, caters primarily to European and American businessmen. It is favorably situated with respect to transportation routes, in the vicinity of the Exhibition Hall. There are several restaurants and stores located on the premises, and services such as a post office and a telex and telegraph office as well as a bank are available.

Baiyun Binguan, White Cloud Guest House, 白云宾馆 Huanshidonglu, tel. 6 77 00, Modern 33-storey hotel which is mostly frequented by tourist groups. Next to it is Guangzhou's new Friendship Store.

Baitian'e Binguan, White Swan Guest House, 白天鹅宾馆 Shamian Nanlu 1, tel. 8 69 68, telex 4 41 49 WSH CN. Luxury tourist hotel.

Liuhua Binguan, 流花宾馆 Renminbeilu, tel. 6 88 00
This reasonably-priced hotel is located directly across from the train station. Because of its good location, it is favored by the individual traveler.

Beijing Fandian, 北京饭店 Yanjiangyilu 105, tel. 2 20 10, 8 94 22

Guangdong Binguan, 广东宾馆 Jiefangbeilu, tel. 3 29 50

Guangdong Lüdian, 广东旅店 Changti 294, tel. 2 16 05, 8 36 01

Guangzhou Binguan, 广州宾馆 Haizhu Guangchang, tel. 6 15 56

Heping Lüdian, 和平旅店 Renminnanlu 17, tel. 2 22 13, 8 91 40

Kuangquan Bieshu, 矿泉别墅 Sanyuanli, tel. 6 13 34

Nanfang Dasha Lüdian, 南方大厦旅店 Yanjiangyilu 49, tel. 8 77 22

Huaqiao Dasha, 华侨大厦 Qiaoguanglu 2, tel. 6 11 12

Huaqiao Lüshe, 华侨旅社 Sanyuanli, tel. 6 12 92

Renmin Dasha, 人民大厦 Changtilu 207, tel. 6 14 45

Shamian Binguan, 沙面宾馆 Shamiannanjie 52, tel. 8 83 59, 8 81 24

Shanzhuang Lüshe, 山庄旅社 Baiyun Shan, tel. 7 17 13, 7 77 83

Shengli Binguan, 胜利宾馆 Shamian Dajie 54, tel. 6 12 23

Shuangxi Lüshe, 双喜旅社 Baiyun Shan, tel. 7 17 12, 7 17 11

Xihao Lüdian, Yanjiangyilu 101, tel. 8 64 61

Xinhua Lüdian, 新华旅店 Renminnanlu 4, tel. 8 64 11

Xinya Lüshe, 新雅旅社 Renminnanlu 10, tel. 8 73 22, 8 82 50

Yanjiang Lüdian, 沿江旅店 Yanjiangerlu 277, tel. 3 31 02

Restaurants and Specialties

Cantonese cuisine is distinguished by its diversity and originality. Thanks to the favorable climate and a location on the coast, fresh seafood, vegetables, fruit and teas are available in abundance.

A typical, delicious specialty of the province is Dim Sum, a type of appetizer which is eaten at breakfast or lunch. Tea is served as the beverage. Many travelers have already become familiar with this dish in Hongkong.

Please make note of the restaurants' hours of opening. Breakfast (Dim Sum) is offered by many restaurants as early as 5:30 a.m., and the restaurant then closes again around 9:00 a.m. Lunch is served from 11:00 a.m. — 2:00 p.m. and dinner from 5:00 — 9:00 p.m.

During fair seasons, making reservations is a must — at well-known restaurants and for large parties, sometimes as much as two days in advance.

The number of people in the party and the

total cost per person, excluding drinks, should be submitted. Below is a selection from the many restaurants:

Banxi Jiujia, Xianyangyilu 151, tel. 8 87 06

This restaurant, with traditionally decorated rooms, is one of the most beautiful in Guangzhou. The prices are acceptable by western standards, and the food is superb. Seafood, chicken in tea leaves, Dim Sum and turtle are among the specialties of the house. Reservations are recommended!

Beixiu Fandian, Jiefangbeilu 899, tel. 3 59 41, 3 22 80

Beiyuan Jiujia, Dengfengbeilu 439, tel. 3 00 87, 3 24 71

A good, large restaurant with a traditional interior that takes visitors by surprise.

Caigenxiang Sushiguan, Zhongshanliulu 167, tel. 8 68 35

An excellent vegetarian restaurant.

Datong Jiujia, Yanjiangyilu 63, tel. 8 59 33

An excellent restaurant that will delight foreigners by its view of the Zujiang, Pearl River, alone. Specialties of the house are roast baby pork, chicken a la Datong and Dim Sum.

Guangzhou Jiujia, Wanchangnanlu 2, tel. 8 71 36, 8 78 40

A restaurant of high quality that offers the entire range of Cantonese cuisine.

Jingji Canting, Shamianerlu 8, tel. 8 87 84, 8 57 90

Jingji restaurant is one of the oldest restaurants in the city. It is located on Shamian Island and offers a large variety of Chinese and western dishes at reasonable prices.

Likoufu Haixian Fandian, Shisanhanglu 86, tel. 2 24 18, 2 13 22

A seafood restaurant.

Liwan Fandian, Xianyangsanlu, tel. 8 89 34

Specialties of the house are carp, shrimp, chicken and pasta.

Moslem Fandian, Zhongshanliulu 325, tel. 8 84 14, 8 89 91

Those who cannot travel in the north have an opportunity to enjoy the specialty, Mongolian hot-pot, here. A change in ingredients has been made, however. In the north, only lamb meat is served, whereas here, chicken, crab or beef are also available.

Nanyuan Jiujia, Qianjinlu 120, tel. 5 15 76

An excellent, tastefully decorated restaurant situated in picturesque surroundings. Magnificent dishes are available at reasonable prices.

She Canguan, Snake Restaurant, Jianglanlu 41, tel. 2 18 11

Taipingguan Canting, Beijinglu 344, tel. 3 55 29

One of the oldest restaurants in the city. Zhou Enlai dined here frequently. He supposedly favored one of the specialties of the house, fried pigeon. The restaurant serves Chinese and western cuisine, both of excellent quality.

Yeweixiang Fandian, Beijinglu 249, tel. 3 09 97

Wild game is prepared here. The menu includes such specialties as wild cat and wild boar, but beef and fowl dishes are also available.

Yuyuan Fandian, Liwannanlu 90, tel. 8 68 38, 8 85 52

One of the specialities of the house is Peking Duck. The Cantonese dishes served here are also excellent. Yuyuan is famous for its desserts, which many customers gladly eat instead of the main meal.

Travel agency

Guoji Lüxingshe, CITS, Huanshilu 179, tel. 3 34 54

Ticket sales, tel. 6 14 51 telex 4 41 50, near train station.
Open 8:30-11:30 am and 2:30-5:30 pm, service desk at Dongfang Hotel, Rm. 2366.

Zhongguo Lüxingshe, Qiaoguanglu 2, tel. 6 11 12

Ticket sales, tel. 3 22 47

Huaqiao Lüxingshe (Overseas Chinese), Qiaoguanglu 2, tel. 6 11 12

Ticket sales, tel. 3 18 62

Gong'an Ju, Public Security Bureau, Jiefangbeilu 863, tel. 3 10 60

Open 8:00 am-12:00 noon and 2:30-5:30 pm, closed on Sundays

Telephone, Long distance, national: 03, information 06

Long distance, international: 08, information 3 00 00

Bank of China, Changti 137, tel. 2 05 43

The Bank of China has branches in numerous hotels, guest houses and businesses.

Baiyun Airport, 3 28 78, 3 19 34

CAAC, domestic 3 12 71, 3 16 00 international 3 40 79, 3 36 84
Huanshilu 181, near train station

Train station, information 3 33 33

Taxis

Central office: 6 12 51
Dongfang Binguan: 3 22 27
Guangzhou Binguan: 3 22 77
Huaqiao Dasha: 6 11 12
Nanfang Dasha: 8 82 50
Liuhua Binguan: 6 88 00
Renmin Dasha: 2 11 99
Baiyun Binguan: 6 77 00

Universities

Jinan Daxue, Shipai, tel. 7 86 72

Zhongshan Daxue, Henan Kanglecun, tel. 5 17 10
Building for foreign experts: 5 12 41

Especially for Business Travelers

Chinese Export Goods Fair, Zhongguo Chukou Shangpin Jiaoyihui Foreign Trade Center, Guangzhou, Renminbeilu, Liuhuahupan, tel. 3 08 49
Central office, tel. 6 16 61
Telegrams and Long distance calls, tel. 3 07 63
Bank and insurance, tel. 3 07 65
Post office, tel. 3 07 66
Dispatch service, tel. 3 07 68
Customs, tel. 3 07 69
Information, tel. 3 07 45

Shopping

The main business streets are Beijinglu, Zhongshanlu, Yanjianglu and Renminlu.

Guangdong Antiques Store, Hongshubeilu 575, tel. 8 76 00

Guangzhou Antiques Store, Wendebeilu 146, tel. 3 12 41, 3 42 29

Youyi Shangdian, Friendship Store, Huanshidonglu, tel. 3 24 03, 3 22 90, near Baiyun Hotel

Nanfang Dasha Department Store, Yanjiangyilu 49, tel. 8 60 22

Nanfang Baihuo Shangdian, Department Store, Huanshibeilu 9, tel. 3 44 41

Xinhua Shudian, Xinhua Bookstore, Beijinglu 276, tel. 3 08 73

Waiwen Shudian, Foreign Language Bookstore, Beijinglu 326, tel. 3 27 34

Conghua 从化

Conghua Wenquan, Conghua Hot Springs
从化温泉

The hot springs are located northwest of the district capital Conghua, 80km from Guangzhou. It is a favorite destination for outdoor excursions and a resort area for both the Chinese and foreign visitors. The 11 springs are surrounded by hills, bamboo groves and fruit orchards. The hottest spring has a temperature of 71°C, the others have temperatures between 50 — 60°C. The water is conducted to the dozens of sanatoriums, hotels and villas. They belong to different categories and prices range accordingly.

A waterfall, Baizhangfeitao, is located not far from the springs. It can be reached easily by car.

Foshan 佛山市

An interesting daytime excursion is a trip to Foshan, about 20 km southwest of Guangzhou. The name of the town means 'Buddha Hill'. A Buddhist meeting place was located here in past centuries. Foshan was an important center of trade for ceramics; this craft has a tradition that reaches back to the Song period. The oldest workshops are outside of Foshan in Shiwan Zhen. They specialize in ceramic figurines. Visitors have an opportunity to learn about the entire manufacturing process on location. Typical factory products are on sale in the factory's own store.

Foshan has also become famous for its artistic paper cuttings. A visit to the Foshan paper cutting workshops can be very interesting to those who collect or simply enjoy paper cuttings. One can see for oneself what care and precision are used in creating these extremely delicate works of art.

Foshan Zumiao, Foshan Ancestral Temple
佛山祖庙

Foshan Ancestral Temple, now a museum,

dates from the Northern Song period but was enlarged and restored during the Ming and Qing periods. It consists of several halls. The temple's most interesting features are its roof decorations: clay figures portraying entire groups and scenes that can not help but astonish the observer.

Guoji Lüxingshe, Travel Agency CITS, Fanxiulu 4, tel. 8 71 21

Arts and Crafts Store, Dongfenglu 85

Zhaoqing 肇庆市

Zhaoqing, west of Guangzhou on the Xijiang's north bank, was founded in the 1st century BC. Today, it is the center of an area used intensively for agriculture, the home of various industrial concerns and a port where trade is conducted with the Guangxi Autonomous Region.

Qixing Yan, Seven Star Crags 七星岩

These crags Qixing Yan lie in the city's northern suburbs, about 100km west of Guangzhou. There are seven stone peaks which are distributed in the same pattern as the stars of the Big Dipper around Xinghu, Star Lake, and which are formed from limestone. Many caves can be found here.

A large gate with the inscription Qixing Yan, Seven Star Crags, written by the revolutionary Zhu De, leads into the park to large Xinghu, Star Lake, and the cliffs which bear the following names from east to west: Langfeng, Yuping, Shishi, Tianzhu, Chanyu, Xianzhang and Apo. The highest one is Shishi, Stone Chamber Rock, at 90 m. A cave containing 270 stone cuttings is located within the crag. Some of them are poems by famous writers. An underground river flows through the cave and can be navigated by boat. From the river, one has a good view of the artificially lighted rocky cliffs. A glance through Shishi Cave's northern exit reveals a tapering rock that seems to touch the sky. This is Tianzhu Yan, Pillar to the Sky Crag. The Seven Star Crag area is being opened to tourists to an ever greater extent. Several hotels and restaurants have already been built. Local specialties such as watercolored rocks are offered in the stores.

Dinghu Shan Mountains 鼎湖山

The Dinghu Shan mountain range is located 18 km northeast of Zhaoqing. It has numerous peaks, the highest of which is 1,000 m. Because of the ancient trees and the large variety of plant life here, the mountains have been turned into a nature preserve. Qingyun Si temple, dating from the Ming era, stands at the southern foot of Dinghu Shan, and the Tang era temple Baiyun Si stands on the mountain's southwestern slope. The temple complexes consist of several halls. A hotel is located in Qingyun Si.

Hotels

Zhaoqing Furong Binguan, Kanglebeilu, tel. 2 32 83

Zhaoqing Dasha, Tianninglu

Xiqiao Shan Mountains 南海西樵山

The Xiqiao Shan mountains are located southwest of Nanhai County, 68 km from Guangzhou. The highest elevation is only 346 m, but there are numerous interesting sights. The 72 mountains, 36 caves, 21 cliffs, 32 springs and 28 waterfalls assure that every outing is a lively experience. The western, eastern and central sections of the mountain are the most interesting. Visitors usually come from the northwest and make their way first to Baiyun Dong valley. A waterfall is located there, and Yunquan Xianguan hall from the Ming period is not far away. The hall used to be an academy, but today it is a museum for archeological relics from the surrounding areas. East of the hall, the path leads past the villages Longyan Quan, Xiaotaoyuan and Shijian Shi and the waterfall Xiaoyun Pu up to Baiyun Shan mountain. Many caves are located in the mountain's southeastern section. Hotels, restaurants and tea houses await visitors on the Xiqiao mountains.

Shaoguan 韶关市

Shaoguan, also called Qujiang, lies on the bank of the Beijiang in the northern part of the city. It is located on the railway line Guangzhou — Beijing. The city was founded in the 1st century BC. It underwent its most prosperous period in the 18th and early 19th centuries. At that time, Shaoguan was a hub of commerce into bordering areas. Water and land routes led to Hunan and over the Meiling Guan pass towards Jiangxi. Even today, Shaoguan is an important redistribution point for agricultural products from the northern part of the province. Since 1949, heavy industry has been established to a greater extent.

Nanhua Si Temple 南华禅寺

Nanhua Si, a complex laid out in 504 that is still in good condition today, is located about 20 km from Shaoguan.

In the imposing hall Daxiong Baodian, three gilded Buddha statues are seated on lotus blossoms the Buddhas of the past, present and future. Five hundred Luohan figures are on the walls in five rows, one above the other up to the skylight. A huge water vessel from 1338, Qianren Guo, Thousand Men Pot, stands behind the hall.

The next pavilion, Cangjing Ge, contains valuable sutras, original decrees from the Tang empress Wu Zetian and emperors from the Yuan and Ming dynasties and copies thereof, as well as a robe from the monk Huineng who used to be in charge of the temple. The robe was a present from Empress Wu Zetian. A brick pagoda dating from the 8th century stands behind Cangjing Ge pavilion, Liuzu Dian hall is dedicated to the monk Huineng.

Nanhua Si Temple

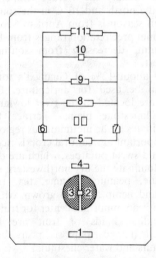

1. Caoxi Men Gate
2. Wuxiang Ting Pavilion
3. Fangsheng Chi Pond
4. Baolin Men Gate
5. Tianwang Baodian Hall
6. Gulou, Drum Tower
7. Zhonglou, Bell Tower
8. Daxiong Baodian Hall
9. Cangjing Ge Pavilion
10. Lingzhao Ta Pagoda
11. Liuzu Dian Hall

Hainan Island 海南岛

Tropical Hainan is the second biggest island in China. It was always an isolated area in such a great country and unbeloved officers, such as Su Dongpo who was obliged to stay on this isolated island for three years, would sometimes be sent here by the Emperor.

One fourth of this island is mountainous. The highest elevation is Wuzhi Shan, 1879 m. The island is rich in mineral resources including iron ore, bauxite and coal. It is also rich in exciting landscapes, which attract more and more tourists.

The island has more than 5 million inhabitants. The original native people of this area were the Li and Miao. They are nowadays mostly concentrated in the center of the island and they number about 740,000 (Li: 700,000, Miao 40,000). The city Tongshi is the political and cultural center of the Li and Miao autonomous region. Some 5000 moslems live at the south of the island, west of Sanya.

Haikou is the main city and the cultural and economic center of the island and is situated in the north. Close to this city you will find various places of historical interest, such as the Tomb of Hai Rui, a famous official of the Ming Dynasty, (in Bintian, west of Haikou); Memorial Temple of the Five officials of the Tang and Song dynasties and Memorial Temple of Su Dongpo (Fucheng Township in Qiongshan County).

On the east coast of Hainan Island, you will find the fascinating beaches Tianshui Wan and Zhilan Wan, which are situated in the vicinity of Wenchang County, and the island's largest coconut plantation. Southeast there is a well-known place for pearl cultivation, 10 km south of the Monkey Island. Further south, near the city of Sanya, you will find the famous Dadong Sea and The Remotest Corner of the Earth, Tianya Haijiao, a beach with giant rocks embedded in the sand and rising up out of the water. Daxiao Dongtian is 10 km further to the west and famous for mysterious caves.

On the west coast, near the city of Zhonghe is Baimajing, a large fishing port. 10 km to the northeast is the site of the ancient Danzhou where Su Dongpo spent some time during his exile. The well and his former residence can still be seen.

Guest House

Haikou: Haikou Binguan, Sanjiaochi, tel. 2 39 72

Huaqiao Fandian

Sanya: Yezhuang Binguan

CITS, Datonglu 17, tel. 2 27 25 (Haikou)

Guangxi Zhuangzu Zizhiqu, Guangxi Autonomous Region of the Zhuang Minority 广西壮族自治区

Area: 230,000 km² / Population: 38.42 million / Capital: Nanning

The South China Guangxi Autonomous Region borders on Guangdong in the east, Beibu Wan (Gulf of Tonkin) in the south, Vietnam and Yunnan in the west and Guizhou and Hunan in the north.

History

Guangxi was always a controversial area. Up into the 19th century, Han Chinese and non-Han-Chinese groups struggled for control of the region. When the Western powers came, they tried to gain a foothold in Guangxi and bring the area under their domain.

The rice-cultivating Zhuang people lived in the area of present-day Guangxi as far back as the Zhou Dynasty. During Qin Shihuang's conquests during the 3rd century BC, the eastern region became part of the Chinese empire. A short time later, with the help of the Zhuang, a Chinese general was able to establish the independent state of Nanyue. The Han rulers came to reconquer the area once again.

During the Han Dynasty, members of the Yao tribes began to emigrate from Jiangxi and Hunan to Guangxi. Unlike the Zhuang, these people were not prepared to submit to Han Chinese rule. The areas which they populated became the centers of unending turbulence. After the decline of the Tang Dynasty, an independent state called Southern Han was created here, but it was soon thwarted by the Song rulers. In 1052, a rebellion arose once more with the goal of founding an independent kingdom. The Zhuang leader Nong Zhigao led the attempt at separation which was successful at first but defeated a year later. The following centuries did not bring peace to this area of China. One of the bloodiest battles in the history of Guangxi took place near Guiping in 1465. It was a clash between Yao warriors and the Ming imperial troops. The Taiping Rebellion also broke out near Guiping in 1850. During the second half of the 19th century, the French and the British fought to assert their claims. The French tried to broaden their sphere of influence from Vietnam while the British made the same endeavor by way of Guangzhou (Canton). Longzhou was forced open to foreign trade in 1889, Wuzhou followed in 1897 and Nanning in 1907. At the beginning of the 20th century, those with power in Guangxi supported the overthrow of the Qing Dynasty and the establishment of the Republic. The Japanese invaded the southern part of the province in 1939 and occupied Nanning and Longzhou. In 1944, they also managed to occupy the north but could not maintain this position.

Guangxi's scenery is scattered with karst formations. Guilin's mountains are famous everywhere. They stand towering and isolated in the middle of the plains and astound the visitor with their picturesque shapes. The mountain ranges in Guangxi run from northeast to southwest. They are formed from sandstone or limestone, schist, porphyry or granite and reach heights from 1,000 — 2,000 m. The lowlands lie at elevations less than 300 m. Guangxi's most important river is the Xijiang, which flows through the land from northwest to southeast.

The climate in Guangxi is sub-tropical. The summers last seven months and are hot and moist. The average temperature in July is 27°C in the north and 32°C in the south. Winters are mild; in January the average temperature is 4°C in the north and 16°C in the south. The monsoon season is from April to September. The annual precipitation ranges from 1,000 — 2,000 mm, decreasing from southeast to northwest.

Only about 12% of Guangxi's total land area can be used for agriculture. Farming centers are located in the river lowlands and in the limestone plains. Terrace farming predominates in the mountainous regions. The most important agricultural crop is rice; corn, wheat and sweet potatoes, which are dry field crops, dominate the dry northwestern regions. Sugarcane, peanuts, sesame, tea, tobacco, cotton and hemp are also grown. Moreover, Guangxi is an important center for fruit crops. The leading kinds of fruit are lichees, grapefruit, mangos, papayas, pears, bananas, citrus fruits and water chestnuts.

The fishing industry also plays a key role, both fishing directly off the coasts and on the high seas, as well as river fishing.

Guangxi is rich in mineral resources. There are large deposits of coal and iron, as well as some tungsten, antimony, tin and manganese. Guangxi's industry has managed to develop considerably since the founding of the People's Republic. Heavy industry has made its way into Nanning, Liuzhou, Wuzhou and Luzhai. Iron and steel works and machine and cement factories have sprung up. Emphasis is given to the area of light industry. Textile, leather, paper and match factories, oil mills, sugar refineries and pharmaceutical concerns have been established during the past three decades.

Nanning 南宁市

Nanning is the seat of the People's Committee of the Zhuang Autonomous Region. It is situated on the north bank of the Yongjiang, about 30 km from the confluence of the Yujiang and the Zuojiang rivers.

The city is connected to the railway line Hengyang, Hunan — Youyiguan, Guangxi. A connection that was made to the part of Zhanjiang in 1957 makes direct access to the sea possible.

History

The history of Nanning goes back more than 1,600 years. As far back as 318, the city was a district capital and a military stronghold. During the Tang Dynasty, it was expanded to a garrison town. The rulers of the Ming and Qing dynasties turned Nanning into a *fu*, prefecture. From 1912 — 1936, the city was the capital of Guangxi. During the Sino-Japanese War, the city was temporarily occupied by the Japanese. Nanning became the capital of the province in 1949, and in 1958, the capital of the Guangxi Autonomous Region. Although Nanning used to be primarily an administrative and trade city, the city has been able to make considerable progress since 1949, especially with regard to industry. Today, Nanning is Guangxi's most significant industrial center.

The most important crops in the surrounding areas are rice and sugarcane. Thanks to the favorable climate, a large variety of subtropical fruits are harvested in Nanning, including lichees, mangos, bananas, pineapples and watermelons.

Nanning is also the cultural center of the region. In 1952, a national minorities institute was opened where members of 12 different national minorities are trained to become teachers and cadres. They are taught politics, Chinese, foreign languages, math, physics and chemistry.

Arts and crafts, theater and puppetry have a long tradition in Guangxi. Visitors are frequently guided to the Gui, Zhuang or Caidiao operas or to shows put on by song and dance ensembles. Those who are in Nanning at the beginning of July can take part in the beloved Dragon Boat Festival. This is an event that entices thousands of visitors to Yongjiang's shores each year. It takes place on the fifth day

of the fifth month according to the lunar calendar. Teams of young women and men rush along the river in long, narrow boats, each of which is decorated with a dragon's head. The winning team is rewarded with a roast for the festival and wine.

Nanning is the city of evergreen trees and blooming flowers. However, it is not only the nature lovers who enjoy themselves here, but also the gourmets. The Guangxi cuisine offers several delicacies, including dishes made with snake and mountain tortoise or fried pigeon.

Nanhu Gongyuan, South Lake Park 南湖公园

South Lake is located in the southeastern part of the city. It is surrounded by park grounds where the special feature is subtropical plants. An orchid garden and medicinal herbs and bonsai displays capture the interest of many visitors.

The South Lake fish restaurant offers typical Guangxi fish specialties.

Renmin Gongyuan, People's Park 人民公园

People's Park is located in the northern section of the city, not far from Friendship Hotel and Mingyuan Hotel. It is a peaceful place with beautiful grounds and quiet walkways.

Museum of the Guangxi Autonomous Region 广西壮族自治区博物馆

This museum was opened in 1954. It offers insights into the general history of the various national minorities in Guangxi. Among other things, the displays include archeological relics and important historical documents. Items of particular interest can be found among the bronze instruments and vessels.

Yiling Yan Cave 伊领岩

Yiling Yan is located 20 km northwest of Nanning. Amidst the multicolored lighted stalactic formations, the visitor is likely to feel as if he is in a fairy tale. The native Chinese sought this cave out for protection in times of war and turbulence. A tour through the 1,100 m long cave takes about 1½ hours. The average temperature is 18°C. For that reason, it is wise to take along something warm to wear even during the warm seasons.

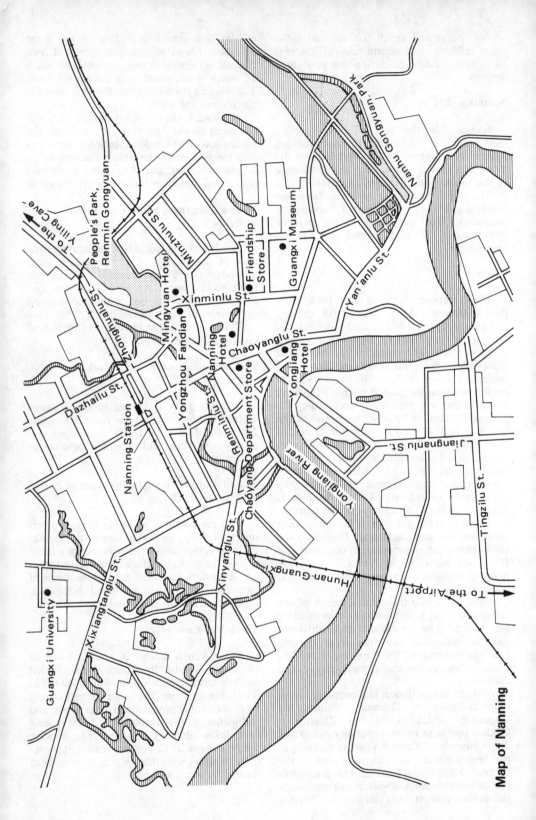

To the Y iling Cave

People's Park, Renmin Gongyuan

Minzhulu St.

Zhonghualu St.

Nanhu Gongyuan Park

Friendship Store

Guangxi Museum

Yan'anlu St.

Mingyuan Hotel

Xinminlu St.

Yongzhou Fandian

Nanning Hotel

Chaoyanglu St.

Yongjiang Hotel

Dazhailu St.

Renminlu St.

Nanning Station

Chaoyang Department Store

Jiangnanlu St.

Yongjiang River

Guangxi University

Xixiangtanglu St.

Xinyanglu St.

Hunan-Guangxi

To the Airport

Tingzilu St.

Map of Nanning

Hotels

Mingyuan Fandian, 明园饭店 Xinminlu, tel. 29 86

Yongjiang Fandian, 邕江饭店 Linjianglu, tel. 39 51

Yongzhou Fandian, 邕州饭店 Minzhulu, tel. 39 13, 31 20

Xiyuan Fandian, 西园饭店 Jiangnanlu, tel. 39 31

Restaurants

Bailong Chating, Bailong Teahouse, Xinminlu, Renmin Gongyuan park, tel. 51 40

Nanhu Fish Restaurant, in Nanhu Gongyuan park, tel. 24 77

Nanning Jiujia, Minshenlu, tel. 24 73

Shopping

The Friendship Store, Youyi Shangdian, is located on Xinminlu street. Books and crafts items can be bought on Xinhuajie. There is an antiques store inside the museum Qiyi Guangchang, July the First Square.

Travel agency

Guoji Lüxingshe, CITS and **Zhongguo** Lüxingshe, Xinminlu, tel. 20 42, 47 93, telex 4 91 92

Gong'an Shi, Office of Foreign Affairs, Guangxi Autonomous Region, Minzhulu, tel. 36 37

CAAC, tel. 33 33, 42 72, 53 77

Train Station, information, tel. 24 68

Liuzhou 柳州市

Liuzhou, located on the Liujiang in the middle of the region, is an important intersection for land and water routes. The railway lines from Guiyang, Guizhou, Huaihua and the Hengyang — Nanning line meet here. Large highways lead away from Liuzhou in all directions. The confluences of various tributaries of the Liujiang favors water transportation. Liuzhou is an old city with a history of more than 2,100 years. During the Tang Dynasty, the prefecture Liuzhou was formed. Primarily, it was a trading center for agricultural products and wood. Today, the city is still an important commercial town. In addition, it has also developed into an industrial city.

Liuhou Ci Temple 柳侯祠

Liuhou Ci is located in Liuhou Gongyuan park. It was built in 821, in honor of a famous literary official from the Tang Dynasty, Liu Zongyuan.

Liu Zongyuan (773—819) was both a public official and a poet. As a high official, he supported the reform plans of Wang Shuwen. For this reason he fell into disfavor, was removed from office and banned to Liuzhou in 815. During the short period that he was in office, he accomplished remarkable things in the fully neglected city. He did away with banditry and slavery, had schools built, fought against superstition and saw to the rebuilding of the dilapidated city wall and the digging of wells. The people's gratitude is reflected in the fact that his name has never been forgotten. The Song emperor Huizong (period of reign 1101—1125) posthumously bestowed the honorary title Wenhui Hou upon him. Thus, Liu Zongyuan is usually referred to as Liu Hou.

The present-day temple was rebuilt in 1729. It still contains a number of Liu Zongyuan's stone inscriptions.

Yufeng Shan, Fish Peak Mountain, 鱼峰山 and Xiaolong Tan, Small Dragon Pond. These two places of interest are located in the southern part of the city near Ma'an Shan mountain, which serves as a good observation point. Fish Peak Mountain and Small Dragon Pond have become well-known due to the following legend:

The third sister of the House of Liu was a beloved singer who, while singing about mountains and shepherds, frequently condemned the greed of a certain lord. One day, the furious lord drove her into a pond. Two carps came to save her. The girl escaped on the back of one, and the other turned into a stone mountain burying the landlord beneath him. The mountain was thus named Yufeng Shan, Fish Peak Mountain, and the pond, Xiaolong Tan, Small Dragon Pond. On the fifteenth day of the seventh month according to the lunar calendar, a mountain songs festival takes place on the shores of Xiaolong Tan. Most of the singers belong to the Zhuang nationality. Yufeng Shan is 80 m high. A stone statue of Liusanjie, the third sister of the House of Liu, can be found there.

Dule Yan Cliff 都乐岩

Dule Yan, 12 km southeast of Liuzhou, has 40 caves. Among these, Panlong Dong, Tongtian Dong and Shuiyun Dong are especially worth seeing.

Hotels

Liuzhou Fandian, 柳州饭店 Wengelu 1

Liujiang Fandian, Longchenglu, tel. 2 52 61

Longcheng Fandian, Jiebeilu, tel. 2 54 65

The Travel agency Guoji Lüxingshe, CITS, is located in Liuzhou Fandian hotel. Tel. 32 29

Guilin 桂林市

Guilin is located in Guangxi's northeastern region on the upper course of the Lijiang, one of the sources of the Guijiang river.
Population: 690,000

History

The two rivers Lijiang and Xiangjiang flow fairly close together not far from Guilin. This natural feature proved advantageous for a noteworthy project more than 2,000 years ago. Emperor Shihuang of the Qin Dynasty (221—206 BC) arranged for a canal Lingqu, to be constructed to join the two rivers together. Since the Lijiang could not be navigated, it had to be canalized up to the point where it empties into the Guijiang. Thanks to the Lingqu canal, it became possible to transport Qin troops from the area along the Changjiang to Guangdong.

Up into the 1st century, this canal remained the major transportation route from Central to South China. Even today, it is still in use, but it can only be navigated by small boats. It is more significant as an irrigation source. Guilin sprang up as the canal was built; it was founded by Qin troops. During the Ming Dynasty, the prefecture *(fu)* of Guilin was located here. The Qing rulers designated Guilin as the capital of Guangxi. Nanning took over the position of capital in 1912. The title was regained by Guilin in 1936, only to fall once more to Nanning in 1949. During the Sino-Japanese War, Guilin became a refuge for thousands of nationalists and intellectuals.

Guilin had always been a center for trade and crafts. This position was strengthened when the Hengyang — Guilin railway line was finished in 1938. Industrial development has been pushed ahead in the last decades.

Autumn is the most beautiful season for a visit to Guilin. At that time the city is filled with the beguiling scent of cassia trees, and the city bears its name 'Fragrant Blossom Wood' with justice.

At home and abroad, Guilin is primarily known for its enticing and unique scenery. Chinese frequently refer to it as the world's most beautiful scenery, and one will acknowledge its beauty once one has taken a relatively tranquil trip down the Lijiang. For that purpose, the cool months during the off-season when tourism is hardly noticeable are probably the best time. Over the course of centuries many poets and painters have been drawn to these parts, and they have all praised the beauty of Guilin in their works.

Guilin represents a typical karstic region. Strangely shaped mountains rise up singly from the plains by the hundreds. Three hundred million years ago, this area was still covered by the sea. A thick layer of limestone settled to the bottom, only to be raised up during geotonic movements and become wonderfully shaped by wind and water. There are thousands of caves; every mountain is hollowed out, and each cave has its own character. Numerous legends, fairy tales and poems are intertwined with each mountain, cliff and cave.

Guilin offers travelers a number of interesting sights. Those who are staying only a single day in Guilin should take a trip down the Lijiang or visit Ludi Yan, Reed Flute Cave, and Qixing Gongyuan, Seven Star Park. A two-day stay allows the visitor to take advantage of both options. Any additional time could be profitably spent visiting Duxiu Feng, Diecai Shan and Fubo Shan.

From the Lijiang Fandian and Ronghu Fandian hotels, it is already possible to see some of the city's attractions, namely Ronghu, Banyan Tree Lake, and Shanhu, Pine Tree Lake. Originally, both of these lakes were part of the moat by the city wall. They were created during the Song period when a bridge was built and were named for the trees which at the time grew by their shores.

Xiangbi Shan, Elephant Trunk Mountain, is located southeast of the lakes that are mentioned above. A cave gives the rock wall the appearance of an elephant drinking from the river. The legend tells of an elephant that belonged to the celestial emperor. When the emperor came down to conquer the earth, the elephant was forced to work so hard and endure so much that he finally became sick. A few farmers saved him, and out of gratitude the animal decided to stay on earth and serve those who had rescued him. The celestial emperor became furious. He killed the elephant, who was drinking water on the banks, and the elephant turned into stone. Puxian Ta pagoda stands at the top of the

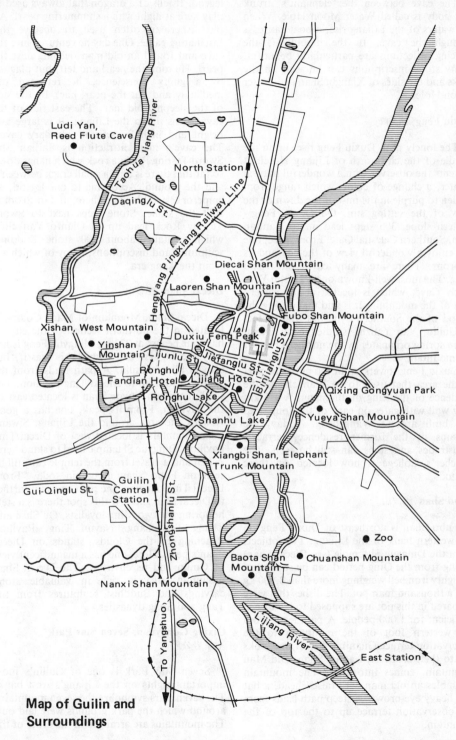

Ludi Yan, Reed Flute Cave

Taohua Jiang River

North Station

Daqinglu St.

Hengyang Pingxiang Railway Line

Diecai Shan Mountain

Laoren Shan Mountain

Fubo Shan Mountain

Xishan, West Mountain

Duxiu Feng Peak

Yinshan Mountain

Lijunlu St.

Jiefanglu St.

Binjianglu St.

Ronghu Fandian Hotel

Lijiang Hotel

Ronghu Lake

Shanhu Lake

Qixing Gongyuan Park

Yueya Shan Mountain

Xiangbi Shan, Elephant Trunk Mountain

Gui-Qinglu St.

Guilin Central Station

Zhongshanlu St.

Zoo

Baota Shan Mountain

Chuanshan Mountain

Nanxi Shan Mountain

To Yangshuo

Lijiang River

East Station

Map of Guilin and Surroundings

cliff. It represents the handle of a dagger. The pagoda was built during the Tang period and restored during the Ming period.

The cave between the 'elephant's' trunk and body is called Water Moon Hole. When the waters of the Lijiang rise, a boat can pass through the cave. In the moonlight, the dancing reflections are particularly beautiful. Many stone inscriptions can be seen on the rocks and the sides of Xiangbi Shan and Water Moon Hole.

Duxiu Feng 独秀峰

The lonely peak Duxiu Feng rises up in the middle of the city north of Lijiang Hotel. It presents the observer with a wonderful natural theater, a change of colors which range from golden to purple in the mist of the dawn or the glow of the setting sun. On Duxiu Feng's western slope, 306 steps lead up to Nantian Men, Southern Celestial Gate. From there, one can enjoy a wonderful view of the city and its environs. There are many caves on Duxiu Feng. The most well-known one is Dushu Yan, Study Cave, which is located at the eastern foot of the mountain. It is said that during the period of the Southern dynasties, the prefect of Guilin, Yan Yanzhi, studied here. Duxiu Quan spring originates by the northern foot of the mountain.

Duxiu Feng towers up in the northern part of the area that used to be Wangcheng, the residence of the King of Jingjiang. A 1.5 km long wall with gates on each of the four sides was built around Wangcheng. Today, the remains of the former residence, terraces, balustrades and steps can still be seen. The Teacher's College is now located on these grounds.

Fubo Shan 伏波山

Fubo Shan is northeast of Duxiu Feng on the western bank of the Lijiang. Two objects from the Dingyue Si temple (see Diecai Shan) dating from the Qing period can be seen here, a mighty iron bell weighing more than 2,500 kg and a thousand-man pot. The dishes that were prepared in this pot are supposed to have been sufficient for 1,000 people. A path leads from the western foot of the mountain to the observation terrace Guanjing Tai. If one looks out to the northwest, Laoren Shan, Old Man Mountain, comes into view. The mountain resembles an old man with raised head, a hat and heavy eye-brows. A steep path leads from the observation terrace up to the top of the mountain.

A very famous cave, Huanzhu Dong, Returned Pearl Cave, is located at the foot of Fubo Shan. The name comes from an old legend. It tells of a dragon that always used to play here at night with a shimmering pearl. An old fisherman often used to observe this fascinating game. One day he ventured into the cave and found an old man sleeping near the pearl. He took the pearl and left, but plagued by a guilty conscience, he returned immediately and put the pearl back by the side of the sleeping old man. The east side of the cave opens up to the Lijiang. It is large and bright and includes several subsidary caves. The cave's main attraction is Shijian Shi, Sword Testing Rock, a rock which hangs down so far that there is only a small crack between it and the ground. According to one legend, an emperor tested his sword here, and in so doing split the stone. Stone steps next to Sword Testing Rock lead up to Qianfo Yan cliff, which contains about 200 stone Buddhist sculptures and inscriptions, many of which are from the Tang era.

Diecai Shan 叠彩山

Diecai Shan, Mountain of Many Colors, is located in the northern section of the city. It has four peaks; at 223 m, Mingyue Feng is not only the highest one within this massif, but also in all of Guilin. A path leads from the southern foot up to Diecai Ting pavilion. The small mountain Yuyue Shan is located east of the pavilion. From its peak, one has a good view of the area around the Lijiang. Siwang Shan mountain is located west of Diecai Ting pavilion. Dingyue Si temple used to stand here. A bell and a vessel from the temple can still be seen on Fubo Shan mountain today. From Diecai Ting pavilion, the path leads up farther to Diecai Men gate. At this spot there is a stele honoring the two Ming loyalists, Qu Shisi and Zhang Tongchang. Nayun Ting, Pavilion Reaching to the Clouds, stands on Diecai Shan's peak. Here, one has a magnificent view of Guilin and its environs. The Diecai Shan mountain area is rich in valuable stone carvings and Buddhist sculptures from the Tang and Song dynasties.

Qixing Gongyuan, Seven Star Park 七星岩公园

Seven Star Park is one of Guilin's most important sights on the Lijiang's west bank. The seven stars symbolize the seven mountains around which the park grounds were laid out. The mountains are arranged in the order of the seven stars in the Big Dipper. The four northern mountains make up Putuo Shan, the three southern mountains form Yueya Shan. Many large caves are located on Putuo Shan. Qixing Yan, Seven Star Cave, is one of these. It is located on the mountain's western foot and is particularly worth seeing. Most tour groups are taken there. The cave was formed by a subterranean river and the movement of the earth's crust. It consists of three layers — only the middle one is open to visitors. The sightseeing tour through the cave covers 814 m. The temperature is around 20°C. Guided tours are conducted on a regular basis and should be taken advantage of so that one does not overlook any of the colorfully lighted forms and figures that are connected with so many legends and fantasies. The monkey gathering peaches, the frog jumping into a pool and two dragons playing ball are only some of the shapes to be discovered. Because the cave has attracted people here for centuries, many sayings and poems by various literary figures have been eternalized on the stone walls throughout the course of time.

Huaqiao, Flower Bridge, is located at the entrance to the park. It is a stone construction from the Song era, but it was extended from five to seven arches during the Ming period. Numerous pavilions and trees and flowers are passed on the path towards Seven Star Cave. After viewing the cave, the visitor may take the path leading to Huoran Ting pavilion and towards Yueya Shan in the west. There are caves and steep cliffs in the area. Guihai Beilin, Stone Tablet Forest, has over a hundred inscriptions, more than half of which were made during the Song period, and is of great interest.

Luotuo Shan, Camel Mountain 骆驼山

Camel Mountain is located in the eastern part of Guilin, south of Qixing Gongyuan. The mountain actually resembles a sitting, one-humped camel.

Ludi Yan, Reed Flute Cave 芦笛岩

Ludi Yan is located in the northwestern section of the city. It is 240 m deep and is probably the largest and most magnificent cave in Guilin. Ludi Cao, reed grass, grows in front of the cave and can be used to make the most wonderful flutes. This was what gave the cave its name. It used to be a favorite place for the local people to hide themselves in times of war or trouble. It had already been discovered by the Tang era, but it was first made into a

tourist attraction in 1959.

A 500-m-long path leads past fantastic, colorfully lighted stalactites and stalagmites which appear to be made of coral, jade, amber and agate. Aided by the untiring, imaginative explanations provided by the guides, flower gardens, magnificent halls, pavilions and wonderful pictures appear before the observers' eyes. A grotto within the cave is roomy enough to hold up to a thousand people. This is the dragon king's crystal palace. A stone column represents the dragon king's magic wand with which he governed the sea. In the famous tale *The Journey to the West*, the king of the monkeys, Sun Wukong, asks the dragon king for his wand. However, the dragon king refused, and the king of the monkeys took the wand by force, defeated the dragon king's army which consisted of snails and jelly fish and laid waste to the palace. The conquered snails and jelly fish are still strewn around the cave today — broken pieces of stalagmite.

Nanxi Shan Mountain 南溪山

Nanxi Shan is located in the southern part of Guilin. It has two peaks facing each other. Several caves are located on the northern slope. Nanxi Gongyuan park stretches along the northern foot and is the location of bamboo and pine trees, flowers and pavilions. A bridge leads to a tea house.

Zengpi Yan Cave 甑皮岩遗址

A Stone Age settlement used to be located at the southwestern foot of Dushan mountain in a southern suburb 10 km from Guilin. The cave was discovered in 1965 and systematically explored in 1973. Excavations revealed tools made of stone, bones and shells, as well as ceramics, animal bones and teeth. Hearths and graves were also found. In 1978, display rooms were built where the relics can be seen.

Boat Trip to Yangshuo on the Lijiang River 漓江游

A visit to Guilin would be incomplete without a trip on the Lijiang river. This experience is one of the highlights of a trip through China. The poet Han Yu from the Tang Dynasty described the Lijiang as a blue silk ribbon surrounded by green jade hairpins. The ship takes the visitor past everchanging rock formations, caves, waterfalls, sleepy villages and narrow bamboo rafts carrying cormorant fishermen. It seems as if one has been transposed into a traditional watercolor painting in another time. Many generations of poets and painters have been inspired by the beauty of the Lijiang and its mountains.

Yangshuo is about 80 km away. The voyage can last up to six hours, depending on the size of the ship. One of the first things the ship passes is Xiangbi Shan, Elephant Trunk Mountain. Baota Shan, Pagoda Mountain, and Chuanshan, Mountain with a Hole Through It, follow on the east bank. A pagoda from the Ming period, Shuofo Ta, stands on Baota Shan. The mountain is surrounded by maple trees whose beautiful leaves offer a special enticement in the autumn. The hole in Chuanshan is called Moon Cave by the Chinese. It resembles a full moon in the evening sky. More mountains follow with wonderful names such as 'Clean Vase' — a nicely-shaped vase seems to lie in the water on the west bank — 'Forest of the Strangely Shaped Peaks', 'Nine Oxen', 'Embroidered Mountain', etc. After the half-way point, Huashan, Picture Mountain, suddenly rises up steeply from the water. It has nine peaks and gives the effect of a huge painting where, with plenty of imagination, nine horses can be seen in different positions. One bends down to drink water from the river, another rears up on his hind legs, etc. As the river comes closer to Xinping, it becomes broader and peaceful. Feather-like bamboo trees line the banks. The water, even clearer than before, mirrors the passing scenery. An unearthly, unique mood arises.

Yangshuo District Capital 阳朔风光

Like Guilin, Yangshuo was founded during the Qin Dynasty (221 — 206 BC). It has held the status of district capital since the Sui Dynasty. For many centuries, the city attracted famous writers, philosophers, poets and painters. Anyone who believes Guilin residents when they say that their scenery is the most beautiful in the world is bound to be set right in Yangshuo. The people who live there hold the view that Yangshuo is far more beautiful than Guilin.

Yangshuo is southeast of Guilin. Evergreen trees, strange rocks, crystal clear rivers and brooks all leave their mark on the landscape. Here, also the Lijiang offers an impressive scene. Numerous peaks rise up steeply from the banks. Their appearance changes with the time of day and will fascinate the visitor time and time again. There are caves in all the mountains. Several of these are very large, such as Jiaoping Dong; others are located

at particularly high elevations, including Mingyue Dong, and still others are connected together, such as the famous eight caves on Zhongling Shan. Yangshuo offers not only a number of interesting sights but also a rich tradition in crafts. The creation of miniature rocks is especially interesting.

Some of the city's most important sights are: Bilian Feng, Green Lotus Peak, Shutong Shan, Mountain of the Studying Child, Yangshuo Gongyuan park, Rongyingudu, Banyan Tree by the Old Ferry, and Yueliang Shan, Moon Mountain.

Bilian Feng, Green Lotus Mountain 碧莲峰

The lush, green Bilian Feng is located southeast of the city on the banks of the Lijiang. Coupled with its reflection on the river, it resembles a lotus blossom. On the mountain slope, the two-story pavilion Yingjiang Ge offers a wide view of the river.

Jianshan mountain, with rock sides as smooth as glass, rises to the north of Bilian Feng.

Rongyingudu, Banyan Tree by the Old Ferry 榕荫古渡

A mighty banyan tree over 1,400 years old grows on the bank of the Jinbao He river about 6 km south of Yangshuo. A ferry used to cross the river at this spot.

Yueliang Shan, Moon Mountain 月亮山

Is located 3 km south of the banyan tree. There is a hole in its peak in the shape of a half moon through which the sky can be seen. A path winds its way up to the hole.

Pingfeng Shan, Screen Mountain 屏风山

Pingfeng Shan mountain resembles a screen. It can be found in Yangshuo Gongyuan park in the western part of the city. Those who climb up to the top of the mountain can enjoy the view from Woyun Ting pavilion. Zhonglin Shan can be seen near Pingfeng Shan. Eight interconnecting caves, each with its own character, are located there.

Xingping Village 兴坪

Xingping, a small city with a long history, lies north of Yangshuo. During the Jin Dynasty (265—420), Xingping was a district capital. This peaceful and romantic spot is an ideal place to observe life in the country.

Hotels (Yangshuo)

Yangshuo Fandian, 阳朔饭店 tel. 22 60

Xilangshan Fandian, 西郎山饭店 tel. 23 12, both are in the center of Yangshuo.

Hotels (Guilin)

Dangui Fandian, Zhongshanzhonglu, tel. 35 76

Guilin Fandian, 桂林饭店 Zhongshan-zhonglu, tel. 22 49

Jiashan Fandian, 甲山饭店 Lijunlu, tel. 22 40

Lijiang Fandian, 漓江饭店 Shanhubeilu 1, tel. 28 81

Ronghu Fandian, 榕湖饭店 Ronghubeilu, tel. 38 11

Xiangshan Fandian, 香山饭店 Zhongshan-nanlu, tel. 28 35

Restaurants

Guilin Jiujia, Zhongshanzhonglu 212, tel. 23 77

Tonglai Guan, Zhongshanzhonglu, tel. 34 49

Yueyalou, in Qixing Gongyuan park, tel. 36 22

Shopping

Zhongshanzhonglu is Guilin's business street. A few of the stores that are located there are an antiques store, an arts and crafts shop, a department store, a Friendship Store and a Xinhua Bookstore.

Travel agency

Guoji Lüxingshe, CITS and **Zhongguo Lüxingshe,** Ronghubeilu 14, tel. 38 26 48, telex 4 84 01

Gong'an Ju, Public Security Bureau, Baguilu, tel. 32 02

CAAC, ticket office, Zhongshanzhonglu 144, tel. 30 63

Train Station, Zhongshannanlu, tel. 31 24

Taxis, Ronghubeilu 3, tel. 20 89

The Autonomous District of the Dong Minority, Sanjiang Xian
三江侗族自治县

Chengyang Fengyu Qiao, Chengyang Wind and Rain Bridge 程阳风雨桥

This bridge located 20 km north of the district capital Sanjiang, was built by Dong minority master builders in 1916. Five pavilions rest upon five stone piles and are connected by covered corridors. The bridge is an excellent example of timber frame construction and the typical style of the Dong minority. This sort of bridge is found frequently in Dong regions. They offer protection from the sun, rain and wind and provide passers-by with an opportunity to rest and chat at ease.

Mapang Gulou Drum Tower 马胖鼓楼

The Mapang Drum Tower, another example of the Dong minority's architectural style, is located in the Bajiang Gongshe People's Commune in Sanjiang district. It is the largest of this type of tower, which can be found in almost every Dong village. The drum tower serves as a place for meetings and events. Performances are frequently held in front of the tower.

Mapang Gulou, made entirely of wood, was constructed in 1928. It reaches a height of 20 m, the nine-tiered roof included. Four mighty wooden columns support the building. The interior walls are decorated with paintings of landscapes.

Flower Fireworks Festival

On the third day of the third month according to the lunar calendar, Dong minority members celebrate the Flower Fireworks Festival in the Fulu Zhen community, located on the banks of the Duliu Jiang river. This festival lasts several days. People come from near and far to gather beside the river, watch fireworks and sell their wares, most of which are hand-made. For the occasion, the Dong dress up in their finest attire.

Jintian 金田市

Qiyi Jiuzhi, The Place where the Taiping Rebellion Began 金田起义旧址

The historically interesting Jintian is located on Zijing Shan mountain, 24 km north of the district capital, Guiping. In 1847, the Taiping rulers Hong Xiuquan and Feng Yunshan founded the Shangdi Hui society here. Thousands of men and women joined together to form a commune where they resided in different camps according to their sex. On January 1, 1851, Hong Xiuquan initiated the Taiping Rebellion. There are still traces of the former commune buildings. Sanjie Miao temple, where Hong Xiuquan first commanded his troops, contains displays of weapons, inscribed tablets and period documents.

Sichuan Province 四川省

Area: 570,000 km² / Population: 99.7 million / Capital: Chengdu

Sichuan is located in the southwestern region of China. It is bordered by Hubei and Hunan in the east, Guizhou and Yunnan in the south, Xizang (Tibet) in the west and Qinghai, Gansu and Shaanxi in the north. The name 'Sichuan' means 'four streams', and it refers to the four most important tributaries to the Changjiang: Minjiang, Tuojiang, Fujiang and Jialing Jiang which flow through the province from north to south. Thanks to the favorable climatic conditions, intensive farming and numerous mineral resources, Sichuan is one of the richest provinces in China.

History

The area of present-day Sichuan was not originally settled by Han Chinese, who did not come to Sichuan until the 4th century BC. During the Zhou Dynasty, the region was named Shu Ba; during the period of the Three Kingdoms (220—280), it became the Kingdom of Shu Han. Up into the 10th century, the region's name, administrative status and also its affiliation were changed many times. Sometimes it was an independent kingdom, at other times it was a regular part of the empire. Its remoteness and secure military position favored separatist movements and called forth a strong feeling of regional identity. The region has been called Sichuan since the Song era. Provincial status was achieved during the Qing period. After the overthrow of the Qing Dynasty, Sichuan became the plaything of individual military rulers, and it was difficult for the national government to maintain control. During the period in which the military rulers were in power, the province was torn apart into separate regions — for a time,

as many as 17. As the national government weakened, preceding the Japanese invasion in 1938, it withdrew to Sichuan, and the province was suddenly pushed into the spotlight of events. To a certain extent, the region profited from this development, as people and capital suddenly streamed from the coastal regions into remote Sichuan. The national government remained in Sichuan until 1946, and the Japanese never succeeded in conquering the region. Since the founding of the People's Republic, Sichuan has once more been brought under the firm control of the central government.

The province can be divided into an eastern and a western half. Numerous mountain chains divide the western region. The highest elevation in Sichuan, Gongga Shan mountain at 7,590 m, is located in this area, about 70 km from Ya'an. In contrast to the eastern half, the western half is sparsely populated. Most of the inhabitants have Tibetan-Burmese ancestry and live in the mountains. They make their living by raising cattle and pasturing, farming or hunting. The Red Basin is located in the east, surrounded by mountain ranges. Several hundred million years ago, an inland sea was located here, and its red deposits led to the basin's name. The basin's surface is hilly and severely eroded. Effective farming became possible only by introducing terrace farming. Today, the basin is also called Land of Millions of Terraces. It is one of the most densely populated areas of China and is inhabited primarily by Han Chinese. The Han make up about 96% of Sichuan's population. Thanks to the long growing period of around 350 days, it is possible to grow two crops a year almost everywhere in the region. In the summer, almost a third of the entire land area is devoted to growing rice; corn, sorghum and sweet potatoes are planted in the rugged areas where it is difficult to irrigate. In the winter, wheat and rape are the dry land crops. Sugar cane, cotton, peanuts and citrus fruits are grown in certain river valleys. Tea is planted in the mountains in the west. Pressed brick tea is a specialty. Chengdu's plains are Sichuan's traditional region for the cultivation of rice. It is the only large area in the region that is relatively level. An irrigation system, Guanxian's Dujiang Yan, was laid out here as early as the 3rd century BC under the direction of the prefect Li Bing and his son Erlang. This system was not only one of the oldest in China, but also one of the most successful. It guarded the basin against floods and droughts.

Due to the high mountains in the north and west which prevent cold air masses from entering the region, Sichuan's climate is mild. In Chengdu, the average temperature is 7°C in January and 26°C in July. In the mountainous western region, it is 20°C. Three-quarters of the annual precipitation falls between June and September.

Sichuan is one of China's most important suppliers of wood. Mineral resources are also significant. There are large supplies of iron-ore, copper, gold, silver, aluminum, salt, coal, oil, asbestos and marble. The leading industrial centers are Chongqing and Chengdu, as well as Neijiang and Yibin.

The capital, Chengdu, is the second largest city in Sichuan. The largest city in the province is Chongqing.

Chengdu 成都市

Chengdu lies in the middle of the province and has 3.89 million inhabitants.

History

Chengdu was founded during the period of Warring States. It was the seat of the prefecture of Shu until the Han Dynasty and was the capital of the Shu Empire during the period of the Three Kingdoms. Chengdu developed into a booming business and trade town during the Tang Dynasty. There were hundreds of lacquerers and jewellers; the silver filigree work of Chengdu is still some of the best of its kind in China today. In 1368, Chengdu became the capital of Sichuan. During World War II, many people streamed into Chengdu from the eastern provinces to escape the Japanese threat. Institutes and universities came with them. After 1949, the city developed into an important transportation junction; the railroad lines to Chongqing, Baoxi and Kunming meet here and highways lead to neighboring regions.

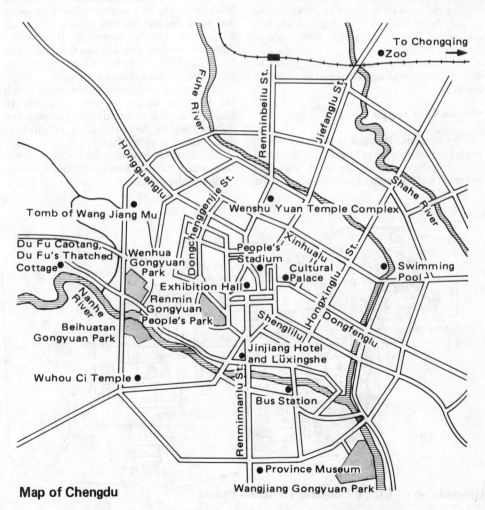

Map of Chengdu

Chengdu has become an important manufacturing city with several factories in light and heavy industry.

Chengdu has always been a cultural center and attracted literary men and scholars. There was a school run by the state here as far back as the Western Han Dynasty (206 BC—8 AD). There are 14 institutions of higher education, including Sichuan University founded in 1927, several research institutes and an institute for minorities.

Chengdu is often called the city of brocade. The breeding of silkworms and the weaving of brocade were highly developed as early as the Han era (206 BC—220 AD). Even today, one-third of the Chinese mulberry spinning-silk is produced on the Chengdu Plain.

Chengdu is also the city of hibiscus. Meng Cheng, King of Shu and a fancier of hibiscus, had it planted along walls and the edges of streets in the 10th century.

Gourmets should not pass up the chance to try out the Sichuan cuisine in Chengdu. It is substantially hotter and spicier than those of the other provinces.

The sights of Guanxian should also not be missed. They can be easily reached by taxi from Chengdu.

Wenshu Yuan Temple Complex 文殊院

This complex, founded in the 6th century, lies in the northern part of the city. The present halls date from 1691. The most important buildings are: Tianwang Dian, Sandashi Dian,

Daxiong Baodian, Shuofa Tang and Cangjing Lou. The more than 100 bronze Buddhist figures in the temple are especially worth seeing; most of them were cast during the Qing Dynasty. Shuofa Tang hall contains 10 iron figures from the Song Dynasty.

Du Fu Caotang, Du Fu's Thatched Cottage 杜甫草堂

The former residence of the famous poet Du Fu (712 — 770) is located in the city's western district on the banks of the Huanhuaxi.

Du Fu resigned from his official position in the capital, Chang'an, and came to Chengdu in 759. He retired to a thatched cottage outside of Chengdu and wrote 240 poems there within three years. One hundred years after Du Fu's death, the poet Wei Zhuang had a thatched cottage built on the foundations of the old grass hut in Du Fu's memory. This compound was expanded and restored again and again in the course of the centuries. It attracted numerous writers and scholars from near and far. After 1949, the People's Government had the entire complex restored.

Several halls are open to visitors in which Du Fu's life and work are portrayed. In addition, statues, stone carvings, paintings and calligraphies by famous writers of different dynasties are also on display.

The complex was expanded into a public park, which includes a bamboo garden, several pavilions and bridges.

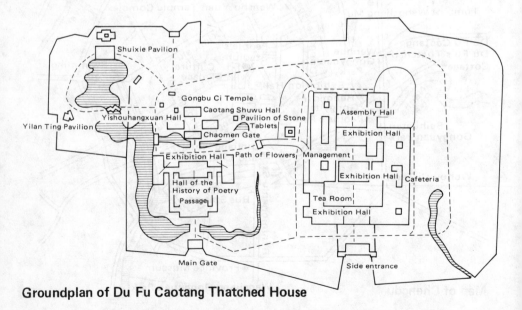

Groundplan of Du Fu Caotang Thatched House

Tomb of Wang Jian Mu 王建墓

A 10th-century tomb is located 2 km west of Chengdu near Sandong Qiao bridge. Wang Jian (847 — 918) was laid to rest here. He was a general who accompanied the last Tang emperor, Xizong, on his flight to Sichuan.

After the fall of the dynasty in 907, he appointed himself emperor of Shu in Chengdu and ruled over Sichuan, Shaanxi, Hubei and a part of the present province Gansu.

The burial place is divided into three areas by 14 stone arches. Its length measures 23.4 m. The coffin rests on an artistically decorated stone terrace in the middle section. In the rear section, there is a stone statue of Wang Jian. The sepulchral finds are displayed in two exhibit rooms on the grounds.

Daci Si Temple 大慈寺

Daci Si on Dongfenglu street dates from the Tang Dynasty. The halls open today are reproductions from the reign of Tongzhi (1862 — 1874).

In past times, the temple was well-known and valued in the entire area for its murals. Tianwang Dian, Guanyin Dian, Daxiong Dian and Cangjing Lou halls still stand today.

Wangjiang Lou Gongyuan Park 望江楼公园

This park, 2 km east of Chengdu on the south bank of the Jinjiang river, owes its reputation to the fact that the famous poet Xue Tao (768 — 831) once lived here. She originally came from the capital, Chang'an, and later moved to Chengdu with her father. After his death, she ran into financial difficulties and became a singer. Her poetic work was acknowledged and admired by her contemporaries.

Xue Tao loved bamboo. She regarded it as the symbol of modesty and self-control, and 130 different types of bamboo were planted on the grounds in her honor. Wangjiang Lou tower, the River View Tower, is located within the park. It is 30 m high and very elegantly constructed. The two lower stories are rectangular and the two top ones octagonal.

Baoguang Si Temple 宝光寺

Imposing Baoguang Si is located in Xindu Xian district, 19 km from Chengdu. The complex is supposed to date from as far back as the Eastern Han Dynasty; however, the remaining buildings are more recent. At the end of the Tang Dynasty, in 881, Emperor Xizong fled to this temple from the rebellious troops of Huang Chao from Chang'an.

This temple was well preserved during the Cultural Revolution. The military troops which were sent by Zhou Enlai in 1967 succeeded in averting a violation by Red Guards, and therefore we can see many treasures, for example a white jade Buddha sculpture from Burma, many paintings and calligraphy. The original painting of 'The big horse' by the famous painter Xu Beihong is hanging in one of the main halls of the inner courtyard. The visitor should pay special notice to the hall of the 500 Luohan sculptures.

Qingyang Gong Temple 青羊宫

Daoistic Qingyang Gong, located in Wenhua Gongyuan park in the western part of the city, was originally built during the Tang Dynasty and later renovated several times. The present halls date from the Qing Dynasty. Bagua Ting pavilion is located in front of the main hall Sanqing Dian. It attracts attention because of its yellow tile roof and eight stone columns with their carved dragon patterns. Sanqing Dian contains a gilded clay figure of the Daoist monk Sanqing.

Ever since the Tang period, a Daoist temple celebration has taken place here on the 15th day of the second month of the Chinese lunar calendar. It is called *Huahui*, the flower celebration. Farmers from near and far come to the city and sell their flowers.

Zhaojue Si Temple 昭觉寺

Zhaojue Si lies 5 km north of Chengdu and is one of the best-known temples of the city. It was built at the beginning of the 7th century. The buildings which are still preserved today are reproductions from 1663. The temple consists of several imposing halls, pavilions and the grave of Yuanwu, a monk.

Wuhou Ci, the Temple of the Duke of Wu (Zhuge Liang) 武侯祠

Wuhou Ci, located in the city's southern district, was built at the end of the Western Jin era (265 — 316) in honor of Zhuge Liang, the chancellor of the state of Shu. Zhuge Liang lived during the period of the Three Kingdoms (220 — 280). He served the emperor of Shu, Liu Bei, as an excellent strategist and politician. After his death, he was honored with the title of Zhong Wu Hou, Faithful Duke of Wu. Today, the name Zhuge Liang is still a symbol of intelligence (see also page 364).

Temple of the Duke of Wu

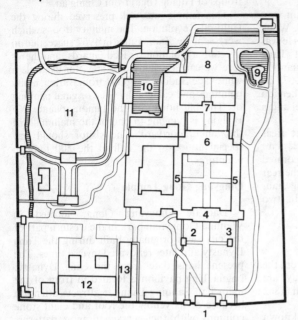

1. Main Gate
2. Stone Stele from the Ming Period
3. Stone Stele from the Tang Period
4. Second Main Gate
5. Walkway
6. Liu Bei Dian Hall
7. Passage Gate
8. Zhuge Liang Dian Hall
9. Lotus Blossom Pond
10. Lotus Blossom Pond
11. Liu Bei's Tomb
12. Exhibition Hall
13. Management

The halls accessible to the visitor date from 1672. Over 40 portrayals of persons from the Shu state can be seen, as well as numerous inscriptions and stone steles. The path to Liu Bei hall, with statues of Liu Bei and his grandson Liu Chen, leads through the main and second gates. In the left and right side halls there are sculptures of Guan Yu and Zhang Fei, Liu Bei's sworn brothers, among others. Representations of 28 of his officials have been preserved in the east and west walkways, each of them with its own short biography. There is a gilded sculpture of the statesman in Zhuge Liang hall. Sculptures of his son and grandson are at his side. Liu Bei's grave lies to the west of this hall. He died in Baidi Cheng on the Changjiang river in 223.

Chengdu Qingzhen Si Mosque 成都清真寺

Chengdu's mosque is on Gulounanjie street. At one time, a magnificent mosque stood here, but it was almost completely destroyed in 1941. Two gilded columns in the present main hall, the prayer hall, have been preserved.

Teahouses, an old tradition of China and typical of Chengdu, survived the Cultural Revolution. Some of them often invite Sichuan Opera singers (amateurs or pensioners) to come and perform. The atmosphere and the spontaneity of such performances in teahouses often outshine professional Sichuan operas. The tourists can find such teahouses through local people or tourguides of CITS.

Sites around Chengdu see page (351 — 355)

Hotels

Jinjiang Binguan, 锦江宾馆 Renminnanlu 180, tel. 44 81

Dongfeng Fandian, 东风饭店 Dongfenglu, tel. 70 12

Restaurants

Chengdu Canting, Shenglizhonglu, tel. 53 38

Furong Canting, Renminnanlu, tel. 40 04

Rongcheng Fandian, Renminxilu, tel. 46 47

Yuehua Canting, Chunxilu, tel. 66 65

Shopping

Antiques, Wenwu Shangdian in Nanjiao Gongyuan park

Friendship Store, Youyi Shangdian, Shenglizhonglu

Arts and crafts, Chunxilu

Travel agency

Guoji Lüxingshe, CITS, and **Zhongguo Lüxingshe and Huaqiao Lüxingshe,** in **Jinjiang Hotel,** Renminnanlu 180, tel. 59 14

CAAC, ticket office, Beixinjie 31, tel. 30 87, 30 38

Train station, Renminbeilu, tel. 9 26 33

Gong'an Ju, Xinhuadonglu, tel. 65 77

Guanxian District 灌县

Dujiang Yan Irrigation System 都江堰

An imposing irrigation plant has been located on the upper course of the Minjiang river in Guanxian, 59 km from Chengdu, for over 2000 years. The prefect of Sichuan, Li Bing, ordered the construction of the system in 256 BC, because the Minjiang frequently overflowed its banks and caused catastrophic floods. Li Bing had a part of Mount Yulei removed to fill in a divide in the river. One-half of the water is diverted into a canal and led onto the wide plains of central Sichuan through a network of tributaries and canals. In this way, floods were prevented and the irrigation of the cultivated areas was guaranteed. Thus, the plain developed into one of the richest grain-growing areas in China. The Dujiang Yan system still plays an important part today. The system is dredged annually to prevent the deposit of mud and the elevation of the riverbed.

Dujiang Yan Irrigation System

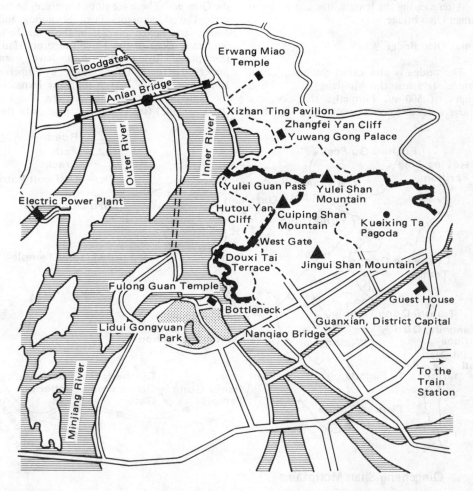

Fulong Guan Temple 伏龙观

Fulong Guan offers the best view of the Dujiang Yan plant. The temple consists of several pavilions and halls. The stone statue of Li Bing, which dates from 168 and is located in the main hall, was recovered from the middle of the Minjiang river in 1974.

Erwang Miao Temple 二王庙

Erwang Miao, the Temple of Two Kings on the east bank of the Minjiang river on Yulei Shan mountain, was erected in memory of Li Bing and his son Li Erlang in the period of the Northern and Southern Dynasties (420 — 589). The present compound dates from the Qing Dynasty. A statue of Li Bing is located in the main hall. Behind it, in a second hall, there is a statue of his son. The compound, arranged on different levels, is very imposing and definitely worth a visit.

After viewing the temple, one can go on to Anlan Qiao bridge.

Anlan Qiao Bridge 安澜桥

The bridge is also called Suoqiao, Chain Bridge. It spans the Minjiang river with a length of 500 m. Formerly, this Song-era bridge was well-known because of its bamboo construction. It was restored and its wooden piers replaced by stone ones in 1974. The former bamboo railing was replaced by chains.

Qingcheng Shan Mountains 青城山

The Qingcheng Mountains, revered by the Daoists, lie about 15 km southwest of Guanxian. A trip to the Daoist complexes and enchanting countryside will appeal to all those who wish to go for a two-or three-hour walk and who love the quiet. The climb begins at Jianfu Gong temple at the foot of the mountain. It was constructed during the Tang era; however, the present buildings are reconstructions from 1888. Room and board are available here. Tianshi Dong temple lies halfway up the mountain and is about a two-hour walk from Jianfu Gong. Master Zhang Daoling, also called Zhang Tianshi, is said to have taught here. The complex dates from the Sui period; the halls were restored at the end of the Qing era. There are stone sculptures of the three Daoist emperors Fuxi, Shennong and Xuanyuan, carved in 723, in the main hall, Sanhuang Dian or the Three Emperors Hall. Inscriptions by famous men have been preserved in this hall, for example, by Emperor Xuanzong (685 — 762) of the Tang Dynasty; the famous official of the Song era, Yue Fei (1103 — 1142) (see Hangzhou, page 244); the

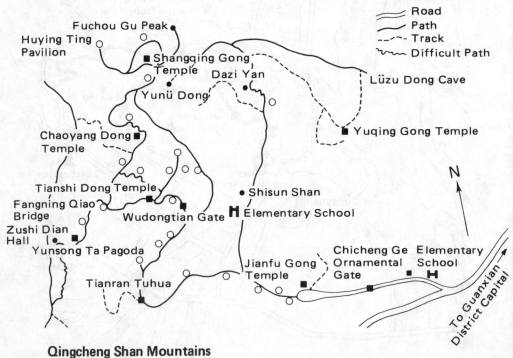

Qingcheng Shan Mountains

painter Dong Qichang (1555 — 1636); and the scholar and painter Zheng Banqiao (1693 — 1765).

Behind the main hall, a stairway leads to a small room in the west that houses a sculpture of Zhang Tianshi.

Two paths lead the way from the Tianshi Dong temple further up the mountain. The path to the northeast leads to Sandao Shi, Three Island Cliff. The one to the west leads to Shangqing Gong temple.

Those who are fond of vegetarian cooking should, perhaps, stay awhile in Tianshi Dong and eat a meal. The vegetarian cuisine of this temple is excellent.

A path leads westward from Tianshi Dong temple to Shangqing Gong temple on the 1,600-m-high main peak Laoxiao Ding. The climb takes another two hours. The view becomes broader and more impressive with each step.

The temple was built in the 3rd century, but the present buildings date from the Qing era. A statue of the Master, Li Laojun, is in the main hall. On the right side of the temple compound is Magu Chi pond, which is supposed to never dry up. Behind the temple, the path continues up for a few hundred meters to the highest point of the mountain and to Huying Ting pavilion. One has a magnificent view from here.

One does not need to return by the same route, rather, it is possible to climb down towards the east. This path is much shorter and also goes by some interesting points such as Yunü Dong, Dazi Yan and Shisun Shan. It takes about an hour to reach Jianfu Gong temple. Here, one can drink a cup of the outstanding Qingcheng Shan tea, a real pleasure — especially when one knows that only the emperor had the privilege of drinking it in former times.

Whoever does not want to climb up to the mountaintop can walk southwest from Fangning Qiao bridge and take a look at Zushi Dian temple. Its surroundings are especially quiet and romantic.

Leshan 乐山市

Leshan lies south of Chengdu on the Chengdu-Chongqing railroad at the confluence of the Minjiang, the Qingyi and the Dadu. This city, formerly called Jiazhou or also Jiading, has a 2000-year-old history. During the Han Dynasty, the district capital Nan'an was located here. The town has been called Leshan ever since the Qing era.

Leshan is an important center of the silk industry. A sight in Leshan's surroundings is the Great Buddha.

Leshan Dafo, the Great Buddha of Leshan 乐山大佛

A huge Buddha statue stands on the rock slope of Lingyun Shan mountain at the confluence of Dadu and Minjiang rivers in the southeast district of the city. It is a 71-m-high portrayal of the seated Maitreya, finished in 803 after 90 years of work. Its head is 14.7 m high, 10 m wide and ends at the tip of the cliff. Its eyes are 3.3 m wide, its ears 7 m long. Its feet rest just above the surface of the water. It was the Buddhist monk Taitong who arranged the construction of the Great Buddha. He was to watch over the dangerously powerful currents in this area and to protect the boats. The sculpture can best be seen from the water. One can take a tourist-boat or ferry from the port of Leshan.

Leshan Rock Cave Tombs 乐山岩墓

Leshan has many rock cave tombs, especially in the city districts Shiziwan, Mahao, Yunzhen Dong and Xiaoba. They date from the 1st to the 6th centuries. The largest is 90 m deep, and even the smallest is 6 m deep (see also page 77).

Wulong Si Temple 乌龙寺

Wulong Si, located on Wulong Shan mountain 1 km from Leshan, consists of Tianwang Dian, Mile Dian, Rulai Dian and Daxiong Dian halls. The latter has three large, gilded sculptures made of fragrant camphor wood: Sakyamuni, Wenshu and Puxian.

Lingbao Ta Pagoda 灵宝塔

The rectangular brick pagoda Lingbao Ta on Lingyunshan dates from the Song era and is 38 m high. It is possible to climb up it and have a look at the surroundings.

Guo Moruo's Birthplace 郭沫若故居

Guo Moruo (1892 — 1978), one of the leading writers of the 20th century and invested with high offices after 1949, was born in Shawan Cheng 35 km east of Leshan. His home is a traditional residence. Guo was born in the left-hand room of the first courtyard. In a small inner courtyard connected to the back garden, there is a small hall in which he was taught by a private tutor. The complex has been restored and opened to the public.

Emei Shan Mountain 峨眉山

Emei Shan is one of the four holy mountains of Buddhism in China. The other three are Putuo Shan in Zhejiang, Wutai Shan in Shanxi and Jiuhua Shan in Anhui. Emei Shan is dedicated to the bodhisattva Puxian. It is located 160 km southwest of Chengdu and 36 km from Leshan. The train travels to Emei County; it is only 6 to 7 km south from there to the foot of the mountain. Here, there is a great ornamental gateway with an inscription by Guo Moruo: Tianxia Mingshan, a famous mountain on earth. It is not far from there to Baoguo Si, a temple from the 16th century. It consists of the four halls Mile Dian, Daxiong Dian, Qifo Dian and Cangjing Lou as well as several decorative pavilions and towers. Of special interest are a colorful ceramic Buddha statue from 1415 and a 7-m-high bronze pagoda. Its walls are adorned with 4700 Buddhist figurines and the text of the Huayan Jing sutra. There is a model of Emei Shan showing the mountain's paths and sights next to Daxiong Dian hall.

The first temples were built as early as the beginning of the Eastern Han Dynasty. They were originally Daoist compounds. The construction of Buddhist monasteries started with the coming of Buddhism to China in the 2nd century. The bodhisattva Puxian is supposed to have taught here at one time. During the Ming and Qing eras, the monasteries and temples numbered 200; today, 20 still remain. It is about 63 km from Baoguo Si temple to the peak. The greater part of this distance can be covered by car so that there are only about 11 km to walk. However, the road is far away from the impressive paths, rugged cliffs and precipices, the waterfalls and mountain streams. There are over 3000 plant species, including a number of rare flowers such as 30 types of azaleas and 14 types of orchids, old gingko trees, cedars and medicinal herbs.

One can make out stone steps and iron chains on the mountain-side while underway. These are the old, narrow paths still used by medicinal herb gatherers. The expansion of the paths was begun as far back as the Song Dynasty.

Fuhu Si monastery lies at the foot of the mountain only 1 km west of Baoguo Si temple. It was founded in the Tang era and redesigned in 1651. Visitors will find a guest house and a restaurant there. Qingyin Ge pavilion is in the middle of an untouched landscape 15 km from Baoguo Si. Two streams, Bailong Jiang, the White Dragon River, in the west and Heilong Jiang, the Black Dragon River, in the east flow past the pavilion and then converge. Two parallel arched bridges span the streams.

The 500-m-long 'Path of 99 Bends' leads from Qingyin Ge towards Hongchun Ping monastery. This path is steep and winding and, therefore, difficult to walk along.

Hongchun Ping monastery lies 10 km from Qingyin Ge at an elevation of 1,100 m. It was built in the Ming era and restored in 1790. The temple's treasure is a tall, bronze lamp with a diameter of 1 m, decorated with over 300 Buddha sculptures, dragons and lotus blossoms.

The Daoist cave Jiulao Dong, the Cave of Nine Immortals, was the refuge of nine old men in ancient times, according to a legend.

Xianfeng Si temple at an elevation of 1,700 m dates from 1612. The halls that are open to the public were built during the Qing Dynasty.

The Elephant Pool, Xixiang Chi, is a hexagonal, 3-m-deep stone basin about 14 km from Xianfeng Si. According to one legend, the bodhisattva Puxian washed his elephants here whenever he passed by. Near the Elephant Pool, there is a temple at an elevation of 2,100 m: Chuxi Yan from the Ming era. It consists of only one hall in which three Buddhist sculptures stand: Guanyin, Dizang and Dashi Zhi. There are many monkeys in this region. A few decades ago, they were threatened with extinction; however, extensive protective measures have been taken that successfully banned this danger.

The highest part of Emei Shan is the 3,100-m-high Jinding, the Golden Peak, also called Qianfo Ding, Thousand Buddha Peak. It is about a two-hour's walk from the Elephant Pool and is surrounded by countless peaks. In the east, the glistening waters of the Qingyi, Minjiang and Dadu rivers can be seen. The special feature of the Golden Peak is 'Buddha's Light', a natural phenomenon that can be observed several times a month and almost daily in October and November. In the afternoon, the sunbeams break through the cloud cover and build a rainbow in the shape of a closed circle. Whoever looks down from Sheshan Yan cliff can see his own shadow in the middle of the rainbow. Many a Buddhist pilgrim who saw his shadow in this circle of light falsely interpreted it as his having achieved illumination and sprang into the abyss.

On the return route, one should go into Wannian Si temple at an elevation of 1,000 m. It was founded during the Jin era (265 — 420) and rebuilt or restored many times afterwards. In 1946, it was destroyed by fire except for a brick hall. In 1953, two halls were rebuilt

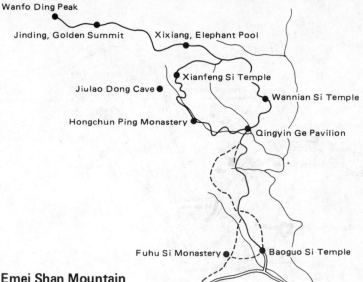

Emei Shan Mountain

according to old plans. The brick hall is the main sight of the temple. It dates from the Wanli period (1573 — 1620) of the Ming Dynasty and has a bronze statue from 980 depicting Puxian riding on an elephant.

Chongqing 重庆市

Chongqing is located at the confluence of the Changjiang and Jialing Jiang rivers in eastern Sichuan. The city was built on hilly terrain. Thousands of alleys, narrow streets and steps lead between the houses down the slopes. Modern apartment blocks, industrial complexes, trees and parks come into view between the black roofs of the old houses. Chongqing has 6.51 million inhabitants and is thus the largest city of the province and the most important manufacturing center in Southwest China. Light and heavy industry have all kinds of manufacturing plants here, including coal mines and shipyards. The city's economy is supported by its favorable location on the Changjiang.

The city's history is over 2000 years old. During the Tang era, the town was called Yuzhou. Yu is still the classic name of the city today. It was renamed Chongqing in the Song period. The city is proud of its revolutionary past. At the time of the Japanese invasion, the southern office of the CCP and the Chongqing office of the 8th Route Army were located here. Chongqing was the war capital of China from 1939—1945. The Nationalist government had retreated this far from the Japanese

invaders. Millions of people from the eastern provinces accompanied the government. Thus, Chongqing, like other cities in Southwest China, prospered economically and culturally. Entire factories, universities and administrative offices were moved here. Chongqing's development could not even be stopped by the Japanese bombardments of 1938—1941, and it continued after 1949.

The city has also been able to develop culturally during the last few decades. In addition to Chongqing University, there are several other colleges and technical schools.

The summer months are hot and humid in Chongqing. The foggy period starts in the fall and lasts from October to April. Whoever wants to undertake a trip on the Changjiang starting at Chongqing at this time has to figure on a delay of several hours when the fog is heavy. The fog lifts as the morning goes by.

Chongqing has few older sights. The hot springs of Beipei and Nanwenquan are worth an excursion. It is possible of late to travel to Dazu and see the Buddhist caves.

Visitors not staying at Renmin Binguan guest house should really go there and take a look at the building, built in 1954. It was designed according to the traditional style and is suggestive of the Temple of Heaven in Beijing. The modern rooms are located in the wings. Local meetings and events take place in the main part of the building.

The city takes pleasure in several parks, including the People's Park, Renmin Gongyuan, in the southwest, Baihuatan

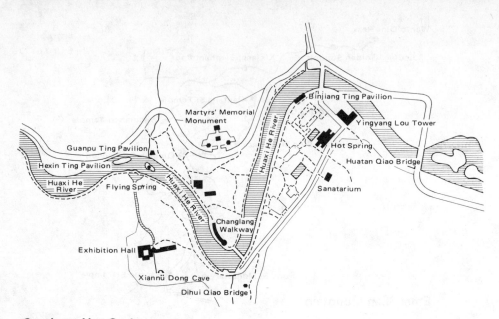

Southern Hot Springs

Gongyuan in the west and the zoo in the northern district.

Beiwenquan, Northern Hot Springs 北温泉

Hot springs are located in **Beipei** northwest of Chongqing. The water temperature averages 32°—37°C. There are plenty of swimming pools and bathing cubicles. The springs lie in the midst of a large park bordered by mountains and canyons on one side and by the Jialing Jiang river on the other. Several Buddhist halls from the Ming and Qing eras can be visited here.

Ziran Chenlieguan, Museum of Natural History 自然陈列馆

The Natural History Museum in Beipei was opened in 1955. The exhibit is comprised of 60,000 objects. Among the most interesting are dinosaur skeletons found during excavations in 1974 and 1977.

Nanwenquan, Southern Hot Springs 南温泉

Another park with hot springs lies 24 km south of the city center. The water temperature is about the same as that of the Northern Hot Springs; the water is sulphurous. The park grounds of Nanwenquan are best-known for their scenic charm. Visitors encounter bridges, cliffs, canyons and lush vegetation. Each of the 'Twelve Landscapes of Nanwenquan', as

this picturesque spot is often called, has its own appeal.

Laojun Dong Caves 老君洞

Because of their agreeable cool temperatures, the Laojun Dong on the south bank of the Changjiang at the foot of Tushan mountain are frequently visited by tourists during the summer. The Daoist temple Laojun Miao, which consists of five halls, is also located there.

Pipa Shan Mountain 枇杷山

The Pipa mountain is not far from the city's center. A private garden that was located here before 1949 was changed into a public park in 1955. The city museum stands on top of the hill. Pipa Shan affords an enchanting view of the city and its surroundings in the evening. The Changjiang can be seen to the south and the Jialing Jiang to the north.

Hongyan Cun 红岩村

Hongyan Cun lies on the banks of the Jialing Jiang, where the 8th Route Army opened an office after the Japanese attacked Wuhan in 1938. In December that year, Zhou Enlai, Dong Biwu and others also withdrew to Chongqing and opened the southern office of the CCP's Central Committee, headed by Zhou Enlai. In August 1945, Mao Zedong conducted peace talks here with the Kuomintang.

No. 50, Zengjiayan 曾家岩五十号

In 1938, Zhou Enlai rented this house in Zhongshansilu street, officially for his private use. Actually, however, other members of the southern office also moved in. Offices were located on the ground floor, the bedrooms of Zhou Enlai and his co-workers were on the third floor. The Secret Service of the Kuomintang had become suspicious and rented the second floor to be on the safe side. When Mao came to Chongqing in 1945, he received foreign and national correspondents here. After 1949, the house was turned into a memorial.

Zhongmei Hezuosuo Jizhongying, Sino-American Cooperation Concentration Camp — Prisons for Political Prisoners 中美合作所集中营

In 1943, the USA and Chiang Kaishek's government founded the above-mentioned organization, which undertook the training of the Chinese secret service in special camps. Later, the training camps were converted into prisons for political prisoners. More than 20 prisons arose, the largest of which were Baigong Guan and Zhazi Dong. Baigong Guan had over 20 cells, each holding several people, and a torture chamber. Zhazi Dong lies 2.5 km from this prison and had 18 cells for men and 2 for women. On November 27, 1949, one day before the Kuomintang troops fled, there was a massacre that only 34 of the 400 prisoners survived. Since then, the dungeons have been changed into memorials.

Hotels

Renmin Binguan, 人民宾馆 Renminlu, tel. 5 34 21

Chongqing Binguan, 重庆宾馆 Minshenglu 235, tel. 37 31

Yuzhou Binguan, 渝州宾馆 Panjiaping, tel. 5 14 86

Huixian Lou, 184 Minzulu, tel. 5 14 86

Chongqing Fandian, 重庆饭店 Xiao Shizi, tel. 4 32 42

Shopping

Friendship Store, Youyi Shangdian, Minzulu

Gongnongbing Bazaar, Qingnianlu

Chongqing Department Store, Minquanlu

Lianglukou Department Store, Zhongsanlu

Arts and crafts store, Zouronglu 107

Lacquered objects, Xietaizi 40

Xinhua Bookstore, Minquanlu

Travel agency

Guoji Lüxingshe, CITS, and **Zhongguo Lüxingshe and Huaqiao Lüxingshe,** Renminlu, tel. 5 14 49 at Renmin Hotel, telex 6 01 87

Gong'an Ju, Public Security Bureau, Linjianglu, tel. 4 39 63

CAAC ticket office, Zhongshansanlu 190, tel. 5 29 61, 5 29 70

Train station, Caiyuanba, tel. 5 26 07, tickets tel. 5 39 27

Changjiang River Traffic Administration, Caiyuanba, tel. 4 19 75, ticket sales tel. 4 28 61

Dazu Xian County 大足县

Dazu Shike, Stone Sculptures of Dazu 大足石刻

Dazu Xian County lies 176 km, about three hours by car northwest of Chongqing. In the last few years, Buddhist cave temples have been restored here that are often part of a tourist program for Chongqing.

Cave temples are no rarities in North China. In South China, the Dazu Shike are among the most beautiful caves of this artistic school. They date primarily from the end of the Tang and the beginning of the Song dynasties and are thus not nearly as old as the ones in North China. The 50,000 stone sculptures of Dazu are spread over 40 locations. The best-known are found on Beishan, the Northern Mountain, and Baoding Shan mountain.

Beishan 北山

Beishan lies 2 km northwest of the county capital Dazu. The stone sculptures here are concentrated in the town of Fowan.

The first ones were carved into the rocks in 892, the last ones 250 years later. The majority of the southern sculptures date from the late Tang and Wudai eras. In the northern area, most of the sculptures are from the Song period.

Baoding Shan 宝顶山

It is 15 km northeast of the county capital Dazu. In this place more than 10,000 sculptures were made during the years 1179 – 1249. The famous monk Zhao Zhifeng had successfully collected the necessary funds for this overwhelming undertaking and he made the Baoding Shan a center of the Mizong school (Tantric Buddhism). There are two main points: Great and Small Buddha Curve, Dafowan and Xiaofowan. The Dafowan is about 500 m long and up to 30 m high. This is where the Sleeping Buddha lies, the most famous stone carving at Dazu. It is a representation of entering Nirvana. The sculpture is 31 m long.

Collective portrayals dominate in Baoding Shan, whereas in Beishan they are mostly of individuals. The numerous Guanyin bodhisattva sculptures are impressive. Each is unique in form and expression and is a work of art. The tender facial expressions, the charm of their posture, the elegance of their clothing and jewelry and the strong feminine character have been greatly admired, but also given cause to a reproach of exaggeration. The artists also emphasized the different qualities of material — silk and cotton clothing can be clearly differentiated, even though carved in stone.

Trip down the Changjiang

Changjiang Sanxia, The Three Gorges of the Changjiang 长江三峡

The 6,300-km-long Changjiang is not only the longest river in China, but also one of the longest in the world. Its source is in the Qinghai highlands and it flows eastward through eight provinces and one centrally administered municipality. At the place where the river reaches the eastern Sichuan Basin, it makes its way deep into and through the Wushan mountains. It becomes narrow and swift and difficult for boats to navigate. Rugged cliffs, steep crags and high peaks line the banks. This incredible landscape is called the 'Three Gorges of the Changjiang'. They extend over 193 km from Fengjie in the west to Yichang in the east. A trip through the gorges is an unforgettable experience for foreign as well as Chinese tourists.

The Changjiang used to be the main transportation route to and from Sichuan. The passage through the gorges was dangerous. Shallows, dangerous bends, rapids and cliffs demanded the utmost attention and a lot of experience from the boatsmen. An additional difficulty was the great variability of the water level — up to 53 m difference in the gorges between the dry and rainy periods. Many people lost their lives or boats and cargo. Boats traveling upstream had to be towed, something that occasionally is done even today. After 1949, the government made funds available to make navigation easier. Dangerous rocks were blasted away, passages dredged and leveled. Today, the gorges are much less dangerous, however, passage through them still requires a high level of concentration from the ship and boat navigators.

The traveller normally begins his trip through the three gorges in Chongqing with a downstream steamer. The trip to Wuhan takes three days; the same trip upstream requires five. Whoever wants to see only the three gorges can get off the boat at Yichang and continue his journey by train. An interesting alternative is to leave the ship at Fengjie west of the gorges and spend a night in the guest house there. It is possible to hire a boat and navigator there and 'conquer' the first gorge slowly. The advantage of this is that the traveler can get off the boat on the way and climb around the cliffs and the path on the north bank. It is also possible to make an excursion to Baidi Cheng from Fengjie. The next day, one can continue the trip through the gorges on the next steamer. Such a side-trip should be arranged in advance with the Lüxingshe in Chongqing.

The trip from Chongqing to Fengjie lasts about 20 hours. The 12 - tiered, red pagoda of Shibaozhai can be seen en route.

Baidi Cheng 白帝城

The City of the White Emperor, lies on the north bank of the Changjiang, 4 km from Fengjie and at the western entrance to the Qutang gorge. It is said that the city was founded by the ruler Gongsun Shu during the Western Han period. Gongsun Shu is supposed to have seen a white dragon in front of his well in a dream one day. He took that for a sign that he would someday become emperor. He declared himself the White Emperor in 25 AD. Ever since, the city has born this name. At the time of the Three Kingdoms, Liu Bei, Emperor of Shu (present-day Sichuan), led his troops in the battle against the state of Wu. He was unsuccessful and the troops were forced to retreat. Liu Bei died here.

The small city lies on a cliff directly on the

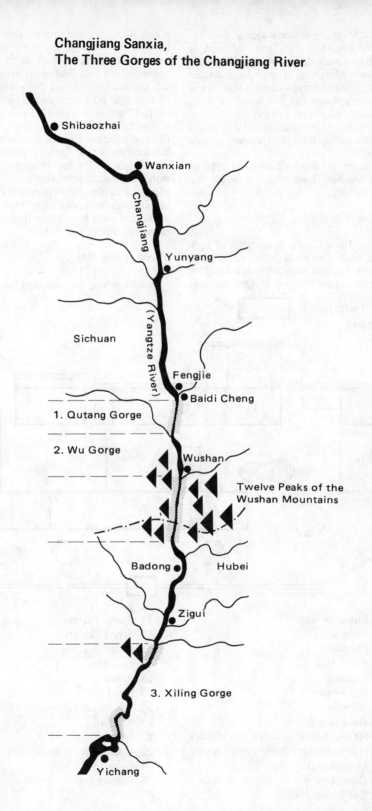

Changjiang Sanxia, The Three Gorges of the Changjiang River

Shibaozhai

Wanxian

Changjiang

Yunyang

Sichuan

(Yangtze River)

Fengjie

Baidi Cheng

1. Qutang Gorge

2. Wu Gorge

Wushan

Twelve Peaks of the Wushan Mountains

Badong

Hubei

Zigui

3. Xiling Gorge

Yichang

river. Baidi Si temple is worth seeing. One has to climb up countless steps from the bank to reach it. It was built during the Qing Dynasty. Its main hall, Mingliang Dian, houses statues of Liu Bei, Zhuge Liang, Guan Yu and Zhang Fei. There are numerous old stone carvings, some of which date from the Sui era.

The residents enjoy making outings to the temple, where they meet for picnics, singing and games.

The area around Baidi Cheng used to be an important military base which guarded the approach to Sichuan.

Qutang Gorge 瞿塘峡

Begins at Baidi Cheng. Steep walls of rock rise more than 100 m high on either side, looking as if they had been cut by a knife. This is the narrowest part of the river. Qutang gorge

is only 8 km long and thus the shortest one, but in spite of that it is the most impressive. A mighty rock formerly rose at its western end against which countless boats were battered. It was blasted away during the work on the river so that it is no longer dangerous to pass this spot. If one looks closely, one can discover remains of coffins in some cracks high in the cliffs. A tribe laid their dead to rest here several hundred years ago. Archeologists were able to recover some of these wooden coffins, along with some swords and other relics. If one walks along the narrow path cut into the rocky cliffs of the north bank, one finds frayed splinters of wood that must have come from the formerly numerous wooden coffins.

Wuxia Gorge 巫峡

Is 40 km long and follows Qutang gorge. It

Baidi Si Temple,
Baidi Cheng

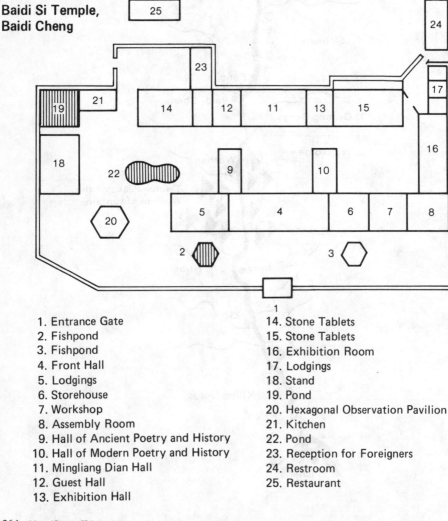

1. Entrance Gate
2. Fishpond
3. Fishpond
4. Front Hall
5. Lodgings
6. Storehouse
7. Workshop
8. Assembly Room
9. Hall of Ancient Poetry and History
10. Hall of Modern Poetry and History
11. Mingliang Dian Hall
12. Guest Hall
13. Exhibition Hall
14. Stone Tablets
15. Stone Tablets
16. Exhibition Room
17. Lodgings
18. Stand
19. Pond
20. Hexagonal Observation Pavilion
21. Kitchen
22. Pond
23. Reception for Foreigners
24. Restroom
25. Restaurant

begins near Wushan in Sichuan and leads to Baodong in Hubei. Twelve high peaks line both banks of the river. The most famous one is Shennü Feng, the Peak of the Holy Woman, named for its graceful shape.

In the Wuxia Gorge the Daning He flows into the Changjian. Some of the travel agencies have recently offered excursions into this side valley, it is a journey in small boats passing through the so-called Three Little Gorges, a distance of about 50 km; a fascinating experience which deepens the impression of this river landscape.

Xiling Gorge 西陵峡

76 km long, is the next gorge. It is possible to make out the most varied objects in the rocks and cliffs, for example, rocks arranged like stacks of books or swords. Xiling gorge was once greatly feared for its dangerous shallows. A trip after dark was perilous. Navigation, even by night, has been made safe by the removal of over 100 shallows and the installation of signal lights. After the last bend of Xiling gorge has been passed, a wide plain stretches out. The river becomes almost 2 km wide. Two small islands not far from the gorge divide the river into two channels. This natural phenomenon was used in constructing the giant hydraulic project Gezhou Ba (see page 320).

Guizhou Province 贵州省

Area: 170,000 km² / Population: 28.55 million / Capital: Guiyang

Mountainous Guizhou Province lies in southwest China. It is bounded by Hunan in the east, Guangxi in the south, Yunnan in the west and Sichuan in the north.

History

The area of present-day Guizhou was originally peopled by ethnic minorities, above all the Miao, who lived in fortified towns and villages under the rule of tribal chieftains. Since the Yuan Dynasty, a road has connected distant Yunnan with the Chinese heartland. Because the road also led through Guizhou, the central government's control and regimentation increased. Immigration movements to Guizhou also started from the Hunan, Jiangxi and Sichuan regions. The province was founded in 1413. During the Qing Dynasty, the central government tried to remove the local leaders and chieftains from power and replace them with appointed officials; however, this met with considerable resistance and led to unrest and rebellions.

The saying: 'Every 30 years an uprising and every 60 years a rebellion' held true for over 200 years.

Since 1949, autonomous administrative authorities have been created in regions with high percentages of ethnic minorities. Large groups of minorities still live in the southeast (the Miao) and the south (the Zhuang).

Guizhou is situated on an enormous plateau that declines from the northwest to the southeast. In the west, it attains elevations between 1,500 — 3,000 m, but in the east it barely rises 600 m above sea level. The plateau mainly consists of limestone, although slate and red sandstone are also present. There are innumerable grottos, underground rivers and lakes in the depressions caused by erosion. There are hardly any large level areas. The Dalou Shan mountains rise to the north and the Miaoling mountains extend in the south and form the watershed of the province. The rivers originating in north and east Guizhou all flow into the Changjiang Basin; the rivers south of the Miaoling mountains belong to the Zhujiang Basin.

Guizhou has a mild, moist climate due to the mountain ranges in the north. The southern and eastern regions are affected by the monsoons. Thus, the summers are warm and the winters mild. In the capital, Guiyang, the average temperature in July is 24°C and in January 4°C. The precipitation level is high: 1,000 — 1,500 mm annually. About 45% of the annual precipitation falls in the summer, and over 20% in the spring as well as in the fall. Blue skies, otherwise typical of China, are rare in Guizhou; the sky is cloudy about 260 days a year.

An old proverb says: 'There are no 3 consecutive days on which the days are clear, there is no piece of land of 3 square feet large that is level, there is no one who owns 3 silver coins.' The latter situation has improved considerably owing to increased industrialization.

Guizhou is one of the Chinese provinces richest in natural resources. There are large deposits of coal, iron ore, copper, bauxite, phosphorous and aluminum, and some gold, zinc and antimony. Industry has developed well over the last three decades. The chief branches are the iron and steel industries, machine manufacturing and the chemical industry. Only 12% of the land is arable. Rice is the most common crop. In the northwest, dry field crops prevail such as corn, wheat, barley and sorghum. The growing of tobacco, cotton, sesame and peanuts is becoming increasingly important. One of Guizhou's best-known products is Maotai Jiu wine, made of wheat and sorghum. It is considered to be the best liquor in China.

About 9% of Guizhou's surface area is covered by forests. In the north, mainly conifers, Asiatic sumac, birch and maple grow, whereas in the south it is cedar, various species of bamboo, willows and conifers.

Guiyang 贵阳市

Guiyang, also called Zhu, lies in the middle of the province hundreds of different plants and herbs along the way. Towering, ancient trees line the path. If one descends on the other side, one walks by the Buddhist temple Hongfu Si from 1672. The compound consists of several imposing halls joined by walkways. It was restored recently. A path leads from this point to the western peak, which offers a pretty view of the city. A path to Qianling Hu lake is behind Qianling Shan. Shengquan, the Sacred Spring, comes to the surface north of the lake. It was honored as a type of fountain of youth in ancient times.

Huaxi Gongyuan Park 花溪公园

Huaxi Gongyuan is 17 km south of downtown. The residents call it the 'flower of Guizhou plateau' because of its enchanting location. Here, there are pavilions, terraces, bridges, islands and teahouses. The park was named after the Huaxi He river. Guizhou University and the teachers' college are located in the vicinity of the park.

Travel agency

Zhongguo Lüxingshe, Bajiaoyan, Sheng Zhengfu Dayuan, tel. 2 51 21, 2 55 10

CAAC, Zunyilu 170, tel. 2 40 00

Zunyi 遵义市

Zunyi, Guizhou's second largest city, lies north of Guiyang on the highway and railroad from Guiyang to Chongqing. The city has a long history. It received its name as early as 642 AD. In recent history it became known as an intermediate station for the Communist troops on their legendary Long March from Jiangxi in southwest China.

Zunyi was only a small market-town completely dependent on the banks of the Nanming He river, a tributary of the Wujiang, on the largest plateau in Guizhou at an elevation of 1,200 m. The railroad and highway networks intersect in the city, and it is also the political, economic and cultural center of the province. The first village was founded as early as the Han Dynasty; however, its sole importance in later centuries was as a military outpost. During the Yuan Dynasty, the locality was expanded to a military base. During the Ming Dynasty, a city wall was built around Xingui, as it was called at that time. In the Qing era, the city was the seat of Guiyang prefecture. Since 1913, the city has been called Guiyang, but it remained little more than the administrative center of a backward province until 1949. Today, it is an important manufacturing center. Since 1960, a large iron and steel integrated plant has hastened the development of machine manufacturing. Guiyang is an important supplier of aluminum. In addition, there are manufacturing plants for industrial and mining equipment, railroad car, textile and chemical factories, glass-blowing workshops and various factories for consumer goods.

Guiyang has various educational institutions. The most important are the University of Guizhou, a teachers' college and a medical school.

Qianling Shan Mountain 黔灵山

Qianling Shan is located 1.5 km northwest of downtown Guiyang. It is surrounded by the grounds of Qianling Shan Gongyuan park and is the most important mountain in southern Guizhou with its height of 1,300 m. A path paved with granite winds up the steep slope to the mountaintop. Experts can find on Guiyang until 1949. At the beginning of the first five-year plan period, it started developing into an industrial center. It has an ironworks, chemical industries, machine manufacturing plants, grain mills, paper factories, silk-spinning factories, etc. Manganese is produced in the vicinity of the city.

Zunyi Huiyi Jiuzhi, Meeting-House of the Politburo of the CCP 遵义会议旧址

A conference of the CCP politburo took place in this house in Zunyi's Old City in January 1935 during the first phase of the Long March. At this meeting, Mao Zedong was appointed the head of the party and the Red Army.

The two-storied house is a national monument and has been made into a museum. The furnishings in the rooms are in accordance with that period. A list of the conference participants is among the exhibits.

In Renhuai Xian County, northwest of Zunyi, the community of Maotai Zhen town is located. The world-famous Maotai wine is produced here.

Zhengning Xian, Autonomous County of the Buyi and Miao Minorities
镇宁布依族苗族自治县

Huangguoshu Falls 黄果树瀑布

Huangguoshu falls on the Baishui He river, 155 km southwest from Guiyang, is the largest and most powerful waterfall in China. It plunges 60 m deep and 30 m wide (40 m during the rainy season) into Xiniu Tan lake. In the rock wall behind the waterfall, there is a 20-m-deep cave. There are more waterfalls in the vicinity of Huangguoshu, for example, the three-tiered Gaotan Pubu in Guangling Xian district 10km from Huangguoshu, as well as caves and bizarrely-shaped rocks.

Yangming Dong Cave 阳明洞

Yangming Dong cave is in Longgang Shan mountain, 1.5 km north of the county capital Xiuwen Xian. At one time, the philosopher and educator Wang Yangming (1472 — 1528), also called Wang Shouren, lived here. He was a high official of the Ming government, but fell into disgrace and was banned to Guizhou.

Stone steps lead from the cave to Junzi Ting pavilion. Wangwenchenggong Ci temple stands not far from it. The temple was built in honor of Wang Yangming, who had taught here.

Yunnan Province 云南省

Area: 390,000 km² / Population: 32.55 million / Capital: Kunming

Yunnan Province in Southwest China is bordered by Guizhou and Guangxi in the east, Vietnam and Laos in the south, Burma in the west and Tibet and Sichuan in the north. The population of Yunnan is two-thirds Han Chinese and one-third minorities, including, as the largest minority groups, the Yi, Bai, Naxi, Hani and Dai. About half of the more than 50 nationalities in China live in Yunnan.

History

Yunnan was originally populated solely by non-Han Chinese nationalities. Power was in the hands of the tribal chieftains. Although they acknowledged the supremacy of the Chinese empire, the region remained largely outside of the Han Chinese sphere of influence. During the Tang Dynasty, the Nanzhao Empire (738 — 902) of the Bai arose. It was succeeded by the state of Dali (937 — 1253) in the 10th century. Yunnan's situation changed abruptly at the beginning of the Yuan Dynasty: the Mongols not only overran the Chinese heartland, but also advanced into present-day Yunnan and destroyed the state of Dali in 1253. They founded Yunnan Province and annexed it to the empire. Moslems from Northwest China moved into the regions that had been depopulated as a result of the battles. During the following dynasty (Ming), the central government supported the immigration of Han Chinese from the Changjiang Plain to Yunnan to strengthen its control over the province. The administration of the separate regions was in the hands of local leaders responsible to high Chinese officials. Separatism, frequently coupled with ethnic and religious differences, resulted in much strife in Yunnan — most noteworthy is the great Moslem uprising (1857 — 1872). At the beginning of the 20th century, Yunnan became the victim of French and British power politics. The French, operating out of Vietnam, tried to bring Yunnan completely under their control. They built the railway line from Hanoi to Kunming in order to exploit the copper reserves. The British acted out of Burma. The period of the Japanese invasion brought Yunnan unexpected progress. Entire factories, universities and government offices were moved from the coastal provinces to the safer province Yunnan. For the first time, govenmental efforts were made to build up industry and tap the mineral resources. However, these attempts were hindered by the lack of an infrastructure.

Since 1949, the People's Government has promoted the development and expansion of industry on a large scale, and the southwest is among the priority regions. The new policy, which also tries to take a well-balanced position towards the minorities question, has brought political unity and stability to Yunnan.

Yunnan's topography is marked by mountain chains and plateaus that continue the Tibetan massif and fan out towards the southeast. The Ailaoshan mountains in the middle of the province divide the area into two great eastern and western regions. High mountain ranges separated by deep river valleys extend through the west. In the northwest, the mountains attain heights up to 6,000 m, torrential rivers flow through the valleys and are only navigable for canoes. In the southern part of this region, the mountains are considerably lower — up to only 2,000 m. Plateaus and broad valleys make intensive farming possible here.

In the east, a broad plateau stretches out, reaching an altitude of about 2,300 m on its western end and 1,500 m on the border to Guizhou. Depression lakes such as Dianchi near Kunming are characteristic of the region.

The climate is mild on the eastern plateau. The summers are cool owing to the elevation and the winters mild due to the protective northern mountain ranges. The growing period lasts at least 10 months. The average temperature is 22°C in July and 9°C in January. In the western part of Yunnan, the summers are hot and humid in the deep valleys. Yunnan lies in the monsoon area and thus receives a lot of precipitation. More than 1,000 mm fall annually, most of it between May and October.

Yunnan's climate and elevation have made it into a botanic garden. There are huge forests in the west and even jungles with typical tropical flora in the southwest. Rice is raised above all else on the plateaus and in the broad valleys. Other important crops are corn, wheat, sweet potatoes, soybeans and tea and, in the southwest, tropical plants such as coffee, sugar cane, tobacco and bananas. Mining is extremely important in Yunnan because of its plentiful mineral resources. The tin deposits of the province are among the world's largest. Yunnan is also rich in copper and, in addition, there are substantial coal, iron and phosphorous deposits.

The ambitious industrialization program, which has already been partly put into effect in Yunnan, has resulted in the expansion of the highway and railroad networks. Not only is Kunming linked to Sichuan and Guizhou by rail, but a star-shaped highway network leads from Kunming to all parts of the province and to the neighboring regions.

Kunming 昆明市

The plane ride from Beijing to Kunming takes less than three hours. The capital of Yunnan lies in the eastern part of the province at an elevation of 1,894 m above sea level in the midst of a fertile high plain. Mountains in the north, east and west protect the plateau from cold winds from the north. Kunming is called the city of eternal spring because of its mild climate and lush vegetation.

History

The city has a long history. Its origins date as far back as the Han era. Its location on the north shore of Dianchi lake was favorable to its economic development. Kunming became the capital of newly-founded Yunnan Province under Yuan rule (1271—1368). Up until recently, Kunming's importance was due to its function as intersection of the trade routes to Burma, Indochina, Sichuan and Guizhou. The railroad line to Haiphong was built from 1906–1910. The city was forced to open to foreign trade in 1908. Kunming strengthened its position as a commercial city during the thirties, after the completion of the roads to Chongqing and Guiyang. During the time of the Japanese invasion, universities and institutes from the coastal provinces were evacuated here so that they would not be destroyed by Japanese troops. Entire factories and workshops were also relocated. Thousands of people from the up-to-date eastern regions of China flooded into underdeveloped Kunming.

The modernization of the city was continued after 1949. Wide streets, modern housing and parkgrounds arose. Modern districts were built next to old ones. Tall buildings tower over older buildings that are usually only two to three stories high. Kunming has developed into a manufacturing city and a center of industrial metal-working with a population of 1.99 million.

Kunming is also the cultural center of the province. It has diverse educational institutions such as universities, medical and technical schools and teachers' colleges, various research institutes and an institute for minorities.

In Kunming, many things differ from the rest of China. Various nationalities live close together — Han, Yi, Hui, Miao and Bai. They lend the city a unique atmosphere. Going for a stroll, one constantly runs across people dressed in colorful ethnic costumes. Arts and crafts products are sold everywhere: gaily embroidered bags, trimming, caps, blouses and dresses.

Dianchi Lake 滇池

Dianchi covers 297 km² at an altitude of 1,885 m above sea level southwest of the city. It is also called Kunming Hu or the 'Pearl on the Yunnan-Guizhou Plateau'. At its longest, it measures 40 km from north to south and at its widest, 8 km from east to west. Its average depth is 5.5 m. The lake is fed by 20 small and large rivers. On Shizhai Shan mountain, on the

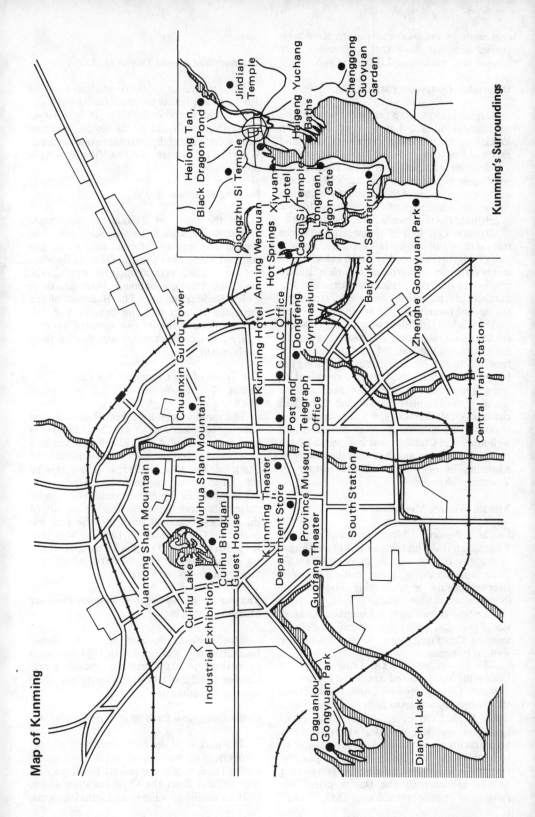

Map of Kunming

Kunming's Surroundings

Heilong Tan, Black Dragon Pond
Jindian Temple
Haigeng Yuchang Baths
Chenggong Guoyuan Garden

Qiongzhu Si Temple
Anning Wenquan Hot Springs
Xiyuan Hotel
Caoqi Si Temple
Longmen, Dragon Gate
Baiyukou Sanatarium
Zhenghe Gongyuan Park

Chuanxin Gulou Tower
Kunming Hotel
CAAC Office
Post and Telegraph Office
Dongfeng Gymnasium
Central Train Station

Yuantong Shan Mountain
Wuhua Shan Mountain
Cuihu Lake
Cuihu Binguan Guest House
Industrial Exhibition
Kunming Theater
Department Store
Province Museum
Guofang Theater
South Station

Daguanlou Gongyuan Park
Dianchi Lake

east shore of the lake, excavations have been carried out that show that settlements were located here more than 2,000 years ago.

Daguanlou Gongyuan Park 大观楼公园

Daguanlu Gongyuan lies on the north shore of Dianchi lake, 2 km west of downtown Kunming. At one time, a private villa and Daguan Lou temple stood here. The present buildings were all built after 1869. The grounds were made into a public park after 1913. Each year on the 15th day of the 8th month (according to the lunar calendar), the mid-autumn festival is celebrated in the colorfully illuminated park.

Daguan Lou hall is noteworthy. To the right and left of the entrance gate, there is a pair of antithetical couplets, set in golden characters on a blue background. Couplets usually consists of only two verses that correspond in number of characters, grammatic structure, rhyme and meaning. They are usually written on the left and right sides of columns or house entrances, although they may also hang next to each other on the wall. Many families attach these scrolls to their doors, above all during the New Year celebration. They are supposed to bring good luck, or may just decorate the house. The Couplets of Daguan Lou hall consists of 180 characters, 90 on each side and is one of the longest, yet most beautiful and well-known in China. It was composed by the poet Sun Ranweng and describes the beauty of Kunming in one half and the history of Yunnan in the other.

Xishan, Western Mountains 西山

The Western Mountains, of which Taihuashan is the highest, lie 15 km southwest of the city on the western shore of Dianchi. Their appearance is often compared to a sleeping beauty or a sleeping Buddha and therefore called Shuifoshan.

The best-known sight is Longmen, Dragon Gate. One can go by bus or car directly to Sanqing Ge. From there, it is a ten-minute walk to Longmen.

The Daoist Sanqing Ge Temple was first built in the Yuan era and completed in the Qing Dynasty. Ciyun Dong cave can be reached from that temple by a narrow path along steep rock walls. Behind the cave, a path leads up to Longmen, the Dragon Gate, which affords a breathtaking view of the lake. It is possible to walk through the gate to the rock pavilion Datian Ge, also called Kuixing Ge. It was built on the initiative of the Daoist priest Wu Laiqing and not completed until 1853, after 72 years.

The Buddhist temple Taihua Si 太华寺

The temple is located at the foot of Taihua Shan. It was founded during the Yuan period and restored in 1688. It is a large, impressive compound — the temple gate and halls were built right into the wooded slope. Wanghai Lou tower, the Sea-View Tower, is on the right.

Huating Si temple 华亭寺

On the north of Taihua Si, the temple originally dates back to the Song era. The present compound is of more recent date and contains Tianwang Dian and Daxiong Baodian halls as well as Zhuangzhong Lou tower. In the main hall Daxiong Baodian, there are three gilded Buddha statues: The Buddhas of the Past, the Present and the Future. The hall became famous for its five hundred Luohan figures, which are crowded together on three levels on the walls.

The Tomb of the Composer Nie Er 聂耳墓

The tomb was built between Taihua Si and Sanqing temples. Nie Er (1912 — 1935) was born in Kunming. After 1930, he worked as a member of Mingyue Gewutuan ensemble in Shanghai. On July 7, 1935, it is said that he was killed in an accident during a stay in Japan. Nie Er composed numerous songs during his short life, including the melody of the Chinese national anthem. His urn was buried on Gaorao Shan in 1938. In May 1980 his grave was moved to this lovely spot. It can be reached by climbing 24 steps, which symbolize the composer's age.

Yunnan Sheng Bowuguan, Yunnan Province Museum 云南省博物馆

This museum, located on broad Dongfengxilu street, was opened in 1964 and owns approximately 50,000 exhibits, including prehistoric fossils, old bronze objects and tools used by the minorities.

Cuihu Gongyuan Park 翠湖公园

The park is in the city's northwest district across from Cuihu Binguan hotel. It surrounds Cuihu Lake, where the private residence of a high official from the Qing era once stood. With its pavilions, willows and lotus blossoms, this park is a restful place, especially for guests staying at the Cuihu Binguan.

Yuantong Shan Mountain 园通山

Yuantong Shan rises in the northern part of the city and is one of Kunming's most beautiful mountains. It is especially attractive when the cherry, wild apple and peach trees are in bloom; at that time, the entire park is enveloped in pink. Yuantong Si temple is located here, built in the Tang era and restored during the Ming and Qing periods. An octagonal pavilion in the middle of a square pool is worth seeing. Imposing Yuantong Baodian hall is to the north of the pavilion. It contains Buddhist sculptures from the Yuan era. Two Ming dragons wind around two columns as if to protect the sculptures. The zoo, Yuantong Shan Dongwuyuan, lies to the north of the complex.

Two old brick pagodas are located in the southeast part of the city: Xisi Ta, the West Temple Pagoda, on Dongsijie street and Dongsi Ta, the East Temple Pagoda, on Shulinjie. Both are reproductions of pagodas that were built here during the Nanzhao era but destroyed during the Moslem uprising. They are rectangular and 13 stories high.

Daliguo Jingzhuang, a pagoda from the Dali Empire on Tuodonglu street, has seven stories and is octagonal. It is decorated with Buddhist figures and texts in Sanskrit and Chinese.

Heilong Tan, Black Dragon Pond 黑龙潭

The pond is located 14 km north of Kunming in the midst of beautiful Heilongtan Gongyuan park. Because Heilong Tan never dries up, even during great droughts, the people used to believe that a dragon must have lived in it, for dragons were thought to be rulers of the water. Thus, the pond was given its fitting name.

The buildings on the park grounds were constructed during the last two dynasties. The main gate of the temple Longquan Guan is noteworthy because of its conspicuously large ornamental bracketing system. However, though the grand buildings attract many people, it is primarily the interplay of architecture and nature which gives the park its attractive worth.

Qiongzhu Si Temple 笻竹寺

Qiongzhu Si is located 10 km northwest of the city on Yu'anshan mountain. Its main hall, Daxiong Baodian, contains three Buddha sculptures dating from the Yuan period. The most important sight of the temple complex are the 500 Luohan terra-cotta sculptures carved from 1883—1890. They are the work of the sculptor Li Guangxiu from Sichuan and his five pupils. The sculptures are very well-known in China, for they are exciting, unconventional creations. The artists seem to have taken their models from all levels of society. Warriors, officials, literary people, peasants, artisans and beggars are portrayed vividly and some of them even in great motion. Their faces clearly mirror their moods. They are among the most realistically portrayed Luohan sculptures in China.

Jindian Temple 金殿

Jindian temple is located on Minfengshan mountain, 7 km northeast of Kunming. The main hall was cast in bronze in 1671. The sculptures, columns, doors and latticed windows are also made of bronze; the terrace, balustrade and the steps of marble. Many camelias were planted in the surrounding area.

Anning Wenquan, Anning Hot Springs 安宁温泉

The hot springs in Anning, also called Biyu Quan, the Jade Springs, are 40 km southwest of Kunming and were discovered and used several centuries ago. Their temperature varies between 42°C and 45°C.

Anning is a simple yet very pretty area. The springs are on the river. There are various baths, shops, restaurants and a teahouse.

Caoxi Si temple, at the foot of Longshan mountain 1 km west of the springs, dates from the Tang era. The present buildings are more recent. Zhenzhu Quan spring, the Pearl Spring, is worth mentioning. It is located south of the temple.

Shilin, the Stone Forest 石林

The Stone Forest, 126 km southeast of Kunming in the autonomous district of Yi at an elevation of 1,750 m, is one of the best-known sights of China. Many millions of years ago, there used to be an ocean here. A thick layer of limestone built up on the sea-bottom. Geotectonic movement changed the sea-bottom to mainland and further land movements caused deep cracks in the rock that were then washed out by rain. In this way, rock formations took shape that resemble pagodas, bamboo shoots, huge columns, camels, etc. The entire Stone Forest covers 26,000 hectares, but tourists usually go to see only about 80 hectares, where there is an accumulation of especially bizarre rocks. A 2-km-long, marked path leads through the labyrinth, past rocks up to 30 m tall, down ravines and up again to vantage points.

After the walk refreshments are available in the guest house or the nearby teahouse. Many visitors spend the night at Shilin Binguan Guest house.

Hotels

Cuihu Binguan, 翠湖宾馆 Cuihunanlu 16, tel. 21 92

Kunming Fandian, 昆明饭店 Dongfeng-donglu 145, tel. 22 40, 52 86

Kunhu Fandian, 昆湖饭店 Beijinglu, tel. 77 32

Shilin Binguan, 石林宾馆 Lunan Xian, near the Stone Forest

Xiyuan Fandian, 西园饭店 Xishan (Western Mountains), tel. 99 69

Restaurants

Guangwei Fandian, 广味饭店 Jinbilu, tel. 29 70

Beijing Fandian, 北京饭店 Xinxiangyunjie 77, tel. 33 27

Shanghai Fandian, 上海饭店 Dongfengxilu 73, tel. 29 87

Yingjianglou Moslem Restaurant, 迎江楼国民餐厅 Changchunlu 413, tel. 51 98

Travel agency

Guoji Lüxingshe, CITS, and Zhongguo Lüxingshe, Huashanxilu 68 — 72, tel. 42 52 Service desk at Kunming Hotel

CAAC ticket office, Dongfengdonglu 146, tel. 42 70

Bank of China, Huguolu 271, tel. 45 29

Mail and Tele-communications Center, Dongfengdonglu, tel. 73 19

Gong'an Ju, Beijinglu 525

Shopping

Department store, Zhengyilu

Nationalities store, Nanbinglu

Antiques, Nanbinglu

Arts and crafts, Qingnianlu and Dongfengxilu

Friendship Store, Dongfengxilu 99

Taxis

Kunming Hotel, tel. 50 11
Cuihu Hotel, tel. 21 92, 23 96
Three-wheeled taxis, tel. 38 98
Train station, tel. 60 42
Day and night service, Jinri Gongyuan park, tel. 62 43

Dali and Surroundings 大理市

Dali lies about 400 km northwest of Kunming in the Bai autonomous district. The city's history reaches back more than 1,200 years. Due to its beauty, the area around Dali is often called the Switzerland of the Orient.

The city Taihe, located 7 km south of present-day Dali, became the capital of the Nanzhao kingdom (738—902) in 741. Pilouge, a Bai tribal leader, united the six tribes of the Erhai region under his control. The kingdom of Nanzhao covered not only the area of present-day Yunnan, but also parts of Guizhou and Sichuan. After Pilouge's son ascended to the throne, a new capital was built in Dali. Dali is also called the city of marble, which was used in the construction of most of the imperial palaces, among other buildings. The city's marble is known not only to the Chinese, but also to connoisseurs abroad. Thus, marble is frequently called Dali shi, Dali stone, in China.

In addition to marble, Dali's tea, camelias and its fish are also well-known.

Shegu Ta Pagoda, the Serpent's Bones Pagoda 蛇骨塔

Shegu Ta is south of Dali near Xiaguan. A legend tells of Chengxian Tai terrace, which existed beyond the village of Yangpi Cun during the Nanzhao period. At that time, it was believed that whoever set foot on the terrace was changed into a saint and entered paradise immediately, for no one who went to the terrace ever returned. A young man doubted this belief and discovered that a giant snake devoured the people waiting on the terrace. Thereupon, he fastened several daggers to his clothing and also stood on the terrace. He did not succeed in conquering the snake, which devoured him, too: however, the daggers wounded it fatally. It was burned and the ashes mixed with lime. Shegu Ta was erected in memory of the brave young man. The present building is 39 m tall and made of brick.

Erhai Lake 洱海

Erhai Lake is located 2 km east of downtown Dali at an elevation of 1,980 m. It measures 41 km from north to south and 4-9 km from east to west and is one of Dali's scenic highlights.

Cangshan Mountains 苍山

The Cangshan mountains, also called the Diancang Shan, extend 42 km from Yunnong Feng peak in the north near Shanguan to Xieyang Feng peak in the south near Xiaguan.

The 19 peaks are lined up one next to the other and resemble a screen. The main peak, Malong Feng, is 4,122 m high, the others are between 3,000 and 4,000 m.

The mountains are beautiful. There are steep cliffs, deep valleys, raging waterfalls, springs and temples on the eastern side.

Santa Si Temple, the Three-Pagodas Temple 三塔寺

This renowned temple is to the northwest of Dali. Its three pagodas date from the Tang era. The main pagoda, Qianxun Ta, is a rectangular, 69-m-tall building that resembles Xiaoyan Ta in Xi'an in its design. The other two pagodas are octagonal and 42 m high. During their restoration in 1978, more than 600 interesting objects from the Tang and Song eras were found in the foundations and roofs of the three pagodas, including bronze mirrors, medications, a valuable 24-cm-tall golden Buddha sculpture and a gilded silver phoenix with widespread wings standing on a lotus blossom.

Yutong Guanyin Dian hall is behind Santa Si. It contains a bronze bodhisattva sculpture. In front of the hall is a large marble stele from 1325.

Sanyuejie, March Festival 三月街

For over a thousand years, the Bai people have celebrated the March festival from March 15-20 of the lunar calendar. It takes place on Diancang Shan mountain in the western part of the city. The Bais are not the only ones to participate in the festival, members of many other nationalities also come from near and far, dressed in traditional festival costumes. There is singing and dancing, competitions are held and wares are sold at small stands.

Jianchuan Xian County 剑川县

Shizhong Shan Shiku, Caves of the Stone Bell Mountain 石钟山石窟

The caves are located 25 km southwest of the county capital Jianchuan Xian. They were made by the Bais of the Nanzhao and Dali eras and can be divided into three groups: the caves near Shizhong Si, the Stone Bell Temple; those near Shizi Guan, the Lion's Pass; and those near the village of Shadeng Cun. The eight caves of the first group contain representations of the kings of Nanzhao and their retinues, as well as religious scenes. Three caves are in the vicinity of Shizi Guan. They house portrayals of the royal families of Nanzhao and religious sculptures. The group near Shadeng Cun has five caves, in which two celestial kings are located.

Lijiang, Naxi Autonomous District 丽江纳西族自治县

Lijiang, the district's government seat, is an old city in beautiful surroundings in northwest Yunnan. It is situated on a plateau at an elevation of 2,600 m and is impressive because of its scenery and lush vegetation.

Yulong Xueshan, the Jade Dragon Snow Mountains 玉龙雪山

The mountains lie about 10 km northwest of Lijiang and south of the Jinsha Jiang river and have 12 peaks, the highest of which is 5,596 m. The mountain tops are covered by snow year-round. Yulong Shan is considered a treasure chest by botanists. It is home to over 400 types of medicinal herbs, 300 sorts of azaleas and many rare types of wood. The color and vegetation of the scenery change with the elevation.

Heilong Tan, Black Dragon Pond 黑龙潭

Heilong Tan, also called Yuquan, the Jade Spring, is located north of Lijiang at the foot of Xiangshan, Elephant Mountain. Actually, it is as large as a lake and enchantingly reflects all of the Yulong Xueshan mountains.

The Naxi people built Longwang Miao, the Temple of the Dragon King, in 1737. Fayun Ge pavilion was erected north of the lake in 1882. It has three stories and is the result of teamwork by Naxi, Han and Tibetan artisans. the 'flying' roof construction gives it the appearance of a group of five phoenix, which is why it is also called Wufeng Lou, the Five Phoenix Tower.

The Baisha Frescoes 白沙壁画

At one time, the temples and palaces of the former Naxi tribal leaders were located in Baisha, 15 km from Lijiang. Many of them have been preserved. The 350 frescoes, created about 500 years ago, are especially valuable. The majority of them depict both Buddhist and Daoist religious scenes.

Jinsha Jiang River 金沙江

The Jinsha Jiang is the upper course of the Changjiang. It flows south to the village of Shigu Cun, where it abruptly turns north again. This place is called the 'First Bend of the Changjiang'. The water flows relatively slowly through this bend. A marble tablet from the Ming era that resembles a stone drum, thus named Shigu, stands on the bank. The village is also named after the drum. During the Long March, the Red Army crossed the river here under the leadership of General He Long in 1935. The residents helped to transport 18,000 soldiers and their equipment from one side of the Jinsha Jiang to the other within two days. This spot is thus also called Shigu Dukou, the Stone-Drum Ferry. The river flows north to Sanjiankou, where it again turns south. Both bends are inside Lijiang district.

Hutiao Xia, Tiger Leap Gorge 虎跳峡

The most dangerous spot on the Jinsha Jiang lies farther downstream about 50 km from the Stone Drum. Here, the river flows between the Yulong Xueshan and Haba Xueshan mountain ranges through a 15-km-long gorge. The mountains tower 3,000 m over the river, which is 30-60 m wide at this point. The residents say that the gorge is so narrow that a tiger can leap over it. It is considered to be one of the deepest gorges in the world.

Xishuang Banna 西双版纳

Xishuang Banna Autonomous District of the Dai minority is located in the southernmost part of the province. Thirteen separate ethnic groups are represented in the population of 620,000, of which the Dais make up the largest share with 34.7%. Xishuang Banna is reached by flying from Kunming to Simao and then traveling by bus from there to Jinghong, the capital of the autonomous district.

Xishuang Banna covers an area of 25,000 km² at an altitude of 1,000 m above sea level on the Lancang Jiang river. The climate is subtropical. High mountain ranges in the north hold back cold air masses and monsoons bring warmth and rain.

The average temperature is above 21°C.

Xishuang Banna is a huge botanical garden. Everything native to the tropics grows here. Flowers bloom the entire year round and exude a pleasant fragrance. Over 100,000 hectares of jungle still exist. Rare woods such as mahagony, camphor, teak and sandalwood are common in this region. The animal world also still exists here in undisturbed areas. It includes wild cattle, elephants, giant snakes, peacocks and rhinocerous, among other species.

The typical bamboo huts can be seen in the Dai villages; pile dwellings standing 2 m above the ground that provide protection from moisture and wild animals. They are usually surrounded by cocoanut palm trees. Visitors will never forget the Dais' hospitality, cordiality, clothing, dancing and music, nor their cooking.

A 330-m-long bridge built in 1964 leads over the Lancang Jiang river to the district capital Jinghong. There is a market here every Sunday. Members of the various ethnic groups such as the Dai, Hani, Bulang and Jinuo come down from the mountains and sell their agricultural and arts and crafts products. Usually, the women farmers come to the market.

In Xishuang Banna, various traditional festivals are celebrated, for example, the Water Festival — the Dai New Year's celebration — which takes place according to the lunar calendar in spring. Between the end of the year and New Year's, there are two so-called 'empty days' that belong neither to the old nor to the new year. During these two days and on New Year's Day, many Dais put on festive clothing. On the first day, dragon boat competitions are held, on the second and third days, everybody splashes everybody else with water as an expression of New Year's congratulations. This is done outdoors, on the streets and rivers and in the villages. It does not matter if it is a friend, an acquaintance, a relative or a foreign visitor — everyone is congratulated, and everyone joins in — men

Xishuang Banna Zone

1. Lancang Jiang River
2. Damenglong Fota, White Pagoda
3. Ganlan Ba Park (Center of the
   Water Festival Activities)
4. Mengla District Capital
5. Luosuo Jiang River
6. Tropical Garden
7. Mengyang Village
8. Jungle
9. Jinzhong District Capital
10. Tea Plantation
11. Menghai District Capital

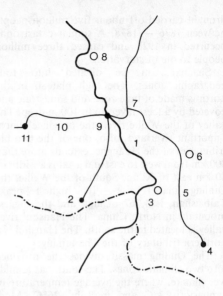

and women, young and old.

Buddhism was widespread in Xishuang Banna. Almost every village had a pagoda and a temple, but few still remain.

Damenglong Fota Pagoda or Feilong Baita, White Pagoda 大勐龙 (飞龙) 白塔

This pagoda is located in the Damenglong People's Commune on Feilongshan mountain in Jinghong district. It was built in honor of Sakyamuni Buddha in 1204 and is one of the most beautiful Buddhist buildings in China. It consists of nine pagodas that all rest on a common base. The main pagoda is 16 m tall, the other eight surrounding it are only 9 m high. Several niches containing Buddhist figures are in the base.

Mengzhen Fota Pagoda 勐真佛塔

This pagoda, 14 km west of the district capital Menghai on Jingzhengshan mountain, is similar to an octagonal pavilion, which is why it is also called Jingzheng Bajiaoting, the Octagonal Pavilion of Mount Jingzheng. It was built in 1701 and is 15.4 m tall. Its special feature is its octagonal, richly decorated roof. According to drawings, Dai architects designed the roof in the shape of Sakyamuni's hat. It consists of several pointed layers with upturned eaves.

Guest House

Xishuang Banna Binguan, 西双版纳宾馆 tel. 1 74

Shaanxi Province 陕西省

Area: 200,000 km² / Population: 28.9 million / Capital: Xi'an

The northern Chinese province Shaanxi is bounded by Shanxi and Henan in the east, Hubei and Sichuan in the south, Gansu and Ningxia in the west and Neimenggu in the north.

History

Finds from the Mesolithic and Neolithic periods prove that the northern part of the province and the Weihe river valley were among the earliest settled regions of China. After the Zhou Dynasty had been founded, its rulers resided in the Weihe valley in the capital city Hao, near present-day Xi'an until they were driven out in 771 BC. The gradual decline of the Zhous was accompanied by the development of the strictly centralized state of Qin in this area. The construction of an extensive, effective irrigation system helped provide the state with prosperous farming. The Prince of Qin was successful in uniting China under his rule and founding the Qin Dynasty. Xianyang, near present-day Xi'an, became the capital. Shaanxi remained the political, economic and cultural center of China into the 9th century, after which time the center of power moved east and north. The entire region deteriorated and was soon one of the poorest in China. Its only real importance was strategic. Numerous wars and rebellions shook Shaanxi into the 20th century. A terrible drought carried off about five million people between 1876 — 1878. A similar catastrophe occurred in 1928 and caused three million people to die of starvation.

Shaanxi can be divided into four geographic zones. The high plateau in the north is made of limestone and sandstone and covered by a loess layer up to 100 m deep. The valley of the Weihe river, the province's most important river and, also, one of the two big tributaries of the Huanghe, extends more than 300 km from west to east and attains a width of 60 km east of Xi'an. South of the Weihe, the Qinling massif rises. Its highest peak, Taibaishan, is 3,767 m high and the biggest mountain in North China. The Hanshui river valley is located in the south. The Hanshui is a northern tributary of the Changjiang.

The Qinling massif divides the province into two climatic zones. The south has a mild, wet climate, where the average temperature in January is 3°C and in July, 26°C. Most precipitation falls between May and October. The climate of the Weihe Valley is cooler and drier. The average temperature in January is 0°C and in July, 26°C; the rainy season is from May to October. In spring and early summer there is little rain and the variability in precipitation is 30%, which is why droughts are not unusual. The amount of precipitation decreases towards the north; the growing period, which lasts 260 — 280 days in the south and 240 days in the Weihe Valley, drops to 190 days in the north. Due to the high fluctuation in precipitation, agriculture is dependent on irrigation. Soil erosion is a big problem. Less than 25% of the entire area can be used for agriculture. In the Weihe Valley, intensive farming is conducted, just as in the valleys of its most important tributaries, the Luohe and the Jinghe. Over one-half of the land in these areas is cultivated. They are also the most densely populated areas of Shaanxi, where over 50% of the population lives. Winter wheat and corn are the most important crops, secondary ones are millet and beans. Three crops in two years can be harvested and, with well-irrigated fields, even two crops a year. Cotton-growing is also important; due to the improvements in the irrigation system, cotton can be planted on 50% of the cultivated land in some areas. In the north, mainly winter wheat and millet are grown; in the southern Hanzhong Basin, rice and winter wheat; and in the Dabashan and Qinlingshan areas, corn and winter wheat. Tea, citrus fruits, apples, apricots and pears come from the south. The most important mineral resources of the province are coal and oil. Xi'an is the

province's manufacturing center. It has the leading textile industry in Northwest China.

Xi'an and Surroundings 西安市

Xi'an is the city that conveys the continuity of Chinese civilization most clearly to the stranger. Three-thousand-year-old Xi'an was the capital of 11 dynasties for a total of 1080 years, the most important of which were the Zhou, Qin, Han, Sui and Tang. It lies in a fertile basin south of the Weihe river, north of the Qinling massif and on the eastern end of the famous Silk Road. Xi'an, which was inhabited by many merchants from Central Asia, already had a million residents during the Tang Dynasty (618 — 907). Today, there are 2.94 million, and Xi'an is considered to be one of the largest centers of economics and culture in Northwest China.

Due to its long history, Xi'an offers tourists many historical sights. About 6 km east of Xi'an, traces of early settlements from the Neolithic era can be observed in Banpo Cun, a village attributed to the Yangshao culture.

In the middle of the 11th century BC, the Zhou king Wenwang made Feng his capital. It was located southwest of Xi'an and on the west bank of the Fenghe. His successor moved the capital somewhat farther east to Hao on the east bank of the Fenghe. Hao remained the political center of the Western Zhou Dynasty until 771 BC. About 500 years later, the founder of the Qin Dynasty and first emperor of China, Qin Shihuang, installed his capital on the north bank of the Weihe in Xianyang, near present-day Xi'an. Qin Shihuang went down in history not only as the founder of an empire and a great reformer, but also as one who commissioned the construction of monumental buildings. For example, he had copies of the palaces of all the princes he had conquered built in Xianyang according to their originals. More than 100 of the richest families from all parts of the empire were forced to move to the new capital. After the buildings of Xianyang became too small for Qin Shihuang, he had Afang Palace built on the south bank of the Weihe. Nothing remains of it. However, even today it is possible to see convincing evidence of the emperor's peculiar projects in Qin Shihuang Bingmayong Museum. The emperor's clay army was discovered in 1974; he had more than 7,000 life-size statues set up in underground shelters east of his mausoleum. They were supposed to make him, the mighty Qin Shihuang, invincible, even in the other world.

After the downfall of the Qin Dynasty, the

Map of Xi'an

Map labels:

To Lanzhou — Main Station — To Luoyang — To Huaqing Chi

Memorial Museum of the 8th Army
Lianhulu St. — Revolution Park — To Banpo Museum

Telegraph and Telephone Building — Lüxingshe, Renmin Hotel

Mosque — People's Theater

Gulou Drum Tower — Post Office — Department Store — Zoo

Airport — Xidajie St. — Zhonglou Bell Tower — Dongdajie St.

Shaanxi Province Museum — Xingqing Gongyuan Park

Huanchengnanlu St.

University Area

Xiaoyan Ta Pagoda

Chang'anlu St.

Shaanxi Province Stadium

Dayan Ta Pagoda

first Han emperor built his capital somewhat farther north of Xianyang and named it Chang'an, Eternal Peace. Nine Han dynasty emperors, including Liu Bang, the founder of the dynasty, were buried north of the Weihe river and two other emperors lie buried south of the Weihe. Liu Bang's tomb is located 20 km east of Xianyang.

Chang'an experienced its heyday under the Sui and Tang rulers. The first Sui emperor had his capital built southeast of the Han Dynasty Chang'an and called it Daxing Cheng, the City of Great Wealth. The Tang rulers took over the Sui capital and enlarged it. Chang'an developed into a city with over a million inhabitants and a world metropolis. It was the beginning and end of the Silk Road, the famous trade route to the west, by which merchants, missionaries and artists from Central Asia, Europe and even Africa came to Xi'an. Excavations in the former trade quarters of the city turned up the widest possible range of foreign coins. Chang'an had a leading position in politics, economy and culture in the 7th and 8th centuries with its population of almost two million.

The most obvious feature of the Chang'an from the Tang era is its chessboard design, largely preserved until today. At that time, there was a total of 112 city districts and 9 north-south and 12 east-west streets. This man-made city design simplified the administration and control of the separate city districts.

The city was surrounded by a 35.5-km-long wall with 13 gates: four in the north and three each in the east, south and west. The Imperial Palace district was located in the north. A part of the southern wall, called Xiwang Tai, can still be seen today 80 m south of Lianhualu street in front of Yuxiang Men gate.

Only the foundations of Taiji Gong,

Daming Gong and Xinqing Gong palaces have been preserved. However, that is enough to provide an impression of their former dimensions.

The inner city, seat of all government offices, lay south of the palace district. The residential quarters, the Daoist and Buddhist temples, the Islamic and Nestorian places of worship and the markets were located in the outer city. After the Tang Dynasty was overthrown, Chang'an began to decline. Not until the Ming era, when a princely residence was built, did Chang'an, now called Xi'an, start to recover. However, the Xi'an of Ming times was only about one-sixth as large as the Chang'an of the Tang era. Due to the walls, its dimensions are still clearly recognizable today. The city walls had been built on top of the foundations of the Tang Imperial City Walls. They were about 3,300 m long in the north and south, about 2,600 m long in the east and west, 12 m high and 15 — 18 m thick at their base. The Ming-era bell and drum towers still exist. The downfall of the Qing Dynasty again resulted in unstable times for Xi'an. Unrest, uprisings and war shook the city. After 1911, Xi'an remained relatively isolated until the railroad line to Zhengzhou was built in 1930. After 1949, the city developed rapidly: new residential areas, schools, sports grounds, parks, department stores, etc. were built, streets were widened and paved and industry established. Xi'an is now the center of Northwest China's textile industry.

Agriculture is an important factor in the city's surroundings. The Xi'an Plain is very well suited to growing wheat and cotton. An excellent irrigation system guarantees good crops.

Xi'an has again become a cultural center with several technical institutes and institutions of higher education. Last, but not least, the excavations of the past years have helped to place Xi'an in the spotlight of international interest several times.

Zhonglou, Bell Tower 钟楼

The Bell Tower is located at the intersection of the main streets in the center of the Old City. Originally, it had been built somewhat farther west. After the city gates in the north and south had been moved and the central axis relocated farther east, the Bell Tower was also rebuilt farther east.

Gulou, Drum Tower 鼓楼

Unlike the Bell Tower, the Drum Tower, located northwest of the Bell Tower, was not moved east. Therefore, it does not lie on the central axis. It was built in 1370 and restored several times in later years.

Dayan Ta, The Large Wild-Goose Pagoda 大雁塔

Dayan Si is located in the city's southern district. While still a prince, Tang Emperor Gaozong had Ci'en Si monastery built in honor of his mother, Empress Wende, in 648. It was a large compound with 10 courtyards and 1897 rooms in which 300 monks lived. It was destroyed towards the end of the Tang era. The present small complex dates from the Qing period. There are three Buddha and 18 Luohan statues in the main hall. Even Du Fu and Bai Juyi sang the praises of the pagoda behind the hall. Emperor Gaozong had it built to protect the 657 volumes of Buddhist writings in 652. They had been brought back from a pilgrimage to India by the Chinese monk Xuanzang (602 — 664), who had set out for India in September 629 and did not return until February 645. After completion of the monastery, he moved to Ci'en Si in 649 and translated a part of the Indian writings. The emperor had the pagoda built at Xuanzang's request, although it was somewhat smaller than Xuanzang had desired. The monk chose the name of the pagoda by referring to an old Indian legend telling of a monastery where the monks were allowed to eat venison, veal and wild goose according to the school of Southern Hinayana Buddhism. One day, a flock of wild geese flew over the monastery. The geese admonished the greedily staring monks to give up eating meat and bade them to teach and missionize according to the school of Mahayana Buddhism. As a warning, one of the geese sacrificed itself by plummeting from the air. The monks then built a pagoda and buried the goose there.

The Wild-Goose Pagoda named after this legend is square, 64 m high and originally had five stories. The greatly decayed building was torn down from 701 to 705 and a much more splendid and higher one was built. It probably had 10 stories at that time. Today, only seven remain. A layer of brick was added to the outer wall to stabilize the building. Otherwise, the pagoda has remained well-preserved for over 1,200 years; it has resisted climatic influences as well as severe earthquakes, unrest and war.

One should not miss climbing to the top floor and enjoying the view of the city and its surroundings.

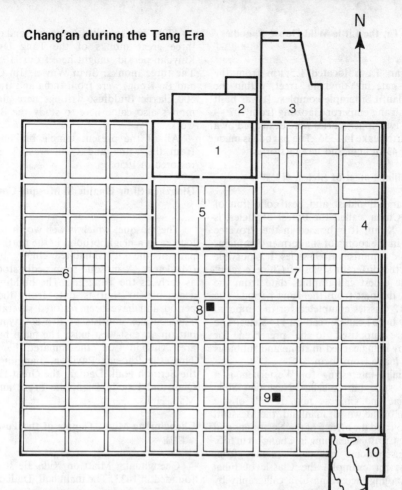

Chang'an during the Tang Era

N

1
2
3
4
5
6
7
8
9
10

1. Palace City, Taiji Gong Palace
2. Imperial Park
3. Daming Gong Palace
4. Xinqing Gong Palace
5. Imperial City

6. West Market
7. East Market
8. Little Wild-Goose Pagoda
9. Large Wild-Goose Pagoda
10. Lotus Park

Reconstruction of the Tang-era
Mingde Men, South Gate

Xiaoyan Ta, the Little Wild-Goose Pagoda
小雁塔

Xiaoyan Ta is located 1.5 km from the southern gate in Youyixilu street, within the former Jianfu Si temple complex. It was built to honor Tang emperor Gaozong from 707 — 709. The two upper stories were destroyed by a strong earthquake in 1555. The pagoda is made of brick, 43 m high and has 13 stories.

Xi'an Beilin, Forest of Steles 西安碑林

The largest, oldest and best collection of steles in China, called the Forest of Steles, is found in Xi'an. It is housed in the Province Museum in the rooms of the former Confucius temple and comprises 1,095 steles. It is possible to study the different styles of Chinese script here. The oldest calligraphies date from the Han era, the best from the Tang period. The texts of 12 classics completed for the Imperial Academy in 837 can be read on 114 steles. The texts were supposed to be preserved for eternity by being carved in stone and rubbings could be made from them.

Especially interesting for Westerners is a memorial stele the so-called Nestorian Stele with Syriac and Chinese text. It tells of the formation of the world, mankind, the Messiah, the mission and the arrival of the Nestorians and about the Christian learning in Chang'an in 635. Some inscriptions originally came from emperors, for example, the Classic of Filial Piety, Xiaojing, according to a calligraphy by Emperor Xuanzong of the Tang Dynasty.

Shaanxi Province Museum 陕西省博物馆

This museum contains one of the best exhibits of Chinese history from its beginnings up to the Qing era. Bronzes, ceramics, metal objects and tools from the various periods, as well as jewelry, documents, inscriptions, grave figures and statues are on display.

Guangren Si Temple 广仁寺

Guangren Si is located in the northwestern part of the city. It dates from 1705 and belongs to the Lamaist Yellow Sect. Each year, on the 24th and 25th days of the 10th month of the lunar calendar, a festival is held in honor of the founder of the sect, Zongkaba.

Daxingshan Si Temple 大兴善寺

Daxingshan Si, located 2.5 km south of the city center, was built during the Jin era (265 — 420). The so-called Kaiyuan Sandashi, the three great monks of the Tang Dynasty's Kaiyuan period, taught here from 716 — 720. The three monks, Shan Wuwei, Jin Gangzhi and Bu Kong, were from India and translated 500 classic Buddhist writings here. Japanese monks also came here to study the Buddhist works.

All of the present temple buildings date from the Ming and Qing eras. They were restored in 1956.

Qingzhen Si or Huajue Si Mosque Complex
清真寺

The mosque, which is well worth a visit, is located in a neighborhood in the northwestern part of the city inhabited chiefly by Huis (Moslems). A mosque supposedly stood here as early as the Tang era. The buildings now accessible to tourists date from the Ming period and have been restored several times. The complex consists of five courtyards laid out on an east-west axis. The main buildings are: Xingxin Lou, the minaret, Fenghuang Ting, the Phoenix Pavilion, Jiangjing Tang, the Sermon Hall, Dadian, the Great Hall and Qian and Houda Dian, the Front and Rear Main Halls.

Chenghuang Miao, Temple of the Town God
城隍庙

Chenghuang Miao on Xida Jie street was founded in 1433. The main hall, Dadian, dates from 1723. Today, a number of small shops are to be found on the temple grounds.

Dongyue Miao Temple 东岳庙

Dongyue Miao, within the East Gate complex, was built in 1116 and restored during the Ming and Qing eras. Dongyue, the Eastern Peak, refers to the holy mountain, Taishan, in Shandong. The compound consists of several halls and an impressive ornamental gate. The main hall contains some interesting murals on the east and west walls.

Banpo Yizhi, the Museum of the Remains of Banpo 半坡遗址

In the northern part of the village of Banpo 6 km east of Xi'an, workers discovered traces of a Neolithic settlement while laying the foundation for a factory in 1953. After five digs from 1954 — 1957, the settlement was uncovered and a museum opened. The excavations showed that a matriarchal tribe lived here on an area of about 70,000 m² around 6,000 years ago, farming, fishing, raising farm animals and hunting. The village was located on a fertile loess terrace on the banks of the Chanshui River. It had about 500 to 600 inhabitants and was divided into three separate areas: a residential area, ceramic workshops and a graveyard. A 4,000-m² area has since been uncovered and roofed over. It makes up a part of the museum. The main attraction is the 45 houses, which were either square or round and had a diameter of 4 — 7 m. Most of them had shallow pits as bases. They all faced south and their entrances were so narrow that only one person at a time could pass through them. Usually, a sloping ramp or several steps led into the dark, low inner room. The fireplace was located in the middle. In the center of the residential area, there was a 160-m²-large building, either a meeting or community house or the living quarters of the tribal leader. Grain storage pits and tool and implement storehouses were located near the houses. The graveyard lay north of the dwellings. It contains 177 graves, in which only adults were buried. Ceramics and ornamental objects were also laid in the graves; and millet remains, a grain that is widely cultivated even today, were found in one grave. The children were buried near the houses. Archeologists suppose that they were to be protected from wild animals in this way. Six kilns for ceramics were located in the eastern part of the village. Painted, reddish clay vessels were produced that are attributed to Yangshao pottery. Representations of fish and human-like masks were the main designs. Scratched symbols on some of the vessels are noteworthy, for it is assumed that they are the primitive beginnings of a writing system. The entire village was surrounded by a 6-m-deep and 6-m-wide defense ditch. In the adjacent exhibition rooms, there are implements, weapons, household utensils and ornaments.

Lishan Mountain and Huaqing Chi Hot Springs 骊山、华清池

Lishan mountain, about 1,200 m high, is in Lintong Xian county. A train goes from Xi'an to Lintong.

The famous Huaqing Chi hot springs are located at the foot of Lishan. They were discovered during the Western Zhou Dynasty over 3,000 years ago. The Zhou ruler Youwang was the first to have had a winter residence built here. Qin emperor Shihuang and the Han and Tang emperors followed suit. Especially during the Tang period, pavilions, towers, terraces and halls were located throughout the Lishan area. In 747, Emperor Xuanzong had Huaqing Chi pond constructed, which was fed by waters from the hot springs. Since that time, the springs have also been called Huaqing Chi. They have a temperature of 43°C.

The halls and pavilions that are on the pretty pond lined by willows and flowers were built in the Tang-era style after 1949. Over 1,000 years ago, Tang emperor Xuanzong spent the winter months here with his beloved concubine Yang Guifei. A reproduction of the Guifei Chi bath, which she is said to have used, is on display.

Lishan charms the visitor with its beautiful scenery. Some paths are steep and safeguarded by chains. A story tells of Lishan's peak, where remains of signal towers from the Zhou era can still be seen. During the Western Zhou period, a fire was lit in these towers whenever enemies in the area posed a threat. In these cases, the princes from the adjoining areas rushed to the sovereign's aid. The story has it that Zhou ruler Youwang (ruled from 781 to 770 BC) loved the pretty concubine Bao Si. In spite of all her charms, she had one fault — she never laughed. The king tried with all

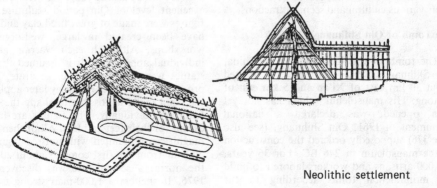

Neolithic settlement

his might to make her laugh, or at least, smile. One day, it occurred to someone to play with the signal-light. The king had it lit and, of course, all the princes hurried to his aid. After seeing that they had been fooled, they returned home angrily. Bao Si, however, laughed maliciously. This filled the king with so much enthusiam that he soon repeated the joke. When enemies really did come a short time later and the signal-fire was lit, nobody came to his rescue. The enemies killed him — the downfall of the Zhou Dynasty could not be prevented.

Huaqing Chi was the site of the well-known Xi'an incident. Chiang Kaishek came here in December 1936 in order to continue his planning to destroy the Communists, who had settled in Yan'an after the Long March. His two generals, Zhang Xueliang and Yang Hucheng, tried to convince Chiang that the Civil War finally had to be ended and an alliance made with the Communist Party to take unified action against the invading Japanese troops. Chiang was taken prisoner after rejecting this course of action. At daybreak of December 12, 1936, the troops called by Zhang and Yang arrived. Upon hearing shots, Chiang fled into the rocky cliffs, but was soon found. Today, a pavilion marks the spot where he was arrested. Zhou Enlai realized that only a peaceful solution to the incident could prevent further worsening of the national catastrophe and therefore had Chiang released on the condition that he agree to a united front against Japan.

Zhongnan Shan Mountains 终南山

The Zhongnan Shan mountains 40 km south of Xi'an are one of the favorite recreation areas for the inhabitants. They extend from Wugong Xian to Lantian Xian counties and are part of the well-known Qinling range. One of the mountains in Zhongnan Shan is called Cuihua Shan. It is located in Chang'an Xian county and offers various cultural and scenic attractions.

The Tomb of Qin Shihuang 秦始皇陵

The tomb of the first emperor of China, Qin Shihuang (259 — 210 BC), is located about 30 km east of Xi'an and 5 km east of Lintong. His mausoleum, which has not yet been opened, was declared a national monument in 1961. Qin Shihuang, (see also page 376) supposedly ordered the construction of the mausoleum in 246 BC. For 36 years, 700,000 artisans and workers labored to build the monumental tomb according to the

emperor's desires, however, they were not able to complete the project, for the early death of the emperor abruptly ended their work.

The pyramid-shaped, graduated burial mound at the foot of Lishan mountain on the Huishui River is 47 m high and covered with pomegranate trees. The grave was built on a north-south axis and is enclosed by an outer and an inner wall. The outer wall was 6,264 m long and had only one gate on the east side, whereas the inner wall measured 2525.4 m with one gate each on the east, west and north sides. Because the tomb has not yet been opened, one can only guess what treasures and valuables are buried there. The descriptions. from the historian Sima Qian (ca. 145 — 86 BC) telling of the glory and dimensions of the tomb have seemed credible since the discovery of the clay army.

While drilling a well about 1,250 m east of the burial mound in the spring of 1974, farmers came upon an underground complex that turned out to contain an army of about 7,000 men. The main body of the army is located in the first section of the underground complex, which is open to the public and protected from the weather by a huge hall. Approximately 6,000 life-size clay warriors and horses stand on an area of 14,260 m² (230 x 62 m) about 5 m below the surface. They face east with the mountain on their right and the river to their left, forming a rectangular combat team. Three rows of 70 warriors each form a vanguard in the eastern transverse gallery, followed by six war-chariots each drawn by four horses and the infantry, which is divided into different units of 11 marching columns according to their arm of service. The outermost rows in the north and south were occupied by archers, who, in contrast to the rest of the army, faced north and south to protect the troops' flanks. The rear guard followed on the western end and consisted, like the vanguard, of three rows of 70 warrior each. Visitors will be able to judge for themselves the excellent level of Qin period sculpture. The figures were made of gray, fired clay and must have been created in large, well-organized workshops. Although each warrior has an individual appearance, it is assumed that the statues were put together of separate, mass-produced parts. A layer of clay later applied to the head made it possible to shape the facial features individually. The figures are hollow except for their feet and legs. All of them were magnificently painted with unfired pigments. Not far from the first complex about 20 m to the north, a second one was discovered in 1976. It shelters a 1,000-man strong unit of war-chariots and mounted cavalry on an area of about 6,000 m². A sort of central command was found on a third spot of about 500 m². It includes the supreme commander and his advisors and escort. A fourth complex, although finished, was found empty, which is a sign that the construction work must have been interrupted at short notice. Qin Shihuang's clay forces, undoubtably copies of that period's military units, provide information about the first emperor's military victories. After all, he had succeeded in conquering the six other states and uniting the entire empire under Qin rule. His army incorporated many military innovations, including the creation of a strong cavalry as the main body of the army. The real weapon that the clay figures carry indicate the high level of weaponry. For example, they already had repeater crossbows with sighting mechanisms and long swords made of a 13 - metal alloy as hard as average strength carbon steel. When the Qin Dynasty was overthrown and the rebel general Xiang Yu and his army conquered the capital, the tomb was partially devastated and most of the weapons of the underground army stolen. The wooden posts and boards in the shelter were destroyed by fire, causing the underground compound to cave in. Many of the statues were smashed and all of them sank down into the mud. It is absolutely forbidden to take pictures here.

The Tang Tombs 唐代陵墓

Nineteen of the 20 Tang emperors were buried near Xi'an. Qianling and Zhaoling are among the largest tombs.

Qianling 乾陵

It is located about 100 km northwest of Xi'an. Liangshan mountain forms the natural tumulus. It is the burial site of the third Tang emperor, Gaozong (ruled from 649 — 683), and his wife, the infamous Empress Wuhou (Wu Zetian, 624 — 705). The compound has a circumference of 40 km and there are seven adjoining tombs in which relatives and high dignitaries were buried. The construction and design of the tombs follow the tradition of solid construction which had been developed after the Han era. The burial site was surrounded by a square wall. Towers stood on each of the four corners; each of the four gates was guarded by a stone lion. Three pairs of stone horses still stand outside the north gate; and ornamental columns, stone figures of animals and people, and steles line the path to the grave outside of the south gate.

Among the secondary graves are those of Prince Zhanghuai and Princess Yongtai.

Tang Zhanghuai Taizi Mu, the tomb of Crown Prince Zhanghuai (654 — 684) of the Tang Dynasty 章怀太子墓

The tomb lies about 3 km southeast of the Qianling tumulus. He was the second son of Gaozong and his wife, Wu Zetian, which, however, did not prevent him from falling victim to the power politics of the Empress. The tomb was opened and explored in 1971 — 1972. The sensational results reported by the scientists staggered the experts. The rooms of the tomb were decorated with mural cycles providing accurate insights into daily life at the

Crown Prince Zhanghuai's tomb

court. officials, foreign princes, officers and soldiers, palace servants and plump concubines are portrayed. The paintings, which are not only informative, but also of excellent artistic quality, are immensely valuable for research into Tang-era painting. The inscriptions were of great importance to historians, for they provide information about the intrigues and chaos of that time. This tomb is also surrounded by a wall, which is rectangular, however. Not much of its is left. In the south, two ornamental towers, *que*, and two stone rams decorate the path to the tomb. The pyramid-shaped tumulus has a truncated apex and covers the 71-m-long burial site.

The tomb had already been plundered before 1971. In spite of that, some funerary objects, mostly of ceramic, were found in the adjoining rooms. The front chamber is 20.25 m^2 large and 6 m high. The starry sky is pictured on the vaulted roof. The rear chamber is 25 m^2 large and 6.5 m high. Its dome is also decorated with constellations, like the ceiling of the front chamber. The stone sarcophagus was in this room. The inner, wooden coffin had already rotted away.

Yongtai Gongzhu Mu, the tomb of Princess Yongtai, 永泰公主墓

It is located southeast of the main grave not far from Crown Prince Zhanghuai's tomb. Princess Yongtai was the granddaughter of Tang emperor Gaozong. She died at the age of 17 in 701 and was laid to rest here with her husband, who died in 706. The tomb was excavated from 1960 — 1962. It turned out to be one of the largest of the previously explored Tang tombs. The underground burial-place is 87.5 m long. It was also decorated with outstanding murals. Archeologists have found gold and silver objects, ceramics and clay figures among the 1,300 funerary offerings. Many of them are on display today in the Qianling Museum.

Zhaoling 昭陵

It lies northeast of the county capital Liquan about 60 km northwest of Xi'an on Jiuzun mountain. It is Li Shimin's (Tang emperor Taizong) burial site, built on 20,000 hectares from 636 — 649. The compound includes the secondary graves of 167 relatives, high officials and generals. Zhaoling Museum, opened in 1979, has a highly interesting collection of colored ceramic figures, paintings and stone inscriptions assembled during various grave excavations.

Hotels

Xi'an Binguan, 西安宾馆 Chang'anlu 6, tel. 5 13 51 located in the south part of Xi'an.

Renmin Dasha, 人民大厦 Dongxinjie 319, tel. 2 51 11, central location

Zhonglou Fandian, 钟楼饭店 opposite the bell tower, tel. 2 20 33, central location.

Jiefang Fandian, 解放饭店 opposite train station

Shengli Fandian, 省立饭店 Hepingmenwai 38 tel. 2 31 84

Xiaozhai Fandian, Xiaozhai, tel. 5 21 31

Shaanxi Binguan, 陕西宾馆 Nanjiao Zhangbagou, tel. 2 38 31

Restaurants

Xi'an Fandian, 西安饭店 Dongdajie, Juhuayuankou, tel. 2 20 37 (Shaanxi cuisine)

Heping Canting, 和平餐厅 Dashikou, tel. 2 47 26 (Beijing cuisine)

Dongya Fandian, 东亚饭店 Luomashi, tel. 2 84 10 (Jiangsu cuisine)

Wuyi Fandian, 武夷饭店 Dongdajie, Anbanjiekou, tel. 2 38 24

Travel agency,

Guoji Lüxingshe, CITS, and **Zhongguo Lüxingshe** in Renmin Dasha, tel. 2 11 91, 5 32 01, telex 7 01 15

Gong'an Ju, Public Security Bureau, tel. 2 51 21

CAAC, airport, information tel. 4 22 25

Ticket reservations, Xishaomen 296, tel. 2 18 55

Train station, information tel. 2 69 76, 2 33 33 Ticket sales in the train station, Lianhulu, tel. 2 58 64

Taxis, tel. 5 15 05

Shopping

Friendship Store, Nanxinjie

Arts and Crafts, Nanxinjie 18

Antiques, Dongdajie 375 and the Drum Tower

Huashan Mountains 华山

Huashan is one of the five holy mountains in China (in addition to Taishan in Shandong, Songshan in Henan, Hengshan in Hunan, Hengshan in Shanxi), where ceremonial sacrifices have been carried out since the Han Dynasty. It is located in Huayin county and is considered to be the steepest of all five mountains. Huashan can be reached by the train to Huayin (on the Beijing-Xi'an line). There is a guest house in town as well as several restaurants and teahouses.

Huashan is known for its steep cliffs and dangerous paths. The saying Huashan zigu yitiao lu, 'Huashan has had only one path since ancient times', reveals the fact that it is almost impossible to avoid these steep paths. Thus, visitors are strongly advised to wear sturdy shoes and practical clothing.

Starting at the train station, one walks 7.5 km east to Yuquan Yuan, the Jade Springs Garden. Here, it is possible to take a short tea break and then start the climb. First, one comes upon Yushi, the Fish Stone, a huge, fish-shaped stone. The 'First Pass', a stone gate, comes shortly thereafter, then, the 'Second Pass', a stone that looks as though it were split by an axe. The 'Eighteen Curves' follow, which is a path affording an impressive

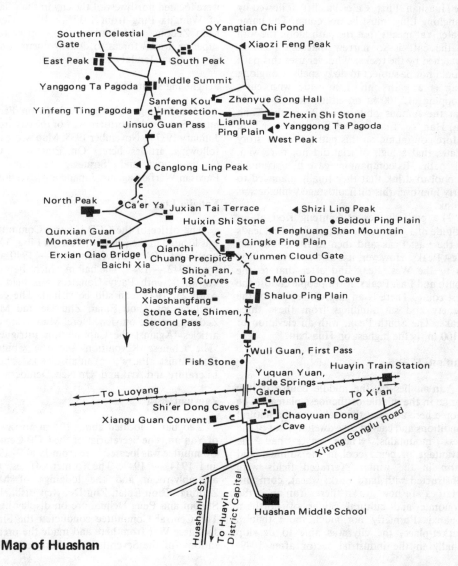

Map of Huashan

view after each bend. Yunmen, the Cloud Gate, is the end of the Path of Eighteen Curves. There is a view of the distant surroundings from here. Qingke Ping, a glorious scenic spot with its streams, waterfalls, springs, old conifers and high peaks. Here, the decision whether or not to continue the climb must be made, for the path becomes steep. In former times, high officials had themselves carried in litters no farther than this point. The following precipice, Qianchi Chuang, is reached by 370 narrow stone steps. Baichi Xia and Laojun Ligou follow it. The North Peak, Beifeng, 1,500 m high, comes next. It drops steeply on three sides. The three other peaks are towards the south. The following path is the most dangerous one on the Huashan. First, Ca'er Ya cliff, followed by Canglong Ling, must be overcome. The name 'Ca'er Ya' means that the path along the wall of the cliff is so narrow that one's ear is scratched by the rocks. Whoever uses this path should not be subject to dizzy spells. Canglong Ling is a path only 1 m wide with cliffs dropping off 100 m on either side. It is said that the famous philosopher from the Tang era, Han Yu, first wrote a farewell letter here before continuing on this path. Another story relates that a high official did not dare walk this path. His companions gave him so much alcohol to drink that they finally managed to carry him over this difficult stage while he was drunk.

The path divides at Sanfeng Kou at an altitude of 1,800 m. The eastern fork first leads to the East Peak and then to the South and West Peaks. However, it is also possible to first go to the West Peak and after that to the South and East Peaks. Most people choose the first route. There is an impressive view of the scenery and surroundings from these three peaks. The South Peak, with an elevation of 2,100 m, is the highest on Huashan.

Yan'an 延安市

Yan'an lies on the middle course of the Yanhe in the middle of the loess plateau. The people here adapted themselves to the natural conditions and carved cave dwellings out of the loess mountains. These caves had the advantage of being cool in the summer and warm in the winter. Terraced fields were constructed with hard work; wheat, corn and potatoes are now grown there. Yan'an is the economic and cultural center of northern Shaanxi. Formerly not much more than a market-place, the city was able to develop rapidly in the industrial sector after 1949.

Yan'an owes its prestige to its revolutionary past. At the end of the Long March in 1935, the army and party leadership of the CCP settled here and made Yan'an their headquarters. The city became a magnet for many intellectuals and patriots in the following years.

The chief sights in Yan'an are the former lodgings and offices of the leaders of the CCP and the army. Due to Japanese bombardments, the lodgings had to be changed frequently.

Wangjia Ping 王家坪

The headquarters of the military commission of the CCP and the 8th Route Army were located northwest of the city in the village of Wangjia Ping from 1937 — 1947. Here, Mao Zedong wrote the article 'Concentrate superior armed forces to destroy enemy units singly' from January 1946 to March 1947.

Fenghuang Shan 凤凰山

Mao Zedong and Zhu De lived on Fenghuang Shan in the northern part of the city from January 1937 to November 1938. Mao wrote the following articles here: 'On Practice', 'On Contradiction' and 'Strategic Problems of Partisan Warfare against Japanese Aggression'.

Yangjia Ling 杨家岭

The office of the CCP Central Committee was located in the village of Yangjia Ling, 3 km northwest of Yan'an, from 1938 — 1940 and from 1942 — 1943. The hall in which the well-known Seventh Party Congress was held on April 23, 1945, can still be visited. The cave dwellings of Zhou Enlai, Zhu De and Mao Zedong are also on view. Here, Mao wrote the articles 'Against the Capitulation Intrigues', 'The Chinese Revolution and the Chinese Communist Party', 'Yan'an Talks about Literature and Art' and 'On New Democracy'.

Zaoyuan 枣园

Zaoyuan is located about 10 km northwest of Yan'an. The Secretariat of the CCP Central Committee was located here from 1940 — 1942 and 1944 — 1947. The former offices, the assembly-room and the lodgings of Mao Zedong, Zhou Enlai, Zhu De, Ren Bishi, Liu Shaoqi and Peng Dehuai are on display here. The Central Committee conducted the Sino-Japanese War from here and made the preparations for the Seventh Party Congress. Mao

Zedong wrote the articles 'Serve the People' and 'On Coalition Government' in Zaoyuan.

Yan'an Pagoda, Baota 延安宝塔

The Yan'an Pagoda is the city landmark and also a symbol of the Chinese Revolution. It dates from the Song Dynasty and was restored in 1950.

Travel agency

Zhongguo Lüxingshe, in Yan'an Binguan guest house, tel. 23 63

Ningxia Huizu Zizhiqu, Ningxia Autonomous Region of the Hui Minority 宁夏回族自治区

Area: 60,000 km² / Population: 3.89 million, including one-third Hui and two-thirds Han, Mongols and Manchus / Capital: Yinchuan

Ningxia, in northwest China, is bounded by Shaanxi to the east, Gansu to the south and by Inner Mongolia to the north.

History

Ningxia Autonomous Region was founded on October 25, 1958. Since the Qin Dynasty, it has been ruled by various administrations. During the Yuan era, parts of Ningxia belonged to Gansu and Shaanxi. For a time during the Ming Dynasty, Ningxia was a prefecture. However, the area soon became part of Shaanxi again and, during the Qing Dynasty, part of Gansu. Ningxia was awarded provincial status in 1928. At that time, however, it was considerably larger than today. In 1954, the area that was inhabited chiefly by Mongols was annexed to Inner Mongolia and the rest again subordinated to Gansu. Not until 1958 was the area populated by Huis united into an autonomous region.

In 1969, parts of Inner Mongolia were added to Ningxia, but they were returned in 1979.

About two-thirds of Ningxia consists of desert. The south is part of the loess plateau. The Ningxia Lowlands of the Huanghe stretch out in the north, one of the most beautiful areas in North China and also the agricultural center of the region.

As early as the 3rd century BC, construction of a network of irrigation canals was begun,

which had to be expanded and improved upon again and again due to the small amount of annual precipitation (200 mm). Wheat and rice are the most important crops, followed by millet, sorghum, cotton, hemp, flax, sugar beets and beans. Livestock is raised in the mountainous areas. Ningxia has mineral resources, above all, coal. There are also iron and copper reserves as well as petroleum, and gold and silver deposits.

There are railway connections from the capital, Yinchuan, to Lanzhou and Baotou (Inner Mongolia).

Yinchuan 银川市

Yinchuan lies west of the Huanghe and east of the Helan Shan mountains. The city was linked up to the national railway network upon completion of the Lanzhou - Baotou line in 1958 and can thus be reached from all parts of China. Earlier, the sole main transportation route was the Huanghe, which connects the city to Baotou (Inner Mongolia) downstream but is only navigable upstream to Zhongning and Zhongwei. The port of Yinchuan lies in Hengcheng, 15 km away. Highways connect Yinchuan to Lanzhou and Wuwei in Gansu, Xi'an in Shaanxi and Baotou.

History

In the 5th century, the capital of the state of Xia, Yinhan, was located about 7 km away from present-day Yinchuan. After the fall of the Tang Dynasty at the beginning of the 10th century, Yinchuan became the capital of the Western Xia Dynasty. The Mongols invaded the area in 1227. Yinchuan had the status of a prefecture *(fu)* during the Ming and Qing eras. In 1928, it was declared the capital of the newly-founded province of Ningxia, but was subordinated to Gansu in 1954. Yinchuan again became the capital four years later, after the founding of the Ningxia Autonomous Region. Ever since the Han Dynasty, the plains around Yinchuan have had an excellent irrigation network, which has been constantly enlarged and improved and makes intensive farming possible. The most important crops are rice, wheat and hemp. The city has always been an emporium for local agricultural and livestock products.

Today, with its population of 640,000, it is prominent in machine manufacturing and the textile industry. Among other industries, there are also chemical and metal - working plants.

Special local products are wool blankets and carvings from Helan Shan stone.

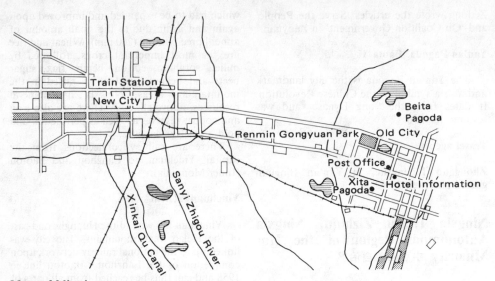

Map of Yinchuan

Yinchuan is now the cultural center of the region. It has a university, several institutes of higher education and academies.

Beita, North Pagoda 北塔

Beita is located in the city's northern district. According to tradition, the King of Xia had a pagoda built here at the beginning of the 5th century. Present-day Haibao Ta is a reproduction dating from 1778. It is 54 m high and has a square ground-plan. However, it appears to be twelve-sided because of its rows of niches. This architectural style is rare in China.

Wooden stairs lead to the upper stories. There is a wonderful view of the city, the Helan Shan and the Huanghe from there.

Xita, West Pagoda 西塔

Xita is located in the southwestern part of the city. It was first built in 1050 and was a part of Chengtian Si temple. The temple and the pagoda were destroyed by a severe earthquake in 1738. The present pagoda was built according to old plans in 1820. It is octagonal and 64.5 m high. The roof is covered with green ceramic tiles. Iron bells hang in the corners of each story. Stairs lead to the top floor.

Xixia Lingmu, Royal Tombs of Western Xia 西夏陵墓

About 30 km west of Yinchuan in the eastern foothills of the Helanshan, there are eight Xia royal tombs and over 70 secondary ones (Western Xia Dynasty: 1032—1227). Not much is left of the buildings that used to stand in front of the underground burial chambers. The only remaining objects of interest are some steles with inscriptions in Han Chinese and the language of the Xixia rulers. The region covers an area of 40 km^2. Each tomb is an independent complex consisting of outer and inner walls, four corner towers and gates in each of the four sides as well as a stele pavilion, altar and memorial hall. The rectangular underground burial chambers were made of rammed earth. Although the chambers had been already looted, archeologists were still able to save many valuable pieces of gold and silver jewelry, bamboo carvings, pearls and ceramic shards.

Travel agency

CITS, Jiefangxilu 150, tel. 47 20

Guyuan Xian County 固原县

Xumi Shan Shiku Caves 须弥山石窟

There are countless large and small caves built between the 5th and 10th centuries at the foot of Xumi Shan mountain about 30 km northwest of the county capital Guyuan. Landslides and earthquakes as well as the robbery of sculptures have caused much damage. Twenty caves are well-preserved, especially caves 2, 3, 6 and 8. Cave 2 is the largest and most typical.

A landslide destroyed the front part of the cave so that the 20-m-high Maitreya statue now stands outdoors.

Cave 3 is the oldest cave and has several valuable carvings. Yuanguang Si monastery, dating from the Ming era, is near it. Cave 6 has a Buddha representation worth seeing and in cave 8 there are masterfully carved bodhisattva figures.

Typical caves from the Northern Wei period are square and have a pagoda-shaped column of several layers in the middle. Niches were worked into each layer. Buddhas and bodhisattvas were carved into the walls.

The caves from the Sui era are similar to those of the Northern Wei period. However, the central column usually has only one layer and the sculptures have fuller and more serious features.

Two sculptures of two followers were added to the Buddha and bodhisattva figures.

The Tang-era caves had no central columns. The collective representations mostly consist of seven sculptures.

Gansu Province 甘肃省

Area: 450,000 km² / Population: 19.56 million / Capital: Lanzhou

Gansu Province in northwestern China is surrounded by the People's Republic of Mongolia in the north, Inner Mongolia in the northeast, Ningxia and Shaanxi in the east, Sichuan in the south and Qinghai and Xinjiang in the southwest and west respectively.

Gansu, once backward and poor, has been able to develop an aspiring industry owing to its rich mineral resources.

History

When Emperor Shihuang of the Qin Dynasty established the great Chinese empire, Gansu also came under his rule. During the Han Dynasty, Chinese power was expanded further westward and control was exercised over the trade routes to central Asia. Gansu's importance is closely connected to the history of the Silk Road. Owing to a belt of oases stretching through Gansu and fed by water from the Qilian Shan, the state was a suitable link between east and west. Camel caravans carried the coveted Chinese silk, porcelain and tea to the countries of the Mid-East, to Byzantium and to Rome. Western wares and many arts, music and dances reached China along this route, as did religions such as

Buddhism, brought to China by foreign Buddhist monks as early as the 1st century BC.

The old commercial cities on the Silk Road: Dunhuang, Jiuquan, Zhangye and Tianshui, developed into centers of Buddhism in the course of time. Buddhist art came to Gansu with the foreign religion. Initially, this art was enthusiastically supported, especially by the rulers of the Northern Wei Dynasty. Thus, a great many cave temples — an Indian type of sacral complex — were built along the Silk Road. Some of these compounds still exist today. The caves of Dunhuang are undoubtably some of the most famous examples of this art. They represent one of the most important cultural monuments in Gansu and even all of China.

Gansu was considerably larger during the Qing Dynasty than it is today. In addition to the present region, it included Ningxia and parts of Qinghai and Xinjiang and was ruled by the governor-general of Shaanxi-Gansu, who resided in Lanzhou.

The desert-like Gansu (Hexi) Corridor, Hexi Zoulang, extends in the west. It is characterized by plateaus at an average altitude of 1,000 m and various depressions. It is bounded by the Qilian Shan mountains in the south. The region east of the Huanghe belongs to the loess plains extending throughout Shaanxi and Shanxi. Their average elevation is 1,500 m.

Gansu stretches 1,500 km from east to west, accordingly, it has different climatic zones. In July, the average temperature in the east is 21°C and in the west 26°C; in January, it is -4°C in the east and -10°C in the west. Precipitation is highly variable. The average annual amount of precipitation is 400-500 mm, however, in the west it is barely 100 mm; 50-70% of it falls during the summer.

Due to the climatic and topographic conditions, Gansu's agriculture is completely dependent on irrigation. In the past, droughts often destroyed the crops and caused catastrophic famines. Thus, the construction and expansion of the irrigation systems has been especially important during the last few decades.

Wheat is the most important crop. About 40% of all cultivated land is covered by wheat. Barley, millet, beans and sweet potatoes are also important crops. Rice, in addition to various dry-field crops, is planted in the Lanzhou Basin in the middle of the province. Fruit is also grown in this area. The pears, peaches, apricots, apples and watermelons of Lanzhou are famous.

Sheep-raising is an important source of

income. It is carried out by minorities on the prairie highlands.

Gansu is rich in mineral resources, of which the oil reserves are the most important. There are also considerable amounts of coal, iron, lead, zinc and copper.

Gansu has changed its appearance in several ways since 1949. The province, with Lanzhou as the leading city, has become the center of the Chinese West owing to the expansion of the transportation network. Railways lead from Lanzhou to Urumqi (Xinjiang) and Golmud (Qinghai), via Baotou (Neimenggu) to Beijing and through Xi'an, Zhengzhou all the way to Lianyungang. The modern transportation network has favored the industrial development of many formerly isolated cities. Today, the following cities are leading industrial centers in addition to Lanzhou: Yumen (oil), Jiuquan (iron ore) and Tianshui. During the period of the first five-year plan, heavy industry was expanded in Lanzhou. The nuclear power industry has been built up since 1960.

Sichou Zhilu, the Silk Road 丝绸之路

The Silk Road was a trade route connecting China with central and western Asia. Not only goods, but new ideas were exchanged between the peoples of the East and West on this road.

The route was named after Chinese silk, which was China's most important export article besides tea. Silk production and processing were wide-spread in China as early as the 2nd millenium BC.

The Silk Road started in Xi'an and led through Gansu to Dunhuang. There, it forked and led through Xinjiang in two directions — to the north and the south of Takla Makan desert, across the Pamir Highlands to Afghanistan. From that point, it went either farther westward to the eastern Mediterranean coast or farther southward to India.

The trade routes probably existed long before the Han Dynasty. Official trade missions were sent to the west starting with the reign of Han emperor Wudi (reigned from 140 — 87 BC). During the Western Han period, an expedition was led by Zhang Qian, an official, and during the Eastern Han era, another by Ban Chao. Both men are still well-known today.

Wars and unrest during the first millenium AD gradually made the routes unsafe and precarious. At the same time, overseas trade expanded. Under Mongol rule during the 13th and 14th centuries, the old trade routes flourished anew. Marco Polo traveled to China on these routes at this time. During the Ming and Qing eras, unrest and wars again made

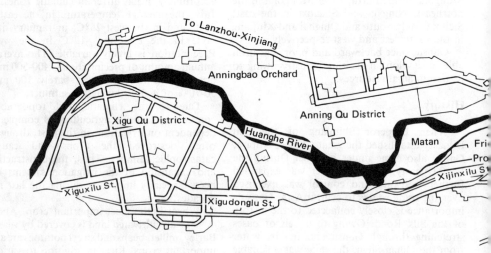

1. Stadium   2. Department Store   3. Dongfanghong Square   4. Lanzhou Hotel   5. Train Statio

overseas trade more attractive, so that the roads lost their former importance.

Today, there are still many sights to be found along the old Silk Road in China, especially in Dunhuang and Jiuquan.

Lanzhou 兰州市

Lanzhou lies on the upper course of the Huanghe, the Yellow River, in the eastern part of the so-called Gansu Corridor. It is the second largest city in Northwest China and has a population of 2.4 million.

Lanzhou has a long history. As early as 81 BC, the city was known under the name Jincheng, Gold City. Like other cities of the Northwest, Lanzhou became an important station along the Silk Road. However, its favorable location had no significant influence on the area around Lanzhou, which thus remained the center of a poor, backward region until 1949. During the last 30 years, the city has been able to make great progress in industrialization and modernization. Lanzhou is the leader of Chinese nuclear power research. The petro-chemical industry, the locomotive engine and railroad car factories, the metalworking shops and the chemical, leather and wool processing industries are of great importance. In addition, Lanzhou is an

important trading center between Northwest and Southwest China and the Central Plains. Since the expansion of the Longhai railway line, which now extends from Jiangsu in the east to Xinjiang, Lanzhou has been an important link between the East China coast and the Northwest.

Wuquanshan Gongyuan, the Five Springs Park, and Baita Shan, the Mountain of the White Pagoda, are among the city's best-known sights.

Lanzhou is well-known for its fruit — its sweet melons are the most famous. In summer, it is pleasantly warm, but in winter, it is very cold, though dry.

Gansu Sheng Bowuguan, Gansu Province Museum
甘肃省博物馆

The museum is across from the Friendship Hotel. A collection of colored ceramic finds partly dating from the Neolithic period is worth mentioning. The best-known exhibit is a bronze sculpture: a horse that appears to fly standing with one hoof on a swallow. The sculpture comes from a grave of the Eastern Han era discovered in Wuwei district in 1969.

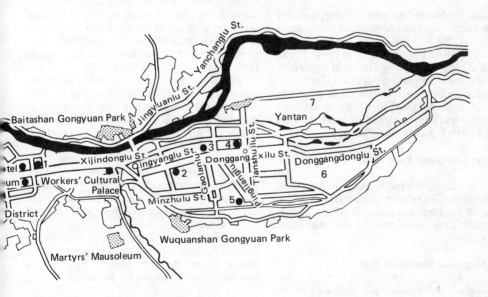

ngguan Qu District   7. Yantang Gongyuan Park

Map of Lanzhou

Wuquanshan Gongyuan, Five Springs Park
五泉山

Wuquan Shan mountain, 1,600 m high and located in the southern part of the city, is a favorite recreation area for Lanzhou's inhabitants. The main sight is Chongqing Si temple, built in 1372 and restored several times. The temple is famous for two things: the iron bell Taihe Tiezhong, cast in 1202, 3 m high and weighing about 5,000 kg, and the bronze Buddha Tong Jieyinfo, over 5 m high and cast in 1370.

Baita Shan Mountain 白塔山

Baita Shan, once a military base, is 1,700 m high and located north of the Huanghe river. It was named after the White Pagoda, Baita, which was built during the Yuan period. It has seven stories, is octagonal and 17 m high.

Various interesting buildings are located on Baita Shan: Luohan Dian, Sangong Dian and Sanxin Dian halls, Yunyue Si temple and one pavilion each on the east, west and north peaks. There is a pretty view of the nine bends of the Yellow River from there.

Huanghe Tieqiao, the Iron Bridge over the Yellow River
黄河铁桥

The Tieqiao is located at the foot of Baita Shan mountain. As early as the reign of Hongwu (1368 — 1398) during the Ming era, a sort of floating bridge had been built. It was called Zhengyuan Qiao. The local chronicles of Lanzhou Prefecture report that this bridge played a decisive part for the trade routes to Qinghai and Ningxia. In 1907, a German company was commissioned to build the Iron Bridge, which was restored in 1954.

Yantan Gongyuan Park 雁滩

At one time, 18 sand banks were located in the Huanghe. They were connected to the city by a 20-km-long causeway in 1958. Today, Yantan is a recreation area for the inhabitants of Lanzhou.

Xinglong Shan Mountain 兴隆山

Xinglong Shan rises 5 km southwest of the district capital Yuzhong Xian, directly opposite Qiyun Shan mountain. It is 2,400 m high and affords many sights, among them caves, springs, temples, tower buildings and gorges.

Hotels

Jincheng Binguan, Tianshuilu 209, tel. 2 79 31

Youyi Fandian, Xijinxilu 14, tel. 3 05 11

Lanzhou Fandian, Donggangxilu 28, tel. 2 29 81

Travel agency

Guoji Lüxingshe, CITS, and **Zhongguo Lüxingshe** in Youyi Fandian hotel, respectively.

CAAC, Donggangxilu 46, tel. 2 34 32, 2 34 31

Jiuquan 酒泉

Jiuquan used to be an important commercial town on the Silk Road and is still of great significance today as a transportation junction and an industrial city. It was founded as a military outpost as early as 111 BC. While still called Suzhou in the 6th century AD, it received its present name during the Tang Dynasty.

It is said that the general of the Western Han Dynasty, Huo Qubing, stationed his troops in the area of present-day Jiuquan after a victory over a tribe of the northern steppe. Emperor Wudi supposedly sent him imperial wine as a reward, which, however, Huo Qubing did not drink alone. Rather, he had it poured into a spring so that everybody could drink of it. The name of the city, Jiuquan, or Wine Spring, is supposed to have its origin in this story. The spring well into which the wine was supposedly poured can still be seen in Jiuquan Park today.

Jiuquan has won great economic importance due to its mineral resources. Iron ore is mined in the Jingdie Shan mountains to the south and coal near Shantan in the southeast. An important oil field is located not far away, in Yumen.

About 14 km southwest of the city, Wenshu Shan mountain is located. One of the most important Buddhist centers was located here for hundreds of years starting in the 5th century, and various caves and temples are still on view today.

Several interesting tombs have been found around Jiuquan. One of them is the tomb of a prince from the 5th century BC that is especially worth visiting for its murals.

Hotel

Jiuquan Binguan, 酒泉宾馆 Cangmenjie 2, tel. 29 43

Travel agency in Jiuquan Binguan

Bingling Si Shiku, Rock Temples of the Thousand Buddhas 炳灵寺石窟

The Buddhist rock temples are located 35 km southwest of the district capital Yongjing on the north bank of the Huanghe, on Xiaojishi Shan mountain. The word *Bingling* comes from the Tibetan language and means 'thousand Buddhas'. This name was given to the rock temple, formerly called Longxing and Lingyan, when it became a lamasery during the Yuan Dynasty. The grottos are scattered over an area of 2 km in the steep rock wall. The first ones were built in the 5th century. In Grotto 169, one of the most representative, murals from the Northern Wei period have been preserved. After the Northern Zhou era, mainly sculptures were carved. Today, it is possible to view 34 grottos, 149 niches, 679 stone figures and 82 clay figures as well as several murals of the 195 caves said to have existed during the Yuan period. The largest statue is over 27 m high (Maitreya), the smallest, about 20 cm. The lay-out of these grottos is similar to those of Yungang and Longmen. About two-thirds of them were built during the Tang period.

During construction of the hydroelectric power plant Liujia Xia from 1964 — 1974, a 200-m-long and 20-m-high embankment was built in front of the temple to protect the cultural monument from the rising water. Boats are available to visitors so that they can also view the sculptures from the water. In 1972, a wooden overpass was built above the 27-m-high Sakyamuni statue in cave 117. It connects the caves and makes them more easily accessible.

The hydroelectric power plant Liujia Xia supplies Shaanxi, Gansu, Qinghai and Ningxia with electricity. The former district capital Yongjing disappeared at the bottom of the reservoir upon completion of the power plant project, which was built to regulate the Yellow River.

Jiayu Guan Pass 嘉峪关

Jiayu Guan Pass, which forms the western end of the Great Wall (see also page 170), was built during the Ming Dynasty in 1372. A square, 12-m-high and 733-m-long wall of packed earth runs around the inner part of the compound. There is one gate each on the eastern and western sides. Towers 17 m high were added in 1506. Loopholes, parapets and corner towers make the wall seem impregnable. The so-called floodgate in the northeast corner and Jiayu Guan gate in the west are the only openings built into the outer walls.

The material calculations for the pass compound were supposedly so exact that only one brick was left unused. It is kept today in a small tower at the west gate.

Weijin Bihua Mu, Tomb Paintings from the Wei and Jin Periods 魏晋壁画墓

In 1972, eight tombs dating from the Wei and Jin eras were opened up 20 km northwest of Jiayu Guan. Six of them have murals depicting scenes from the life of that time.

Hotel

Jiayuguan Binguan, Beixinhualu 1, tel. 58 04

Travel agency in Jiayuguan Binguan

Tianshui 天水

Tianshui is a city on the Weihe river on the old Silk Road. Today, modern transportation routes from Xi'an and Lanzhou lead into it.

The area around Tianshui has been settled since the Neolithic age. Throughout the course of its long history, the city has always been of great strategic and commercial-political importance. Various industrial plants have been constructed since 1949, among them machine manufacturing, wool textile and match plants. An old but effective irrigation system has made farming possible around Tianshui. Millet, sorghum, winter wheat, cotton and tobacco are grown.

Near Tianshui are some of the places where Buddhism succeeded in establishing itself in China.

The lacquer carvings of Tianshui are familiar to experts in Chinese arts and crafts. They are well-known not only within China, but also abroad.

Hotel

Tianshui District Guest House, 126 Jianshelu, tel. 36 21

Travel agency

CITS in Tianshui District Guest House, tel. 36 21

Maijishan Shiku Grottos 麦积山石窟

The famous grottos on Maiji Shan mountain are located 45 km southeast of Tianshui. Construction of the grottos was begun during 384 — 417. As late as the Northern Wei Dynasty, a large and flourishing Buddhist center is supposed to have arisen here. The grotto compound was further expanded during the course of the following dynasties up to the 19th century. A strong earthquake destroyed the center part of the Maijishan cave temples in 734. Only the eastern and western groups of grottos were spared. Today, there are still 54 grottos in the eastern part and 140 in the western part. In all, 7,200 clay and stone figures and over 1,300 m² of murals have been preserved. Most of the grottos were cut out of the rock wall at a height of 20 — 30 m or 70 — 80 m. Paths totalling 1,200 m have been improved or newly laid out in the recent past, so that it is possible to easily reach the separate parts of this area.

Unlike the Dunhuang grottos, which are known for their murals, those of Maijishan are interesting because of their clay figures. The most beautiful ones are located in the caves dating from the Northern and Western Wei eras — numbers 44, 74, 121, 123, 127 and 133. The 16-m-high figure of Maitreya from the Sui Dynasty, carved directly into the rocky mountainside, is visible from afar.

Lamasery of Labrang 拉卜楞寺

Labrang, once known as the most magnificent and powerful lamasery of China, today is still one of the six most important monasteries of the Yellow Sect. It is located at a distance of 1 km from Xiahe river, a tributary of the Huanghe. It is situated at an altitude of 2,600 m with the Mandala Hills to the south and the Dragon Hills to the north.

The monastery was founded in 1708 during the reign of Emperor Kangxi. Previously, up to 4,000 monks had been living there and their scholastic learning and discipline were praised throughout the country. Today there are about 1,000 monks. There are two halls which especially attract the visitor's attention: the Big Golden Tiled Temple, also called the Maitreya Hall and the Small Golden Tiled Temple, also called Sakyamuni Hall.

To the experts the monastery is mainly known for its extraordinary library which houses one of the best sections of Buddhist writings in China. Nowadays religious feasts which attract pilgrims and merchants from the whole area are once more celebrated. In the past Labrang was famous for its masked dances. On the 13th day of the first lunar month a huge metre cloth with a painted portrait of Buddha will be unrolled at the mountain side. The following day masked dances will be performed and on the 15th day the butter festival will be celebrated, its main attraction being an exhibition of lanterns and sculptures made of Tibetan butter.

Travelers will be accommodated in Labrang Binguan which is designed in Tibetan style.

Dunhuang Gucheng, Dunhuang, the Ancient City 敦煌古城

Dunhuang lies at the western end of the Gansu Corridor, called Hexi Zoulang. One travels by train in the direction of Ürümqi, gets off in Liuyuan and reaches Dunhuang by bus or car after a 120-km drive south.

The name *Dunhuang* originally meant 'prospering, flourishing' — a hint that Dunhuang must once have been an important city. Old Dunhuang is located about half a kilometer west of the present district capital Dunhuang on the west bank of the Danghe river. Old records indicate that Dunhuang became a prefecture in 111 BC under the rule of Han emperor Wudi; it was one of four prefectures in the Gansu Corridor. The three others were Wuwei, Zhangye and Jiuquan. The famous Silk Road forked to the north and south here. The southern route led to Yangguan Pass, the northern route to Yumen Guan Pass. This position at the intersection of the two trade routes was what made Dunhuang flourish. The coming and going of the horse and camel caravans carried new thoughts, ideas, arts and sciences to the East and West.

Old Dunhuang was laid out rectangularly. The east-west axis measured 718 m, the north-south axis 1,132 m. Parts of the south, west and north walls still remain today.

Mogao Ku, Thousand Buddhas Grottos 莫高窟

The famous grottos of Dunhuang the first Chinese center of Buddhist art, lie 25 km southeast of the district capital on the banks of the Danghe. They are located in a small oasis facing Sanwei Shan mountain, with Mingsha Shan to their rear. Throughout many centuries, monks cut grottos into an approximately 1,600-m-long sandstone wall and decorated them with paintings and sculptures. They are an unparalleled example of the development of Buddhist art, especially of sculpture and painting. In addition, they provide valuable clues to a great variety of aspects of the cultural, political and economic life of those times, e.g., rites, clothing, architecture trades and agriculture.

The first Buddhist communities were founded in the 1st century AD, however, they mainly consisted of immigrated Buddhists. Missionary activities started in the 2nd century, which were not successful until the

A River Scene of Kuilin, Guangxi

Beautiful Sunset in Kuilin, Guangxi

The Great Buddha of Leshan, Sichuan

Qutang Gorge, Sichuan

Two of the Five Hundred Arhats in Qiongzhu Si Temple, Kunming, Yunnan

The Stone Forest of Lunan, Kunming, Yunnan

The Large Wild-Goose Pagoda in Xi'an, Shaaxi

Mingshashan Mountains of Dunhuang, Gansu

The Potala Palace in Tibet

A Tibetan Woman

The Heavenly Pond on Tianshan Mountains, Xinjiang

3rd and 4th centuries and then made Buddhism increasingly influential. Dunhuang became a Buddhist center, for monks and missionaries from the central Asian countries gathered here. In 366, the first grottos were built. According to an inscription from the Tang era, a monk landed in Dunhuang in 366 on his way to the west. When he arrived, at sunset, the Sanweishan mountains are said to have suddenly begun to sparkle as if they were lit up by a thousand Buddhas. The monk took this for a holy sign and built a grotto in the sandstone wall opposite the mountain. This is supposedly the first Buddhist grotto of Dunhuang. In the course of the centuries more and more were added. Dunhuang remained a prominent Buddhist place of worship until the 11th century. However, as trade was reduced on the Silk Road the city declined in importance. The monks abandoned the cave temples in the 15th century and they were gradually forgotten. Not until 1900 did a man called Wang Yuanlu rediscover them. He had fled from a famine in Hubei, heading for Gansu, and settled in Dunhuang. As it happened, Wang was cleaning grotto 16 when he came upon a collection of valuable books, silk paintings and embroidery, and bronze figures — about 60,000 objects of art in all. This collection probably belonged to monks living in the cave temples during the 11th century who had hidden it from the approaching enemy before fleeing. The oldest pieces date from the 5th century, the most recent from the 10th century. The authorities were told of Wang's discovery, yet the officials of the Qing government did not recognize the value of the find and shrank from the costs of recovering it. Wang was ordered not to touch the discovery and to conceal the cave. A few foreigners, who by this time had become curious, very quickly recognized the immeasurable worth of this discovery, in contrast to the Qing officials. The latter's fatal decision made it possible for the foreigners to buy valuable writings and paintings from Wang at ridiculously low prices and send them out of the country. In this way, the greater part of the collection went to England, France and Japan and has been lost to China to this very day. Finally, at the beginning of the forties, the Chinese government decided to call a halt to this 'clearance sale', but not until the founding of the People's Republic were efforts made to restore and care for this cultural inheritance. The grottos have been a focal point of governmental policy of protecting monuments since 1961. An institute was founded in Dunhuang dedicated solely to their investigation.

Many caves have been destroyed by erosion and drifting sand. Only 492 grottos dating from the 4th to the 14th centuries have been preserved.

The caves have a total of 45,000 m² of murals, 2,450 colored sculptures from the 4th to the 13th centuries as well as artistic decorations on the ceilings and pillars. The paintings have now been covered with a protective coating. The largest grotto is 40 m high, the smallest less than 1 m. The sculptures were carved of clay and sandstone; the biggest is 33 m tall, the smallest only about 10 cm. They are arranged singly or in groups.

The grottos have square or rectangular layouts. Each has a tablet listing its number, date of origin and dynasty. Balconies, first built during the Song era, link separate rows.

Early Phase

The Buddhist murals depicting the whole life of the real Sakyamuni Buddha from his birth to his enlightenment, his wandering and preaching years and his entering nirvana, and also showing scenes of earlier lives and legends, are characteristic of the older grottos of Dunhuang. They tell of great suffering, self-sacrifice and boundless charity. In addition to the Buddhist themes, there are scenes from the lives of hunters, fishermen and artisans. Portrayals of wild animals in the mountains and forests creatures from the world of Chinese myths and legends, musicians and dancers, geometric patterns and lotus blossoms are also to be found. The artists continued in the tradition of Han painting with their simple compositions and natural shapes and coloring. The Indian influence is clearly noticeable not only in the Buddhist choice of themes (the painters' models were central Asian cult images), but also in the way people are portrayed. They wear light garments, usually only a skirt and flowing scarf, and are bare-breasted. The eyes and noses are accentuated with red and white colors. The faces and movements are life-like. Twenty-three caves have been preserved from the early phase of rock temple art. Cave 275, built between 340 — 380, is among the oldest at Dunhuang. The murals tell of the wanderings of Sakyamuni and King Sivi, who sacrificed his own flesh to feed an eagle and thus save a dove from the claws of this bird of prey. Several well-preserved Maitreya sculptures are in this cave.

Northern Wei Dynasty (386 — 534)

Cave 259 contains an interesting sculpture

of Buddha. Its smile is often compared to Mona Lisa's by Chinese experts. Cave 257 contains fantastic paintings depicting the life of the Stag King. The horse on which he is riding is noteworthy. It was portrayed so gracefully and vividly that it seems as if it will run off at any minute.

Cave 254 tells, among other things, of Prince Sudana, who sacrificed himself to a weak, hungry tiger as food. The story of King Sivi is also repeated. Other beautiful examples of painting and sculpture from this period are to be found in caves 248, 260, 263, 272, 431, 435 and 439.

Western Wei Dynasty (535 — 557)

The elegance of the sculptures is the striking characteristic of the style of the Western Wei period. The faces became narrower, the smiles more delicate, the bodies thinner. Interesting painted ceilings and murals are in the well-preserved cave 285. The colorful bodhisattva representations painted in the niches should not be missed. Cave 249 contains the noteworthy painting of a hunt: mounted hunters shooting at gazelles and tigers with bows and arrows. In this cave, motifs from both Buddhist and Chinese mythology are portrayed side by side. Cave 432 is worth seeing for its chromatic scheme, in which black, green and white predominate. The patterns on the ceiling, for which the colors of the murals are again used, and the richly decorated pillars are interesting.

Northern Zhou Era (557 — 581)

Cave 428, which has been restored very well, contains a central pillar opulently adorned with sculptures. The murals depict scenes of Prince Sudana's self-sacrifice, among others. The ornamented ceiling is just as splendidly colored as the paintings and sculptures in this cave.

Representations of events along the Silk Road and its caravans of traders can be seen in cave 296.

Sui and Tang Eras

After the protracted division of the empire, China was reunited in the 6th century. A time of stability began in which the economy and cultural life revived. Buddhism was at the peak of its development, as was Buddhist art. The teaching of Amitabha and his Pure Land doctrine had found many followers and was a frequent motif in Buddhist art. This doctrine

maintained that the invocation of Buddha Amitabha is sufficient by itself to be reborn in the Pure Land, the Western Paradise. Buddhist art, which had by then been thoroughly permeated by the Chinese spirit and sense of form, brought forth a style during the Tang period that became the ideal for all of East Asia.

Sui Dynasty (581 — 618)

A total of 95 caves from the Sui period have been preserved. Cave 419 is typical of the art of that time. It contains interesting murals and a group of clay sculptures: Buddha surrounded by two bodhisattvas, his cousin and favorite pupil Ananda and the monk Kasyapa.

Caves 420, 427 and 244 are just as noteworthy for their sculptures. Murals of scenes from Chinese mythology are found in cave 423. Other caves worth mentioning are numbers 295, 305 and 404.

Tang Dynasty (618 — 907)

The 213 grottos remaining from the Tang era comprise the largest group. The artists of this period also frequently chose their themes from Buddhist writings. The works of those who portrayed worldly problems — scenes from commercial life, the trades and farming — are noteworthy. The visitor to the Tang grottos is usually overwhelmed by the magnificence of the paintings and sculptures. Two giant sculptures are impressive: a 33-m-tall Buddha sculpture created at the beginning of the Tang Dynasty in cave 96 and a 26-m-tall statue from the mid-Tang period with a glorious ornamental ceiling in cave 130. The most imposing of the Tang grottos is cave 220. It contains the now famous painting of a group of musicians. The portrayal of the dancers and the Buddhist layman Vimalakirti, who is engaged in a heated debate with the emperor in his black and red robe and the emperor's ministers, make viewing this painting an experience. Cave 329 will fascinate the visitor with its imaginatively painted ceiling of scenes from the Pure Land. It is possible to draw conclusions about the architecture and clothing of the Tang period from it. The sculptures and large painted niches of cave 328 are quite interesting. Cave 322 contains the sculpture of a celestial king and pretty bodhisattva figures. Lovely dancers, musicians and feitia, flying apsaras, are to be found in caves 320 and 321. They soar and dance with flying sashes and scarves. One more portrayal of the Pure Land is in cave 217. It is very informative about Tang era architecture. Another famous painting is in cave 445: The Tonsure of the Concubines. The representations of musicians and marriage ceremonies are no less interesting. Cave 112 contains paintings of song and dance groups. Finely worked sculptures are located in cave 45, including once again Ananda and the monk Mahakasyapa. Cave 158 houses one of the most famous sculptures in Dunhuang, the sleeping Buddha. The paintings in cave 156 were done during the late Tang period. One painting is called 'Zhang Yichao conquers Hexi'. Over 100 warriors are portrayed going to battle under waving flags. China was again divided after the fall of the Tang Dynasty. The trade routes became unsafe and overseas trade more attractive. Dunhuang lost its importance. What is more, the events of 845 — the persecution of Buddhism — had grave consequences, above all for Buddhist art, for they robbed it of all creativity (see page 394). This persecution initiated the downfall of Buddhism in China. The only school which was ever to flourish again was Chan Buddhism. But, it rejected religious sculptures and developed Chinese watercolor painting entirely according to its own interpretations.

Wudai, the Period of Five Dynasties, (907 — 960) and the Beginning of the Song Dynasty

Cao Yiquan's family ruled over Dunhuang for three generations. It supported Buddhism as best it could and had many of the existing caves expanded or restored. Due to lack of space, no new caves could be built. A painting academy was founded at which artists were trained solely for the caves of Dunhuang. A special chromatic harmony characterizes their style. Thirty-three caves from this period have been preserved. The most remarkable one is cave 61 from 981 AD. It contains a 13-m-long painting: a pictorial description of the landscape of the Wutai Shan mountains. Over 170 buildings are depicted, including famous temple complexes, bridges, settlements, people, mountains, plants and animals. It is the area extending from Taiyuan in Shanxi to Zhengdian Xian district in Hebei. This painting is one of the oldest Chinese geographic maps preserved up to the present. Cave 98 is also noteworthy and contains a portrayal of the King of Yutian, Li Shengtian. This painting provides valuable insights into the style and clothing of the Period of Five Dynasties.

Xi Xia, Western Xia (1032 — 1227) and Yuan Period (1271 — 1368)

The work done during the Western Xia Dynasty was mainly limited to touch-ups of old paintings or imitations of styles from past dynasties (caves 328 and 97). A few new caves were built during the Yuan period. Their murals were noticeably influenced by various schools of Buddhism, among them the Esoteric School. Two Yuan-period caves are 465 and 3.

During the Ming Dynasty, Dunhuang steadily declined in importance and finally sank into oblivion.

Mingsha Shan, Ringing Sand Mountain 鸣沙山

Mingsha Shan is located 5 km south of Dunhuang. The mountain was formed by drifting sand. It is 40 km long from east to west and 20 km wide from north to south. If one slides down its sides, the friction causes a whistling sound.

Hotel

Dunhuang Binguan Dongdajie, tel. 24 92

Travel agency

Zhongguo Lüxingshe, Dongdajie tel. 24 92

Xinjiang Weiwu'er Zizhiqu, Xinjiang Autonomous Region of the Uigurs Minority 新疆维吾尔自治区

Area: 1,646,800 km² / Population: 13 million / Capital: Ürümqi

Xinjiang is the largest and northwestern-most of the Chinese autonomous regions and provinces. It covers about one-sixth of the entire area of China. Xinjiang borders on Gansu and Qinghai Provinces in the east, Xizang Autonomous Region (Tibet) in the south and on India, Kashmir, Afghanistan, the Soviet Union and Outer Mongolia. Starting in the 1st century BC, Xinjiang was an important intermediate station for China's trade with central Asia, India and the Roman Empire. Cultural and religious ideas were exchanged here. Buddhism found its first followers in Xinjiang on its way from India and music and dances were integrated.

History

In the 1st century BC, the rulers of the Han

Dynasty succeeded in defeating the Xiongnu, who had ruled over the area of present-day Xinjiang. They founded a governor-generalship. As the Han empire weakened, the area was lost. The individual oasis states were successful in their repeated attempts to preserve their autonomy in spite of Tibetan, Mongol, Hun and Turkish foreign rule. In 657, Xinjiang became a part of the Tang empire. The Uigurs settled in east and south Xinjiang during the 10th century. They were able to preserve some measure of autonomy only until the 13th century, when the area was conquered by the Mongols.

The Manchus extended the sphere of power of their Qing Dynasty as far as Xinjiang. They broke Mongol dominion over the Dzungarian Basin and that of the Islamic peoples in the south. In the middle of the 19th century, the Islamic peoples took advantage of the central government's weakness and started a rebellion. As a result, the empire lost the greater part of Xinjiang, which was not won back completely until 1878 by governor-general Zuo Zongtang. In 1884, Xinjiang was proclaimed a province. Times of unrest followed the fall of the Qing Dynasty, leading to endeavors for autonomy and uprisings. In September 1949, the local government of Xinjiang sided with the new government in Beijing. The area was granted the status of autonomous region in 1955 as a part of the minorities policy. Various autonomous prefectures and districts were formed where the minorities could develop according to their traditional, ethnic cultures.

The Tianshan massif is the dividing line between north and south. The Dzungarian Basin lies in the north with an area of about 700,000 km² and borders on the Soviet Union and Outer Mongolia. The Altai Shan massif rises on the border to Outer Mongolia. The Dzungarian Basin consists mainly of steppe and deserts surrounded by a ring of oases and mountains. The Tianshan mountains take up about one-quarter of the area of Xinjiang. The highest points are Hantengri Feng, 6,995 m, and Shengli Feng, 7,439 m. About half of Xinjiang is made up of the Tarim Basin, which is encircled by the Pamir and Kunlun mountain ranges in addition to the Tianshan. It lies at an altitude of 1,200 m in the west and 760 m in the east and consists of the 700,000-km²-large desert Takla Makan, which is surrounded by alluvial land and a ring of oases. The Kunlun Shan mountains mark off Xinjiang to the south. Mountain passes in the east and west lead to neighboring Tibet.

The Tarim He is the most important river in Xinjiang. It flows eastward through the region.

Xinjiang has a dry, continental climate in which it is a bit more humid north of the Tianshan massif. The average temperature in January is -15°C in the north and -7°C in the Tarim Basin. In July, the temperature in the north averages 21°C. The lowest point in Xinjiang is the Turpan Depression, which is 154 m below sea level. The average July temperature there is 32°C, the highest recorded temperature 48°C. The average annual amount of precipitation in Xinjiang is low — less than 250 mm in the Dzungarian Basin and less than 100 mm in the Tarim Basin.

Thirteen different minorities live in Xinjiang. The largest group are the Uigurs, followed by the Kazakhs and Kirghiz. The Uigurs make up the greatest portion of the population in the Tarim Basin, whereas the Han Chinese predominate in the Dzungarian Basin. The Uigurs are settled farmers, as are most Tadzhiks and Uzbeks. The Kazakhs are a nomadic tribe like the Mongols.

Because of the dry climate, 90% of the cultivated land is fully dependent on irrigation. The most important crops are wheat, corn, rice, sorghum and millet. After 1949, the People's Liberation Army took part in the cultivation and irrigation of large desert areas. The fruit of Xinjiang is famous throughout China: apples from the Ili Valley, sweet melons from Hami and grapes from Turfan. About 60% of the Chinese demand for wool is met by Xinjiang-home of 25% of the country's sheep.

Xinjiang can be reached by train from Lanzhou, Gansu. The railroad runs through Hami to Ürümqi and Korla. Many new main and secondary roads have been built around the Tarim and Dzungarian Basins. One connection runs through the Tianshan mountains to Ürümqi. The junction Kashi, the legendary Kashgar, lies to the west — once one of the most important stations of the silk trade between Asia and Europe. There is a road south to Tibet in the west and a road to Qinghai and Gansu in the east.

Xinjiang has developed into an important industrial center since 1949. The expansion of the transportation network made possible the mining of the province's abundant mineral resources. Petroleum, coal, iron ore and gold are among the most important. Uranium deposits are very important and have made Xinjiang the center of nuclear power research. A large number of uranium works have been built during the past 20 years.

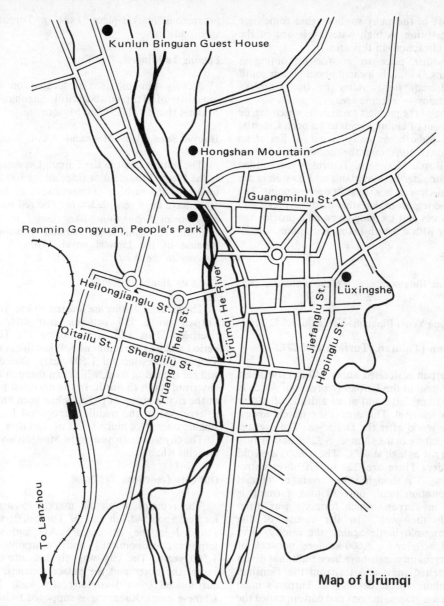

● Kunlun Binguan Guest House

● Hongshan Mountain

Guangminlu St.

● Renmin Gongyuan, People's Park

Heilongjianglu St.

Qitailu St.

Shenglilu St.

Huang helu St.

Ürümqi He River

Guangminlu St.

Jiefanglu St.

Hepinglu St.

● Lüxingshe

To Lanzhou

Map of Ürümqi

Ürümqi 乌鲁木齐市

Ürümqi, which lies at the northern foot of the Tianshan mountains is connected to the internal Chinese transportation network and thus easily reached by plane, train or bus. Ürümqi means 'Beautiful Meadow' in the Uigur language. The city is located in an oasis surrounded by mountains and is inhabited by members of 13 nationalities in addition to the Uigurs: the Hui, Mongols, Han, Kirghiz. The 1.11 million inhabitants are Moslems. Therefore, the city is characterized by many buildings in the typical Islamic style as well as 30 mosques.

Ürümqi used to be an important stop on the Silk Road. Thanks to its rich mineral resources (coal and iron ore), it has developed into a modern manufacturing city in the last few decades.

There is a beautiful view of the city from Hongshan, the Red Mountain. A nine-storied pagoda stands on top of the mountain. People's Park is located not far from Hongshan on the west bank of the Ürümqi He river.

A popular recreation area located south of the city is called Yan'er Wo, 'Swallows' Nest', because of the many swallows that come here in the spring. A high waterfall is one of the main attractions in this area.

Another place to go for an outing is Baiyang Gou. It is located about 60 km south of Ürümqi in a valley in the Tianshan mountains — a scenic area.

One of the prettiest excursions which can be taken out of Ürümqi leads to Tianchi, Celestial Lake, three hours away by car. It lies at an altitude of 1,980 m at the foot of the 5,400-m-high Bogda Mountain. Tianchi is surrounded on four sides by mountains and its waters are crystal-clear. It is 90 m at its deepest point. The snow-covered peaks, the many cypress and pine trees and the jade-green lake provide the visitor with a breath-taking panorama.

Hotels

Kunlun Binguan, 昆仑宾馆 Fanxiulu, tel. 33 60

Xinjiang Youyi Binguan, Yen'anlu, tel. 2 39 91

Turpan (Tulufan, Turfan) 吐鲁番市

Turpan is situated about 140 km southeast of Ürümqi in the Turpan Depression, which is 50,000 km² large and at an altitude of 154 m below sea-level. This area is the second lowest in the world after the Dead Sea. The average temperature in the summer is 32°C and in July it can rise as high as 47°C. The winters are cold and dry. There are 220 to 270 days above freezing. Although the average annual precipitation totals only 10 mm, farming is done in Turpan, which formerly was often called 'the oven'. In the course of the centuries-old battle against the aridity, over 1,000 wells and a 3,000-km-long network of underground canals have been built that divert the melted snow and ice from the Tianshan mountains to the depression. Turpan's main crops are grapes, melons and cotton, called the 'three treasures of the Turpan Depression'. The best-known grape is the seedless Turpan grape, which has a sugar content of 20%. They are dried in the sun and then sold as Xinjiang raisins throughout China and abroad. The sweet Hami melons, grown for over 1,000 years, are also known in all of China. They can weigh up to 15 kg. During the summer months, field work can only be done at dawn and dusk.

Turpan lies on the north branch of the Silk Road and was an important trade, cultural and political center over 2,000 years ago. Cultural influences from the East and West blended here. Even today, the ruins of formerly prosperous market-places exist in Turpan's surroundings.

Sugong Ta Minaret 苏公塔

A very famous sight is located on the outskirts of Turpan: beautiful Sugong Ta Minaret (built in 1779) and Mosque.

Huoyan Shan, Flame Mountain 火焰山

The hottest point in the Turpan Depression is the Flame Mountain, a ridge about 100 km long and 851 m high. Temperatures of over 50°C have been recorded here. The red rocks of Huoyan Shan shine like flames in the sunlight. The Chinese are familiar with them because of the famous novel *Xiyou Ji, A Journey to the West*.

Old City Jiaohe 交河故城

The ruins of Jiaohe are located 10 km from Turpan on a hill between two dried-up riverbeds. This city arose during the Han period and was the center of political life in the Turpan Depression for 1,500 years. One can still see the trunk road, which ran through the city from south to north. In the northern part of the city, a group of pagodas had been built: a large one in the middle surrounded by 25 smaller ones. Not much is left of the latter.

The city was destroyed by the Mongols under Genghis Khan.

Old City Gaocheng 高城故城

The remains of an old market town are located about 40 km east of Turpan. It was founded in the 1st century AD and was important economically and culturally for 1,500 years. The city was divided into the inner, the outer and the palace districts, all surrounded by a 5-km-long city wall. The Chinese monk Xuanzang is supposed to have taught here for a month after his return from India. During the 14th century continuous feuding between the aristocratic families shook the fortunes of the city. In the course of this process the subterranean irrigation system was destroyed, and the destruction of the city quickly followed.

About 15 km east of Gaocheng, in the eastern and western parts of Tuyugou Valley, the Caves of the Thousand Buddhas are located. They date from the 3rd and 4th centuries. The eastern caves are interesting; the design of some of them resembles that of the caves at Dunhuang.

Astana Graves

The Astana graves are northwest of ancient Gaochang. There the dead of Gaochang were buried at the period between the 3rd and 9th centuries. Three of the tombs are open to visitors.

Qianfo Dong, Cave of the Thousand Buddhas
千佛洞

It is another group of caves, which are located 50 km northeast of Turpan and were built between the 6th and 14th centuries.

The Qianfo Dong are known in the west as the Caves of Bezeklik, place of the frescoes. These witnesses of the flourishing time of Buddhism had to endure a sad fate. Moslems and exterior influences had already brought about serious destruction but it was a real catastrophe when the German explorers Albert von Le Coq and Theodor Bartus arrived and systematically removed the precious mural paintings from the stone walls to transport them to Berlin. During the first quarter of this century explorers from different countries, mainly Sweden, England, France, Germany, Russia, Japan and the United States – claiming whatever moral right–brought the treasures of the temples, graves and ruins of Chinese Turkistan to their countries. Many of these are nowadays lost, destroyed or scattered across the world in museums in India, Japan, Taiwan, South Korea, the United States, Germany, England and France.

In 1905 Albert von Le Coq discovered the frescoes of Bezeklik that had been buried by the sands of past centuries. Le Coq and his expedition team dug them out and realized their outstanding condition. They were huge wall paintings that bore unique witness of the time when they came into being; Buddhist monks from India and East Asia with their names in their respective languages, Indian princes, Brahmans, Persians, Europeans, hunters, horsemen, noble men and women, Indian gods. Le Coq decided to saw the biggest and most beautiful paintings from the walls and to transport them to Berlin where soon after he was an honored man. There these paintings formed the so-called Turpan-Exposition of the Ethnological Museum. But most of it was destroyed by allied bombing in World War II, 1943 – 1945. Only the empty walls of Bezeklik survived.

Kashi, Kashgar 喀什噶尔

The well-known oasis of Kashgar, situated on the Silk Road and the most western city of China, is the destination of every Xinjiang traveler. Kashgar is situated on the western edge of the Tarim Basin. Once one of the most important stations on the Silk Road, the city, like the rest of Xinjiang, had to endure many riots and wars. Although the glamor of the legendary Kashgar is long since lost, the city still has an extraordinary attraction.

Lying at the southern edge of the Pamir, it is an 3.5 hour flight away from Urumqi. Most of the 120,000 inhabitants are Uigurs, with a minority of Han-Chinese, Tadzhiks, Uzbeks, and Kiriz. The best impression of this mixture of peoples can be got while visiting Sunday's market which is the biggest in the world and attracts up to 150,000 people from near and far. Merchants on donkey carts, camels, mini-tractors and bicycles flow into town to offer their goods. Apart from business, the market is also a meeting point for young and old people exchanging news and rumors, discussing problems, matching-making, giving advice, settling medical questions or just getting a new haircut. It is here that the visitor from afar can see the typical traditional handicraft of Kashgar which is known even beyond the borders of Xinjiang. Metalware, jewelry and the well-known Yengisar knives, earthenware, woven carpets, musical instruments and embroidery.

Besides the market there are several other important places of interest: in the center of the city the big Id Kah Mosque, in the eastern part of the oasis the Abakh Hoja (Xiang Fei) tomb.

Hotels

Remin Binguan, 人民宾馆 in the center of the city.

Kashgar Binguan, 喀什喀尔宾馆 in the eastern part of the city.

Qinghai Province 青海省

Area: 720,100 km² / Population: 3.89 million (35% Tibetans, 30% Han, 20% Hui, 10% Mongols) / Capital: Xining

Qinghai is a northwest Chinese province located in the northeastern part of the Tibetan plateau. The average altitude is 4,000 m above sea-level. The area is bordered by Gansu in the north and east, Sichuan and Tibet in the south and Xijiang in the west. The province was named for Qinghai Hu, the Blue Lake. This lake, also called Koko Nor, is at an altitude of 3,040 m and is China's largest inland lake.

History

Qinghai was formerly inhabited chiefly by Tibetan and Mongol nomadic tribes. Parts of the region were under central government rule as early as the 3rd century BC, however, the settlements of the Han farmers were concentrated in the northeast corner of Qinghai, in the area around Qinghai Hu lake. Han influence increased during the Sui Dynasty as local headquarters were established and the region duly controlled. In the 8th century, Qinghai was invaded by the Tibetans; later, the northern part came under the power of the Tanguts and Uighurs. Qinghai belonged to the region of the Tangutan Western Xia Dynasty from the 11th to the 13th centuries and did not become a part of the empire again until the Tanguts were annihilated by the Mongols. Qinghai has had the status of a province since 1929.

Over 90% of its area consists of mountains and plateaus. The Qilianshan mountains lie to the north. Qaidam Pendi basin, at an altitude of 2,700 m, stretches out between the Qilianshan and the Bayan Harshan mountains further south, which form a divide for the sources of the Huanghe and Changjiang rivers. In the south, the province borders on the Tanggulashan mountains.

Qinghai has a typical continental climate: the summers are hot and the winters cold, dry and windy. Annual precipitation is low — in the northeast 250 mm, in the west 100 mm. Most of the precipitation falls in the summer months. Intensive farming is practised in east Qinghai, in the Huanghe river basin, where wheat, rye, oats, corn and sweet potatoes are the most important crops. In the west, stock-raising — sheep, goats, yaks, horses and cattle — is carried out chiefly by Tibetan and Mongol tribes. Their most important products are leather and sheep and yak wool.

The province is rich in mineral resources that have hardly been tapped yet. In the Qaidam Basin alone, there is petroleum, coal, iron ore, borax and salt. The province has been able to make rapid progress industrially during the past few decades; textile, food-processing and chemical plants have been built.

Xining 西宁市

Xining lies on the banks of the Huangshui, a tributary of the Huanghe, on a fertile plain 2,200 m above sea-level. It is 200 km away from Lanzhou, Gansu, and can be reached from there by rail.

Xining, which existed under the name of Lingju Zhai as early as the time of the Han emperor Wudi, has always been strategically important throughout the course of its history.

Since 1949, Xining has gradually developed into a manufacturing city; among others, there are chemical, textile and metalworking plants there today.

Xining is only 70 km from Qinghai Hu lake (Koko Nor), the largest Chinese inland lake. The special attraction of Xining — indeed, of all Qinghai — is the lamasery Ta'er Si (Kumbum), 19 km southwest of Xining. It is the largest monastery complex in Qinghai and a sacred place for the Yellow Sect. As Tibetan Lamaism became increasingly important after the 7th century, Xining developed into an important religious center.

Ta'er Si Lamasery (Kumbum) 塔尔寺

Ta'er Si lamasery, one of the largest and most famous ones of the Yellow Sect, is located 19 km from Xining in the community of Lusha'er in Huangzhong district. It is said that Zongkaba was born there.

Zongkaba (1357 — 1419) was a reformer of Lamaism and the founder of the Yellow Sect. He was given into the care of a Lama when he was only two years old. His thirst for knowledge and intensive studies at different monasteries and under excellent teachers made him a very learned man. His first followers gathered around him in 1392, forming the beginning of the so-called Gelugpa Sect. Owing to his influence, Lamaism was purified from all superfluous practices, from faults and misuse. The strict rules drawn up by Zongkaba demanded discipline, faultless conduct and fervent religiosity. He also produced note-worthy literary works.

Construction of the monastery was begun in 1560. It was designed in the Tibetan style. Over the next centuries, more buildings were added, among them various ones in the Han Chinese style. An extensive renovation was carried out in 1979. The grounds cover 142,000 m². Formerly, 4,000 monks lived at Ta'er Si; now there are said to be about 50.

The 14-m-high Great Stupa stands at the entrance to the lamasery. It bears a horseshoe-shaped monogram that faces the monastery and combines seven syllables and three symbols, which in this arrangement symbolize the relation of the microcosmos to the macrocosmos. There are eight white stupas between the Great Stupa and the forecourt of the lamasery. They were erected in 1776, supposedly after eight lamas had been murdered. The stupas are 5 m high and made

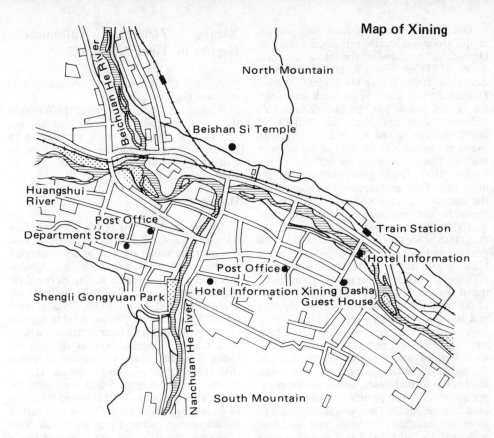

North Mountain

Beishan Si Temple

Beichuan He River

Huangshui River

Post Office

Department Store

Train Station

Hotel Information

Post Office

Shengli Gongyuan Park

Hotel Information

Xining Dasha Guest House

Nanchuan He River

South Mountain

of brick.

The main building in Ta'er Si is Serkhang Chenmo, Great Golden House, commonly called Gold Roof Hall. It is an imposing hall in the Han Chinese style. Its origin is directly connected to Zongkaba. It is said that at the place where he was born and his mother's blood seeped into the ground, a sandalwood tree grew three years later. Its leaves and bark showed wonderful pictures of deities and Tibetan letters. After Zongkaba had become a famous man, his old mother wished to see him. He sent her a message from Tibet telling her to erect a stupa above the sandalwood tree; that would be the same as a reunion. His mother is supposed to have fulfilled his wish. In 1560, a lama and 10 monks settled at the stupa and built the first cells. In 1577, a temple was erected close to the stupa. It contained a statue of 12-year-old Maitreya.

The hall covers about 210 m². The outer walls are covered with glazed tiles. The double roof was renovated in 1883 and is covered with gilded metal plates. The ridge of the roof is decorated with several lucky signs made of gilded bronze. The center one is a gandshir, a type of vase. The front of the hall faces east.

Believers worship in front of the gates leading into the hall by throwing themselves to the floor according to certain rules. A 12-m-high stupa is inside the hall, surrounded by an impressive cloth structure. This is the stupa under which Zongkaba is said to have been born and the sandalwood tree grew. The cloth covering hardly permits a glance at the exterior of the actual building, a stupa covered with silver. A 1.3-m-high statue of Zongkaba, clothed in a silk coat, is located in a niche; Buddhist scripts and objects of worship are stored on the shelves and in the cupboards of the hall.

South of the main hall, Jokhang Maitreya Hall is located, a temple from 1577 containing a gilded statue of the 12-year-old Maitreya, portrayed as the Buddha-to-Be. In addition, there is a gold and silver sculpture of Zongkaba and two of his followers. The Temple of Dipankara, the Buddha of the Past, is north of the main hall. It is also called the House of Prayer because of the prayer-wheels built into the gallery surrounding the temple. The gallery contains a gilded statue of Buddha, a statue of the bodhisattra Guanyin and one of seven-year-old Maitreya.

One of the most important halls on the temple grounds is located east of the Temple of Dipankara; it contains the most beautiful statue of Ta'er Si — a gilded statue of Zongkaba. It stands on a low pedestal, holds a khadak, a ritual scarf, in its hands and wears the typical yellow hat. Because Zongkaba's followers wore this hat, his school of Buddhism was named the Yellow Sect. The sword of wisdom is to the right of the statue, a stack of Tibetan books to the left.

The 'Holy Trees' grow northeast of the main hall. They are supposedly shoots from the legendary sandalwood tree that was the reason for the construction of the monastery.

To the east, opposite the main hall, the Great Hall of Meditation is located, which is the meeting and sutra hall and a typical Tibetan building with its flat roof. It was built in the 17th century and is the largest religious building of the temple complex. The monks gather in this hall to study the holy writings together and to pray. The hall's ground-plan is rectangular. Numerous so-called tshaltan, emblems of victory, and gandshir decorate the roof. A gilded gandshir about 4 m tall stands in the middle of the temple roof. A gilded wheel, the symbol of Buddhism, stands on the parapet of the roof. The statues of a gazelle and a hind face the wheel. They admonish people to listen to Buddhist teachings just as these animals did — tradition has it that they were the first to follow the sermons of Buddha in Benares. The interior of the hall resembles a sea of columns: 108 of them, covered by valuable carpets with dragon patterns, divide the room. Low benches formerly provided seating for up to 3,500 monks.

The room is decorated with religious scroll paintings, the Tanggas, and appliqué and patchwork pictures. These, along with the sculptures of Tibetan butter, are called the three wonders of Ta'er Si.

Colorful individual and collective sculptures made of Tibetan butter are created for the sacrificial ceremonies, also called the Butter Festival, which takes place on the 15th day of the first month according to the lunar calendar. The sculptures, which vary in size, portray people, deities, landscapes, animals, plants, buildings, etc. The festival marks the end of a 15-day period beginning on New Year's Day, when the monks commemorate the legendary happenings in Buddha's life.

Hotel

Xining Binguan, 西宁宾馆 Qiyilu, tel. 2 39 01

Xizang Zizhiqu, Autonomous Region of Tibet 西藏自治区

Area: 1,220,000 km² / Population: 1.89 million / Capital: Lhasa

Xizang, or Tibet, the Roof of the World, is the second-largest of China's autonomous regions and provinces. It is surrounded by Yunnan, Sichuan, Qinghai and Xinjiang as well as by Kashmir, India, Nepal, Sikkim, Bhutan and Burma.

History

During the first half of the 7th century, a state with a central government, uniform laws and an army under the rule of King Songzan Ganbu already existed in Tibet. An alphabet from India was introduced during his reign. He was successful in extending his realm to Nepal, West Tibet and North India, among other places. Tang emperor Taizong tried to appease him by giving him a Chinese princess to wed — Wen Cheng Gongzhu, who is still famous today. Songzan Ganbu's successors expanded their sphere of power into present-day Gansu. It was a time of tension and wars with the Chinese Tang empire. Tibet achieved the zenith of its military might during the second half of the 8th century, when it received tribute from China and the Tibetans had advanced to the Chinese capital, Chang'an.

As the kingdom gradually declined, the realm split into small princedoms at the end of the 9th century. The situation quieted down in the course of the 10th century and the monasteries gained economic as well as political and cultural influence with the increasing political stability. Buddhism had probably reached Tibet from India by the 3rd century, but it did not spread until the 8th century. Several schools of Buddhism developed: the Gelugpas sect, the Yellow Caps, achieved absolute political supremacy in the 17th century. Under the Mongol Yuan Dynasty, Tibet became a type of satellite state of the Chinese empire. Kublai Khan declared a lama ruler of the land. The lama and his successors lived at the Chinese court. After the fall of the Yuan Dynasty, a new monarchy arose in Tibet — the Phag-mo-gru Dynasty, which was to rule for 100 years. A rapprochement between the Mongols and the hierarchs of the Yellow Sect occurred towards the end of the 16th century; the powerful Altan Khan awarded the leader of the Yellow Sect the title of Dalai Lama. During the course of these developments, the Mongols converted to

Lamaism. Under the leadership of Gushi Khan at the end of the Ming period, the Mongols invaded Tibet. The Dalai Lama became the ruler and Gushi Khan the king of Tibet. The new rulers declared Lhasa their capital, Potala Palace was built and a number of existing monasteries enlarged and magnificently furnished. During the early 18th century, the Chinese emperor regained control of Tibet after expelling the Mongols.

As the Qing government became weaker, Tibet became more independent, although it still acknowledged the supreme rule of the Chinese empire. England first attempted to negotiate with Tibet during the 19th century. During 1903 — 1904, a British-Indian military expedition advanced to Lhasa and forced Tibet to sign a British-Tibetan treaty. However, soon after, in 1906, Great Britain acknowledged Chinese supremacy in an agreement. On the strength of that agreement, the central government sent a 2,000-man-army to strengthen its territorial sovereignty.

After the fall of the Manchu Qing Dynasty, the Dalai Lama proclaimed the independence of Tibet. The young Chinese republic did not recognize this declaration. After the People's Republic had been founded, Beijing sent troops to Tibet to safeguard the western border in October 1950. China and Tibet signed an 'Agreement on Measures for the Peaceful Liberation of Tibet' in May 1951, which was recognized by the Dalai Lama in August. In 1954, the Dalai Lama and the Panchen Lama were representatives to the First National People's Congress in Beijing. The Preparatory Committee for the Autonomous Region of Tibet, which was headed by the Dalai and Panchen Lamas, was formed in 1956. Shortly thereafter, democratic reforms announced at the same time were postponed until 1962. Unrest and uprisings occurred from 1957 — 1959. The Dalai Lama fled into exile in India, the local government was dissolved and the Preparatory Committee with the Panchen Lama at its head took over the functions of government. In 1965, he was removed from office. Tibet was declared an autonomous region in the same year.

Tibet is a high plateau surrounded by mighty mountains. A barren, high plain stretches out in the north and northwest, where there are no rivers, only brackish lakes. The average altitude is 4,900 m. The high plateau is bordered by the Kunlun Mountains in the north; their highest peak is Muztag, 7,723 m high. In the east, there is a river basin that receives a lot of precipitation where the inhabitants can farm. The Yarlung Zangbo Jiang (Brahmaputra) flows through southern Tibet. The important cities Lhasa and Xigaze are located there. Tibet is bordered by the Himalayas to the south. Their highest peak, Mt. Everest, rises 8,848 m on the border to Nepal.

The climate is mostly dry and varies according to altitude. The high mountain ranges in the south and west prevent the passage of the wet monsoon winds. In the high-lying areas, it is cold and precipitation low; in the low-lying areas, it is mild and precipitation is abundant. It is humid in the Yarlung Zangbo Jiang Valley and in the east. Traveling is most pleasant during late spring and early autumn.

Tibet has little vegetation. About three-quarters of its surface is covered by grass or snow. Richer vegetation is only found in the river valleys and low, wet regions of the south and southwest. Farming is possible here. Wheat, barley, rape-seed and peas are the most common crops. Fruit is also harvested, for example, apricots, peaches and apples. Huge areas of valuable virgin forests, about 44,000 km^2, are located in the southeast. The largest cities are Lhasa, Xigaze and Qamdo. About half of the population of Tibet lives in Lhasa and the neighboring cities in the south.

The land is rich in minerals such as gold, silver, copper, uradium, iron and salt. Up to now, only little of it has been mined: the main hindrances are non-existent transportation routes, impassable areas, shortages of technical equipment and a raw climate. Formerly, the people believed that the deities would be disturbed by mining and therefore hardly mined at all.

Most Tibetans are farmers and livestock-raisers. Until 1951, there was hardly any industry, rather small workshops where traditional Tibetan art was created. Since then, various heavy and light industrial plants have been built, for example, electric power plants and coal mines, machine manufacturing, construction materials and chemical factories, and wood-processing, match and food-processing plants. Tibet has experienced great changes in its transportation system. Formerly, whoever wanted to travel had to do so on foot or on the back of an animal. During the last three decades, four main transportation routes have been built that connect Tibet to Xinjiang, Qinghai, Sichuan and Yunnan. The network of roads, with Lhasa at its center, is 21,000 km long and is being expanded. Lhasa is a part of the internal Chinese air traffic network via the cities of Golmud, Xi'an and Chengdu.

Persons interested in traveling to Tibet

should remember that it lies at a very high altitude, a condition which may affect travelers, especially those with high blood pressure. A doctor should be consulted beforehand.

Lhasa 拉萨市

Lhasa was the center of Tibetan theocracy for 300 years, right into the 20th century. Much has changed in Lhasa during the last 20 years. The city has grown considerably; modern houses and streets have been built. Some sacred buildings have had to make way for modernization projects such as road construction whereas others have been restored at great cost and attract pious Tibetans and interested tourists today.

Lhasa lies at an altitude of 3,600 m on the banks of the Lhasa He river, a tributary of the Yarlung Zangbo Jiang. Lhasa's population consists of both Tibetan and Han peoples.

Since 1980, foreigners have been able to easily travel to Lhasa; the city is readily accessible by plane. The central airport of Tibet, one of the highest in the world, is located 120 km outside of Lhasa. It is possible for foreign visitors to stay at Guest House No. 1 near Dazhao Si monastery, in the heart of the old City. A comfortably furnished hotel of the Lüxingshe travel agency is 7 km outside the city.

Dazhao Si monastery in the center of the city is one of the holy places of Tibetan Buddhism. It is surrounded by the lively business section, which consists of small shops and markets. Recently, it has been possible to see pious Tibetans walking clockwise around

the grounds of Dazhao Si on the holy circumambulatory path Barkhor. Walking around a sacred object expresses reverence for it and is a type of purification. In addition, there is another, outer circumambulatory path called Lingkor.

Potala Palace 布达拉宫

The most famous building in Tibet is located in northwest Tibet — the Potala Palace. It is the former residence of the Dalai Lama and used to be the center of all the Tibetan theocracy's religious and political activities. With an area of 130,000 m² and a length of 360 m, it covers the south wall of Maburishan, the Red Mountain, which is consecrated to the bodhisattva Avalokiteshvara (Guanyin). Nine kings and ten Dalai Lamas have resided on this mountain. In the 7th century, King Songzan Ganbu had a type of fortification built which was said to resemble a sleeping elephant. Another building later called the 'Red Palace' was added upon the arrival of the Chinese princess Wen Cheng.

The word *potala* originally comes from Sanskrit. It is the name of a mythical mountain in southern India, where the bodhisattva Avalokiteshvara is supposed to have lived. The monk Xuanzang brought the story of the mountain and its myth to China during the Tang era. Because the Tibetan Buddhists considered King Songzan Ganbu to be an incarnation of this bodhisattva, the Red Mountain and its former residence were later called Potala. The fifth Dalai Lama, also worshipped as an incarnation of Avaloki-

Map of Lhasa

teshvara, continued this tradition in the 17th century. He had another residence, the White Palace, built on the eastern part of Potala Mountain and modelled after the Tang era Red Palace. It was completed in 1648 and later expanded by his successors. From 1690 — 1693, the Red Palace was built in memory of the fifth Dalai Lama. It makes up the central part of the complex and is surrounded by the buildings of the White Palace. Some of the architects were Han Chinese, whose influence is clearly reflected in the sloped roofs and the beam and bracket constructions.

The highest building in Potala Palace is 13 stories — 117 m — high. Its walls are up to 5 m thick. One defense tower, each in the east and west symbolizing the sun and moon, frame the compound. A wide stairway leads up the mountain to the east gate and the Eastern Terrace, where ceremonies and dances took place. The entire palace complex supposedly has about 1,000 rooms. The Red Palace contains mainly prayer halls and eight chortens decorated with gold leaf and precious stones in which the embalmed bodies of the dead Dalai Lamas rest in a meditation position. The statue of the fifth Dalai Lama is the oldest (1690) and also the largest, 14.8 m high. About 3,700 kg of gold went into its construction. The largest hall in the Red Palace is the West Hall. It contains wonderful murals including portrayals of episodes out of the life of the fifth Dalai Lama, e.g., an audience with the Qing emperor in 1652.

The lodgings and administration rooms are located in the White Palace. Its largest hall is the East Hall, where the ceremonies of the Dalai Lama's inauguration into office took place. It was built in 1645. The Dalai Lama's private chambers were located in the western part of the White Palace. The divine kings lived here with a following of 500 lamas, usually sons of the foremost families in Tibet.

The oldest part of Potala Palace is the Avalokiteshvara Chapel in the northeastern part of the Red Palace. It is also called the bridal chamber of Princess Wen Cheng and King Songzan Ganbu. The chapel contains a statue of thousand – armed Avalokiteshvara.

Potala Palace is a unique museum for every visitor, where excellent examples of Tibetan art can be seen. In addition to valuable sculptures, calligraphies, colorful columns, brackets and beams decorated with the most delicate of carvings, precious brocades and silks, gold and precious stones, the murals especially will remain unforgettable for the visitor. They can be divided into two categories: portrayals of real people with biographic accounts and motifs from Buddhist writings.

Longwang Tang Park 龙王塘公园

A park extends north of Potala Palace. In its center, Dragon King Lake and Dragon King Temple are located. The lake supposedly was created during construction of the White Palace in the 17th century when the earth needed for building was taken from here.

Dazhao Si Monastery, or Jokhang, House of the Master 大昭寺

Dazhao Si, the oldest complex in Lhasa, was built when the marriage between the Tibetan King Songzan Ganbu (617 — 650) and the Chinese princess Wen Cheng took place in 641. This marriage is still considered to be an important event in the history of Chinese-Tibetan relations.

This Buddhist holy place, now a national monument, is located in the center of Lhasa. After 1966, it was used for purposes other than those originally intended as a guest house and movie theater. It underwent extensive renovation from 1972 — 1975 and has served its original purpose again since March 1979. Dazhao Si was enlarged and remodelled considerably after its original construction. The complex's four Chinese roofs were probably added in the 14th century. The complex, which is built on an east-west axis, has a total of 24 halls. The stone and timber construction is in the Tibetan style; but the Chinese influence is clearly recognizable, just as elements of Nepalese and Indian architecture can be found.

An old willow grows at the entrance to Dazhao Si, said to have been planted by Princess Wen Cheng. North of the willow, the stone tablet Dang Fan Huimeng Bei, dating from 823, is located, which commemorates the pact of 821 between China and Tibet. The inscription was written in Tibetan and Han Chinese.

A wheel of the law and two Buddhist emblems of victory are above the entrance, the west gate. A gilded bronze statue of 12-year-old Sakyamuni stands in the central chapel of the main hall. Princess Wen Cheng is said to have brought this statue from the Chinese capital at that time, Chang'an, as a wedding gift from the Chinese emperor. Today it is the most valuable Buddhist sculpture in Tibet. In the course of the centuries and after various disturbances, it has probably had to be restored and even replaced several times. It is thought that the present statue dates from the

12th century. Wen Cheng is also supposed to have brought various classical Buddhist writings and a handbook of geomancy with her. She introduced the Tibetans to Chinese knowledge of this art.

The increased dissemination of Buddhism in Tibet is thought to be due in part to the influence of Wen Cheng and the Nepalese wife of the King, Princess Bhrikuti (Chi Zun).

In the main hall, as well as in the others, one should not miss the glorious carvings, ornamentation and painted decorations on the pillars, beams and brackets. Three sculptures frequently shown to visitors today are those of Songzan Ganbu, his Chinese consort Wen Cheng and his Nepalese consort.

Xiaozhao Si Temple (Ramoche) 小昭寺

Xiaozhao Si, once the second most important Buddhist holy shrine in Lhasa, is located in the northern part of the Old City. It is reported to have been built by order of the Chinese Princess Wen Cheng in the middle of the 7th century. The complex was destroyed several times. Supposedly, only a few monks still lived there at the end of the 19th century.

Luobulinka Summer Residence (Norbulingka) 罗布林卡

This compound is located in what is called the Tibetan 'Treasure Garden' in a western suburb of Lhasa, 4 km from Potala Palace. It was built during the first half of the 17th century as Summer Residence for the Dalai Lama. Few buildings from that time have been preserved; the present ones date from 1954 – 1956.

Only the latter two of the three largest monasteries in Lhasa — Gadan Si, Zhebang Si and Sela Si — still remain.

Zhebang Si is about 10 km west of Lhasa. It was founded by one of Zongkaba's followers in 1416. Most of the remaining buildings, all of them strictly in the Tibetan style, date from the 17th and 18th centuries. Zhebang Si was not only the largest and most important monastery, but also the political center of the Yellow Sect, where 8,000 monks once lived. The fifth Dalai Lama resided here until he moved to Potala Palace.

The monastery's printing shop was of great consequence. It specialized in editing the works and biographies of the Dalai Lamas.

One of the most important sights in the monastery is a large, gilded bronze statue of Maitreya Buddha, who is considered the protector of Zhebang Si.

Nechong is located about 1 km from Zhebang Si. It was the seat of the state oracle created by the fifth Dalai Lama and consulted in all important political questions until very recently. It expressed itself through the medium of a Lama in a trance.

Sela Si monastery, 5 km north of Lhasa, was also founded by a follower of Zongkaba. It dates from 1419 and became famous due to its academy. At one time, 6,500 monks lived here. The statues of the monastery are noteworthy. Renovation work started a few years ago.

Xigaze (Shigatse) 日喀则

The second-largest city in Tibet, which lies at an altitude of 3,800 m, is about 10 hours by car from Lhasa. Xigaze was the residence of the governor of Zang under the Dalai Lamas. His palace stood on Zongshan mountain. Its design resembles that of Potala Palace in Lhasa. However, it was built earlier, at the beginning of the 17th century, and therefore must have been a model for Potala's architects. The palace was destroyed during the Cultural Revolution.

Zashilunbu Monastery 扎什伦布寺

The monastery is the most prominent sight in Xigaze, which is founded in 1447 by a follower of Zongkaba, Gendunzhuba, who was posthumously declared the first Dalai Lama. The monastery became the residence of the Panchen Lama in the second half of the 17th century. The fifth Dalai Lama declared the abbot of Zashilunbu to be the Panchen Lama in 1650, who was thereafter honored as the incarnation of Buddha Amitabha. Thanks to extensive restoration during the past few years, the monastery is in very good condition. It offers an abundance of very valuable religious objects, sculptures and precious objects. The oldest remaining buildings on the grounds are the Great Assembly Hall from the early 17th century and the first Dalai Lama's burial chapel with its excellent murals. The tallest building is the Temple of Maitreya, erected at the beginning of the 20th century. It contains a 26-m-high bronze statue of Maitreya.

Jiangzi (Gyangze) 江孜市

The monastic city Baiju Si, dating from the 14th century, is located about 300 km from Lhasa in Jiangzi. Since the 17th century, 16 monasteries belonging to the most varied sects had existed here side by side. The three-storied Sutra Hall, which is shaped like a mandala and dates from the late 14th century, forms the focus of the city. It contains choice examples of Lamaist art in its main hall and adjacent secondary halls — including a bronze statue of Maitreya, the Buddha-to-Be, extending into the second story and flanked by Sakyamuni and Dipankara, the Buddhas of the Present and Past. The second story houses, among others, the rooms in which questions concerning the entire monastic city were debated. The unique Mandala Chapel, with valuable mandala paintings from the 15th century, is on the third floor.

The Daputi Pagoda, a monumental chorten from the 15th century, is the second important attraction in the monastic city. It is a unique work of Tibetan architecture. It has a mandala-shaped floorplan and dozens of niches containing hundreds of sculptures and paintings. They are among the most beautiful in Tibet and have brought fame and honor to the monastery. Their diversity provides an impression of the variety of the Lamaist pantheon.

The ruins of the fortress on the mountain opposite the monastery are remarkable. They were constructed in the 14th century. This complex, where the rulers of Jiangzi once lived, was destroyed by British bombardments in 1904.

Taiwan Province 台湾省

Area: 35,788 km² / Population: 18.27 million / Capital: Taibei

China's largest island, Taiwan, is about 100 km from the coast of the southeast Chinese province Fujian. The Nationalist government, under the leadership of Chiang Kaishek, fled there after the collapse of Guomindang rule in 1949 — 1950. As a result, the island went its own political, economic and cultural direction. The description of Taiwan's development and attractions is reserved for a separate account.

Appendices

List of Maps and Groundplans

List of Monochrome Illustrations

List of Tables

Expressions Frequently Used in Descriptions of Cities and Countryside (Chinese/English)

bówùguǎn	博物馆	museum
cángjīng diàn	藏经殿	sermon or instruction hall
chéng	城	city, wall
chí	池	pond, pool
cí	祠	ancestral temple
dǎo	岛	island
dàxióng bǎodiàn	大雄宝殿	Hall of the Great Heroes
dī	堤	dike
diān	颠	summit
diàn	殿	hall, palace, temple
dǐng	顶	peak
dòng	洞	cave, grotto
fēng	峰	peak
Fó	佛	Buddha
gé	阁	pavilion
gōng	宫	palace
gōngyuán	公园	park
guǎn	馆	hall
gǔlóu	鼓楼	drum tower
hǎi	海	sea, big lake
hé	河	river
hú	湖	lake
jiāng	江	river
líng	陵	mausoleum, imperial tomb
lóu	楼	tower, multi-storied building
mén	门	gate, door
miào	庙	temple
mù	墓	grave, tomb
pùbù	瀑布	waterfall
púsa	菩萨	bodhisattva
qiáo	桥	bridge
quán	泉	spring
shān	山	mountain, hill, mountain range, massif
shāngǔ	山谷	mountain valley, ravine
shānmén	山门	mountain gate
shěng	省	province
shí	石	stone, rock
shì	市	city
shíkū	石窟	grotto, cave
sì	寺	temple
tǎ	塔	pagoda
táng	堂	hall
táng	塘	pond
tiānwáng diàn	天王殿	Hall of the Celestial Kings

tíng	亭	pavilion
xī	溪	brook, small stream
xiá	峡	gorge
xiàn	县	district
xuān	轩	pavilion
yán	岩	rock, cliff
yuán	园	garden
yuàn	院	courtyard
zhōnglóu	钟楼	bell tower

Vocabulary and Idioms

Good day; Hello.	你好	Nǐ hǎo.
Goodbye.	再见	Zàijiàn.
I	我	wǒ
you, you (formal)	你，您	nǐ, nín
he, she, it	他，她，它	tā
we	我们	wǒmen
you (plural)	你们	nǐmen
they	他们	tāmen
friendship	友谊	yǒuyì
I'm an American.	我是美国人。	Wǒ shì Měiguórén.
I'm an Englishman.	我是英国人。	Wǒ shì Yīngguórén.
I'm a Canadian.	我是加拿大人。	Wǒ shì Jiānádàrén.
I'm an Australian.	我是澳大利亚人。	Wǒ shì Àodàlìyàrén.
Wait a moment, please.	请等一等。	Qǐng děng yī děng.
Do you understand English?	您懂英文吗？	Nín dǒng yīngwén mā?
I'm looking for...	我找…	Wǒ zhǎo...
I would like to have...	我要…	Wǒ yào...
I'd like to go to...	我要去…	Wǒ yào qù...
I'd like to buy...	我要买…	Wǒ yào mǎi...
Please sit down.	请坐。	Qǐng zuò.
Let's go.	走吧。	Zǒu ba.
thank you	谢谢	xièxie
rest, pause	休息	xiūxi
restaurant	饭店、饭馆	fàndiàn, fànguǎn
hotel	旅馆、饭店	lǚguǎn, fàndiàn
guest house	宾馆	bīnguǎn
Bureau of Public Security	公安局	Gōng'ān Jú
post office	邮局	yóujú
bank	银行	yínháng
Friendship Store	友谊商店	Yǒuyì Shāngdiàn
department store	百货大楼	bǎihuò dàlóu
train station	火车站	huǒchēzhàn
airport	飞机场	fēijīchǎng
taxi	出租汽车	chūzū qìchē
bookstore	书店	shūdiàn

English	Chinese	Pinyin
embassy	大使馆	dàshǐguǎn
hospital	医院	yīyuàn
entrance	入口	rùkǒu
exit	出口	chūkǒu
ladies' room	女厕所	nǚ cèsuǒ
men's room	男厕所	nán cèsuǒ
hairdresser	理发	lǐfà
coffee	咖啡	kāfēi
tea	茶	chá
soft drink	汽水	qìshuǐ
orange juice	桔子水	júzishuǐ
mineral water	矿泉水	kuàngquánshuǐ
beer	啤酒	píjiǔ
fruit	水果	shuǐguǒ
cigarettes	香烟	xiāngyān
fire	火	huǒ
make a telephone call	打电话	dǎ diànhuà
mail a letter	寄信	jì xìn
0	零	líng
1	一	yī
2	二	èr
3	三	sān
4	四	sì
5	五	wǔ
6	六	liù
7	七	qī
8	八	bā
9	九	jiǔ
10	十	shí

Index of Names, Places and Subjects

Z